THE

BIG
BOYS

THE
BIG
BOYS

POWER AND POSITION IN AMERICAN BUSINESS

Ralph Nader and William Taylor

PANTHEON BOOKS · NEW YORK

Library of Congress Cataloging-in-Publication Data
Nader, Ralph.
The big boys.
Bibliography: p.
Includes index.
1. Big business—United States. 2. Businessmen—
United States. I. Taylor, William, 1959–
II. Title.
HD2785.N33   1986   338.6'44'0973   85-25979
ISBN 0-394-53338-0
ISBN 0-394-72111-X (pbk.)

Book design by Joe Marc Freedman

Manufactured in the United States of America
First Paperback Edition

*To former or retired corporate executives
who write their memoirs.*   R.N.

*To Chloe, who will never really know how
much her support means.*   W.T.

Contents

FOREWORD

In Search of Arrogance

by Thomas J. Peters

Newsweek devoted two columns of its June 2, 1986, business section to this book. In an article entitled "Has Nader Gone Soft?" the reporter as much as snickered as he concluded: "[Nader] sets off in search of corporate pestilence but finds excellence instead."

Not in the eyes of this beholder. After reading the book, I was left deeply shaken. I would not have supposed that possible, given my long-standing indictment of the performance of the Fortune 500 chieftains.

No portrait of the nine business leaders Nader profiles in his book is entirely pretty. U.S. Steel Chairman David Roderick abandoned his industry, using time and money largely gained by protectionist policies to acquire Marathon Oil and Texas Oil and Gas, valued at $9 billion. Part of the move out of steel may have been necessary, but his insensitivity is shocking. Roderick explains his repeated failure to meet with community leaders who wanted to develop an alternative use for the about-to-be-closed South Works in Chicago: "Look, I don't want one of these goddamned committees coming in here—a priest, a Boy Scout, and a housewife—telling me what to do. We're here to make money."

General Motors Chairman Roger Smith was equally insensitive about the destruction of Poletown, the impoverished Detroit community that made way for a new GM plant. He also publicly humiliated on television (on *Donahue*) seven governors who groveled to get him to locate GM's Saturn operation in their state, a setup former United Auto Workers President Douglas Fraser called "obscene." Smith gave speech after speech about forthcoming car models that would have seven onboard computers featuring 38,000 instructions. But now he can't get the cars

Thomas J. Peters is co-author of In Search of Excellence *and* A Passion for Excellence.

to work and GM is losing its market share each quarter to Ford, Chrysler, and the imports.

Northrop Chief Executive Thomas Jones is a supersalesman, having led his defense contracting firm to outperform the industry by a wide margin since 1960. But are we well served by an exchange that Nader describes during the most recent annual shareholders' meeting? "Jones was asked by our correspondent to reflect on the deadly impact of the product his corporation manufactures. Admiral Hyman Rickover, in his farewell testimony to Congress, told legislators that he would sink all the nuclear-powered ships whose construction he had sponsored were they not a necessary evil. Has the Northrop chairman ever had similar reservations about the wisdom of his work? 'I've not had similar thoughts,' Jones said with a smile. The auditorium rang with a chorus of approving shareholder laughter." I sadly acknowledge the need for weapons, as did Rickover, but I find the topic far short of amusing and I am saddened that any chief executive would behave so flippantly regarding this grave topic.

Even giant-slayer Bill McGowan, head of MCI and humbler of AT&T, is somewhat tarnished. His cause was noble and his outspoken demeanor most refreshing. Nonetheless, Nader suggests that McGowan has simply created one more long-distance telephone company that soon will be part of a new oligopoly of a half-dozen companies in place of AT&T's monopoly.

Then there is William Norris of Control Data Corp. Nader admires his vision, which epitomizes the CEO's power to extend the corporation's aims. Inner-city and farmland ventures dot the CDC agenda, along with the billion-dollar PLATO (Programmed Logic for Automatic Teaching Operations). But Nader's profile depicts at least as much ego and arrogance as thoughtful application of power. Surely shareholder wealth-creation is not all there is to life, but Norris has run roughshod over his board of directors in pursuit of grandiose visions, crippling his balance sheet in the process and making the firm vulnerable to takeover. Specific practices such as the "Shark Club," which celebrates occasionally unscrupulous sales victories, further blur the picture.

Is this the excellence *Newsweek* claims Nader has found? In fact, only one of Nader's chief executive officers comes through with tiny blemishes —Dow Chemical boss Paul Oreffice. Oreffice faces a transition that equals Smith's or Roderick's in autos and steel. However, he has stayed with chemicals and quickly transformed the firm from a sluggish, basic-commodity producer to a faster-moving specialty-chemical producer that emphasizes pharmaceuticals and consumer products. Moreover, the wrenching transition was accomplished while maintaining, at great expense, a "no layoff" policy. Nader even praises some, but not all, of Dow's environmental policies.

Nader's avowed objective is to weigh the use and abuse of power among American leaders of giant businesses. He observes that chief executive officers are granted exceptionally wide latitude. Ironically, they are granted especially wide latitude when business performance is poor; though they are arguably to blame for such malaise, the historic American tendency has been to leave them alone to oversee the recovery when things get tough.

Nader digs deeper and asks a broader set of questions, to my knowledge, than has ever been asked of chief executives. Even in the case of Roger Smith, for whom there is doubtless little Nader fondness (Nader was once trailed by GM-hired private eyes), his reporting is scrupulously balanced. He draws heavily upon secondary sources and interviews with numerous current and former colleagues and industry participants. Moreover, six of the nine principals granted Nader extensive interviews (Smith and Jones did not). But even in the three cases where the CEOs did not participate, the story Nader pieced together is extensive.

Nader's portraits are complex. His chief executive officers are not simple villains or heroes. They are not one-dimensional men. All are intelligent and a few are strikingly intellectual (Oreffice, Roderick). While some do hide from public view (notably Roderick and Smith), some, even in beleaguered industries and on sensitive topics, are outspoken to the point of bellicosity (Oreffice, McGowan, and Norris).

Though lush with compelling data, the book often rambles. Moreover, Nader never really answers his question: Do these men abuse power? Numerous vignettes, sprinkled throughout the profiles, hint that they do; as many anecdotes suggest they don't. The result is that the complexity of these men is revealed. But Nader's steadfast refusal to draw inferences ultimately frustrates his purpose. The nine profiles are presented back-to-back without analysis, other than a concluding paragraph at the end of each fifty- to eighty-page sketch. Even the introduction and conclusion to the book are skimpy.

In these few analytical lines, Nader's primary concern is not whether the chief executives abuse their power, but that they fail to use it toward the broad social ends Nader would like. He cites, for instance, Harold Willens, a southern California executive and author of *The Trimtab Factor,* for his support of anti-nuclear policies, and wonders why none of the chief executives he profiled took proactive positions about such vital public issues.

There are limitations to this line of argument. Nader restricts his analysis of the companies to their chief executives. He does not discuss corporate governance—in particular, the fast-changing relationship between CEOs and their boards of directors. In fact, in today's environment of increasing director liability, chief executives arguably have a much shorter leash than Nader infers. Boards have long been accused of existing only to rubber-stamp the decisions by the incumbent chief executive and preserve his power. This is much less the case today than in the past. But even to the extent that it is true, the board provides the rubber stamp only because it and the chief executive agree upon a relatively narrow agenda. I suspect that few boards would stand still for a CEO who became a pro-freeze activist, for instance, even though a modestly active civil rights posture might be admired. The thoughtful stance of James Burke of Johnson & Johnson in the case of two Tylenol tragedies is widely admired. On the other hand, one cannot forget the laughter of Jones's audience at the annual meeting; pro-nuke activism is apparently okay among southern Californian aerospace firms.

Among Nader's profiles, Norris is the only CEO who did appear blatantly to manipulate his board. However, CDC's performance has been so problematic in the last six years that signs of board restlessness have been widely evident. In fact, many analysts suggest that the recent and belated appointment of a Norris successor was done over his strenuous objection.

In some areas, these executives are not shy about the bald use of their power. Nader cites the strong opposition to Political Action Committees (PACs) of Irving Shapiro, former DuPont chairman and top Democratic businessman-advisor to the Carter administration. But the view of Oreffice is much more common: Oreffice loves PACs. Businesses' purchase of politicians via the PACs is an increasingly prominent—and questionable—feature in the political landscape.

In addition to PAC power, business is openly exercising a new-found power. In the face of regional transitions in the manufacturing sector, anything now goes in the name of saving jobs. Once again, problematic past performance leads to more power, not less—the power to decide where the shrunken job base will reside. And along the way, so much for airbags, and gas mileage, safety, and environmental standards. Public officials regularly make spectacles of themselves in relentless pursuit of new jobs. And businessmen have learned to play the game.

Though the business agenda is much narrower than Nader wishes, business activism is at an all-time high. As it should be. The stakes are awesome. The current tax code resulted in a negative 1 percent tax rate for the chemical industry, compared to 27 percent for pharmaceuticals and 26 percent for computers. Sadly, I feel, victories in Washington,

D.C., on even minor tax-code issues achieve the biggest return on a chief executive's investment of time. Lobbying will determine more of a CEO's legacy than whether or not his company's car or phone system or computer works effectively. McGowan of MCI, the closest to a Nader hero in this set of profiles, is an exemplar of the new priorities. The MCI founder, Jack Goecken, wished to create a company that provided innovative services; since his ouster by McGowan, for instance, he has become the founder of Airfone. McGowan's forte is very different: he is MCI's master of litigation and regulatory strategy.

Nader does not provide any framework to deal with how businesses ought to use the power they have—the power to create jobs, to capriciously shift jobs about, to shift industry focus, to affect the Washington agenda regarding the industry, to affect a broader social agenda. Vignettes on the use, abuse or shunning of power dot the book, but no systematic conclusions are reached.

Robert Reich, in *The Next American Frontier*, coined the phrase "paper entrepreneurship." He chronicled the growing tendency of managers to value manipulating paper over constructing quality products and delivering quality service. The paper entrepreneurs' game is the number-one business power game, and Nader chose to neglect it. Its cost, in terms of failure to attend to business basics, is huge. In addition, economists Barry Bluestone and Bennett Harrison, in *The De-industrialization of America*, estimate that 27 million people have been dislocated because of the heartland's economic trauma. How many of the uprootings could have been avoided by attention to business basics is, of course, not calculable. But Nader's failure to examine this abuse of power—the failure to use it in pursuit of sound products and services—is unfortunate.

Roderick's answer to steel's problems is to get out of steel as fast as he can. He steadfastly denies most of big steel's shortcomings. But it is a fact that there are highly profitable (more profitable than even IBM), fast-growing, and sizeable (billions of dollars) companies in the U.S. steel industry, such as Nucor Corporation, Chaparrell, and Worthington Industries. Thus there are steel strategies that would have worked, or at least would have lessened the agony of transition, which could have paralleled those Oreffice followed in the chemical industry. Why didn't Roderick follow them? Moreover, Nucor's (et al.) strategies are consistent with the emerging and clear-cut shape of American competitive winners—flatter, less flabby, closer to the customer, more flexible, more innovative, more service-oriented, and more quality-oriented.

General Motors still can't make cars that work, and virtually all of its models look alike. And it has not deigned to go after new market segments. The most profitable car company in the world is one of the smaller ones—BMW, which follows an equivalent strategy to that of the American winners in the steel race. Smith rests his claim to fame on more abstract notions—computerization of cars, factories, and car distribution systems (the Japanese won't move as fast as Smith does, because of their concerns with reliability) and some questionable acquisitions such as the $5 billion purchase of Hughes Aircraft. In fact, some say that Smith is after bigger game, with rumors up to and including giant American Express.

American business, especially its manufacturing core, desperately needs a new vision and a bold one—and quickly. What is it? I know what it is not. Nader approvingly explains that Norris of CDC "distinguishes the Control Data strategy from the traditional corporate approach to social responsibility, which he said emphasizes greater concern for employee welfare, product quality and participation. 'Social responsibility thus defined was an appropriate place to start 25 years ago. But it is not nearly good enough, because our society has been going downhill.'" Perhaps our society has been going downhill, but there is dubious merit to the argument that attributes the problem to businesses' failure to move beyond quality and worker participation. We are getting clobbered in more than 75 percent of our manufacturing businesses, from semiconductors to steel. And we are getting clobbered on the basis of quality and service. In turn, quality and service stems from emphasizing human rather than financial capital, and from wholesale worker participation and partnership. We can sadly say that we have not yet achieved success with the more limited agenda, regardless of the merits of the broader one.

And to listen to Nader's CEOs, we aren't even trying the limited agenda. It is so distressing to read page after page of commentary on Smith, Roderick, even Norris, and find no mention whatsoever of an altered view of working with people and the unions. (The unions, and Nader makes this abundantly clear, have no bold vision either.) A bit shines through in McGowan's case and with Oreffice. But even those two do not articulate a broader vision. This, clearly, is a distressing failure to use power that could be readily exercised within the confines of the most conservative board of directors imaginable. Few boards would fight decent product quality brought about through widespread employee involvement, though, tragically, few demand it.

My criticism of Nader is unfair in part. Nader's agenda is not mine. He ranges far beyond the commonplace business analysis as he probes business participation across a broad agenda. Above all, Nader has convincingly demonstrated that even a non-ally of business can write an incredibly detailed and thoughtful book about chief executive officers. Only Ken Auletta's study of Schlumberger's former CEO, the late Jean Riboud, in

The Art of Corporate Success, matches these Nader portraits. It's the kind of analysis that should be done. Big business performance is more vital than ever to America's social as well as economic performance. (And perhaps geopolitical, too, as transnational business activities increasingly dominate economic and political affairs.) The study of business leaders, especially in industries amid wrenching transition, has been shamefully limited. The only appropriate closing word about this Nader undertaking is: Bravo!

Acknowledgments

It would be impossible to list by name all of the persons who lightened the load during our work on this book. We would, however, like to cite the contributions of a handful of friends and colleagues. Jean Highland offered much-needed support and editorial guidance. John Greenya made substantial contributions to the chapter on David Roderick. James Musselman, Mike Westfall, and Clarence Ditlow provided welcome assistance on the Roger Smith chapter. Susan Smyser attended Northrop's 1984 annual meeting on our behalf. Karen Branan, Karen Lehman, and Randall Rothenberg offered their insights into the career of William Norris.

Julie Strawn and David Dana gathered many file drawers' worth of valuable data. Joseph Ryan and Kate Winton offered their hospitality to Andrew Moore during an extended research stay in Minneapolis, while Michelle Haueter was an equally gracious host in Los Angeles. The following individuals reviewed preliminary drafts of certain chapters: Gordon Adams, Ronald Brownstein, Don Clark, Joan Claybrook, Richard Gilmore, Robert McIntyre, Jack Metzgar, Jack Newfield, Philip Simon, Samuel Simon, Cathy Trost. While they all offered valuable insights and comments, responsibility for errors and omissions is ours alone.

Finally, we would like to recognize the very important role Andrew Moore played through out this project. Andy visited many cities, reviewed thousands of pages of documents, and conducted scores of interviews. His research was always as thorough as his documentation was meticulous.

Introduction

Wherever I go, people ask, "What is it like to take on General Motors or the steel industry or the chemical fraternity?" Seldom do they ask, "What is it like to face Roger Smith or David Roderick or Paul Oreffice?" If they did, the answer would have to be, "I don't know." For corporate leaders are as remote to their critics as they are anonymous to the general public. How many Americans can name the chief executive officer (CEO) of Exxon, Procter & Gamble, Du Pont, Sears, U.S. Steel, General Electric, Citibank, Metropolitan Life, General Mills, IBM, or Xerox? Some company bosses do crave the limelight—Lee Iacocca and Frank Perdue come to mind. But most of their colleagues yearn for anonymity or, at least, for a public profile that is modest and retiring. Most CEOs could write a book with the same title as the collection of essays by James Baldwin, *Nobody Knows My Name*.

It was not always this way. Around the turn of the century, many people recognized leading businessmen by name and discussed their latest doings and musings. J. P. Morgan, Andrew Carnegie, John D. Rockefeller, and Jay Gould did not enjoy the comforts of anonymity so relished by industrialists of the late twentieth century. In an age of instant, mass communications, Madison Avenue produces Morris the Cat, who is far better known than the leader of the company that manufactures the cat food. But there is one overriding similarity between today and 1900: These giant enterprises neither animate nor direct themselves; they are run by the men at the top, those distant executives whom blue-collar laborers and office workers alike refer to as "the big boys."

For years, as legislative and regulatory struggles raged over critical issues of health, safety, quality control, community relations, and the other dimensions of corporate accountability, I wondered about these business leaders. What were their thoughts about the course of the economy and society? What bureaucratic rot were they anxious to excise from their companies? Did they genuinely believe what they were telling Congress and the press about their inability to achieve or afford even modest advances in environmental and workplace health and in product safety? Why did they not make more creative use of their privileged positions to raise and address issues that fall outside the conventional parameters of business discourse?

The sources consulted offered few answers to these and other important questions. I would observe the rare CEO testifying before a congressional committee with a stiff demeanor. I read many features in the major business periodicals—profiles that dwelled relentlessly on short-term forecasts and the other predictable formulae of financial journalism. I also perused the limited company-generated literature on these executives that was available to the public: annual reports, transcripts of shareholder meetings, and documents filed with the Securities and Exchange Commission. Once in a while, a CEO would ask to meet me, or there would be a chance exchange at one of the formal correspondents' dinners in Washington. I eventually concluded that the culture of communication had given these men a decidedly one-dimensional image—to their flatterers, critics, and the media alike. CEOs and other leading corporate power brokers are viewed as the ultimate bottom-line functionaries whose careers are judged by that one, essential dollar yardstick. This was troubling, because such images are often reciprocated, as in a self-fulfilling prophecy. People tend to gravitate toward the standards by which they are judged.

It is certainly the case that the road to the top of a giant corporation can narrow as well as concentrate the mind. John Kenneth Galbraith has elaborated on the costs of these tight norms:

> The counterpart of the modern executive's disciplined commitment to the job at hand is an extremely severe sacrifice of the right to personal thought and expression. . . . What he says is required by the rule and ethics of organization to be both predictable and dull. He does not speak for himself; he speaks for the firm. Good policy is not what he wants but what the organization believes it needs. . . . Executive expression is ignored [by the public] because, by the nature of organization, it must be at an exceptionally tedious level of organization stereotype and caution.

What is, is not what has to be. I am not inclined to accept *a priori* the Galbraith description. The mere thought that the men running these vast business empires are simply organizational automatons invites objection. Galbraith may be right, but coals, too, can appear to be dormant until they are fanned.

A glimmer of what may be lurking beneath the platitudinous surface of the Organization Man emerged from a one-to-one television interview I conducted in 1980 with John Nevin, chairman of Firestone Tire & Rubber. His public insight and candor were close to astonishing. Here was a man who had worked as vice-president for marketing of Ford Motor Company, and then as chairman of Zenith, telling his audience that "Washington is probably more a scapegoat than it should be in American business"; that he thinks "most of the wounds that are suffered by American business . . . are self-inflicted"; and that he is glad that the auto, tire-safety, and job-safety laws are on the books.

Nevin also commented that manufacturers are far behind department stores in how they treat their customers and that it is "absolute nonsense" to blame workers for product defects. "There is no major [product] recall, or no major product defect, that I can recall in the last ten years of American business history, that could be blamed on American workers," he explained. The Firestone 500 radial tire "was a design error. It was a management error. The men and women who worked in the plants that put that tire together did their job exactly the way they were told to do it."

The Nevin interview intensified my interest in developing a more extensive focus on residents of the executive suite, whose thoughts and judgments appear so camouflaged by patinas of programmed expression. There were some obvious barriers to overcome. I was not the most likely candidate to get access to corporate leaders and their associates. Moreover, these years are quite turbulent for American business. Unthinkably huge deficits in the federal budget and foreign trade, a roaring merger and takeover wave, bank failures and business bailouts, the perils of deregulatory adjustment, military-contract scandals, public outrage over toxic-waste hazards, and upheavals in company-union and company-community relations do not create an inviting atmosphere for searching interviews. Nonetheless, with my coauthor, William Taylor, and researcher, Andrew Moore, I embarked on the journey.

We examined the beliefs and careers of business executives with reference to several criteria. Executives were selected from companies operating in vital sectors of the economy—from automobile production to agriculture to Wall Street. We wanted a measure of regional diversity; our subjects direct enterprises headquartered in Pittsburgh, Los Angeles, New York, Detroit, Minneapolis, Washington, D.C., and Midland, Michigan. Another criterion was diversity of individual history and mission. We wanted to probe the motivational and operational distinctions between company men, entrepreneurs, and executives who move outside the conventional corporate structure. We also approached prominent figures on the business scene—including Firestone's Nevin, who consented to another long interview, and Mesa Petroleum chairman T. Boone Pickens, neither of whom was finally included as a profile subject. These individuals elaborated on themes developed in the various chapters and offered fresh insights on executive behavior.

We typically made contact with our subjects by writing a long letter that described the book, the reasons we wished to interview them, and the issues we wanted to discuss. Reactions to our letters and follow-up approaches varied widely. General Motors chairman Roger Smith was a closed door from the beginning, and he remained one despite what even his associates in the public-relations department must concede were our heroic attempts at gaining access. We tried everything short of renting the Goodyear blimp to pass his office with a banner invitation. At one point we telephoned Keith Crain, publisher and editorial director of the influential *Automotive News,* who acknowledged that Smith should talk to us. He also agreed to relay his opinion to Smith. Crain later reported that the GM chairman had said he "did not trust" us. Sometime after that Smith-Crain conversation, the GM leader received a public letter from me criticizing GM for its campaign to roll back property-tax assessments on its factories in several Michigan communities. "Now do you see why I don't trust him?" Smith told Crain when they next met. Ultimately, William Taylor traveled to Detroit for GM's 1985 annual meeting and posed questions from the floor to the reluctant chairman.

David Roderick was also a steely predicament for us. Everyone in the Pittsburgh media with whom we spoke lamented the U.S. Steel chairman's reluctance to grant individual interviews, as opposed to fielding questions at company press conferences. Telephone calls to his office and his Washington representatives produced no change in his position. Then came a breakthrough—after we informed U.S. Steel that we had completed a draft chapter despite the chairman's refusal to cooperate. Roderick granted two long interviews in his office high over Pittsburgh, followed by a final telephone conversation. He proved to be clear and perceptive, but he banned any interviews with his company colleagues.

Not all of our executive communications were so involved. Prompted by his iconoclastic reputation, I asked an associate to dial William McGowan's number at MCI Communications. The chairman answered the telephone himself. "Will you take a call from Ralph Nader?" my associate asked. "Why not?" McGowan quipped. "I took one from you." Soon thereafter came the first of four conversations that totaled more than ten hours. Dow Chemical president Paul Oreffice placed a call to us just seven days after we mailed off our interview request. He agreed to a personal interview in his Midland office and participated in a second conversation during a trip to Washington.

We considered including a number of other business leaders before arriving at the final nine. Aetna Life & Casualty chairman John Filer, whose study on philanthropy attracted attention in the 1970s, immediately rejected our interview request. Filer was still smarting from what he considered unfair editing of an interview with NBC correspondent Chris Wallace, who anchored an April 1982 documentary on the insurance industry, "Protection for Sale." After much prodding, however, Filer agreed to reconsider—if we agreed to a strict set of conditions for the interview. Negotiations reached an impasse when he insisted upon reviewing the chapter about him before publication. This impasse soon became moot. In August 1984, Filer startled the insurance world by announcing his early retirement, a decision that most analysts attributed to Aetna's troubled financial performance during the 1980s.

More amusing than our fruitless talks with Filer were our brief encounters with John Welch, the young chairman of General Electric. Welch demurred at our interview request when he was approached in March 1984. He argued that he had a "short tenure as CEO"—he had assumed the helm at GE three years earlier—although he did give us a rain check. In a telephone call to him several months later, I received a more animated reaction. I was making a final entreaty for an interview when suddenly Welch's voice changed to a mixture of rapid pleading and a "lemme outta here" tone. "I don't need this," he cried. "I'm just a boy with knickers and a lollipop. I don't want to be part of a book. I'm just a grungy, lousy manager. . . . You can have access to the company on any other basis. . . . I don't want a high profile. . . . I'm just a grunt. . . . I'm just a man in a room." No combination of written words could capture the wonderfully off-the-cuff, ingenuous voice of this supercharged general of GE.

Throughout preparation of the book, William Norris remained in office at Control Data. His comments, and comments about him, reflect his active status. He announced his retirement early in 1986 and was replaced by Robert M. Price. In the eighteen months since the book was first published, there have been important developments in the lives and careers of two other profile subjects. William McGowan suffered a serious heart attack in December 1986, and underwent heart transplant surgery the following April. Although he remains chairman and chief executive of MCI Communications, and reports indicate that his recovery is proceeding, it is uncertain whether he will return to active duty. Dow Chemical president Paul Oreffice has announced that he will step down as CEO in December 1987, in keeping with the company's policy that no chief executive can hold the office past age sixty. Oreffice will remain chairman of the board, and a major presence at the company.

The chapters on McGowan and Oreffice, as well as the remaining profile subjects, have not been revised to reflect these and other recent developments. Our analysis of these executives is intended to describe the use and ongoing impact of power acquired over long careers. Individual events—whether an impending retirement, a major acquisition or divestiture, a temporary increase or decrease in company profits—have not altered their leadership visions and patterns of conduct developed and deployed over decades. The book's concluding chapter reflects on the implications of recent developments involving several of the profile subjects.

. . .

Our studies of these executives are not designed to produce results as if they were a scientifically representative sample of powerful businessmen. This is not a book of quantitative findings; it is a look at nine men of power who are important in their own domains, each analyzed in the context of the company and industry of which he is an integral part. Our interest is to broaden the public appraisal of their personalities, policies, and business judgments by sharpening the focus on the complexity of their work and deployment of their power. Books are written on politicians far less important than major executives. If we can encourage reporters to look upon businessmen as denizens of a *terra incognita* in need of extensive exploration and evaluation, this effort will have succeeded in its initial purpose.

When corporate leaders express their views on subjects they are rarely, if ever, asked about, the public dialogue is enriched and the influence they wield becomes more public. Breaking their mutual codes of silence regarding other persons of power (stay out of my backyard and I'll stay out of yours) can only be healthy for a democracy. Abuses of authority can come from not using one's power—as in holding back criticism of the president or ignoring the broad public debate over the arms race—as well as from the affirmative application of influence. In our conversations with these executives, we elicited their views on traditional business matters. But we also pressed them on conditions and issues quite removed from their daily work habits. What are the most pressing social problems in the United States? Do they favor a verifiable freeze on production and testing of nuclear weapons? How do they evaluate the quality of the business press? How do they explain the explosion of reports on waste in the defense industry and misconduct by large corporations in civilian areas?

We think it fair to say that our interview subjects enjoyed these meetings, if only because the questions were not as narrow and predictable as the inquiries they are used to fielding. Their replies often indicated that they had given some thought to these subjects, but were surprised to be asked about them. We were sometimes surprised by what they said. U.S. Steel's Roderick offered detailed criticisms of irresponsible lending to the Third World by major commercial bankers. He also wondered whether most bankers had learned their lesson, given various bailout proposals being floated on Capitol Hill. Control Data chairman William Norris told us he would be willing to sell all but the most advanced weapons to the Soviet Union. MCI's McGowan said he favored decriminalizing heroin and distributing it free to current addicts. The list of unconventional observations goes on and on.

Throughout these chapters—including the chapters on Northrop chairman Thomas Jones, GM's Smith, and Cargill chairman Whitney MacMillan, all of whom refused to grant interviews—we made it a point to give our subjects their say directly. In the case of the three CEOs who declined interviews, we relied on their public speeches, occasional press-conference transcripts, and their published articles and essays. In poring through hundreds of speeches by our nine subjects, we could sympathize with the description of this category of literature by the nameless hero in George Lee Walker's recent novel *The Chronicles of Doodah*—a satirical story about the travails of a megacorporate speechwriter. Explaining his task to a company seductress, he says,

> Well, all the speeches are about the same length, twenty to thirty-five minutes. They cover pretty much the same ground, too —economic forecasts, the state of the industry, a description of the Company's activities, and so forth. You don't read much about them in the newspapers or hear them on television because—to be quite frank—they rarely say anything worth reporting. Oh, once in a while there will be an announcement of a plant expansion or a new product, and that kind of thing will get into the newspaper. But for the most part, these speeches are dead the moment they are given. The fact is, they're dead even before they are given.

However, taken together over a span of many years, these speeches, albeit mostly ghostwritten, begin to reflect an executive's mind-set, his sense of limits, humor, candor, flattery, and priorities. Once in a while, if you mine them carefully, you find tiny grains of gold or at least of silver lining the lode of humdrum. One obtains a sense of how an executive handles his responsibilities to various external constituencies and how he treats the concerns of the day, whether government regulation, union relations, foreign competition, corporate subsidies, or controversial economic policies. In choosing to profile executives who did not cooperate, we wish to demonstrate, however modestly, what can be gleaned about business leaders from third-party interviews and written sources.

These are all men with power. But each of our subjects has his own distinctive *style* of power in using the authority, networks, and leverage afforded him by his company, his industry, and his character. For David Roderick, it is the power to deny that accrues to giant companies whose principal product is on the decline, supplemented by the nonnegotiating style that derives from Roderick's personality and financial background. For Roger Smith, the dynamic reactionary, it is the power of an unleashed CEO riding a resurgent sales curve to block, break, or co-opt the countervailing forces of labor, government, and competitors. Paul Oreffice reflects the impact of the single-minded corporate ideologue. Felix Rohatyn, the investment banker, and Charls Walker, the Washington lobbyist, refine, direct, and steer the inherent power of their clients to entrench their clients' standing even further; theirs is the derivative power of corporate intermediaries. Cargill's MacMillan wields the unique background power of a giant privately held corporation, shielded from many of the forms of accountability and disclosure required of publicly held enterprises. Thomas Jones demonstrates the power of persistence and resiliency—of personally being there again and again when it counts. William McGowan and William Norris are entrepreneurs and company founders whose reach extends beyond that of their relatively modest firms.

Writing about nine very different men of position and influence in our political economy demands more than patience. By and large, we were not dealing with publicity-seekers. Nor were we able to tap deep reservoirs of scholarship and journalism on these men or their colleagues in the business world. We chose to view their careers much as one views a large jigsaw puzzle—a challenge in finding and piecing together a wide variety of oral and documentary sources into a coherent appraisal of their thoughts and actions. We conducted a thorough search of primary and secondary materials, including speeches, court records, congressional hearings, corporate reports, and regulatory-agency files. Through requests under that essential Freedom of Information Act we obtained correspondence with government officials and pertinent memoranda. We logged thousands of miles visiting corporate headquarters, touring plants and communities, and attending annual meetings.

By far the best leads and insights came from interviews with the colleagues, subordinates, competitors, and critics of these executives. We spoke with over 650 people for this book. There were several hundred individuals whom we approached, but who refused to be interviewed. As any probing business reporter knows, there are, regrettably, still more incentives for keeping mum than for contributing to the flow of public information about decision-makers in the upper reaches of big business. But we were pleasantly surprised on more than one occasion by the willingness of individuals with no axes to grind to speak forthrightly.

Our interviews with most of the principals of this book found them predictably guarded at first. But as the first, second, and, in some cases, third interviews unfolded, they became more relaxed and were more forthcoming. Still, there was no illusion that we were coming ever closer to eliciting their real business confessions. We did develop a more precise appreciation, though, of one central truth that all reporters, scholars, and publishers ought to keep in mind: Beneath the tip of the iceberg that business executives reveal of themselves, there are stories, revelations, opinions, and desires that would make front-page news every day of the year. Like capped oil wells in a time of gasoline scarcity, these valuable raw materials warrant more searching inquiry by both the media and independent researchers, for there is much that everybody needs to learn about the workings and lurchings of our gigantic economy.

RALPH NADER
August 1987

THE
BIG
BOYS

DAVID RODERICK

Ice Ingot

On November 10, 1983, in a major address before the National Press Club, David Roderick, chairman of United States Steel Corporation, announced that "contrary to rumors" he did not intend to abandon the company's South Works complex in Chicago. His assurances were meant as an upbeat conclusion to an otherwise stern and sobering presentation. Roderick disclosed that U.S. Steel was filing suits charging unfair trading by state-owned steel producers in Argentina, Brazil, and Mexico. He endorsed legislation introduced that same day by the Congressional Steel Caucus to impose a five-year quota that would limit foreign steel shipments to the United States to 15 percent of the domestic market. And he warned of the escalating threat to his industry posed by imported steel from the Third World.

"It's said that every developing nation wants its own steel industry and its own airline—even if it's only one mill and one plane—and even if they suffer losses *ad infinitum*," Roderick noted with visible disapproval. "They seemingly serve the purpose of national identity. And all the while some of us in the steel industry thought a flag and a national anthem could serve that purpose, with much less anguish for everyone."

South Works, a sprawl of blast furnaces, basic oxygen furnaces, and finishing mills extending for two miles along Lake Michigan on Chicago's South Side, was once the crown jewel of one of the world's great steelmaking centers. Tens of thousands of Swedes, Poles, Germans, and Hungarians flocked to South Chicago and built their homes in the shadows of the giant plant. Its original blast furnaces and steelmaking facilities were installed in 1881, two decades before the formation of U.S. Steel itself. The mills supported a way of life that was as stable and important as it was grimy and dangerous. At the height of World War II, South Works employed 16,000 people. Since then, like the rest of the industry, it has experienced a steady erosion in the market for its products, the condition

3

of its equipment, and the size of its workforce. By the late 1970s, employ-ment had been slashed to 6,000. Roughly 1,100 workers were on the job when Roderick delivered his Press Club remarks.

But South Works was poised for a modest comeback. U.S. Steel had issued a challenge in April 1981. The company announced that it was prepared to invest hundreds of millions of dollars—the ultimate figure was $225 million—to modernize three electric furnaces and build an advanced mill to manufacture train rails if unionized employees and Illinois public officials met three conditions. First, members of United Steelworkers Local 65, an institution with a militant tradition that once ranked among the largest locals of any union in the country, would have to ratify a concession package that relaxed work rules at the rail mill. The member-ship approved the agreement in August 1982 by a vote of 1,795 to 305. Second, the Illinois legislature would have to abolish a 7 percent excise tax on rails shipped from the state. That transpired in September 1982, and Roderick flew in for the signing ceremony. Finally, regulators would have to be persuaded to stretch out the costs of a water pollution accord signed by U.S. Steel several years earlier; they were.

The 1977 consent decree, under which the company paid a $4 million fine because of its failure to meet previous cleanup deadlines, actually applied to the massive U.S. Steel complex in nearby Gary, Indiana. U.S. Steel agreed to spend $70 million to reduce hazardous emissions from the Gary Works, which pumps ammonia and cyanide, among other toxic chemicals, into Lake Michigan and the Grand Calumet River. Production at South Works and Gary had been coordinated since 1982. Illinois attorney general Neil Hartigan proposed that the state create a Jobs Trust Fund to allow U.S. Steel to invest $33 million in South Works that it had earmarked to meet the terms of the pollution-control agreement at Gary.

The Hartigan plan was unveiled in the summer of 1983. All the pieces were in place for a modest renaissance in a region whose residents were accustomed to grim economic news. A modernized South Works would produce a million tons of raw steel each year. That steel would be proc-essed into structural beams at an existing mill or into train rails at the new mill. South Chicago was about to reclaim a portion of its heritage as a thriving source of steel for the Midwest.

Or so it seemed. Members of the luncheon audience unfamiliar with the intricate maneuvering around the plant might not have appreciated the gray lining in the billowy cloud of optimism in Roderick's November pledge. "We intend, subject to the full cooperation of labor and local, state and federal governments, to proceed with construction of a rail mill there," he had said. "The feasibility study is continuing, and we are hopeful that we will be able to put together the necessary elements to make South Works competitive once again. It will be smaller, but with the addition of the rail mill we can save jobs, turn a loss operation into a profitable one, and keep South Works as a vital part of the economy of Chicago and Illinois."

Roderick's talk of "full cooperation" from labor was an oblique reference to the fact that U.S. Steel in the fall of 1983 had gone to Local 65 and demanded another set of concessions. These new demands applied not to the rail mill but to the remaining facilities at South Works. Management insisted on unprecedented autonomy to contract out a range of union jobs—cleaning, bricklaying, trucking, pipefitting, mobile equipment repair, and others—to independent companies. It demanded the right to work employees ten hours a day and on Sundays and to limit wage premiums. This grueling schedule would allow U.S. Steel to use cheap electricity available late at night and on weekends. It also proposed limits on incentive pay and the immediate resolution of outstanding grievances.

The new demands tested the patience of Local 65. Not only did they follow upon the heels of the August 1982 agreement, but the United Steelworkers of America (USWA) had already ratified a national concession package in March 1983. That contract, which of course applied to South Works, slashed union wages by $1.25 an hour, scaled back cost-of-living allowances, and eliminated one week of paid vacation for most workers. It represented an unprecedented sacrifice by a union whose members were accustomed to steady wage and benefit improvements.

"The company wanted complete jurisdiction to contract out at will without allowing the union to file grievances," complained Michael Ally, chairman of the Local 65 grievance committee. "They wanted any pending grievances to be withdrawn. The only reason they came back to us was that they wanted to blame the union for why the rail mill didn't go. They were not naive enough to believe we would ever go along." Ally and his colleagues calculated that the new concessions could eliminate as many jobs as the rail mill created. On December 21, 1983, the leadership of Local 65 officially rejected the company's demands. U.S. Steel announced on December 27 that it was canceling plans for rail production and would abandon most of its other facilities at South Works. The decision meant permanent termination for 3,100 workers, 300 of whom were still on the job. Roderick's soothing words of seven weeks earlier became another agonizing footnote in the history of the demise of South Chicago.

Joseph Cardinal Bernardin, the archbishop of Chicago and one of the most eminent Catholic leaders in the country, sent a letter to the U.S. Steel chairman on January 18, 1984. "The [South Chicago] area is made up predominantly of stable and industrious working-class families whose very livelihood is now in serious jeopardy," he wrote. "Because of the state of our economy, the steelworkers who would lose their jobs might find themselves permanently unemployed. The entire community would suffer grievously with the closing of this plant." Bernardin suggested that Roderick form "a coalition of government officials, politicians, union officers, and community leaders, as well as representatives of the churches and synagogues" to explore strategies to maintain production at South Works or develop alternative uses for the equipment.

Roderick responded two weeks later. His letter complained about the "confusion and misunderstanding" surrounding the shutdown. He fixed responsibility for the closing squarely on the shoulders of Local 65. Roderick did not respond to Bernardin's proposal to form a coalition or to his offer of a meeting to discuss the future of South Works. Several months later, the U.S. Steel chairman traveled to Dearborn, Michigan, to address the second National Conference on the Dislocated Worker. Reporters asked about his response to the cardinal's pleas. (Roderick's letter had not been made public.) He praised Bernardin and mentioned that the religious leader had asked him, "Why can't we keep [South Works] going longer even though we might suffer some minor losses? Well, we kept it going for $324 million in losses. We are not a welfare agency. In a corporation, the surest way to destroy jobs for everybody is to sit there and try to operate something that in effect is not competitive in the marketplace."

Cardinal Bernardin issued a terse response. "I regret the decision [to close the plant] and regret, too, that no effort was made to form the coalition that I had recommended," he said. "No one ever suggested that a business should be run as a welfare agency. However, businesses too must be concerned about the well-being of their employees. I still hope that attempts will be made to find alternative uses for the productive facilities at U.S. Steel's South Works."

.   .   .

David Milton Roderick, a former schoolboy boxer and marine, has spent more than three decades as a loyal employee of the most powerful institution in Pittsburgh, Pennsylvania, the city of his birth. He turned sixty-one on May 3, 1985. Roderick is short, somewhere in between stocky and portly, and when seen or photographed from the front appears to be totally bald, which he is not. He wore a tan summer suit with a bright yellow tie to our first conversation. Roderick generally favors dark no-comment suits, white shirts, and dark striped ties. He is said to have a sense of humor, which did surface briefly during our interviews.

Does U.S. Steel have acquisition designs on cereal giant Kellogg—a rumor that has been given wide circulation in Pittsburgh? "I can absolutely assure you that we never seriously in any way, shape, or form considered buying Kellogg," he replied. "That is a story that persists. And it persists enough that one time I had our people send Kellogg a message to assure them that we were not, as Jimmy Carter said, lusting for them."

The most distinctive feature of the Roderick character and personality is the sense of iron discipline he communicates. He said his years as a marine during World War II were a watershed in his personal development. Roderick served as a platoon sergeant in the Fifth Amphibious Corps of the Fourth Marine Division and saw action at Midway and Iwo Jima. He was not on the front lines in the battles for control of these islands. He would land several days after a beachhead was established, to take prisoners and maintain order in the American camps. "There is no question about it," he told us. "It is probably different for different people. But that discipline at that stage of my life turned out to be a very good thing for Dave Roderick."

The U.S. Steel chairman has a strong voice, and, unless angry, he speaks slowly and deliberately. There is an uncanny precision to his speech. The rigorous grammar of his sentences is matched only by the economy of their construction. Not a word is wasted when Roderick answers a question. He began our first conversation with an unsolicited oath of veracity. "We will answer any questions that you have to the best of our ability," he declared as we turned on the tape recorder. "That may be good, or it may not be good, but at least it will be the best that we can do." He grew noticeably less stiff as the interview wore on. But he was seldom lighthearted or jocular—even when his questioners raised subjects that might be considered suitable for such treatment.

The 1942 yearbook of Oliver High School portrays a David Roderick almost unrecognizable today. He was a thin-faced youth with a high, sweeping pompadour. Young Roderick was a member of the Go-To-College Club and the Etiquette Club. It was reported that he "disliked snobs and two-faced women." His favorite celebrities were Bob Hope and Glenn Miller. The vital statistics in Roderick's yearbook entry also include a slogan meant to describe his ethos as a student: "Livin', lovin', laughin'." Surprised by this information, we asked the chairman about his boyhood days.

"I was very active in high school and I always enjoyed it," he said. "Maybe one of my problems in high school was that I enjoyed it too much. I had a great time. . . . I really looked forward to going each day. . . . And I think that 'livin', lovin', laughin' ' was the way I felt about a lot of things at the time. However, I came out in June 1942, and by that fall I was in the Marine Corps. After three years, that 'livin', lovin', laughin' was long gone." Was the U.S. Steel chairman a studious lad? "No," he replied. "I was probably a C-plus to a B student in high school. I never took homework home. I don't think in the four years I went to high school, I ever brought a piece of homework home. Whatever had to be done, I just did in a study period because I was too busy enjoying myself."

The carefree days at Oliver High are indeed long gone. David Roderick is a tough and resolute corporate leader—a disposition underscored by his actions at South Works. But his no-nonsense demeanor should not obscure the depth of his intellect. Roderick reads widely and makes it a point to stay abreast of the business literature. "I read the *Wall Street Journal*, the *New York Times*, the *Pittsburgh Press*, and the *Pittsburgh Post-Gazette*," he told us. "I read most of the national [business] publications, although I don't say, 'I have to read *Business Week.*' I'll be on the [corporate] aircraft this afternoon. We keep the latest publications on there, and I will read those publications."

His nonbusiness reading is devoted primarily to what he calls historical novels. Roderick is a devoted fan of James Michener and has read all of his books. "I can read Michener till the cows come home," he told us. "Even though the first hundred pages usually can be quite boring." He also enjoys memoirs by politicians and diplomats who have recently left office. "I've read Haig's book," Roderick said. "I've read Cy Vance's book. There is a history to them. They have something you can identify with. I mean, when Haig was secretary of state, you recognize the events [he is writing about] and how they evolved."

Our conversations with the U.S. Steel chairman, which extended for six hours over three sessions, were not restricted to the fortunes of his company or the future of his industry. Roderick was at ease with a wide range of topics: the Soviet Union and the nuclear arms race, the future of organized labor, even abortion and the return of a peacetime draft. It would be an overstatement to suggest that he demonstrated much imagination or curiosity. He simply answered the questions he was asked. But Roderick did not hesitate to criticize other segments of the business community, an exercise in candor that most chief executives prefer to avoid. He came down hard on New York commercial bankers and the wisdom of many of their loans to the Third World. He argued that borrowers such as Brazil, whose foreign debt in 1985 approached $100 billion, are not subjected to the same rigorous tests of creditworthiness that U.S. borrowers must endure.

"Part of the problem with Brazil repaying its [foreign] debt is that part of the principal on which they are paying went to build steel plants that are clearly uneconomic," he told us. "I think that with a lot of these loans bankers weren't acting as bankers. They were shuffling money rather than acting in a responsible way. These loans are not just bad today. They were bad when they were made."

Roderick made specific reference to a massive iron ore project in the Brazilian Amazon. U.S. Steel controlled 49 percent of the development, which is situated in the Carajas region, until it sold its interest in 1977. Carajas reportedly contains the world's richest deposits of high-quality iron. Roderick complained that New York banks continued to pour money into the Brazilian venture even after U.S. Steel demonstrated that the project was uneconomic. What explains such imprudent behavior?

"Let's face it," he said. "There were very high interest rates, very attractive, and it was a good way [for banks] to grow very rapidly. Everybody with an MBA from Harvard was running down to Brazil to throw money at them. . . . I think it was crazy. And I don't think the American taxpayer should be called on to pay for what was clearly bad judgment [by commercial lenders]."

The U.S. Steel chairman also spoke openly about the business press, which he gave "pretty high marks" for overall quality and fairness. But he did offer two criticisms. He complained about reporters who insist on interviews with high-ranking corporate officials even though they don't need the information to write their stories. "We have had this happen a number of times," Roderick said. "People have written an article, and our suspicion is that they can't get it printed unless they get an interview with the chief executive. They come in wanting an interview and take one or two hours of your time, the article comes out, and there is nothing in the article from the interview. There is some theme that clearly was preconceived that [the reporter] couldn't get by his editor without an interview. That's the type of thing that irritates."

Roderick also expressed frustration with sloppy reporting. "They just too often make tremendous factual errors where just a check, a phone check, [would correct them]," he told us. "Not even giving the person a sense of the article, but [just saying], 'Here are thirty facts that are going to be in my article; are these facts accurate?' We would be very happy to say yes they are or no they aren't. Because they're facts. . . . We have seen articles about our company in major publications, where within the course of the article they have ten or fifteen absolutely factual errors. Not in a book. I'm talking about maybe two columns in the *Wall Street Journal*. Now that's what bothers us."

What has been his worst experience with the business press? "Again, I would have to say it is inaccuracies," Roderick replied. "And I would have to say the biggest have tended to be in the *New York Times*. There have been a number of articles there that just plain have not been factually correct. And I think they are therefore damaging to our company, damaging to our shareholders, and to an extent damaging to our employees."

Roderick cited a lengthy article that appeared two weeks before our second conversation as an example of journalistic carelessness. In September 1984, the *Times* examined the crisis of the domestic steel industry and described a decision by the Reagan administration to negotiate "voluntary" quotas with foreign steel producers. The article contained at least two unambiguous errors. It recalled the outrage of government officials and union leaders when U.S. Steel spent $6 billion to acquire Marathon Oil "after it got concessions on labor costs, environmental controls and imports." But the United Steelworkers did not approve wage concessions until March 1983—one year *after* the Marathon deal was finalized. It also reported that "many steel companies, particularly U.S. Steel and LTV's Jones & Laughlin, already import [semifinished] slabs" from abroad for finishing and sale in the United States. Although U.S. Steel did participate in controversial negotiations with the British about striking such a deal, those talks fell through months before the Reagan plan was announced. U.S. Steel had not imported any foreign slabs.

"I don't think it's malicious," Roderick said of the mistakes. "I think it's human error. I think it's the pressure of time. I think it sometimes is a preconceived position that the facts don't support, so therefore, you know, you don't try to dedicate yourselves too much to checking the facts. For example, if it helps the story to say that we negotiated concessions with the union and then went out and bought Marathon, which indicates a double cross, it's convenient to say that's the way it was. Even though that wasn't the way it was. But that's not convenient. That doesn't go into the tone of the article."

These and other errors in the *Times* piece were so "glaring" that U.S. Steel felt compelled to write executive editor A. M. Rosenthal. "We put [the letter] in with the idea that we would get a correction," Roderick told us. "But instead we got a phone call. So I don't think we'll ever see the correction. I think it would be too embarrassing because it was just so damn inaccurate." The *Times* did publish an abridged version of the letter, which was signed by Donald Clay, general manager of public affairs at U.S. Steel, twelve days after our conversation. It ran less than 100 words of a 527-word letter.

These matter-of-fact criticisms of the banking establishment and the business press are compatible with Roderick's style of corporate management. He approaches his job, and the protest and hostility he has inspired, with a single-minded resolve that does not leave room for second-guessing or self-censorship. Roderick has no stomach for judicious understatement. An aide to a Pennsylvania congressman who has clashed with U.S. Steel described his perception of the chairman's personality. "Roderick is a real hard-ass, hard-boiled kind of guy," he said. "He hurries toward controversy. He is the type of guy who is real aggressive, out front, not timid in any way. And he has antagonized a lot of the steel industry."

We asked the chairman whether the intellectual and emotional demands of leading a corporation as troubled as U.S. Steel had affected his health. He seemed to relish the question. "I can't really say I feel that at all," Roderick assured us. "I started working when I was seventeen years old. I am now sixty. And I think during that period of time I have missed three days of work, including a three-and-a-half-year stint in the Marine Corps. I started today at five o'clock in the morning. I had a driver pick me up at a quarter to six and I am here by seven. I'll probably get home tonight at about nine or ten." His day at the office began with a meeting at 7:15 A.M. with vice-chairman Thomas Graham. It included a flight to New York for a political strategy session with other chief executives.

.   .   .

David Roderick became chairman of U.S. Steel on April 24, 1979. The corporation, and the industry with which it is synonymous, have not been the same since. Roderick assumed command shortly before he turned fifty-five. He plans to remain as chief executive until age sixty-five—longer than all but three past chairmen of a corporation that took shape in 1901 as the world's first billion-dollar enterprise. Roderick is also one of the few chairmen to have climbed to the top at U.S. Steel by scaling the financial bureaucracy. Edgar Speer, his immediate predecessor, learned his trade by working in the mills. He was not even a college graduate. Edwin Gott, Speer's predecessor, was an engineer trained at Lehigh University. He did time at Clairton Works, outside of Pittsburgh; Gary Works, on Lake Michigan; and Youngstown Works, in northeastern Ohio. Gott was named chairman in February 1969 and retired four years later.

The man who today runs the nation's largest steel producer has not spent one day as general manager of a steel mill or superintendent of an open hearth. Roderick joined U.S. Steel in 1953 when he signed on as an accountant with two of its railroad subsidiaries. His first appointment with the parent corporation came in 1959, when he was named assistant to the director of statistics. This rather unglamorous job had definite benefits for Roderick's future advancement. His responsibilities included collecting information for the annual report and gathering data for meetings of the board of directors. Both assignments required that the young executive work closely with members of the U.S. Steel finance committee and the chairman of the board. Roderick was transferred to Paris in 1962 as an accounting consultant for international operations. He also worked on-site with construction crews that were building a manganese mine and railroad in central Africa. The mine is located in Gabon, a small country on the Atlantic coast. U.S. Steel still controls 36 percent of the corporation that mines the ore.

It is difficult to picture today's David Roderick—proper, serious, at home with the comforts of life at the top—navigating the jungles of Africa. But his performance in Gabon was an important chapter in his climb to the top. We asked about his work on the mine. "They were interesting days, and I did spend a great deal of time there," Roderick said. "This was during the de Gaulle period, when the [French colonists] from Algeria were trying to assassinate him. So there was some political instability in places like Algeria and certainly in France itself. They were exciting days. You really learned that life in Africa was still pretty basic. It didn't unduly impress me one way or the other, because I had seen some of that same standard of living on the [Pacific] islands during the war. So it didn't come as any great shock to me that things were still as backward as they were. The areas were very remote. Transportation was by roads that you built yourself. There was no communication other than radio."

Did Roderick indulge his fancy for hunting? "No," he replied. "I had the offer, but when I was in Africa, I was always so busy trying to get the operation turned on that I just never wanted to take two or three or four days to get out to one of the good locations. You can get awfully remote when you get down there. I remember when my wife was living in Paris with the kids and I was in Africa. I came home, one time, after about three weeks. My wife said, 'I was getting worried. I didn't know whether you would be able to get home.' I said, 'Why were you worried? I told you I would be home in three weeks.' She said, 'I thought the war might interfere.'" Here the chairman laughed. "I said, 'What war?'" The war in question was the 1967 Arab-Israeli conflict.

Roderick made it back to Pittsburgh when he was named vice-president for international accounting. His ascent to the executive suite was underway. He was named chairman of the finance committee, the third most powerful job in the corporation, in 1973. He was elected president in August 1975 and chairman less than four years later.

This unusual road to power has produced in Roderick a leadership style that most of his predecessors would not recognize. He does not consider himself a hands-on "steelman." He has surrounded himself with three vice-chairmen—U.S. Steel has no president—who supervise day-to-day operations at the company. Thomas Graham, whom Roderick persuaded to leave Jones & Laughlin in 1983, is vice-chairman for steel and related resources. Harold Hoopman, who was president of Marathon before the 1982 acquisition, stayed on to run the oil business. W. Bruce Thomas, a Roderick loyalist who has worked for U.S. Steel since 1952, is vice-chairman for administration and chief financial officer. David Roderick plays the role of grand strategist. He is an asset deployer. He is a dealmaker. He is a political tactician who does not shrink from rough-and-tumble lobbying or media controversy.

"I have no interest in going over to Marathon and telling them which well they should drill next," he explained. "That is their job. The same with Tom Graham. I am not going to tell him which blast furnace he should take off and which one he should leave on. I'm not interested in that. Now, that's a change. . . . When I was president, our chairman was still interested in which blast furnace you would take on and which one you would take off. He wanted to be part of that decision because he was a general superintendent at one time. That's a natural thing. [Plant operators] want to be part of the process because they were part of it at one time. My philosophy is substantially different."

The chairman's background has also contributed to the radical strategic departures he has engineered at U.S. Steel. Roderick has closed mills that his predecessors struggled to save. He has shed product lines to which others were committed. He has sold assets and businesses that Speer and Gott were content to maintain.

Staughton Lynd, the prominent labor historian and attorney, has faced off against Roderick in litigation. He argued that Roderick's policies as chairman can only be understood with reference to his path to power. "The critical thing to remember is that Roderick's background in the corporation is on the money side, not the steel side, and that he is the first CEO to be essentially an accountant," Lynd told us. "He hired two steelmen—Bill Roesch"—who served as president until he retired in September 1983—"and Tom Graham—and Roderick sees himself as a financial overseer. If you have a steel executive who is sentimentally attached to a mill where he worked, and replace him with someone who couldn't care less, it might appear to management that there could be some advantages in the short run to closing plants."

David Roderick bristled at the suggestion that his strategies and management style are rooted in his background as a bean counter. He even took exception to the idea that he has spent most of his career as an accountant. "Do you manage differently with a financial background as opposed to an operating, engineering background?" Roderick asked. "You probably approach problems differently. You probably approach them from a different angle. But keep one thing in mind. People say I am a 'financial man.' And let me tell you why they say that. I was associated with the accounting department for a good bit of my career. And I was chairman of the finance committee." Here Roderick became unusually animated. "But I have never closed a set of books in my life. I have never been in general accounting in my life. I have never worked in a treasury department in my life. So am I a financial man? It's a good question. . . . My whole background in so-called accounting or financial was as an analyst. Analyzing operations as to how we could improve them, either from the standpoint of getting more output or improving the quality. Lowering the cost and improving the profitability. So all of my accounting life has been spent with operators. I really don't consider myself a good accountant. I am not an accountant."

However his background is described, it is undeniable that David Roderick has set in motion a dynamic of change and planned shrinkage at U.S. Steel that will permanently transform the character of the corporation. That transformation is affecting in profound ways the lives and futures of people not unlike those with whom David Roderick grew up.

The John Morrow School area of Pittsburgh is situated in the city's North Side. It is a very long walk, and light years away, from the sixty-four-story tower that dominates the Pittsburgh skyline and serves as headquarters for the corporation Roderick now commands. The old neighborhood, like the green-and-white two-story house on Bainton Street where Roderick and his sister and brother grew up, appears a bit ragged around the edges. It could use a coat of paint and the attention of a carpenter. One suspects that his father, who worked for the post office, kept it in better shape. The home next door is being remodeled. And the neighborhood, despite the changes, remains neat and quiet. Very quiet.

Around the corner from Bainton Street, before the Saint Francis Xavier Church near the top of California Avenue, there is a grand view of the Ohio River Valley and its industrial basin. Up the river sits a Jones & Laughlin steel plant. Within walking distance are factories owned by companies that produced barges, bathtubs, and turbines. All the plants are closed today.

It is midweek, ten-fifteen on a spring morning. The bartender in a tavern on California Avenue, whose parking lot overlooks the silent plants, is already serving beer drinkers. All the patrons are men—and almost all are either retired or unemployed. Few of the customers questioned at random remember the young David Roderick. But several are aware that the chairman of U.S. Steel once lived "somewhere around here." Those who did recall him had, for the most part, words of high praise. They also spoke well of his parents, especially his mother, who did charity work during the Depression. Both of his parents are now deceased.

"One thing about being sixty years old and being raised in Pittsburgh, in an Irish Catholic neighborhood on the North Side, you know what unemployment is all about," Roderick told us. "We were the people in those days on our street that in effect made up the baskets of food. Mother would go out on her Sunday afternoon trips and distribute food because Dad was making eighty bucks every two weeks. And [his job] was certain. But a lot of the people in the neighborhood were not that lucky. . . . We have seen [unemployment]. We have seen it with our friends, our neighbors. We understand the problem. I was raised with the problem. People think that because you're on the sixty-first floor you were born on the sixty-first floor. I wasn't born on the sixty-first floor."

Mrs. Sophia Vaughn, whose father built the handsome red-brick home across from the Roderick house, was several years ahead of the U.S. Steel chairman in school. She still lives in the old neighborhood. Mrs. Vaughn remembered a few incidents from Roderick's youth quite well, such as when the industrialist-to-be broke a pane in one of her mother's basement windows playing ball. Instead of running off, he offered to pay for the damage at a rate of ten cents a week from his allowance.

"Some years later Dave Roderick came back from the [military] service and was applying for a job with Gulf Oil," Mrs. Vaughn told us. "He gave them my mother's name [as a reference], and someone came out and talked to her. She told them the story about the broken window, and when they hired him, they said that had impressed them greatly. So we used to say that mother had gotten Dave Roderick his start. When we heard the news on TV about his becoming head of U.S. Steel, mother had me write Dave a letter reminding him of this. I did, and he sent a very nice acknowledgment. Mother was elated. She kept the letter and used it as a bookmark. When she died, we put it in the casket."

North Pittsburgh is largely a memory for the chairman of U.S. Steel. He and his wife, Bettie, whom he married in 1948, live in a well-appointed home in the affluent Fox Chapel suburb. Roderick socializes and hunts with the leaders of other giant corporations, including John McKinley, chief executive of Texaco, whom he considers "probably his closest" business friend, and William Hutchison, chairman of Texas Oil and Gas. He has played golf with the chairmen of Nippon Steel and British Steel. And Roderick is a dominant presence in his hometown. On May 30, 1983, the *Pittsburgh Post-Gazette* published a special section on Pittsburgh and its future. A straw vote of twelve editors declared the U.S. Steel chairman the most powerful figure in the city.

David Roderick told us he does not agree with that assessment. "You have to tie things together," he insisted. "In other words, what is power? Power usually is not the individual. It's the position that you hold. First you have to segment what is the power base. Well, the power base is chairman of United States Steel Corporation. It isn't David Milton Roderick as an individual entity. So I think, first, I don't view the power as mine personally. I believe the power is the influence of this corporation in this community. That's the power. Now, when they say 'the most powerful individual in the community,' I really don't agree with that. I think in our community the real power is in the political body. I think we have an excellent mayor. Mayor [Richard] Caliguiri does just an outstanding job. Clearly he is the catalyst within the total community."

.   .   .

There is more to this response than the rush of modesty that seems to infect all corporate leaders who are asked about the power they wield. David Roderick is an executive under siege. In 1979 he inherited control of a corporate empire whose formidable industrial legacy had withered under the misguided policies and sheer incompetence of his predecessors. Youngstown Works, which Roderick ordered closed in November 1979, was a decrepit giant that had not received a major infusion of modernization capital since the 1940s. Even when U.S. Steel did allocate capital for modernization and expansion, management often found ways to waste it. The company spent tens of millions of dollars in the mid-seventies to build a rod mill at South Works. It abandoned the facility, whose output could not compete with products manufactured by smaller and more nimble competitors, when it mothballed the Chicago operation in 1983. U.S. Steel spent $70 million to design and build a huge blast furnace at Gary Works that went into operation in 1974. But Blast Furnace Number 13 was plagued by so many technical problems that Roderick summoned consultants from Japan's Nippon Steel to rebuild it. The additional cost reportedly came to $100 million.

As chairman, David Roderick has embarked on a course that might be described as simultaneous rationalization, diversification, and confrontation. Soon after he took office he moved—and he has remained firm in the face of protest, fear, and organized opposition—to guide U.S. Steel away from dependence on the commodity it was formed to manufacture, steel, and to focus its manufacturing operations on the sale of fewer products made in fewer locations by fewer employees. *Rationalization* involves a dramatic reduction of the company's steel capacity. U.S. Steel could produce 38 million tons of raw steel in 1978. By 1984 it could produce only 26.2 million tons. This reduction in capacity has wreaked a devastating toll on the company's employees. U.S. Steel employed more than 166,800 workers in 1978. By 1984 employment had been slashed to 88,753—a decline of 47 percent. No segment of the workforce has been spared. U.S. Steel began a campaign in 1982 to prune its huge and unwieldy bureaucracy. At the end of 1984 white-collar employment had shrunk by 53 percent. Members of the United Steelworkers, who comprised 65 percent of the U.S. Steel labor force when Roderick assumed power, now account for only 35 percent. Their ranks have withered from 108,000 in 1978 to 31,000 in 1984.

Much of the shrinkage at U.S. Steel has been achieved in two waves of plant shutdowns. The first, announced less than nine months after Roderick became chairman, meant permanent termination for more than 13,000 employees. U.S. Steel shuttered a group of mills that stretched from New Haven, Connecticut, to Torrance, California. The decision to abandon the Youngstown Works in northeastern Ohio, which meant permanent layoff for 3,500 employees, came on the heels of a major plant closing in 1977 by Youngstown Sheet and Tube Company and the 1978 shutdown of a steel complex owned by Jones & Laughlin. The community has yet to begin to recover from this devastating triple blow.

South Works fell victim to the second wave. When U.S. Steel's board of directors met in 1983, two days after Christmas, it voted not only to cancel the Chicago rail mill but to close more than seventy other facilities. Hardest hit, in addition to South Works, were the U.S. Steel complex in Gary, Indiana, which lost 2,500 employees, and the collection of plants in the Monongahela Valley, outside Pittsburgh. Employment at the Mon Valley Works declined by 3,800. The 1983 closings reduced total employment at U.S. Steel by 15,400. Nearly 4,600 of these workers were on active duty, while more than 10,800 were already on layoff.

Diversification is shorthand for Roderick's crusade to inspire fealty to the bottom line in a corporation whose leadership for decades worshiped at the altar of production and volume. The shutdowns of 1979 and 1983 mean that U.S. Steel can now generate higher profits by producing less steel. Roderick has strengthened the company's "strategic planning" apparatus in order to search out new investments and apply rigorous standards of return on investments in existing lines of business.

Roderick has also devoted considerable personal energies to disposing of assets that were long part of the U.S. Steel empire. He sold Universal Atlas Cement, once the nation's largest cement producer, to a West German company for $138 million. He sold 49,000 acres of timberland in southern Alabama to International Paper for $28 million. He collected a cool $550 million when he sold 842 million net tons of coal reserves to Standard Oil of Ohio in 1981. Roderick's asset-disposal campaign raised a staggering $3 billion between 1980 and 1984. That cash war chest was used to finance a huge transaction that shook the steel industry to its core.

On November 18, 1981, U.S. Steel announced it was intervening as a white knight to rescue Marathon Oil from the unwanted clutches of

Mobil. The $5.9 billion deal, which generated howls of protest in Pittsburgh and Washington, transformed U.S. Steel overnight. A giant enterprise that in 1978 generated 80 percent of its $11 billion in revenues from the sale of steel and related products generated only 34 percent of its $19.1 billion in revenues from steel in 1984. Marathon makes an even more dominant contribution to profits. Oil and gas operations generated $3.7 billion in operating earnings between 1982 and 1984, whereas steel was in the red. *Fortune* now classifies U.S. Steel under petroleum refining when it compiles its annual survey of industrial corporations. The characterization seems apt. Four years after the Marathon deal, the company unveiled a second huge merger. Roderick offered U.S. Steel stock worth $3.6 billion to acquire Texas Oil and Gas, one of the country's largest independent producers of natural gas. Texas Oil and Gas has been a financial superstar among U.S. energy companies. But on the heels of declining profits in 1985, after twenty-seven consecutive years of higher earnings, William Hutchison, Texas Oil's chairman and Roderick's hunting companion, agreed to sell out to the steel giant.

Roderick told us that he has studied the mechanics of institutionalizing this diversification by reorganizing U.S. Steel as a holding company. Each of its lines of business—steel, oil, chemicals, and other manufacturing—would be operated on an independent footing. Were such a reorganization to take place, he suggested, U.S. Steel might even change its name.

"I have no mental block to changing the name," Roderick explained. "However, U.S. Steel is a name we think has an excellent reputation in business circles around the world. We think it has great asset value commercially. So I have no desire at the moment to dispose of the name U.S. Steel. . . . [But] at some point in time, and I haven't reached that point up to now, if we go more into letting each of our lines of business be reasonably independent and adopt more of a holding-company structure, I think then at that particular time you might want to consider whether U.S. Steel would be the proper name for the parent-type company. You could still retain the name U.S. Steel for your steel subsidiary and the resources related to that."

Is the movement to a holding company under active consideration? "I have not talked to the board about it," Roderick replied. "We have studied it. What are the implications of it from a management point of view and a tax point of view? What would be the legal ramifications of trying to make that kind of a name change? We have studied it, as we study many things. But I am not at the point that I would be willing to recommend its adoption."

The third defining element of the Roderick tenure has been *confrontation.* This has been a conscious pursuit, particularly with respect to the

United Steelworkers of America, as well as a by-product of the twin strategies of rationalization and diversification. By most estimates, steelworkers are the best-paid industrial workers in the United States. Their average compensation in 1982—before the March 1983 concession agreement—was $14.50 an hour. This figure, provided by the United Steelworkers, includes wages, incentive pay, and premiums for overtime, weekends, and nightwork. Auto workers earned an average of $13.03 an hour, and aluminum workers $13.82. Roderick claimed his blue-collar employees still command a wage 100 percent over the average manufacturing wage. The steelworker premium during the 1950s and 1960s was about 33 percent. His objective is to shrink the existing premium, over a period of ten years, back to its level of three decades ago—a goal that is bound to unleash bitter resistance.

One enduring challenge for corporate leadership is whether change as radical as the course Roderick has set in motion can be accomplished with support for and by production workers—labor and their communities as allies of renewal—or whether it must only move forward by means of raw conflict. It is clear which course U.S. Steel has chosen. The company has been quick to close facilities where union givebacks over and above the 1983 agreement are not forthcoming. U.S. Steel resumed operations in February 1984 at steel-making facilities in Birmingham, Alabama, only after employees approved new manning agreements at the mill. Workers at a mill in Johnstown, Pennsylvania, effectively voted their jobs away in March 1984 rather than accept a third round of concessions that reportedly included a 25 percent cut in wages and benefits.

Phillip Cyprian, president of Local 1014 at Gary Works, told us in March 1985 that labor relations at his plant "are right now at an all-time low." The flashpoint issue at Gary, as it was at South Works, centers around management's determination to contract out jobs traditionally performed by union members. Cyprian's troops have become so enraged that they have voted twice to wage unauthorized strikes—a dangerous course, on which they eventually chose not to embark—unless the company modified its practices.

David Roderick has played an undeniably critical role in this deterioration of morale. There is a pervasive antipathy and mistrust directed at the chairman on the shop floor and in the communities where U.S. Steel operates. To be sure, other large corporations have inspired bitter resentment when they insist on labor concessions and taxpayer subsidies as a condition of investment. But the depth of the anger expressed by union members and their advocates toward Roderick was unlike anything we encountered during research on the leaders of General Motors or Dow Chemical or Control Data. One unemployed steelworker, whom we met in a popular tavern that sits in the shadow of U.S. Steel's massive complex in Homestead, Pennsylvania, described the chairman's standing in the Mon Valley. "Roderick wouldn't dare walk into Homestead," he declared. "He wouldn't get out alive."

Jack Metzgar, an assistant professor at Roosevelt University and editor of the *Labor Research Review* who has advised union leaders at several U.S. Steel plants, spoke with us at length about developments at Bethlehem Steel and other domestic producers. His tone changed markedly when the conversation turned to David Roderick. The chairman of U.S. Steel "is a classic villain," he said. "Bethlehem has tried to save what [steel capacity] it could. They are really committed to steel. They have not been all that successful, but at least they are committed to steel . . . . Roderick is about the worst thing to come along since Attila the Hun."

What is truly unsettling about the U.S. Steel chairman is that he has done so little to counteract these bitter feelings. Roderick seems to question the value of ongoing communications between the man at the top and workers on the shop floor. He certainly has no real program for improving his standing among blue-collar workers or community residents. He told us he would be willing to debate a prominent critic of his industry or appear on the *Phil Donahue Show* to defend his policies.

Would it be too great a risk for him to convene public meetings in towns and cities with major U.S. Steel plants to explain his business agenda and respond to worries and fears about the future? "I don't say it's a risk," he replied. "I just don't think it's productive. There's no risk. I mean, after all, every time we get an opportunity we tell it like it is. That's all you're going to do in that public forum. You're not going to say anything different there than you say in a press conference and you get asked the questions. You say, 'This is the way it is.'"

U.S. Steel provided a broad selection of speeches delivered by Roderick during his tenure as chairman. We were hard pressed to find any mention of detailed proposals to create new structures of dialogue between management and labor—let alone any indication that he has lost the confidence of his rank-and-file. Is Roderick tougher in his public speeches than in private so as not to suggest a lack of resolve? "I think to a degree, yeah," he replied. "I think you have to be firmer in any group presentation, or in a speech, than if you were sitting down eyeball-to-eyeball with the head of a local and talking cold turkey."

Roderick told us he makes it a point to visit U.S. Steel mills across the country. He meets with plant managers and major customers and may speak to the local chamber of commerce or some other civic forum. Does he use these visits to address groups of production workers and respond to frustrations and complaints?

"I have done it when I was president," he replied. "We have not done it recently. And for a lot of reasons. These plants are massive. And if you are not going to spend a lot of time really trying to do it in an organized way, if you do it in an impromptu fashion, I am not convinced it is overly productive. The advantage of it is, it lets the guys see you. That's about the extent of it . . . . But I think the honest answer to your question is no. We don't do that very often. And given your druthers, would you like to talk to every employee on a one-to-one or on a one-to-ten basis? The answer is yes, I'd love to."

U.S. Steel chairman Benjamin Fairless, who served from 1952 to 1955, used to travel with United Steelworkers president David McDonald to tour plants and meet with workers. Has the current chairman thought of adopting a similar communications strategy with current Steelworkers president Lynn Williams? "No, we really haven't," he replied. "Again, during this period we are going through, I don't think the union would be too receptive to that. And I'm not sure it would be too productive. One of the problems that you have, and I say this because I believe it—it may not be true, but I believe it—is that the labor leader is a politician. And he has got to be reelected. For example, [Lynn Williams] is going to have to run in 1985. I don't think it is going to help him get reelected if he gives the image to his workers that he and Dave Roderick see eye-to-eye on things. I don't think that's going to help . . . . I think his people expect him to be confrontational during these difficult times. I think they expect that of him."

These comments illuminate the limits of Roderick's creativity and flexibility with respect to labor. The national contract with the United Steelworkers expires on July 31, 1986. Management will be pressing hard for more concessions and wage restraint. But Roderick told us he would not consider assigning a seat on the board of directors to a union representative in return for major revisions in the labor pact. Giant corporations like Chrysler and Eastern Airlines have successfully pursued this formula for renewal.

Would he exchange a block of shares in U.S. Steel for wage reductions by blue-collar workers? "I don't think so," he replied. "At least it would be sort of a last-resort technique. And here's the reason. We're a multiproduct company. We have oil and gas. We have chemicals. We have steel. So if you begin to get a group in a particular sector whose pay is out of line, let's pick steel, and then you say, 'If you make concessions, we will give you common stock,' well, what you're really doing is giving them part of an asset to which they directly have no ties whatsoever. You're giving them an investment in oil and gas. You're giving them an investment in chemicals. Why should they get that investment? I think if you're a pure steel company and they say we will make concessions if you give us stock in the company, that's very direct. I think in the case of U.S. Steel it would not be appropriate."

Roderick's talk of the "confrontational" posture of the United Steelworkers is also disquieting. The union is on the defensive on all fronts. The March 1983 concession agreement, which was negotiated by Williams's predecessor, Lloyd McBride, was an unprecedented retreat on wages and benefits. Wheeling–Pittsburgh Steel, the country's seventh largest producer, filed for Chapter 11 protection in April 1985 and moved to slash its labor costs. Weeks later, industry executives announced that they would dissolve the Steel Companies Coordinating Committee, the forum through which negotiations had been conducted for nearly thirty years. The demise of coordinated bargaining is expected to fuel still more concession demands in 1986 and weaken the union's capacity to resist.

One indication of the eroding strength of the United Steelworkers was the reaction of its president to our request for an interview. Roderick spoke freely about Lynn Williams and the future of organized labor. We thought it only fair that Williams have an opportunity to respond. He agreed to do so—provided he could answer our questions in writing. "Lynn is concerned about doing [a personal interview] for a mix of reasons," explained general counsel Bernard Kleiman. "It's incredibly complicated for the union. We are facing probably the worst year in the existence of the union. We are bargaining with four major sick, distressed industries. Lynn is torn between saying, 'Well, the best thing is to do nothing.' But he really wants to cooperate. He really does. He just thinks that a spontaneous thing could cause some problems."*

Williams limited his answers to the substance of labor policy at U.S. Steel. His letter was extremely measured and cautious. He refused to comment on Roderick's personality or his style of corporate leadership. Despite Roderick's claim, Williams said he would have "no objection" to the chairman "meeting with or speaking to groups of his employees, provided that he does not violate his moral and legal duty to deal with

---

*The Steelworkers president echoed Kleiman's comments in his letter to us. "It is a cardinal rule of collective bargaining that negotiators must avoid the personalization of issues and disputes," Williams wrote. "If we were to permit ourselves the luxury of becoming angry, antagonistic or abusive toward our bargaining counterparts, we would do great harm to those we represent, because such indulgences can enormously complicate the otherwise difficult task of negotiating a collective bargaining agreement with a huge company or industry. I would, therefore, prefer not to enter the arena contemplated by your questions. Having decided to do so, however, I will answer honestly, but the scope of my answers will to some degree be limited by the considerations I have mentioned."

our union as the exclusive bargaining agent of
sent." He also said he would be "willing to accompa
these meetings "for the purpose of enabling our memb
about the future of the company." Williams offered a ser
observations:

- *On the general relationship between U.S. Steel and the Un
  Steelworkers:* "The overall state of relations between the Union
  and U.S. Steel is not good. The major issues of contention are
  an outgrowth of what the Union perceives as an increased disregard on the part of U.S. Steel management and supervision for
  the provisions of collective bargaining agreements and an unwillingness to recall laid-off employees because of the cost of renewed eligibility for insurance, pension, supplemental unemployment and other benefits. As a result, we see an increased
  level of sub-contracting, plant and departmental closures, job
  combinations, crew cuts, failure to follow established practices,
  and assignment of bargaining unit work to non-union, supervisory and management employees."
- *On the labor policies at U.S. Steel as compared with those of its
  competitors:* "Relations between the Union and U.S. Steel are
  currently more difficult than are relations between the Union
  and many other steel companies. I cannot attribute this to Mr.
  Roderick or to any other specific individual. We in the union
  have no way of knowing how corporate policies are formulated
  [or] who is responsible for their development . . . . U.S. Steel
  appears to be pursuing the approaches outlined in my [previous]
  answer to a greater extent than are most other major producers."
- *On the long-term intentions of chairman Roderick vis-à-vis the
  union:* "I have no way of judging Mr. Roderick's intentions or
  motives. He has denied any interest in injuring or crippling our
  Union and its members. For my part I have made it clear to all
  who will listen that while our Union seeks and prefers cooperative and mutually constructive relationships, we will not shrink
  from confrontations that are forced upon us and will, if challenged, do whatever is required to prevail."

David Roderick inspires grudging respect and a degree of fear
among constituencies touched by his business agenda. But he elicits little
warmth or genuine admiration—even among executives in his own industry. Lewis Foy, who retired on May 31, 1980, as chairman of
Bethlehem Steel, declined to be interviewed for this profile. He said

the employees we repre-
ny Mr. Roderick" to
rs to question him
es of additional

unbalanced. It was not positive.
of a small midwestern steel com-
major producers and their Wash-
t-for-attribution appraisal of Rod-
d at dealing with the union," this
ood at dealing with his top execu-
rtainly has not endeared himself to

he history of U.S. Steel under its
opposition to its corporate evolu-
number of constituencies: unem-
rough the misery and despair of
forced to choose between wage
concessions and losing their jobs, communities where plant closings have touched off a ripple effect of economic stagnation, members of Congress who balked at the acquisition of Marathon Oil just months after Roderick and his corporate allies pressured them to approve lucrative tax breaks in the name of steel modernization and competitors who worry that Roderick's visibility jeopardizes the entire industry's standing in Washington.

What is notable is the relative impotence of this usually impressive constellation of forces. Only once, in March 1984, when U.S. Steel abandoned its proposed acquisition of the steel-making operations of National Intergroup, a $900-million deal to which the Justice Department objected, has Roderick retreated from a course of action solely in response to the power of a countervailing institution. David Roderick has not made many friends since he became chairman of U.S. Steel. But his adversaries have been powerless to reverse or modify the policies to which he is committed.

. . . .

The residents of Chicago's South Side are one such constituency. U.S. Steel's decision to scrap its rail project and close most of South Works was not unexpected in light of the rejection by Local 65 of the company's major concession demands. But the formal decision unleashed an outpouring of rage and despair. It was interpreted as a mortal blow to a community that had already suffered through the demise of Wisconsin Steel, whose South Side plant once employed 3,400 workers, as well as drastic cutbacks at a complex owned by Republic Steel. A January 1985 study by the Steelworkers Research Project reported that South Chicago lost 11,000 jobs in the steel industry between 1980 and 1984. The South Chicago Development Commission estimated that layoffs and shutdowns in all industries claimed 28,000 area jobs between 1980 and 1983. On March 30, 1984, when U.S. Steel officially closed all but an electric furnace and structural mill, members of Local 65 organized a procession to commemorate the death of the plant. They drove to South Works, were allowed entry by a guard, and surveyed the blast furnaces and finishing mills. Later that day as many as a thousand workers gathered at union headquarters for the equivalent of an industrial wake. "This community is basically dead," despaired Michael Ally, with whom we spoke a year after South Works closed. "People here realize this is not the thriving southeast side of the city any longer. Steeltown. I think all hope has been given up. The rate of [small] business closings, home foreclosures, the separation rates of marriages, everything around here is in a very sad state."

The rage that accompanied the death of integrated steel production at South Works reflected the sense of betrayal among community residents. U.S. Steel received what it had originally asked for in April 1981. But Roderick and his associates raised the ante in the final hours when they went back to Local 65. Robert Mier, Chicago's economic development commissioner, helped to assemble a package of tax breaks for South Works worth tens of millions of dollars—incentives over and above the April 1981 demands. He complained bitterly to the *Chicago Tribune* about U.S. Steel's negotiating posture. "Every time their demands have been met, they've upped the stakes," he said. "I can certainly understand the union's reluctance to make further concessions."

Congressman Dan Rostenkowski, chairman of the House Ways and Means Committee, echoed Mier's anger. He told us in March 1985 that he had extracted "a total commitment" from Roderick that the rail mill would be built. Rostenkowski worked with the late congressman from Indiana, Adam Benjamin, and Congressman John Murtha of Pennsylvania in 1981 and 1982, when tax legislation of grave importance to U.S. Steel was wending its way through Congress. Of particular significance to Roderick was a controversial provision called safe-harbor leasing. This tax preference was approved by Congress in 1981 as a result of intense business lobbying. It was repealed in 1982 in the face of heavy criticism. Safe-harbor leasing allowed firms with more tax breaks than they could use, a segment of corporate America that included U.S. Steel, to "sell" their credits and exclusions to corporations with taxable income. Rostenkowski and his congressional allies worked hard in 1982 to pass "transition rules" and make sure that certain industries, including steel, would be able to use leasing for one year beyond the repeal deadline for other sectors. South Works figured in the bargaining.

"It was to me somewhat of a breach of promise," Rostenkowski said of the decision to close the plant. "I truly believed when we worked out those transition rules that Adam Benjamin, John Murtha, and I had an agreement that there was going to be some investment at South Works." The Ways and Means chairman estimated that he met with the U.S. Steel chairman "maybe four" times from 1981 through 1984 in connection with the rail mill. How did Rostenkowski react to the mill's cancellation? "Well, it put Roderick in cold storage with me for a long period of time, I'll tell you that much."

Other reactions were not so restrained. R. C. Longworth, a business writer for the *Chicago Tribune,* captured the general mood of the city in a January 11, 1984, column. Longworth and others were indignant that U.S. Steel had spent $19,500 to purchase a full-page ad in the *Tribune* on the day the newspaper reported the closing and had pinned the blame on Local 65. His impassioned comments warrant extensive quotation:

> U.S. Steel lied to the workers, to the State of Illinois, and to the South Side neighborhood where South Works stands. It said it planned to expand operations there with the rail mill, but it is clear now that the company never had any such plans. It toyed with the workers, many of whom gave decades of their lives to U.S. Steel. And when it finally opened the trap door under them, it had the gall to claim it was the workers' fault.
>
> Through all this, U.S. Steel chairman David M. Roderick and vice chairman Thomas Graham seemed to take delight in the misery, since it contributed to what they saw as a good cause— the breaking of a union that not only had agreed to contract concessions but had helped the firm win government protection from foreign imports.
>
> Say what you will about the turn-of-the-century robber barons, they were builders, pirates on a rising sea, who caused plenty of hardship but also left behind the railroads, mines and mills that generated American prosperity. Roderick operates in the same rapacious spirit but will leave no legacy other than padlocked mills and decaying neighborhoods.

The U.S. Steel chairman felt compelled to respond to the Longworth column. He argued that U.S. Steel had spent nearly $80 million on engineering, site preparation, and the purchase of materials—evidence of its commitment to the mill. He complained that Attorney General Hartigan's proposal to reduce the cost of pollution-control equipment at Gary was slow in materializing. And he said that labor concessions extracted by other rail producers meant that U.S. Steel needed another round of givebacks from Local 65 to remain competitive.

"Were the economic factors coming together—Yes!" Roderick wrote. "Was the environmental issue on the road to being resolved—Yes! Would the plant be cost-competitive—that depended on discussions with the union. Without a cost-competitive labor agreement there would be no chance for a viable and profitable South Works."

The letter did little to calm the passions. Nor has U.S. Steel's behavior since December 1983. The shutdown at South Works, like U.S. Steel's 1979 decision to abandon Youngstown, Ohio, and recent cutbacks in the Mon Valley, soon generated proposals for a community-employee buyout of the plant or its sale to another corporation or entrepreneur. The United Steelworkers, a public-interest group that represents unemployed workers, and city and state officials pooled their financial resources and expertise to study alternatives to permanent shutdown. No one with whom we spoke would declare unequivocally that South Works could be revived. But certain facts could not be ignored. U.S. Steel spent $80 to $90 million in 1982 to rebuild Blast Furnace Number 8 at South Works. This investment in modernization was never tapped because the company closed the plant before it relit the furnace. Even though the plant itself dates back to 1881, much of the equipment, including efficient basic oxygen furnaces, is in working order. South Works will never again produce the millions of tons of steel it once turned out each year. But with creative application of the plant's modern equipment, as well as wage or work-rule concessions, which employees might approve if they controlled the plant, the complex could perhaps enjoy a limited rebirth.

This at least was the scenario. But its soundness could not be tested unless U.S. Steel granted access to cost and production data and allowed an on-site inspection of the plant. Instead of cooperating, the company adopted an attitude of unrestrained hostility. Members of the feasibility team were allowed inside the complex only at the point of a court order. The union and its allies filed for an injunction against destruction of Blast Furnace Number 8. The complaint charged that an outside contractor had begun to assemble a 300-foot boom crane next to Blast Furnace Number 8, presumably to be used in its dismantling. The plaintiffs won their court order in August 1984. The injunction remained in effect until August 1985.

Attorney General Hartigan also opened a second legal front. He filed a suit in July 1984 to compel U.S. Steel to live up to its pledge to build the rail mill. He also argued that the physical dismantling of South Works, as opposed to its sale, would constitute anticompetitive behavior on the part of Roderick's corporation.

"U.S. Steel has been totally resistant and uncooperative," said Douglass Cassel, general counsel of Chicago-based Business and Professional People for the Public Interest (BPI). BPI represents unemployed workers from the plant. "They have taken extreme and ridiculous positions in litigation. And I have never run into a major corporation that you can trust as little as U.S. Steel in court. Nothing, but nothing, is guaranteed unless it is nailed down by court order. I have no doubt that if we had given them an opening, they would have gone in and smashed parts of the plant. None of us assume any good faith on their part."

Cassel said that one proposal, admittedly tentative, was to operate South Works as a source of semifinished slabs for other mills in the region. David Roderick dismissed that idea out of hand. "There is no market for the product," he protested. "I mean, it can go to Gary, that's a semifinished situation." Here he whispered for emphasis. "We don't need the semifinished. So you are going to take that and do what with it? *Do what?* I mean, if you operate the blast furnace and operate the steel shop and operate the primary mills. To do what? Who wants the semifinished product? The answer is nobody. So what the hell are you going to do with it?

"What surprises me is that some people are saying, 'We want to take over the total complex,' " Roderick continued. "I tell you if they do, those eleven hundred people won't be working two years from now. I don't know what people are thinking about. I sort of shake my head. We are keeping a very low profile on that because we think the lower the profile right now the better. People are a little angry. And you can understand that. You've shut down a major facility out there. But believe me, we have lost I think it is $450 million at South Works in five years. Now somebody thinks they are going to come in there? And keep in mind, we lost that while using the semifinished at other locations ourselves. There's no way. There's no way."

Attorney Cassel was not satisfied with the chairman's explanation. "David Roderick may be absolutely right when he says there is no market for semifinished slabs," he told us. "We are not sure he is right or wrong. . . . I would not want to give the impression that South Works could be reopened on a very large scale. But it is so important to the community that we are not willing to simply accept U.S. Steel's pronouncements. If the economics [of the plant] are so demonstrably bad, why not let the community look at it? Why the hell won't he cooperate with the people in the community who want the information?"

The bitter divisions over South Works dragged on into the summer of 1985. Mayor Harold Washington formed a Steel Task Force, chaired by former Commerce secretary Philip Klutznick, to explore proposals to rehabilitate the complex. Congressman Rostenkowski hosted a meeting in his Washington office with Roderick and Attorney General Hartigan. They discussed a "legal truce" on the part of Hartigan and his allies in return for a degree of cooperation from U.S. Steel on the Klutznick report. Whatever the final outcome at South Works—and the future of the mill may well be debated for months and years to come—distrust of U.S. Steel and its chairman has been etched permanently into the collective memory of South Chicago.

"I tell you what, if I owned a business I would want David Roderick to be chairman of the board," said union leader Mike Ally. "He's got fucking balls. He's not afraid to make decisions. And he's ruthless and conniving. That's what you need if you own a very big business. Those are the kind of people who succeed."

. . .

From his spacious office on the sixty-first floor of the U.S. Steel building, whose view includes the North Pittsburgh neighborhood in which he was raised, David Roderick must believe he has succeeded. He presides over an industrial empire as vast as it is troubled. U.S. Steel's total assets of $19 billion in 1984 exceeded the combined assets of its four largest steel industry competitors: LTV, Bethlehem, Inland Steel, and Armco. Gary Works, which can produce 7.5 million tons of raw steel per year, has reputedly poured more steel over its lifetime than any other plant in the world. The coke ovens at Clairton, one of six plants in the company's Mon Valley Works, can still produce more of that critical steel-making commodity than nearly any coke plant outside the Soviet Union.*

*Most integrated steel plants include the following facilities: iron ore yards, coal yards, coke ovens, blast furnaces, steelmaking furnaces, primary mills, and finishing mills. The basic raw material for steel is iron ore. Ore is transformed into molten iron in a blast furnace, whose other key inputs are coke (metallurgical-grade coal that has been baked in coke ovens) and limestone. Molten iron is then transported to steel-making furnaces, of which there are three basic categories. The open hearth was for decades the dominant steel-making technology. It has since been displaced—although open hearths do continue to operate—by the basic oxygen furnace (BOF), also known as a BOP shop. This process is radically different from, and more efficient than, its open-hearth predecessor. Steel can also be produced in electric furnaces. These facilities melt down steel scrap rather than use molten iron.

Molten steel is next transformed into semifinished shapes: slabs, which can be rolled into sheets, strip products, and plates; blooms, which can be rolled into finished shapes, such as structural beams and rails; and billets, which are finished into simple products, such as bars, rods and light structurals. Two different processes govern the movement from molten steel to finished shapes. The steel can be loaded into a ladle and then poured into molds and allowed to cool as ingots. The ingots are then

These manufacturing operations are fueled by a raw-materials base of unrivaled scale. Roderick's corporation owns or leases billions of tons of iron, coal, and limestone. If its 4.3 billion tons of iron reserves were sold at the average market price for iron in 1984, U.S. Steel would have collected $118 billion. Such a calculation is hypothetical, but it does suggest the enormity of the holdings. U.S. Steel controls enough coal to meet its steel-making needs for the next one hundred years, even after its massive sale of reserves to Standard Oil. It mines manganese in the Gabon and copper, zinc, and iron ore in South Africa.

U.S. Steel's oil and gas holdings are comparably vast. But the defining characteristic of the corporation during the Roderick tenure has been the erosion and decline of its steel operation. One reminder of the continued vulnerability of this giant enterprise is the fact that U.S. Steel no longer owns the steel and glass tower in which its chairman labors. The building was sold for $250 million in 1982 as part of Roderick's asset-disposal program, and the company leases its office space. From 1979 through 1984, U.S. Steel recorded net operating losses of $1 billion through the sale of steel and related products. The corporation as a whole, including the results of Marathon, generated only $259 million more in total profits than losses over this same period. Sales of steel in 1984 brought in $6.5 billion. Sales of steel in 1979 generated revenues of nearly $10 billion. Most telling of all, the volume of steel manufactured in 1984—14.8 million tons—was only 35 percent above U.S. Steel's production volume in 1902, its first full year of operation. Steel production in 1973 was nearly 35 million tons.

"What I think I am willing to be judged by, by my peers and by history, is to say there were six major integrated steel companies going into the 1980s," Roderick told us. "Now, during Roderick's tenure, did he get U.S. Steel through the eighties better than his competition? Because, keep in mind, those are the circumstances I have to deal with. I mean, I can't be somebody else. I started out in the steel business, and that's the job I have to manage. So how well did I manage it compared to my competition? If I come out of the decade with a healthy, vibrant, growing entity that is head and shoulders above my competition, then I would hope people would say that [my legacy is] the development of a strategic plan, the commitment to it, the development of a philosophy that we

reheated and passed through a series of heavy rolls to produce semifinished shapes. Alternatively, through application of the continuous-casting process, molten steel can be poured into a tundish positioned above a set of molds and transformed directly into slabs, billets, and blooms. Continuous casting reduces energy costs, minimizes generation of scrap, and increases labor productivity.

were going to bite the bullets that needed to be bitten rather than try to bury them. . . . I'm not saying they will conclude that. They may conclude something substantially different. But I would like to bring this corporation out of this decade as a growing, financially healthy entity that is well placed in corporate America. I do not want to leave this job with an entity that is clearly in a declining or liquidating mode. I don't want to do that."

The ongoing plight of U.S. Steel and its domestic rivals is a case study in the long-term hazards of oligopoly. When David Roderick joined U.S. Steel in 1953, the company ruled the world in the production of a commodity whose strategic and economic value was unquestioned. U.S. Steel produced two-thirds of all the steel consumed in the United States when it was formed in 1901. By 1950 its market share had declined to 31 percent—still enough for effective price leadership of the U.S. market. Dominance at home meant world supremacy as well. The United States accounted for more than 45 percent of global steel production in 1950. American blast furnaces and mills were larger and more efficient than their overseas rivals. U.S. steelworkers were so much more productive than their foreign counterparts that management willingly granted premium wages and benefits.

But profitable dominance during a period of buoyant economic expansion had its costs. By the 1960s, the steel industry had evolved into a closed club of entrenched and lethargic giants. Donald Barnett, a former chief economist of the American Iron and Steel Institute (AISI) and coauthor of *Steel: Upheaval in a Basic Industry,* described four strategic blunders that continue to haunt domestic producers. Industry executives ignored promising new technologies in the late 1950s and 1960s in favor of massive investments in familiar production techniques. These same executives sprinkled limited capital over too many plants. An obsession with restraining competition from foreign steel through political clout in Washington weakened management resolve to cut costs and shed uncompetitive product lines. An all-consuming fear of import surges during strikes by the United Steelworkers—as well as industry enthusiasm for cementing a political alliance with labor on import restraint—encouraged domestic producers to accept wage agreements whose costs were not offset by increased labor productivity through modernization.

"The structure of the industry has no bearing whatsoever on how the industry should be structured for efficient production," Barnett told us. "There is no particular advantage to having more than two or three plants [per company]. These [integrated] companies have grown up over a period of years in totally irrational locations. The product mix in different plants seems to have no bearing on what particular market areas require. The organization of technology in specific plants is not geared to any particular product strategy. It is just a hodgepodge. If some czar were to come along and say, 'Wait a minute, let's reorganize the whole industry,' it would not bear any relationship to where the industry is now. . . . You are dealing with a corporate structure which goes back to 1900 and cannot stand the test of the 1980s."

Is it fair to say that workers and communities are suffering more today because steel management is making adjustments in the late 1970s and early 1980s that it should have initiated in the early 1970s? "Yes," Chairman Roderick replied. "I think you could say that. Maybe some of the pain gets more concentrated from a time-frame point of view. But I think you have to be very careful when you draw the conclusion. If you go back into the 1960s and early 1970s, steel was making money. [Management] wasn't forced to do some of the things we have been forced to do in this very highly competitive market, in both the domestic and the international arenas. You could still operate a plant like South Works in the early 1970s and make money. So obviously, you are not going to begin to shut off product lines if you are making money or generating cash flow. But by the time you hit the 1980s, it was very, very clear that unless you had a low-cost operation and were well situated to the market, and had facilities that could produce a satisfactory quality product, you either had to face up to that problem—and quickly—or you were going to suffer massive deterioration of your [cash] surplus. And worse, you in effect were going to be using your cash to sustain operations rather than improve facilities."

The historic pressures bearing down on David Roderick have been immense. These burdens of the past are magnified by two external challenges over which he has no control. First, the American economy simply consumes less steel relative to its gross national product than it did twenty or thirty years ago. Plastic, aluminum, and other materials have displaced much of the steel used in automobiles, appliances, and containers. According to estimates cited in the *Wall Street Journal*, the United States will consume roughly 97 million tons of steel in 1985. But if steel were used with the same intensity in 1985 as it was in 1965, demand would stand at 175 million tons. The second threat comes from abroad—the relentless growth of foreign competition. Steel imports totaled 15.2 million tons, 12.4 percent of the U.S. market, when David Roderick was plucked from corporate obscurity in 1973 to become chairman of the U.S. Steel finance committee. Imports captured more than 26 percent of the domestic market in 1984. Roderick and his industry colleagues are battling for a declining share of a stagnant market.

These inherited pressures condition and constrain Roderick's management freedom with respect to steel. He must spend as much time responding to the accumulated errors of his predecessors as he spends devising strategies for the future. But the vulnerability of his corporation has an ironically sustaining effect on his power to extract from outside constituencies—organized labor, government, communities, competitors—the concessions or subsidies or political alliances he demands as a condition of future investment and renewal. The decline of U.S. Steel creates new reservoirs of power from which its chairman can draw to work his will in the public realm. These reservoirs are fed by the desperation and heavy dependency of steel communities and Roderick's authority to pick and choose among them when he allocates scarce modernization capital. The ultimate power of David Roderick is the power to deny. It is a form of power he has not been loathe to deploy.

Congressman Peter Kostmayer represents the Bucks County area of Pennsylvania. He crossed swords with the chairman in 1983 when Roderick proposed that U.S. Steel import semifinished slabs from Britain. Kostmayer described the hardships of doing battle with Roderick's firm.

"People in private and public life seem to be more frightened of [U.S. Steel]," he told us. "Frightened at the prospect that they will close up. That's what they made clear in Bucks County. They were going to leave if they didn't get their way. We just decided that we couldn't knuckle under to them. We took a chance. But they have more and more leverage. That's why they intimidate the [Congressional] Steel Caucus. Nobody talks back to Roderick. You know how members of Congress often berate witnesses. That doesn't happen when Roderick comes up [to testify]. Nobody gives him a hard time. He's too powerful. Or there is a perception that he's too powerful."

The proposal to import slabs from British Steel may well qualify as the single most controversial episode of Roderick's tenure. It provoked condemnation from the United Steelworkers, other industry executives, and politicians who had carried the ball for years on behalf of U.S. Steel. The deal fell through nine months after the negotiations were made public. But it was economics—not politics—that mothballed the proposal. David Roderick managed to pursue his plan over the objections of nearly every segment of the industry.

Members of the tightly knit steel fraternity were stunned to learn in March 1983 that the chairman of their largest producer had been negotiating for several months with Ian MacGregor, chairman of British Steel Corporation, to strike a deal with grave implications for the structure of the industry. Roderick and MacGregor proposed that the British ship between 3 and 3.5 million tons of semifinished steel each year to the United States from a plant in Ravenscraig, Scotland. The slabs would be delivered for finishing at Fairless Works, the last integrated steel plant built by U.S. Steel, whose open-hearth furnaces are technologically out-moded. An alliance between British Steel and U.S. Steel would have combined the efficient steelmaking facilities at Ravenscraig with newly modernized finishing equipment at Fairless.

The economics of the proposal were enormously complex. British Steel planned to spin off its Ravenscraig operation so that it could function independent of government control. Roderick also insisted that the British commit a substantial investment—between $150 million and $600 million—to renovate the finishing end at Fairless. The politics of the proposed alliance were less involved. Word of the negotiations leaked out days after the United Steelworkers had approved their national concession package. The news generated understandable anger and charges of betrayal. Had workers sacrificed billions of dollars in wages and benefits so that the industry's largest producer could import foreign steel and eliminate one thousand to three thousand jobs at Fairless? Roderick's competitors were no less bitter. The industry had for years maintained a united front in the campaign to restrict imports. How could U.S. Steel demand quotas on subsidized European steel even as it imported slabs from a British corporation that by certain estimates had received $6 billion in direct government assistance since 1975?

The opposition mobilized within days. The United Steelworkers began a national media blitz. Bethlehem Steel chairman Donald Trautlein condemned the proposal before the Senate Judiciary Committee and announced that thousands of Bethlehem employees had mailed him union-sponsored postcards to express their opposition. Trautlein pledged that if the U.S. government did not sue to block the deal, Bethlehem would. Peter Kostmayer cosponsored a resolution that detailed congressional reservations about the trans-Atlantic venture.

How did Roderick respond to this outpouring of opposition? Congressman Kostmayer met for several hours with the U.S. Steel chairman at the height of the controversy. He described the tone of their discussion: "Roderick said, 'Listen, this is what we have to do to protect our shareholders and to earn money. That place is antiquated, and we are going to bring in the slabs [from Scotland].' I said, 'You're not going to bring them in. We're going to stop you. It's illegal to import that [steel] and we're going to stop you. We'll see who wins.' " Kostmayer also informed Roderick that workers at Fairless had considered not unloading the slabs when they arrived. Roderick's response to that scenario? "He said, 'I'll fire them all,' " Kostmayer reported. "I think he may have used those exact words. 'I'll fire them, and we'll hire new steelworkers.' "

The congressman then proposed that Roderick form a committee to examine competitive problems at the plant. "He said, 'Look, I don't want one of these goddamn committees coming in here—a priest, a Boy Scout, and a housewife—telling us what to do,' " Kostmayer reported. " 'We're here to make money. You guys can't get that through your head.' "

Having failed to conclude a deal with British Steel, Roderick turned to the Far East. In December 1985, he announced a joint venture between U.S. Steel and the Pohang Iron and Steel Co. of South Korea. After 1989, Korea will provide all the hot-rolled steel used by U.S. Steel's finishing plant at Pittsburg, California, which until now has been supplied by the U.S. Steel Geneva mill near Provo, Utah.

.   .   .

Such muscle-flexing by David Roderick is curt testimony to the durable power of a large steel company in the process of sizable liquidation. The revenues of the entire steel industry in 1985 were less than the sales of IBM alone. But U.S. Steel's ability to press its demands in Washington or in the communities where it operates compares favorably with the power of much larger and more robust companies. Steel management made costly blunders in the 1950s and 1960s that continue to exact a heavy toll on workers and the economy. Roderick has pursued a political agenda riddled with inconsistencies. But his credibility in Washington has not been damaged.

The U.S. Steel chairman inherited deep-seated problems when he took office in 1979. He also inherited an infrastructure of power that magnifies and concentrates the leverage of his industry. There are several distinct elements to this formidable political base. The Congressional Steel Caucus, which was convened in September 1977, provides a bipartisan legislative coalition through which the industry can sponsor bills, put pressure on the executive branch, and rivet public attention on its program for relief. More than a hundred members of Congress are affiliated with the Steel Caucus. The Washington alliance between major producers and the United Steelworkers also enhances the industry's power. Business demands for tax breaks or import quotas become more palatable to Congress when they are echoed by labor representatives. The American Iron and Steel Institute is yet another forum of influence. Political coordination among rival steelmakers allows them to pool financial resources and geographic reach for maximum advantage. The importance of maintaining this united front inspired much of the anger other steel companies showed over the British Steel negotiations.

This long-standing network of alliances offers any chairman of U.S. Steel an ample supply of visibility and influence in the political realm. As the largest and best known member of the industry, U.S. Steel is in a unique position to lead and benefit from its infrastructure of power. And Roderick has worked diligently to embellish the influence he inherited. He is a seasoned political operative with a history of personal activism on Capitol Hill and in the White House. Roderick does not delegate crucial lobbying to Washington representatives or hired guns, although he makes ample use of both. He told us that he ranks in the "upper ten percent" of Fortune 500 executives in terms of the energy he devotes to "public policy." He estimated that he routinely spends 10 to 15 percent of his time on political affairs—even more in 1983 and 1984, when he also served as AISI chairman.

Albert Monnett, who retired from U.S. Steel in August 1981, served as vice-president for corporate planning under chairman Edgar Speer and as assistant to the chairman under Roderick. Monnett told us that Roderick consistently "took the initiative" on Washington strategy and that it was the one area of corporate policy where he exercised "unilateral" authority. "And that's a difference between Dave and Ed," Monnett said. "Ed didn't like Washington. He didn't understand it. We had [Vice-president] Bill Whyte down there at the time. Whatever Whyte said kind of went. Dave was his own man."

Roderick was "his own man" during our conversations when he was asked to evaluate President Reagan. He offered some preliminary words of praise. "I think the president is a fine, strong international leader," he said. "He is a very sincere man. I think he's doing a very good job overall."

But he proceeded to offer unexpectedly harsh criticisms on two fronts. Roderick became deadly serious when he raised the specter of runaway budget and trade deficits. "I think in the area of the budget deficits I would give him failing grades," Roderick told us. "Most people are hesitant to say that, but it is absolutely true. The budget deficit is unsustainable. You have a hard time justifying something that is unsustainable. We can't just sit here. I believe what [Federal Reserve chairman] Paul Volcker says. I believe what Marty Feldstein [former chairman of the Council of Economic Advisers] and those fellas are saying. You can play this game short. But you can't sit there with a $180 billion budget deficit, a $130 billion trade deficit—a $310 billion pull of available capital sources in this country. That is unsustainable. I talked to people who were over here for the IMF [International Monetary Fund] meeting. I talked to the chancellor of the exchequer of the U.K. They are all saying the same thing. You are in an unsustainable mode. I agree with that."

Would he agree with commentators who suggest that these long-term threats have created a time-bomb economy? "It is," Roderick said. "If you don't do something, it sure in hell is."

Roderick also chastised the administration for its lack of progress on arms control. We raised this issue in October 1984—before resumption of the Geneva talks. The U.S. Steel chairman described himself as a "hawk." He said he did endorse the administration's weapons buildup. But he was clearly uneasy about the lack of dialogue with the Soviets.

"I think the president has handled it badly," Roderick said. "I don't think he's handled it well. The very fact that you're not talking would indicate that it hasn't been handled too well from a diplomacy point of view. Some of the rhetoric, I think, was unnecessarily sharp. . . . You can get so violent in your rhetoric, even if it is true, that for diplomacy, as a world leader, it is probably more disruptive. So a lower level of rhetoric and name-calling probably was desirable. I would say that a good job has not been done there."

We asked Roderick to discuss his perspective on the roots of Soviet foreign policy. Does he agree with certain foreign-policy moderates that much of Soviet behavior can be traced to the memories of repeated invasion from Europe and the millions of casualties in World War II? Could the Soviet Union be motivated by a protect-the-motherland impulse as opposed to grand imperial designs? "I understand the logic of the position," Roderick said. "And if you say, Can you show clear-cut historical evidence that Russia has been a very aggressive force, trying to take over Europe, or have they been more or less in the 'defense-of-the-motherland' concept? Of course the answer comes out that historically they have been defense-of-the-motherland. My only argument against that is that I think there is enough evidence that suggests that this is not what they are content with today. Poland isn't the motherland. East Germany is not the motherland. Hungary is not the motherland. When they get a hold of something, they don't let it go. So I do think they have more aggressive desires if they could get away with them."

David Roderick spoke at length with us about power and politics in Washington. He demonstrated an intimate familiarity with Capitol Hill that few of his business peers could match. He discussed his access to the Carter White House and his conversations on tax policy with cabinet members G. William Miller and Michael Blumenthal. Roderick protested mildly that he "was listened to more [under Carter] than I am today" on the subject of tax reform. He complained that "inter-agency play" often cripples decision-making in the executive branch. And he was open about various tools used to increase business influence in the political process.

The U.S. Steel chairman described as "absolutely great" the explosion of political action committees (PACs) as a source of funds for congressional campaigns. He acknowledged that PACs allow contributors to focus donations for maximum impact. He said that U.S. Steel prefers to finance individual candidates rather than political parties. He did not obscure the narrow criteria on which legislators are judged. Would Roderick support a congressional candidate with whom he agrees on nearly every issue but who opposes U.S. Steel on a crucial bill? "If I were advising our PAC, and I don't, and somebody was doing something detrimental to the steel industry, I would say he would not warrant any support," he replied. Would he counsel active opposition? "It depends on what his opponent was advocating. If his opponent was advocating things that you felt were in the interest of the industry, and obviously not going to do anything detrimental to the nation—yeah."

These comments are more than idle speculation. Roderick's corporation and its affiliates make aggressive use of PAC donations as a weapon for political influence. PACs sponsored by U.S. Steel, Marathon Oil, and Bessemer Railroad, a transportation subsidiary, contributed a total of nearly $410,000 in the 1982 and 1984 congressional elections. Their donation patterns are consistent with many of the familiar techniques used to build reliable access. The U.S. Steel Good Government Fund is more concerned with congressional loyalty than partisan affiliations. It contributed to 125 Republicans and 65 Democrats in 1982—and 105 Democrats and 85 Republicans in 1984. The donations went exclusively to candidates as opposed to political parties. Virtually all of the $410,000 was channeled to incumbents.

Two exceptions to the incumbent bias demonstrate how PAC financing can be used to punish legislators who buck their patrons. The U.S. Steel Good Government Fund made donations in seventeen of Pennsylvania's twenty-three congressional campaigns in 1984. In only one of these races—the reelection bid of Peter Kostmayer—did it support a challenger over an incumbent. Two years earlier, the U.S. Steel PAC made donations to twenty-one congressional candidates in Pennsylvania. Its only $5,000 contribution, the largest permitted under law, was to Ted Jacob, a hard-driving Republican who was running to unseat Eighteenth District congressman Doug Walgren. Why Jacob? It seems that Rep. Walgren, who had demonstrated the expected loyalty to steel interests since his election in 1976, sided with environmentalists in the Ninety-sixth Congress during debate on amendments to weaken the Clean Air Act.

Walgren's behavior even caught the attention of Roderick, who dashed off a message to company executives less than one month before the 1982 election.

Dear Fellow Employee:
 This letter is being sent to certain management employees of
U.S. Steel who live in the 18th Congressional District to discuss

an opportunity race in the November General Election that is important to U.S. Steel. It's an opportunity to change things for the better for our company and for the industry.

Ted Jacob is the Republican candidate for the 18th Congressional District seat, now held by Congressman Doug Walgren. Simply stated, I believe that Mr. Jacob shares the viewpoint and concerns of business and Congressman Walgren does not.

Since he was elected in 1976, we have tried very hard to work with Mr. Walgren. These efforts were made with the hope that he would be understanding and helpful concerning issues which bear heavily on our industry. Further, to demonstrate our confidence, he has received contributions in the past from our Good Government Fund.

To no avail. For instance, in almost every vote on the Clean Air Act amendments he has voted contrary to our interests. In recent months, he voted for a very unwise and damaging amendment which resulted in killing any chance for significant changes in the Clean Air Act this year. He was advised before he cast his vote of its importance to us, but we were unable to persuade him to support us on this issue of vital importance at a time when our company and our industry badly need relief from excessive governmental regulation. On this vote, especially, his was critical because the total count was so close that a vote for our position would have changed the outcome.

We have concluded that there is no longer any hope that Mr. Walgren will support our position on clean air legislation. Neither do we believe that he will be supportive on energy legislation—another issue of major importance to us—which is also handled by a Committee on which he serves. . . .

Congressman Walgren should be replaced. It won't be easy. Ted Jacob has a difficult fight against an incumbent whose party has a registration majority, but we are sure he is up to the challenge. And I think you and I are up to the challenge, as well, to work hard to elect Ted Jacob to replace Congressman Walgren. Of course, this includes casting your own ballot on Election Day.

Walgren was returned to Congress by an overwhelming margin. He received no PAC contributions from U.S. Steel in 1984.

David Roderick is less retributive when he clashes with large corporations that oppose his Washington agenda. Few issues in recent years have been lobbied as fiercely as was the 1982 congressional battle over safe-harbor leasing. U.S. Steel and its business allies worked feverishly—and unsuccessfully—to retain this controversial loophole, which in effect allowed corporations to buy and sell tax breaks. Leasing had channeled billions of dollars to companies that were not profitable enough to take advantage of all the loopholes approved the year before in the Economic Recovery Tax Act (ERTA). But many other large corporations lined up to oppose leasing; the provision fueled such a public backlash that other business preferences were threatened with repeal. Moreover, companies that for years had specialized in leasing did not look favorably upon competition generated by the safe-harbor provisions.

Paramount among safe-harbor opponents was General Electric— "Greed Electric" to business lobbyists who were dismayed by the company's position. GE had managed to make such creative use of the Reagan tax package that it paid no federal income tax in 1981 and 1982, despite having earned profits of more than $4 billion. But the company worked hard in 1982 to defeat leasing. It considered the provision a grave threat to the more conventional leasing operations of its General Electric Credit subsidiary.

Did Roderick telephone GE chairman John Welch to protest that Welch's company was battling to kill a provision of grave importance to the steel industry? "No," Roderick replied. "Everybody has his own viewpoint. And keep one thing in mind. GE Credit was in the leasing business —right? Now, if that's your business, would you be in favor of safe-harbor leasing? They were adamantly opposed to it" when it was approved in 1981. "Adamantly opposed to it. Why the hell did they want nine thousand other companies out there getting into the leasing business? And that's what you could do with safe harbor. Everybody all of a sudden could sell from one company to another. When [leasing] was created, they opposed it. But it went in anyway. So what did they do? They said fine, we'll cream it." Here the chairman paused for emphasis. "And they *creamed* it. And then people said, 'We ought to rescind it.' So they said yes, we ought to rescind it. So they were consistent. GE opposed it from the very beginning. They were better off without it."

There is no more dramatic illustration of the power of U.S. Steel and its industry allies than President Reagan's decision in September 1984 to impose "voluntary" import quotas. The Reagan program represented a decisive victory in the steel industry's two-decade campaign for protection. Never before had a president agreed to so comprehensive a system of restrictions on foreign steel. The long-term goal of the quotas, which extend through 1989, is to limit imports to 18.5 percent of the domestic market—a dramatic reduction from the 26 percent that imports claimed in 1984. Protectionism under earlier administrations had been limited to quotas on steel imports from specific countries or to so-called trigger prices that in effect set a minimum price for steel sold in the United States.

The Reagan program evolved under sustained pressure from industry and labor. Bethlehem Steel and the United Steelworkers staked out the legal front in the campaign for quotas. They filed a petition for relief in January 1984 with the International Trade Commission (ITC). Section 201 of the Trade Act of 1974 provides that the president can restrict imports, even if they are being sold at fair prices, if the ITC concludes that foreign shipments are causing serious harm to domestic producers. Bethlehem and the Steelworkers timed their suit so that President Reagan would be forced to reach a decision just weeks before the November 1984 election. Roderick took a different approach. He worked side-by-side with the Congressional Steel Caucus to press for legislative approval of the Fair Trade in Steel Act. This bill, which was introduced on the same day that U.S. Steel filed countervailing duty suits against three South American countries, would have limited imports to 15 percent of the domestic market. The full-court press had its desired effect on the White House. The Reagan administration announced a system of "voluntary" quotas that won immediate industry approval. Reagan defended himself against cries of protectionism by pointing to the likelihood that Congress would approve even stricter limits.

David Roderick was summoned to Washington several days before the White House reached its decision. He worked closely with Bethlehem Steel chairman Donald Trautlein, who was then chairman of the American Iron and Steel Institute, and various administration officials. Roderick understood that the administration would not accept the ITC's recommendation that it adopt stiff quotas and tariffs. He even knew the margin by which the cabinet had voted to reject the ITC proposal: twelve to one.

Roderick described the course of negotiations from that point. "The process went something like this," he told us. "By word of mouth from various people we were told that the [ITC solution] was from a philosophy point of view not going to be accepted [by the administration]. They didn't want to impose limitations on trading partners, especially where there was fair trade. . . . We were told that it would not be viewed favorably—which was the way we evaluated it from the very beginning. We never joined" the 201 petition "because we didn't feel it was a good way to go.

"We worked on Friday, Saturday, Sunday, and Monday and finally agreed that there was a voluntary approach that was workable," Roderick continued. "The cabinet reviewed that on Tuesday. It was not unanimous. I don't know what the vote was; no one has ever told me. . . . But the president attended [the cabinet session]. He was right there. And he agreed that the voluntary program was consistent with his philopsophy.

. . . Once they reached their decision, [U.S. Trade Representative] Bill Brock had his press conference and revealed it to the public. We did not know what the final decision was. In other words, once we had our say, the process disappeared into the bowels of the administration. Then the president called. The AISI suggested four or five people, a representative segment of the industry, to go over to the White House and meet with the president in the Cabinet Room. He explained why he had turned down the 201 [relief], why he had found this to be a more acceptable remedy. Mr. Brock was there, and he instructed Mr. Brock to carry out the program."

The way in which the Reagan plan evolved sheds light on many of the political weapons at the disposal of Roderick and his industry. The trade laws not only provide judicial relief but can be used as leverage to force the hand of administration officials. U.S. Steel's hard line on the legislative front, derived in collaboration with the Congressional Steel Caucus, created a climate where "voluntary" protectionism of unprecedented scale could be sold as an alternative to mandatory quotas.

One final element in Roderick's Washington clout has been his ability to remove from the political agenda issues on which his company was on the defensive in Congress and before the courts. His decisive break with the past on environmental policy is an instructive example of the virtues of selective retreat.

Under chairman Edgar Speer, U.S. Steel maintained a virtual state of war with regulators charged with enforcing the Clean Air and Clean Water acts. Speer dismissed officials of the Environmental Protection Agency (EPA) as "those nuts down in Washington." His company once commissioned full-page newspaper ads hinting that it would leave Pittsburgh if negotiations over pollution at Clairton Works were not resolved to its satisfaction. Overall, U.S. Steel pursued a legal strategy of maximum resistance to environmental regulation. The company paid millions of dollars in fines during Speer's tenure for violating pollution-abatement agreements at Gary, Clairton, and other plants across the country.

The bitter confrontation between U.S. Steel and Washington regulators came to a rhetorical boil on February 5, 1976. John Quarles, deputy EPA administrator, delivered a widely publicized speech on environmental policy at a seminar sponsored by the Conference Board. Quarles praised by name several corporations that had unveiled innovative conservation and pollution-reduction programs. He then directed a tongue-lashing at U.S. Steel. Quarles cited five different episodes—from U.S. Steel's behavior during an air-pollution emergency in Alabama to its shutdown under protest of a steelmaking furnace at Gary—that demonstrated a pattern of resistance to and disregard for federal regulation.

Quarles complained that U.S. Steel's behavior "tends to give all of industry a black eye." He concluded that Speer's corporation had "compiled a record of environmental recalcitrance second to none."

U.S. Steel has made important progress under its current chairman from its days as an environmental renegade. Much of that progress can be explained by the depressed state of the industry. Steel mills do not generate much pollution when they are not operating. But it is also the case that as soon as Roderick took office, he moved to put behind him the costly and diverting confrontations that had so occupied his predecessor. He signed a consent decree in June 1979 that governed company operations in the Mon Valley. He reached agreement with EPA in 1980 on a timetable to reduce emissions from the Geneva (Utah) Works. He went so far as to bargain personally with environmentalists when the Carter administration drafted legislation to allow steel companies, under certain conditions, to defer investments required to meet the terms of the Clean Air Act.

The thought of Edgar Speer negotiating a legislative compromise with officials of the EPA and the Natural Resources Defense Council is amusing, to say the least. But that is precisely what Roderick did to win passage of the Steel Industry Compliance Extension Act of 1981. Nor would Speer likely have agreed publicly with his successor's unqualified declaration that workplace and environmental standards have made employees more healthy and their communities more livable.

"Oh, there is no question about that," Roderick told us. "There's no question about that. A lot of the things we did we would not have done other than by legislative requirement. We were required to do it. . . . Do we have a healthier atmosphere? I think you have to say yes. Are there less pollutants around the plants? Are there less pollutants in the community? The answer is yes. I mean, there is just no question about it."

Roderick chuckled softly when he was reminded of the Quarles speech. "That was Quarrelsome Quarles," he joked. "Mr. Quarrelsome." But he stood up for Speer against the 1976 attack. "That was something," Roderick said. "I will be very candid. We never could figure out why Quarles did that. It was undeserved. It was uninvited. It was unproductive. . . . We never could figure out why. I'm sure he had a good reason, but we never could get the reason. He seemed to single out U.S. Steel all the time. Maybe because we were the biggest. And therefore, if you are going to pick on somebody, pick on the biggest."

Roderick's defense of his confrontation-minded predecessor points to a final dimension of his use and accumulation of power. David Roderick has broken with the past in his approach to environmental compliance. Yet he is careful not to criticize the executives whose policies he has overturned. Retroactive condemnation amounts to an admission of management fallibility that could jeopardize the standing of current leadership. It is no mystery why John Quarles and his regulatory allies were so enraged for so many years over the behavior of U.S. Steel. But even as the current chairman reverses course, he proclaims his fealty to the ancien régime.

.   .   .

The gulf between Roderick's break with the past on environmental policy and his reluctance to speak critically of the confrontational posture adopted by Edgar Speer raises a caution about interpreting his tenure. It is possible to overstate the depth of change at U.S. Steel since its current chairman assumed office. Roderick's career and rise to power do set him apart from his predecessors on the sixty-first floor. But in many respects he continues to reflect the attitudes and world view of the hard-boiled men who have ruled this industry since the turn of the century. He told us that he believes strongly in peacetime conscription, with a choice of military duty or civilian service. He said he disagrees with the auto industry on the wisdom of mandatory seat-belt legislation. (He believes such laws violate free choice.) And he has grave misgivings about the legal status quo with respect to abortion.

"I really am against abortion," he told us. "Again, there are exceptions. I think you have to deal with it intelligently. Obviously for incest or rape, or for the mother's safety, I can clearly understand when a doctor recommends it. I just in principle am against it. . . . I would oppose [abortion] other than in very defined circumstances. I don't think you ought to be able to get abortion on demand."

Roderick demonstrated similar traditional instincts with respect to this book. Although he was quite generous with his time, he agreed to participate only after we told U.S. Steel that we had prepared a draft chapter *without* his input. We had spent nine months soliciting Roderick's cooperation through letters and telephone calls. It was not until August 1984, when we informed Washington vice-president Earl Mallick that we had conducted extensive research on his chairman that the company changed its position. Still, Roderick would not allow us to interview other U.S. Steel executives. He was the only CEO we profiled who agreed to be interviewed but denied us access to subordinates. Reporters in Pittsburgh said this unusual policy was in keeping with a history of tight executive control at the top of the steel industry.

Eileen Shanahan, a veteran *New York Times* correspondent who spent nearly three years as senior assistant managing editor of the *Pittsburgh*

Post-Gazette, complained that Roderick was aloof and uncooperative with the local media. In an era of plant closings and economic uncertainty, she said, public accessibility is an important dimension of social responsibility. (Shanahan left Pittsburgh in June 1984 to accept a position in Washington, D.C., with Northwestern University's Medill School of Journalism.)

"In the years I was at the newspaper, we never had an [exclusive] personal interview with Roderick," she told us. "We are told to submit written questions. It's absolutely incredible. As long as I've known that company, starting back in the early fifties, they've been the worst I have ever seen. 'A real public-be-damned attitude' is what I once told a top U.S. Steel flack. . . . You can't get through to any of their top people, except possibly Tom Graham. Roderick goes to the National Press Club and answers questions. He goes to Vienna, Austria, and has a press conference. But he won't give interviews here."

The U.S. Steel chairman expressed puzzlement when we presented Shanahan's complaints. He insisted that he maintains a policy of maximum accessibility. "I don't understand that," Roderick said. "I don't think there has been any person in the history of Pittsburgh that has been interviewed more than I have." What about one-on-one interviews with local reporters? "Now, keep in mind, that's a problem," he conceded. "I agree with that. But again, the one-on-ones, I mean, when you're in this job, if you start going one-on-one, I'm going to spend four hours a day giving interviews. I can't do that. What I do say is—I'll have a press conference. Have at me as long as you want. I'll answer any questions you have, no subjects barred." Roderick initiated a system of quarterly press conferences in July 1984 that are held in Pittsburgh and beamed to locations across the country.

Shanahan is not the only media figure in Pittsburgh to have remarked on Roderick's aloofness. Peter Leo, a *Post-Gazette* columnist, wrote a humorous piece on October 5, 1983, that was headlined "It's Hard Work to Say Nothing." His column was meant as a message of protest. "If U.S. Steel really wants to get something off its chest, it sends chairman David Roderick on the road to say something important in places like Cleveland or, as was the case yesterday, Vienna," Leo wrote. "Why does U.S. Steel do this? Maybe it thinks we in Pittsburgh won't be paying attention if Dave drops a bombshell in Vienna. Also, it is tough to dispatch a couple of busloads of picketing steel workers to Vienna on a moment's notice. I prefer to think that U.S. Steel is simply recognizing the intense interest of the Vienna press in Pennsylvania steel mill closings."

Roderick also revealed a bit of a temper as our conversations wore on. Haruki Kamiya, executive vice-president of Nippon Kokan, Japan's second largest steel producer, criticized his American counterparts in an interview with the *Los Angeles Times* in May 1984. Nippon Kokan purchased 50 percent of National Steel after the Justice Department objected to Roderick's acquisition proposal. Other Japanese producers, including Sumitomo Metal Industries and Kawasaki Steel, have demonstrated enthusiasm for the American steel market by investing in it—even as companies such as U.S. Steel have diversified out of it.

"I don't understand the thinking of American steel executives, particularly Roderick of U.S. Steel," Kamiya said. "While saying that the American industry needs leeway to carry out equipment investment he is using all that money to buy Marathon Oil. If U.S. Steel has enough money to buy Marathon Oil, why doesn't it spend that amount to modernize its own [steel] facilities?"

Did Kamiya apologize for the remarks? "No, but Pete Love, the chairman of National Intergroup, apologized for them as being out of line," Roderick sidestepped adroitly. "Number one, you know that gentleman is not very knowledgeable about this country. As you can appreciate. He may be very knowledgeable about Japan and about his own company. I would say he borders on being ignorant of the affairs of U.S. Steel. And you would expect him to be. How could he be an expert on U.S. Steel any more than I could be an expert on Nippon Kokan? . . . He has not learned to keep opinions to himself."

David Roderick has internalized many of the personality traits that animated his predecessors at the helm of U.S. Steel. He is traditionalist. He is the man in charge. He has little tolerance for barbs hurled by competitors. We wanted to probe the limits of Roderick's candor with respect to his disagreements with old-guard management at U.S. Steel. Many of the strategies he has championed—closing millions of tons of capacity, selling billions of dollars of assets, shedding product lines—are implicit repudiations of the policies of Edgar Speer and Edwin Gott.

Would either of these chairmen have pursued this strategy of rationalization and diversification? "That's hard to say, of course, whether I am doing things they would not have done," Roderick replied. "Keep in mind that when they managed, they had a different set of circumstances than I have. . . . Sure, we had an import problem. But we didn't have an industry in crisis. During the whole time that Ed Gott was chairman, we probably never had a year where the industry [as a whole] had a loss. We have had two consecutive years [1982 and 1983] when the industry lost $3 billion. It is a totally different set of circumstances. Therefore, it is very difficult to say, what would they have done had they been faced with my circumstances? I can't answer that and I don't think anyone else can either."

Roderick is of course correct. But it is undeniable that his tenure as chief executive would have been much less traumatic for workers and communities had his predecessors responded more nimbly to forces over which Roderick now has little control. The demise of the integrated steel industry has been documented and dissected in countless books, articles, and monographs. What is remarkable is not that management has come in for criticism, but that the criticism has been so universal and uniform. Roderick spoke at length with us about charges of incompetence and shortsightedness leveled against his predecessors.

His initial response was one of extreme caution. "I want to make sure as a matter of record that I am not second-guessing [management]," he insisted. "I am second-guessing, but I am not questioning the judgment of the people who had to make those judgments at the time they were made. They had to deal with the facts and circumstances at that time, not as you view them twenty years later."

Roderick then launched into a detailed examination of the legacy of his predecessors. First, he took exception to the most damaging insights served by critics of the industry. The chairman denied that steel operated as an oligopoly for several decades before and after World War II or that the tightly knit structure of the industry retarded adjustment. "I don't want to get into a long historical argument," he told us. "You know, there are all sorts of cases before congressional committees and so forth on that old question of administered prices. The industry has never been found guilty of any improper practice in that area on any broad basis. They have been accused by people . . . but there never has been any guilt."

These comments etch the boundaries of what Roderick considers acceptable revisionism. The steel industry has been the target of government sanctions on pricing behavior since at least 1924, when the Federal Trade Commission (FTC) prohibited U.S. Steel and its subsidiaries from selling under the Pittsburgh Plus system of pricing. Pittsburgh Plus meant that steel marketed in Texas or Minnesota would be priced to reflect the cost of production plus transportation costs from Pittsburgh to Texas or Minnesota, even if the steel was manufactured at an in-state mill. This pricing scheme reduced competition by eliminating the price advantages of producing steel closer to the customer. The FTC intervened again in 1951 to ban other forms of deceptive and anitcompetitive behavior by steel manufacturers.

Michael Borrus, deputy director of the Berkeley Roundtable on the International Economy, examined more contemporary pricing behavior in a 1983 essay on the decline of the steel industry. "The largest producers have consistently advocated full-cost pricing in the domestic market as well as in foreign markets," Borrus wrote. "This advocacy has held even when competitive pricing could drive imports out of the U.S. market, or could increase U.S. shares of foreign markets, and even when under-used capacity exists to accomplish either of these objectives. . . . Their actions suggest a long-run explanation of their behavior: as oligopolistic producers, the major integrated firms seek over the long term to refrain from any activity that might unnecessarily destabilize respective market shares."

U.S. Steel's anticompetitive instincts have even crossed into the realm of criminality. It has been found guilty of price-fixing or illegal rebating on several different occasions. Roderick's company was one of nine corporations fined a total of $566,000 in 1976 for having conspired to set prices on reinforcing steel bars sold in Houston and Dallas–Fort Worth. U.S. Steel pleaded no contest to the charges. (The FTC also fined four of the companies, including U.S. Steel, a total of $440,000 in connection with the Texas price-fixing scheme. The agency said their behavior violated the 1951 consent decree.) A U.S. Steel railroad subsidiary was fined $150,000 in September 1982 after pleading no contest to criminal charges that it conspired between 1956 and 1978 to eliminate competition from private truckers shipping iron ore from Lake Erie to steel mills in a four-state area. And federal judge Miles Lord fined U.S. Steel $3.6 million in 1980 for civil violations of anti-rebating laws on shipments of coal to mills in Duluth, Minnesota. An appeals court vacated the judgment in 1981, and the case is now under review by the Interstate Commerce Commission (ICC).

Chairman Roderick also disagreed that technological backwardness is an important source of the industry's competitive dilemma. U.S. steel-makers continue to trail their overseas counterparts in the adoption of the two most dramatic steel-making breakthroughs since World War II: the basic oxygen furnace and continuous casting. Wall Street analyst Charles Bradford has estimated that continuous casting can shave thirty dollars off the production costs of a ton of steel—more than 5 percent of the average cost of production. But the industry in the late 1960s and early 1970s failed to appreciate the profound competitive implications of this new technology. By the time steelmakers woke up, they were no longer making enough profits to finance the massive investments needed to meet their foreign rivals. Japanese producers continuously cast more than 80 percent of the steel they turned out in 1983. American producers used continuous casting on 25 percent of their output. The figure for U.S. Steel was just over 14 percent.

Have domestic producers been laggard in applying important technologies, such as basic oxygen furnaces and continuous casting? "I think that's not as valid as it may sound," Roderick said. "It's a good theme for people to [advance] because they confuse technology with the ability to apply technology. I don't think there has ever been a technology lag in the American steel industry. Because a technology lag means that you don't have the knowledge to really put in place the latest practices. That just is not the case. We had continuous-cast [steel] out in Gary before three-fourths of the casters now in the world [were operating]. There is no question what a caster does. There is no question what a BOP shop does. It's quicker. It's cheaper. If you have to replace an open hearth, you are going to put a BOP shop in. But if you have a very, very good open hearth, it is surprising that you may be making more money, and have lower costs, in a good open hearth, when scrap prices are low, than in a BOP shop." (Open hearth furnaces can accept either molten iron or steel scrap. Basic oxygen furnaces operate largely on molten iron.)

Roderick eventually turned from his differences with steel industry critics to areas of agreement. In a rare display of corporate self-analysis, he cited four specific issues that management—with hindsight—should have addressed more decisively. These observations merit detailed exposition:

- *Targeted investment.* "I think steel investment should have been more targeted. In other words, if you had six steel plants, you should have recognized twenty years ago—using the [consumption] trends, and the international importation [trend], and the clear evidence that exists today that there is tremendous over-capacity in the steel industry around the world—that you should not have tried to maintain the capacity of six plants. You should have concentrated all of your investment on, let's say, three plants. So that those three were totally modern and effective. The worst position to be in is to have six plants that are half modern. That means you are mediocre in six places rather than excellent in three. . . . You could specialize in certain product lines. In other words, do not try to be a [steel] supermarket anymore. That day clearly was ending. I guess part of the job I have had to do in the last five years was really an accumulation of things, some of which, if they would have been anticipated —if the circumstances could have been anticipated—would have happened over a much longer period of time, and probably should have."
- *Blue-collar wages.* "We have been too quick to accept labor settlements on the assumption that the cost could be passed through into our product. And you should never make that

assumption. I don't think you should ever give a labor settlement that you can't afford to absorb, because it's very presumptuous to assume that your product is going to be able to pass it through. . . . One of our problems has been that the leadership of the union and the companies, in effect, have been too good to one another. I have heard people in this industry brag that we haven't had a strike since 1959. And when you look at the result, you have to say that's too bad. We shouldn't be bragging about that. There should have been some [labor] confrontation, somewhere along the line, so we didn't work ourselves into this dilemma."

• *Bureaucratic streamlining.* "I think we could always say, looking inward at ourselves, that if we had everything to do over again, one thing we would not have done is that—we became perhaps too fat. We didn't operate lean enough. Could we have operated with fewer administrative people? Well, we are today so I guess we could have then."

• *Global expansion.* "Probably this industry should have internationalized and followed the trend" of the electronics industry and other high-technology companies. "In other words, global sourcing . . . I think you could have done some of that. If you look back on it, there was no real effort by the basic steel industry to do that. The aluminum companies did it. The aluminum companies did it in spades. But the steel companies really did not. . . . We should have been more venturesome, let's say, in maybe taking some of that money we were investing and, in effect, looking at a broader market than the United States and looking at a broader economic base for making the product than the United States." Roderick then explained the roots of this failure with respect to foreign expansion. "The reason is, a lot of the industries we are talking about—some of the high-tech industries—you go over[seas] and you build a roof. The machinery is light. The investment—you put down twenty-five million bucks and you are in business. When you are in the steel business and you want to go to Timbuktu, you maybe go in for openers and start talking about half a billion dollars. Well, if things don't work out in five years, you can't just pick up your half a billion and walk away with it. And you can't afford to write it off. Where this [high-technology] guy, he tries a place, and if it doesn't work out—ah, it's four million bucks. Forget it. He goes to another place and builds another roof. [The steel industry] is not as mobile. The capital intensity

is much greater. The political profile in these [foreign] countries is horrible. You are invariably competing with the government."

.   .   .

David Roderick's candid retrospective on the demise of the steel industry
suggests the intensity of the pressures under which he is operating. His
resolve in the face of opposition, a trait that has animated leaders of the
industry for generations, has inspired a take-no-prisoners deployment of
power in Washington and Chicago and Bucks County, Pennsylvania. But
Roderick's power to deny also brings certain costs. He has encountered
widespread protests against and challenges to his rule. The intensity of
these protests would confound his well-insulated predecessors. The personal strains on Roderick that have accompanied U.S. Steel's corporate
transformation should not be underestimated. His response to these
strains offers important insights into his leadership and character.

Many of the "rebound consequences" of change have been relatively
benign. Roderick has received letters from unemployed steelworkers and
their spouses that communicate the fear and misery of economic dislocation. How does he respond to these missives of pain? Roderick told us that
he answers personally when a letter from the chairman is the only appropriate response. Otherwise, he routes the correspondence to various departments—personnel, employee benefits, labor relations—for follow-up action.

"I don't know how many letters we received," Roderick said. "We
never tried to tally them. But I think it would be reasonable to say, on
the total closings [in 1979 and 1983], a couple of hundred. They [usually]
write and say they feel bad about this or they feel bad about that. A lot
of them are concerned that their husband was discriminated against. You
know, 'Charlie was kept on, but my Harry was terminated. I think he was
mistreated. He's loyal, he's dedicated.' I would process those over to our
personnel department and say look into this. In other words, is this a
legitimate grievance? Others say, 'I would like your views,' and so forth.
We would clearly answer that letter."

Other experiences for Roderick have been unpleasant—but conducted within the legal and corporate framework in which he normally
operates. The Youngstown closing of 1979 inspired a lawsuit that challenged U.S. Steel's freedom to abandon the mill. The suit was filed by the
Tri-State Conference on Steel, a community organization formed in response to earlier plant closings, a number of United Steelworker locals,
and Republican congressman Lyle Williams. It charged that U.S. Steel
had breached repeated verbal commitments to maintain production at

Youngstown so long as the plant operated profitably. The lawsuit was lost after an emotional trial before a U.S. District Court judge in Youngstown that attracted national attention.

Roderick was compelled to sit for a deposition and testify during the course of the proceedings. The transcripts suggest he did not enjoy the scrutiny to which he was subjected. He refused to answer all questions in his four-hour deposition as to whether he would sell the Youngstown facilities to the employees and their community. He reported that U.S. Steel had not made major investments for modernization at the complex since the 1940s. He conceded that he was unaware, prior to U.S. Steel's decision to close, of plans drawn up by William Kirwan, superintendent of the Youngstown Works, to rehabilitate the mill by installing electric furnaces. Roderick was also asked why he had declined to see Robert Appleyard, Episcopal bishop of Pittsburgh, who requested a meeting three weeks prior to the Youngstown closing to discuss with the U.S. Steel chairman and members of the Tri-State Conference future plans for capital investment in northeastern Ohio:

Q: Was there any reason for not meeting with Bishop Appleyard?
A: You mean why I will not meet with him?
Q: Yes.
A: Well, I would assume that Mr. Appleyard being a bishop of the church, I just didn't think that, I guess, he could give me a whole lot of advice on how to run [a] steel business and how to run any chemical plants and that I couldn't give him a lot of advice as to how to run his church. I guess I just didn't feel there would be any purpose for such a meeting.

Nowhere have the "rebound consequences" of U.S. Steel's corporate transformation exploded more dramatically than in the burgeoning protest movement of unemployed workers in the Monongahela Valley outside of Pittsburgh. The Mon Valley is a collection of mill towns and plants that was at one time the center of steel production for the giant corporation headquartered nearby. Seven of the eight companies that combined in 1901 to form U.S. Steel had operations in and around Pittsburgh. The valley now accounts for only 15 percent of the corporation's total production capacity. If there is one community that captures the glorious past and troubled future of the Mon Valley it is Homestead, the birthplace of modern steelmaking in the United States.

In the summer of 1892, while Andrew Carnegie was vacationing in England, the Amalgamated Association (forerunner of the United Steelworkers) called a strike at the Carnegie plant in Homestead. Henry Frick, the tough steel boss who was in charge during Carnegie's absence, hired three hundred Pinkerton guards and floated them up the Monongahela River on barges. The angry strikers gathered on the dock and refused to let the Pinkertons land. Shots were fired. In the riot and battling that followed, thirteen men were killed. The governor of Pennsylvania dispatched seven thousand national guardsmen, who occupied the region for four months.

Homestead today survives largely on memories. U.S. Steel employed nearly 6,500 workers at its giant mill as recently as 1980. By 1985 barely 1,000 workers were on the job. The company employed more than 22,500 workers in all of its Mon Valley operations in 1980. Five years later the figure was 5,000. Homestead and the surrounding communities are not ghost towns—at least not yet. Coal barges still ply the Mon River. Tractor trailers still rumble down East Eighth Avenue, Homestead's main thoroughfare, twenty-four hours a day. But their numbers are so small that they seem conspicuous by their presence.

The Mon Valley is caught in a vise grip of economic forces over which its residents have no control. Steel markets have moved westward, which means higher transportation costs for products shipped from these plants. Stagnation in the heavy construction and capital-goods sectors, to which most of the valley's output is directed, has reduced demand. And an investment focus by U.S. Steel on plants further west and south has left the network of mills that comprises the Mon Valley Works starved for modernization capital.

The quiet desperation of this region produced a grass-roots protest movement that has struggled to reverse this dynamic of decline. The Mon Valley Unemployed Committee, which was formed in October 1982, has worked vigorously to cushion the social and economic impact of chronic joblessness. The Unemployed Committee has lobbied for a moratorium on home foreclosures and in favor of extending benefits to jobless workers. The Tri-State Conference on Steel, which has been organizing against U.S. Steel shutdowns since 1979, has developed an economic and political program to revive steelmaking in the valley. Its agenda revolves around the use of eminent domain by local officials to take control of abandoned mills and financial support from state and federal authorities. But the two organizations that have riveted national attention on the Mon Valley—and that direct their protests most directly at Roderick himself—are the Denominational Ministry Strategy (DMS) and the Network to Save the Mon-Ohio Valleys. We spoke to a number of DMS and Network activists about the future of their region and the tenure of David Roderick.

Mike Bonn, the burly former president of United Steelworkers Local 2227, which represents employees at U.S. Steel's Irvin plant, described the situation in March 1985. Irvin is better off than most of its Mon Valley counterparts. The plant produces sheet steel from slabs shipped from the nearby Edgar Thomson mill. Its major customer is a modern appliance plant in Louisville, Kentucky, owned by General Electric. Irvin also ships large quantities of steel to the beverage-can industry. But better-than-average is not good enough. Bonn said that four members of his local have committed suicide in the past thirty months. He links their deaths directly to the bleak future of the Mon Valley. His son-in-law, who was not employed by U.S. Steel, lost his job through the ripple effect of decline. He also took his own life.

"I had a fella here that was laid off and got accepted into a computer school," Bonn told us. "He was a personal friend of mine. We worked so hard to get him into this computer school because he was so down at that time. He went through there and he aced the course. But he came out and found out he couldn't get a job yet. Now here's a guy who was single, no wife and kids to worry about. He was living with his parents. But after completing computer school, and still not getting a job, he shot himself."

Mike Bonn has become a prominent figure in the Mon Valley. He is a leader, with Ron Weisen, president of Homestead Local 1397, of the Network organization. The Network has worked closely with DMS, an organization of Protestant ministers that was formed in 1980, to sponsor a series of militant nonviolent protest actions. One of their basic goals is to pressure U.S. Steel to install continuous casters in the region. The Mon Valley Works is the only U.S. Steel operation outside of its Utah complex without a continuous caster. The company announced in 1980 that it would spend $100 million on a caster at the Edgar Thomson plant that could produce 1.3 million tons of steel per year. But it abandoned those plans in 1982 after the onset of a recession from which the region has yet to recover. These activists argue, with little dispute, that without a caster, steelmaking in their milltowns may disappear forever.

As that dark reality looms larger and larger, the tactics of the Network have become more and more desperate. Bonn and his colleagues have disrupted services, including the 1984 Easter mass, at churches in affluent neighborhoods where leading steel executives and bankers worship. They have printed Roderick's home telephone number on leaflets and urged sympathizers to call him and voice their opinions on the future of the valley. Network members have driven a church bus loaded with activists to Roderick's home in Fox Chapel.

"I think after that day he realized we were legitimate," Bonn told us. "We just drove the bus right up the driveway to his house. We showed him that he can't hide from us. He can't feel safe." Network members even claim to have sprayed skunk oil—a substance of which they have made liberal use—in a U.S. Steel helicopter. "Roderick knows that if we can do that, we can do anything to his helicopter," Bonn said. "They know that we know where they are at all times."

Bonn and Weisen seem to have gotten under the skin of the U.S. Steel chairman. Would Roderick allow members of the community to ask questions at his press conferences in Pittsburgh? "No," he declared. "When we are holding a press conference, it is our press conference. If Ron Weisen wants to have a press conference, he can have his. And I am going to have mine. But I'm not going to have a [press conference] in order for him to have one. I'm not interested in that."

Roderick was asked why he has refused all invitations to meet with leaders of the Network or DMS. The organizations have offered to abandon their protests in return for promises of new investment in the valley. "These people belong to two organizations, the bulk of them," Roderick told us. "They belong to a union and they belong to a company. And we think we have a legitimate concern [for their welfare] and an ongoing concern and a sensitivity. Now, the union, of course, has its own structure to deal with us and to deal with the employees. Those lines of communication are open. We do dialogue with [United Steelworkers president] Lynn Williams and the international officers. Our local people of course dialogue with the district director and the local presidents. But what we try to do is keep it reasonably well structured so that we do not undermine the union leadership itself.

"Now, what happens is that people get frustrated with that mechanism—it's either not working the way they want it to work or they figure it does not represent them," he continued. "So they splinter off. They go off and form this group and that group. And it is quite obvious that you can't deal with all those groups. If you attempt to deal with them, you find out very quickly that if there are five of them, they have five different objectives, five different approaches, and conflicting approaches. And usually conflicting interests. So what we try to do is to stay within some mechanism so that we can deal with it in a more orderly way. Now, does this mean that we don't hear what they're saying? Of course, the answer is that we do hear what they're saying."

Roderick spoke at length during our conversations about the Mon Valley protest movement: its impact on the community, its effects on him, his opinions of its organizers. Throughout the discussion he remained remarkably composed. He also made it clear that while he is aware of and may understand the roots of the protests, they will in no way influence investment strategies at the Mon Valley Works. What follows are excerpts from our conversation:

- *What does Roderick think of Homestead leader Weisen, who has achieved national attention as a union activist?* "Let me put it this way, I think his reasoning is extremely poor. I would not give any ulterior motive [to his actions]. I have to believe he believes, sincerely believes, in what he is doing. But I don't think he is helping the people at Homestead one iota. And I don't think he is representative of the steelworkers. I don't think he is representative of steelworker leadership . . . . He has run for [national] office two or three times to try and get a broader [constituency] and he has been trounced every time."

- *How would Roderick characterize the impact of the Mon Valley protest movement?* "They have raised the visibility of the issue. They have raised the communication level, demonstrating the frustration of an unemployed, dislocated worker. I think they have raised the awareness that all is not right with the world. In other words, maybe you're fat and happy, but by Gad while you're fat and happy and hitting chip shots onto the eighteenth green, there are a hell of a lot of people out here who aren't working—and we're not happy about it. I think it's made a broad segment of our community more aware of it than they otherwise would be. And I think that's good. . . . But when you make people aware of the problems, you want to accomplish two things. You want to make them aware of it and you want them to try to become part of a solution. The worst of all worlds is to communicate the problem but do it in such a way that you polarize people into not helping you. . . . Some of the tactics used, as you say, may have been necessary to get whatever attention they have gotten and maybe for communications reasons were necessary to vent their frustrations. And compared to some of the other ways they might have vented it, it was a good way. But I think that when you get into breaking up people's church services on Easter Sunday, what you do is polarize opposition to you."

- *How does Roderick react to the protest tactics aimed directly at him?* "I don't think anybody should ever get mad at somebody who's mad because they want to work. I think you ought to get mad at people where there is work and they don't want to work. But you shouldn't get mad at people, or frustrated by people, who are protesting and are irritated because they had a job, they are willing to work, they are able to work, and in effect you don't have work for them. So my feeling is you have to be patient. You have to be sensitive. I think anybody who enjoys . . . making the

very difficult decisions to close plants that are no longer economic and are inflicting tremendous financial losses over an
extended period—anybody who enjoys inflicting that pain on
the employees and the community is someone I would not want
working for me. I wouldn't want as part of this corporation. So
I think you maintain a sensitivity. You [also] maintain your
resolve. You have to have a strategic plan. You have to have a
philosophy. And you have to stick to it. Otherwise you go here,
and then you go there, and then you go there. So with a good
strategic plan, a good philosophy, I think a clear conscience that
you have done what could be done under the circumstances, the
important thing is to maintain your patience."

It would be easier to accept Roderick's claims of patience and sensitivity if he had demonstrated more creativity in his response to the Mon
Valley protests. The chairman of U.S. Steel cannot simply wave a magic
wand and resurrect overnight the bustle and prosperity that once characterized life around Pittsburgh's steel mills. But workers and community
residents have organized campaigns to salvage what they can of their
plants. As with South Works in Chicago—and Youngstown before it—
U.S. Steel has chosen not to endorse community proposals. Roderick's
decision to demolish the Dorothy Six blast furnace, a huge facility that
once turned out five thousand tons of steel per day, is typical of his
reaction to sincere and reasonable strategies advanced by local residents
to revive their communities.

U.S. Steel announced in June 1984 that it would shut down Blast
Furnace Number 6 and associated steelmaking facilities at Duquesne
Works in the Mon Valley. The news was another devastating blow to area
residents. Duquesne employed 3,200 workers in 1979 and 2,000 workers
in early 1984. Dorothy Six, named after the wife of a former U.S. Steel
president, was only twenty-one years old when the company condemned
it to death. It thus qualified as a relatively modern facility. Only months
before Dorothy Six was closed, members of USWA Local 1256 had been
presented U.S. Steel's "Ironmaster" award for breaking production records at the furnace. Dorothy was an operable facility that fell victim to
the profit and production calculus of the corporation that owned it.

A "Save Dorothy" movement soon emerged. Roderick was persuaded
to postpone destruction of the furnace for sixty days. The steelworkers and
local governments raised $150,000 to finance a feasibility study on the
future of Duquesne. The results were made available on January 28, 1985.
Locker-Abrecht Associates, a New York-based consulting firm, reported
that with an investment of $90 million over three years, Dorothy Six and

its companion facilities could remain a viable source of semifinished steel for other mills. Revival of steelmaking at Duquesne would save between 550 and 600 jobs.

U.S. Steel announced that it would consider the Locker-Abrecht plan. On April 15, David Roderick issued his verdict: The blast furnace would be closed as planned. "I think we all have to realize that it can't be business as usual, that we're in a highly competitive market," the chairman told reporters. "We want to be friendly, but we're not Santa Claus."

.   .   .

Through a combination of iron determination and a fixed sense of corporate direction, David Roderick has become the nonnegotiable man. By refusing to bend, he makes others break. In a bargaining situation between contestants, each of whom has some chips, a hard line to victory may be considered shrewd or brilliant gamesmanship. But when your adversaries or supplicants are almost literally on their knees, when all they want is what little they have left by way of employment, a nonnegotiable straight-arm is unbecoming a responsible chief executive—particularly one so possessed of additional intellectual resources upon which to draw and so conscious of the economic circumstances that predated his drive to the sixty-first floor.

How to handle what a company considers to be uneconomic manufacturing facilities is not ruled by a single standard written in stone. There are adaptive or transitional approaches that can be debated and discussed with the affected community. Aging industrial properties can be put to uses more suited to sustaining community morale and revival than leaving empty hulks with broken windows through which the wind can howl. The painful decline of U.S. Steel is not the first time that factories have been closed on a large scale. But the abruptness of Roderick's plant closures, the feeling of betrayal or manipulation that pervades the afflicted townspeople, and, above all, the negation of their voice cannot be justified as the hardheaded workings of free enterprise. U.S. Steel has benefited from the rescue of so many public subsidies, through trade, tax, and other protections, that reposing total decision-making authority in the private hands of its subsidized executives robs the public of its stake in the company and ignores the larger national policy behind laws passed to assist the troubled or mismanaged business.

Many people within and without the corporate world insist on reciprocity from the poor who are on the public dole. They call it workfare. Corporations, rich and nonrich, have been on a growing public dole for years in our country, albeit in a more camouflaged manner. Accordingly, the word "welfare" is not used; its replacement is the softer terminology of "incentives." A wide variety of protections from the inroads of more efficient competitors, tax-free industrial bonds, waivers from pollution-control requirements, loan guarantees, property-tax abatements or reductions, company patents of publicly funded innovations, income tax credits and allowances are some of the ingredients in the public-subsidy brew. U.S. Steel has sipped generously from this trough for a long time. The fact that Roderick's corporation long ago became a private enterprise held together by public taxpayers and public concessions raises basic questions of reciprocity. What is the community's, the taxpayer's, the consumer's *quid pro quo* for their contribution beyond the recovery of the corporation's ability to restore to itself its private profits? In their expressions of anguish and outrage, the people in the declining steeltowns of South Chicago and the Mon Valley have given the answers: the right to information in a timely way, the right to participate before final decisions are made and the opportunity to negotiate the least damaging solutions.

There is very little indication that Roderick recognizes the existence or validity of this kind of "corporate workfare" for subsidies received. He makes decisions as if he were operating in the days of Andrew Carnegie —who, by the way, did not trundle down to Washington looking for relief. Roderick may reply that the vastly greater number of regulatory standards imposed on U.S. Steel merits public "incentives." To control pollution, industrialists argue, companies should be given the benefit of tax-free pollution bonds. But when laws prohibit dangerous conditions, as did fire codes or boiler codes decades ago, why should compliance with these requirements demand a subsidy through the tax system? The argument becomes even stronger when applied to a much larger brace of subsidies arising out of laws lobbied through Congress by the steel industry and its allies. Why shouldn't he who pays the piper help to call the tune? After all, taxpayers are not supposed to be paying for something without conditions and procedures intended to achieve the mutually-agreed-upon objectives of the subsidy.

It is not yet clear whether Roderick is willing or capable of the "lateral growth" that would contemplate a broader array of corporate responsibility to mitigate the disruptive consequences of company decisions. He came into office single-minded, not broad-minded. He moved quickly to shrink the company's steel operations, to dispose of fixed assets for flexible cash, and to use the money to diversify the company through acquisitions of nonsteel firms such as Marathon Oil. He has done this with deliberate precision, waiting for just the right opportunity. But is there anything in Roderick's future except another large acquisition or two? Now that he is running out of plants to close—a depletion of assets that also weakens his power to deny—can he amass new leverage over outside constituencies to achieve his ends? There is a gap between the perceptions of U.S. Steel's power and the reality of its scaled-down presence. Against this shrinking background, Roderick seems to have few plans for or commitment to a resurgence through more innovative and dynamic modes of steel production and marketing. He certainly displays little empirical attachment to or sentiment for steel mills—which perhaps is understandable for one who never managed a plant.

There are many worried observers, such as the Tri-State Conference on Steel, who have long argued that David Roderick's ultimate goal is "to get U.S. Steel out of the steel business." They point to the massive reductions in capacity since 1979. They argue that the acquisitions of Marathon Oil and of Texas Oil and Gas are an obvious signal that scarce investment dollars will be diverted away from steel. If U.S. Steel could borrow $3 billion to purchase Marathon, why didn't it borrow those funds to modernize its steelmills?

Economist Donald Barnett is unsure of the company's long-term profile. "I can't say for sure that Roderick has made a conscious decision to get out of steel," he told us. "But the facts are that everything U.S. Steel is doing suggests that they are getting out of steel. If you are getting back into steel, you better have one healthy [integrated] facility. They haven't got one. They haven't got one facility that's worth anything."

The U.S. Steel chairman has heard these criticisms before. He assured interviewers that they are misplaced. His company could not have borrowed $3 billion to invest in steel plants even if it wanted to—the returns on new investment in steel simply would not have supported the cost of the loans. U.S. Steel has made substantial investments in modernization at certain plants. Did not the attempt to acquire National Steel, which would have cemented his firm's position in the critical flat-rolled segment of the market, provide proof of intent that he does not want to abandon the industry?

But what Roderick does not say—and what suggests that his dedication to steel might well be described as a strategy of profitable decline—is that he did not tap the one source of investment funds that could have produced dramatic steel modernization. U.S. Steel has raised at least $3 billion since 1980 through the sale of idle or low-return assets it has owned for decades. Much of that cash was used in acquisitions or to reduce long-term debt incurred to finance the Marathon deal.

Cannot unemployed steelworkers legitimately claim that these funds would be better spent on modernization and that their use elsewhere represents an abandonment of steel? "A steelworker could logically say that because he is looking at it in his own interest," Roderick told us.

"He's not looking at it from the standpoint of the shareholders. He is not looking at it from the standpoint of management, which has to manage assets in the best interests of the shareholders, but with total sensitivity to employees. Let's say all of our other assets—some of the ones we are selling are earning eight percent. To, in effect, sell them and reinvest them in a business that is earning four percent when I can take them and put them in a business that is earning twelve percent. . . . I mean, why would I do that? I don't get paid to do that. That's not what shareholders expect."

There are some members of Congress who led the drive for steel industry assistance, some advocates of the national interest in a resurgent steel industry, and many workers now stuck in occupational obsolescence who would have liked to have heard that Roderickian business philosophy expressed so precisely in earlier years. It would have clarified matters so much.

ROGER SMITH

Detroit Iron in Orbit

The atmosphere was tense in the office of the boss. While Roger Smith did not become chairman of General Motors by making waves, he understood, after the losses of 1980, that to remain in command he would at least have to rock the boat. That to Smith meant concessions from the United Auto Workers (UAW)—a demand without precedent in the union's forty-three years of collective bargaining with GM. The UAW president, soft-spoken Douglas Fraser, and his deputy, Owen Bieber, met with Smith in the fall of 1981 to discuss the touchy subject. A labor contract signed in 1979 was not due to expire until September 1982. But for months Smith and his counterparts at Ford had been insisting that negotiations begin ahead of schedule. The meeting with Fraser took place on the fourteenth floor of GM's Detroit headquarters, behind two sets of regularly locked doors, in Chairman Smith's corner suite.

The UAW leader described the encounter with a telling tone to his chuckle. "We got into quite an argument," Fraser told us. "Smith wanted us to reopen the agreement, and we didn't think so. He got tough with us, and I got tough with him. As Owen and I were walking out of the office, I said to him, 'A lot of people wondered why this guy became chairman of the board. Well, now you know. He's a tough little son of a bitch.' "

Doug Fraser was not alone in wondering about Roger Smith's character and personality. The GM chairman was not viewed as a prepossessing figure. Raymond Peck, who as President Reagan's first National Highway Traffic Safety administrator acquiesced in nearly all of GM's major deregulatory demands, told us that upon meeting Smith he could scarcely believe this was the man in charge of the world's largest automobile company. Michigan congressman Dale Kildee sat with the chairman during an August 1983 celebration at a GM truck factory in Flint. "He talked more about hunting and fishing than about trucks," Kildee recalled.

"He's really kind of a low-key guy." How would the congressman appraise Smith's personal qualities? "He reminds me of a manager of a nice friendly hardware store . . . really like a manager of the local hardware store."

His appearance and demeanor notwithstanding, Roger Smith is a powerful man if only because of the corporation he now leads. General Motors—the colossus of the global auto industry—had produced 235 million cars and trucks before Smith took the helm on January 1, 1981. It accounts for more than two of every five cars sold in the United States and nearly three of every five built in North America. It also produces locomotives and turbine engines and is the world's largest manufacturer of control computers. With a labor force of 750,000 and sales of $83.9 billion in 1984, GM represents a corporate empire of unrivaled scale. It has facilities in twenty-six states, Canada, and thirty-seven other foreign countries. No manufacturing enterprise employs more workers than General Motors. GM is as potent a buyer as it is a seller. It purchased 6.5 million tons of steel in 1984, more than 8 percent of all domestic shipments, and was the single largest steel consumer in the United States. When Smith decided to push his suppliers to lower prices for the 1986 model year, steelmakers as formidable as U.S. Steel and LTV had little choice but to go along.

General Motors is also a vertically integrated giant. It controls its own finance company, the largest such operation in the United States, and its own insurance company. General Motors Acceptance Corporation (GMAC), which finances wholesale and retail sales of cars and trucks, had assets of $54 billion and revenues of $8 billion in 1984. GMAC also ranks as the country's second largest mortgage banker, with a loan portfolio of more than $18 billion in 1985. This immense financial, dealer, and market power has long given the corporation undisputed reign over the domestic automobile oligopoly. Henry Ford II volunteered an appropriate metaphor to a student team interviewing him in the early 1970s. When asked how it felt to contend against General Motors, Mr. Ford, who was then running the world's fourth largest industrial company, replied, "It's like going to bed with an elephant."

A decade later the metaphor was extendable but in a different way. By 1981 the "elephant" was drifting. GM was mired in a swamp of waste, mismanagement and product defects. During Smith's first year as chairman, GM recalled 5.8 million Chevrolets, Buicks, Pontiacs, and Oldsmobiles manufactured between August 1977 and December 1980. There was a possibility that on certain cars the bolts that attach the lower rear control arm to the frame might eventually fracture, causing a loss of control. Total GM recalls for safety defects or emission problems in 1981 exceeded 7 million—more than all the cars, trucks, and buses the corporation turned out that year. In 1980, a fully foreseeable but even more dreaded statistic had floated across the Pacific. Japan for the first time surpassed the United States as the leading automobile-producing nation in the world. That same year GM reported its first annual loss ($763 million) since 1921.

Many analysts outside General Motors viewed the company's troubles in early 1981 as nothing more than the domestic industry's trauma arising from the doubling of gasoline prices in 1979 and the quicker exploitation of that opportunity by hordes of more fuel-efficient Japanese cars manufactured by lower-paid and more pliant workers. With the moderation of oil prices, imposition of the auto-import quota in April 1981, and President Reagan's promised tax advantages to business, it was considered only a matter of time before General Motors righted itself and reclaimed its position among the elite of industrial America. This view was certainly not challenged by GM spokesmen, practiced as they were in pointing to external conditions as the source of the company's problems. The inside diagnosis was yet to come.

Enter Roger Smith as chairman. The new leader's personal background and rise through the ranks could not have prepared GM's tradition-bound bureaucrats for the fury he would unleash. Smith's career had been almost perfectly in tune with the corporation's cardinal rules of management training and promotion. He had observed those rules with consummate skill and attention. He received undergraduate and MBA degrees from the University of Michigan, the alma mater of numerous GM leaders. His studies were interrupted by a hitch in the Naval Reserve during World War II. Smith's Wolverine classmates remember him as decidedly one of the boys. He was accomplished in mathematics—Smith was said to have taken a course in differential equations to boost his grade-point average—but there were few signs that he was destined for life at the top. He drank beer, played softball, and went to Michigan football games.

Hugh Hanson, now president of a Buick dealership in Bay City, Michigan, was a Phi Delta Theta with the chairman-to-be and his older brother, E. Quimby Smith. Hanson described Roger as "an active fraternity member, not a real outgoing person but well liked and respected." He participated in fraternity sings and even cut an album with his Phi Delta Theta brothers. Hanson conveyed the ambience of the days at Ann Arbor.

"Those were our glory years because of Michigan athletics," he told us. "Hell, we had All-Americans in our [fraternity] house. That was when Michigan was the national champion in football. So it created a lot of fun. And it was a good atmosphere. You know, we had won the war. We were back. We were back in college. And we had girls in the sororities. It was a great time, and Roger was involved with the rest of us. Most of us were all regular people. What I'm saying there is, the Phi Delta Theta house was not a real moneyed one. In fact, a lot of us were athletes. We waited on tables and things like that. So we had a good common bond. In fact, that was our fraternity slogan—Yours in the Bond."

Did Hanson sense a future for Smith as head of one of the world's most powerful corporations? "Everyone knew he was a good student," he replied. "And in that fraternity we had several fellows go on to become successful business people, doctors and lawyers and so forth. But if you had told me that Roger Smith was going to be chairman of the board of General Motors, I would have said, 'You've got to be kidding me.'"

Smith left Ann Arbor in 1949. He was inclined to move to southern California to work in the nascent aerospace industry, but his father urged him to take a stab at landing a job with General Motors. And why not? The giant corporation was under the rule of the legendary Alfred P. Sloan, Jr., who had been president since 1923 and chairman since 1937. GM already accounted for more than 40 percent of all the automobiles produced in the United States. It was even the largest U.S. defense contractor, a position it would maintain through the Korean War. Young Smith's talents with math and his unabashed self-confidence made a good impression on his GM interviewer. He was promptly hired as a general accounting clerk in the Detroit central office. One of his first assignments involved the demanding, if dreary, task of consolidating financial statements from GM's foreign subsidiaries. Smith's various projects also required that he log many evening hours on the telephone with an accountant in New York by the name of Thomas Murphy, who had signed on with GM after graduating from the University of Illinois in 1938. Murphy would become chairman in 1974 and eventually transfer power to the current CEO.

Roger Smith's thirty-two-year ascent through the GM hierarchy is impressive if only because it demonstrates his ability to recognize where the power brokers in the company were situated. Here is a man who rose to the top of the world's largest car company without ever having worked a single day for a car division. Instead he devised his own advancement strategy composed of several ingredients: Outwork everyone, even at the expense of family life. Become known as the man with the numbers. Attach yourself through specific assignments to executives at the top or almost certainly on their way to the top. Specialize in the financial side of the company, which is the breeding ground for CEOs at General Motors. Press your superiors enough to gain their respect, but don't shake them so much as to earn their irritation. Above all, be a loyalist. This became the evolving formula for promotion. Smith was dispatched to

New York in 1960 for the requisite tour of duty at GM's financial nerve center. He returned to Detroit after eight years and was soon made corporate treasurer. He was named one of four executive vice-presidents in 1974, his last elevation prior to his election as chairman.

John T. Connor, an outside director for nineteen years, did not stand for reelection in 1985. He described his first impressions of the future chairman. "Smith had a good running start," Connor told us. "As a young man, he was sort of an assistant to each CEO in succession. He worked closely with Fred Donner, and then with Jim Roche, and then with Dick Gerstenberg, and then with Tom Murphy. So he had a pretty good idea of what the job involved. . . . He was one of those young people who sort of gets marked for greatness early in his career. He was so damn bright and ambitious and hardworking and aggressive and impatient and willing to do what was necessary to get a job done."

Arvid Jouppi, the prominent auto analyst, worked with Smith for a few years during the 1950s. Jouppi was one of three officials who drafted the GM annual report. Smith was a liaison between the financial staff and Jouppi's group. What were his impressions of the aspiring executive? "Roger just outworked everybody," Jouppi said. "He seemed kind of immune to rank, but he worked within the system." Jouppi also relayed comments attributed to Richard Gerstenberg, much repeated since Smith's rise to power, that underscored the sheer tenacity with which the young manager approached his job. Gerstenberg, then a vice-president, is reputed to have told GM chairman James Roche during the late 1960s that if he asked Roger Smith to move the GM headquarters building across the street, his only question would be, "Which way do you want it to face, onto [West Grand] Boulevard or Second Avenue?"

Smith's willingness to go anywhere or do anything for GM did come at the expense of a certain human touch. The cold imperatives of balance sheets and project evaluations often left little room for humor or creativity. University of Michigan professor David Lewis, an expert on the auto industry, worked on GM's public relations staff in the 1960s. He dealt with Smith on several occasions. "All that mattered in the world to him was that briefcase he had in his hand," Lewis told Anne Fisher of *Fortune* in 1984. "He was a cold s.o.b." Lewis conceded that Smith did his job. "He was a storehouse of facts. He knew a hell of a lot, and you never had to go anywhere else to verify what he told you."

There were no brilliant proposals, nimble responses to crises, or high-visibility marketing triumphs that can be considered turning points in Smith's career at GM. He came to learn that galloping up the financial trail was a more secure way to reach the top than making a daring race along the product highway. Ever since the reign of Harlow Curtice, a free-spending product man who served as GM's president and chief executive from 1953 to 1958, the company's financial kingpins swore they would never again cede such authority to a president. Indeed, Curtice remains the last GM president who also held the title of chief executive. The presidency is now reserved for an engineer, with oversight responsibilities for manufacturing. The chairman's position belongs to someone with a financial pedigree. And the chairman at GM is decisively numero uno.

It is also important to understand that the upward climb to the chairmanship poses fewer external risks and observable challenges beyond an executive's control than does the push for the president's job. The journey through GM's car divisions involves being enmeshed with defect controversies, the ups and downs of styling and sizing decisions, political struggles with regulators and citizen groups, interactions with workers and union leaders, occupational health and safety conditions, and community relations. The financial side of the company involves the manipulation of numerical symbols and analyses, evaluations and forward planning of investments and financing techniques, organizing and reorganizing departments and subsidiaries. Few outsiders come into extensive contact with this brand of executive. Few outside forces interfere with his plans. An engineer may sink or swim based on market reaction to the product. The aspiring financial manager is judged largely by his personal relationships with executives above him. His career ascent can be clear in focus and splendid in its isolation. Roger Smith's personality, confidence, and steadfastness made climbing the ladder a task of securing incremental advances.

Certain episodes did catch the eye of Smith's superiors. When the Senate Subcommittee on Antitrust and Monopoly embarked during the 1950s on what would become an historic investigation of concentration in the auto industry, the initial reaction of senior GM management was to look the other way. But Smith urged that GM submit an exhaustive defense to the panel. He worked closely with top executives to prepare them for their grilling in Washington by Sen. Estes Kefauver and his colleagues. GM president Curtice appeared before the panel in 1955 and 1958.

"Estes Kefauver sent Harlow Curtice a letter asking him to appear," recalled Arvid Jouppi. "Curtice wrote back and said it wasn't a convenient time for him to testify. No one at General Motors took [those hearings] seriously except one man: Roger Smith. Roger quarterbacked the whole thing. He put up a factually strong defense for GM. All Harlow had to do was read [the statement] into the record."

A few years later Smith was one of a small group of officials who assisted Alfred Sloan on his book, *My Years with General Motors.* Smith was able to appreciate Sloan's management experiences and philosophies and understand the strategies behind the formation and rise to dominance of GM. He took special notice of how the GM of millionaire founder William Durant grew by acquiring other companies—a strategic awareness he has carried to his present position. "Other automakers had built their businesses by expanding existing facilities," Smith told a New York audience in 1983. "Durant built General Motors by bringing together many small automobile producers and component and parts manufacturers in a single holding company. It was an idea that worked very well."

Roger Smith was transferred to the treasurer's office in New York eleven years after he signed on with GM. This was the period when he demonstrated his unshakable commitment to the enterprise. It was also the period when he forged his special bond with Thomas Murphy, who spent nearly three decades in New York until his return to Detroit as GM comptroller in 1967. Smith's New York assignments—first as director of the financial analysis section, then as assistant treasurer—were both positions once held by Murphy. When Smith came back to Detroit in 1968 as general assistant comptroller and, later that year, general assistant treasurer, he served under Murphy. When he became treasurer in 1970, Smith replaced Murphy, who had been named a vice-president and group executive for the Car and Truck Group. Murphy became vice-chairman in 1972 and chairman less than three years later. If Thomas Murphy was not Roger Smith's mentor, he most certainly cleared a path to the chairmanship to which Smith stuck closely.

· · ·

Like many other aspiring managers with a facility for numbers, Roger Smith remained largely unencumbered by the sometimes simple, sometimes complex questions of corporate product and social responsibility. Presiding over the distribution of billions of dollars of shareholder dividends or issuing hundreds of millions of dollars worth of public debt, two of Smith's responsibilities during his seven-year tenure as a GM executive vice-president, can be exhilarating and challenging. But such assignments also create a managerial cocoon in which GM's financial guardians insulate themselves from customer dissatisfaction, poor automobile performance, or even from frequent contact with their peers running GM's manufacturing divisions. This insulation was common to many of Smith's predecessors in the chief executive slot. And with each decade the power of GM's chairman (finance) over the corporate president (engineering) became more pronounced.

Auto companies were usually started by engineers—Henry Ford and Walter Chrysler only being the most famous—but as they merged or matured, the "bean counters" came to dominate. Engineering investment and innovation for product, as opposed to manufacturing facilities, suffered. Factories became more automated, while the cars and trucks they turned out suffered from technological stagnation. Styling became more important in marketing automobiles than engineering. By the 1963 model year, GM's Fisher Body division produced for the company's five car divisions—Chevrolet, Pontiac, Buick, Oldsmobile, and Cadillac—140 body styles and 843 trim combinations.

"Dynamic obsolescence" was the phrase coined by GM styling pioneer Harley Earl to describe the commercial value to the company of slight appearance changes in front ends, rear ends, hoods, ornaments, rear decks, rear quarter panels, tail lamps, rocker panels, wheel covers and lugs. By 1964 the reign of styling over the shrinking province of engineering began to trouble some executives at Ford Motor Company publicly. Ford vice-president Donald Frey delivered an address that year in which he complained about these misguided priorities. "I believe that the amount of product innovation successfully introduced into the automobile is smaller today than in previous times and is still falling," he said. "The automatic transmission"—adopted on some cars before World War II—"was the last major innovation of the industry."

Frey's chief, Henry Ford II, expanded on these sentiments: "When you think of the enormous progress of science over the last two generations, it's astonishing to realize that there is very little about the basic principles of today's automobile that would seem strange and unfamiliar to the pioneers of our industry. . . . What we need even more than the refinement of old ideas is the ability to develop new ideas and put them to work."

In the late 1960s a series of federal laws and regulations responded to this stagnation by pressing the auto industry into making its cars safer, less damage-prone in collisions, less polluting, more fuel efficient, and more accountable through warranty and recall obligations. But the elephant from Detroit turned from its parochial environs to establish its presence in Washington for the purpose of regulating the regulators. But unlike his peers who were rising inside the car divisions, Roger Smith was not professionally shaken by these pressures and demands. He stayed among the financial analysts. Their visions remained narrow and unperturbed. They continued to shuttle between Detroit and New York and to evaluate the bottom-line performance of the car division managers.

One of those hands-on managers was John Z. DeLorean. Whatever his personal crises and legal troubles since leaving GM, DeLorean was a spectacular success during his seventeen years at the corporation. He ran the Pontiac Division to record sales in 1967 and 1968. He was named general manager of the troubled Chevrolet Division in February 1969 and by model year 1972 had taken it to record sales of 3.1 million vehicles. But the rising star left GM in April 1973, at age forty-eight, seven months after he became vice-president and group executive for cars and trucks. Roger Smith, who was then forty-seven, was one of three other group executives at the time DeLorean left GM. He supervised the company's nonautomotive and defense segments, which generated less than 10 percent of total domestic revenues. DeLorean had tired of the petty demands for social conformity emanating from top executives. He had become frustrated with the stifling myopia of the financiers. He had developed a series of detailed objections to prevailing corporate policies and practices that he realized could not be seriously addressed, let alone adopted, from within GM.

As related to J. Patrick Wright, author of *On a Clear Day You Can See General Motors,* Delorean's criticisms were prophetic. He condemned the increasing centralization of management on the fourteenth floor at the expense of decision-making power in the car divisions. He worried that operating decisions were being made more and more by bureaucratic, unimaginative executives who rose to positions of power through personal loyalties. He recoiled against the numbing impact of GM's myriad task forces and committees.

Measured by Roger Smith's speeches and organizational changes since his election as chairman, the current head of GM quietly shared many of these insights and criticisms. Smith likes to trumpet the virtues of what he calls the three Rs—risk, responsibility, and reward—and frequently exhorts his troops to abandon their bureaucratic traditions. He reorganized GM's North American car operations in 1984 by consolidating the five car divisions into two integrated units. Each unit has responsibility for design, engineering, and manufacturing. The CPC Group (Chevrolet-Pontiac-GM of Canada) is to specialize in small-car production. The BOC Group (Buick-Oldsmobile-Cadillac) is to turn out large cars. Unlike the flamboyant DeLorean, however, Smith bided his time. He did not buck his superiors or make known his frustrations with the received corporate wisdom. He was coldly indifferent to the questions of design flaws and wasteful styling being raised in Washington and elsewhere. Such detachment, Smith learned years ago, was the stuff from which acceptable executive timber came.

John DeLorean simply could not maintain the degree of loyalty demanded by the upper reaches of GM's corporate culture. He became increasingly restless. It was this frame of mind that led him in December

1972 to sit down in his well-appointed office and compose a stunning memorandum to Thomas Murphy, then GM's vice-chairman. DeLorean told us that Murphy was so taken aback by its contents that he returned the memo without any response or comment. It was just too hot to remain in the vice-chairman's files. (Murphy declined by letter to grant us an interview.) What precipitated DeLorean's forthrightness was a meeting with Murphy and GM president Edward Cole. The two executives had cautioned their junior colleague about his lack of single-minded focus and dedication to the immediate welfare of the corporation. DeLorean, it seems, was showing a distracting concern over minority rights, urban poverty, and other social issues.

The vice-president's formal response, which ran to nineteen double-spaced pages, is worth recounting at some length. It provides an altogether rare inside evaluation of GM's impact on its customers. It is important to keep in mind that DeLorean was considered a leading candidate to assume the presidency of GM one day. These were not wild claims from a disgruntled middle-level bureaucrat. Had it been released at the time it was written, DeLorean's memo could have exposed many executives to serious law enforcement actions. Now the document serves to illustrate a chapter of company history that has been too long in darkness. It also provides a description of the company climate in which Roger Smith was steeped before he came to prominence.

The memo began with a preamble. "I honestly feel that most of our executives are a product of corporate inbreeding and as a consequence lack a real perspective [on] the relationship of General Motors to America," DeLorean wrote. "I might recount a few incidents in my own career that illustrate the point that GM lacks social responsibility and conversely that a strong sense of social responsibility and a genuine concern for our fellow man are not only the proper posture for General Motors but actually would make her more profitable and certainly help to eliminate the controversies which are now ripping our cities apart."

Then the executive crossed the Rubicon. DeLorean cited a number of examples of inhumane engineering and disregard for human life that are chilling in their straightforward portrayal. What follows are excerpts:

- In 1958, most GM cars went to the wasp-waisted "cruciform" frame despite my (and many others', including Lou Lundstrom's) admonitions that this frame was not safe since it offered no side impact protection. Not long afterward we saw accident after accident in which cruciform frame equipped cars literally broke in half spewing helpless occupants all over the streets. A great deal of expense was incurred by GM in 1961 to get back to a safe design.

- Early in my GM career I remember asking and hearing many others (again including Lou Lundstrom) plead with Oldsmobile to stop using the long, sharply-pointed rocket ornament on their hood which was at the perfect height to impale a child's brain or spear out an eye in even a minor accident—Olds would not hear of dropping their rocket hood ornament which they felt was a commercial identification feature until threatened safety legislation forced it. Olds also continued to use extremely dangerous cookie cutter instrument knobs long after it was obvious these were causing grave, often fatal injuries.

- The swing axle Corvair was put into production despite the strongest, most vocal pleading against it by the Engineering Staff experts on vehicle handling and suspension. Von Polhemus and Max Ruegg, head and assistant head of GM suspension development, both protested that the proposed swing axle was unsafe and they made elaborate functional models to demonstrate how the rear suspension would "jack" and the car flip over. Mr. Knudsen told me that, as Chevrolet General Manager, he had to threaten to quit before the corporation would approve replacing the dangerous swing axle with a slightly more expensive, safer design in 1965. All of this data was removed from the files prior to Corvair litigation. In my opinion, if you must destroy a file because the contents are embarrassing, you are not acting responsibly as a public corporation. I don't think the last has been heard of Corvair handling; much more time consuming and expensive litigation is in the offing.

- The same was true of the Corvair heater—many people (Chuck Hughes for one) objected violently to a direct engine air heater without an intermediate safety shield. Because it is well known that all engine gaskets and exhaust systems will deteriorate and leak in time—so that the car would eventually, inevitably become a carbon monoxide death trap. There is no telling how many people have been injured or killed by these deadly fumes —either dulling their reflexes so that their safe driving ability was impaired or actually causing a monoxide inhalation death. This would have been avoided with a sense of responsibility and concern for our public; certainly we were forewarned by many of our engineers. Once again we can expect much more expensive litigation—so that the few cents the shield might have cost will be insignificant.

In stark contrast to DeLorean's reports on the Corvair's instability and the leakage of carbon monoxide fumes, GM's expert witnesses and lawyers, during the large volume of litigation brought by victims or their next of kin, asserted under oath that there were no safety problems and that no relevant documents had been destroyed. GM's legal strategy on the Corvair stretched over a decade from the early 1960s to the 1970s. It was developed and discussed at the highest levels of management. Discipline and company loyalty were strict under the regime of Frederic Donner, the iron-willed chairman. It remained that way after his retirement from active duty in 1967. To be a public whistle blower at GM would have required personal courage and a willingness, at the least, to be ostracized and excluded from any business that was remotely vulnerable to the auto company's displeasure.

DeLorean then focused attention on a major defect case:

When I first became aware of a Pontiac motor mount failure which stuck the throttle and resulted in a serious accident I sponsored the interlock type mount that would not permit the engine to move out of position even in a mount failure. It was my insistence that put the mount in production on the 1959 Pontiac. At that time all of the other car divisions were made aware of the problem and our solution to it. While most divisions had experienced the same problem they refused to spend the small amount required for a safety interlock. This was brought up to various Chevrolet managements many times through the years by various engineers and engineering change requests (ECR's), which have since been removed from the files and destroyed, again—these were always rejected on the basis of cost. Finally, when I got to Chevrolet I insisted on the interlock mount—which was put in the 1970 model—or we would be campaigning those cars also. Once again concern for humanity would have saved both money and lives in the long run.

Indeed, in December 1971, under pressure from the Department of Transportation, GM recalled nearly 6.7 million Chevrolet cars from model years 1965 through 1969 and trucks from model years 1965 through 1970 for precisely this kind of motor mount slippage, causing throttles to stick, cars to crash, and people to die or be maimed. Prior to the recall, Edward Cole, GM's president from 1969 through September 1974, was asked during a news conference about these faulty engine mounts, which were breeding tens of thousands of warranty claims. He tried to downplay the hazard, saying, "It is no different than having a flat tire or a blowout where you don't expect it."

DeLorean also objected to management stonewalling on air bag technology. He wrote,

> This device was first demonstrated by GM Research [GMR] about 10 years ago. I became very enthusiastic about its life saving potential as did Bill King and others of GMR. They were not provided funding for continuing work on the air bag hence I sought many times over a period of years to promote the development of the device inside of GM—when this failed I requested permission to let outside researchers (perhaps U of M) do some low cost development work on the air bag. This was also rejected. About a year and a half ago when I asked Steve Malone of Pontiac for copies of this correspondence (to be used to make a point with corporate management on the lack of social responsibility) he told me that all of my (and his) correspondence promoting air bags was taken from the files and destroyed.

John DeLorean was not the only high-ranking General Motors executive persuaded of the effectiveness of the technology. GM president Ed Cole was a strong advocate of air bags. He set out his position in a January 20, 1977, letter to William Haddon, president of the Insurance Institute for Highway Safety. "I don't think there is any question where I stand on passive restraint systems," Cole wrote. "I firmly believe the air cushion system can be made to work at a reasonable cost. . . . The technology is available and the need is there. I think the only way passive restraints are going to get to first base is making them mandatory."

Sitting on engineering innovations and destroying documents are themes that recur again and again in GM's postwar history. Roger Smith is no exception to portions of this dark tradition. As executive vice-president, and certainly as chairman, Smith has been a party to and leader of GM's disinformation campaign against the air bag. In 1976, General Motors filed documents with the Department of Transportation estimating that air bags would cost $220 per car. Smith and his GM colleagues now routinely toss around estimates of up to $1,100 per car—a five-fold inflation of costs in less than ten years. Smith presided over the shutdown of GM's air bag development unit in April 1981 and the shredding of some of the unit's files.

DeLorean next turned his attention to air pollution:

In the area of air pollution our record is, if anything, even worse. In no instance, to my knowledge, has GM ever sold a car that was substantially more pollution free than the law demanded —even when we had the technology. As a matter of fact, because the California laws were tougher, we sold "cleaner" cars there and "dirtier" cars throughout the rest of the nation. This approach of just doing the "bare bones" minimum to just scrape by the pollution law when GM could do much better by spending a few dollars is not socially responsible. With our virtual monopoly position in the industry we also, in effect, control our competitors—who would be economically devastated if they tried to do better socially but at greater product cost.

We of Chevrolet proposed to the EPG [Engineering Policy Group] that we make our cars cleaner than the law demanded— we were told that the other divisions did not need a $15.00 air pump to meet the law—we were to take it off of our cars. Our next proposal was to have all optional engines exceed the law (do the best we knew) since the customer would pay the extra cost anyhow —once again we were not permitted to do so for fear we would lose a few sales. . . .

One final thought on emissions. Our corporation has lost credibility with the public and the government because each new emissions standard has been greeted by our management's immediate cries of "impossible," "prohibitively expensive," "not economically responsible"—usually before we even knew what it involved. The remarkable thing is that with all of our resources and the amount we tell the government we are spending on emissions research that most of the significant developments in this field have come from someone else—for example, our first answer, the "Clean Air Package," was developed by a handful of engineers at Chrysler, the manifold reactor which meets the 1975 standards now (and should be in production) was developed by duPont with less than 10% of our facilites and manpower. The other 1975 answer, the catalytic converter with EGR, was developed by a small grant given by Ford, several oil companies and several Japanese manufacturers. Not a very good record for a corporation that professes to be vitally interested in emissions. When we tell the government about our large expenditures for emissions controls we don't bother to tell them that very little is being spent on R and D and that most of our money is spent on adapting hardware to our wide variety of engines.

John DeLorean was sensitized by the turbulent politics and street protests during the late 1960s and early 1970s. His range of friends and social contacts widened his horizons beyond the tight-knit fraternity of GM officials and business acquaintances in which most rising executives circulated.

Near the end of his memo he questioned the overall direction of GM priorities: "Over the years we have wasted millions of dollars on executive whims and petty novelties and [spent] virtually nothing on safety research until we were forced to by our cities and the government. . . . The point of all this is that while these are just a few examples (there are many more I could mention) they demonstrate that GM in policy or actuality has never demonstrated real social responsibility."

Roger Smith occupied the other end of the management spectrum. Smith perfected the practice of seldom separating himself from his peer group either professionally or socially. His delicate balancing act was never to stand apart, but always to stand out. DeLorean told us that he and the chairman-to-be seldom crossed paths during their years together as group executives, even though only four officials in the entire corporation held the title. Smith told an interviewer in December 1982 that he was "sorry" DeLorean was "in the difficulties" he was in. "I knew John, sure," he said. "I used to sit next to him at the administration committee and shared some offices."

.   .   .

Roger Bonham Smith, who turned sixty on July 12, 1985, seems to have been preparing all his life for the high command at General Motors Corporation. He was one of four children born to a family that traces its ancestry not only to the *Mayflower* but to a signer of the Magna Carta. His father, E. Quimby Smith, was a bank president in Columbus, Ohio, who moved to Detroit after his bank failed during the Depression. His mother was assistant superintendent of schools in Columbus. Despite the trauma of Depression-era failure, the Smith family was by no means impoverished. Smith senior settled his wife and children in a fashionable Detroit neighborhood. Roger graduated from University School, now University Liggett School, and enrolled at the University of Michigan in 1942.

Brock Yates, editor-at-large of *Car and Driver,* etches the social setting of the typical Michigan auto executive in his 1983 book *The Decline and Fall of the American Automobile Industry.* Yates ridicules the conformity and in-breeding rife in communities such as Bloomfield Hills, a wealthy Detroit suburb that is home to nearly everyone who is anyone among automakers:

Life in Bloomfield Hills is a group activity, played out in lush cultural isolation from the nonautomotive society. "They live together, they work together, they drink together, they play golf together, they *think* together," said a former GM executive. He was speaking of the highly structured life-style of General Motors management, which insists on weekends of golf and gin rummy games at the Oakland Hills Country Club and back-lawn barbecues dominated by conversations about the automobile business.

"It's like entering the priesthood," remarks another local observer. "They get out of college and go into the system at the zone level. From then on the Corporation takes care of everything; it sells their houses when they move, invests their incomes, provides them with new cars every few thousand miles, gets them memberships in the right clubs and so on. They even retire together in GM colonies in the South and Southwest. You talk about a cradle-to-grave welfare state. They simply have no concept of the real world."

Roger Smith has thrived for years in this rarefied world. He lives with his wife, the former Barbara Ann Rasch, and teenage son, Drew, on Rathmoor Road in Bloomfield Hills. The Smiths also have three adult children, two daughters and a son, who are now on their own. The GM chairman enjoys the requisite hobbies and maintains the proper club memberships. He is said to own a 1923 Buick touring car and a 1959 Corvette—emblems of executive identification with vintage cars and company heritage. He owns a vacation home on Burt Lake, south of Cheboygan, close to where Lake Huron meets Lake Michigan. He also has an interest in a fishing and hunting preserve in northern Michigan that is frequented by many prominent business executives. Smith belongs to the Orchard Lake Country Club, the Bloomfield Hills Country Club, the Detroit Athletic Club, and the Detroit Club. He is a member of the Links Club in New York City. It was here that the GM leader met for dinner in the winter of 1982 with Japanese auto mogul Eiji Toyoda to initiate discussions that led to the GM-Toyota joint venture in Fremont, California.

James Evans, chairman of the Union Pacific Corporation and a GM director since 1980, is a close friend of Smith. The two went salmon fishing in 1983 on the Miramichi River in New Brunswick, Canada. Evans and Smith were accompanied by the late J. Stanford Smith, a retired GM director and former chairman of International Paper, as well as by active executives of the giant paper and wood-products company. International Paper owned the land on which the businessmen relaxed. Evans says

Smith is skilled at gin rummy, a favorite pastime of the auto establishment.

"He's a wonderful cardplayer," Evans told us. "He loves to play cards of all kinds. He's a great raconteur, a great storyteller. He has lots of humor and doesn't take himself too seriously." Evans appreciated the fact that Smith flew in from Europe in April 1984 to attend his wedding in Manhattan. "He came all the way from London or Amsterdam," the Union Pacific chairman noted. "Back to New York in time for him and Barbara to be at a five-o'clock wedding at the Brick Presbyterian Church. He attended, and we had a reception afterward at the River Club. He was very much a part of the whole thing."

Columnist Ann Landers, whose husband, Jules Lederer, founded Budget Rent-A-Car in 1958, has known Roger Smith for six or seven years. Landers described the GM chairman as "not an overwhelming personality like Walter Annenberg. He's so easygoing that after you've seen him a few times, you feel like you've known him forever." But the advice columnist has yet to make known to Smith her attitudes on passive restraints. "I have not talked to him about safety features," she told us. "I would like to tell him that every car should have an air bag. Now they're talking about teenagers drinking and driving. I don't think that was their best effort. They are talking a lot about safety, and they have to do more. . . . The [automobile] companies could do a better job. I would not hesitate to tell him that."

Landers went on to recount a story meant to illustrate Smith's willingness to do a favor for a friend. "In 1983 I called and said I had a 1980 Cadillac limousine," she told us. "I wanted a new car. Baby blue, everything on it. A glass window separating passengers from the chauffeur. He said, 'They're hard to find, but I'll get you one.' The next morning—and I had called him late in the day—he had a car for me. A 1983 Cadillac. He said it was in a suburb and that he could have it to me by three P.M." And it was delivered. "It was perfect. He phoned all over the country and found precisely the car I wanted. There is no detail too small for him."

The venerable axiom that "social is political" was not lost on the rising Roger Smith. While ambition drives the career, it must not be too forward lest it breed antagonism among colleagues. So Smith also tried hard to be one of the boys in his social activities. Yet another fishing buddy told a story to the *Detroit Free Press* in 1981 meant to capture the lighter side of the chairman's personality. Earlier in his career Smith attended a conference of GM managers at the Greenbrier resort in West Virginia: "He had thirty minutes between meetings, so he ducked down to a trout stream on the property where nobody else was having much luck. He had brought a special lure from Detroit. He made ten casts and caught eight trout, and went back to his meeting. He absolutely wiped everyone else out."

The GM leader likes to project this "just a regular guy image." At times such efforts by this multimillionaire can appear rather overwrought. At a 1982 House Ways and Means Committee hearing, Congressman Don Bailey asked Smith whether he owned his own home. His reply: "With the help of a mortgage, I own my own home. I guess I have to say, the bank and I own it." GM president James McDonald explained to author Brock Yates that company executives should communicate their status as mere mortals. "Letting the public know and see what kind of people run General Motors—just *ordinary* people, and that's a big revelation to a lot of people—is vitally important."

Roger Smith is frequently compared to former GM chairman Frederic Donner, who ran the company from September 1958 through October 1967. David Cole, director of the University of Michigan's Office for the Study of Automotive Transportation, and the son of former GM president Edward Cole, told us that "Donner was an ultimate financial guy. I suspect Roger looks on him very admiringly." There are undeniable similarities between the two executives. Donner could be stern, intimidating, humorless, and cold—traits that the current CEO has been known to demonstrate. But Smith has also tried to break with the taciturn and autocratic style of past GM chairmen. He likes to cover his decisive and determined personality with a congenial, folksy, gung-ho overlay. Profile after profile reports that Smith is fond of expressions such as "holy Toledo" and "man, oh Manischewitz." This aw-shucks gloss, as union leader Doug Fraser came to appreciate, says less about the man than about his public relations tactics.

Frederic Donner ran GM in a period of relentless sales growth and limited foreign competition. He could get away with management by intimidation. Roger Smith was perceptive enough to appreciate that his ruling period was quite different. His personal leadership would have to exude more motivation and excitement around the challenges of technological and organizational change than any previous GM chairman could or wanted to muster. But this management style supplemented rather than displaced the traits he shared with Donner. Roger Smith was entirely capable of keeping an iron fist of intransigence and insensitivity inside his velvet glove.

Smith's reaction to our requests for an interview is a case in point. Of all the executives approached in connection with this book, none was more dismissive and aloof than the GM chairman. We initiated contact with Smith in April 1984 by sending a letter describing the project and our interest in an interview. We specifically asked that Smith "not delegate this attempt to establish a direct dialogue to the GM public-relations office." That is precisely what happened. A few weeks after our interview request was mailed, we received a letter from GM vice-president John McNulty, who oversees the company's public-relations staff. His entire letter was composed of only one sentence: "Roger Smith has asked me to tell you that, in view of your long history as an adversary of General Motors, he does not want to lend to your book the cooperation you request."

A number of veteran industry observers said they were surprised by this abrupt dismissal. David Cole told us he thought Smith should cooperate with us and suggested that we contact two other GM public-relations officials, which we did. More letters and a brief meeting in Detroit failed to budge the company. Keith Crain, publisher and editorial director of the influential weekly *Automotive News*, who told us he sees Smith "every two or three weeks," also said he thought the GM boss should grant an interview. He even said he would write an editorial to that effect. When that column failed to appear after several months, we called Crain back. He explained that other issues had demanded his editorial attention. He also said that he had seen Smith soon after our initial conversation and asked why he would not cooperate. Crain told us Smith replied, "I don't trust him." The *Automotive News* publisher also said he saw Smith on the very day Michigan newspapers were reporting on a press conference convened by the authors to describe the adverse potential consequences of a campaign by GM to appeal its property-tax assessments across the state. "Now do you see why I don't trust him?" Smith asked Crain, who again told the chairman that he thought he was making a mistake but that he was entitled to his position. In defense of Smith, Crain told us, "He is not a coward."

Indeed, Smith has never been fully at ease with or in command of the public dimension of his job. Part of the problem is out of the chairman's hands. He does not measure up physically to the traditional image of an auto mogul. He is rigid and ill at ease behind a podium—nothing like the brash and exuberant Lee Iacocca or the cool, patrician Thomas Murphy. *Automotive News* offered this description of the GM leader in a special issue commemorating GM's seventy-fifth anniversary.

"Smith has been subjected to putdowns entirely unrelated to his activities as chief executive of the world's largest manufacturing corporation," the publication noted. "His stature has been mentioned. So has his voice. Smith is short, about 5-feet-8; he's sandy-haired and would not be mistaken for a matinee idol. He is not a compelling speaker; his voice is rather high-pitched, lacking the timbre and resonance of the born orator.

It does not shatter glass. On the other hand, Paul Newman is handsome, but could he run GM?"

The chairman's diminutive presence has even inspired commentary from GM insiders. "Roger's great strength is his brain," one of his advisers told the *Detroit News* in 1982. "I don't think Roger will ever be the image of a chairman. He hasn't got the stature (short and unassuming). He's got the wrong hair color (sandy). He's got the wrong squeaky voice. And when you get under his skin, which you can pretty quickly, he can bite."

Smith has worked hard to develop a more captivating presence outside the corporation. It has not been easy. General Motors provided us with more than 140 prepared speeches delivered by Roger Smith during his years as a major GM executive. The transcripts extend back to 1971, when as corporate treasurer he unleashed a polemic against citizen activism and proposals that institutional money managers adopt criteria of social responsibility when they decide where to invest their funds.

"Some want to move in this direction, others in that direction," Smith told the Colorado Bankers Association. "We skip from crisis to crisis. Minorities, women's liberationists, ethnic groups, youth, environmentalists, consumer advocates, the poor, the hawks, the doves, all press their individual causes—and all with great heat and passion. Television and other channels of instant communication have helped feed this kind of social competition. The combination has led to the emergence of a new force in our society—the professional critic."

The stridency of the 1971 lecture gave it a spark, a certain spontaneity, that at least makes for interesting listening or reading. Smith also exhibited a modest taste for candor in a March 1975 speech at a conference of GM managers in New Orleans. He discussed various external challenges to the continued autonomy of General Motors:

> We expect public confidence in the economy to improve substantially before the year is out. But public confidence in business is another matter. This has declined alarmingly in recent years. Especially disturbing is the indication that mistrust has now spread to the large segment of the public that regards itself as conservative. Far too many people who are not opposed to profits as such now believe that business is putting its own interests ahead of serving the public. Far too many people are concerned about what they regard as misleading advertising, poorly made products, and unfairly high prices. Our challenge is [to] be sure we are not guilty of any of these—and then making sure our customers and the general public know the positive story of what General Motors is doing to maintain our good reputation.

A typical address by Chairman Smith demonstrates little of the plain talk of these two early speeches. His lectures gush with visions of robots and artificial intelligence and "factories of the future." They most certainly are not drafted by the CEO himself. Smith's speechwriters have also tried to inject some humor into his remarks. But the purported jokes come across as something less. He opened one address with the standard pleasantries and then declared, "Well, I better get to the 'meat' of the talk before Clara Peller asks, 'Where's the beef?' " Speaking before the Michigan Auto Dealers Convention in 1984, he quipped, "Actually, coming up just for lunch, I feel a little like one of Zsa Zsa Gabor's husbands: I know I'm only going to be around for a little while . . . so I plan to enjoy it while I can!"

He began a written keynote speech to a 1984 management conference at the University of Chicago on this strained note. "I chose my subject for today on the basis of several factors," Smith declared. "First, my letter of invitation asked for a talk on 'a subject of current interest.' Well, there is certainly no dearth of those. I could offer you my views on school prayer . . . or I could debate the merits of tennis versus racquetball . . . or perhaps I could present a critical analysis of the latest album by Michael Jackson."

Smith's humor has at times crossed the boundary between the inept and the grossly insensitive. In February 1981, during the controversy over GM's displacement of a large Detroit neighborhood called Poletown for a Cadillac plant, the press was covering the bitter opposition to the project by Polish Americans who were long-time residents of the area. During a conversation at a convention of the National Automobile Dealers Association (NADA), Smith told a Polish joke to a reporter for the *Detroit News* that would have caused an uproar back home had it been made public: "There is a Polish guy who runs a tree farm. He is selling Christmas trees. His friend asks him, 'How is business going?' He says, 'it costs me ten dollars to produce each tree and I sell them for nine dollars apiece.' His friend asks, 'How are you going to make a profit?' He says, 'I'll make it up in volume.' " The young reporter, worried about continued access to Smith, chose not to file a story on the chairman's remarks.

Ann Landers told us that she attended a speech Smith delivered early in his tenure. "He wasn't assertive enough in either the speech or the questions," she recalled. "He was too stern, not open. His approach did not match the personality I knew. He is actually a very warm guy. This was a humorless, rather wooden presentation. I took it upon myself, when I saw him, to say, 'Roger, you need to work on your public speaking.' I suggested that he smile more, use more humor in his speeches."

When the GM chairman was scheduled to appear on the *Phil Donahue Show* in May 1982, Landers once again offered some advice. "Roger called and asked if I would have dinner with him the night before," she reported. "We ate in the Prince of Wales Room at the Knickerbocker Chicago Hotel. We talked about some of the things I had mentioned [before]. He was grateful. . . . I taped it so I could watch it again. I wrote a long letter and evaluated him carefully. People asked needling questions, but he never lost his cool."

. . .

Roger Smith became chairman of General Motors on January 1, 1981. His rise to power elicited a collective yawn from industry veterans in Detroit and analysts on Wall Street. Here was a man who had spent three decades earnestly working his way along GM's well-trod routes of advancement. He appeared to be a younger, and less engaging replica of his monolithic predecessors. Smith himself did not seem to take offense at the lack of inspired reaction to his appointment.

When the *Detroit News* interviewed him in September 1980, after he had been named chairman but before he took office, a reporter asked whether his expected decade at the helm, a lengthy tenure by GM standards, would allow Smith to "leave his mark" on the corporation. "Well, the ten years is the factor, obviously, because whether you want to or not, you probably will," he replied. "But I'm not looking with any great desire to leave a mark on anything. That's not the be all and end all. There are other goals that are certainly more important than that. That is, to have the corporation be successful, to have it grow, to provide the jobs and be a world force. If I get all that done, I wouldn't really care if someone said I left my mark."

Smith's nonchalance obscured more grandiose ambitions and much deeper understandings—both in terms of his latent power and of the overdue need for change at General Motors. Times were tough for domestic auto makers when he took control. Not only was GM coming off its first annual loss in sixty years, but there were few signs that business would get much better in the near future. Profits remained extremely depressed in 1981 and 1982 by historical standards. The company earned $1.3 billion over the two years on revenues of $123 billion. GM had earned $3.5 billion in 1978 alone, the most recent period of peak auto sales, on revenues of $63.2 billion. The number of vehicles shipped from GM factories also reflected this downturn. General Motors shipped nearly 7 million cars and trucks in the United States in 1978. It shipped just over 4 million vehicles in 1982.

Commentators questioned whether the new chairman was up to the task of straightening out a stumbling giant. Better than anyone else, however, Roger Smith understood that red ink and decline at General Motors presented as many opportunities as it did challenges. The failure of major corporations to maintain employment levels or respond to foreign competition rarely leads to enhanced public accountability or the erosion of the autonomy of inept managers. In times of economic crisis, the dependency of people with neither power nor capital motivates them to lean desperately on the very corporations that embody the crisis. GM's short-term difficulties created a deep reservoir of windfall power from which its leader could draw. Roger Smith wasted little time deploying the clout born of others' despair.

Congressman Dale Kildee discussed with us how corporate power increases during periods of economic decline. He should know. His Flint, Michigan, constituents, who are highly dependent on the auto giant for their livelihoods and tax base, have faced an ongoing campaign by GM to slash its property-tax payments. "They are able to play on fears," Kildee said. "There's no question. . . . The community has to keep people working there. They're afraid to say no, even if they should say no, for fear that maybe they are going to build a plant or move a plant someplace else. So the corporation plays upon those fears. Now, the law"—in 1976, in Michigan—that was passed "on the [tax] breaks left it up to the local city councils to decide whether they wanted to give the breaks or not. But the pressure put on the local city council is very severe. . . . If they miscalculate and say no we're not going to give [the abatement], and [GM] does close down a [production] line, whether the line would have closed down or not, the city council is afraid they're going to be blamed for not having given the tax abatements."

An unprecedented confluence of forces took shape in 1981 that freed Roger Smith from constraints that had limited, however modestly, the management autonomy of his immediate predecessors. The United Auto Workers, reeling from layoffs and plant closings, quickly withered as a meaningful check on the power of the fourteenth floor. When Smith took office, 90,000 blue-collar employees were on indefinite layoff at GM. By the spring of 1982, when the union agreed to concessions, indefinite layoffs at GM had climbed to 150,000. The auto import quota, which was imposed just three months after Smith became chairman, provided breathing space against the Japanese and allowed GM to raise car prices even as sales declined. Smith's domestic competitors— flirting with bankruptcy in the case of Chrysler, nursing deep economic wounds in the case of Ford—nearly disappeared as variables in his strategic calculus. Deploying this windfall power, the chairman moved to transform his reservations about how GM had been managed during the 1970s into a series of radical strategic departures and bitter confrontations with workers, consumers, and communities. Roger the Blah became Roger the Bold.

Smith worked to redirect General Motors on several related fronts. Internally, he moved to slash manufacturing costs and overhead expenses by muscling the union, further automating assembly lines, and computerizing administration. He has bought into small enterprises specializing in artificial intelligence and machine vision in his quest to promote the "factory of the future." Smith has also begun to transform the world's largest producer of cars and trucks into a global conglomerate. The reported goal of GM's acquisition strategy, code-named Star Trek, is to increase nonautomotive revenues to more than 20 percent of the company's business by 1990. Nonautomotive operations accounted for only 7.3 percent of GM revenues in 1981. Smith paid $2.5 billion in 1984 to acquire Electronic Data Systems (EDS), the giant data-processing outfit established by Ross Perot in 1962. He exchanged $5 billion in cash and securities in 1985 for Hughes Aircraft, the country's largest producer of military satellites. GMAC has purchased mortgage companies and mortgage portfolios worth billions of dollars. By 1990 GM will be a massive conglomerate with operations in automobiles, computer technologies, telecommunications, aerospace, and banking.

Another element of the Smith agenda has its roots in the threat from across the Pacific. He has responded to the price and quality advantages of his international rivals by forging joint ventures and import alliances with them. Smith's Asia Strategy began to take shape when GM announced in March 1982 that it would not build a replacement for the Chevette, its aging and increasingly unpopular subcompact. Instead the corporation sealed one of several new contracts with hungry Japanese and Korean manufacturers. GM is importing, or has plans to import, Asian cars under three different arrangements:

- *Suzuki Motor Company:* GM bought 5 percent of the Japanese manufacturer in August 1981, and began importing its Suzuki Cultus in June 1984 for sale as the Chevrolet Sprint. The Sprint —twelve feet long, five feet wide and only 1,500 pounds—is the smallest car Chevrolet has ever sold. While the Cultus retails for less than $3,000 in Japan, GM is marketing the Sprint for a base price of nearly $5,000.
- *Isuzu Motors:* Smith agreed to invest $200 million in Isuzu, in which GM has held an equity interest since 1971, to design and build in Japan a new subcompact that GM began marketing at home in November 1984. The corporation plans eventually to import 200,000 cars per year for sale as the Chevrolet Spectrum.

The first Spectrums carried a suggested retail price of $6,295 for a two-door hatchback and $6,575 for a four-door sedan.

- *Daewoo Group:* GM reached an agreement with this South Korean conglomerate in June 1984 to participate in a $427 million joint venture to manufacture front-wheel-drive subcompacts for sale in the United States and Korea. The joint venture will build two models of a new small car designed by GM's West German subsidiary, Adam Opel AG. More than eighty thousand Korean cars are expected to be shipped each year to the United States and sold under the Pontiac nameplate. The first shipments are expected to arrive in model year 1987.

The most significant plank in Smith's bridge overseas was nailed down in February 1983. Toyota announced that it would invest $150 million and team up with GM to produce a small car for Chevrolet based on a popular model sold in Japan. The joint venture, called New United Motor Manufacturing Inc. (NUMMI), would assemble an Americanized version of the Toyota Sprinter, to be marketed as the Chevrolet Nova, in a mothballed GM plant in Fremont, California. Production schedules call for NUMMI to reach its maximum output of 250,000 cars per year by 1987. The Nova sells for a base price of $7,200 and is the most expensive model in GM's line of small cars.

Smith's Asia Strategy serves several purposes at once. General Motors has in effect acquired a line of small cars without having to invest hundreds of millions of dollars to design new models and tool up for production. GM's subcompact line was moribund in 1984. The company built fewer than 175,000 Chevettes and just over 25,000 Pontiac 1000s. GM is now in a position eventually to import from Japan and Korea, and to build in cooperation with Toyota, more than 500,000 subcompacts a year and to earn large profits in the process. Coopting the competition also allows Smith to funnel capital and engineering resources into the segment of the market to which he is really committed—enormously profitable large cars, sports cars, and luxury models.

General Motors during the 1980s has poured billions of dollars into building state-of-the-art plants across the Midwest. Its new factory in Wentzville, Missouri, which became operational in March 1984, ranks among the largest automobile assembly facilities in the world. The $600 million plant is a monument to high technology and automation. It can turn out seventy-five C-Body luxury cars—the Oldsmobile Ninety-eight, Regency, Buick Electra, and Cadillac DeVille and Fleetwood—per hour. GM's Lake Orion (Michigan) plant, another robot-intensive marvel, also assembles C-Body cars. While Chairman Smith likes to point to these ultramodern facilities as GM's response to Japan, they in fact manufacture high-profit large cars that the Japanese do not sell in the United States. GM's Asia Strategy allows Chairman Smith to boast about beating Japan even as he joins it.

The implications of the Asia Strategy extend well beyond the perimeters of the GM empire. Consider what Smith has accomplished by forging his *entente cordiale*. The world's largest car manufacturer is producing subcompacts in a joint venture with the world's third largest manufacturer. The corporation that sets prices in large cars is acting as a distributor for two of its most aggressive price competitors in the small-car segment. Roger Smith responded to the first real emergence of competition in the postwar auto industry by snuffing it out before it had a chance to spread.

Few understand the grave implications of these alliances with Japan, in particular the GM-Toyota joint venture, more fully than Chrysler chairman Lee Iacocca. His corporation filed an antitrust suit against GM soon after the Federal Trade Commission (FTC) made a halfhearted investigation of the deal and voted not to oppose it. (In April 1985, Chrysler settled the suit for minor modifications in the GM-Toyota agreement.) Iacocca also traveled to Washington in February 1984 to testify against NUMMI before the House Subcommittee on Commerce, Transportation, and Tourism. His testimony will be remembered for its candid warnings about the concentrated power of General Motors:

> What, really, is the issue here? Size and power. GM's sales are bigger than the GNP of all but 25 countries in the world; add Toyota and their combined sales are bigger than all but 20 countries. In the U.S. market, which is the one at stake, they are bigger than all the other automotive companies in the world put together. But you know that, and so does the FTC and the Justice Department. But they continue to feel that this combination will increase, not diminish, competition in the U.S. market, and I say that they are standing the world on its head when they come to such a conclusion. Why? One reason is prices. Everybody knows —even the FTC figured this out, by the way—that GM is the domestic price leader and Toyota is the import price leader. Ford and Chrysler target their domestic prices on GM. . . . It has been the head-to-head competition between Toyota and GM that sets the pricing pattern for the entire industry. Do you think that pattern is going to stay the same when GM and Toyota sit down together and set prices, as they already have, and when this competition disappears, do you think the American consumer will have lower prices? I don't.

FTC Commissioner Michael Pertschuk dissented from the panel's three-to-two approval of the joint venture. His formal statement emphasized the industry-wide implications of Roger Smith's deal with Toyota.

> In addition to the serious antitrust violations this joint venture appears to represent, it signals an ominous trend of American manufacturers conceding that they cannot compete on their own in small cars. . . . GM has now found a way to sell small cars, not by manufacturing them itself, but by assembling cars which are made primarily in Japan. The staff estimates that sixty percent or more of the value of the [Nova], including the engines and transmissions, will be built by Toyota [in Japan]. Not only does this represent a white flag by GM, but there will be powerful incentives for Ford and Chrysler to follow. The result of this trend is likely to be the precise opposite of what is desirable for the long run health of the industry and for vigorous competition—production of high quality small cars in the U.S.

Pertschuk proved to be prescient. After the GM-Toyota deal was approved, Ford announced a joint venture with Mazda and Chrysler agreed to one with Mitsubishi.

It has become routine to suggest that Roger Smith's ten years as CEO will represent as significant a juncture in the history of General Motors as the tenure of Alfred Sloan, the late chairman whose memoirs the current chairman helped prepare. John Nevin, chief executive of Firestone Tire & Rubber, is not given to whimsical reflections on the impact of his peers. But he emphasized the scope of GM's evolution under Smith. "I think the guy has brought changes in General Motors that would have been hard for anyone else to make," he told us. "He will be the most revolutionary chief executive since Sloan."

Nevin has witnessed some of those changes firsthand. Firestone ships millions of dollars worth of tires to General Motors every year. It has had to adjust to tough new conditions governing the automaker's business with the thousands of companies that manufacture steel, plastics, parts, and electrical components for GM cars. "Basically, what we're looking for is that supplier who can deliver 100 percent good quality *all* the time, not just *most* of the time," Smith told an industry luncheon in February 1984. "We're going to be 'family' with those companies who have *company-wide* quality assurance control. What we are saying is that the *products* the company makes must be perfect, and in addition the company must develop quality in *every* aspect of its business—in its management techniques, financial controls, labor relations, and relations with its own suppliers. That company must eliminate wasteful practices wherever it finds them. . . .

"Our ultimate goal is to reach the point where our suppliers have their businesses so finely tuned that we won't need to inspect incoming material," he continued. "There'll be no need to count parts and double-check work that's already been done. Our suppliers, in effect, will be an extension of our production lines. They'll be on line with our scheduling computers, and we'll have a truly 'paperless' receiving system. At the same time, quality and just-in-time delivery will be assured."

Roger Smith is demanding of his suppliers a pattern of efficiency and reliability that he has set for General Motors itself—and has not come close to achieving. His call for "100 percent good quality all the time" has its corollary in television ads that trumpet GM's commitment to quality, and in speeches by president James McDonald, who seems to preach the gospel whenever he steps down from the fourteenth floor. But Smith and McDonald have been singularly unable to translate their self-proclaimed goals into reliable products. GM recalled more than 17.5 million cars and trucks for safety defects or emission problems from 1981 through 1984. The recalls involved rear-brake lockups, leaking fuel systems, inadequate welds in suspension support assemblies, and other dangerous defects.

Industry-sponsored research organizations also confirm GM's ongoing quality problems. J. D. Power & Associates, a respected market research firm, surveys new car buyers twelve to fourteen months after they take delivery of their vehicles. The survey covers problems on delivery, problems during the first year of operation, dealer service and warranty experiences, and other measures of quality and performance. Power & Associates then develops a Customer Satisfaction Index (CSI) with an average score of 100. Ratings above 100 indicate above-average performance, under 100 below-average. Mercedes-Benz led all automobile nameplates in the 1984 CSI with a score of 161. Honda rated a 134, and Toyota 129. Only one GM nameplate, Cadillac, was declared above average in the 1984 survey. Cadillac's rating was 102. Chevrolet and Pontiac each had a satisfaction index of 81.

General Motors can set goals for suppliers it is unable to meet internally by wielding its market leverage. John Nevin discussed Firestone's experiences under this new regime. "I would describe GM as having in the last five years become an enormously more sophisticated and more long-term buyer," he told us. "Their supply people are in our plants talking about the investments we're making in new technology. They're in our plants rating us on quality capability. They're talking about the importance of them not having five suppliers spend their money trying to design a tire for the new Cadillac when they only need one or two suppliers for the new Cadillac. They need relationships with suppliers that will let them say, 'Hey, Firestone, you and Uniroyal do this car; Goodyear, you and General Tire do this car.' They're becoming much more Japanese in the sense that they are very demanding. They want very efficient suppliers but they also want long-term relationships. They are looking at the total cost of the system. They're saying, 'Firestone, if you spend five million dollars trying to design a tire for a new General Motors car and then don't get the business, you either go bankrupt or you get that five million dollars back by overpricing the other tires.' "

Has GM become more demanding in terms of supplier warranties? "The warranties are almost *de minimus,*" Nevin replied. "They will literally shut you down. If they find that your tires are not meeting their quality standards when they come into the plant, they'll just shut you down. They had one supplier that was out of business with them for two months [in 1984]. They just told them to stop shipping until we've been in your plants and are certain that the quality is coming in. We are very aware that they think the horse has been stolen if they have to tell us that a Firestone tire is failing in the field. They want to know what our [manufacturing] process is. They want to know what our quality control checks are at the end of the line. They want a certification from us as to whether the tire meets specs. And then they do the statistical checks in their plants. And if we flunk, we get told damn fast."

. . .

One of Roger Smith's first steps in the restructuring of General Motors was to define his own role at the summit of its management hierarchy. The new CEO was determined not to have his time consumed with details, with rushing to Washington to lobby, with immersing himself in the intricacies of GM's AC Spark Plug plant in Milwaukee or its assembly operations in Lordstown, Ohio, or its foundries in Illinois and Michigan. Thomas Murphy, who was a visible public spokesman and Capitol Hill activist for corporate America, sighed near the end of his term that soon it would be a relief not having every minute of his day programmed. Chairman Smith wanted to control his time himself. Policy, strategic planning, and future directions were going to be his areas of concentration. He would be the Grand Vizier, mapping out the long-term evolution of his company. He would be Chief Cheerleader, in charge of rhetorical motivation and media exposure. He would be the Diplomat, opening dialogue and negotiations with the oncoming Japanese.

Smith rules GM with the advice and counsel of a group of advisors who are steeped, as is the chairman, in the management rituals and

troubled recent history of the corporation. James McDonald, who oversees manufacturing and serves as emissary to the GM dealer network, is
a forty-five-year company veteran. Vice-chairman Howard Kehrl, Smith's
engineering guru, joined General Motors in 1948 and has been a member
of the board since 1974. F. Alan Smith, executive vice-president for
finance, is considered the leading candidate to succeed the chairman in
1990. Only one member of Roger Smith's inner circle, strategic planner
Michael Naylor, seems not to have been cut from the true-blue GM cloth.
Naylor remains a rather mysterious figure inside the company. He is
young, about forty-five, born in Britain, and did not join GM until 1967.
It is Naylor's job to peer into the future and amend Smith's master plan
for the corporation. "He literally has a letter from the chairman giving
him immediate access to any and all information within General Motors,"
a former Naylor associate told the *Detroit News*. "He's probably got the
most sensitive job in the company."

This rule-by-committee approach should not obscure Smith's determination to have the sprawling GM empire feel his presence right down to
the plant floor. The new chairman made it clear that he was going to
reduce his company's blubber, cut its costs, and begin to jolt managers
who spent more time looking over their shoulders than planning the
future. GM's market power since World War II had created a recurrently
profitable corporation with seeds of complacency throughout. Why
change when the status quo is so profitable? Why disrupt the decades-old
formula of price leadership, the broadest line of car models in the world,
and the volume to define the styling environment in which the rest of the
industry had to maneuver?

The *Detroit News*, in a remarkable 1982 series of articles based on
many off-the-record interviews with current and retired company executives, described GM's management tradition in ways quite contrary to its
carefully honed image. "At GM, you respected your elders, you didn't
rock the boat, you didn't seriously criticize, you didn't take risks, innovate
or do things differently," the *News* reported. "And, most of all, you paid
your dues: picking up superiors at airports, carrying bags, making sure the
right brand of booze was in their hotel rooms. There was more caring for
not only executives, but sometimes their wives and children as well. And
sometimes, it went to excess."

Roger Smith knew these traditions quite well. He had employed them
on his way up and benefits from them now that he is on top. But the
flattery and cloying deference that animated GM's executive corps were
also important ingredients in the management paralysis of the 1970s. A
company that resented all criticisms from the outside, and was filled with
layers of executives who shunned criticism on the inside, was not a com-

pany prepared to respond to changing markets and an unstable economic environment. So ingrained were the behavioral rituals of this sluggish mammoth that even when the boss came to grips with external challenges, little could be changed. The *News* cited a comment from retired chairman Richard Gerstenberg, made soon after he retired in late 1974, that captured his sense of impotence: "I am like an ant on the front of a log heading downstream toward a treacherous bend and all I can do is stick my foot in the water to try to steer us clear and yell, 'Whoa, you s.o.b., whoa.' "

The new chairman planned to act with more authority than his predecessors. His determination was supplemented by the windfall power at his disposal. Smith first took aim at the UAW. Union leader Peter Kelly, whose Warren, Michigan, local represents highly skilled employees at the GM Technical Center, obtained a confidential document in February 1984 that made all too plain GM's objectives on labor. The report, a script of a presentation to personnel directors by Alfred Warren, the company's labor-relations czar, described an "aggressive productivity" scenario under which GM could slash its U.S. hourly workforce to less than 300,000 by August 1986. Compare that with the more than 500,000 hourly workers employed by GM in 1978.

Automation, robotics, and global sourcing would combine to allow General Motors to produce more cars with fewer workers. A 1985 report by researchers at Harvard Business School suggests that Smith is making substantial progress on his labor-saving agenda. "By the fourth quarter of 1983, GM was making vehicles with far fewer workers than ever before," the authors note. "In the fourth quarter, 137 man-hours were used in each vehicle in contrast to 141 during the first quarter of 1983 and 142 in 1978, the most recent year of peak sales. At an annualized rate, GM was producing 5.6 million vehicles with 369,000 [hourly] employees. In 1972 when GM produced a comparable number of vehicles (5.7 million), it employed 413,000 workers. Thus, those fourth-quarter figures imply that a permanent reduction in the workforce of somewhere between 50,000 and 75,000 is already under way."

Smith's determination to shrink GM's blue-collar workforce was in keeping with the initial thrust of his speeches and interviews as chairman. The new CEO hammered away at the union. From the moment he took power, the cry went forth that autoworkers were overpaid and that their compensation accounted for the bulk of the competitive disadvantage with the Japanese. Smith even made his case privately to President Reagan in a January 18, 1982, letter congratulating the president on his first year in office. The chairman complained that his company's labor costs "are approximately 80 percent higher than those of our Japanese competitors."

Personally, however, Smith knew his problems ran much deeper than GM's contract with the UAW. Even before his letter to Reagan, Smith had begun to imply as much publicly. He delivered an important speech before the Society of Automotive Engineers in October 1981 in which he discussed the Japanese challenge and the management roots of his industry's competitive malaise. "If I were to make a pile of all Japanese advantages and try to reduce them to absolute essentials, I think I would distill out three," he said. "Outstanding product quality, impressive manufacturing efficiencies, and an amazing degree of cost-effectiveness. The third is a direct result of the first two—but the three together represent a potent force to compete against. . . . There is hardly a scrap of technology in Japan today that we in America didn't originate. The difference is that too many American manufacturers tended to keep that valuable technology on the shelf, while the Japanese were smart enough to put it to use —and they used it very effectively."

Smith was less forthcoming before an audience of millions. He appeared on *Face the Nation* in March 1981 and was asked whether Japanese and German cars had better workmanship than U.S. vehicles. "Well, not better workmanship," he insisted. "They have had a gain on us in the fit, finish, and trim items. But the American cars exceed the foreign cars in what I think are the much more difficult areas of corrosion, durability, customer service. We have a definite edge in those. If I had one area I would like to catch up in, it would be the fit and finish, because that's the easiest to do. We had an expression around the industry that they had a fifty-mile advantage on us. For the first fifty miles they looked better. But we know how to do that and we're dedicated to fixing it. We're going back over all our old dies and we're going after it."

First and foremost among the problems at General Motors were problems of management. UAW members did not prevent GM from making more fuel-efficient cars. UAW members did not prevent GM from building superior vehicles in terms of repair frequency and reliability. UAW members did not enjoin their management from just-in-time inventory controls and other cost-saving techniques. Roger Smith was shrewd enough to recognize that the scapegoating jig against labor was up. It was time to change his style and grind down his suppliers, workers, and communities with the cry, "The Japanese are coming, the Japanese are coming!" The price of this tactic was turning inward, announcing major corporate redirections, and exuding everywhere a willingness to change, to shake things up.

When John DeLorean communicated his criticisms of General Motors to author Patrick Wright, he was explicit, illustrative, and did not shy away from using proper names or citing specific product failures. Roger

Smith sends signals with generalities. He spoke to *Fortune* in March 1984, shortly after GM announced its North American reorganization. He discussed the costs of excessive layers of management. "As facts are traveling up the organization, some of them fall off," he said. "That's because a guy can't convince his boss that some fact is important, so his boss substitutes another fact that wasn't there before, and his boss does the same. By the time the information gets up here to the fourteenth floor, you're not seeing what the first guy way down there sees."

The solution? "We sat down and increased almost every authorization limit we had on what individual managers and supervisors could approve," Smith explained. "And that means salaries, projects, and almost everything else. We made a desperate effort to get rid of all those reports. And for my money we still have too much paper flowing."

These comments amount to quite a negative reflection on GM management under Smith's predecessors. Even before he became CEO, Smith was hinting at his misgivings—but always within the realm of accepted discourse. In a March 2, 1979, address at the LBJ Library in Austin, Texas, he declared, "I can say that, at least in GM, we acknowledge that one antecedent of regulation lies in our own shortcomings in satisfying our customers." By 1984, in the midst of swelling profits, Smith rhetorically asked a National Press Club audience in Washington, "Can the American auto industry survive prosperity without falling back into the bad habits that helped bring on the hard times?" No reporter bothered to ask Smith to provide examples of the "bad habits" about which he warned. A few months later in Anderson, Indiana—a GM town—the chairman pronounced "the days of the autocratic top-down leadership style" to be "finished." About the same time, GM president James McDonald was describing quality as an "explosive concern" at GM—as the company's product defect record certainly warranted. He said GM learned from studying quality-control programs at other companies that "the most effective quality systems start at the top; that organizational achievement follows only after management commitment is in place."

Public speeches by GM executives contain a kind of language code. Those who are accustomed to wading through the platitudes, the boasting, the exhortation, the jeremiads against government, and the audience flattery are sometimes rewarded by sentences that jump out and signal an executive's awareness of some deep problems inside the company. In a May 1985 address, President McDonald happily declared that "through the active cooperation of our rail and truck partners, costs for transportation damage per unit shipped have been reduced by almost eighty percent in the last four years!" One wonders what the manager in charge of this damage control was doing before 1981.

Roger Smith also had to be wondering about many people in GM who have been too smug, too unchanging, and too willing to pass the buck in the face of the growing Japanese import wave. His acquisition of EDS amounted to a direct repudiation of the GM bureaucracy and a recognition by Smith that his company could no longer survive as an autarkic empire. The EDS purchase set off a torrent of media speculation about GM's evolution as an integrated computer-communications-finance conglomerate. But the immediate rationale behind the deal was much less glamorous. GM's chairman came to recognize that computerized administration—instantaneous communication between factories and dealers, more efficient processing of insurance claims, global coordination between automobile factories and offices—was emerging as a significant competitive factor in the industry. He also understood that GM's well-paid troops were incapable of responding to the challenge on their own.

MCI Communications chairman William McGowan, who has thought deeply about the competitive implications of computers and telecommunications, discussed Smith's EDS decision. "GM paid $2.5 billion for a religious sect because that religious sect was into the information technologies," he quipped during a conversation in the summer of 1985. (EDS is governed by a strict set of rules on everything from employee beards—none are permitted—to a prohibition against discussing salaries with fellow workers.) "GM knew they desperately needed it, and they couldn't do it. The day GM acquired EDS, they put ten thousand of their own [data-processing] employees in EDS, which has got to give [the employees] some indigestion for some period of time. Because GM gave up on them. They said they couldn't do it."

What convinced Smith to give up on his own data-processing operation? " 'Not invented here,' " McGowan told us. " 'Too established. We know better. The world is going in the wrong direction if it's not going in our direction'—and their direction was nowhere. [Retired chairman] Phil Caldwell did it at Ford. He really moved that company. They never gave him credit because you didn't see it in [Ford's] revenues and profits. . . . But Phil Caldwell really did a fantastic job there for two or three years. And I think other people like GM recognized they were way behind. Way behind Ford. Still behind Ford."

Ross Perot seemed to confirm McGowan's observations in a July 1985 interview with the *Washington Post.* The EDS founder was asked why Smith felt compelled to acquire his company:

Well, his problem is that they were way behind the curve in automation—whether [with] traditional financial information or [on] the factory floor. He didn't have the numbers of people that he needed or the management organization that he needed in order to accomplish what he wanted to do. . . . General Motors had its EDP [electronic data processing] departments broken up and split up in the organization. There was no single EDP organization, it was just a bunch of little cottage industries. Now Roger could stand up some morning and say, "by golly this is the wrong organization," and he'd pull all this together into a single unit. . . . And the elephant might not even bat its eye. Now this is my reading—and I've never even discussed this with Roger—but I think Roger has figured out how to trick you all. And buying EDS was part of tricking you all. See, in one fell swoop he can move all those little pieces over into EDS and suddenly he had a single EDP organization.

Two internal documents prepared by GM executives in the early 1980s illustrate the sloth and deep-seated inefficiencies rampant in the corporation Roger Smith inherited. Industry apologists often point to wage differentials between U.S. workers and their Japanese counterparts as well as the yen-dollar imbalance in order to explain why American production costs for small cars remain $1,500 to $2,000 higher than automobile costs in Japan. In his 1982 letter to Reagan, Smith claimed that labor costs represent "about three-fifths" of the Japanese landed-cost advantage. These documents suggest that GM understands full well management's role—through inadequate inventory controls, poor shop-floor layout, inadequate coordination with suppliers—in contributing to its cost disadvantage.

The first document, dated July 25, 1980, is a memorandum on GM's S-Car. Joseph Godfrey, group executive for Body and Assembly, dispatched a four-page overview to future president James McDonald of the proposed subcompact, which was scheduled to be introduced in the fall of 1984 and compete head-on with Japanese imports. Godfrey reported that the goal of the project was to assemble each vehicle in ten hours. "If successful, this 10 hour S-Car will put us closer in line with our Japanese competition, although they will probably make considerable progress between now and 1984," he wrote. He also explained that GM's *best* assembly performance to date was the eighteen hours required to assemble a normally equipped Chevette in its Wilmington, Delaware, plant. Thus, to catch up with the Japanese, GM would have to shave nearly 45 percent off the required assembly time of its pace-setting Chevette. Godfrey described the radical changes in accepted management practices required to meet the ten-hour goal:

> The job has to be designed, engineered and processed simultaneously to reduce the late change syndrome. A team approach must be used to bring this car to production. Coordination and commonization should be basic objectives of this program, including such items as common wheel base, windshield and door openings, common sheet metal for all body styles. . . . New concepts in parts packaging, shipping and related inventory disciplines must be a part of the program to increase inventory turns and reduce inventory investments. Automatic load at source plants with automatic unload at assembly plants must be implemented on a cost effective basis with new concepts of shipping containers.

Roger Smith eventually abandoned plans to produce the S-Car in the United States. Instead he negotiated his agreements with Suzuki, Isuzu, and Toyota.

A second document, this one from 1983, described plans to introduce new pickups in 1987, GM's first all-new line of light-duty trucks in fourteen years. The bulky report, which went on for more than one hundred pages, outlined the threat to GM's profitable trade in pickups posed by Ford and overseas competitors. It reported with some concern that GM had lost six points of market share to Ford in the half-ton segment between 1979 and 1981. "The competition is successful for two reasons," the document argued. "They force cost, quality and reliability efficiencies by up-front interactions between engineering, processing and manufacturing . . . and they pay great attention to details. There's no romance in the way they develop vehicles, but it works. It will work for us, too, if we discipline ourselves to do the same."

This internal evaluation determined that to produce a competitive new pickup, GM would have to shave 25 percent off current manufacturing costs. Meeting quality goals would require that the corporation reduce average defects in a 1987 pickup by 92 percent compared with defects in 1982 models. The report was candid enough to concede that without existing trade protection, GM's current S-Truck models were in a vulnerable competitive position.

"Historically, when quality was stressed, cost would increase . . . and when cost reduction was emphasized, quality or features would suffer," the study noted. "The S-Truck is a good example of this . . . high quality but only competitive pricewise because it benefits from a 25 percent tariff on imports. We can't compete with the foreign manufacturers in a free market. We've looked. This can no longer be tolerated. We must both increase quality and decrease cost."

. . .

Stripped to its essentials, Roger Smith's strategy to resurrect General Motors runs on two feet—keeping company costs down and product prices up. The first foot increases the pace of automated production; controls wages and salaries for employees below upper management; squeezes suppliers; enlarges community subsidies; and brings federal safety, emissions, and fuel-efficiency regulations to a standstill, if not a rollback. The second foot involves responding to the Asian challenge through joint ventures and distribution agreements, thus reasserting GM's across-the-board hegemony in its home market. By maintaining a product mix skewed more toward larger cars than its domestic rivals, and at least staying even on small cars by selling captive imports, GM hopes to demonstrate that no other mass automobile producer has an interest in engaging in sustained price competition with the industry giant. With a new brew of constants, Roger Smith wants to reclaim GM's role as price leader. New, functional vehicle engineering for the motorist's benefit would wait for another executive era.

This strategic agenda required that the GM chairman square off against constituencies such as blue-collar workers, whose bargaining power had been sapped by unemployment and economic stagnation. It also hinged on the disposition of the one remaining institution—the federal government—with the wherewithal to reverse or moderate the course he had set in motion. That potential lever of resistance self-destructed even before Smith took office.

It is difficult to overstate the windfall power that fell into Roger Smith's hands as a result of the 1980 election. The rise of Ronald Reagan meant the demise of antitrust enforcement, a prospect that for decades had restrained GM leaders from conglomeratizing their corporation or aggressively expanding their already dominant share of the auto market. Smith made news during the first year of his tenure just by mentioning that he wanted GM to build 70 percent of all the cars produced in the United States. In the past such an aspiration would have been considered unduly provocative by the Justice Department's antitrust division. The acquisitions of EDS and Hughes, a $7.5 billion exercise in diversification, were made without so much as a hint of disapproval from Washington.

Freedom from the prospect of antitrust sanctions was reinforced by protection from international competition. In April 1981, when the Reagan administration negotiated a three-year Voluntary Restraint Agreement (VRA), placing a quota on Japanese imports, it erected a paper wall behind which GM could maneuver to reclaim lost market share. Chairman Smith coyly remained at arm's length from this blatant protectionism. Why carry the ball on so controversial an issue when the White House is prepared to do the unpleasant work for you?

Three months after Smith took office, he appeared on *Face the Nation* and was asked how he could reconcile the proposed import quota with his crusade for deregulation of the auto industry. He responded with the improbable argument that a negotiated quota was an alternative to permanent trade protection. "I don't want to see a trade war start," Smith said. "It would be the worst thing in the world. So if we can have a voluntary program by the importers, I think that would help. And the government should do that. The industry can't do that. . . . I don't know anyone that wants to see legislation enacted that could start the trade war. . . . I don't want to see anything permanent. So I think it would be in the best interests of the Japanese and our country to do this voluntarily."

This self-serving logic notwithstanding, there can be no question that GM greeted the auto import restraints with unrestrained enthusiasm. General Motors submitted a prepared statement to the Senate Finance Committee in March 1981 endorsing "initiatives to persuade the government of Japan to . . . take action which would result in a voluntary, immediate and substantial reduction in passenger car exports to the United States." Smith personally endorsed the VRA at GM's 1981 shareholders meeting. At his Orwellian best, the GM chairman hailed the quota as being "in the interest of open world trade."

Domestic automakers faced two choices as cars from Japan began to flood the U.S. market during the late 1970s: lower their prices in response to the competition or sacrifice market share to maximize short-term profits. George Washington University professor John Kwoka, a consultant to the FTC in its GM-Toyota investigation, has argued that U.S. manufacturers went for the latter option. GM and its counterparts "chose to yield up market share by pricing in a fashion that permitted continued [Japanese] entry into the small-car market," Kwoka wrote in a 1982 paper. "That is, they deliberately kept prices high enough to permit continued imports, because by doing so they maximized their profits. To deter entry, prices would have to be held so low that the profit return was inferior. Thus, the preferred strategy for the dominant firms was to sell off market share even at the expense of future sales, production and employment."

Kwoka paid specific attention to the pricing behavior of General Motors in the 1978 model year on its Chevette subcompact. Gradual devaluation of the dollar compelled Japanese producers to raise the price of cars shipped to the U.S. every few months—a perfect opportunity for aggressive price competition by GM and other domestic manufacturers. That did not take place. Kwoka concluded,

> What GM in particular proceeded to do was to behave like a dominant firm maximizing the present value of profits without regard to ultimate market share. It raised prices nearly in lockstep fashion with the Japanese, resulting in a Chevette costing $3734. Chevettes began the model year two or three hundred dollars above the Japanese models; it concluded [even after the dollar devaluation] at $250 above both. Relative prices were virtually unchanged and so, not surprisingly, were market shares. . . . Each [pricing] round was led by Toyota, quickly followed by Datsun, and typically within two to four weeks matched by General Motors. No opportunity to raise prices was missed by GM.

The VRA was a convenient resolution of the choice between profits and volume. Japanese imports totaled 1.9 million cars in 1980. In 1981, as a result of the quota, shipments were scaled back to 1.86 million. They remained roughly at that level for three years. The Japanese then agreed to extend the VRA to April 1985 in return for a modest increase in the limit. Four years of protection had its desired effect. While the share of U.S. car sales claimed by imports rose from 17.7 percent to 27.9 percent between 1978 and 1982, the foreign share had actually declined to 22.5 percent by the first six months of 1984. This reduction in competition fueled an increase in prices and profits. Japanese manufacturers, who were now shipping fewer cars than consumers were demanding, could charge more for their products. U.S. manufacturers, who were making sales to buyers who could not find scarce Japanese vehicles, increased their revenues. For General Motors, windfall power led to windfall profits. Smith in turn applied much of those windfall profits not to improving vehicle quality and performance, but to advancing his Star Trek agenda for conglomeratizing GM.

The demise of antitrust enforcement and imposition of the VRA created an economic environment in which Roger Smith could unleash the full force of GM's market power and financial leverage. A third consequence of the Reagan victory—the assault on auto industry regulation—lifted from the chairman's shoulders pressures to produce safer and more reliable cars that had infuriated, and at times obsessed, his predecessors. Six days after President Reagan took office, GM submitted a wish list of proposed or existing regulations it wanted scrapped or postponed. The company claimed that eliminating or delaying safety Standard 208, the passive-restraint rule, would save GM $285 million. It offered no estimate of the number of lives that would be lost. GM urged the Reagan government to roll back standards in force since 1978, requiring that bumpers protect cars against damage in collisions at a mere 5 miles per hour. The company wanted to install cheaper 2.5-mile-per-hour bumpers. The proposals went on and on. Roll back emissions standards on heavy-duty engine exhausts. Rescind the particulate emissions standard for diesels.

General Motors was playing to a sympathetic ear. Chairman Smith met in early February 1981 with Transportation secretary Drew Lewis and White House advisor Ed Meese to preach his deregulatory gospel. Two weeks later he spent four hours in Detroit with the Transportation secretary and continued his wildly exaggerated drumbeat. "We showed Lewis a list of 1,500 regulations on the government schedules and especially those that aren't cost-effective," he boasted to a reporter after his meeting. "The five-mile-an-hour bumper is an $800 million load on the consumer."

The chairman's concern about a "load on the consumer" was disingenuous at best. GM's own filings pegged the purported cost savings of 2.5-mile-per-hour bumpers at $50 per car. Unless Smith was expecting the industry to ship 16 million vehicles in 1981—twice as many as it turned out in 1980—his $800 million figure is difficult to understand. But accuracy and reason were not the guiding imperatives in Detroit or Washington during the early Reagan years. The name of the game was crippling agencies and gutting standards. And on this objective Roger Smith and Ronald Reagan were in complete agreement.

Smith gushed about the president to reporters in the spring of 1981, saying that "so far, I haven't seen the guy say one thing that I don't agree with. And I don't even agree with my wife one hundred percent." He also began corresponding regularly with Secretary Lewis, the official charged with unshackling GM from its alleged regulatory chains. The leader of the U.S. auto industry and a top member of the Reagan cabinet became two of the most powerful pen pals in America.

"It was good to meet with you last week," Smith wrote Lewis on February 9, 1981. "Our discussions with you and then with Ed Meese were most valuable in getting a sense of the priorities and interests of the new Administration." Smith also added a P.S.: "We just learned of your announcement today on passive restraints and are pleased by your recognition of our competitive problem with full-sized cars and by your decision to review the entire matter of passive restraints." (Lewis had proposed suspending Standard 208 for one year as a prelude to the October 1981 decision to rescind the rule entirely.)

Six weeks later, Smith reported on his work as a Reagan cheerleader. "As you and I have discussed, I am taking every opportunity to support the President and his program," he wrote. "The attached clip reflects that effort and I thought you might find it of interest. It was good to see your remarks about the lack of need for further fuel economy standards and your plan to revise the bumper standard. . . . As you know, we want to help the President and you wherever we can."

Roger Smith received a friendly note from Drew Lewis in May describing an "atmosphere of closer cooperation between government and industry than either of us has seen before." By the end of 1982 the GM chairman could point with satisfaction to a number of specific regulations that his friends in Washington had eliminated or emasculated. The list of rescissions, delays, and suspensions is far too long for detailed discussion. Two examples out of many suggest the scale and implications of this antiregulation frenzy:

- *Bumper standards:* The National Highway Traffic Safety Administration (NHTSA) announced in 1982 that it would roll back the 5-mile-per-hour bumper standard. A survey by the Center for Auto Safety indicated that roughly 50 percent of all 1983 car models had been equipped with the inferior 2.5-mile-per-hour bumpers. The Center also concluded that "no difference in sticker price could be found between those GM models which had 5 MPH bumpers and those with degraded bumpers. . . . Industry's claims [on price savings] proved illusory at best." The Highway Loss Data Institute later reported marked increases in the frequency of insurance claims on four 1984 GM models—Pontiac Phoenix, Buick Regal, Buick LeSabre, and Buick Electra—that had been equipped with degraded bumpers.

- *Passive restraints:* In October 1981 NHSTA rescinded Standard 208, which would have required automakers to install either air bags or automatic seat belts in new cars beginning with 1982 full-size models. But it was forced to reconsider after the Supreme Court ruled in June 1983 that the rescission was "arbitrary and capricious." Transportation secretary Elizabeth Dole reissued the standard in July 1984 but also announced that she would revoke it if states representing two-thirds of the U.S. population enact laws on mandatory seat belt use by April 1, 1989. The *Washington Post* reported in February 1985 that auto makers would spend $15 million in 1985 to lobby state legislatures in support of mandatory seat belt laws.

The Reagan-Smith assault on regulation for efficient and humane automobile performance did not end after the administration's initial flush of rule crushing. GM and Ford petitioned NHTSA in March 1985 to roll back the fuel-efficiency regulations on 1986 model cars from 27.5 miles per gallon to 26 miles per gallon. It seems the two largest U.S. automakers could not market a fleet of vehicles that could meet schedules for improved Corporate Average Fuel Economy (CAFE) approved by Congress back in 1975. Chrysler, the smallest of the Big Three, claims to have invested close to $4 billion to downsize its fleet to meet CAFE schedules. Its executives, including Chairman Lee Iacocca, vigorously opposed the petitions of its more powerful brethren. But misinformation and raw political influence carried the day. NHTSA announced in July 1985 that it intended to bow to the wishes of GM and Ford and roll back the CAFE standard. In September 1985 it did.

GM's failure to comply with long-established fuel-efficiency goals is a troubling reminder of its continued intransigence with respect to engineering for real value as opposed to styling and expensive gadgetry. When the Energy Policy and Conservation Act was passed in 1975, the average fuel economy of GM cars was approximately 12 miles per gallon, the lowest of any major auto manufacturer in the world. This performance was a consequence of management's drive for large-car profits and decisions to ignore any number of available conservation technologies. The 1975 law established a timetable to raise CAFE requirements from 18 miles per gallon in model year 1978 to 27.5 miles per gallon in 1985. GM and Ford have been out of compliance with CAFE standards since the 1983 model year.

Equally troubling is the argument by GM representatives during agency proceedings, congressional hearings, and media interviews in defense of its NHTSA petition. Company officials, including Chairman Smith, warned that without a CAFE rollback, GM would be forced to restrict production of full-sized cars. The simple matter of meeting fuel-efficiency regulations was transformed into a choice between continued prosperity in automobile towns such as Flint and Pontiac and the return of unemployment and despair. GM submitted a thirty-three-page statement to a Senate subcommittee in May 1985 that illustrated its tactics on CAFE.

"There would be a multiple impact if General Motors is forced to restrict production of some of its best selling cars," the document argued. "First, it would lead to an immediate reduction in the number of General Motors employees, a reduction in the number of people employed by GM's suppliers, and eventually a reduction in the number of people distributing General Motors cars. The Department of Commerce has estimated that between 80,000 and 110,000 auto industry and supplier jobs would be lost if Ford and GM reduced production by between 750,000 and one million units due to the current CAFE standards, and this number does not include lost distribution jobs."

The claim that Ford and GM would be compelled to restrict large-car production in response to CAFE requirements was patently false. Under the Energy Policy and Conservation Act, GM could have continued to turn out its high-profit gas guzzlers even if its fleet did not meet the 27.5-mile-per-gallon standard. The company would have simply had to pay a civil penalty of five dollars per car sold for every one-tenth of a mile by which its fleet exceeded the standard. GM's penalties for the 1986 model year would have amounted to an estimated $400 million. Chrysler executive vice-president Robert Miller, in testimony before the subcommittee to which GM submitted its statement, sharply denounced the threat to close large-car assembly lines.

A Chrysler brief submitted to NHTSA elaborated on Miller's testimony. GM's "line of argument is apparently intended to increase the pressure on NHTSA and Congress to roll back the standard," the petition explained.

> After all, how could anyone oppose a rollback if that is the only way to avoid enormous economic dislocation and hardship? But the argument fails because, in the real world, *there is no possibility that GM and Ford would close their factories instead of paying the civil penalties.* The act does not bar them from selling a mix of vehicles that fails to meet the standard. If they pay the penalties and establish a program for bringing themselves back into compliance, the risk of a successful [shareholder] derivative suit is minimal—certainly, much too small to convince Ford or GM to forgo the penalty option in favor of the far more damaging consequences of witholding products and closing factories.

Such well-reasoned statements apparently have little place in Ronald Reagan's Washington. When Transportation secretary Elizabeth Dole responded to a letter from us inquiring about the CAFE rollback, she simply parroted the gloom-and-doom scenario set out by GM and Ford. She even repeated GM's estimate that maintaining the CAFE standard would result in "the potential loss of 110,000 American jobs."

.   .   .

The aggressiveness displayed by Roger Smith during the early stage of his tenure as chairman of General Motors—his face-off with the UAW, his assault on federal regulation—was not unlike the power to deny exercised by U.S. Steel chairman David Roderick. In the short run, the symptoms of an industry such as steel plagued by structural decline resemble the symptoms of a viable industry such as autos suffering the effects of a deep recession and management incompetence. The misery and community despair that accompany layoffs have certain fundamental power-enhancing consequences for the companies, whether that misery is centered in Detroit or in Pittsburgh. But the power to deny is inherently self-limiting. A CEO can extract only so much in wage concessions or community subsidies or regulatory relief by closing plants before he runs out of plants to close. Roger Smith has managed to sustain his windfall power by launching a permanent offensive against countervailing organizations and institutions.

The transition from windfall power to offensive power is reflected in the shifting media perception of Smith's performance over his five years in office. During the period of economic stagnation—1981 and 1982— the GM chairman was subjected to a barrage of criticism, even ridicule, in the business press. Eugene Jennings, a veteran business professor at Michigan State University, told the *Wall Street Journal* in April 1982 that "Roger Smith reminds me of a guy running around stamping out ants who doesn't see the elephants coming." This front-page article was so stinging that retired chairman Thomas Murphy felt compelled to write the *Journal* and defend his beleaguered successor. The *Journal of Commerce* reported in August on hearsay, both inside and outside GM, that the struggling leader might be ousted.

The GM chairman's rocky start can be traced partly to a series of controversies early in his tenure that were widely interpreted as costly management blunders. GM's J-Cars—Chevrolet Cavalier, Pontiac 2000 Sunbird, Buick Skyhawk, Olds Firenza, and Cadillac Cimarron—were unveiled in May 1981 as the first "new" vehicles to go into production under the Smith regime. The cars debuted with much public-relations fanfare, but from the start they attracted little but criticism. The J-Car was said to be overpriced and underpowered for its size, which was larger and heavier than the popular Honda Accord. Production delays caused GM's plans for a massive national media campaign to fizzle. The cars also reflected Detroit's less-for-more pricing policies: Cut the weight (the J-Car was four feet shorter and 50 percent lighter than GM's big family cars of the 1970s) but keep the price up. This embarrassing product flop dogged Smith for much of his early tenure.

If the J-Car was an institutional blunder, Smith's performance during the 1982 UAW negotiations was strictly the boss's doing. General Motors received in March 1982 the wage concessions its chairman had been demanding for more than a year—but not before Smith incurred the wrath of blue-collar workers, editorial writers, and even his major competitor. Shortly after the negotiations began in January 1982, the GM chairman and union chief, Douglas Fraser, held a press conference to announce that any savings generated by the agreement would be passed on to consumers in the form of reduced sticker prices. This public-relations gimmick backfired almost immediately. Customers postponed new GM car purchases until the labor agreement had been sealed, thus assuring themselves a discount. Dealers were less than enthusiastic about the chairman's posturing—particularly when the promised discounts failed to materialize.

Ford chairman Philip Caldwell was livid. GM had worked up its discount plan after a meeting held months earlier between Fraser, Smith, Owen Bieber, and Al Warren. The day before Smith made his public announcement, he and his labor advisors convened a session with their Ford counterparts to plot strategy for the upcoming negotiations. But Smith did not mention one word about the bombshell he was about to drop.

"We were scheduled to meet with both companies on a Monday," recalled Doug Fraser. "I went over to GM on Monday morning and Ford on Monday afternoon. We found out later from the Ford guys, who were furious, that they met with GM on Sunday, the day before, to outline their strategy as to what they should demand of us in the opening session. And Roger did not tell the Ford boys [about the pass-along concept]. So they went through this charade. The fact of the matter is, a Ford guy told me, Roger said, 'We're really not asking the UAW for enough. We should up the ante.' He said that knowing all the time that GM had an [understanding] with us that we were going to go a different way. Ford was furious for a long period of time. I never would have gotten over it."

Fraser was later told that Smith did not inform Ford of his plans because of possible antitrust sanctions; GM could not legally discuss pricing strategy with its largest rival. The union leader's response? "If that was the excuse, then what he should have done was cancel that meeting and not misled Ford the way he did."

Smith's preagreement hassles with Caldwell were merely a prelude to the outrage he would encounter after the new contract was signed. The chairman was confronting a rather sticky problem in the spring of 1982: how to reduce blue-collar compensation and simultaneously increase executive pay. Thus was born the great Bonus Fiasco. GM's bonus policies must be ratified at least once every five years by shareholders. It so happened that the existing plan had been approved in 1977, which meant that it was up for renewal or revision at the May 1982 shareholder meeting. Smith had been receiving internal reports for some time that GM's unprecedented failure to distribute bonus payments in three consecutive years, a direct result of the severe downturn in the industry, was making it more difficult to hang on to talented young managers. The Bonus and Salary Committee of the GM board had begun to review existing payment schedules in early 1980. On March 1, 1982, the committee proposed a very generous increase in executive compensation. The General Motors Bonus Plan, the major incentive program, was made much more lucrative. The committee also proposed to expand by 5 million the number of shares available for executive stock options. It even created a whole new program, the Performance Achievement Plan, under which five hundred top managers would be eligible to share in an annual bonus pool worth millions of dollars.

This major increase in executive compensation would have been controversial no matter when it was proposed. The salaries paid to auto moguls traditionally attract wide coverage in the press and certainly do not go unnoticed by UAW activists. But Smith's 1982 salary grab could not have been timed more ineptly. The proxy statement describing GM's new bonus formula hit the street on the very day General Motors and the UAW were initialing their concession agreement.

Doug Fraser described to us how he reacted to this monumental blunder. "We didn't know a goddamn thing about it," he said. "We read about it in the paper. Owen was screaming at Al Warren. He was really beside himself. Owen came into my office, and the first thing we thought was that Smith should call off the stockholders meeting. He said they couldn't do that because they had already sent out millions of proxies . . . . So then we looked at the GM bylaws. They said that while the stockholders could vote on the new bonus plan, the board of directors did not have to implement it. We thought that was the key, so we arranged a meeting with Al Warren and Smith. We called a press conference for five P.M. that day and we went over [to GM headquarters] at two P.M. We told them we were going to blow them out of the water unless we could solve this issue. Smith said this was not done with malice aforethought, that they had in fact adopted this bonus plan in September 1981, before they knew we were willing to negotiate. He even offered to show me the board minutes."

Fraser proposed that Smith agree to adopt the new bonus plan, but not to implement it for the life of the 1982 labor contract. The agreement was scheduled to expire in September 1984. "Then we had a long discussion," Fraser continued. "He said, 'I'll issue a press release saying that we won't implement it during the life of the agreement.' I said, 'Well, I don't want a press release, we've got a press conference already. I want you to give me a letter.' He said okay. I remember this well, because he said, 'I'll give you a letter. I'll say, Dear Doug—' And I said, 'Don't give me that Dear Doug shit! Just write me formally, and just tell me that you're not going to implement the bonus plan that's been adopted by the board of directors. We're having a press conference at five P.M., and I'll release your letter.' That's the way we wanted to do it. So he said okay. He also said he was going to have a hell of a time with his board, that he can't just unilaterally reverse the board's decision. He had to get on the phone [with GM directors] right away."

The bonus fiasco touched off a flood tide of public criticism. The normally adoring *Automotive News* wrote that Smith's miscalculation demonstrated that GM executives "live and work . . . far, far away from the real world." The company "could not have done more to infuriate the rank and file of its workforce if it had set out to do just that." Still, Roger Smith seemed not to appreciate the lessons of his blunder. "If they"— the contract signing and the bonus announcement—"hadn't happened on the same day," he sighed to reporters, "I don't think there would have been a problem."

The real problem in Detroit was a history of excessive salaries and bonuses in an industry whose leaders seldom fail to compare wages earned by UAW workers with wages on Japanese assembly lines. These same managers almost never juxtapose the greater than thirty-to-one difference between top-management salaries and assembly-line wages in the U.S. auto industry with the comparable differential—no more than ten-to-one —in Japan.

Roger Smith's personal compensation is a case in point. As a result of the furor over the 1982 bonus plan, GM's return to profitability in 1983 did not allow its chairman to take advantage of its sweetened terms. He had to make due with the meager provisions of the 1977 formula. Smith still managed to command a salary of $625,000 along with a cash bonus, stock bonus, and company-financed stock purchases that raised his total compensation to $1.5 million. Not only did he become the first GM chairman ever to break the $1 million threshold, but four other GM executives joined him as members of this elite club. Bonus payments to 5,800 eligible managers exceeded $181.5 million in 1983, more than the value of the company's investment in its joint venture with Toyota. Smith increased his compensation to $1.86 million in 1984. Aggregate executive bonuses topped $224 million in cash and stock.

Retired UAW president Fraser offered an approving chuckle when we asked whether labor relations in the auto industry would improve if the ratio of executive salaries to blue-collar wages in the United States reflected the Japanese differential rather than the prevailing gap. He went on to explain what he considered to be an important contributing factor in these lavish salaries and bonuses. "A lot of it is not the money," Fraser told us. "It's status. I ran into that a couple of times. I remember talking to Roger Smith and saying, if we go to the bargaining table, because it was time for the stockholders' meeting, don't you guys dare give yourselves an increase in salary. And he starts complaining, almost whining, 'Phil Caldwell gets more than me and he only has one-half the size of company that I do.'"

· · ·

The post-1982 Roger Smith has been almost completely free of the criticism and second-guessing that followed him during his first two years as chairman. It did not require a computer-generated report from his strategic-planning confidant, Michael Naylor, for the chairman to appreciate that continued public focus on his personal blunders and GM's product flops would sap his standing in Detroit and his influence in Washington. Smith understood that the press felt obligated to report with great frequency on the world's largest car producer. So he decided to sieze the initiative, set the agenda for the media, and keep reporters occupied with *his* business. The results, for the time being, have been stylistically successful. Smith has been praised, almost glorified, in virtually every major newspaper and business periodical in the country. He honed a public-relations strategy based on offering resurgent hope and high-tech promises and on raising the media's horizons, with extraterrestrial metaphors such as the Saturn project. He has thus managed to disarm his media critics and replace any taste for the brand of aggressive and independent reporting that characterized much of the coverage of the auto industry during the late 1960s and early 1970s.

There is an uncanny similarity between the media techniques perfected by the GM leader and the techniques used so effectively throughout the career of his political hero, Ronald Reagan. Smith has become a master of the colorful photo opportunity, the big event, the subtle deception, the touching personal gesture staged to attract maximum coverage. While he still cannot come close to Reagan's ease behind a podium, Roger Smith must rank as a consummate corporate media handler. His Janusfaced performance on the question of adding a third brake light to GM cars is a case in point.

The National Highway Traffic Safety Administration sponsored research studies as early as 1976 documenting that a stoplamp installed in the rear window of an automobile could sharply reduce the incidence and repair cost of rear-end accidents. The agency opened a rule-making docket just before the Carter administration left office, proposing to require these high-mounted stoplamps on new cars beginning in September 1983. For sometime, GM raised doubts about them and discouraged NHTSA from requiring them. Many delays ensued, but NHTSA eventually did require automakers to install the brake light on 1986 model cars.

Once the regulation was passed, Smith launched a little campaign to adopt the light as a pet innovation. He decided to move ahead of schedule. He pressed GM's production managers to install the lights on 1985 models, which they were able to do on some luxury models, such as the Cadillac DeVille and Fleetwood, and to ship high-mounted stoplamps to dealers. "I wanted them to put those lamps on the cars a year ahead of schedule, and they all agreed to do it," Smith told reporter Cary Reich· in 1985. "Well, golly, I came back two months later and asked about it, and they told me it's gonna be six months for the tooling and so many months for production—my Lord, it was something like 11 months." Reich cited this episode in his *New York Times Magazine* article to illustrate Smith's impatience and aggressiveness. The chairman had offered another rationale for his enthusiasm several months earlier. In a June 1984 speech in Anderson, Indiana, the town which is host to the GM Fisher Guide factory that manufactures the light, Smith claimed he wanted to use the stoplamps to underscore his favorable disposition toward worthwhile safety standards.

"I also spent some time today with the people at Guide," he told his chamber of commerce audience. "They're hard at work now on the new high-mounted stoplight. This is government-mandated on new cars, starting in 1986, and optional on some 1985 models, but Guide is already shipping the new lights to dealers so they can be installed on some vehicles currently on the road. We're moving more quickly than required on this to demonstrate our support for the regulation. We think it should reduce the incidence of rear-end collision in heavy urban traffic, and we're eager to put it to work."

What Roger Smith did not say, and what Reich did not report, was that GM for years had argued in documents filed with NHTSA that the stoplamp's effectiveness had not been proven, would cost far more than what NHTSA estimated, even that it might be technologically infeasible to install the light inside small hatchback cars. A former high-ranking NHTSA official under Reagan told us that GM was "the most adamant" of all the automakers in opposing this regulation. "They are the only company that went out and committed serious research funds in an effort to disprove the efficacy of the light," this official said. "They went out around the beltway in Detroit. They submitted to the docket research studies purporting to contradict the conclusions we had drawn."

. . .

It is the birth of Saturn Corporation in January 1985 that will be remembered as the decisive chapter in Smith's tactical use of the media to give his policies a momentum that displaces critical analysis and investigation by the press. Saturn is a new GM subsidiary established to design, manufacture, and sell an American-built small car that can compete on price and quality with Japanese imports. It was initially capitalized at $150 million and is expected to command assets of up to $5 billion. GM plans to manufacture up to 500,000 Saturn automobiles per year, although it has set no firm date in the 1990s for when the yet-to-be-built assembly plant will generate its maximum output. GM estimates that Saturn itself will employ six thousand workers and generate up to twenty thousand additional supplier jobs.

Saturn could have been treated as another, although no doubt important, chapter in the history of General Motors. But from the very beginning Saturn was packaged with an overriding public-relations imperative, a high-technology aura, that turned it into one of the most widely covered projects in business history. Smith presided over the introductory Saturn press conference in Detroit with much verve. He unveiled and spotlighted the themes that have dominated coverage of the project ever since. Saturn was "truly an historic occasion," he declared. It was a "clean-sheet" effort to develop a whole new way of building cars. "We believe Saturn is the key to GM's long-term competitiveness, survival, and success as a domestic producer." He promised to drive the first Saturn off the assembly line personally before he retires in 1990. But according to Cary Reich, the chairman remained dissatisfied with the day's hoopla. John McNulty, GM's public-relations czar, described Smith's reservations to the journalist.

"The photo in the press kit has too many reflections on the hood," Smith complained to McNulty. "You don't have anybody who can take pictures right. And that thing out in the courtyard"—Smith took a prototype for a test drive—"was like a Chinese fire drill. Nobody seemed to know who should get in the car with me. And the press was all over the place. Shouldn't they have been behind a rope?"

Such sensitivity to detail comprises only one strand of the broader communications tapestry Smith uses to project public perceptions of General Motors and to convey indirectly, but unmistakably, GM's diverse power over any group thinking of challenging its hegemony. Unlikely as it may have sounded a few years ago, Roger Smith's media role has become a thematic pursuit for continued political and economic dominance.

Theme One is to exude a rhetorical Reagan optimism, an upbeat swell of the excitement and growth that lie ahead, an effusive portrait of the workers and managers of the future equipped with ultramodern equipment beyond the dreams of Buck Rogers. Smith addressed a three-day forum on the auto industry sponsored by the University of Michigan in August 1984. His keynote lecture was titled "Saturn, Jupiter, Venus and Beyond: Automaking in the Age of Aquarius." It was typical of the wide-eyed tone that now dominates his public discourse.

"We talk about Saturn rising out of a clean-sheet-of-paper, and it did," he told the audience. "It is our space-age approach to making a new line of subcompact cars—cars that will be cost-competitive with small foreign cars. These will be highly advanced cars, with all-new parts, including a revolutionary new engine and new transmission. But even more than it is a car, Saturn will be an advanced manufacturing process for an automobile."

Smith then launched into a galactic preview of the future. "Jupiter will be the next step—and after it, no doubt, will come Venus or another project," he promised. "Jupiter will be GM's next-generation car, the Car-of-the-Future, to take us to the year 2000. But, at the same time, Jupiter will require new manufacturing facilities even beyond those developed for Saturn. . . . We have some exciting times ahead of us—virtually a whole solar system of projects yet to explore."

One effect of this interplanetary optimism is to redirect the scrutiny of reporters away from the here and now. Reporters deluged with talk of Saturn, Jupiter, and Venus can easily lose sight of the earthly defects and inefficiencies that continue to plague GM's products and production lines. Few of the articles that gush over GM's rebirth under Smith mention that the company has been losing market share since 1982 to Chrysler and Ford. Another dividend of persuading the media to look forward is that it then seldom bothers to look back, a phenomenon that obscures a trail of broken promises and inaccurate projections that might otherwise weaken the chairman's credibility.

Consider Smith's rhetorical performance with respect to CAFE standards. On April 9, 1976, in a speech to a seminar in Washington, D.C., the future chairman warned that the fuel-economy law passed four months earlier would devastate the auto industry. "Barring a technological breakthrough that nobody at GM knows how to achieve, the law will limit your choice of a new car in ten years from now to something the size of a Vega or Chevette," he predicted. "It will make a shambles of customer choice for motor vehicles as we know it today." GM actually managed to surpass CAFE standards for four years after the law took effect. Its primary "technological breakthrough" was shaving hundreds of excess pounds off its cars. By early 1981, in Smith's first annual report to shareholders, the fuel-economy tune had changed considerably.

"GM expects its fleet average fuel economy to exceed the Government-mandated fuel economy by an ever wider margin as it intensifies its programs to satisfy the demands of the marketplace," the 1980 annual report pledged. "At a press conference on July 9, 1980, GM announced its intention to achieve an estimated fleet fuel economy of 31 mpg for the 1985-model fleet, nearly a 160% improvement over 1974 and well above the mandated 27.5 mpg average." This projection was off the mark again. Smith and his Washington representatives were back at NHTSA by 1985 petitioning for a rollback of the CAFE standard.

The chairman's forecasting skills with respect to diesel-equipped cars have been even less inspiring. In 1981, soon after he assumed power at GM, Smith predicted with some confidence that diesels would eventually account for 25 percent of the company's sales. Then came defects, consumer outrage, and the formation across the country of organizations representing thousands of dissatisfied diesel owners. GM announced in December 1984 that it would no longer manufacture diesel engines for passenger cars. For the first ten months of that year, it sold only 26,200 diesels.

On certain occasions Smith's rhetorical excesses have truly gone into orbit. During a June 5, 1985, press conference in which he announced the $5 billion acquisition of Hughes Aircraft, Smith was asked by a reporter about how the deal would affect GM's ability to compete technologically with its international rivals. "I think if you look at what has happened, our foreign competitors have been basically content to take what has been developed in the United States and duplicate it in their products," he bragged. "Where did the automatic transmission come from? It came from right here. If you look at all the major advances, the only one I can think of that we should give them credit for is the coin holder."

No reporter bothered to ask Smith why GM was offering as an option on 1986 Corvettes electronic antiskid brakes, an important new safety technology, developed and produced by Robert Bosch GmbH, a German company. No reporter mentioned the fact that Saint-Gobain Vitrage, a French firm, has pioneered in the development of antilacerative windshields. GM has started offering the windshields in its luxury models.

Saint-Gobain's 1982 estimates suggest that more than 300,000 people sustain lacerative injuries from windshield glass each year. As of March 1983, Saint-Gobain Vitrage's Securiflex inner-guard windshield had been installed on fifty thousand European cars, including vehicles manufactured by GM's Adam Opel subsidiary. The reporters might also have reminded the overzealous chairman that the automobile itself is not an American invention. As Smith told a different audience in 1985, the car "traces its roots back to Germany in 1885 and the early work of Daimler and Benz."

Theme Two is to keep the media in a state of anticipation and high expectation. Smith likes to drop factual nuggets to induce reporters to scramble among themselves for mini-scoops about the GM agenda. This tactic manages to lend the company's conventional secrecy an aura of titillating mystery. In 1984, the chairman began referring to a "lulu" he was trying to put together for GM. Reporters soon began searching for a new product, a new engineering feature, a new manufacturing process, all to no avail. When Smith announced the Hughes acquisition, he buoyantly declared, "Lulu is home now." The press-conference auditorium erupted with approving laughter.

Media anticipation was transformed into frantic behavior over the Saturn project. Saturn spawned a number of rings, each with its tantalizing anticipations. Where will the plant be located? Just what will Saturn do? Can the operation really function as the "paperless company" that Smith has promised? Two *Detroit Free Press* writers went so far as to rummage through garbage bins outside Saturn Central looking for whatever clues the refuse might hold.

Smith helped to raise Saturnmania to absurd dimensions. He appeared on the *Phil Donahue Show* in February 1985 complete with a very general prototype of the Saturn vehicle and his standard high-tech themes. "Saturn goes beyond the car and this company," he declared. "We're going to Saturnize our whole corporation. . . . We have a brand-new distribution system, a brand-new set of dealers. And we hope, and this is our fondest hope, to run a paperless company. I say all the information should flow through on computers."

The GM chairman left the program after fifteen minutes and turned the stage over to seven state governors, tumbling over one another in their zeal to land the project. This televised public auction was only the most visible in a series of gimmicks and stunts through which GM gained much favorable publicity. Pennsylvania bought time on Detroit radio stations so that golfer Arnold Palmer could tee off on behalf of the state. Missouri spent several thousand dollars to erect "Give us a ring . . ." billboards on Detroit highways. Residents of the Youngstown, Ohio, area wrote 200,000 cards and letters, mainly from schoolchildren, urging GM to build the plant in their troubled community. A Youngstown radio station even broadcast a jingle to inspire the troops: "Don't just sit awishin', stand behind Saturn today, let Roger Smith hear us say, 'We're the force that can do it, so bring Saturn our way.' " The avalanche of mail and attention from Youngstown prompted Smith, ever tuned to a new public-relations advance, to write the editors of two area newspapers in response to the correspondence:

> I have had the opportunity to read some of the thousands of letters regarding our Saturn project that your area realtors delivered to General Motors recently. I only wish I had time to respond to each of them individually. . . .
> Among the letters I did read were at least two that touched on points I think typify so much of what Saturn is all about. One of the letters, from LaChelle Owens of Youngstown, noted that Saturn will mean more jobs—which is one of the prime reasons we want to do this project in the United States. Another letter, from Bob Reece of Warren, mentioned that the Mahoning Valley already has some GM plants located there. He is absolutely right. . . . While we must base our decision on the Saturn plant location on hard technical and economic data, I do thank you all for your letters. Be assured that we at GM are proud to be part of the Mahoning Valley and look forward to your continuing support in the future.

The bidding for Saturn was serious business. Twenty-seven governors, as well as the economic development officials of nine other states, journeyed to Detroit to plead for the project. They carried promises of free land, cheap electricity, low-interest loans, tax holidays, taxpayer-financed job training—in all, the most extensive and expensive bidding war over an industrial project in American history. New York governor Mario Cuomo hand-delivered a SATURN-1 license plate and a proposal for cut-rate power that would save the GM plant $1 billion over two decades. Minnesota's Rudy Perpich offered GM a tax-free existence for thirty years, free daycare for the children of Saturn employees, and low-interest mortgages for the division's top one hundred executives. And the million-dollar, sometimes billion-dollar, subsidy packages just kept coming. GM finally announced in late July 1985, after several delays, that Saturn would wrap its rings around Spring Hill, Tennessee, a town of 1,100 situated thirty miles south of Nashville. A straight-faced William Hoglund, Saturn's president, told reporters that "the single biggest economic factor" in the choice was freight cost. Spring Hill is said to be about one and a half day's shipping time from 75 percent of the U.S. consumer market —a geographical reality that subsidies and tax breaks could not change for many of the other potential sites.

Saturnmania also had a less visible, but no less troubling, impact on political power and debate. Elected leaders in states considered prime contenders for the project simply lost all critical faculties with respect to GM's behavior outside the Saturn orbit. We encountered an unprecedented degree of self-censorship among public officials who in the past had not always shrunk from speaking their mind about one of America's most powerful economic institutions. Congressman Dan Rostenkowsi, the chairman of the House Ways and Means Committee, told us he did have certain reservations about the bidding war over Saturn. Would he be willing to convene hearings on the issue? "I'd be a hell of a lot more enthusiastic about doing it after GM makes its decision," came the reply.

There was no more dramatic episode of Saturnized self-censorship than the behavior of elected officials from Michigan. We contacted both of the state's U.S. senators and several members of Congress. It soon became clear that GM and Roger Simth were immune from scrutiny— on any issue—until the Saturn location had been chosen.

Congressman Howard Wolpe, who was more forthright than most of his colleagues, explained why he felt uncomfortable when we asked about the excesses of the bidding process. "That's obviously a very tough question," he said. "As a member of the Michigan delegation I am obviously very keen on locating Saturn in Michigan and, if possible, in southwestern Michigan. . . . People aren't teeing off at GM at this point on site selection because on the issue Michigan has a vested interest and a decided tax disadvantage in terms of Texas." (Michigan and Texas were long thought to be the two chief Saturn candidates.) "The interest of the Michigan congressional delegation is seeing that Saturn is located in Michigan."

By far the two most thoroughly muzzled Michigan officials were Sen. Donald Riegle and Gov. James Blanchard. Riegle refused to speak with us in person. He asked instead that we send prepared questions. We did submit six questions that ranged from the Saturn bidding to the auto import quota to Riegle's impressions of Smith's lobbying presence in Washington. The reply? A one-page testimonial:

> For the 9 years I've served in the Senate, I have had a very good working relationship with the heads of all the U.S. auto companies. My relationship with Roger Smith has been positive

and constructive. I have commented before on my strong support of GM's decisions in recent years to build or establish several new state of the art facilities in Michigan. These are vital investments in the job future and economic future of Michigan and the country. . . . Michigan also has a good chance of winning the Saturn competition, which would mean additional job creation and new multi-billion dollar capital investments . . . . While we have had differences of opinion on the trade issue—and Japanese imports —we have worked cooperatively on numerous issues over the years. I consider Roger Smith a man of vision and daring in reshaping GM for the global economy of the 1980's and beyond. Michigan is fortunate to be the home of the American automobile industry and of General Motors Corp.

Governor Blanchard avoided an interview of any kind, although early in the summer of 1985 his scheduling office did promise that he would participate in a telephone conversation. Blanchard's press secretary, Rick Cole, explained his boss's reticence. "It is not likely that the governor is going to discuss this with you until the [Saturn] decision is made," Cole told us. "Saturn is of critical importance for people in this state." You mean Governor Blanchard could say something that would provoke GM into locating the plant in Texas? "Someone could construe some comments he would make. . . ." But even after Saturn located in Tennessee, the governor would not talk to us.

Theme Three is to play the role of "Good News Roger." Smith has made an art form of the splashy celebration and the feel-good gesture. President Reagan participated in the July 5, 1984, dedication of GM's $600 million Lake Orion assembly plant outside Pontiac, Michigan. He also visited the GM Tech Center, which, flush with the spirit of the occasion, he mistakenly called the High-Tech Center, and took a widely televised spin in a Saturn prototype.

But not even Ronald Reagan could match the GM leader's patriotic drumbeat. "This is a great day in the history of our corporation," Smith announced. "It may be the fifth on the calendar, but the feeling is the Fourth of July—red, white, and blue; baseball, hot dogs, apple pie, and Chevrolet; the whole bit." Smith then introduced the assembled dignitaries: GM president McDonald, Congressman William Broomfield, Senators Donald Riegle and Carl Levin, Governor Blanchard, and, of course, the president.

Smith is less talkative when he is asked to—or compelled to—respond to criticism from victims of his corporate redirections. In September 1983, the GM chairman participated in a gala celebration in Flint, GM's "hometown," to mark the corporation's seventy-fifth anniversary. There were banners, parades, bands, the governor, UAW leaders, and local celebrities. It was a colorful and important day in the city's history. The *Flint Journal* went so far as to publish a special "Salute to GM" edition. After an effusive introduction by *Journal* publisher Robert Swartz, Roger Smith was even more effusive.

He praised the cooperative attitude of UAW vice-president Donald Ephlin, director of the GM Department. He gurgled over Governor Blanchard for "saying such nice things about General Motors. I just love it when he says yes to business like that." He thanked the entire gathering "because GM owes all of you a great debt of gratitude for your generosity and friendship." Smith did not mention that GM was in the process of mounting a challenge to its property-tax assessments in Flint that could cost the small city tens of millions of dollars each year, not to mention a rebate to GM of $33 million in back taxes and interest. Nor did he return to Flint when invited by residents in 1985 to participate in a forum in order to explain the demand for such draconian tax reductions.

Theme Four is to shift the media's attention and curiosity away from the corporation's impact on people to corporate manufacturing processes. Saturn is also an instructive lesson on this score. Of the millions of words written and spoken about the project, of the dozens of interviews Smith has granted in which Saturn was discussed, there has been virtually no inquiry about nor detailed elaboration of the automobile itself. What are the design improvements and new technologies that make Saturn safer than current subcompacts? Are there engineering breakthroughs to improve the car's handling, operating efficiency, and reliability? Nearly all of the focus has been on the technological systems that will produce Saturn—the means—rather than what kind of car will roll out of the factory—the end.

Smith goes out of his way to encourage this focus. "I know this is going to sound crazy to you," Smith told Cary Reich. "But do you know what really impresses me? I saw a robot pick up an *egg!* You show me a robot that can pick up an egg and I'll show you . . . well, it's fabulous! Picking up an egg! You know, most robots go *squish* like that. That's what most robots do. They clamp on to pick something and they, they *got* it. But you show me a robot that can literally pick up an egg . . . that's tremendous."

The GM chairman's hyperbolic musings at the June 1985 Hughes Aircraft press conference represent the ultimate example of his unchallenged focus on the means of production rather than on what is produced —a tactic that camouflages a profound gap between promise and performance. "This is truly a great day for General Motors," he exclaimed in celebration. "I'd say it's a super-historic day for us. . . . Our interest in [Hughes] was that we felt they were the premier electronics company in the entire world. And, of course, electronics, we believe, is going to be the key to the twenty-first century." Smith was later asked to elaborate on this point. "I think we've made the major developments already in terms of road and handling and safety and emissions and fuel economy," he declared. "The big thing left is electronics. It's the new frontier."

What contrasted so remarkably to Smith's talk was its jarring inconsistency with the company's performance. GM has made all the "major developments" that are to be made in fuel efficiency? Even as Smith was speaking, his company was petitioning the Department of Transportation for a rollback of CAFE regulations because it could not market, with ten years' notification, a fleet of cars that would meet a modest fuel efficiency standard. Safety? Smith has made no secret of his desire to block the air bag. Innovation? Imagine the reaction the owner of a GM diesel would have to the claim that electronics is the last frontier. GM has proven itself incapable of manufacturing a reliable diesel engine for passenger cars. Road and handling? By 1984, GM's troubled X-Cars, which were phased out of production ahead of schedule in 1985, had been recalled again and again for various defects since they were first produced in 1979. General Motors even faced a Reagan administration lawsuit filed in August 1983 charging that the company knowingly sold 1980 X-Cars with a hazardous brake defect.

. . .

In any evaluation of a chief executive's leadership and record, what counts are the kinds of products that are manufactured at what price and under what working, environmental, and community conditions, not Reagan-style rhetoric or changes in organization charts. By conditioning the media and setting their agenda and expectations, Roger Smith has managed to fill newspapers and the air waves with answers to the wrong questions.

The GM chairman has received help from an unexpected source in his strategy for media dominance: the leadership of the United Auto Workers. Since the rise to power of UAW president Owen Bieber, the union, largely by its own choosing, has abandoned its traditional role as a loud and expert voice countervailing GM outside the collective-bargaining realm. Not only has its economic research arm been less visible, but its silence allows the media to become entranced by the Smith agenda.

Victor Reuther, one of the celebrated founders of the union, expressed to us a number of reservations about its current direction. He worries that the new Saturn labor agreement, in which the UAW accepted a 20 percent reduction in base pay in return for certain guarantees of job security and additional compensation tied to productivity, represents "a return to piecework and the pitting of one worker against another in terms of actual output." He is concerned, more generally, that the union has no master plan to counter the increasing power of GM management. "The biggest problem is that GM has a strategy and knows where it's going," Reuther told us. "I think at this moment the UAW has no strategy. It is merely reacting, not developing a counterstrategy."

The inertia of the UAW is evident on any number of fronts. The union failed to take a position on the rollback of CAFE standards, even though fuel economy requirements are one of the forces working to retain at least some small-car production in the United States. It has made only token efforts to cultivate grass-roots opposition to GM's Asia Strategy and Smith's program to export U.S. jobs to low-wage countries, such as Korea. UAW president Bieber made no public statements of dismay during the destructive bidding war over the Saturn project, even though the union was involved from the beginning in discussions with management over where the plant would be located. And despite months of letter-writing and telephone calls to Solidarity House, the UAW chief refused to share his insights on the GM chairman for this profile, even after an aide asked us, and we agreed, to put our questions in writing and leave Bieber adequate time to respond in writing.

The UAW's silence is especially deafening given the strong opinions expressed by former UAW officials and international union leaders. Consider the Saturn project. Robert White, the hard-hitting president of the Canadian UAW, who led his membership out of the U.S.-based union after the 1984 round of collective bargaining, described the Saturn spectacle as "unreal." The bidding "says something to me about the power of corporate investment," he told us, "about what's wrong with society in terms of full employment. And it says something to me about what I would call respect for politics. You wouldn't have the same kind of thing in Canada." Doug Fraser, the retired UAW president, labeled the entire affair "obscene."

· · ·

General Motors owns assembly plants, foundries, and warehouses in twenty-six states across the country. In many of the towns and cities in which it operates, particularly the automobile-dependent Midwest, GM is the largest employer, the largest taxpayer, and the engine of much regional economic activity. One important test of the character and leadership of a CEO is how he balances community needs for stability and adequate services with corporate cost reduction and profit maximization. Roger Smith leaves no doubt about how he resolves this sensitive balancing act: total control.

Smith has presided over a string of crises and controversies in which the weight of General Motors has been pitted against outraged and defenseless residents of GM communities. His first test of strength began to take shape in 1980, before he became chairman, when the corporation insisted that Detroit raze a section of the city called Poletown to make way for a highly automated plant to produce luxury cars. Although the planned destruction of Poletown was initiated under the regime of Thomas Murphy, it was Smith's job after January 1, 1981, to face down the protest, spurn pleas for compassion, and forge ahead until the deed was done. His approach to the year of agony and publicity can be summarized in a single phrase: hide behind the mayor.

The collision between General Motors and Poletown had its roots in a site search for a plant to replace aging Cadillac and Fisher Body factories in Detroit scheduled for shutdown. Mayor Coleman Young and his political allies wanted the new plant inside the city limits. So did GM—if the city could meet the company's conditions. Young eventually offered nine potential locations, and GM selected Poletown. In July 1980 the Detroit City Council voted to acquire the site by eminent domain, utilizing a Michigan "quick-take" statute. It sent its agents into the neighborhood to tell residents their homes had been condemned and that they could negotiate compensation in subsequent weeks. In the past, Young had seen a number of Detroit areas taken for urban renewal purposes. He believed this case would be routine.

Mayor Young was mistaken. Poletown was more than a section of eastern Detroit; it was an integrated lower-middle-class community with a sense of tradition, a sense of place and of history. Here much of the early agitation leading to the formation of the United Auto Workers took place, around the giant Hamtramck Chrysler plant. Polish immigrants started to settle the area in 1872, and by the 1920s a thriving ethnic community had formed. In succeeding years, the more upwardly mobile children and grandchildren moved to affluent suburbs. The arrival of black families in the post–World War II period was gradual and uneventful. By the time Thomas Murphy and Roger Smith tapped Poletown for their new plant, there were some rundown streets but there were also 3,438 residents, living in 1,176 houses serviced by 117 commercial and industrial buildings, 12 churches, a 278-bed hospital, and 2 schools. Some 1,000 people found gainful employment in the area.

Anna Constanti was seventy-three years old and her sister, Mary, was sixty-nine in 1980. They lived in the eight-room house into which their parents had moved back in 1913. The two women kept their home in very good condition and tended a backyard filled with sixty rosebushes. The city of Detroit offered them $8,000 for their property after condemning it. Mrs. Josephine Krajewski, a Poletown resident for the past fifty-seven years, regularly attended the Church of the Immaculate Conception, which was majestically situated in a corner of Poletown. The city of Detroit condemned both her home and the church.

The Church of the Immaculate Conception was a community center as well as a house of worship, and many a memory of good and sad times reverberated through its basement gathering rooms. The pastor, Rev. Joseph Karasiewicz, found himself tragically torn between obeying the diocese, which had agreed to sell the church to the city for $1 million, and his devotion to his church, built lovingly by the efforts of Polish immigrants earlier in the century, and the fearful families who looked to him for succor and leadership. It was here that the newly formed Poletown Neighborhood Council gathered once a week in those foreboding fall months searching for a way to stop the storm clouds from engulfing their community.

Meanwhile, across town, the Murphy-Smith-Young juggernaut was gaining momentum. GM knew the deal had to be concluded promptly, both to speed up the city bureaucracy and to head off opposition. Company executives informed Mayor Young that the city had to acquire title to the site by May 1, 1981. GM announced publicly that it planned to build and open the plant by May 1, 1983—a timetable that had not been met over two years later. Young knew his overriding political argument was the need to retain six thousand out of fifteen thousand jobs once provided by the two facilities scheduled for shutdown. He made this jobs-retention argument over and over again during an extraordinary process of collecting a plethora of subsidies from federal, state, and local sources that totaled about $220 million. These funds were used to acquire the area, relocate the residents, demolish the structures, build roads and rail facilities, and for other site preparations. A twelve-year, 50 percent property-tax abatement brought a total subsidy package to General Motors of $350 million. GM was to receive this massive ready-made industrial park for a mere $8 million. Under this one-sided agreement GM was not legally bound to build the plant.

Top GM executives were quite content to remain shielded from the growing attention of the media and let Mayor Young and the city council take both the spotlight and the heat. But there was little doubt about who was pulling the strings and making the demands. In his dissent to a Michigan Supreme Court decision upholding the city's condemnation power, Justice John Fitzgerald observed, "Behind this frenzy of official activity was the unmistakable guiding and sustaining, indeed, controlling, hand of the General Motors Corporation. The city administration and General Motors worked in close contact during the summer and autumn of 1980 negotiating the specifics for the new plant site." Fitzgerald concluded that "the evidence then is that what General Motors wanted, General Motors got. The corporation conceived the project, determined the cost, allocated the financial burdens, selected the site, established the mode of financing, imposed specific deadlines for clearance of the property and taking title, and even demanded 12 years of tax concessions."

The Michigan jurist was not the only authority to look unfavorably upon GM's silent orchestration. Harvard Business School professor Joseph Auerbach wrote an article for the May–June 1985 issue of the *Harvard Business Review* in which he examined the Poletown episode as a case study in business-community relations. Auerbach listed six steps a corporation should follow in meeting its community responsibilities when undertaking a project as contentious as Poletown. He then evaluated GM's performance.

"The corporation must . . . disclose the terms to all the social communities involved and to their representatives," the professor wrote. "There may be many host communities involved from a social standpoint, in both number and political sovereignty. In this case, General Motors singled out the city for disclosure of terms and establishment of communication and thus effectively foreclosed the significant participation of other affected social communities."

Nestled in his comfortable home in Bloomfield Hills, Roger Smith was pleased with the dispatch of the negotiations and the consummation of this unprecedented taxpayer subsidy to the world's largest manufacturing enterprise. The people of Poletown felt differently. Many of them simply gave up. Others resolved to fight. Poletown began to be a regular television news story in late 1980. By 1981, with the rise to power of Chairman Smith, it became at times a daily story for the local evening news.

Sad things were happening in Poletown. Families broke up; some people committed suicide. Arson became a regular topic of conversation, as did the indifferent police protection, while vandalism and the burning of homes of the evicted continued nightly. The community was besieged. It cried out for help. But such are the imperatives of a one-crop city that even those who were so inclined found it in their interests to remain apart. Not the UAW, nor the diocese, nor any community group reliant on the city for grants or other assistance lent a hand. Associates of the authors went to Poletown in early 1981 in response to requests for help. They found a community trying to save itself in the courts while its opponents were engaged in virtual street warfare and siren psychology to evict the holdouts. They found small-businesspeople, families, and churchmen wondering aloud if this was still America. Father Joe was telling the press that destroying churches and a community to build a factory would not even happen in communist Poland. Charles Mistele, owner of a fuel-supply company in Poletown, was forced to close down because the city would not grant him six months to relocate his firm. Pressed by GM, City Hall said there was no time. GM wanted to have the plant ready in two years. By August 1985 the plant was *still* not producing cars. Mistele shut down, eliminating seventy-two jobs.

"I'm bitter," he said. "I've been in business longer than GM's been in business. I'm a private corporation and I've been put out of business for them."

Actually, Mistele's complaint was one part of the legal question that the Michigan Supreme Court decided, by a vote of five to two, in favor of the city and GM. The majority opinion was three and a half pages of sterile redundancy known as defining one's way to a predetermined conclusion. In a far lengthier dissent, Justices Fitzgerald and James Ryan took apart the majority's ruling, which they summarized as deciding "that the power of eminent domain permits the taking of private property with the object of transferring it to another private party for the purpose of constructing and operating a factory, on the ground that the employment and other economic benefits of this privately operated industrial facility are such as to satisfy the 'public use' requirement for the exercise of eminent domain power."

On that basis, wrote the two dissenters, "there is virtually no limit to the use of condemnation to aid private businesses. . . . No homeowner's, merchant's or manufacturer's property, however productive or valuable to its owner, is immune from condemnation for the benefit of other private interests that will put it to a 'higher use.' " The majority "has altered the law of eminent domain in this state in a most significant way and, in my view, seriously jeopardized the security of all private property ownership," the dissent continued.

Avarice aside, this bold takeover of private properties, with its large taxpayer subsidy, must have unsettled privately at least some of the purer private-enterprisers on the fourteenth floor of GM headquarters. Roger Smith, who has written and spoken vehemently against government involvement in or regulation of the auto industry, maintained a total silence on this rather fundamental irony except to say that management would be remiss to its shareholders if it turned down the city's presentation. All through the year of Poletown's agony, GM made clear that the company could have gone to a "greenfield" site in a rural area to build its facility. But out of concern for Detroit, company executives claimed, they were entertaining offers from the Motor City. What Smith and his associates did not mention were the great advantages of not going to a "greenfield" location: trained workers, connection to a rail spur, a tremendously valuable piece of real estate that could accommodate other projects and some valuable subsidies available only for urban construction.

Testimony at one of the Poletown trials by architect-planner Richard Ridley argued that the whole question of jobs versus the community was not valid because the jobs could have been available in the alternative, largely vacant site. But GM insisted on going first-class, with Mayor Young running interference and collecting welfare payments for the corporation from all three levels of government.

The Poletown Neighborhood Council, furious with the hypocrisy of GM and the city government, demonstrated, picketed company headquarters, and one Saturday led a small caravan to Smith's house to ask him to give up *his* home and acreage for the plant. Smith was not home. Residents also invited Smith to meet with them and discuss the project. To no avail. The land where the church was located was to be used as the shrubbery-adorned corner of a vast GM parking lot.

"Please, do save at least our church, which is both an architectural gem and an historical structure as well," Father Joe wrote Smith in February 1981. "While I am aware of the fact that his eminence, Cardinal Dearden, made it known that he would not oppose your project, I dare to presume more 'on the spot' appreciation of the situation here in our parish. If our church should be demolished, the resulting harm inflicted on our people would be absolutely devastating, causing, as I can envision it, irreparable personal harm."

The pastor offered to give the corporation chairman a tour of the church. Smith neither responded to nor appointed anyone to respond to Father Joe, but he let it be known that the cardinal wanted the church sold and abandoned. That was the GM leader's tactic—refer all demands to the mayor or the diocese as if they were the principals.

When it became apparent that Smith was ducking the controversy, Poletown citizens began to focus more on GM and less on its City Hall agents. One woman revealed her pride and her insight when she told a reporter, "We are neighbors, we help and love each other. I'll bet those General Motors executives don't have neighbors who love them." Another resident exclaimed, "GM is using my taxes to evict me." Others expressed themselves in pathos. Every week one elderly man came back to his vacant house and sat on the front porch weeping.

With the Detroit media becoming more attuned to Poletown's plight, and with arson and vandalism escalating to frightening levels at night, the GM–City Hall collusion moved toward climax. At five o'clock on a July morning, dozens of police cruisers descended on the sixty-two-year-old Church of the Immaculate Conception. A chain was tied to the door and a tow truck ripped it out. Police in full gear rushed into the church basement and arrested a dozen parishioners, half of them elderly, who had assumed a vigil there to protect their church.

Within a few hours the steel ball of the giant wrecker crashed again and again against the Twombly Street side of the rectory while several of the onlooking parishioners cried out in spontaneous unison as if they had been struck. The police did not like this job; many openly sympathized with the residents. "You've got to feel bad for the little people, a big corporation like General Motors coming in and pushing them all out," said one policeman.

Justices Fitzgerald and Ryan put the same thought in more jurisprudential language in their dissent: "Eminent domain is an attribute of sovereignty. When individual citizens are forced to suffer great social dislocation to permit private corporations to construct plants where they deem it most profitable, one is left to wonder who the sovereign is."

After most of Poletown was bulldozed into rubble, Smith traveled, on May 1, 1981, to the future site of his factory. With Mayor Young by his side, the GM chairman received title to the properties and symbolically broke ground. In a twenty-minute address, Smith made two very brief references to the community that once stood there. He praised Mayor Coleman Young for taking "a lot of flack to help us . . . in spite of pressures generated by perennial out-of-town critics of General Motors." And he described the pending lawsuits by "well-intentioned people with real concerns about their property" as groundless. After the bulldozers had torn Poletown to piles of debris, Smith tardily observed that "this is certainly a time for compassion and understanding of their needs."

The more affluent environs of Detroit seemed relieved that the groundbreaking had finally taken place; the Poletown demolition was attracting national media attention and was beginning to give Michigan a bad image. After a visit to the community in its last gasps for survival, Rep. Barbara Mikulski, a Maryland Democrat, told reporters, "If this was occurring in Poland, there would be an international uproar and demands for a United Nations inquiry." The people of Poletown invited Mikulski because they were unable to find any members of the Michigan congressional delegation willing to visit them, much less speak up for better treatment. When Congressman John Conyers wrote a mildly questioning letter to Mayor Young, he was told to stay out of the situation.

Roger Smith's reaction to community protest and resentments illuminates a part of his character that even otherwise supportive acquaintances find troubling: his insensitivity and coldness toward the innocent losers in GM's wars. At the May 1, 1981, groundbreaking ceremony for the Poletown plant, he described the factory-to-be as "a big plant, with about seventy acres under roof, but a plant that is . . . well landscaped." It was precisely the taking of 465 acres for a GM plant of 70 acres that infuriated the residents of Poletown.

The insensitivity persisted. On the *Phil Donahue Show* in 1982 a member of the audience said, "Mr. Smith, I was born in Poletown, so you're not my fan." Smith replied, "You ought to go back and see it now." The controversy came up repeatedly at stockholders meetings. In the May 1981 meeting, Smith claimed that "most of the people were delighted to be rescued from homes they couldn't sell. A few were not, of course." After several persistent questions from Poletown residents, the chairman became exasperated and cut off debate. At one point he shouted, "We've had all the discussion we're going to have on Poletown today."

During the 1982 meeting, a shareholder who had been active in the Poletown resistance asked Smith for a moment of silence in memory of Father Joseph Karasiewicz. Father Joe had died of a heart attack (some would say of a broken heart over his fallen church) the previous December at age fifty-nine. Smith agreed, but not before he launched into a diatribe against the shareholder's assertion that the pastor was a "victim of General Motors." Smith called Poletown a "decaying community that was a problem to the city of Detroit."

These words were uttered by a man whose company required the destruction of twelve churches to make room for that one-level parking lot. Then, asserting that most Poletown residents were better off now, Smith reverted to his sovereign role: "Now, I'm sorry that people had to get displaced. . . . We have to build freeways; we build power lines. People do get displaced in the name of progress."

The Poletown plant was still not finished by February 1985. It was nearly two years behind schedule—despite the terrible rush to evict residents from their homes. By year's end, consultants from other automobile companies flocked to the plant trying to help GM solve immense technological difficulties. A *Detroit Free Press* columnist, Neal Shine, toured the facility and was impressed by its modernity. But he could not shake the past. "For much of the tour, I kept thinking about other things, seeing other faces," he wrote.

Like Josephine Jacubowski, gray-haired and 70, on the top step
of the police van following her arrest for protesting the demolition

of Immaculate Conception Church . . . or Stanley Danieluk, 91, who stayed behind for several days after relatives had moved all but a sofa out of his house. . . . I wondered if anybody had ever suggested to GM that the location of some Poletown landmarks, great and small, be honored with a stenciled marker on the new cement floor. Things like: "On this spot, Stella Borowski operated her grocery store on Kanter for 50 years," or "This marks the location of the Famous Bar-B-Q Restaurant on Chene near Grand Blvd. where Roman Karolewski and Al Azar played their last game of gin rummy in 1981."

Shine's sincere musings did not embrace the alternative that both the plant and the community could have coexisted with a modest location shift and a more sensitive industrial site plan. This did not have to be a zero-sum game between the opponents. Unless, that is, one opponent wanted it all. But his column did poignantly depict how, even in victory, the GM of Roger Smith, who gives the company its public personality, was determined to prevent the lingering on of any artifacts that could nourish a remembrance of what once stood.

· · ·

The needless destruction of Poletown will be remembered as a cruel chapter in the annals of Detroit. But the agony was not an idiosyncratic accident of GM history. Roger Smith eventually launched for Saturn a nationwide squeeze play on communities with a fervor that might have shamed Alfred Sloan and even tough-minded Frederic Donner. First, Saturn was dangled before the nation, and a widely reported state and local bidding war erupted. Smith claimed on several occasions that GM was not asking cities and states to engage in the bidding war. At the 1985 shareholders meeting, he said, "We are not asking for a handout."

Smith's posture begged obvious questions. Was there no way General Motors could have structured its search to diminish the bidding frenzy? If an overriding variable was geography—one day's access to the bulk of the Saturn market—could not GM have publicly limited its search to states that met the condition? Did not Smith's own behavior over the frantic several months indicate that he was quite pleased with what was happening? The answer to all three questions is yes. The chairman seldom missed an opportunity to boast about how the bidding war demonstrated the abiding national interest in Saturn and how this race to throw tax breaks and subsidies at GM would improve the "business climate" for other corporations as well.

There was a time when corporations weighed factors such as access to a skilled labor pool, availability of raw materials, transportation and energy costs, and distance from markets when they had to choose a site for a new factory. These are still the critical selection factors, as numerous studies of plant location have demonstrated. But now major corporations are demanding windfalls, asking for bundles of welfare subsidies and tax breaks, from communities anxious to land whatever new jobs they can. Roger Smith is exploiting this auctioneering environment to new extremes.

Consider the turn of events in Kansas City, Kansas. The question: Would General Motors replace its 1940s Fairfax assembly plant, scheduled for closing in 1988, with a new factory in Kansas City or would it locate the operation in some other state? All officials from the local chamber of commerce had to do was mention that Louisville, Kentucky, was in the running to induce panic in City Hall. The local government concluded that it had to make a dramatic gesture of fealty. On December 27, 1984, the city council voted to close Fairfax Municipal Airport and offer virtually all of the land to GM for its new plant. The property was across the street from the old GM facility and near a $17-million city-funded wastewater treatment plant.

The airport was no desolate tract. Used by commercial and private pilots alike, this spread of 580 acres housed fifty-four businesses and individuals holding sixty-five leases, some of which ran to the year 2000. Recent investments in airport improvement totaled $2.5 million. Then came the race for additional subsidies. GM soon applied for low-interest bonds. The state established an enterprise zone on the airport site, which exempts a builder such as GM from sales, use, property, and *ad valorem* taxes. Status as an enterprise zone also gave GM the right to request that the state provide equipment and instruction for job training. Then came the big money. On March 14, 1985, the county of Wyandotte, the city of Kansas City, the Kansas City–Wyandotte Joint Port Authority, and General Motors entered into an inducement agreement. The deal followed weeks of intensive secret negotiations brokered by the local chamber of commerce. The city agreed to issue $775 million in economic-development revenue bonds, including up to $50 million in pollution control bonds. It provided 568 acres of land. It drained a $10 million city account funded with a special 2 percent sales tax. The account was intended for industrial development—but presumably its original sponsors had more than one project in mind.

In return for these singular preferences, GM announced on April 30, 1985, that it would build a $750 million, 2.3 million-square-foot assembly plant on the airport site. A jubilant Mayor Jack Reardon boasted that "no city in America sweats the decisions like Kansas City, Kansas." If General Motors changes its mind about the plant, it need only pay the city $1,000 in liquidated damages, plus $250,000 in expense reimbursement. Not much sweat there. GM can also terminate the agreement with thirty days notice.

Modest attempts by *Kansas City Star* reporters to explore the larger dimensions of the negotiations with GM earned them a sharp rebuke from the newspaper's ombudsman. "The day of this kind of advocacy reporting ought to be over," his memorandum protested. The paper thereafter became predictably calmer. But the *Kansas City Times* weighed in with a cartoon depicting grass-skirted natives preparing to drop a human sacrifice into a set of massive smokestacks labeled "GM." The caption read, "Ever get the feeling that our efforts to keep them happy are getting *slightly* out of hand?"

Roger Smith watched all this from behind his desk at GM headquarters. The deal was struck with a minimum of bad publicity and, indeed, almost total anonymity for the company personnel who negotiated the massive subsidy package. It was enough to give the jaunty Mr. Smith even greater airs of institutional confidence for the next drive—a series of appeals filed in March 1985 with the tax assessors in cities and towns across Michigan demanding unprecedented reductions in the assessed value of GM properties. The move stunned local assessors and political leaders. Smith himself had told a Tokyo audience in April 1984 that " 'old' GM factories have been updated to the point that the only really old things in them are the doorknobs and the windows." In Michigan, his company was telling assessors that these ultramodern plants were not worth very much at all.

It is difficult to make the case that General Motors is overtaxed. The company has made extensive use of a Michigan statute, Public Law 198, that permits local governments to approve 50 percent abatements on certain categories of industrial property in the interests of job creation. A March 1985 report in the *Flint Journal* estimated that GM received a staggering $700 million in taxpayer-financed incentives in Michigan over the past decade. More than $500 million of those subsidies involved tax abatements approved under PL 198.

Congressman Howard Wolpe was a member of the state legislature when the law was passed. "I believe PL 198 is one of the worst pieces of tax legislation to be enacted," he told us. "It invites the kind of competition [over new investment] we are seeing. There is no evidence that tax incentives increase investment or employment. It has produced windfalls for a number of companies that would have made the investments anyway. I really regret what we did. It has been very harmful for the state overall. It has really invited this kind of competition."

But Roger Smith got more than he bargained for. After years of compliant behavior, leaders and residents of the affected communities became indignant and felt betrayed. Steve Nagy, the tax assessor for Genessee Township, spoke with us shortly after GM filed its appeal. Genessee Township is home to a Fisher Body plant with a real-property assessed value of $24.5 million. GM already has a twelve-year, 50 percent abatement on the plant's personal property, which is valued at $10 million. The company's appeal targets a new valuation on real property of $10 million, a reduction of 59 percent.

"Roger Smith just wants to stomp us [into] the ground," Nagy complained. "All he wants to do is make more money. He doesn't care who he steps on to get it. He's a finance man. . . . GM is shifting the burden from the large industrial taxpayer to local people, individuals, who are already up to their neck in taxes."

Nagy was not alone in his outrage. The historically loyal and boosterish *Flint Journal* printed the first of several critical editorials on June 10, 1985. Its headline, "How Can GM Bully Friends This Way?" captured the mood of the community. "GM's campaign for tax relief at the expense of residents and smaller businesses is coming to be seen as intimidation," the newspaper declared. "In effect, GM is saying it can take its payroll elsewhere if local jurisdictions don't cry uncle."

This is the same *Flint Journal* that two years earlier published its special "salute" to GM. Its June editorial touched off a barrage of critical letters directed at the automaker and its chairman. "As a UAW representative, community member and a GM employee for the past 20 years, I am appalled that General Motors would even suggest it wants its fair share of taxes further reduced," wrote a member of UAW Local 598. "GM wants to take our tax dollars and spend them on its new automated plants, which have substantially fewer workers. . . . A revolt is beginning to brew against GM in Flint."

Soon other local papers and political leaders began voicing similar disbelief. The mayor of Warren, Michigan, declared that GM facilities in his town were *undertaxed.* And as the summer months of 1985 wore into the autumn, the protests spread beyond the councils of government and the press into the ranks of workers, teachers, school superintendents, small businesses, and other segments of the community. The calls for Roger Smith to visit these towns and face people affected by his policies began to increase. It seemed like an opportune time for Smith to put into practice a point he made in a May 21, 1985, speech to the International Association of Business Communicators (IABC). The GM chairman had just received the group's Excellence in Communication Leadership Award.

"From extensive research we have conducted inside GM and from reviewing IABC research we are convinced that we must put much greater emphasis on face-to-face communication at all levels," he said. "Face-to-face is the best form of communication because it is much more personal and allows for a two-way exchange of information. It heightens credibility."

But Smith did not abide by his own standard in the property-tax dispute. Lower-level GM spokesmen handled all communications with the press and outsiders. A Detroit law firm, Honigman Miller Schwartz & Cohn, known for its aggressive tactics in property-tax disputes, together with GM community operatives, managed the appeals, negotiations, and the various games of hardball with local officials. Even when an associate of ours, who was assisting the protest movement, attended GM's 1985 shareholders meeting and invited Smith to attend a "responsible" forum that included elected officials, the chairman would not budge.

"We have people meeting with them continually," he insisted. "And those people are more skilled and understand property taxes better than I do. And those are the ones conducting the negotiations. The people who can do the job the best are meeting with them and will meet with them and will continue to meet with them."

He then launched into a defense of his tax-reduction demands. "We're not out to bankrupt anybody," he insisted. "There are millions of communities around this world that operate with a reasonable tax system and provide [for] the schools and the police forces. So this is not some disastrous situation. . . . I told you what our position is. I think you've got the situation blown entirely out of context. But I'm telling you, we are not going to pay more than the taxes we are legally required to. I could not face the stockholders and ethically say to them, 'Well, we're paying more taxes than we're supposed to.' Why? 'Well, we just decided to give your money away.' It's not my money. It's the stockholders' money."

GM has also begun to move its tax-reduction campaign to other states. One very high-ranking company official, who supports the substance of the GM policy, told us that "politically GM made a mistake going national and trying to do it all at once to be efficient. Now we are trying to go to the communities, one by one, and say to them, 'We don't intend to bring you to your knees, we can do a phase-in.' We should have done this over time."

When Union Carbide's chairman, Warren Anderson, heard the news of Bhopal, India, he flew, at the risk of personal exposure, directly to that shaken city of tragedy. Roger Smith is not that kind of man. He would not go to Poletown at the invitation of the parish priest, his neighbor. He declined to go to Pontiac or Warren, Michigan, a few miles away, at the invitation of the townspeople. His conflicts with communities demonstrate more than an overdose of power or an absence of empathy. They trace backward through years of monetized thinking that carried Chairman Smith to his present position. Attracting money and making money are the performance yardsticks of all CEOs. But there is more than a modest distinction to be drawn between those who go to extremes at the expense of innocents and those who wield exceptional influence to increase economic and safety risks for millions of people.

The more one studies the GM chairman's actions, statements, and policies, the more it becomes apparent that while he is indeed making quantitative changes inside the General Motors conglomerate, his qualitative objectives as far as what kinds of vehicles motorists receive for their dollars are very much in the tradition of Alfred Sloan and Frederic Donner. Smith's ample record of written and spoken words includes few references to desirable or coming progress in safety, energy efficiency, emissions reduction, improved bumper protection, superior maintenance and repair performance, and greater durability. Instead, his recitations of GM's looming technology are restricted largely to its plants and offices, to its dealers and customer ordering systems, to its inventory control and standards for suppliers. He exults in the future automation of production while he rejects the presently-available automation of crash protection.

Roger Smith often punctuates his public statements with talk of the "mini-revolution" inspired by GM's new technologies. "In our plants, the technological revolution is marked by welding and painting robots, flexible machining, automated vehicle guidance systems, and statistical process control," he noted in 1985. "And the full utilization of artificial intelligence machines in our factories is not far off. In the management of the business itself, technology is creating new and advanced management information systems to link all our people by computer, leading eventually to paperless systems for running the company."

But what about the car, the van, and the truck? Smith predicts that within the next decade, "every single device and function in the motor vehicle will come under computer control," including the "entertainment systems." Electronics "will govern every system, not just the radio, emissions, and fuel-economy functions we're used to seeing run by a computer today. Electronics will also govern the transmission, steering, suspensions, braking, and navigation systems. And there will be a resultant improvement in the safety, reliability, and durability of our vehicles."

There is a ring of déjà vu to these exuberances. In the mid-1960s, during a tour of GM research facilities in Michigan with high company executives, we were informed about the computer leadership of General Motors and its beneficial impact for the consumer. Tens of millions of vehicle recalls later, one wonders. Years of glacial slowness in functional automotive engineering later, one wonders. Mitsubishi Motors, a leader in new technology concepts for the automobile, notes the proper measure of caution. A company official told *High Technology* in 1985 that "with the current state of electronics, we can build complex systems for experimental use, but for commercial use we must be sure that electronics improves performance and function without becoming too complex or difficult to maintain."

John Noetl, an independent consulting engineer and former Missouri Automobile Club official whose expertise is in diagnostic and repair problems, believes that overly complex car electronics used for redundant or trivial purposes sets the motorist up for larger repair bills. He discussed with us the potential for ever greater consumer dependency on ever more skilled—and therefore ever more expensive—repair garages, except where modular systems require total replacement for the deficiency of even one small part. Smith seems to share few of these concerns.

"It's entirely possible that the travelers of tomorrow will go to their Triple A office and receive maps on a cassette or laser disk," he told an Automobile Association of America audience in 1985. Smith described how these cassettes would plug into the vehicle's "satellite navigation system," an on-board computer than picks up readings from a network of satellites. "The electronic map would be projected on a display screen in their vehicle, and a dot on the screen would show their location."

It is superficial only to characterize this electronic fascination as mere hype and more hope springing eternal for customer titillation. There is a merchandising strategy here that is sure to evolve in the coming decade. The GM chairman understands that the inexorable growth of automobile production in Asia and South America means his company's share of the global market will necessarily shrink. Cars will thus have to fetch higher relative prices if the corporation is to maintain its relative profitability. Styling changes once served to keep prices up and car turnover high. Styling defined modernity in a car, and GM pioneered in the use of style for the pursuit of profit. While style is still a factor, especially with the more sporty cars, it can no longer carry such a heavy marketing burden. Electronics—what critics call gadgetry or junk technology—will emerge as its replacement.

Roger Smith's new pricing strategy is more than GM's traditional formula of a "target rate of return." It is more than accommodations with Asian producers through joint ventures and distribution agreements. Pricing GM's "car of the future" will reflect a new annual "sizzle factor" from the razzle-dazzle world of space-age automotive gamesmanship. During the June 5, 1985, press conference in which Smith discussed the Hughes

Aircraft acquisition, one reporter listened to his ravings about how the research prowess of Hughes engineers would help GM's technology efforts and asked, "Is this going to create cheaper cars in the future?" The GM chief replied, "More value in the car, that's it. You don't want cheaper cars, you want more value." He gave an illustration of his definition of "more value" when he told a management conference in April 1984, "We expect some of our cars will have as many as seven computers on board and they'll provide an estimated 38,000 command instructions." It is quite likely, however, that these cars and their computers will experience a crash with the same collision-force patterns as the cars of 1974.

Because the GM leader, as noted earlier, has pronounced that the major developments in road handling, safety, emissions, and fuel economy have all been made, and that electronics is the "new frontier," it is possible to envision Smith's car of the future. And because no engineer or scientist, even in his own company, can take seriously, as a technical proposition, Smith's claims of definitive achievement in these areas, one cannot help but suspect that his statements embrace a political message. Basically, Smith wants us to believe that previous GM executives and engineers were prevented from concentrating on the international vehicle electronics race because of the time they had to devote to meeting government standards.

"The fact is, we have the best scientific and engineering talent in the world," he told the National Academy of Engineers in May 1985. "But up until recently they haven't had the freedom to be fully competitive. They've been tied up meeting regulation after regulation. But now that we have a little more stability in the regulatory climate, we've been able to free up available talent—and we're ready to roll."

Smith's statement sounds as if GM's thousands of scientists and engineers have some calling higher and more important than to create a vehicle they would be proud to warrant on the highway or in a crash. It suggests that the bulk of these technical officials were occupied with proposed and issued regulations that have in fact been both few and exceedingly modest over the past fifteen years. Very few significant crash-safety regulations have been implemented from Washington since 1970. But the chairman's view of Washington has its own magnifying lens, which sometimes functions like a funhouse mirror. In 1976 he complained about "over 1,500 federal agencies whose major province is the regulation of business." He told a television audience six years later than GM had spent $2 billion in 1981 "on government regulations, not for the hardware on the car, but just for filling out forms and doing all that." Although the factual bases for these assertions are not apparent, they do provide additional insight into Smith's state of mind. He wants all this "Washington" business behind him, ignoring the recognition by his own engineers that federal pressure advanced the rate of innovation and computerized processes in cars.

On August 7, 1984, Roger Smith elaborated on the factors, besides size, that he believes consumers consider when choosing a car. He listed the variables in order of importance before a convention of Michigan auto dealers:

- First, there's design and styling—the shape and form of the vehicle, its paint, trim and general image.
- Just as important are the car's economics—its price, miles per gallon, financing and warranties.
- Right behind economics we have the engine and drive train options—front- or rear-wheel drive, engine size, fuel, and turbo or supercharging.
- There's a three-way tie for third place: first, comfort—the feeling of plushness, the quality of the ride, the sound control, and the options; second, utility—vehicle function, range, safety, overall performance; and third, durability—in other words, reliability, corrosion resistance, and serviceability.
- Finally, there's technical innovation—electronics and aerodynamics. You know, aerodynamic styling can give you tremendous gains in fuel efficiency. And that's just got to be a factor in the shape of tomorrow's cars. It may make them more similar in appearance than they'd otherwise be.

Smith did not disclose the basis for his rankings, nor did he refer to the many professional and company polls that demonstrate very high preferences for safety, low repair and maintenance costs, and fuel efficiencies. Three internal customer polls conducted by GM in the 1970s, which were released under prodding from a congressional committee, showed very strong consumer demand for air bags despite an estimated $300 price that was generous to say the least. Pollsters routinely caution that survey results depend on how the questions are phrased, what questions are asked for comparative purposes, and what scenarios of engineering and cost savings are presented. A safety feature becomes attractive when its costs are not exaggerated and when its life-saving benefits and insurance premium savings are described. But before the Michigan auto dealers, as usual, Smith was relaying the battle cry GM chairmen have been relaying since Alfred Sloan. It was Sloan, after all, who declared that customers want "comfort, convenience, power, and style."

Contentions over style, safety, and unfettered manufacturer control

of vehicle engineering were thought to have been significantly settled with
the passage of federal legislation between 1966 and 1975. New laws
established as national policy the need for safety, health, and fuel efficiency standards. As a dynamic reactionary, Roger Smith wants to restore
the halcyon days of the 1950s and 1960s, when auto executives made
life-and-death decisions on safety and pollution without worrying about
Washington. These federal safety programs have worked. The U.S. Department of Transportation estimates they have saved over 100,000
American lives and prevented many more injuries. Cars are less polluting;
Smith himself conceded the point in an address before the National
Petroleum Refiners in 1981: "There's no question that the nation's air is
cleaner today than it would be without this [Clean Air Act] legislation."
And the 1975 Energy Policy and Conservation Act has led to the nation's
most successful official energy-conservation program, saving motorists billions of dollars. But at almost every juncture, the fuller promise of these
programs has been dimmed by delays, intransigence, and opposition from
the auto companies. Since the rise to power of the Reagan administration,
GM and its allies have been unable, through congressional lobbying, to
weaken the laws themselves—but they have virtually stalled the enforcement and new standards process at the agency level.

One piece of unfinished business continues to plague Smith: the air
bag. To his nettled mind, this technology must seem like the safety device
that refuses to die. Admittedly, the air bag does present unique challenges
to Smith's determination. He has been boxed in from top to bottom, from
one side to another. First there is the predecessor factor. In 1970, GM
president Ed Cole notified the Department of Transportation that "approximately one million 1974 model General Motors cars could be
equipped with the air bag cushion. . . . In the fall of 1974, the air bag
would be made standard equipment on all 1975 General Motors passenger
cars." Although that pledge never came to pass, ten thousand GM cars
with optional front-seat air bags were sold in the mid-1970s, with very
little promotion, and provided successful highway experience in actual
crashes.

Then there is the engineer factor. For years a crack crew of GM
scientists and engineers made the air bag ever more effective and flexible.
There is also the lateral pressure of the insurance industry, led by Allstate
and State Farm, whose former leaders, Archie Boe and Edward Rust, were
long-time enthusiasts of the air bag. Some large insurance companies have
declared premium reductions of $40 to $50 annually for cars equipped
with the system, which turns the $250 price of the standard-equipment
device into a good economic investment.

There is more. One competitor, Mercedes-Benz, began offering the air bag as a driver-side option in 1981 and made it standard equipment in November 1985. The Ford Motor Company started selling air-bag-equipped Tempos and Topazes to government and corporate fleet buyers, once a federal agency announced in 1984 that it would purchase five thousand such cars for its drivers. Four major insurance companies followed with fleet orders from Ford. In late 1985, Ford announced optional availability of driver-side air bags for Tempo and Topaz lines by March 1986. Supplier companies, including Rockcor, Allied Chemical, and Morton Thiokol, believed in the technology and even formed a trade association to push it, until the delays atrophied their interest. The Department of Transportation supported research that produced safety vehicles demonstrating practical air bag deployment in compact cars up to a collision speed of 50 miles per hour, far beyond the 30 miles-per-hour level of the federal passive-restraint standard issued in 1977, but still not in effect. A host of medical and public-health associations, including the American Medical Association, have endorsed the air bag. Even the AAA finally announced its support in the late 1970s. Finally, a New Jersey company has received high praise for a new and cheaper mechanical air bag system from both GM and federal government engineers.

Nonetheless, Roger Smith remains opposed and is without doubt the chief obstacle to the widespread deployment of these automatic lifesavers. That is power. The source of his opposition lies in the mid-1970s, when Chairman Richard Gerstenberg reversed GM policy from the Cole years as part of an all-points resistance to federal regulation of the automobile industry. Whatever the mounting competition from more fuel efficient imports, whatever the capabilities of GM engineers or the consequences to motorists going through windshields, the men on the fourteenth floor were not about to let successful federal crash-protection standards give credibility to other government safety, efficiency, and emission-control proposals.

During the Carter years, GM paraded various technical objections to the air bag, but agency reviews showed them to be without substance. By 1980 GM president Pete Estes was telling us in an interview that the air bag was technically effective but that it was too expensive to sell. The price factor then became the company's lead objection to marketing the product as an option, and its estimates zoomed from $350 in 1977 to $1,000 in 1981. When questioned, GM would admit that the latter figure was based on a limited production run of well under 100,000. A more realistic analysis of the cost to consumers of air bags for the full front seat came in 1981 from the Automobile Occupant Protection Association (AOPA), an organization of manufacturers of the safety system's components. Based on annual volumes of production, the AOPA released figures of $185 for a 2-million production volume, $240 for 1 million, $280 for 500,000, $500 for 100,000 and $1,100 for 10,000. These prices cover the entire air-cushion system, including both automaker and dealer profits. The AOPA went on to say that "since domestic automobile production runs 6 to 8 million cars per year, the cost of air cushions as options should be about $300, based on sales to one in 12 to 15 car buyers. (The Department of Transportation's 1983 price estimate for an air cushion is $320.) In smaller production volumes, they should cost up to $500—still less than options such as luxury interior trim, removable roof panels, special bucket seats, and power windows. As successive generations of air cushions are developed, their cost will be even lower." To make the air bag more economically attractive, New York State passed a law in mid-1984 that requires insurance companies to reduce annual insurance premiums for cars with air bags an average of $67 per car.

But merits no longer decide air-bag debates. The issue has become freighted with political, symbolic, and facesaving value for Smith. As a man who, friends say, has few private or public tendencies toward regrets or self-recrimination, he is in a position to have his way. Other major auto sellers in the United States have waited on GM to move first on air bag and other major safety changes. The Ford breakaway, partial though it is, stands as historically rare. Should Ford move to a more aggressive marketing effort, the GM elephant could begin to take notice. Indeed, at a 1981 Transportation Department hearing, Raymond Peck asked GM's David Martin, "If foreign manufacturers in direct competition with your luxury-line vehicles would introduce air cushion restraints or passive restraints on an optional basis, would GM do likewise?" The corporate safety official replied, "We will always respond to competitive forces in the market-place, and if we perceive that we were at a disadvantage because somebody else utilized that technology which we believe is viable from a technical point of view in full-size cars, we would certainly respond to that competitive pressure."

But about the same time, his boss, Roger Smith, was feeling confident enough about the Reagan government to dispatch a spokeswoman to Congress to urge full rescission of the Carter-issued passive-restraint rule. She also announced that GM was closing down its air-bag development program, signaling the decline in the company's crash-protection-research commitment and the disbanding of a spirited group of engineers and scientists who dreamed of making a major contribution to saving lives. Her consolation to the audience that day was to assure them that GM "can demonstrate that we produce a highly effective device." For the approximately sixty Americans a day who die in GM vehicles, such an assurance is not a little remote and tardy.

In 1984 Smith saw an opportunity, given him by the Department of Transportation's peculiar reissuance of Standard 208, to block the air bag decisively. If states containing two-thirds of the nation's population pass seat belt laws by 1989, the standard reads, then the department would revoke the entire passive-restraint regulation. Smith decided to suspend his antipathy to government regulation if the states would regulate 150 million motorists in order to revoke the federal regulation of some fifteen auto manufacturers. In 1984 and 1985 he spent millions of dollars for a state-by-state lobbying drive to enact mandatory seat-belt-use laws, funneling much of the money through an industry advocacy group called Traffic Safety Now. As Senator John Danforth pointed out during a Senate hearing, GM was not averse to dangling the prospect of Saturn (backed by the powerful GM dealer associations) to persuade state legislators to support legislation that would be used to undermine the adoption of automatic crash protections in future cars.

While the air bag is superior to the shoulder harness at higher collision speeds, better suited for large and small persons unable to wear belts, and more protective against head injuries and flying glass, its principal advantage is the near 100 percent frequency of instant use when needed, in contrast to the modest compliance rate for shoulder belts even where use is mandatory. However, for GM and its chief executive, just to lobby for belt-use legislation is a long journey from Smith's early years, when GM refused to install lap belts and then later, in 1967–68, vainly opposed the government's proposed standard to require manufacturer installation of the full shoulder-and-lap-belt system in their cars.

For Smith, the cloud remains; the air bag won't go away. CBS's *60 Minutes* twice in 1985 played a highly favorable report on air bags. GM refused to be interviewed. There is support in Congress for legislation requiring auto companies to provide installation space in their cars so that aftermarket suppliers can sell air bags to those consumers who want them. GM opposes this idea as well.

The air bag issue—to the extent that it challenges Smith's power—throws light on how the character and personality of the man is imposed on the corporation. The company produces and proves the safety device; the man at the top says no, and everything stops. Internal technical dissent and social consciousness, public opinion, on-the-road experience, the approval of important professional associations and membership groups—all these factors are given no weight and afforded no forum, except for a few brief questions at an annual shareholder meeting. Smith's highly centralized authority is obviously formidable when displayed against the backdrop of the widespread appeal of this twenty-nine-pound technological savior poised automatically to rescue his customers from death and injury. Consider the direct and indirect control that Smith exercises over numerous dissenters inside his own company where, David Cole observes, the air bag has become a very touchy, emotional subject.

The moral and marketing incentives to speak out, to protest, to blow the whistle, are as nothing when compared with the sanctions and peer-group pressures that the corporate culture can place on any employee or retiree who pursues such a route. More dissent erupts publicly from military organizations than from major corporations. One of GM's most successful dealers would not go on the record in his interview with us even to praise: "If you say anything with those guys, it takes a year to get out of trouble with them, at least, regardless," he cautioned good-naturedly. "When you're saying Roger Smith, you're saying General Motors, because the two are just synonymous right now. That hasn't been true with every chairman," he added. This dealer, bursting with growth and upbeat ideas, believes that if you have a useful or important product, such as air bags, the rest is up to marketing ingenuity. "I haven't seen any marketing innovations [under Smith]. The problem still remains with General Motors and the pecking order. Everybody's protecting their ass, and that's always true. . . . That hasn't changed."

·   ·   ·

The pressure to conform, to avoid saying what one knows from skill and experience, can become increasingly inescapable within the corporate organizational labyrinths. It is leadership's prerogative to relieve this pressure or not. More than exhorting phrases are needed; affirmative action, provocation, rewards and forums for such expressions are called for. Jack Welch, chairman of General Electric, believes that making a large corporation work requires a more enabling climate of freedom to take chances and to disagree with policy. "It's really the heart of the issue," Welch told *Forbes:* "Can we take the punitive aspects out of having our people tell us the truth?"

Smith has more than the routine reasons to take this question seriously. He has made much news and many headlines announcing a massive corporate reorganization, acquiring EDS, Hughes Aircraft, and several other firms, joint-venturing with Toyota, and purchasing the vehicles of one Korean and two Japanese manufacturers. Now he has to make these transitions and readjustments work for tens of thousands of employees and thousands of managers. Few outsiders realize the extent of the difficulties and preoccupations that drain the time and energy of the bosses when such moves occur. Incorporating the changes, acquisitions and automation systems he has pushed during the first five years of his tenure may take Smith's remaining years as CEO. If so, it does not augur well for much top-executive attention to improving the vehicles themselves.

What does Roger Smith dream of leaving behind when he retires in 1990 besides a company that is making money in more and more sectors of the economy? What roles and specific directions does he envision for GM toward improving the surface-transportation system—its balance with mass transit, its safety, its pollution control, its fuel efficiency, its handling of consumers caught in the lemon groves of poor construction and service? His many public statements hardly touch on these considerations, which have an impact daily all over the country. This is why we especially regretted not being able to discuss such matters with him directly. He aspires to head a paperless company of maximum feasible automation. This is what he tells all who listen. But does he aspire to lead an ethical management concerned with creating a technology that serves the needs and respects the rights of affected people? Or will he become increasingly embroiled with internal structure and more and more resentful of external forces that demand accountability? There are those inside General Motors who feel his official coldness, who nod quietly when they read in the *Detroit News* of acquaintances describing Smith as "Wall Street's kind of guy," or "brilliance unimpeded by humanity." Are those the descriptions by which he will be remembered after he retires? That prospect may not displease the head of General Motors, whose career, while hierarchically at its peak, may be developmentally on a plateau. Smith has in his possession remarkable powers, many yet unused, that could shake up the automotive world for people's sake and apply technology as if people mattered.

The prospect that he will reorient his position does not seem probable. For all the characterizations of Smith as "bold," "innovative," and "a man of vision" that have filled the business press, the chief of the world's largest manufacturing corporation remains quintessentially conventional in his view of executive purpose and accountability. From his suite in the GM headquarters building, Smith can survey what was once Poletown, can peer at the automotive pollution, and at times may observe a pile-up of cars that could have been crashworthy. It is likely that he would see these cityscapes in a detached manner, for it was Roger Smith himself who told a local reporter not long ago, "What the board [of directors] tells me is what counts, and they tell me I'm doing a good job. I don't worry about the other stuff."

PAUL OREFFICE

Chemical Warrior

Paul Oreffice was enjoying a vacation in Arizona, where he often travels to play tennis and escape the rigors of life as chief executive of a major corporation, when his company found its name splashed across the front pages of newspapers throughout the United States. It was not the type of publicity relished by the president of Dow Chemical Company. On March 15, 1983, Congressman James Scheuer disclosed that Dow officials had been allowed to review and edit prior to its release an Environmental Protection Agency (EPA) report on the health effects of exposure to dioxin and sources of dioxin contamination in the Great Lakes region of the United States and Canada. Scheuer's charges were destined to attract a swirl of media attention. They were made less than one week after the forced resignation of EPA administrator Anne Burford, who left the agency with a track record of sweetheart deals with industry, and less than one month after EPA announced it would relocate residents of Times Beach, Missouri, a small town west of Saint Louis, whose health was threatened by dioxin-laced waste stored there for more than a decade.

Another chief executive might have rushed back to the home office —in this case, Midland, Michigan, where Dow has been headquartered since it was incorporated in 1897—to preside over a period of crisis management. But Dow Chemical is no stranger to the fear, anguish, and worried questions accompanying nearly any discussion of dioxin. The compound, an unwanted contaminant generated in the production of certain herbicides, was at the center of a massive lawsuit filed in 1979 against Dow and other corporations that supplied the U.S. military with the herbicide Agent Orange for use as a defoliant in Vietnam. The well-publicized litigation became emblematic of the physical traumas and sense of abandonment experienced by many Vietnam veterans. It was resolved out of court in May 1984 when the corporate defendants agreed to contribute $180 million to a relief fund.* Dow for years had been waging a costly and controversial regulatory struggle against an emergency EPA ban of most applications of the herbicide 2,4,5-T, a component of Agent Orange. The EPA moved in February 1979 to suspend use of the compound, and Dow halted production soon thereafter. But the company continued to defend the safety of 2,4,5-T and spent more than $10 million in subsequent regulatory proceedings. Dow withdrew its objections to the suspension in October 1983, although company executives insisted that the preponderance of scientific evidence indicates 2,4,5-T is not harmful. Given this background, Paul Oreffice took the unfolding dioxin controversy in stride. "I found out what eight hours' work is," the Dow president quipped when asked how he reacted to initial reports of Scheuer's allegations. "Four hours on the tennis court, four hours on the telephone with Midland."

Oreffice did cut short his vacation by one-half day—he was invited to New York for an appearance on the *Today* show. Asked during the program to discuss the dangers of dioxin, he proceeded to make the sort of statement for which he has become notorious. "There is absolutely no evidence of dioxin doing any damage to humans except for causing something that is called chloracne," Oreffice declared with some conviction. "It's a rash." That abrupt dismissal of the hazards of dioxin ignored compelling evidence of its extreme toxicity when applied to laboratory animals. Minute amounts of the substance have induced cancer and birth defects in mice and guinea pigs. It also ignored more limited, albeit contested, evidence of its possible association with soft-tissue sarcomas, a rare form of cancer in humans. The most respected studies suggesting a link between dioxin exposure and soft-tissue sarcomas have been published by Swedish epidemiologist Lennart Hardell.

Dr. Vernon Houk, a top official of the Centers for Disease Control, testified at a congressional hearing just days after Scheuer issued his charges about the EPA report. He responded to testimony by Dow officials that minimized the potential health effects of dioxin exposure. "Birth defects are only one of the many documented adverse effects of dioxin in the animal model," he told the legislators. "Again, the correct statement is that there are no acceptable human studies [on birth defects] done as

---

*The seven corporate defendants were: Dow Chemical, Monsanto, Diamond Shamrock, Hercules Inc., Uniroyal, T. H. Agricultural & Nutrition Co., and the defunct Thompson Chemical Co. According to a May 1984 report in *Business Insurance,* the terms of the $180 million settlement, which are confidential, require that Monsanto contribute 45.5 percent, or nearly $82 million, and Dow contribute 19.5 percent, or just over $35 million. The remainder of the relief fund was capitalized by the other defendants, whose individual shares ranged from 12 percent to 2 percent.

yet, and the reason for that is because they are difficult and have not been done. There is no evidence that dioxin causes adverse human effects at the low-level chronic concentration. But there is no evidence that it does not. Most of us believe, very strongly, that dioxin is a severely toxic chemical with very low chronic toxicity. I can't help but disagree with some testimony you heard this morning. That in the absence of chloracne there is no possibility, or the possibility is remote, that low-term dioxin contamination or exposure is harmful. I believe that 99.99 percent of the scientific community who is not associated with industry would take exception to that statement."

More to the point from Dow's perspective, Oreffice's comments did little to temper the perception of his company as being cavalier about public health and unwilling to concede the potential hazards of its products. "The Dow name doesn't give people a warm feeling," said George Whitesides, a chemistry professor at Harvard University and a long-time student of the industry. It is difficult to quarrel with Whitesides's speculation. One lingering stain on the Dow reputation resulted from the protests and demonstrations that accompanied its role as a producer of napalm during the Vietnam War, protests that remain very fresh in the minds of many company executives. "The change in the public's perception of Dow's leadership in pollution control occurred before Oreffice [took command], and he inherited it," said retired Dow chairman Carl Gerstacker, who made specific reference to Vietnam as a factor in the company's ongoing problems. "Somewhere along the line it got out of joint. I don't think it's Paul's fault." But it is also the case that since Oreffice became chief executive on May 3, 1978, the company time and again has found itself—or, on occasion, situated itself—at the center of the national debate on the risks to workers and consumers posed by the materials his company and industry produce. It is a debate played out in medical journals and the media, on shop floors, in the halls of Congress, the courts, and the regulatory agencies.

The events of March 1983 also underscore the highly charged, and often unpredictable, environment in which the leader of any major chemical producer operates. The report on dioxin over which Scheuer and his congressional colleagues became so exercised was a modest effort by EPA staff in Region V, headquartered in Chicago, to review existing studies on the health effects and sources of dioxin contamination—hardly a research enterprise that warranted the torrent of newspaper articles and television reports it generated. What is more, on the very day Scheuer's allegations first became news, testimony in a case with far more direct implications for human health came to a conclusion on the West Coast. That case went virtually unremarked upon.

On March 16, 1983, jurors in a state court in San Francisco began to consider evidence presented during the five-month trial of a lawsuit filed by workers at an Occidental Chemical plant in Lathrop, California. The employees charged that Occidental, Shell Oil, and Dow Chemical had failed to warn them adequately of the hazards of exposure to DBCP, a soil fumigant produced by Dow since 1957 whose use on most crops was suspended by EPA in September 1979. Occidental had purchased DBCP from Dow and Shell and then formulated it for resale. Dow voluntarily ceased production in August 1977 after it discovered that a number of workers in its Magnolia, Arkansas, plant had developed depressed sperm counts following exposure to the compound. After eleven days of deliberation, the jury returned its verdict. Dow was found guilty of failing to warn employees adequately of the effects of DBCP; it was acquitted of concealment and charges that Dow and Shell conspired to restrict access to health information. The jury awarded the plaintiffs $4.9 million to compensate for sterility, fear of cancer, and fear of birth defects. The damages were reduced to $2.5 million in a subsequent out-of-court settlement under which Dow agreed not to appeal.

Paul Oreffice has remained personally aloof from most of the product-specific lawsuits and regulatory disputes into which Dow has been dragged or injected itself. But he has played a leadership role in several bitter political battles over the fundamental directions of regulatory policy. He was a central actor in a $2 million industry campaign against a "generic cancer policy" proposed by the Occupational Safety and Health Administration (OSHA) under President Jimmy Carter. This cancer policy, which Carter OSHA director Eula Bingham considered among the most significant initiatives of her tenure, would have accelerated and made more systematic regulation of cancer-causing chemicals in the workplace. The proposed regulations were shelved after the election of the Ronald Reagan. Oreffice was also one of the chemical industry's most vigorous opponents of "Superfund" legislation, designed to clean up hazardous waste sites across the country. On that particular issue, he clashed not only with his traditional adversaries—environmental activists and federal regulators —but with several other leaders of the chemical industry, who considered it unwise to oppose a bill whose passage was virtually certain.

The Dow president may well be the most visible—and controversial —chief executive in the chemical industry today. But it is often the style and intensity of his public presence, rather than the substance, that distinguishes him from colleagues at Monsanto, Du Pont, or Diamond Shamrock. More so than any other chemical industry leader, Oreffice has made his company's battles in the area of health and safety regulation a personal affair. Dow's assault on the regulatory apparatus is *his* assault.

And Oreffice has focused his political activism almost exclusively on the regulatory arena. He has delivered standard business sermons on the threat posed by budget deficits and the overvalued dollar, but his speeches and interviews return again and again to the evils of big government. Soon after he became president of Dow's U.S. operations in August 1975, Oreffice began to fashion a one-man crusade on regulatory policy: lecturing to college and civic audiences, cajoling fellow executives to take up his call, lashing out against the environmental community. Dow USA even canceled in January 1977 the construction of a $500 million petrochemical complex in California after the project experienced what Dow considered to be fatal regulatory delays. Though he has scaled back his direct political activism and public advocacy since the election of Ronald Reagan, Oreffice continues to set the tone and broad outlines of Dow's dealings with official Washington.

Eula Bingham, the former OSHA chief, told us the Dow president brought a "religious fervor" to his dealings with the agency. "Oreffice really made it a crusade," she said. "My impression from him was that [he believed] people were overstating the toxicity of chemicals rather than that [regulating them] cost too much. He is a rare person in terms of being a chief executive officer, really very singular. You never got that impression with Shapiro. He was a much broader person." Bingham's reference is to Irving Shapiro, who retired in April 1981 as chairman of Du Pont, the only chemical firm in the United States larger than Dow. Shapiro and Oreffice are perhaps the two leading personalities of recent chemical industry history. They make for an instructive study in contrast. Shapiro is urbane and consensus-minded, a corporate Democrat who was President Carter's point man in the business community. Oreffice not only endorsed Ronald Reagan in 1980, but a year earlier sweepingly accused Carter of "leading the country down the same centrally controlled economic path that has brought many dictatorships to power."

Dow officials who work closely with Oreffice characterize him as a hard-nosed political fighter. "Paul is a black-and-white guy; he gets very committed to what he believes is right," said Dow executive vice-president Joseph Temple. "You know, politicians never end up on one side of a problem or the other. They are always weaseling around in the middle. So if you say, could [Oreffice] have been more politically sensitive? Yeah. I don't know that he'd make a great politician."

Former president Herbert Dow "Ted" Doan, grandson of the legendary company founder, told us he agreed with positions Oreffice has taken over the years, but offered reservations about the Oreffice style. "There does come a criticism I can offer of Paul," Doan told us. "I think his approach to these things is not as good as it could be publicly. The reason is part ego, part pride. Paul is inclined to push his line to the point where some people say he is arrogant. His passion comes out as too strong, and I don't like that. I think there has been a backlash."

．　．　．

Paul Fausto Oreffice is only the seventh individual to serve as chief executive of Dow Chemical since it was founded nearly nine decades ago. Oreffice is trim and strongly built, a sports enthusiast who once described himself to a reporter as a "frustrated jock." His current athletic passion is tennis, a game he takes very seriously and plays quite well. "When I'm on the tennis court, I forget what company I work for," he joked during our conversations. His hair is short and combed straight back, close to his scalp. His speech exhibits traces of an accent—he was born in Venice, Italy, and lived there until the age of twelve—and is punctuated with occasional mild expletives for emphasis. Oreffice speaks in crisp, almost skeletal sentences and uses frequent, and frequently overblown, examples and analogies to make a point. In a January 27, 1978, speech criticizing the regulatory policies of the Carter administration, Oreffice claimed,

These regulators and ultraenvironmentalists are leading us down a path that says

- We are not completely sure chemicals are safe, so let's stop making chemicals.
- We are not completely sure that all foods are safe, therefore let's stop eating.
- We are not completely sure our drinking water is safe, so let's stop drinking it.
- We are not completely sure the air we breathe is safe, therefore let's stop breathing.

At an October 5, 1983, ceremony in New York City where he received the prestigious Chemical Industry Medal, Oreffice delivered an address on "Law and the Threat It Poses to the U.S. Chemical Industry." He complained to his colleagues about the rise of attorneys specializing in product liability—the "new opportunists," he called them—and warned against "meekly heading into a legal slaughter that will cripple, if not devour, all of our companies." He also took aim at the U.S. jury system. "It is getting harder and harder for a company to be tried by a true jury of its peers," Oreffice complained. "People with important jobs are often disqualified from serving on a jury, and the more difficult and lengthy the case, the more juries tend to be made up of people of lesser means. In a recent case [Dow] lost, the judge told all of the prospective jurors before selection that the case was going to be a long one, and anyone could be excused if they did not think they had the time to dedicate to the case. The result was that only people without other responsibilities, the unemployed, for example, remained to serve on the jury. I doubt that many in the chemical industry would consider that a 'jury of their peers.' "

This tendentious rhetoric reflects two important dimensions of the Oreffice personality. First, he is not a deep or incisive thinker outside the confines of business. Oreffice said he was so swamped by the reading demands of his job that he "only reads a serious book once in a while." He has not reviewed many of the books and reports published over the years by critics of Dow and the chemical industry, although he does on occasion read excerpts. When asked to discuss his intellectual roots, Oreffice named three individuals: an elementary school teacher who inspired in him a love for mathematics, a retired Dow chairman, and Ayn Rand, the late prophet of "objectivism." Second, the Dow president embraces a reflexive and abrasive conservatism that can alienate allies as well as perceived adversaries. One former company executive, who retired after more than twenty years with Dow and who worked closely with top company officials in Europe and Midland, complained bitterly to us about the Oreffice perspective on government regulation and political dialogue. "If you wanted to get along with people in government, you were some kind of communist," he said.

The Dow president's personal combativeness also means he is willing, even anxious, to represent and defend his corporation in public. His media accessibility during the dioxin scare is one example. Oreffice freely granted newspaper interviews, appeared on network television, and presided over a June 1983 press conference where he unveiled a set of scientific initiatives aimed at defusing the escalating controversy. He had no reservations about cooperating with this project. He responded within one week to our request for an interview and participated in two extensive face-to-face conversations—one at company headquarters, one in Dow's Washington, D.C., office—as well as several telephone interviews. The Dow president expressed himself on a broad range of topics.

Oreffice's accessibility generated as many frustrations as it did insights. He is not so much candid as he is opinionated, and his opinions more often resemble articles of faith than reasoned conclusions. Whenever he was asked to address issues that reflect badly on his own industry, such as the decision by Manville Corporation to declare Chapter 11 bankruptcy in the face of massive potential liability over worker and consumer exposure to asbestos, Oreffice dodged the questions. "I've got to admit to you I've never quite understood just how that works," he said. "I've always felt that Chapter 11 is an escape for individuals and companies, which has always bothered me. . . . Chapter 11 bothers me as a total thing. I don't know enough about the whole Johns Manville situation. I've never looked at it that closely."

Oreffice did talk freely on subjects from the Vietnam War to the roots of inflation and the role of organized labor. What are the lessons of Vietnam, a conflict that caused so many problems for Dow? "First of all, you don't go into a war to tie," he replied. "I've never heard of anything, whether it's war or a football game, where if you go in to tie, you don't lose. I think it was criminal to have U.S. kids die when you don't intend to win. I think that is the bitter thing of the Vietnam experience with the American people. And it should be. That we sent kids to die and we never intended to win." Should the U.S. have sent them at all? "No," he replied. "Probably not."

The Dow president is also at ease as a speaker in more formal settings, a talent he cultivated with much effort. Oreffice told us he was "the shyest guy in town" as a college student. After graduation he joined the Toast-masters Club, where members gather for dinner and make speeches to improve their delivery. Today, one of his favorite outside pursuits is to lecture to college students, and he plans to lecture extensively when he steps down as chief executive. He set a goal when he became president of Dow that he would address, preferably in groups of thirty to fifty, at least five thousand employees each year. He has met that target without exception. He writes all of his own lectures. Dow frequently distributes videotapes of speeches by Oreffice as well as question-and-answer sessions he conducts with company employees. The Dow president has also begun a practice at shareholder meetings that he intends to make permanent in which he delivers brief prepared remarks and then steps away from the podium to speak extemporaneously to the audience.

"I don't mind them," he said of annual meetings. "I sort of get a boost out of them. I think the adrenaline starts flowing. I see some of my cohorts [in industry] and they look at [annual meetings] like taking castor oil. I have never let it bother me that way."

Oreffice can be overbearing, even heavy-handed. A case in point is his celebrated confrontation with Jane Fonda in the fall of 1977, one of the first public controversies of his career. Fonda was paid $3,500 to address students at Central Michigan University, which is located less than thirty miles west of Dow's Midland headquarters. During a lecture entitled "Politics in Film," she made several statements critical of corporate power in general and Dow in particular. Her remarks prompted questions from the audience on pollution, business tax breaks, and Dow's role as a supplier of napalm. Fonda's comments were reported by a local newspaper and elicited an immediate response from Oreffice, then president of Dow's U.S. operations. In a letter to university president Harold Abel, Oreffice called Fonda "an avowed communist sympathizer" who had come to "spread her venom" to college students.

"While inviting Ms. Fonda to your campus is your prerogative, I consider it our prerogative and obligation to make certain our [corporate] funds are never again used to support people intent upon destruction of freedom," he wrote. "Therefore, effective immediately, support of any kind from the Dow Chemical Company . . . has been stopped, and will not resume until we are convinced our dollars are not expended in supporting those who would destroy us." Dow had made $73,000 in cash grants to Central Michigan the previous year. CMU officials later reported that Fonda's honorarium had been paid out of the university's general fund. It was unlikely that Dow money was involved, since the company normally earmarked contributions for specific purposes.

The missive attracted extensive public attention. Oreffice said he received three thousand letters in response to his action, of which fewer than one hundred expressed opposition. Columnist George Will applauded the Dow president and argued that "there should be some limits to intellectual frivolousness" on campus. The student newspaper offered a different perspective. "Some people, it seems, just have not learned money cannot buy everything, especially the rights to freedom of expression," said one editorial.

Time seems not to have mellowed Oreffice on the episode, especially on the serious issues of free speech and academic freedom it raised. "They can have all the freedom they want, but not with our money," he bristled. "If you look at the list of speakers [at Central Michigan] who were paid, they all came from one side of the spectrum. . . . I don't think we should give discretionary money to somebody who comes back and throws it at us." What if every corporate donor adopted this attitude? "It would be fine with me if every company withdrew their support from universities who then go out and spend it on only one side of the aisle," he replied. "Why should we spend our discretionary money to support people who are against us?"

Actually, Oreffice's charges of bias are not accurate. A member of the Central Michigan administration provided us with the names of many paid speakers at the university who appeared prior to the Fonda lecture. The list included conservative columnist James Kilpatrick, journalist Hugh Sidey, and retired General William Westmoreland. As it turns out, Oreffice never made good on his threat to discontinue funding. The episode came to a conclusion eighteen months after it began when the

Dow president traveled to Central Michigan to address the student body. "Standing room only," he reported with obvious satisfaction.

.   .   .

Dow Chemical is a driving force in an industry that by any measure rates as one of the economic spectaculars of postwar America. Chemical production was in its infancy prior to 1945. The industry in 1983 turned out more than 30 billion pounds of basic plastics—materials such as polyethylene, polypropylene, polystyrene—nearly 2 million metric tons of synthetic rubber, and more than 9 billion pounds of man-made fibers, such as nylon and polyester. These materials have become ubiquitous elements of the food we eat, the clothes we wear, the cars we drive. They have also stood the test of foreign competition. Unlike their troubled corporate brethren in Detroit and Pittsburgh, U.S. chemical makers remain the envy of the business world. The United States in 1973 exported $3.3 billion more in chemicals than it imported. A decade later, the trade surplus stood at nearly $9 billion.

Enormous scale and technological sophistication are the basis of much of the industry's—and Dow's—operations. The company in 1984 sold nearly $230,000 worth of chemicals, plastics, and pharmaceuticals for every person in its workforce—more than twice the sales per employee of General Motors or AT&T. Its Midland operation employs roughly 4,500 people and turns out hundreds of products. Dow's manufacturing complex in Freeport, Texas, is one of the largest single-company chemical facilities in the United States. More than seventy individual plants in the complex together produce in excess of 10 billion pounds of chlorine, ethylene, salt, and nearly one hundred other products each year. The power plant at Freeport, which began operation in October 1982, generates enough electricity to supply 170,000 homes and enough steam to heat 20,000 more.

Dow Chemical recorded total sales in 1984 of nearly $11.5 billion and employed nearly 50,000 people. Its traditional strength has been production of the chemical building blocks of the industry—materials such as polystyrene and vinyl chloride that are shipped by tanker or pipeline to other chemical companies and transformed into more familiar synthetic fibers and plastics. Dow's position in the "upstream" segment of the industry explains why for decades it has been known as "the chemical companies' chemical company." Its business also underscores one of the unusual qualities of the structure of chemical production. Because it is a process industry, where raw materials and intermediate chemicals are broken down and then recombined to produce new substances, companies can be competitors and customers simultaneously. Du Pont, for example, which for years has been described in the financial press as Dow's most bitter rival, is also one of its largest customers. When Oreffice was asked to name his closest friends among industrial leaders, he named three senior officials of other chemical companies: Edward Jefferson, chairman of Du Pont; H. Barclay Morley, chairman of Stauffer Chemical; and Dexter Baker, president of Air Products & Chemicals, whom Oreffice described as "another tennis nut." Does the Dow president think Edward Jefferson acted wisely when Du Pont acquired Conoco in 1981 for nearly $8 billion? The deal at the time was the largest merger in corporate history. "Don't ask me," Oreffice said with a laugh. "That's his decision. We took a look at it and thought it was not good for us."

It is also important to understand that size and market position alone do not begin to describe Dow's standing in its industry. Unlike Allied Corporation, Diamond Shamrock, or Du Pont—firms whose chemical identities have been blurred through a series of mergers and divestitures pursued in the march toward diversification—Dow has never strayed from the basic mission of its chemical-minded founder. Of the top five chemical producers, only Monsanto claims a higher percentage of its total revenues from chemicals than Dow. The company is far and away the most international member of the U.S. fraternity. Its reach extends to Europe, where it operates massive plants on the Dutch coast and in Stade, West Germany. It is the largest producer of pharmaceuticals in Brazil and owns a major chemical complex in the northeast region of that country. All told, more than half of Dow's sales in 1984 and 40 percent of its assets were outside the United States.

This international presence is a critical dimension of Dow's power and prosperity as a corporation. It is also of enormous personal significance to its current president. Oreffice joined Dow in 1953 as the company was beginning to transform itself from an unstructured enterprise with roots planted firmly in the Midwest to a tightly knit operation with outposts on every continent. His career, and his rise to the position of chief executive, are bound inextricably to this evolution. He served for fifteen years in foreign assignments that took him to Italy, Brazil, Spain, and then to Coral Gables, Florida, where he supervised Dow's operations throughout Latin America. Oreffice said the international roots of his career distinguish him from most chief executives.

During our conversations, we explored the pressures and possibilities of business conducted on a global scale. Oreffice was asked about a famous address delivered in 1972 by Carl Gerstacker, who retired as Dow chairman in 1976 and was a prime architect of the company's thrust overseas. "I have long dreamed of buying an island owned by no nation, and of establishing the World Headquarters of the Dow company on the truly neutral ground of such an island, beholden to no nation or society," Gerstacker told the White House Conference on the Industrial World Ahead. He then explored the implications of these "anational" corporations. "One of the principal concomitants of this anationalism will be the blurring of a corporation's national origins," Gerstacker reasoned. "Parent boards of directors will gradually become genuinely anational vehicles, with personalities of varied origins and residences sitting about the table and making decisions affecting worldwide operations. They will be in a sense junior counterparts of the United Nations Security Council."

Oreffice said Gerstacker's comments were delivered "off the cuff" and that they have been "widely misinterpreted" ever since. "What Carl was trying to say at the time was that Dow had become, or hoped to become, a company that, while its headquarters are in the United States, did business the same way all over the world," he told us. "Therefore, if it was in Britain, it lived under British law. If it was in Brazil, it lived under Brazilian law, rather than being a U.S. company that felt it had to follow U.S. law in each country. His concept, then, was that the only way to do that would be to be on an island. . . . It was then interpreted widely through the years to mean that he wanted to have no allegiance to any government, which really was not [his intent]." The Dow president then offered a more concrete objection to the Gerstacker vision. "I have had a difficult time in my mind knowing how an anational company would find its stockholders," he said. "Maybe you could figure it out, but I just don't know how you would do that."

Oreffice also discussed at length the subject of bribery, an unavoidable topic when one examines the conduct of U.S. business overseas. Dow was never implicated in the foreign payoff scandals that rocked corporate America in the mid-seventies and led to passage in 1977 of the Foreign Corrupt Practices Act, which circumscribes most illicit payments.

Has Oreffice ever encountered demands for payoffs by foreign officials? "This is something I learned early in the game when I was in the international business," he said. "I can claim that it's because I'm moral or such a fine person, but that's not it. It's just a practical thing. One day in one of these Latin American countries, a tax guy came and said, 'Unless you pay me so much, we're going to shut you down while we audit your books.' I said be my guest, shut us down. When he saw we weren't going to pay, he left. I happen to know another American company down there who paid, because they got scared. And they paid, and they paid, and they paid. Because the tom-toms start beating. This one tax guy told the customs guy, 'That company is a bunch of suckers.' "

Oreffice also provided a more contemporary example. "You know, we did a lot of business in South Korea," he said. (Dow sold off most of its Korean holdings, including a wholly owned subsidiary, in October 1982 after a dispute with the government.) "Everyone says you can't do business in South Korea without bribing. But we never bribed anybody, and we did a lot of business."

For all of his company's global power and influence, however, Paul Oreffice approaches his role as chief executive of Dow with a decidedly nonimperial style. He promotes extensive decentralization of management decisions and avoids rigid hierarchy. He eats lunch every day in the company cafeteria. His speeches to and sessions with employees are designed to familiarize himself with thinking and worries at all levels of the company. "A company, like a government, like any other institution, has all kinds of filters," he explained. "Every level of management is a filter. And so, sometimes, when people just give me a presentation officially, I get stuff filtered. I like to get it unadulterated. In fact, I have said more than once that the day I don't know what's going on in the rumor mill, I'm in trouble. . . . I eat in the cafeteria just about every day unless I have some kind of commitment. I just grab a tray and go sit with a group of people. Maybe four or five people. I learn more about what's going on in the organization there, or on the tennis court, than I do in a formal setting."

Oreffice is also a family man. Photographs of his wife, the former Franca Giuseppina Ruffini, and two children, both in their twenties, occupy prominent places in his office. During our conversations, he talked at length about the strains placed on families by the demands of a business career. "I believe you need to lead a balanced life," he said. "I preach this to our young people [at Dow] all the time. If they become workaholics and their family life breaks up, they are not a success." On the day of our Midland interview, the Dow president planned to leave work at five o'clock for two hours of tennis and dinner at home with his wife. Oreffice seldom comes into the office on weekends; he usually plays tennis in the morning, and then does paperwork or light business reading at home.

"I trust my managers here," he explained. "When I go on vacation, I will spend a whole week without hearing from anybody. It doesn't make me nervous at all. I'll never call them, they have to call me, unless something very unusual happens or is on. I can go away for two weeks and talk to the office maybe once, or twice."

The office in which Oreffice labors, like the brick and glass building in which it is housed, is noteworthy more for its modesty than anything else. His most eye-catching possession is a paper shredder he keeps close to his desk—not evidence of an obsession with secrecy, he assured his visitor, but as an active sign of his aversion to paperwork, which he considers, along with meetings, "one of the two enemies of corporate life." The shredder may well be symbolic on both counts. Oreffice has made paperwork reduction a central theme of his tenure. As president of Dow USA, where he served from August 1975 to May 1978, he insisted that subordinates limit memos to him to two pages. "That changed the whole reporting [system] in this company," he told us. Early in 1984, Oreffice issued with much fanfare a decree that abolished monthly financial reporting inside the company—a practice he dismissed as wasteful and a drain on staff productivity. "Let the jungle drums that beat through the organization carry the message that this most sacred of reporting requirements has been overturned and that all sacred cows can be overturned," he told employees in a videotaped address that was circulated throughout the corporation.

At the same time, Dow Chemical has for years been known to guard jealously any information that it considers trade secrets, a policy with which Oreffice has been closely associated. This commitment to corporate secrecy has been the source of several public confrontations with regulatory authorities. For example, Dow filed suit on March 15, 1978, against EPA after the agency hired a private firm to conduct aerial surveillance of Dow's Midland complex and photograph emissions from two coal-burning power stations. EPA took the step after Dow refused to allow on-site photographs the agency needed to complete a Clean Air Act investigation. Dow did allow EPA investigators to inspect the power plant and provided them with schematic drawings. But company officials claimed that the high-resolution aerial photographs could be obtained from EPA under the Freedom of Information Act and that outside access would compromise proprietary technologies.

One month after the suit was filed, Oreffice, then president of Dow USA, appeared before a congressional subcommittee to testify on regulation of industry. He discussed with characteristic fervor the EPA flyover, which he described as "a clandestine spy operation conducted by the federal government against its own people." Dow's complaint was upheld by the U.S. District Court for the Eastern District of Michigan, which enjoined EPA from conducting further aerial surveys of the Midland operation. But that decision was overturned at the appellate level in November 1984 when a three-judge panel ruled that the agency had acted within its statutory authority. "Dow has described no trade secret or confidential relationship outside its building walls that the observer from above would compromise," the judicial panel wrote, "and Dow's objective behavior does not indicate an expectation to be free from the aerial spectator." The U.S. Supreme Court has agreed to hear Dow's appeal.

Among the most celebrated examples of Dow's protection of data is a memorandum, unearthed from company files in the course of litigation, that was signed by Oreffice and distributed to "all Dow USA supervisors" on September 15, 1977. Oreffice at the time was still president of Dow's domestic operations. The memo emphasized company practices on records retention and disposal, practices that were in keeping with Oreffice's aversion to paperwork. But the language and timing of the document suggest a darker motivation. It was distributed less than one week after OSHA issued an emergency temporary standard on occupational exposure to the soil fumigant DBCP, and six weeks before workers at Occidental Petroleum filed their lawsuit against Dow and other companies over exposure to the compound. The memo has become a trophy of sorts among attorneys who have sued Dow, because they believe it highlights the company's secretive ways. The body of the memo is reproduced here:

Recent events have dramatized the need for reemphasis of guidelines for the creation and retention of records.

Briefly stated, those records which are useful to our business, factually reported, and which accurately portray a situation should be created. Conversely then, records which contain more feelings or opinions than fact, which contain phrases, paragraphs or subjects of dubious value or are readily capable of misinterpretation should be avoided. Today's memo may be tomorrow's headline only because we have not anticipated the consequences when we generated the paperwork. Too frequently, words are taken out of context by people who want to embarrass us, especially in a time frame of 10 years or more after the writing. Reasonableness and discretion should accompany our words.

The maintenance of records is also a costly proposition and today, more than ever, we cannot afford the luxury of retaining useless or obsolete data in our files. We face tremendous costs in filing and handling papers. Not long ago, one document retrieval exercise, required by a court order to disclose documents to a plaintiff, turned up more than 50,000 documents in various company and *personal* files. The cost of complying with that order was in excess of $10 per document.

We have a records retention program, with a policy manual containing schedules for retention and destruction. We need to apply them more strictly to our activities.

Dow business matters belong in Dow's official files—not in *personal* files.

Your effective leadership in this area is needed.

WHEN IN DOUBT, THROW IT AWAY!!!

We asked Oreffice about the memo and suspicions of trial attorneys. He denied that its distribution was timed to coincide with the DBCP controversy or that it was designed to promote destruction of damaging documents. "It has nothing to do with that," he said heatedly. "Our records retention [policy] is something [about which] we periodically remind people. And the question is very simple. Very often [internal memos] express opinions of one individual. They have nothing to do with what the company wants to do. We had a case, which we wound up winning, on magnesium. It was an antitrust thing. The most damaging piece of paper was from one guy, way down in the ranks, who said, 'You know, maybe we ought to lower the price so so-and-so doesn't get into the business.' Now, in actual fact, when you look at Dow management, Dow for years hoped we would have a competitor in magnesium because we couldn't grow as we wanted to. The automobile companies wouldn't buy when there was only one producer in the country. The only way we could get a market is if we had a competitor. . . . That's what this [memo] is all about. It is not about [health] records. It is about all these opinions, all these copies that float around, people who make a note, 'I really think we ought to do this or that.' . . . When in doubt, throw it away—I have nothing to say that is any different."

The most striking dimension of the Oreffice character is that the qualities he brings to the business side of his role as chief executive—creativity, flexibility, a certain earthiness—disappear completely when he directs his attention beyond the walls of company headquarters. This curious dichotomy is not just of interest from the standpoint of personal insight. It represents a grave leadership shortcoming when one considers the mandate under which the chief executive of any chemical producer must function: To reconcile the growth and financial prosperity of his company, which depend in fundamental ways on the introduction of new products, the conquests of new markets, and cost reductions in the production of existing materials, with demands for environmental and health protection for the individuals who labor in the plants, live in nearby communities, or consume products composed of or treated by these chemicals. More so perhaps than the managers of any industry save nuclear power, chemical executives must mediate between the conflicting imperatives of short-term profit and the long-term fitness of non-shareholder constituencies. Biologist Barry Commoner articulated the singular burdens of chemical production in a 1977 essay in the *New York Times Magazine*.

"The quandary of the petrochemical industry is that the unique reasons for its success and growth—that it can produce a growing variety of new man-made substances, and can sell them cheaply, but only in very large amounts—are themselves the sources of its growing threat to society," he wrote. "Pressed by its economic structure to create ever more chemically complex man-made products on huge scales, the industry now confronts a hard fact of nature—that the more complex these products, the more likely they are to harm living things, including people, and the more widespread they are, the greater their toxic impact."

The horror and agony of Bhopal, India, where a Union Carbide plant unleashed a cloud of poison gas in December 1984 that claimed the lives of thousands of innocent residents, is only the most graphic example of the daily threat inherent in the manufacture and distribution of petrochemicals. The rise and demise of DBCP and ethylene dibromide (EDB) —soil and grain fumigants that for decades were injected into the ground to fight crop destruction by rootworms or sprayed on citrus and grain after harvest to prevent infestation—underscore less dramatically the human stakes involved in the leadership of a major chemical manufacturer.

Studies demonstrate conclusively that EDB causes cancer in laboratory animals and interferes with reproduction. It became a source of national panic in the fall of 1983, and EPA acted in September to ban or phase out most agricultural applications. The decision to announce an emergency suspension of EDB for use as a soil fumigant, which was issued in response to concerns over potential groundwater contamination in several states, was only the second time in the agency's history that it issued such an order. The first such emergency suspension was for 2,4,5-T. Dow Chemical is one of three principal U.S. producers of EDB, and the suspension order came as no surprise to company officials. Dow had actually halted production of the chemical for use as a grain fumigant in 1976, after toxicological studies convinced company officials it was destined for regulatory nightmares. Dow today produces ethylene dibromide for use only as an additive in leaded gasoline—a permissible application, since human exposure at the gas pump is so minimal—to which 90 percent of annual EDB production is directed.

But the suspension of EDB is as much the beginning of the story as it is the end. Dow began marketing EDB as a soil fumigant in the 1940s but scaled back after it pioneered the development of DBCP, which was even more effective against the deadly worms that prey on plants. Application of EDB as a soil fumigant increased dramatically after DBCP was suspended. And several of the proposed substitutes for EDB as a soil or postharvest fumigant—methyl bromide and carbon tetrachloride are two examples—are themselves under investigation as potential carcinogens. Moreover, Dow settled in April 1984 an $11 million lawsuit filed against the company six years earlier by two Wisconsin grain workers who claimed that exposure to yet another liquid grain fumigant, known in the industry as 80-20, produced chronic fatigue, shivers, weakness in the limbs, and other ailments. The terms of the settlement forbid disclosure of its size, but one of the plaintiffs told the *Milwaukee Journal* that it "involved millions of dollars." The settlement, Dow says, is not an admission that its products were responsible for the condition of the workers.

Paul Oreffice is in many ways in a unique position among chemical industry executives to reconcile the demands for health and profit under which they all operate. He can make important contributions to institutionalizing new corporate and regulatory practices that can prevent the panic, chaos, and human suffering that has been associated with DBCP and other dangerous chemicals. When he was named president of Dow, Oreffice inherited a lingering public-relations challenge—the legacy of napalm. But he also inherited an institutional commitment to certain health and environmental practices that even Dow's most animated critics agree rank the company as an industry leader in sound hazardous waste disposal and extensive use of recycling and toxicology research. These practices are in large part the result of policies pioneered in the 1970s by Carl Gerstacker, who retired as chairman of Dow in 1976. As early as 1972, Gerstacker was featured in *Business Week* as a profit-minded apostle of recycling and pollution control. His perspective at the time attracted doubt and ridicule from industry colleagues. Dow is today a leader in the incineration of hazardous waste—a disposal method that is more stable, and much more costly, than storage in landfills or injection in deep wells. The company stores in landfills less than 1 percent of the hazardous waste it generates. It has abandoned altogether the use of deep wells. According to a 1983 article in *Fortune*, this pattern compares quite favorably with disposal practices at other companies. Du Pont, for example, stores 30 percent of its waste in landfills and 50 percent in deep wells.

What is so puzzling about Oreffice is that he has done so little as chief executive to build on this institutional legacy and use his power as president to inspire further qualitative advances in industry standards for safety and accountability. He has in many ways done precisely the opposite. Oreffice has brandished Dow's position as a leader in toxicology research and its "product stewardship" practices (another Gerstacker initiative) to bludgeon government officials and environmental activists in his campaign against federal regulation. Rather than build on the Gerstacker legacy, the Dow president has used it as a weapon.

Dr. Samuel Epstein, an authority on workplace cancer who has clashed repeatedly with Dow, described this dimension of the Oreffice tenure. "I don't think there is any question that technologically, Dow is far ahead [of its industry rivals] in many ways," he told us. "It has been a pioneer in high-temperature incineration of hazardous wastes, for example. But there is an overwhelming ethos at Dow that the company can do no wrong. There is a disregard for any information that contradicts the company's interests. It is a question of mind-set."

The distinction between sound technology and the "Dow mind-set" prevailed at the company long before Oreffice became its chief executive. This is a relentlessly inward-looking firm. In an era when major corporations routinely choose half of their directors from outside management ranks, only three of Dow's eighteen directors are neither current or retired executives nor members of the Dow family. Attorney Victor Yannacone, who studied the company for years during his participation in the Agent Orange lawsuit, despaired over the unquestioned loyalty that pervades its ranks. "I have never seen such a monolith," Yannacone complained. "People join Dow straight from college and stay their entire careers. They love it. There are no whistle blowers at Dow because nobody believes there is anything to blow the whistle on."

Dow's base in Midland, a small community whose residents and political leaders react to any criticism of their corporate patron with outrage and disdain, promotes a siege mentality that trickles back into the firm. Wayne Schmidt, staff ecologist for the Michigan United Conservation Clubs, described what it was like to attend a hearing in Midland on a water pollution permit for Dow that his organization had challenged. The session took place in April 1984, one year after the onset of the dioxin scare. "The hearing was in a large auditorium," Schmidt recalled. "It was standing room only. It was the only public hearing I've ever been to where I felt physically intimidated. I was glad to see a police presence at that hearing. This is no exaggeration. We were careful where we parked. These people were fearing for their jobs."

This degree of corporate insularity has produced its share of troubles for Dow as well as for those affected by its policies. Perhaps the most revealing example of this dynamic came to light as a result of the Agent Orange litigation. Attorneys for the plaintiffs discovered that on March 24, 1965, Dow convened a meeting of Agent Orange producers to discuss the health hazards of dioxin and urge their rivals to adopt manufacturing practices that would reduce the level of dioxin contamination in the 2,4,5-T component. Attorneys for the veterans agree that of all the Agent Orange manufactured for use in Vietnam, the herbicide produced by Dow was the least contaminated. Four months later, a toxicologist for Hercules who had attended the meeting received a telephone call from a Dow official. He then wrote a memorandum that summarized the conversation. The Dow executive "stated that Dow was extremely frightened that this situation might explode," the Hercules toxicologist wrote. "They are aware that their competitors are marketing 2,4,5-T which contains 'alarming amounts' of [dioxin] and if the government learns of this the whole industry will suffer. They are particularly fearful of a congressional investigation and excessive restrictive legislation on manufacture of pesticides which might result."

A similar point was made in an earlier memo from V. K. Rowe, toxicology director at Dow, to a Dow Canada executive. Rowe was concerned that dioxin-contaminated 2,4,5-T might produce chloracne among users of the herbicide. "If this should occur, the whole 2,4,5-T industry will be hard hit and I would expect restrictive legislation, either barring the material or putting very rigid controls upon it," Rowe warned. "This is the main reason why we are so concerned that we clean up our own house from within, rather than having someone from without do it for us."

As it turns out, not all of Dow's competitors acted on the company's warnings. Indeed, the telephone call to Hercules, another low-dioxin producer of 2,4,5-T, was placed to express Dow's concern that "no one else has done anything" to reduce contamination. Still, Dow executives chose not to notify federal regulators—a decision that has since come to haunt the company, although Oreffice steadfastly denies that Dow should have done otherwise. On April 15, 1970, Julius Johnson, who was a Dow vice-president and research director, told a Senate subcommittee that "in retrospect, it would have been much preferred" had the company notified the Department of Agriculture of its health concerns. When the *Wall Street Journal* asked Oreffice in 1983 about the Johnson testimony, he replied, "Julius would say yes to anything."

We asked whether Oreffice believed that those competitors who failed to reduce their dioxin contamination acted irresponsibly. "Twenty years later, for me to judge what they did is very easy," he said. "You have to put yourself in the times then, whether they believed what we told them. We think we had a compelling story to tell people. All we had seen was chloracne, no other ill effects, but that was enough for us to say we had better lower the concentration of this impurity. And we told everybody [in the industry] what we found. It's very hard to put yourself in their shoes and say, were they responsible because they didn't react? I don't know what their findings were internally. Did they have a chloracne problem or didn't they?"

All told, the Oreffice tenure has served to magnify long-standing resistance at Dow to government oversight and outside intervention of any sort—largely because he simply does not agree with Dow critics on the toxicity and dangers of many of the chemicals Dow produces. Time and again during our conversations, Oreffice minimized, almost dismissed, the potential hazards of the compounds his company and industry manufacture. He erected a wall of intellectual avoidance that was impossible to topple. "Frankly, I think you and I have exposed ourselves this morning to more carcinogens by drinking a cup of coffee and a cup of tea than we do from most things that come out of [chemical] plants," he declared at the end of a long conversation in Midland on workplace exposure to chemical hazards. During a telephone conversation in December 1983, he said that he could not name a single substance aside from tobacco against which federal regulators had been too slow to protect the public. "The only two things I know of where cause and effect"—between exposure and cancer in humans—"has been proven are tobacco and asbestos," he said.

On this score the Dow president is simply wrong. According to the *Third Annual Report on Carcinogens,* issued by the Department of Health and Human Services one month prior to our first interview with Oreffice, there are at least twenty-three chemicals or manufacturing processes "for which the evidence from human studies indicates there is a causal relationship" between exposure to the substance and human cancer. Samuel Epstein put the number of *proven* human carcinogens at closer to thirty. "This is an extraordinary joke for Oreffice to make that statement," he remarked.

What is also clear about the Dow president is that the rigidity he brings to the health and safety debate affects his thinking on other issues as well, from freedom of speech to nuclear war. Our first conversation took place during a period of turmoil for U.S. foreign policy. Days before, 241 U.S. servicemen had been killed by a suicide bomber in Beirut, Lebanon. As we spoke, U.S. troops were mounting an invasion of the Caribbean island of Grenada. When Oreffice was asked to discuss the most pressing issues facing the United States, the conversation turned immediately to world affairs.

"One [issue] is the whole international situation—the role of the U.S. not only in its own defense but as the Big Brother if you will in defense of the world, the free western world," Oreffice responded after a brief pause. "How to carry out that policy. I happen to be in complete agreement with President Reagan that we need to have a stronger America. That's the only way to keep people from chipping away at us. I don't necessarily agree that we have to spend, spend, spend on defense, because there are a lot of efficiencies we can carry out. But the whole question of defense—where do we step in, like Grenada? I don't have enough data to make a judgment, but my first reaction is that they [the Reagan administration] are probably right. There is a *definite* conspiracy to set up Communist countries just along our southern border. And if we let them have too many Cubas, we've got problems."

Oreffice's voice rose as he talked about the "definite conspiracy" that threatens the United States. He is a fierce anticommunist and considers himself well informed on affairs of the Southern Hemisphere as a result of his early Dow career. He is fluent in both Spanish and Portuguese. Soon, the conversation turned to the issue of nuclear war—an issue on which Oreffice was less informed, but no less opinionated.

"I do not support a [nuclear] freeze by *any* stretch of the imagination," he said. "I think it would be an absolute disaster to have a unilateral freeze, and that's what it would be. I don't trust the Russians at all. I think the Russians only understand strength. . . . The biggest mistake this country could make is to disarm, or to unilaterally freeze, or to be weak. The lessons of history keep getting lost. Mr. [Neville] Chamberlain in England wanted to appease, appease, appease, and the result was Hitler marching on everybody. And I think the Russians would be about the same way if we tried to appease them. This is a very, very tough subject on which there is much rhetoric, so much said by people who don't know a damn thing about it. Like me. I don't know a damn thing about it. But I don't go around making statements that we must do this or that. The rhetoric is just incredible without data."

Overall, Oreffice is a man open to few doubts because he has categorical explanations of issues from chemical toxicity to the legitimacy of particular social movements. This could be the mind of an ideologue— or it could be the mind of a canny bargainer, especially on the regulatory front. Oreffice may have calculated that taking the hard line rhetorically and in Washington will eventually win the more limited concessions he has wanted all along. When pressed, the ideological rigidity in which Oreffice cloaks himself does begin to erode. He acknowledged that the United States must accept a certain responsibility for the turmoil in Central America, given its decades of neglect of the region. "You are absolutely right," he said. "We neglected them. We had a Marshall Plan for Europe, which was fine, we should have done that. But at the same time we completely neglected Latin America for decades, let it deteriorate, let them get friendly with others. There is also a complex in Latin America we have to recognize. They are so afraid of Big Brother, Uncle Sam, that sometimes they don't want our help. But we could have worked much better with them." Oreffice even voiced approval of certain forms of regulation and intervention: gun control, mandatory seat belt laws, guaranteed shelter for the homeless.

Carl Gerstacker, who sponsored Oreffice's rise through the company, portrayed the Dow president to us as something of a big-business populist. "We are all somewhat complex, but I think [the two sides] of Paul are consistent," he said. "Paul is willing to attack people his own size or bigger. But he never wants to attack little people. He's for employees and communities. He will never seem tough with those little people. But if it's big government, if it's the head of another country, he's quite willing to do battle."

A different, and more satisfying, analysis comes from a lengthy profile of Oreffice written more than five years ago by Wil Lepkowski, a veteran chemical industry reporter. Upon interviewing Oreffice after his appointment to the Dow presidency, Lepkowski offered this observation in *Chemical and Engineering News:* "Paul Oreffice gives one the impression of a man . . . who sees the world with a breadth circumscribed by his experience as a Dow company man. His perception [is not] the world for the world's sake, but the world for Dow's sake, with little questioning as to whether the two concepts are compatible. The comment is not criticism so much as an observation of Oreffice's value frame."

At bottom, Oreffice is a man of simple beliefs. Family. Country. Dow. Thirty years with Dow have instilled in its current president an unshakable faith in a set of values that have propelled the company since its earliest days: a relentless drive to create new products and conquer new markets; a management style that minimizes hierarchy and puts a premium on flexibility; a reflexive conservatism on public policy and vigilance against government intervention in internal affairs.

Oreffice is also a bare-knuckles political fighter. He is willing to inject himself, and his company, into political battles that less hard-boiled chief executives might avoid. There was no compelling business need for Oreffice to touch off the storm that he did over the Jane Fonda lecture. And even Oreffice conceded that Dow's combative position on certain issues, such as the EPA suspension of 2,4,5-T, may not have served the company well from the perspective of public confidence. "We fought the 2,4,5-T battle, frankly, to our detriment long after we decided we had a much better product," he said. "We fought it not to make 2,4,5-T but [because] we felt we had lots of scientific data which said this product really was not as unsafe as they [EPA] were saying. And if we give in on a product which we think is safe, what happens when the next one comes along where we don't have as much scientific data on it?"

Oreffice might have added that the 2,4,5-T campaign also sent a warning signal to regulators—be prepared to weather months and years of legal challenges when you choose to act against one of Dow's products.

.   .   .

Paul Oreffice's long career at Dow has shaped and reinforced his perspective on the chemical industry and the limits of government regulation and public oversight. But the hard-boiled conservatism of the Dow president has its roots much earlier in life, when as a young boy he fled with his family to escape persecution in fascist Italy. The Oreffice family left Italy shortly before that country officially entered World War II, and spent the next five years in Ecuador, where Oreffice's father, Max, became unofficial leader of the Italian émigré community. The Dow president recalled this period to us with deep feeling and a remarkable narration of detail, testimony to its enduring significance. He has also made reference to his immigrant background in speeches, articles, and other interviews over the years. And his discussions of his youth are often repeated by other company executives.

Jack Jones was a member of the project team that supervised Dow's aborted effort to build a major petrochemical complex in California between 1975 and 1977, a controversial episode that became one of Oreffice's most publicized confrontations with regulatory authorities. During a telephone conversation, Jones explained the roots of the Oreffice perspective on industry-government relations. "Paul was born in Italy," he said. "His father was arrested and tortured by Mussolini. Paul developed an intense, personal hatred of fascists or anyone else who takes a dictatorial or arrogant approach [to government]. During the Carter years, during the years of the Ford administration, you saw a lot of people get into power . . . [who] made decisions in a way very similar to the way decisions were made in Germany or Italy. Paul saw a lot of similarities there."

Paul Oreffice was born in Venice on November 29, 1927. His father was an "agricultural engineer" who took unproductive land situated in coastal areas, built dikes to protect it from the destructive effects of the ocean, and transformed it into productive acreage on which he raised corn, wheat, and other crops. The family was well-to-do. Oreffice called his father a "gentleman farmer" because he hired laborers to work the thousands of acres he controlled in Tuscany and other parts of northern Italy. He also raised horses, which Oreffice called a "passion" of his youth. "I started riding horses when I was four years old and I started breaking in horses when I was about ten," he said with obvious pride. "In fact, when I was twelve years old, I won an international jumping competition in Italy with a horse that nobody else had ever ridden." But this comfortable life began to unravel as Mussolini tightened his grip on Italy and demanded conformity from prominent citizens.

"My father was a very independent thinker," the Dow president recalled. "Essentially his crime was that he did not join the Fascist party. It was obligatory in Italy to join the Fascist party. One day he was invited by the head of the Fascists in Venice to come and visit. He made a date to go, and when he arrived, there were four men with guns who took him into a room where he was beaten severely for several hours. He was fed castor oil, which was the Fascist way of 'cleansing,' and thrown in jail. We didn't even know where he was for eight days. My mother had all these inquiries going, but he had disappeared from the face of the earth. Finally we got a leak . . . that he was in jail. Once she knew that, she could get a lawyer and get going."

After more than a month in prison, Max Oreffice was released and forced to stand trial. He was charged with twenty-five counts of treason, for which the prosecution initially sought the death penalty. With testimony from a number of witnesses, including the mayor of Venice, whom Oreffice called the "strongest" witness on his father's behalf, the trial resulted in dismissal. The verdict ended the immediate threat to the Oreffice family, but it ushered in a period of harassment, constant surveillance, and restrictions on travel. Max Oreffice would not leave the house after dark and could not venture out of town under any circumstances. The police would visit the Oreffice home two or three times each evening to check on his presence, and he went so far as to install a bell by his bed that he would ring to confirm to the authorities that he was there.

"You never knew when they might mug him again in a dark alley or take him in," Oreffice said. "So we started asking for visas from around the world. The war had started. Italy was not in the war yet, but the war had started. We had a very difficult time obtaining permits to leave. My father could not move from town, so my mother did the running to Rome to try and get visas. We finally got temporary visas to the U.S. and caught the last ship to leave before Italy entered the war. It was supposed to have eight hundred passengers. On this trip it had more than two thousand. We slept on cots in the ballroom. We were in New York harbor, as a matter of fact, at the first sight of the Statue of Liberty from way out, when someone said, 'Italy has just entered the war.' So we were in the U.S. without a permanent visa, still working on someplace to go. We spent a few months here while we were doing that and through some friends of friends got visas to Ecuador. The only reason we went to Ecuador was because it was a place to go."

The flight from Italy devastated the Oreffice family from a financial perspective. Citizens could leave the country with only $500 per person and all the baggage they could carry. The Oreffices tried to take their furniture, but there was no room on the ship. So it stayed—and was eventually destroyed by bombs—in the port of Genoa. But the young Oreffice's war-inspired travels did not interrupt his education. In fact, they helped him acquire skills, especially a facility with languages, that paid off handsomely once he joined Dow. By the age of eighteen, Paul

Oreffice was fluent in Italian, French, and Spanish, which he learned in order to attend high school in Ecuador. Upon his return to the U.S. in 1945, he enrolled in Purdue University and added English to his verbal repertoire.

These experiences have clearly left a strong impression on Oreffice. He said it was one aspect of his life that distinguished him from most chief executives. He made it plain that his rise to the presidency of Dow is a source of deep pride and personal satisfaction. Oreffice received cash compensation from Dow in 1984 of nearly $1.2 million and owns Dow stock with a market value in the spring of 1985 of more than $2 million, a far cry from his days as a Purdue undergraduate who studied with a book on one side of his desk and a dictionary on the other.

"I came to this town really as an outsider," Oreffice replied when asked how he hoped to be remembered. "This was a very closed, midwestern WASP community. And I was strictly a strange guy. I combed my hair straight back. This is something I tell some of the minority groups today if they say, 'Well, I'm different.' I say you don't understand what different means. I stood out much more when I first came into this community than any group can stand out today. I *never* thought I would be on the board of this company much less be its chief executive. Things just happened. I say that because in the same way, I don't look at myself and say, 'How do I want to be remembered historically?' All through my career, I would have to say that it was only in the last three to five years before I became [president] that I even entertained the thought that I could possibly be chief executive some day."

Oreffice's background as an immigrant—or, more precisely, as an immigrant who rose to a position of wealth and power he had never dreamed of attaining—has also produced a less charitable streak. He displays such a blind faith in the enduring virtues of the American Dream that he often equates critics of his company with enemies of his way of life. Dow published as a pamphlet in 1980 the transcript of an address by Oreffice characteristically titled, *Let's Break Up Washington.* As an introduction to the lecture, the pamphlet included a brief biography of the Dow president that is testimony to the importance of those early days. "Paul Oreffice was born in Italy, and fled to America as a boy to escape the ravages of fascism," the biography read. "He and his parents arrived in this country with little money and no influential friends, so his rise to become President of The Dow Chemical Company is a classic 'Horatio Alger' success story. . . . Paul Oreffice has lived in many parts of the world, and has had a chance to see this country from inside and outside its borders. That experience has made him an unabashed patriot, a man who dearly loves this country and the ideals on which it is built."

Oreffice the patriot is not averse to questioning the loyalty of those with whom he disagrees. "Lenin said that capitalism would be destroyed from the inside," he warned the Arizona Business Forum on March 29, 1979. "Well, if a weapon was needed, it was indeed found in the so-called environmentalists who have now made a profession of standing in the way of any progress. . . . We are facing a well-organized, often unscrupulous, professional force. . . . We are dealing, let me tell you again, with fiendishly clever people."

Less than five months after that speech, Oreffice wrote a letter to the *Midland Daily News*, his local newspaper, in response to an editorial. The letter criticized economic policies recently unveiled by President Carter. "Fascism came to power on the wings of economic excuses," he wrote. "You yourself state that under Fascism, 'all aspects of national life were strictly regimented, including economic activity.' That is exactly the direction of President Carter's recent proposals for setting up more bureaucracies and ignoring the free market. . . . This administration may not be Fascist-oriented in the World War II sense of the word, but it is certainly leading the country down the same centrally-controlled economic path that has brought many dictatorships to power."

It might be possible to dismiss these statements as verbal flights of fancy were it not for the fact that Oreffice has made similar comments time and again over the past seven years. These antifascist analogies have also become a standard point of reference for Dow executives who discuss their leader. What makes this vitriolic rhetoric so remarkable, though, is the simple fact that the realities of Oreffice's first fifteen years as a Dow executive contrast so vividly with his oratory. Oreffice joined the company in 1953 because his background as a European and his skill with languages dovetailed so conveniently with Dow's objective to become a global force in chemical production. He received job offers from six chemical companies, including industry giants DuPont and Monsanto, but chose Dow even though the salary he was offered was fifth lowest out of six. "Until 1952 Dow was really a domestic company," Oreffice said. "So I thought I had something special to offer. I spoke five languages. I had an international knowledge that most people didn't have. I felt that the opportunities were great—the starting salary was lousy, but the opportunities were great—to grow and do it rapidly."

This is precisely what transpired. Until 1970, when he returned to Midland as financial vice-president, Oreffice worked in or supervised, and often pioneered, Dow operations in countries that were beginning to open their economies to foreign investment and nurture development of the petrochemical sector. Oreffice succeeded in this role because he was prepared to do what had to be done in order to build and expand Dow's presence abroad. That often meant that his responsibilities were as much social and political as they were commercial. He managed to win the confidence of powerful civilian and military leaders in countries that were anything but models of democratic and open societies.

Oreffice's experiences in Spain, when it was still under the harsh rule of dictator Francisco Franco, are an example of his work during this period. He relocated to Spain in the spring of 1963, just as the government was emerging from fourteen years of economic isolation and turning away from state-owned enterprise as its engine of development. Soon after Oreffice arrived, the Franco regime unveiled a four-year development plan that took effect on January 1, 1964, and targeted the petrochemical industry for 11 percent annual growth, faster than any other industrial sector. Oreffice worked for three years in Spain and set the stage for Dow's expansion there. The company broke ground in 1964 on a $20 million plant to produce polyethylene and soon expanded its capacity to produce polystyrene and formaldehyde. He also thrived on a social and political level. He became Spain's bridge champion in 1965. He was awarded in 1966 the Encomienda del Merito Civil, the country's highest civilian honor, for his contributions to the development of the petrochemical sector. A retired Dow executive, who served in Europe with the company for more than fifteen years, discussed with us the Dow president's career. Oreffice "really made it in Spain by being close to Franco's Falangist officers," he said. "In all fairness to Paul, it couldn't have been that easy for him to wind his way through those thugs."

. . . .

Oreffice's years in Spain underscore his role as a player in Dow's evolution as a chemical producer of global significance. But their importance to Dow—or to Oreffice's career and rise through the company—pale in comparison with his years of service in South America. From 1956 to 1963, and again from 1967 through 1969, the business world of Paul Oreffice revolved around the economic and social turbulence of countries such as Brazil, Chile, and Argentina. This is where Oreffice made his mark at Dow. His performance first as architect of Dow's Brazilian operation, later as general manager of Dow Latin America, set the stage for a triumphant return to Midland in 1970 and a rapid rise to the corporate presidency. The legacy of these years also underscores his demonstrated capacity to maintain cordial relations with dictatorial regimes and enhance Dow's business in the process.

Oreffice was dispatched to São Paulo, Brazil's industrial heartland, at the age of twenty-eight. This was his first major assignment for Dow, and

Brazil was the first country outside the United States and Canada where Dow marketed its own products rather than act through local agents. The business was marginal. Dow generated sales in Brazil of roughly $1 million, and Oreffice told us he began his operation with a market survey and two employees. "I did everything," he explained. "I used to go out and sell the product. After I sold the product, I had to do the [paperwork]. I had to do all the [currency] exchange things to import the goods. Once we billed the goods, I went and collected the money."

But it was Oreffice's creativity as a borrower and lender, not as a salesman or bill collector, that made his reputation. In a country where inflation hovered, at the time, between 25 percent and 80 percent, the way a company financed its business was just as important to the bottom line as the amount of business it conducted. Oreffice quickly appreciated this fact of life and designed a financial strategy that proved extremely successful. One such innovation, called a swap loan, involved simultaneous loans by Dow in U.S. dollars to the Banco do Brazil and from the bank to Dow Brazil in cruzeiros, a set of transactions that expedited the import process. Oreffice's exploits did not go unnoticed in Midland.

"The first time I ever heard the name Paul Oreffice was when one of our people told me that Dow had in Brazil one of the most creative financial minds he had seen," said retired chairman Gerstacker, himself a legend among chemical hands for his aggressive approach to corporate borrowing. "So I went out of my way to get to know Paul. I was impressed. He is a natural financially."

The Dow president evidently takes great pride in his accomplishments as a financier. When the company was asked, after our final interview, to provide a brief explanation of the mechanics of a swap loan, Oreffice himself took the time to compose an extended reply. It read in part: "The Dow Chemical Company loaned the Banco do Brazil (Brazil's government bank) dollars in the U.S. and the Banco do Brazil loaned our Brazilian company cruzeiros for the same length of time. The two loans were made simultaneously and were repaid on the same day—one, two, or five years later. In other words, we swapped dollars for cruzeiros. . . . Although many other companies soon joined in these swap loans, the financing we obtained ahead of the others was really the catalyst for what became our great growth in Brazil."

Earl Barnes, who retired in 1982 as chairman of Dow, told us that Oreffice's exploits in Brazil were a critical factor in his selection in 1970 as Dow's financial vice-president—even though he believed Oreffice's later performance as general manager of Dow Latin America was subpar. "I would have to say that Oreffice didn't distinguish himself in Latin America," Barnes explained. The division "had some debacles that were the result of changes of [Latin American] governments. Things didn't really go that well. I wouldn't say that Oreffice was considered as having done anything fantastic there. In fact, the fact that he got the financial vice-president's job was based more on his reputation from his days in Brazil that anything he did [as general manager of] Latin America."

While Gerstacker and other top Dow executives were getting to know Oreffice, Dow's man in Brazil was getting to know influential Brazilians who were impressed by his command of Portuguese, the fifth language he had mastered. Those connections paid off in 1964 when a group of Brazilian generals overthrew the democratic government of President João Goulart, a pro-labor populist whose political agenda included large wage increases and restrictions on foreign capital. Oreffice had been stationed in Brazil when Goulart assumed the presidency. But he had already relocated to Spain by the time political instability began to reach critical mass. Dow executives in Midland then directed Oreffice to return to Brazil in February 1964 and investigate developments.

He discussed the ensuing turn of events with us at some length. "One of the things I had achieved in Brazil is that I speak the language like a native," he said. "Because of that I had been accepted by some Brazilian businessmen as one of them, if you will. In fact, just about every Wednesday I used to go to lunch at the country club [in São Paulo], not to go to the country club but because there was this table—to which one day I got invited, and I was the only foreigner invited to this table—where there were always ten or twelve of these top Brazilian business people. Sometimes they would talk to me about 'those foreigners.' " Here Oreffice smiled. "But it was really a place of honor to be invited to this table. Through them, I knew what was going on in Brazil. These were very influential people. . . . It was interesting when I went back to Brazil, two months before the Revolution. These people all knew that if things got real bad, they said, 'Don't worry about this country going Communist, because we are not going to, the army's not going to let it.' The army would step in if it had to. It happened just the way they described."

It is hardly surprising that Oreffice's friends knew so much about what was to transpire. The business community in Brazil, in particular leading executives from the São Paulo region, rather than the army, did the bulk of the planning for the coup. An ecstatic article that appeared in *Fortune* magazine just months after the March 31 "Revolution" described in intricate detail the role of the Institute of Social Research and Studies (IPES), a business-funded think tank, in first distributing propaganda against the Goulart administration and then opening lines of planning and communication with the military. "Much of the inspiration and planning [for the coup] was provided by business executives and professional men, aroused by Brazil's leftward drift," *Fortune* reported. "Not only were they aroused, they organized to do something about it. Most of these leaders were from the state of São Paulo, and the March 31 uprising can justly be called 'the Paulista's revolt.'"

Years later, no less an authority on the events of March 31, 1964, than General Golbery do Couto e Silva acknowledged the vital role of the business "think tank" *Fortune* had described. Golbery was the chief intellectual architect of postcoup Brazil and founder of its National Intelligence Service, Brazil's combination FBI and CIA. He was described to us by a former U.S. embassy official as "probably the single most important force in Brazilian politics" during the 1960s and 1970s. "The Institute was really a facade for the observation of the political situation and the organization of a front to block any attempt from the government to go more and more to the left," Golbery told an interviewer. "This was really the idea. We made some important economic studies about the agrarian reform, the tax laws, and so on. But the main idea was to organize a front, civilian and military. I went to the Institute to be a liaison man between the military people and the civilians. . . . It was impossible to remain watching such a situation until the end of the government. And there was a revolution in 1964. The Social and Economic Research Institute provided the focal point for communications between civilians and the military."

Golbery's comments are undeniably interesting, but even more interesting is the forum in which they were made. The discussion appeared in a chapter on the general that was part of a Dow-sponsored corporate history, entitled *East from Brazosport,* published in 1974. The reason? Soon after Oreffice left Spain permanently to become general manager of Dow Latin America, the company announced that the general would accept a position with Dow Brazil. Golbery had resigned earlier from the government over a policy dispute. He began as a consultant to Dow Brazil and then spent six years as chairman of the subsidiary. When he left the company in 1974, it was to become chief of staff in the military government of President Ernesto Geisel.

"We always felt that in a country like Brazil we needed some top-notch local advisors," Oreffice explained when asked about Golbery. "We had an advisor who was a financial man—very bright—but he was put in the government. As a member of the government, he couldn't be an advisor, so we asked for some suggestions. He suggested General Golbery, and we found him to be an exceptional individual. I have always found him to be a tremendously well-read type of fellow. . . . He was a real patriot. In my experience the number one patriot I have ever met for [any] country."

Golbery's status also proved to be of exceptional value to Dow. His six years as president of Dow Brazil were perhaps *the* decisive period in the company's expansion there as it transformed itself from an importer of certain bulk chemicals to a Brazil-based manufacturer of a range of commodities and specialty chemicals, such as the powerful herbicide 2,4-D. David Schornstein, who succeeded Oreffice as general manager of Latin American operations, described the decade 1968–78 as one of "hellish growth" for Dow in Brazil. Revenues increased from roughly $15 million per year to $250 million. Today, Dow routinely generates Brazilian sales of more than $300 million, and the country is one of six independent regions into which the company divides its global operations. Dow has become Brazil's largest exporter of industrial and agricultural chemicals and it owns a manufacturing complex in the northeast city of Aratu that is situated on 1,300 acres and employs more than five hundred workers.

It is difficult to discuss with precision the role of General Golbery in this explosion of Dow's sales and investment. What can be said is that prior to the 1964 coup, Dow had been slow to develop a presence in Brazil —and many other parts of the developing world—as a result of its preference for exporting products from the United States rather than building plants abroad. Andrew Ventura, a Brazilian who reported on the petrochemical industry for the U.S. embassy in São Paulo, recalled a meeting with Oreffice in the late 1960s. "We had lunch alone, and I told Oreffice I was puzzled that Dow was not more active in Brazil," he told us. "He didn't really say much, but I knew he would report our conversation to headquarters." Dow eventually began a game of catch-up—precisely where General Golbery entered the business equation. The company stepped up its operations in two stages: expansion in the late sixties of terminal facilities in Santos Bay, one of Brazil's most important ports, and construction in the mid-seventies of its manufacturing complex in Aratu. This brand of rapid expansion was difficult to achieve in Brazil, where powerful local business leaders resisted penetration by foreign capital, and military rulers, although they welcomed U.S. investors, often demanded concessions in the form of technology exchange or participation by Brazilian corporations in foreign-owned operations. Dow managed to increase its Brazilian presence while making few concessions along these lines.

According to Schornstein, the Santos Bay terminal was the only such facility owned and operated by a foreign corporation—and it was constructed under the terms of a law that was repealed soon after the port was built. "We would bring in chemicals by ship, drum them, and sell them to the market or just reship them," Schornstein told us. "We were the only company that had such a facility, which gave us a unique advantage, and thus started to expand our sales quite a bit. At the same time, and at the same location, we got a permit to build a polyether plant for making one of the main ingredients of polyurethane foam. This plant was built, and we also got a permit to build a polystyrene plant." Schornstein explained that construction of these facilities not only increased sales of the products they produced but bolstered Dow's overall Brazilian presence. "Most people prefer to buy imports from people who they know are going to be" in the country, he said. "And if you have a plant there, even if it's not the product they're buying, they feel better about it because they know you're not going to pick up and go home. This allowed us to increase our sales rapidly."

All told, Dow's expansion in Brazil was meteoric, especially considering the maze of regulations to be met and permits to be acquired in the course of plant construction. Schornstein gives much of the credit to General Golbery. The general "really knew the Brazilian government, and where he really helped us in getting permits was that he could lay out a program of how you should go about getting that permit, in what sequence you had to see various ministers, things like that," he observed. "That was one of the things that really helped us. Not that he ever did anything wrong. He was just imparting knowledge—who to see first, who to see second, who to see third." Could Dow have expanded as it did without the assistance of Golbery? "No chance," said Andrew Ventura. "There was no way they could have done it. They had great difficulty even *with* Golbery."

This pattern of expansion raises an obvious question for Paul Oreffice: How could a man who accused Jimmy Carter of leading the United States down the road to "dictatorship" work so closely with a dictatorial government that jailed and exiled opposition leaders, smashed independent trade unions, and was accused by Amnesty International in 1976 of having tortured nearly two thousand people during its first decade in power?

"There is more gross exaggeration in that," Oreffice replied, when asked about reports of torture and arrests of opposition leaders by the military regime. "It's something that really bothers me having lived in Italy and having seen torture firsthand. The way we have distorted things in this country. Every time a government of the right does this much" —here Oreffice opened a small space between his thumb and forefinger —"it gets built into this," as he spread his hands. "When a government of the left does something, nobody bothers. . . .

"Now, the military did get in and did get tough with a few people early on," he continued. "But if you look overall at what they have done, they have been really mild as overall supervisors of Brazil. One of the things I think we have to accept in the United States, and we're never willing to accept, is that not every country can have exactly the same form of government that we have. Brazil under a pure democracy was failing. So what are the alternatives? The last thing you want is to have a dictator. With Brazil's way of going, the military [leaders] were really sort of supervisors. One man could not be president for more than a certain number of years. No one man could become a dictator. So you had a group that essentially named the president. Mexico has what you could call the dictatorship of a party. Is that bad? I can't condemn that. I think that each country has to find its own way, and if you can, avoid *a* man becoming a dictator, because that's where you really run into a problem."

For all of Brazil's failings prior to 1968, is there not some intrinsic value to democratic rule that should be protected? "What if the country had gone communist?" he protested. "Would that be a democracy then? Furthermore, once they go communist, have you ever seen one come back? At least when you get guys relatively from the right, from the military, change is possible. Once you get a Castro, change is never possible. And Brazil was on the verge of going Red."

·   ·   ·

Paul Oreffice returned to Midland in 1970 after fifteen years abroad with a reputation as a master financier and a manager who was able to navigate the political and social turmoil of the Third World, a market that Dow executives continued to target for rapid growth. He would emerge in less than ten years as chief executive of the corporation, a speedy rise to the top that rested on two pillars of advancement: competent performance by Oreffice and an ability to persevere amid the understated turmoil of Midland, where tensions and rivalries among top managers and their lieutenants produced a string of executive casualties that eventually propelled Oreffice to the presidency. He inherited control of the company at a period when the chemical industry was poised to enter a long slide into overcapacity and reduced profits.

When Oreffice was named president of Dow Chemical on May 3, 1978, the company was riding the crest of a twenty-year wave of prosperity. Revenues that year approached $7 billion and had been rising for a decade at an average annual rate of 15 percent. Profits had been increasing even faster. Sales in Europe, where Dow conducted more than one-fourth of its total business, reached record levels, and construction of a massive plant on the island of Krk, Yugoslavia—the first petrochemical joint venture between communist Yugoslavia and the West—was proceeding apace. Business got even better in 1979. Dow not only managed to weather that winter's OPEC oil price shock, but thrived on it. Revenues increased by 34 percent, profits by 36 percent, as Dow took advantage of its strength as an "upstream" producer to pass on to its customers the higher cost of petroleum. *Forbes* was giddy over the company's performance. "Dow is supremely self-confident, ready to take on world markets against all comers," the magazine exclaimed.

Oreffice himself was less buoyant. He long suspected that Dow and the rest of the industry had misinterpreted the structural fallout from the OPEC price shock of five years earlier. He understood that the second round of oil price increases would change forever the environment in which Dow and its competitors operated.

"I started forming my thoughts about a decade ago," Oreffice said during our conversations. "When they really jelled was around the time of the oil price increase of 1974. We were right in the midst of the business being very, very good. But it was apparent to me that you couldn't quadruple the price of oil in one year without it bringing some massive economic dislocations." Operating under the pressures of a second price shock, Oreffice then began to fashion a strategic response. That meant revising, even reversing, the strategy that had carried Dow to its preeminent position in the industry.

Under the direction of a powerful management triumvirate—President Herbert Dow "Ted" Doan, Executive Vice-president C. B. "Ben" Branch, and Chairman Carl Gerstacker—Dow in the 1960s and early 1970s conquered the chemical world by making masterful use of a two-pronged strategy for growth: rapid expansion abroad in search of new markets and an aggressive use of borrowed money to finance that expansion. In a climate of stable demand for chemicals and high inflation (which lowers the real cost of borrowing), the Doan-Branch-Gerstacker approach reaped huge financial rewards.

"During the sixties and early seventies Dow was aggressively leveraging itself through debt," said one Wall Street analyst. "The game was super then. They were borrowing money at 5 percent and getting returns of 15 to 20 percent. What happened all of a sudden [after the OPEC shock] was that Dow started borrowing money at 20 percent and getting returns of 5 percent." This may be a slight exaggeration, but it captured the new realities of life in the chemical industry.

Oreffice's basic insight was to recognize that the world had changed. The emergence of OPEC meant not only higher oil prices but potential competition from new Third World producers of petroleum-based chemicals that were important to Dow. Economic growth was destined to slow down, creating less demand for Dow's products as well as worldwide overcapacity—all of which could then fuel ruinous price competition. Moreover, the tight money policies adopted in the West to combat OPEC-fueled inflation were bound to raise interest rates, increasing the financial burden of Dow's massive long-term debt. This radical new environment demanded a drastic strategic response: (a) a reduction of capacity in basic chemicals; (b) a decisive push to develop higher-margin specialty products, such as pesticides and pharmaceuticals; and (c) a reduction of Dow's debt.

"Oreffice was way out ahead of most managers of chemical companies" in appreciating the new facts of business life, said Wall Street analyst John Henry. "He saw things happening in the world that he didn't like and he got increasingly vocal about them." Since 1981, when the redirection of Dow began to gather steam, Oreffice has presided over a series of critical financial and production decisions:

- *Withdrawals from joint ventures.* Dow in 1982 pulled out of joint ventures in Saudi Arabia, Yugoslavia, and Japan. It also canceled plans to build a $360 million complex in Argentina and sold off its Korean operations.
- *Asset disposal.* Dow announced the sale in March 1982 of its U.S. oil and gas properties for more than $400 million. The sale was part of a program announced by Oreffice the year before to shed $1 billion worth of assets by the end of 1983. The company in early 1984 announced that it would sell for $440 million 50 percent of its oil-well servicing operation to Schlumberger, a French corporation with which it conducts joint ventures around the world.
- *Debt reduction.* Assets sales have permitted Dow to rebuild its balance sheet, a goal of Oreffice since the mid-seventies. At Dow's 1983 annual meeting, Oreffice announced that total debt had been reduced by $1.3 billion from an all-time high of $5.1 billion the year before. Largely as a result of reduced interest payments, Dow posted its first cash surplus in two decades.
- *New operations.* To bolster its move into specialties, Dow in 1981 acquired the ethical drug business of Richardson-Merrell. (Ethical drugs are promoted primarily to members of the medical profession and usually require a prescription.) Oreffice personally negotiated the $260 million acquisition, which was paid for in Dow stock and pursued over the objections of several Dow directors. The company in November 1984 announced it would acquire the Texize division of Morton Thiokol, which makes household chemical products such as Fantastik, Spray 'n Wash, and Glass Plus. The transaction is designed to bolster Dow's position in this segment of the consumer market. It was agreed to after Dow purchased roughly 1.4 million shares of Morton

Thiokol, a turn of events that several Wall Street analysts said resembled the greenmail tactics of corporate raiders such as Carl Icahn and Saul Steinberg.

Carl Gerstacker, an architect of Dow's postwar thrust overseas, said the redirection Oreffice is engineering compares in scale and significance to the changes he introduced. "Any company must re-create itself periodically," Gerstacker told us. "As you look around the country, you see corporations, sometimes whole industries, who stayed in the same mold and were left behind. The steel industry is a good example. Dow has gone through these changes before. In the 1930s the company went from being a producer of inorganic chemicals to manufacturing organics and plastics. That was a major change. In the 1950s Dow became an international company. I think this is another major change. Now is the time for a redirection, and Paul is leading it."

Indeed, Oreffice began articulating the case for redirection just a few years after his return to Midland. Debate inside the company over the wisdom of continued reliance on debt as the fuel for rapid expansion began to heat up during the mid-seventies, and Oreffice was a critical figure by virtue of his membership on the finance committee of the board of directors. "There were recurrent arguments at board meetings on [the corporate] sense of direction," said Gerstacker, who was chairman of the board as well as of the finance committee. "Should the company continue to build massive plants or should it emphasize the specialties more? Paul did lead in that [debate], yes. I remember lots of votes on the board where one vote made the difference. It really came to specific authorizations— should we build this plant or not? Some votes were closer than others." Oreffice in fact pushed Gerstacker so hard to scale back the company's debt burden that the then-chairman described his protégé to *Forbes* as "a little old lady in tennis shoes"—a tongue-in-cheek remark Oreffice never forgot. At Gerstacker's retirement party several years later, he disappeared during the course of the black-tie affair and reemerged dressed in women's clothing and a gray wig, clutching a copy of the *Wall Street Journal*. He said he had come to lecture his chairman "about being such a wildman on capital spending."

But not all of the managerial differences at Dow during this period were so good-natured. For several years during the mid-1970s the company was rocked by unprecedented infighting among its leadership corps. The source of the turmoil was Zoltan Merszei, a Hungarian-born, Swiss-educated firebrand who was named president and chief executive in 1976. It was Merszei's "promotion" to chairman—a promotion in name that really represented a dismissal from power—that created the opening for

Oreffice to be elevated to president and CEO in May 1978. Oreffice would not speak on the record about Merszei, who left Dow after nine months as chairman to join Occidental Petroleum and be groomed as a possible successor to corporate patriarch Armand Hammer.

Neither, for that matter, will any executive currently associated with Dow, although several retired managers did speak with us about the episode on the condition that they not be identified. One former executive, who labeled Merszei a "con artist" because of his ability to ingratiate himself with superiors as he rose through the organization, said there was open tension between President Merszei and Oreffice when Oreffice ran Dow USA. "Zoltan is the kind of guy who expects people to—let me put it this way—kiss his feet," this executive said. "He was determined to make Oreffice knuckle under [to his leadership], and this led to very serious consequences. Something had to give. My feeling is, if Merszei had not been ousted, Oreffice would have left the company. It was that serious." Merszei remains bitter about his forced departure from Dow—although he, too, after taking a week to consider our interview request, declined to discuss the episode.

"This is quite a controversial subject," Merszei explained. "There are a lot of fantasies about Oreffice, and no useful purpose would be served" by talking about them. He then offered a parting shot at his successor and fellow immigrant to the United States. "There is a saying that when somebody becomes a Roman Catholic [through conversion], they try to be more like the pope than the pope. There is some of that here— immigrants who come to this country and act more patriotic than they are. Maybe that has to do with insecurity."

By nearly all accounts, part of the chaos associated with Merszei's brief reign was the personality and life-style of the brash new chief executive. Merszei had a hot temper. "I get my best ideas out of the shouting at my staff meetings," he told an interviewer in 1977. He also reportedly was a bit of a womanizer, something that simply was not tolerated in upright Midland. One former executive, a Merszei partisan, was amused by his decidedly nonmidwestern ways. He described Merszei to us as "a Count Dracula-type." He "looks like he should be wearing a cape," this retired manager quipped. "He was also quite a lady's man."

But the differences between Merszei and Oreffice had a substantive dimension as well. Within the rivalry between the two men operated a broader struggle for the future of Dow: a choice between a course of business-as-usual and a new approach that reversed the strategy on which Merszei's rise to power was based. Until Merszei arrived in Midland in 1975 (he was made an executive vice-president and then quickly appointed chief executive), his twenty-six years with the company had been spent largely overseas—and mainly in Europe, where he built Dow's business from next to nothing into a billion-dollar enterprise. Merszei's career, as was Oreffice's, was wed from the first to Dow's international expansion. Soon after he joined the company, Merszei convinced then-president Leland Doan to dispatch him to Japan, where he established Dow's first overseas joint venture. Shortly thereafter, Merszei opened a small office in Zurich, from which he directed Dow's assault on the continent. He presided over the construction of Dow's first chemical plant outside the United States (in Terneuzen, Holland) and compiled a record of increased sales and profits that Midland could not help but notice.

Wall Street analyst Leonard Bogner offered us an overview of Merszei's rise to power. "Zoltan Merszei built Europe for Dow," he said. "He was probably the most successful manager in the company. He adopted the Dow marketing, distribution, and pricing philosophy in an environment that didn't know anything about it and then ran circles around the European industry. . . . Merszei had built up such a tremendous track record, and at that point Dow was so concerned about its multinational image, that picking a non-American to run the company was very appealing. You could not deny him the opportunity." Thus was born Chief Executive Merszei.

When Zoltan Merszei was running Dow Europe, so the story goes, he carried with him a plastic card that contained his five-year targets for sales and profits on the continent. He seldom failed to meet those objectives. After he became CEO, Merszei reportedly fashioned a new card and distributed it to top management in Midland: a physical reminder of the boss's commitment to continued expansion. Paul Oreffice was named president of Dow USA about the time Merszei first arrived in Midland. But the initiatives of Dow's American boss began to run directly counter to the strategic wisdom of the new chief executive. Oreffice scaled back investment in massive new plants and beefed up Dow's limited lines of consumer products. He made a strong financial commitment to Dowell, the oil-well servicing business. That move proved extremely profitable.

Meanwhile, the performance of the company as a whole was disappointing. During Merszei's first year as chief executive, net income dropped 3 percent, a troubling turn of events for a company used to uninterrupted prosperity. After net income dropped by nearly 10 percent in 1977, Dow's directors decided they had seen enough. In May 1978 the board named Oreffice CEO and offered Merszei the position of chairman. If the displaced president had any doubts about the real meaning of his "promotion," Oreffice soon made clear who was in charge. Asked by *Chemical Week* to explain the division of responsibilities at Dow,

Oreffice replied, "I run the company; Zoltan runs the board." Zoltan Merszei resigned the chairmanship in February 1979.

· · · ·

Whether or not Paul Oreffice meets the objectives he has set for Dow—his basic goal is for the company to derive half its profits from traditional products, half from specialty chemicals by the late 1980s—his efforts to date are noteworthy on at least two fronts. First, Oreffice is repositioning a major corporation without presiding over a traumatic series of plant closings and layoffs, although he has used early retirement and other incentives to reduce Dow's workforce by 11,000 since 1981. What is more, he is responding to a changing economic environment without abandoning the industry his firm was weaned on. Unlike David Roderick of U.S. Steel, or Edward Hennessy of Allied, Oreffice is not trying to diversify Dow out of its problems. We asked him to discuss the pressures that accompany such a profound corporate redirection.

"It has been a lot of fun all along," he said. "It has been lot of fun because although the most visible parts of this restructuring are the things we are cutting back, there has been a lot of building. For example, when I took over, I said there are certain businesses we either have to be in or out of. Number one was pharmaceuticals. We had a small presence in the United States, but we did not have the critical mass to do the kind of research we should be doing. It wasn't enough [for Dow] to be a really good pharmaceutical company. So I set myself a five-year target—I did not tell everybody I had a five-year target—and I set up a pharmaceuticals acquisition team. . . . Fortunately, we found Richardson-Merrell, which I personally negotiated in great part. Now we have a critical mass, we now have a presence, we now will be able to play with the big boys.

"I realize a lot of these decisions affect a lot of people—inside and outside the company," he continued. "To me the most difficult part of the job is when we have to make a decision that involves reducing [the numbers] of people. That is why we have taken an attitude within Dow, and I feel very strongly about this, that at least while I'm around, we will try to be as humane as we can. We have a no-layoff policy. I just don't consider it proper management for us to have layoffs and rehires."

In a spring 1982 speech to Midland employees, Oreffice made a not-so-veiled reference to the Michigan auto industry and accused the automakers of using an "inhuman approach" to labor policy. "Some of the companies I have seen, not far from us, think it is perfectly fine to hire a bunch of people today and lay them off tomorrow," he said. "They are using an inhuman approach. It is not the Dow approach." During our conversation, Oreffice compared Dow's labor policy with that of a direct competitor. "We just had to reduce people in our oil-well services division, at Dowell," he said. "I know that one of our competitors one day just gave pink slips to 28 percent of their employees. They just said good-bye. What we did is offer some incentives for retirement. We didn't have a layoff. It cost us a lot of money, and it took us a good year to make the reductions. But from the human standpoint, it's the only way to do it."

The "human standpoint," of course, is precisely what Dow critics argue is ignored by the company when Oreffice and his colleagues resist and challenge modest efforts by federal regulators to monitor and control workplace and environmental exposure to the products Dow manufactures. It is tempting to argue that the business evolution Oreffice has set in motion—the drive, through acquisitions and new product development, to become a force in specialty chemical production—is related to his vigorous activism against health and safety regulations. Dow becomes even more sensitive to regulatory authority as it evolves from a company whose prosperity depends on process innovation (making the same chemicals more cheaply or in greater volume) to one that depends on product innovations, such as the introduction of new chemicals and pharmaceuticals. But this interpretation is too mechanistic. Oreffice's antiregulatory activism predated the development of a firm commitment by Dow to transform its product mix. It even predated Oreffice's rise to the position of chief executive.

The Dow president has become a visible and controversial figure in Washington by virtue of his combative personality and his preference for debating his adversaries directly—and in public. But it is safe to assume that even if Oreffice had a more reserved demeanor, or more temperate opinions, he could not have escaped completely the wrath of the environmental movement or the attention of a suspicious press. The reason goes to the essence of the industry to which he has devoted his career. Chemical production is an inherently hazardous undertaking and is thus subjected to a much greater degree of federal intervention and public scrutiny than most other industries. No hazard associated with chemical production is potentially more deadly, or politically more explosive, than cancer. At the turn of the century, cancer was the tenth leading cause of death in the United States. It now ranks second only to heart disease. An estimated 440,000 Americans died of cancer in 1983—1,205 people every day, about one every seventy-two seconds. Most public health experts agree that 80 to 90 percent of all cancer is "environmental" in origin and thus largely preventable. Where they disagree—and what is at the root of the battles over health and safety regulation—is on the relative responsibility of such "environmental" factors as cigarette smoking, diet, sunlight, natural radiation, workplace carcinogens, factory emissions, and food additives.

We began our discussion of cancer with Oreffice by reading a passage from *The Politics of Cancer*, a book by Dr. Samuel Epstein of the University of Illinois Medical Center in Chicago. Epstein is a prominent corporate critic on the cancer issue. He argues that incidence rates of certain forms of cancer are rising even after the figures are adjusted to reflect longer life spans and that exposure to workplace and environmental carcinogens is a key factor in the increase.

"Oh God . . ." Oreffice moaned as we mentioned Epstein's name. He interrupted as we began to read the passage. "Excuse me, let me stop you right there," he protested. "That statement is *false.* Age-adjusted cancer has gone down in this country consistently with the exception of lung cancer. Go ahead."

When we completed the Epstein statement, Oreffice offered his perspective on cancer in America. "Plainly false. Mr. Epstein has made a profession out of this. He writes books like *The Politics of Cancer.* The statistics show absolutely the opposite. Furthermore, experts agree [cancer is] environmentally caused, but most of it is from food and life-style. That's part of my problem. We seem to concentrate on where 5 or 10 percent [of cancer] comes from and forget about a lot of other things."

Oreffice's cause célèbre on the cancer question is cigarette smoking—a justified concern, but one that has been used by the chemical industry to deflect attention from the threat posed by workplace carcinogens. The Dow president returned to smoking again and again during our discussion. When asked to project to the year 2000 and discuss the three most compelling threats to the environment, a serious question meant to gauge his ecological sensitivity, Oreffice answered glibly: "Cigarettes number one, number two, number three," he said. "Now, what environmental problems?" In response to a question about the tens of thousands of past and future cancer deaths attributed to asbestos exposure, he quickly changed the subject.

"You know, the numbers on asbestos you have mentioned, I assume them to be true . . ." he said. "We also found that asbestos and smoking together make a tremendous difference. And when one thinks of smoking —if we want to regulate something, why aren't we doing anything about the thing that is killing more Americans than anything else? . . . Government regulators have been completely unwilling to tackle [smoking] *because they smoke.*"

Of course, federal officials have not been "completely unwilling to tackle" smoking. Twenty years have passed since the landmark surgeon general's report on the hazards of smoking. Per capita cigarette consumption has declined every year since 1974. If there has been a persistent obstacle to more vigorous federal action on cigarettes, it is to be found in the Washington offices of the Tobacco Institute, the industry's powerful lobby. The Tobacco Institute, as part of its defense of cigarettes, argues that regulators pay inadequate attention to the cancer-causing potential of workplace chemicals.

Oreffice was asked about the role of this politically powerful industry and whether it was misrepresenting or underrepresenting the hazards of its product. He chose again to blame the regulators. "Sure, the tobacco [industry] has influence," he declared. "But when I had the head of a large regulatory agency sit there for two hours during a lunch and smoke about ten cigarettes in my nose and tell me about the terrible smoke here and this troubling thing there, I just couldn't swallow it. . . . I think we should stop being such hypocrites. We tackle little problems that maybe don't even exist, where just because some rat had a little result of a carcinogen, we set up a whole [regulatory] apparatus. Yet when there is something that we *know* is harming a lot of people, we let it go on unabated. That's really hypocritical."

It is with this perspective on cancer and regulation that Oreffice set out in 1975 to "go after" the regulatory establishment. "Somebody had to say something," he explained. "It might as well have been me." The opening round in the crusade was a study entitled "The Impact of Government Regulation." Oreffice commissioned the report shortly after assuming control of Dow USA. He presented his findings to Congress three years later, when he testified alongside Murray Weidenbaum, the high priest of regulatory "cost-benefit analysis." Dow's expenditures to meet regulations had risen from $87 million in 1975 to $268 million by 1977, the report claimed. Of these costs, $50 million in 1975 and $115 million in 1977 were deemed "excessive" by company officials. The Dow study made no effort to quantify the value to the corporation of government handouts—tax preferences, price controls on Dow raw materials, export subsidies—or the numbers of lives saved as a result of workplace and pollution regulation.

Oreffice was asked to explain why his study, and nearly all similar corporate-sponsored reports, fail to calculate the *benefits* of regulation— lower medical bills as a result of fewer illnesses, higher productivity as result of a healthier workforce, cleaner air and water—with the same precision they calculate its cost. He responded by begging the question. "Our study was only designed to do one thing: to determine the cost of overregulation. . . . We are not, and never have been, against basic government regulation," he insisted. "What I call overregulation is a regulation that really does not provide much benefit but costs a lot of money. I'm sure there have been a lot of benefits out of regulation."

Armed with his home-grown facts and figures, Oreffice embarked on a speaking tour of sorts that took him across the country to preach his gospel. Before the Commonwealth Club of California, he challenged the "growing dictatorship of the regulators." At the Economic Club of Detroit, he likened the U.S. government to a "banana republic." If the United States differs from a banana republic, he continued, it is only because "EPA wouldn't let us produce the pesticides necessary to grow bananas successfully." In Indianapolis, during a speech to the state chamber of commerce, Oreffice chastised a government that "turns populist and screams that the fat cats are guilty, that they pay no taxes, that their companies make obscene profits, and that the 'little' people are being trod upon." And in Arizona, he labeled leaders of the Environmental Defense Fund and Friends of the Earth, two leading environmental organizations, "professional merchants of doom" who practice "a deadly profession."

Paul Oreffice was by no means the only business voice raised in the late seventies in opposition to the regulatory advances of earlier years. Corporate executives streamed to Washington to dismantle a regulatory apparatus that they blamed for every difficulty, from stagnating productivity to high interest rates. Among the most ambitious assaults on regulation was waged by the Business Roundtable, a Washington lobbying force composed exclusively of chief executives from the most powerful corporations in the United States. One of the architects of the Roundtable was former Du Pont chairman Irving Shapiro, and the organization reflected his approach to politics: a distaste for public controversy and a preference for operating quietly on Capitol Hill, a bipartisan attitude that did not exclude cooperation with probusiness Democrats, and a willingness to compromise on thorny legislative issues.

The Roundtable style stood in distinct contrast to the Oreffice approach, which was often rhetorically shrill and intensely partisan. In the 1980 and 1982 congressional campaigns, for example, Dow's political-action committees contributed a total of $485,000 to congressional candidates. Eighty-six percent of the funds went to Republicans. But the Oreffice campaign was also conducted in the open—with opportunity for rebuttal by those with whom he disagreed. Of all the battles before Congress and the federal agencies that Oreffice and his company waged, none generated as much controversy, or such lasting public fallout, as the struggle over creation of a "Superfund" to clean up and monitor hazardous waste sites.

On December 11, 1980, President Carter signed the Comprehensive Environmental Response, Compensation and Liability Act after its passage by a lame-duck Congress and his thrashing at the polls by Ronald

Reagan. That this bill became law represented a stinging rebuke for the Chemical Manufacturers Association (CMA), the industry's powerful Washington lobbying arm. More to the point, it was a defeat for Paul Oreffice, one of a group of CMA directors who pushed the association to adopt a stance of hard-line opposition to the bill, a stance that backfired in no uncertain terms. Superfund, of course, was designed in response to the unsafe storage and disposal of hazardous chemicals, a problem that by 1980 had come to be symbolized by the tragedy at Love Canal and the spectacular explosion and fire at the Chemical Control Corporation in Elizabeth, New Jersey. The final bill created a $1.6 billion clean-up fund, financed in large part (87.5 percent) by industry, through excise taxes on forty-two specific chemicals and petroleum products.

Congress passed the legislation after three years of maneuvering. On the surface, the bill represented a struggle between the chemical industry and Superfund sponsors over several technical considerations: the size of the fund, how it would be financed, the legal liability of chemical companies. But the real battle was within the industry itself, and it centered on one question: how to respond to a political climate that made some form of government action on hazardous wastes inevitable.

Oreffice, by most press accounts, led the CMA faction that counseled all-out opposition to any proposal other than a $600 million fund, which was dismissed by most members of Congress as inadequate. When a Senate committee approved a $4.1 billion Superfund proposal, it seemed that the time had arrived for negotiation and compromise, behavior Oreffice and a majority of the CMA executive committee were unwilling to engage in. On November 19, 1980, however, Du Pont chairman Shapiro broke ranks with his colleagues and told the *New York Times* he could support a $1.2 billion Superfund passed earlier by the House of Representatives. Shapiro's position served as the basis of negotiations between the House and Senate (which was considering a $2.7 billion fund) that eventually produced a compromise at $1.6 billion.

Final passage of Superfund touched off a torrent of criticism of the CMA and its anticompromise posture. *Chemical and Engineering News* called the episode "a gross miscalculation by some segments of the chemical industry . . . a bitter lesson in how not to lobby." *National Journal*, the respected weekly on government affairs, argued that the bill "reflects a major miscalculation by the [CMA], which had fought for two years to prevent just such a law."

To this day, Paul Oreffice remains defiant about the events of late 1980—and the course charted by Irving Shapiro. "I think the chemical industry was had on Superfund, and it was had for one reason," he told us. "Superfund [tax] payments are based not on what you waste but on how much raw material you take in. And he [Shapiro] was the architect of that. I think it was awful for the chemical industry. . . . That was a very fundamental difference." The Dow president also discussed broader disagreements with the retired Du Pont chairman. "I think in the industry we had fundamental differences," Oreffice said. "In part maybe he looked at things from a lawyer's standpoint, which is what he is."— Shapiro spent more than seven years in the Justice Department before he joined Du Pont in 1951—"I looked at them from the standpoint of someone who grew up in the industry."

At bottom, the disagreement between Oreffice and Shapiro lies in their varying personal approaches to politics, rather than in any differential commitment to environmental protection. In fact, on the specific issue of hazardous waste, Dow's performance with respect to sound disposal continues to surpass that of Du Pont. Where Oreffice was a fighter, Shapiro was a compromiser. Where Oreffice was an ideologue, Shapiro was a pragmatist who bowed to political realities and cut the best deal he could for his company. We interviewed Irving Shapiro several months before our conversation with Oreffice. What emerges from the discussions with the two corporate heads, and from speeches they have delivered over the years, are two very distinct perspectives on the proper role of business in society. The following observations, culled from speeches or, where noted, personal interviews, highlight the distinct approaches of these industry titans:

- *On government:*
  Shapiro: The only practical course [for businessmen] is to regard as essentially permanent the system that has evolved. Call it what you will—"quasi-public," "half-free enterprise," "the mixed economy." By any name, it is a system in which heavy government involvement will remain a fact of life for business.
  Oreffice: Early Americans seemed to know that if their economic freedom was lost, their political freedom would be next. But have succeeding generations learned? The so-called liberals don't seem to have. It's interesting that those who talk the most of individual freedoms are doing the most to stifle these freedoms by pushing the government into our daily [business] activities. They don't deserve the name "liberals," they should be called "socialists," which is what they are.
- *On President Carter:*
  Shapiro: A lot of businessmen learned to work with the Carter administration. Some became very good friends of the president. They came to accept the premise that every president

of the United States has to have the support of key people in the country. I think many of them have learned to separate their personal partisan views from their role as CEO of a corporation. [Personal interview, July 27, 1983]

Oreffice: I think the period of Mr. Carter's [presidency] internationally was the worst period this country has gone through. We became whipping boys that anybody could beat at. . . . Irv Shapiro was really Carter's representative in the business community. I just think Mr. Carter was a very weak man, who wanted to do everything himself. If you want somebody who absolutely didn't know how to delegate, he is the prime example. [Personal interview, October 26, 1983]

• *On political-action committees:*

Shapiro: Common experience tells you that when there's a lot of money being passed around [in politics], bad things happen. You can't demonstrate a cause-effect relationship in the sense that anybody is being directly bought. But common sense tells you that if a man is going to run for office, and he knows he is going to solicit a lot of business PACs, he is going to want to have a platform, a program, that is appealing to those business PACs. I feel very strongly that this is a counterproductive development, that it is polluting the system. . . . The PAC program is about the least desirable thing that has happened in this country in my adulthood. It is an invidious thing, it's corrupting, it does pollute the system. [Personal interview, July 27, 1983]

Oreffice: Congressmen have a very tough time voting against programs which make them seem to be against the poor, or against education, or against the aged. But . . . we must not relax our efforts to get Congress to take a more responsible attitude. One powerful force which has emerged in the last few years is the Political Action Committee. If you don't have one in your company, I encourage you to start one. . . . I truly believe PACs have allowed many Americans, including our employees, to participate in the political process. This should be encouraged at every step of the way.

For Paul Oreffice, the time-consuming activity of crusading against regulation in Washington came to a close on January 20, 1981, when Ronald Reagan was inaugurated as the fortieth president of the United States. Reagan came to Washington with a pledge to "get government off the backs of business." When implemented, that pledge revolutionized the way business was conducted at OSHA, EPA, and the other regulatory agencies. The Reagan administration ushered in an era of regulatory freezes, cost-benefit analyses that accommodate the imperatives of industry, and programs of "cooperation" between federal agencies and regulated industries that meant in practice sharply reduced enforcement and minimal sanctions against violators.

Paul Oreffice is exuberant about Ronald Reagan. He called his 1980 election "a second Declaration of Independence for free enterprise," and "the biggest change in America in forty-eight years." In March 1981, as the president's tax and spending proposals were winding their way through Congress, Oreffice and three other Dow executives signed a letter to employees urging them to write their representatives in support of the Reagan package. Several months later, Oreffice was one of six corporate chief executives who met with Treasury secretary Donald Regan to reaffirm their support of administration economic policies.

Actually, however, Ronald Reagan was not Paul Oreffice's first choice to be president of the United States. That distinction went to former Texas governor John Connally, whose quixotic campaign for the Republican nomination raised millions of dollars, collected endorsements from some of the most powerful executives in America—and won exactly one delegate to the Detroit convention. Many business leaders embraced Connally because of his unwavering commitment to the corporate agenda for tax, defense, and regulatory policies. But their support was not nearly as deep as it was wide. Once the Texan's presidential bid showed signs of faltering, corporate executives abandoned him en masse to join the steamroller campaign of the man who would eventually enter the White House.

Not so Paul Oreffice. His endorsement of Connally represented the fulfillment of a promise made nearly a decade earlier, when the presidential candidate was Treasury secretary under Richard Nixon. "I made up my mind [about Connally] eight years ago," Oreffice told an interviewer in 1979. "I would have supported him as a Democrat or Republican." Not only did Oreffice commit his own money to the Connally campaign, but he organized a fundraiser in Midland that the Texan attended and stumped for him in Florida—a key primary state where Oreffice lived for three years as head of Dow Latin America.

Oreffice's close ties to Connally grew out of discussions the two men had had in the summer of 1971, just months before President Nixon unveiled his New Economic Policy and introduced profound changes in the global system of trade and finance. "I had made some comments to the *New York Times* about the international monetary system and some of the things we needed to do," Oreffice explained. Connally read the article, and when he saw Carl Gerstacker at a party, invited him and Oreffice to Washington for a meeting. "I came away with great admiration for the man," Oreffice said. "He was incredibly adept at getting every bit of knowledge I had of the international scene. One of the things I told Connally was that one of the problems with the U.S. balance of trade is that we keep paying for the defense of Europe. In fact, I said, if I were in the U.S. government, I'd give them hell. I still have a note Connally wrote back to me. He said, 'I agree with everything you said [about Europe], except I wouldn't give them anything.' "

This was Oreffice's first experience as a Washington insider. It was a status he no doubt hoped to enjoy under a President Connally. Though that was not to be, the Dow chief executive had reason enough to be cheered by the verdict delivered at the polls in November 1980. Even before President Reagan took the oath of office, Oreffice was enjoying the new realities in Washington. On January 9, 1981, the Dow president met privately with soon-to-be White House personnel czar E. Pendleton James to discuss candidates to head the Environmental Protection Agency. Several days later, the *Washington Post* reported that Oreffice had "spoken against" the appointment of Gordon Wood, a lobbyist for Olin Corporation who adopted a moderate position in the Superfund battle which ended just a month before the meeting.

Oreffice denied to us that he opposed the lobbyist's appointment at his session with James. "I had never even *heard* of Gordon Wood," he said. But the attention generated by the James meeting should have alerted Oreffice to a problem that has plagued Dow throughout the Age of Reagan. As Washington pursues the very policies Oreffice has advocated for years, his company finds itself on the defensive in Congress, in the press, and before the courts. The price of Dow's newfound intimacy with regulatory officials has been a public-relations nightmare of monumental proportions.

Nothing has caused Paul Oreffice more anger or frustration than the furor over Dow's discharges of dioxin into Midland's Tittabawassee River. For weeks after Congressman James Scheuer went public with his claim that Dow had been allowed to edit an EPA report on dioxin contamination, the company was portrayed in the press as a reckless polluter of its own backyard that could flex its political muscle to sidetrack regulatory initiatives. During a March 23, 1983, congressional hearing, for example, Scheuer said of Dow's review of the report, "It was a sorry, low point in the history of the regulatory process for this interference, this invasion, by censorship, by deletion . . . to have taken place." Oreffice, in an April 4 letter to shareholders, responded to Scheuer and other critics: "For those who have heard allegations that Dow has been 'cozy' with the EPA,

I say flatly those allegations are not true. Dow applied no 'pressure' at EPA, and I know of *no* improprieties in our relationship."

On the specific question of the dioxin report, Oreffice may have a point. Documents obtained under the Freedom of Information Act make clear that pressure for the report's premature release to Dow came not from company officials but from John Hernandez, who eventually replaced Burford as EPA administrator on an acting basis and then himself resigned. Throughout much of 1981 (while the report was being prepared), Hernandez waged something of a one-man crusade against the study. Valdas Adamkus, administrator of the EPA regional office that prepared the report, told investigators that Hernandez had called it "trash" and had "questioned [the author's] professional and technical" competence. "Whenever there was a disagreement on a key issue," Adamkus continued, "the comment of [an EPA task force that reviewed the report] was 'John won't accept it,' 'John doesn't want to see it,' or 'John won't release it.'" Hernandez himself told EPA investigators that he released the report to Dow after he saw Charles Sercu, one of the company's Washington lobbyists, "in a hallway at EPA."

The real point in all of this is that Dow did not *need* to exert pressure at EPA. The agency's highest-ranking officials were so eager to do the company's bidding—even when it brought them into conflict with long-time EPA employees—that Oreffice and his lobbyists could assume that Dow's business before the agency would go the company's way.

Especially instructive as a lesson in the nature of Dow's dealings with its Washington regulators was the personal relationship between Paul Oreffice and EPA administrator Burford. Oreffice did not know Anne Burford prior to her appointment to head EPA; he told us he was surprised by her nomination and did not meet her personally "until a year after she was named administrator." That might explain why May 1982 marks the beginning of a series of letters, memos, and telegrams between Burford and Oreffice that captures nicely the spirit of "regulatory cooperation" fashioned under Ronald Reagan. (We obtained the correspondence under the Freedom of Information Act.)

"It was a pleasure to meet you at the luncheon last Friday," Burford wrote in May 18, 1982. "This is a channel of communication that I hope will be used frequently. We share many issues of concern."

That shared concern became evident a few months later, when Oreffice penned an article for *Chemical Week* defending Burford's performance and criticizing the magazine's coverage of EPA affairs. Oreffice's article prompted an editorial reply the following week, and that reply prompted a note from Burford to Oreffice. "After reviewing *Chemical Week*'s 'Editor's Memo' of July 14, there indeed are days when one cannot help but think one step forward equals two steps back," she wrote. "Much appreciation for your ongoing support. Too bad Jack Campbell [managing editor of *Chemical Week*] buys ink by the barrel."

Unfortunately for Burford, she would never make good on a promise in her final note to the Dow chief executive. "It was great seeing you again, and I am so pleased to have had the opportunity to meet your lovely wife," she wrote on February 8, 1983. "Please accept my apology for having to cut our visit short, but I promise to make it up next time we get together, when lunch will be my treat." Almost a month later to the day, Burford resigned her position at EPA.

·　·　·

The career and personality of Paul Oreffice present a temptation to separate the man from the manager. As a person, he possesses some attractive characteristics—he is comparatively open to interviews, to questions from audiences, to debates. Despite his position as chief executive of a major corporation embroiled in ongoing controversies, he chooses not to hide behind company spokesmen and other bureaucratic shields. Unlike Roger Smith's modus operandi of being cloistered and sheltered, Oreffice is up front. He is what he appears to be—a devoted family man; athletic; and without personal addictions to alcohol, tobacco, or drugs. One on one he does not like to throw his weight around against individuals less powerful than he or under his control. For example, he continues to support and implement Dow's little-publicized no-layoff policy, a policy whose financial burdens are especially taxing in an age of many industrial layoffs. An exile from his native land, he bears the imprint of an immigrant's patriotism toward the country that gave his family another chance.

But as the ruler of what he seems to view as the sovereign state of Dow, situational ethics tend to reshape the Oreffice personality. He loves his country, but he rarely misses an opportunity to excorciate that part of the government whose purpose is to protect vulnerable and powerless citizens from the ravages of corporate pollution. His views on the nonhazards of chemicals would have been outdated twenty years ago, but he persists in pushing them with fervor. To be so insulated intellectually from the best available scientific and ecological evidence is either to be surrounded by sycophants or to have removed the in-box years ago. Oreffice is an open personality with a closed mind comparable to the executives of tobacco companies who continue to question the link between smoking and cancer or heart disease—a comparison the Dow leader would no doubt find abhorrent. Perhaps the helmsman of a global chemical company grappling with the unknown effects and known dangers of hundreds of complex chemicals needs such a rigid ideology in order to concentrate on his daily imperatives of expanding sales and increasing profits.

When pressed in personal conversations, however, the Dow president relents, as if to expose more of Oreffice the man. Yes, he avers, the United States has ignored the compelling needs of the suffering masses of South America; yes, good has and can come from government regulation. Oreffice supports gun control, legislated bans on smoking in public places, and mandatory seat belt laws. But it takes some very sensitive mining by the questioner to elicit even these modest droplets of recognition.

One continues to wonder whether his postures are truly fixed positions or, in part, bargaining chips for the settlement of specific issues on attractive terms. His all-out support for John Connally in 1980—the co-architect with Richard Nixon in the early seventies of wage-price controls, a form of government intervention that the free-market Oreffice must abhor—shows that the Dow president is not an unforgiving man. We could not determine if his hard line on health and safety controls on the use and disposal of chemicals would change if he exposed himself through field trips to various contaminated communities and their residents: Love Canal; Times Beach; Nitro, West Virginia; or Bhopal, India. In this respect, Oreffice insulates himself. We asked the Dow president whether he planned to mend fences with Vietnam veterans after the Agent Orange settlement by appearing at conventions of veterans' organizations or by seeking other forms of human reconciliation. He observed that Dow received more support from veterans during the Agent Orange affair than it did criticism. We found this response implausible.

To be sure, the suave, agreeable tongue of an Irving Shapiro does not assure exceptional corporate performance. By comparison, Dow is ahead of Du Pont in its handling of chemical waste and in its institutional commitment to recycling and reduced waste generation. Much of the credit for this leadership position in environmental technology must go to Carl Gerstacker, the retired Dow chairman who in the early seventies infuriated and puzzled his industry colleagues by insisting that Dow could profit by recycling chemical waste. It is clear that Oreffice has benefited from Gerstacker's foresight and legacy. But it is not apparent how much, if at all, the current president is building on that foundation. He is not presiding over the deterioration of this corporate imperative, but he seems astonishingly reluctant or uninterested in blazing new environmental trails.

Paul Oreffice, under Dow's rules, must step down as chief executive when he turns sixty. He will then become chairman of the board and likely remain an influential force in the company's operation and a visible public spokesman. Because of its recent acquisitions, Dow will come increasingly into direct contact with consumers through a range of pharmaceutical and chemical products. The hard-edge style of the company's chief management will create still more controversy and continued public backlash unless it is changed, a prospect Dow may have begun to recognize. Since the fury over dioxin reached its height in the spring of 1983, Dow has slowly begun to smooth over some of its roughest corporate edges. The company signed a consent decree with EPA in April 1984 to settle a long dispute with the agency over authority to sample water and obtain access to other environmental data at the company's Midland complex. Dow hired Hill & Knowlton, the public relations firm, to advise it on its image problem. It published, in November 1984, the first of what will become regular reports on Dow's "public interest" activities. The glossy brochure has all the requisite images of corporate responsibility: smiling children, breakdowns of charitable contributions, pronouncements about the paramount importance of safety in the corporate hierarchy of values. But all of these departures are first and foremost matters of style rather than substance. The Oreffice-reinforced ethos of suspicion of regulators and of opposition to outside intervention will not be so easily refined. And if Dow wears the fashionable glove of public relations, might the fingernails become less clean? In a sense, the confrontational style of Oreffice may be good for corporate behavior. When the boss is ideologically hard-line and highly visible, there may be an incentive for his company to exceed industry norms in terms of environmental performance.

Oreffice's postretirement ambitions are rather modest. They embrace living in Arizona and playing tennis, lecturing to students, and serving on the boards of a few corporations. He told us he would consider writing his memoirs, although it does not seem he has given the idea much serious thought. Under the surface, however, there is a post-Dow potential for Oreffice that invites realization. One who knows so much about government and corporations around the world—for example, Oreffice can demonstrate with case studies the counterproductive effects of overseas bribery—may decide there is an imperative of sorts to share that knowledge with a broader public. Just as Nixon reached out to China, this rigid ideologue can speak very credibly about corporate self-discipline and innovation as a pathway to social responsibility. We left our conversations with Dow's doyen not a little uncertain of the measure of the man once he moves onto a new playing field. A prideful company man, Oreffice has inevitably had to leave a portion of his self on the shelf. Whether he will permit another calling to beckon that self toward new directions and initiatives depends on how many hours of Arizona sun and tennis he can absorb before rebelling against the passivity of corporate retirement.

FELIX ROHATYN

The Interstitial Man

Thirty-two floors above Rockefeller Plaza, in the offices of Lazard Frères & Company, Felix Rohatyn is seated at the head of a small conference table. An atmosphere of reserve dominates his surroundings. The telephones seem to ring more quietly than most, secretaries speak in hushed tones, and a visitor soon loses sight of the frenzied Manhattan traffic from which he has emerged or the rush of high-stakes transactions that occupy the days of those who labor here. The environment is well suited to the personality of Lazard's most illustrious partner. Felix Rohatyn is a soft-spoken man, polite without being warm, who doodles with geometric precision on an unlined white pad through hours of conversation about politics, economic policy, and the wave of billion-dollar mergers that has been sweeping corporate America since the late 1970s. He is especially well qualified to address this last subject. As a partner since 1960 in one of Wall Street's most prominent—and profitable—investment banks, Rohatyn has engineered some of the most expensive corporate takeovers in history.

This track record comes to life when a secretary interrupts with word of a telephone call. "You will have to excuse me for a minute or two. I've got this merger," Rohatyn says as he walks from the table to an adjoining private office. "Would you like something to read, the *Wall Street Journal?*" The front page of the January 1984 newspaper carries details of the transaction that demands Rohatyn's attention. Texaco, the nation's third largest oil company, has made a $10 billion offer for Getty Oil, whose management has been crippled by an ongoing feud among the heirs to the fortune of tycoon J. Paul Getty. Lazard Frères represents neither Texaco nor Getty, but Pennzoil Company, which days before reached an agreement with Gordon Getty, who controlled 40.2 percent of the company's 80 million shares, and the Getty board, to take the petroleum giant private in a buyout worth $5.4 billion.

When Texaco then stepped forward with a more lucrative offer, Gordon Getty and the company's directors simply ignored their tentative deal with Pennzoil and approved the $10 billion merger. The agreement produced headlines, lawsuits (Pennzoil, the jilted suitor, filed for punitive and compensatory damages of $14 billion; in November 1985 a Texas jury awarded Pennzoil $10.53 billion in damages, the largest civil award in U.S. history), and predictions—quite accurate, as it turns out—that it would set the stage for even more massive combinations in the oil industry. It also generated enormous fees, totaling some $50 million, for the five investment banks that counseled and coaxed the gladiators during the brief period in which the struggle unfolded.

"I think a lot of this has become show business," Rohatyn despaired when asked about the proliferation of such corporate "megadeals"—many of them hostile, many of them involving bidding wars between competing suitors for a target company. As for the remuneration members of his profession garner, Rohatyn said simply, "The fees are crazy. They are much too big. There is no conceivable reason why an [investment] bank should make $10 million on a merger."

For all of the boardroom intrigue and avarice that is routine in the world of investment banking, Felix Rohatyn has become known as widely for his exploits beyond Wall Street as for the merger-making pursuits to which he devotes most of his time. He is a transatlantic celebrity whose intimate dinner parties and annual Easter egg hunt, attended by the likes of Oscar de la Renta and William Paley, are chronicled with suitable reverence in the *New York Times* and elsewhere. He is a counselor to senators, governors, and leaders of foreign countries. Rohatyn has traveled to Paris for a number of private meetings with French president François Mitterrand and has entertained the Socialist leader in his Park Avenue duplex. He has journeyed to South Africa as a guest of gold and diamond baron Harry Oppenheimer. He also serves with Oppenheimer (who retired in 1982 as chairman of mighty Anglo American Corporation) as a director of Minerals and Resources Corporation (Minorco). This obscure, Bahamas-based firm, with assets of close to $2 billion, functions as a financial conduit for Anglo's penetration of North America.

Rohatyn has also helped to conclude important and controversial deals outside the conventional parameters of investment banking. Lazard Frères brokered a complex wage-concession and financial-restructuring package that gave birth to Weirton Steel in September 1983. With eight thousand employees and annual revenues of more than $1 billion, Weirton is the largest worker-owned corporation in the United States. Months later, the investment bank played a role in labor negotiations at Eastern Airlines that produced an unprecedented agreement in which unionized employees exchanged wage and productivity concessions worth $370 million for 25 percent ownership of the corporation and extensive representation on the board of directors. Lazard has since advised the United Steelworkers of America in confrontations with U.S. Steel and Wheeling-Pittsburgh Steel, and unions representing employees of TWA, who teamed up with investor Carl Icahn to thwart a takeover bid for the airline by Frank Lorenzo, whose antiunion history has made him a bête noire to organized labor.

Felix Rohatyn lives, works, and plays in a circle of powerful friends and unlimited praise. "Felix is enveloping the world," said Raymond Troubh, a former partner at Lazard Frères who worked alongside Rohatyn on many of his most publicized mergers of the late 1960s and early 1970s. "He is sort of the Henry Kissinger of the financial arena. He is stepping into politics as Kissinger is stepping into finance. . . . But I don't think his [public role] was a calculated decision. He never said, 'I'm going to be prominent on the public scene.' He wanted to be a great investment banker. That brought him into the eyes of the kingmakers in different arenas, in New York and Washington, and from then on his ability pushed him. . . . I equate him with Kissinger, who I think is an outstanding example of a combination of brilliance, power, and will to win. I put Felix in the same basket, exactly the same basket."

Bernard Vernier-Palliez, French ambassador to the United States from January 1982 to November 1984, spoke at length about Rohatyn. "There are very few men in the world who really are competent people, whose advice is valuable, who have influence even if they don't have direct responsibility for this or that policy," he told us. "Felix is obviously one of those people." Is there a contemporary figure whose style of influence resembles Rohatyn's? "On matters of foreign policy in this country, I would [say] Henry Kissinger."

The Kissinger-Rohatyn comparison was invoked with unnerving frequency by other friends and colleagues of the investment banker. We asked Rohatyn why. "Oh, because we are foreign-born," he said, somewhat put off by the question. "Because we are negotiators. Also, we are friends. But Henry has wielded levers of power that I haven't come close to." Rohatyn is more comfortable with comparisons with figures out of contemporary European history. In a 1982 commencement address at his alma mater, Vermont-based Middlebury College, Rohatyn summoned the memory of Jean Monnet, the French financier whose years of political activism figured decisively in the birth of the European Common Market. "Monnet played the roles of negotiator, agitator, propagandist, tactician, and strategist, which are needed to effect fundamental political change in a democratic society," Rohatyn told the graduates. An apt description of the role of the commencement speaker? "Sure, absolutely," he replied. "It is the only role I can play. It is the only role a private citizen can play as long as you have some kind of platform. That's why Monnet was always my role model. He was never a member of a government. He never held a cabinet position. He never ran for office." Yet he transformed the structures and politics of postwar Europe.

Felix Rohatyn's political star began to ascend in 1975 when New York City, poised between the burden of servicing $11 billion of short-term and long-term debt and the reluctance of major banks to extend further credit, teetered on the brink of bankruptcy. The investment banker and an elite corps of businessmen assembled by Gov. Hugh Carey designed a response to the unfolding crisis. Their prescription was based on a substantial redirection of political power away from elected leaders in the city to two new institutions: the Municipal Assistance Corporation (MAC) and the Emergency Financial Control Board (EFCB). Rohatyn, who soon became chairman of MAC, emerged as the most powerful figure in the effort to "save" New York. This involved a series of intricate compromises and concessions—brokered by the Lazard partner—between municipal labor unions, wealthy commercial bankers, and state and federal officials, and the refinancing by MAC of billions of dollars of New York City debt.

Rohatyn's role as chairman of MAC was a watershed in his career. It was one of the few times he has exercised direct authority outside the rarefied arena of high finance. It introduced him to the worlds of politics and unions. The years of pressure and triumph served as a platform for celebrity status. They also shaped a vision of politics—and an approach to political power—that has created a base from which the investment banker aspires to new levels of influence and impact. There is a roving dimension to Rohatyn's presence on the public scene. He has written, spoken, and testified on a range of public issues. And he has made it plain that he is available to participate in their resolution. Two particular areas stand out. Rohatyn has warned about the threat to global financial stability posed by the massive foreign debts of the developing world. And he has championed proposals to reverse the ongoing collapse of the U.S. industrial base through reincarnation of the Depression-era Reconstruction Finance Corporation (RFC). The RFC would direct financial assistance, perhaps as much as $50 billion, to distressed industries and companies and demand concessions from management and labor in return.

In essence, the story of Felix Rohatyn is the story of the rise of a master of the ways of Wall Street and of his subsequent efforts to transplant skills and expertise perfected in the negotiation of billion-dollar mergers to an agenda of public issues that continue to defy solution.

We asked Rohatyn whether his prowess as a negotiator could be applied to arms control or world trouble spots such as Central America and the Middle East. He demurred at the suggestion. But he went on to discuss scenarios in which he *could* play a role. "I think that I could only get the benefit of the doubt [as a negotiator] in economic or financial situations," he explained. "To get into something like arms control— there's a whole body of institutional memory. I mean, Paul Nitze has been doing this all his life. The people know each other. There's a whole vocabulary. I came into the New York City thing without knowing any- thing. But I knew finance. I knew numbers. I knew techniques. The fact that I didn't know municipal finance or politics helped me in a way because it made me more the ultimate technician.

"Where the benefit of the doubt came in" during the New York crisis "was on know-how," he continued. "If I spoke, if I said, 'We're going to restructure this,' people said well, he must know what he's talking about. I couldn't do that in the nuclear weapons field. I could, someday, if there is something to do, redo the Third World debt. Or do some kind of National Development Bank. Or do another Bretton Woods"—a refer- ence to the international conference that produced the postwar global monetary system—"things of that kind, sure, I could do those."

Eugene Keilin, a Lazard partner who joined the firm in 1979 after more than two years as executive director of MAC, offered an assessment of Rohatyn's political philosophy. "I think Felix sees a pattern in a lot of these situations," he told us. "If you have a problem that is solvable—and not all problems are solvable—the approach you take is to get all the parties together, preferably in the same room, and get them to agree on the facts. Get them to agree that there is a problem. Then you suggest, or volunteer, the contribution each party might make to arrive at a solution. That is the art of it. Felix is not an ideologue. He has principles, and he thinks there are principles worth dying for. But interests are not worth dying for."

This is, of course, precisely the formula Rohatyn pursued as chairman of MAC—and the formula he has applied for two decades as a Wall Street deal maker. As MIT economist Robert Solow has written, "A typical Rohatyn solution usually calls for institutionalized wheeling and dealing on behalf of society at large, to be performed by small groups of people very much like Mr. Rohatyn himself." Others are less skeptical. "Felix is badly misunderstood by the progressive community," said an aide to a U.S. senator with whom Rohatyn has worked closely. "He would be very comfortable in Mitterrand's government. He is an elitist, but he is also a Social Democrat. . . . We have confused Felix's aloofness and elitism and raised it into an ideological attack. He is a decent, generous guy who does believe that people like he and Mitterrand ought to run their countries like Social Democrats."

The rise of Felix Rohatyn is also the story of the maximization of limited political resources through a careful cultivation of friendships in the political world; the formation of alliances with unlikely constituencies, such as organized labor; and the maintenance of close ties with those who shape public opinion and perceptions. Rohatyn has learned how to transform celebrity and fame into power and influence.

"Felix is constantly drawing people to him and being drawn to others," said Theodore Kheel, the New York attorney and labor mediator. "He is very careful about his relationships. He thoroughly enjoys being associated with people of prominence. Felix was a great buddy of Mike O'Neill when he was editor of the *Daily News*. He is friendly with many of the people at the *New York Times*. It is all part and parcel of a very astute program on his part to achieve what he wants to achieve. And he has been very successful at it."

Unlike the chief executives of the giant corporations he serves as an advisor, Rohatyn does not control billions of dollars of assets or employ tens of thousands of workers, a material base that translates directly into economic power and political leverage. His influence is of an invitational character. Rohatyn must be called into a situation and be granted authority by the principals to design and broker long-term accommodations. The role of indispensible intermediary requires familiarity with and trust by the principals, as well as a reputation for unrivaled expertise.

"My power in the public arena arises by invitation," Rohatyn told us. "When [in late 1983] we created an extra billion dollars for the city of New York,"—by refinancing outstanding MAC bonds—"and there came a time when we had to negotiate with the mayor and the governor on how to dispose of that money, at that point I had a certain amount of power because it was *our* billion dollars. When Governor Cuomo asked me to co-chair a committee to make recommendations on the state income tax, I had influence by invitation of the governor. . . . Every four years, when people think there might be a Democratic president and I might be in a Democratic administration, people say, Ah." Rohatyn laughed softly. "That isn't power. That's potential power, which creates a little ripple. And when it turns out not to be, then it's over. I think that's about the way it works."

The nature of Rohatyn's power means that his influence in corporate America—as in Washington or Paris—is of an unusually personal character. It grows out of his role as a broker for the powerful and out of the sheer volume of friendships and acquaintances this role has generated in four of the power centers in American society: big business, organized labor, the political establishment, and the press. It is also inherently fragile. Rohatyn's prowess as a mediator takes on particular gravity during times of crisis—the bankruptcy of a city or, as was the case in 1970, the impending collapse of the New York Stock Exchange. From the perspective of personal impact, Rohatyn thrives when others are suffering. Otherwise, he must bide his time and maintain and expand his accumulated stock of reputation and credibility. This is where the comparison with Henry Kissinger becomes relevant. Like Kissinger since his departure as secretary of state, Rohatyn has in a sense been "out of power" ever since New York City emerged from the brink of insolvency and regained access to the capital markets.

"I had real influence at the height of the New York City fiscal crisis because I was, and still am, head of an agency that was financing the city," Rohatyn conceded. "Now, we still raise a lot of money. But the city can finance itself. Therefore, to the extent I had any direct power, that was eliminated, or diminished, when what I was providing—namely, money —was no longer a monopoly that I had."

Unlike Kissinger, however, who is perceived to miss no opportunity to thrust himself into a position to reclaim his former authority, Rohatyn has adopted a more restrained approach to his future role. "You see, I know Henry, so I watch this," he told us. "I have never been in power to the extent he has. Therefore, I don't have the same withdrawal symptoms—which must be very real. I mean, I wasn't in his league, but I did have my own little withdrawal symptoms" after the New York crisis passed. "I think power is something you can't run after. First, I don't think you should because it's not that attractive. And secondly, even if you really want it, the last thing you should do is run after it. It's demeaning. I also think it's self-defeating. Power is not something that is given to you. It seems to me, in today's world, with the amount of disclosure, and the number of lights that shine on you from everywhere, that power is not something you are going to exercise unilaterally. It is something that, if it's real, it is because it is entrusted to you by the public or whomever. And you can exercise it because you are seen to exercise it as fairly as possible. The moment you don't do that, the moment it becomes kind of a personal thing, it appears to other people to be your personal property, it will be taken away from you."

. . .

Felix George Rohatyn, who turned fifty-seven on May 29, 1985, looks and acts the part of the Wall Street financier. He has a genteel, almost patrician, manner. He speaks in precise sentences and measured tones. Rohatyn is married to the former Elizabeth Vagliano, a socially prominent East Sider who is active in civic affairs, and has three children, all boys, from an earlier marriage. Although he is the most famous partner of Lazard Frères, and may be the most eminent investment banker in the world, he does not hold the title of managing partner, Wall Street's equivalent of chief executive officer. This is of his own choosing. For years he resisted the efforts of André Meyer, the late patriarch of the investment house, to persuade him to assume control of Lazard Frères. The title of managing partner has been held since 1978 by Michel David-Weill, who also plays a commanding role in Lazard operations in London and Paris.

Rohatyn talks about his vocation—dealmaking—much as a painter might discuss his latest canvas. He uses words like *symmetry* and *seamless* to describe the characteristics of successful mergers. His greatest professional disappointment was a proposal he engineered in the mid-1970s to restructure the faltering Lockheed Corporation, which was, at the time, the largest defense contractor in the United States. The rescue plan involved significant concessions by the company's lenders and the injection of close to $100 million by Textron, a high-technology conglomerate. The deal collapsed under the weight of lingering reservations by Textron management and reports of rampant overseas bribery by Lockheed that were beginning to surface on Capitol Hill. The restructuring proposal "was aesthetically [my] most interesting," Rohatyn said. "I thought it had the most elements of, I don't know if you can use the term *elegance.* It never went through, and it should have. It was an artistic success, but not a practical success."

Rohatyn's reserved demeanor, and the spare, almost drab, offices in which he and his colleagues conduct business, capture many of the qualities that distinguish Lazard Frères from most of its Wall Street rivals. The firm occupies four floors (thirty through thirty-three) and parts of others at 1 Rockefeller Plaza. It moved to this choice location in 1969 after Meyer was able to secure the space at fire-sale rental costs. Prior to the move, Lazard functioned out of offices at 44 Wall Street, which Meyer's biographer, journalist Cary Reich, has compared to a Dickensian countinghouse. "Exposed pipes were everywhere," he wrote in his 1983 book *Financier.* "If a partner decided his office needed painting, someone would come around to check which of the walls looked the worst and would only paint that one, ignoring the other three. The bathrooms were dingy and dark, with the men's room sporting a window that couldn't be closed, turning the lavatory in the dead of winter into an icebox." Meyer died in 1979, and Lazard's current quarters are a significant improvement over conditions at 44 Wall Street. But the firm remains in many ways the antithesis of the swashbuckling deal factories that are now the rage of the business world. Lazard is a small and secretive partnership that until recently shunned participation in such speculative ventures as leveraged buyouts, where public corporations are taken private with heavy use of borrowed funds, or junk-bond financings, where takeover artists float high-risk, high-return securities, that raise the profile of Wall Street powerhouses such as First Boston Corporation and Drexel Burnham Lambert.

Rohatyn values Lazard's standing as a partnership. "We have a whole different view as to the type of business we run and the validity of public ownership for a firm like ours," he said when asked about First Boston. "I would be very uncomfortable being in a public corporation in our business. . . . I don't want to have to worry about whether we should take on a particular piece of business because the next quarter looks a little lean. We want to run our business so that over the long haul it does what it is supposed to do. Secondly, I don't think our business is a business that lends itself to public ownership. We may have bad quarters. We may have good quarters. We may have people retiring."

He also ridiculed many of the rituals of life on Wall Street. Rohatyn chuckled when asked to comment on a full-page advertisement placed in the *Wall Street Journal* by First Boston. The ad trumpeted First Boston's expertise in defending against hostile takeovers, much as a used-car dealer might boast of his inventory. "Yesterday's poison pill may be tomorrow's placebo," he read from the ad. "Well, I think it's very imaginative."

He went on to say that he and David-Weill have seriously discussed discontinuing advertising with tombstones, the black-bordered notices placed in newspapers and magazines by investment banks to boast of their participation in mergers, underwritings, and other financial transactions. "It used to be that you ran a tombstone," Rohatyn said. "And then you ran two tombstones. Now, people are running entire pages of tombstones. I am absolutely convinced that no tombstone brought us a piece of business ever. That it makes no difference. And we are spending a lot of money [on advertising]. I just think this is a childish thing. And the only thing you think about in making the decision [not to run tombstones] is whether somehow it hurts your relationship with the financial press."

If Rohatyn and his colleagues differ in style from most of their competition, there is one area of substance where traditions at Lazard Frères are very much in keeping with the prevailing Wall Street ethos—the relentless accumulation of profit. Put simply, Lazard is a money machine. On May 18, 1984, as a result of a complex series of transactions designed to coordinate the operations of Lazard offices in New York, London, and Paris, the firm disclosed its five-year financial performance to British regulators. The numbers were staggering. The New York offices reported pretax earnings in 1983 of $80 million, compared with earnings of $46 million in 1980. The *Wall Street Journal* later reported that earnings in first half of fiscal 1984 (Lazard's fiscal year ends September 30) were running at an annual rate of $110 million. These profits were generated by a firm that has fewer than forty partners and four hundred total employees. Although the character of Lazard's ventures has begun to change under the leadership of David-Weill—the firm today participates much more deeply in securities trading and real estate than it did under André Meyer—fees collected by advising on mergers and acquisitions, Felix Rohatyn's area of expertise, remain a focal point of Lazard's operations and profitability. The investment house reportedly helped to engineer mergers with a total value of more than $14.5 billion during the first nine months of 1984, a record for Lazard.

Lazard Frères distributes nearly all of its annual profits to its partners. Thus, it is not unreasonable to assume that many of these partners, including Rohatyn, earn millions of dollars each year. A friend of David-Weill told the *Wall Street Journal* in September 1984 that he "earned more than $50 million" in 1983, with "over half of that directly from Lazard Frères." David-Weill controls a 35 percent stake in the investment bank. Rohatyn is said to control between 6 and 8 percent. A *New York Times Magazine* profile by writer David McClintick reported in August 1984 that Rohatyn's annual income "well exceeds $2 million." *Institutional Investor* speculated in December 1984 that he could have earned $6 million that year. Rohatyn does not like to discuss his own income. We asked him to confirm McClintick's figure, which appeared prior to our final conversation. "He said, 'Look, I am going to write this, am I wildly off?' " Rohatyn told us. "I said, 'Look, I'd prefer that you not write about it at all, because I don't think it's germane. But are you wildly off? The answer is no.' "

Although he is soft-spoken, and clearly uncomfortable with inquiries about his income and life-style, Rohatyn obviously enjoys the attention he receives as a result of his presence on Wall Street and his experiences in New York City. The walls of his outer office, where he holds conversations and conducts negotiations around a small conference table, are decorated with a sampling of the awards he has collected since 1975 from business associations, charitable organizations, and universities. His inner sanctum, where he takes telephone calls and reviews the stream of papers and reports that are an inevitable part of his job, is stuffed with still more plaques and proclamations, editorial cartoons, photographs, and other evidence of his public prominence.

Rohatyn also has a casual way of mentioning activities with which he is involved—a low-key, almost dismissive style—that actually heightens the impact of what he says by giving it such a matter-of-fact quality. "I had a call from [Israeli prime minister] Shimon Peres the other day," he told us in January 1985. "He asked me to be part of a small group to go over there and help them with some of the economic plans they are [developing]. It's a basket case, and of course I will do that. I like Israel, and I think it's something interesting and challenging." During an earlier discussion, he casually ran down a list of friends and acquaintances in the media that would be the envy of any politician. Syndicated columnist Joseph Kraft "has been a friend of mine for twenty-five years," he said. "George Will is a friend, even though we look at the world somewhat differently. So is [David] Brinkley, so is Max Frankel," who runs the editorial page of the *New York Times*. "So is Mike O'Neill," former editor of the *Daily News*.

Rohatyn's public standing offers him a platform available to few figures in the business world to write, speak, and testify on critical issues facing the economy and the society—and to affect the course of events beyond the world in which he operates day to day. But it also injects his influence with a self-limiting quality. Rohatyn always runs the risk of alienating friends and allies if he speaks or acts on positions that directly challenge their interests.

The investment banker, during our conversations, was churning with criticisms of his own profession. He has deep reservations about developments on the merger and acquisition front. He is convinced that many of the fees collected in recent years have been excessive, that the fee structure may promote the completion of large deals rather than the provision of objective counsel, and that many of the offensive and defensive tactics used in merger battles should be prohibited.

"The compensation structure really should be that we get paid as much for *not* doing a deal as for doing a deal," Rohatyn said. "I have tried to push it in this direction but have been utterly unsuccessful, but that is also the fault of the clients as much as anything else. I believe it might be worth ten times as much to a client of ours if we tell him not to do a deal that he's involved in. But nobody wants to do this. So you get these crazily skewed fees, where you get $4 million if the deal goes through and $250,000 if it doesn't. That's all wrong. . . . I think, in many cases, if somebody is going to be paid $10 million, it should come from telling the client not to do [the deal]."

Rohatyn's objections to prevailing merger practices are genuine. And they are shared by few of his colleagues on Wall Street. But they are also limited in scope and by the degree of activism in which he is willing to engage to reform his profession. We asked the Lazard partner about the human consequences of the transactions he helps to engineer. The enormous mergers of recent years, and the conglomerate binge of years past, have precipitated dislocation and decay in communities affected by "rationalization" of the resulting combinations. They have burdened otherwise healthy companies with huge amounts of debt, forcing them to sell off subsidiaries and plants to meet interest charges. *Business Week,* in a remarkable June 1985 cover story, described in graphic detail the disastrous consequences when giant corporations pay too high a price or stray too far afield or assume excessive debt in the process of acquiring another giant corporation. The *New York Times,* surveying the wave of mergers in 1983, posed this question: "The basic issue is whether America's corporations should be spending millions—often through the clever use of special tax breaks—to acquire other companies or whether they should instead be investing more in new machinery and factories. . . . In short, was the $73.5 billion spent [in 1983] on mergers—and the countless more spent on professional fees to lawyers and investment bankers—well spent?"

Rohatyn is agnostic in the debate over the implications of the merger wave, whose value exceeded $122 billion in 1984. "The question with these mergers is, is there greater concentration, is there less efficiency, is capital being allocated improperly?" he said. "I don't know what the answer is. There have been a lot of studies done on these things, and they are fairly inconclusive. Whether the deal is contested or not may have some implications with respect to the top ten people in the company, but in terms of the economy I don't think it has any. It has maybe some implications with respect to interest rates, since these deals tend to be more cash deals than the others. And when you get to the 'megadeals,' it means that more money is being borrowed and more capital is being taken out of the economy. So from that point of view, especially the 'megadeals,' they may have some impact on interest rates."

As to whether the deals turned out badly or well, "I would say that many of the so-called winners in these big deals probably wish they never came close to them. Some of them have turned out probably okay. But my guess is that because a lot of these deals, especially where the so-called white-knight rescuer deals under enormous time pressures, with a lot of people pushing numbers at him that are overoptimistic, with the lawyers and investment bankers getting huge fees if the deal goes, and very little if it doesn't go—the so-called winners, looking back, will probably find that they were overoptimistic and they overpaid."

Even within his own narrow frame of reference, Rohatyn has not risked his personal standing or economic interests to pursue a reform agenda. He has testified before Congress about his reservations. He has written articles and delivered speeches. But he has done little else to seriously rock the investment-banking boat. He told us he once tried to organize a summit meeting of the heads of the major financial houses and Wall Street's most prominent merger attorneys. Few of them were interested. Part of the reason was that nearly all of them disagree with Rohatyn's perspective on the merger wave. Another reason, which Rohatyn confirmed indirectly, is that there exists a certain envy in financial circles of the prominence and influence he commands. "There are a lot of jealousies" directed at Rohatyn, said Democratic party power broker Robert Strauss. "He's not the most popular guy on Wall Street."

We pressed the Lazard partner on why he has not done more to move from the realm of opinion to the arena of activism. "Several of the major [investment] houses have gotten together to lobby in Washington against any changes [in takeover rules]," he said. "They have very deliberately kept us out of the process because of the positions I have taken. I can't marshal any support for my position, or any really significant support for my position, in the industry. So what are my choices? My choices are to step out of the industry and change it from the outside. I do not think that would be successful."

A skeptic could argue that Rohatyn has not even managed to change the conduct of his own investment bank. The fees collected by Lazard Frères are no less staggering than the fees collected by its brethren. It continues to spend for page after page of tombstones, a gimmick Rohatyn dismisses as wasteful. And Lazard in recent years has participated in many of the speculative transactions, such as leveraged buyouts, about which he has expressed reservations.

Is there not an obvious contradiction between what Felix Rohatyn preaches and what Lazard Frères practices? "Look, what I am concerned about, or what I think are excesses in our business, I am concerned about because I think fundamentally that our business is a very good one, and I would like to keep it that way," he replied. "And obviously, [Lazard Frères] plays a very active role in all aspects of this business. . . . I haven't said that all leveraged buyouts are bad. I have said that excessive use of credit is bad. I haven't said that all fees are bad. I have said that excessive fees are bad. I believe we have conducted ourselves very much within the framework that I am comfortable with, otherwise I wouldn't be here. We have participated in leveraged buyouts [which] I think were very conservatively financed. . . . Clearly, we are not going to stop doing business because I think some aspects of the business are troublesome. And I think to the extent that my criticisms have any validity, I can probably be more effective by doing it from the inside."

Rohatyn also spoke ominously, and at great length, about the rise of rampant speculation on Wall Street. He warned in no uncertain terms about the dangers of junk bonds, which have been used with increasing frequency to finance hostile raids. He described as "destabilizing" the enormous amount of arbitrage activity that surrounds most takeover attempts. And he criticized as imprudent the proliferation of interest-rate swaps, commodity straddles, and other financial techniques, whose annual volume runs into billions of dollars. Rohatyn argued overall that increased speculation on Wall Street has been fueled by the emergence of compensation structures that emphasize growth and profitability over sound investment practices. He worries that the individuals who are engaging in these expensive new games of chance have made poor evaluations of the long-term risks they pose.

"The thing that strikes me in a lot of this is how little real professionals understand risk," he told us. "The whole notion that there might be a risk in lending to foreign countries was considered crazy a few years ago. You know, 'sovereign risk.' There's no risk in lending. The leveraged buyout is a risk evaluation. People take a pedestrian company with 20 percent debt and 80 percent equity, and then turn it into 80 percent debt and 20 percent equity, and all of a sudden you have a terrific business. It doesn't make any sense. So you have a lot of deliberate, and mostly not deliberate, speculation [because of] poor evaluation of risk."

Why the popularity of junk bonds? "I have always felt that if the bonus structure of [financial institutions] was geared to their credit rating instead of their earnings per share, you would have very different" investment and lending behavior, Rohatyn said. "I mean, why does an insurance portfolio manager buy a junk bond? He buys a junk bond because he gets an extra one percent return [on investment], and he thinks that is going to look good at year end when he has to report his earnings per share, or whatever. The fact that someday, the whole thing may go falling down on him—well, he doesn't worry about that so much."

Rohatyn is gravely serious about his commentary on the prevailing norms of behavior on Wall Street. He cited the 1984 federal bailout of Continental Illinois Bank—intervention he supported as necessary to prevent more widespread financial collapse—as an example of how the risks that accompany speculation continue to be ignored. Rohatyn told us he was surprised that the huge bailout, which cost the federal government $4.5 billion, could have proceeded without congressional hearings prior to its extension. "This was $4.5 billion," he said. "We asked for a $1.5 billion [federal loan] guarantee for New York City, which was completely secured, and I had to go every day on my knees to Congress."

What accounts for the difference between New York City and Continental Illinois? "Because everybody said, 'Gee, it's a big bank, don't rock the boat. If we make too much noise, we're going to have a banking crisis.' That may have been true. But I thought that was one of the great failures [of the Continental crisis] because there were some lessons to be learned." The near-collapse of Continental Illinois also produced a startling revelation from Comptroller of the Currency C. Todd Conover. The U.S. government, Conover told a congressional committee several months after the Continental rescue, was not prepared to permit the collapse of the country's eleven largest banks. Rohatyn agreed that policies such as these suggest the United States is evolving a two-tier economic structure, where one group of banks and corporations becomes too large and powerful to be allowed to fail, while the vast majority of enterprises must survive the rigors of the market. He also said that based on Conover's testimony, investors and depositors in these major commercial banks may well have legal standing to *demand* federal protection against financial loss. The no-collapse policy "was just a statement," Rohatyn noted. "But I bet you that if I bought securities [in a major bank] which then defaulted, that I would have a reasonably good [legal] case that I could rely on the statements of the secretary of the treasury or the head of the FDIC [Federal Deposit Insurance Corporation] that this [guarantee] was so."

When discussing these and other issues, one comes away with the impression that Felix Rohatyn believes it is his responsibility to save capitalism from itself—that greed, ideological rigidity, or the simple lack of competence outside their narrow arenas of expertise can blind the movers and shakers of the business world to the risks of financial instability they are promoting. Rohatyn told us he is worried that a jolt to the financial system could threaten its structural stability. Where does he expect such a debilitating shock to originate? "It is going to be somewhere where we don't expect it," he said. "I mean, I can give you the weak points—the speculation, the junk bonds, the price of oil, Third World debt, and the domestic energy loans—but it will happen in Hong Kong or it will happen somewhere else. But it will happen."

These are precisely the circumstances that first lifted the Lazard partner to public prominence. As chairman of the New York Stock Exchange's Surveillance Committee, better known as the Crisis Committee, Rohatyn worked feverishly to prevent a collapse of the stock market in 1970. Speculative excesses and inadequate record keeping threatened to overwhelm Wall Street's capacity to process its millions of daily transactions. The stock market, business writer John Brooks wrote in his history of this period, *The Go-Go Years*, "had become a mindless glutton methodically eating itself to paralysis and death." Rohatyn supervised a grueling rescue process that required several brokerage firms to be merged out of existence—a painful and risky exercise that made him one of the most powerful figures on Wall Street.

The near-collapse of Wall Street, and the near-default of New York City, are precisely the kinds of episodes into which Felix Rohatyn can step and perform a service that can be performed by few others. But his talents as a mediator and negotiator have broader implications as well. Any crisis presents the possibility of radical change—in the case of New York, for example, a dismantling of the political dominance of the city's financial establishment and the emergence from the ashes of fiscal despair of a reform political movement to challenge the prevailing distribution of power. By intervening in these situations and brokering long-term accommodations that are acceptable to all parties, Rohatyn not only defuses the immediate crisis but adapts the resolution of the crisis to prevailing values and power arrangements. Ultimately, Felix Rohatyn functions as a conservative force—a force for negotiation and accommodation in circumstances where collapse or chaos loom as alternatives. This may help to explain why Rohatyn can maintain the trust and confidence of the corporate elite even as he offers observations with which they are not in total agreement.

A good example on this score is Rohatyn's activism on Third World debt. Latin America alone owed Western creditors, mainly U.S. and European commercial banks, $350 billion in 1984. The sixteen largest Third World debtors had liabilities of $520 billion, which required annual interest payments of $55 billion. Rohatyn has been writing and speaking since 1982 about the threat to world financial stability—and the solvency of commercial banks—posed by these staggering obligations. He has proposed international negotiations to stretch out the loans, reduce interest rates, and secure commitments on investment and trade from borrowers to avoid bankruptcy by a major debtor nation and a resulting financial panic. Rohatyn has urged Western bankers to declare Poland in default on its outstanding loans. He has argued that future credits to Soviet bloc countries be handled on a government-to-government basis rather than as commercial transactions.

Rohatyn was unprepared to speak with similar certainty about loans to right-wing dictatorships. But he was willing to contemplate restrictions. "I am very clear in my mind about the fact that when you are dealing with governments that operate under a totally different legal, political, and social structure, like the communist governments, anything other than self-liquidating commercial credits should be handled on a government-to-government basis," he said. "I am not sure of the question that you pose, [but] it is a question I would like to see discussed. I would like to see a debate about what is the proper activity for commercial banks in making, in effect, long-term loans to governments? What kind of standards should you put on them? Should you put political and moral standards? Should you just say that when you make long-term loans to another government, you are inevitably getting into foreign-policy questions and therefore it should be handled by a central bank? Frankly, I don't know what the answer is. . . . There is also the question of whether you should lend money to Idi Amin, people like that. Clearly the answer there is no. The question is, where do you draw the line? How do you do it?"

Rohatyn has thought deeply about the debt crisis and he is clearly interested in playing a role in its resolution. But he seldom raises fundamental questions of accountability. Who is responsible for the precarious situation in which the banks find themselves? Did Western bankers behave imprudently by throwing billions of dollars at governments in Brazil, Argentina, Zaire, and the Philippines? Did the thirst for quick and easy profits distort bankers' evaluations of creditworthiness?

Rohatyn said his proposals for global refinancing have "been very sharply criticized in the banking community" by executives who do not share his forecasts of the potential for instability or collapse. Still, as retired Citicorp chairman Walter Wriston explained in a telephone conversation, disagreement on even as pressing an issue as Third World debt does not threaten Rohatyn's standing among his corporate peers. "I think he is completely wrong, and I don't think he has the skill in that area that he brings to others," Wriston said. "But you know the way the world works, whether it's a Saturday night party or something like that. You're still friends. I disagree with him intensely on the subject. I don't believe he has either the facts or the background in this area to make those judgments. On the other hand, he thinks I'm wrong. That's fair enough. And I'm still delighted to have dinner with him and his bride anytime. They're wonderful people. We don't start a fight. We just disagree. You see, I think Ronald Reagan is a great president. He thought Walter Mondale was terrific. So what?"

.   .   .

In the beginning, there was simply Felix Rohatyn, investment banker. Rohatyn, who was born in Austria, arrived in the United States in June 1942 after a harrowing flight from Nazism that took his family from Paris to Casablanca to Lisbon to Rio de Janeiro. Once in the United States he enrolled in a New York City high school and then attended Middlebury College. He graduated in 1949 with a degree in physics. Through the intervention of his stepfather, Rohatyn was offered a job soon after graduation by another refugee from fascism, André Meyer. With the exception of a few years in the 1950s spent, at Meyer's suggestion, as a trainee with European banks closely tied to Lazard Frères, Rohatyn has spent his entire career with the Wall Street firm.

For much of his early career, Rohatyn labored in the shadows of Meyer and Lazard's more senior partners. That began to change in the late 1960s, however, when he dazzled Wall Street with his work as a merger adviser to Harold Geneen, the acquisition-hungry chairman of ITT, and as chairman of the New York Stock Exchange Crisis Committee. It is as a broker of corporate combinations worth hundreds of millions of dollars—on occasion, in recent years, billions of dollars—that the Lazard Frères partner continues to spend the majority of his time. Most of these deals are reached with the mutual consent of the participants, and Rohatyn functions largely as a financial advisor and counselor. He advised Ross Perot, the enigmatic founder of Electronic Data Systems, on his company's June 1984 acquisition by General Motors. The transaction was first broached by GM officials, and much of the negotiating over terms was conducted directly between Perot and GM chairman Roger Smith. Lazard still collected a fee of $4 million on the deal. One month earlier, Rohatyn advised James Dutt, chairman of Chicago-based conglomerate Beatrice Foods, on his $2.8 billion acquisition of Esmark. The deal produced a powerful new force in the food-processing industry—and a fee of $4.5 million for Lazard. Beatrice has since been taken private in the largest leveraged buyout in U.S. history. Rohatyn initiated a meeting between RCA chairman Thornton Bradshaw and General Electric chairman Jack Welch that in late 1985 resulted in the largest non-oil merger in U.S. history.

Lazard Frères has also been a major player in less polite transactions over the years—bitter, contested deals that demand skills as a street fighter and battle strategist that belie the genteel demeanor Rohatyn likes to project. In 1981 Rohatyn came out on the losing side of a $1.4 billion bid by Penn Central, which had emerged from bankruptcy three years earlier, to acquire Colt Industries, a New York–based conglomerate. Rohatyn suggested the deal to Penn Central, and executives of both companies approved it. But a group of dissident Penn Central shareholders, led by company director Howard Terry and members of the Hunt family of Texas, campaigned against the deal and ultimately convinced shareholders to reject it. That vote cost Lazard Frères a fee of $4 million, which was contingent on completion of the transaction. It also generated lingering distrust on the part of the victors.

"I can't blame Felix [for the proposal]," said Howard Terry, who remains a member of the Penn Central board. "His business is making money. But the dollar sign stands in the way of the truth. And Felix has no more respect for the truth than a tomcat has for married life."

Rohatyn is also a trusted advisor to United Technologies chairman Harry Gray, whose acquisitive tendencies and aggressive tactics earned him the nickname "Gray Shark" in Wall Street circles. Rohatyn counseled Gray in 1982 when he entered the frenzied takeover battle between Bendix Corporation and Martin Marietta, a struggle for control that became so intense that the ultimate victor, Allied Corporation chairman Edward Hennessy, who entered the picture soon after Gray, labeled the entire affair "a pretty sorry spectacle for American business." Another sorry spectacle, a $4 billion takeover attempt of Allied by United Technologies, may well have been averted two years later as a result of an unusual leak to the *Wall Street Journal*. The financial community was stunned when the *Journal* reported in November 1984 that it had acquired a copy of a confidential Lazard report, which had been commissioned by Gray, on the merits of a move to acquire Allied.

Rohatyn told us that Lazard launched an unsuccessful investigation to determine the source of the leak. "I think there were three people in this firm who had access to that report," he said. "We satisfied ourselves, as much as you can ever satisfy yourself, that it didn't come out of here. We turned the place upside down."

There is an undeniable, if difficult-to-quantify, connection between Rohatyn's prowess as a merger-maker and the position he enjoys in politics. The two dimensions of his career nourish each other. Edgar Bronfman, chairman of the Seagram Company, said Rohatyn is "definitely" one of the best-connected Wall Street figures he has ever met. "Felix has, of course, a big advantage," Bronfman told us. "He has enormous connections in Europe, which most of our business people have, but not of the character or style of his. They are not only reasonably personal, but Lazard has access to the top people in every country. In this country he seems to know just about everybody." The breadth of Rohatyn's contacts became evident during a conversation in January 1985. One day earlier, the French government had dismissed Bernard Hanon, chairman of Renault, the state-owned automaker, after Renault suffered its worst year in memory. Rohatyn had been a close advisor to the deposed chairman. But he was not troubled by the coup. Hanon was replaced by Georges Besse, chairman of Pechiney Ugine Kuhlmann, the French aluminum giant on whose board Rohatyn has sat for more than twenty years. "Besse is totally professional," Rohatyn said of the change in leadership. "It is clear that this was not some whimsical decision of the government. Renault did lose a billion dollars [in 1984], a great deal of money, and Hanon was not replaced by some political hack."

Rohatyn's most enduring form of business association has been his role as a director of major corporations. He spends about 20 percent of his time attending to his directorships. Rohatyn serves, or has served, on the boards of no fewer than thirteen foreign and domestic firms—giant, powerful enterprises that include Eastern Airlines, ITT, Pfizer, and Schlumberger, a dominant force in oil-field services. It is, of course, an overriding mission of the investment banker to develop and expand relations with powerful members of the business community. A conversation over lunch, a bit of news at a board meeting, a telephone call from a well-placed friend—these are the mechanisms that allow a merger-maker to stay abreast of the wants and needs of potential corporate clients.

Such business connections can also bear fruit, at times almost effortlessly, in the political realm. One of Rohatyn's earliest ventures into national politics came in 1972 when he became involved in the presidential campaign of Edmund Muskie at the urging of an executive of United Artists, a Lazard client. Rohatyn's introduction to the politics and finances of New York City also came through a business friendship, in this case, an informal relationship with Robert Strauss. It was Strauss, during his tenure as chairman of the Democratic National Committee (1972–1977), who suggested to New York governor Hugh Carey that he call on Rohatyn in connection with the city's fiscal problems. Rohatyn and Strauss now serve together on the board of MCA, the entertainment conglomerate whose chairman, Lew Wasserman, is well connected politically. Former Senate majority leader Howard Baker is also an MCA director.

"I knew Felix professionally," Strauss said during an interview in his Washington law offices. "Professionally and socially through mutual friends and business transactions . . . I had been active in assisting Carey in securing the nomination and then being elected governor. We were talking about [New York City], and I said, 'You ought to get Felix Rohatyn.' And he said, that's a good idea. Shortly after I hung up the telephone with him, I called Felix to tell him what I told Carey. . . . Later, Felix called me back and said, 'I got the call from Carey, what should I do about taking this thing?' . . . I said, 'Take it, it's just six months out of your life, you'll learn a great deal, and you'll make a contribution.' " Needless to say, Strauss's advice changed Rohatyn's life. Such is the fortuity that comes about through powerful friends.

In turn, Rohatyn's political exploits generate a higher public profile for him and Lazard and foster a certain star quality that potential clients find attractive. Rohatyn's public visibility "has been a tremendous asset" for Lazard, said former partner Raymond Troubh. "There is no one else in the firm who is a cult personality, as it were. I think it has been an enormous drawing card. But he merits it, because Felix is such a fantastic investment banker. It's very important to know that. This guy has enormous substance beneath the form." A Lazard partner who is a close friend of Rohatyn put it another way. "Felix working half-time [on business] is clearly the most productive member of the firm. Even working 20 percent of the time, he is the most productive member," he told us. "This has given him an unassailable base in the firm. Felix is our principal window on the world. There is no question that this brings us business, from business firms and from government agencies. But he did not calculate this."

· · ·

If Rohatyn's status and contacts as an investment banker are the foundation of his political influence, his emergence as a leading Lazard partner is tied inextricably to the legacies of two individuals: the late André Meyer, the managing partner of Lazard; and Harold Geneen, for two decades chief executive and master conglomerateur of ITT. His relationships with these men also underscore a trait that has characterized Rohatyn's career from the beginning—his ability to fasten himself to and serve with complete loyalty corporate figures who are feared, loathed, or vilified outside the world in which they operate, yet remain thoroughly unsullied by the reputations or misdeeds of his mentors. If Ronald Reagan can be dubbed the Teflon President for his capacity to distance himself from charges of impropriety directed at members of his administration, Felix Rohatyn might well be called the Teflon Investment Banker.

André Meyer, the dominant personality at Lazard Frères for more than three decades, died on September 9, 1979, at the age of eighty-one. David Rockefeller has called him "the most creative financial genius of our time in the investment banking field." Others called him cruel, greedy, and autocratic. But no one doubted his abilities as a generator and acquisitor of great wealth.

Cary Reich, executive editor of *Institutional Investor,* has penned a biography of Meyer that examines the banker's career from his early days on the Paris Bourse through his rise to riches on Wall Street. In a chapter titled "Friends," Reich sketches some of the personal acquaintances and business alliances Meyer cultivated: RCA founder David Sarnoff and his son and successor, Robert, for whom Lazard arranged a number of mergers; CBS chairman William Paley, who was an intimate friend of Meyer, although Lazard did no business with CBS; David Rockefeller, who told Reich that he met with Meyer 139 times over the course of their professional relationship; and Giovanni Agnelli, a titan of the Italian auto industry.

Meyer's network extended to politics as well. He was an informal advisor to Lyndon Johnson (Meyer visited the White House twenty-four times between 1964 and 1968, according to Reich) as well as to French president Charles de Gaulle. He was even a close friend of Rohatyn's "role model," Jean Monnet. "I have been to see [Meyer] every time I go to the United States," Monnet wrote in his memoirs.

During his discussion of the Meyer network, Reich poses an obvious question: Just how useful were these friendships? His answer applies equally well to the career of Felix Rohatyn. "Some of them added substantially to his fortune, and to the success of Lazard Frères," Meyer's biographer concluded. "Others didn't bring him much in the way of direct business, but gave him something equally precious: information, the kind of information that not only produces business ideas but that tends to churn up more ideas in its wake. As Meyer knew well, when it came to information, the rich really do get richer—the more you have the more you are likely to be attractive to people who can give you an even greater supply of it."

It is impossible to understand Rohatyn's network of business relationships without an appreciation of how Meyer helped to shape it. A direct example of this phenomenon is his ties to Harry Oppenheimer, South Africa's minerals baron. Rohatyn became a director of Minorco in 1979. He traveled for the first time to South Africa in the spring of 1984 as a guest of Oppenheimer. He was accompanied by his wife; New York union leader Victor Gotbaum, his closest personal friend; and Gotbaum's wife. This relationship with Harry Oppenheimer did not develop overnight. Prior to his affiliation with Minorco, Rohatyn spent more than ten years (January 1970 to May 1980) as a director of Englehard Minerals & Chemicals, in which Anglo American, through Minorco, held a substantial interest. Rohatyn chose to leave the Englehard board to become a director of Minorco. But it was André Meyer's vision that gave rise to this firm, which took shape in 1967 through a merger of Englehard Industries, at the time, the world's largest fabricator of precious metals, and Minerals & Chemicals Philipp Corporation, born of another Meyer-inspired combination. Meyer's ultimate dream, his biographer reported, was to merge this new creation with Anglo American, giving birth to a minerals combine of inestimable power. Though that deal was not to pass, Anglo did purchase a substantial block of Englehard stock. And Rohatyn, through his seat on the Englehard board, inherited a connection to one of South Africa's most influential figures.

"Everyone recognized the preeminence of André Meyer, even during the time Felix was on our board" as a financial advisor to Englehard, said Milton Rosenthal, former chairman of Englehard Minerals & Chemicals. "Mr. Meyer was the person whose counsel we sought. After Felix joined the board, he played an important role. I don't want to denigrate that at all. But that did not cut off the relationship we had with Mr. Meyer as well."

That relationship has also generated millions of dollars of fees for Lazard Frères in recent years. Englehard Minerals & Chemicals has participated in a dizzying array of spin-offs, mergers, and proposed management buyouts—transactions in which Rohatyn, by virtue of his history with the firm, has participated as a paid advisor. In May 1981, Englehard executives decided to break the company in two and separate the oil and minerals trading arm, known as Philipp Brothers, from the manufacturing and metals-processing side of the business, which was reborn as the Englehard Corporation. Rohatyn counseled Milton Rosenthal, who initiated the spin-off, and Lazard produced a report on the transaction's fairness to shareholders.

"Naturally, I discussed the [divestiture] concept with my colleagues to obtain their reactions," Rosenthal told us. "I first discussed it with one of my senior colleagues, my most senior colleague. The next person I discussed it with was Felix Rohatyn." Five months later, Lazard helped to arrange a $554 million merger between Salomon Brothers, the largest private investment banking firm in the United States, and Phibro Corporation, the new name of the newly independent trading arm of Englehard. Minorco at the time owned more than 27 percent of Phibro. The merged corporation, called Phibro-Salomon, generated revenues of nearly $30 billion in 1983 and profits of close to $500 million. During the summer of 1983, when Minorco decided to reduce its holdings in Phibro-Salomon by six million shares, Lazard co-managed the sale and pocketed a substantial underwriting profit.

Needless to say, there is a troubling dimension to Felix Rohatyn's lucrative dealings with Harry Oppenheimer and his U.S. colleagues. The sales and profits of Anglo American, and not an insubstantial amount of the minerals processed and traded by Englehard, have been generated through the labor of black employees working under one of the world's most discriminatory social and political systems. Protest in the United States over South African apartheid exploded in late 1984. Civil-rights and congressional leaders endorsed a range of economic sanctions against the minority government and proposals to curb U.S. trade and investment with the regime. There were campaigns directed at a number of corporations, including General Motors and Control Data, who continue to do business in the country. Yet Rohatyn's years of profitable collaboration with Oppenheimer have gone largely without notice. And Rohatyn himself, who recognizes the sensitive position he is in, offered little in the way of specific proposals to promote the demise of apartheid or to limit foreign investments that bolster the minority regime.

Rohatyn said the South African connection made him uneasy when he was invited to join the Minorco board, whose directors have included Walter Wriston, Anglo chairman Oppenheimer, and prominent bankers from Canada, Germany, and Brazil. "The easy thing for me to do was to say no," he told us. "Or to put one of my partners [at Lazard Frères] on the board, because the business relationship is there whether I'm on or a partner of mine is. But I admire Harry Oppenheimer. I think he is a very fine human being who is trying to do something very difficult in South Africa. And if I am going to give him financial advice, I should be willing to sit on the board of his company."

Rohatyn was less forthcoming when the discussion turned to U.S. policy. His comments underscore how business relationships can temper his candor or creativity in the public realm. When asked whether he favored a prohibition on new loans by U.S. banks to the South African government, Rohatyn answered, "I don't know." He offered the same response when asked if he favored a ban on the sale of South African Krugerrands in the United States. Both proposals were included in trade sanctions approved by the House of Representatives during the summer of 1985. President Reagan later implemented a ban on Krugerrand sales.

On whether he would prohibit further direct investment by U.S. corporations, Rohatyn said, "It depends on what our interest is, if we desperately need some raw material that we have to develop, or whose development we have to finance. I would not stop or permit investment across the board. I would make the investment conditioned on certain behavior. In fact, I would rather encourage the investment with the behavior conditions than simply prohibit it altogether. But it's a very close call. It's a very difficult question."

· · ·

Felix Rohatyn was named a partner at Lazard in 1960. But it was not until several years later, when he developed an intimate working relationship with Harold Geneen, an emerging force in the corporate world, that his status as an investment banker really began to climb. A driven, callous man who ruled ITT with an iron fist, Geneen had an insatiable appetite for acquisition. Rohatyn's frantic efforts to satisfy that appetite not only established his presence within Lazard as one of the firm's most productive members (in 1968, Rohatyn's first year as an ITT director, fees from

Geneen accounted for nearly 30 percent of Lazard's merger revenues) but attracted the attention of outside forces—the business press, other potential corporate clients, the governors of the New York Stock Exchange, who invited Rohatyn to join their board.

By now, the outlines of the story of Harold Sydney Geneen and his tumultuous two decades at the helm of ITT are familiar. He took control in 1959 of a floundering telecommunications firm, with the bulk of its assets situated outside the United States, and soon developed an overriding mission: to diversify ITT away from its primary lines of business and to guard against expropriation by acquiring assets in the United States. Geneen formally articulated his vision for ITT in March 1963, when he presented a memorandum to the company board simply titled, "Acquisition Philosophy." His moves had begun as early as 1961, when ITT made its first acquisition under its new boss—the purchase of Jennings Radio Manufacturing Corporation, a modest electronics firm based in San Jose, California. Rohatyn became involved in the deal after he invited himself to lunch with Geneen and Albert Hettinger, a more senior partner. But it was not until 1968, when Felix Rohatyn began his service as a director, that the merger spree hit full stride. As the staff report of the House antitrust subcommittee concluded, "The major thrust in ITT's acquisition program came after Mr. Rohatyn's appointment and election to the ITT board. ITT's acquisition activity greatly accelerated, both in terms of numbers and size of companies acquired."

Rohatyn himself recognizes that his election to the ITT board, which was pushed by Geneen over the objections of senior company directors, was a turning point in his career. He maintains an intense loyalty to his corporate mentor. Rohatyn defended Geneen against claims that he engineered the demise of his successor, Lyman Hamilton, after Hamilton began to reverse the strategic course for which Geneen had become famous. Hamilton was deposed by the ITT board in July 1979, less than two years after he succeeded Geneen as chief executive. Outside observers, from business reporters to Geneen biographers to Wall Street analysts, agree that a bitter Geneen had a hand in the turn of events.

Felix Rohatyn disagrees. "I am not going to discuss that in detail because no great purpose can be served by it," he said. "I would just limit myself to saying that the decision to replace Lyman Hamilton was made unanimously by *all* of the outside directors. I would also say to you that if one or two or three of the outside directors had been against this proposition, it wouldn't have happened. And I think it would be unreasonable to think that every last outside director was just at the beck and call of Harold Geneen. If this had just been a Geneen ego thing, it could not have happened. Because you could not have gotten every one of these directors, some of whom were quite close to Lyman Hamilton, to support the decision."

Rohatyn also defended Geneen against the allegations of ruthlessness and misconduct that have hounded the former ITT chairman since the early 1970s—in particular, with respect to ITT's behavior in Chile during the Allende years and the campaign to secure Justice Department approval of its acquisition of Hartford Insurance, a scandal that touched Rohatyn directly.

"Look, I think when things happened the way they did, there were clearly some bad decisions made," he replied when asked whether he believed Geneen was guilty of any wrongdoing in connection with the ITT scandals. "On the other hand, Harold Geneen was a friend of mine. He still is. Harold Geneen was extremely supportive of me when I was a young man who wasn't going anyplace, at a time when ITT was a big, prestigious American company and I was a relatively young, Jewish, not-terribly-elegant investment banker trying to make a place for himself. He taught me a great deal. He got me involved with lots of very interesting and very profitable things, where I learned a lot, and where I made my mark. He put me on the board of his company when lots of people said that some older, more elegant people should go on. And when he got in trouble, I was never able to find anything that convinced me he had committed a crime or had done anything except maybe made some mistakes in judgment. Therefore, I felt that for me to walk away from him at that time would have left the implication that I knew or thought he was guilty, and would be at the human level a terrible thing for me to do."

Although modest by contemporary "megadeal" standards, ITT's acquisitions in the two years that followed Rohatyn's election to the board —they proceeded at a rate of two new companies per month—dazzled Wall Street. Among the company's fifty-odd acquisitions were Levitt & Sons (price: $92 million), the leading U.S. residential construction firm; Sheraton Corporation (price: $194 million), the giant hotel chain; Continental Baking (price: $280 million), the country's largest producer and distributor of baked goods; Rayonier (price: $293 million), the principal manufacturer of cellulose and a producer of paper pulp and lumber; and Pennsylvania Glass Sand Corporation (price: $113 million), the largest U.S. producer of silica and clay products.

Rohatyn also arranged during this period a deal that nearly stopped ITT's acquisition spree dead in its tracks—and threatened to undermine the investment banker's "public" career before it began. On December 23, 1968, ITT made a $1.5 billion offer for the Hartford Insurance Group, one of the largest property-casualty insurers in the United States. The merger was immediately rejected by the Hartford board, which backed down under intense pressure from Geneen and approved the deal months later. Less willing to back down on its opposition was the Justice Department, which filed suit in August 1969 to block the takeover. The antitrust action, one of three filed against the giant conglomerate by Assistant Attorney General Richard McLaren, prompted a massive lobbying campaign by ITT—a campaign in which Rohatyn played a critical role, meeting on numerous occasions with top Justice Department officials and twice with Peter Flanigan, a White House aide. In July 1971, McLaren announced that Justice had reached an out-of-court settlement of the Hartford suit. ITT agreed to divest itself of Avis and all or parts of several other acquisitions and to refrain for ten years from acquiring any company with assets of more than $100 million.

The settlement immediately elicited bitter objections from congressmen and antitrust activists. But it was not until winter 1972, and the publication of a series of reports by investigative columnist Jack Anderson, that the Hartford agreement exploded into a front-page scandal. Anderson obtained a memo written by Dita Beard, who worked as an ITT Washington lobbyist, that linked the antitrust settlement to a $400,000 pledge from ITT to help finance the 1972 Republican convention. Rohatyn soon found himself at the center of a brewing political storm. For four days in March 1972 he appeared before the Senate Judiciary Committee alongside McLaren and recently confirmed Attorney General Richard Kleindienst, who requested a second round of confirmation hearings after the Dita Beard scandal broke. Rohatyn told us that his decision to stick with Harold Geneen, and sit through intense Senate scrutiny, was one of the riskiest decisions of his business career.

Throughout the Senate hearings the loyal investment banker stuck to one line: He knew nothing of the $400,000 pledge, or the Dita Beard memo, other than what he read in the newspapers. This proposition was hard to swallow: How could the individual who had initiated the Hartford acquisition, lobbied Justice Department figures, and worked so closely with Geneen as a director be in the dark about such a significant development? But Rohatyn's testimony was never demonstrated to be false or misleading. To this day he says he had nothing to do with Dita Beard—before, during, or after the Hartford episode. "I never met Dita Beard," Rohatyn insisted to us. We asked about Beard's strange illness during the Kleindienst hearings. Several senators were forced to fly to Denver to take testimony from the ITT lobbyist. They found her in a hospital bed, strapped to an electrocardiograph. Subsequent newspaper accounts reported that she was kept on the ITT payroll, with no responsibilities, for several years after the controversy ended. "I don't know what they did to her," Rohatyn told us. "I don't know what happened to her. I don't know how sick she was. So, I really can't answer that."

Whatever the real story of Rohatyn's role in the Hartford Insurance episode, there is no question that he played a decisive role in promoting and giving concrete form to Harold Geneen's urge to merge—and that these deals were the decisive chapter in his career as an investment banker. The sheer volume of the transactions he brokered on behalf of ITT generated millions of dollars in fees for Lazard. But a single-minded focus on the profitability of Rohatyn's dealings misses an equally important point: His status as Harold Geneen's right arm allowed Rohatyn to display and perfect talents as an investment banker that distinguished him from lesser Wall Street personalities. By 1973 a *Business Week* cover story could label him, "the archetype of the new generation of investment bankers that is taking over Wall Street." He "has shown an uncanny skill in developing new business for his firm by capitalizing on his clients' ambitious plans for expansion."

"The merger business," André Meyer had been known to say, "is ten percent financial analysis and ninety percent psychoanalysis." Working alongside Geneen, Rohatyn demonstrated that he was a master number cruncher as well an accomplished diplomat.

To begin with, the pace of the merger spree put a premium on an agility with figures—a talent especially valued by Geneen, given his roots as an accountant and his legendary obsession with detailed financial reporting from the outer reaches of the ITT empire. Acquisition targets had to be sized up, an appropriate price determined, and the fallen company merged seamlessly into the ITT web.

"The thing that struck me about Felix was his quickness with figures. His quickness with taxes—the tax implications of things," said Robert Townsend, who served first as president and then chairman of Avis Rent-a-Car until it was sold to ITT in 1965. Townsend went on to write *Up the Organization*, the pithy best-seller on business management. "Harold Geneen was an accounting machine. But he was 50 percent of Rohatyn." The Avis deal was a turning point in Rohatyn's relationship with ITT. He, along with Townsend and Donald Petrie (who today is a limited partner at Lazard), rehabilitated the ailing company after Lazard bought a controlling interest for $5.5 million in 1962. The investment bank then sold its Avis holdings to ITT, at a profit of more than $15 million. This successful enterprise further enhanced Rohatyn's stature in the eyes of André Meyer—a man who never hesitated in taking a profit—as well as with Geneen, since Lazard offered him control of a company with substantial prospects for growth.

The ITT chairman's distaste for hostile takeovers of the kind so common today also put a premium on a different, and perhaps more important, talent: a certain capacity to charm. The troubled CEOs of acquisitions targets had to be soothed so as not to resist the advances of Geneen, their egos massaged, and worries about their future roles as managers in the ITT network allayed. In short, Felix Rohatyn had to play the role of nursemaid.

Robert Townsend offered a comparison with Geneen. "Harold Geneen only understood numbers," he told us. "The only thing he understood about people is that if you paid them too much, much more than they're worth, you've got them under your power. You can order them around, browbeat them. Felix was very sensitive to every aspect of a person's needs, desires, wants, ambitions. He was quiet. He had humor. He didn't overpower you with talk. He let *you* talk until you talked yourself into a trap. . . . Everybody he talked to felt that Felix was his personal friend and that whatever was done was going to be done with that personal friend's best interest at heart. Felix could see five people and make them all feel that way."

Raymond Troubh described Rohatyn as a psychologist. "He understands the motivations of other people," he said. "He was always ahead in being able to cope with the personalities and prima donnas. You make your money in investment banking by handholding or pushing people into a deal they are not sure they really want to make. It is a great trauma to sell your company or to buy a big company. And you need someone in the middle who is pushing and shoving and thinking primarily of the fees for his firm."

How did Rohatyn's skills as a "psychologist" manifest themselves? "Felix understood the use of humor," Troubh said. "The use of self-deprecatory humor when necessary to put people in a mood to be— manipulated is a harsh word—to be sculpted and molded to the deal. In any environment, in any room full of people, sooner or later Felix would say something that would focus attention on him."

Rohatyn's furious work on behalf of ITT elevated him to a position of prominence within Lazard Frères, and on Wall Street that set the stage for still more lucrative relationships with other corporations and a degree of public attention that served him well in the New York City fiscal crisis. But what earlier discussions of Rohatyn's years with ITT have failed to address—and what goes to the heart of Rohatyn's capacity to attach himself to the achievements and power of others without being touched by their shortcomings or failures—is the one dimension of this period that should be of central interest to those examining the career of a Wall Street operator. The ITT deals generated headlines, enormous fees for Lazard, and a not insubstantial amount of suspicion and scorn in political circles. But for the constituency on whose behalf they were engineered—ITT shareholders—a good number of these mergers proved disastrous. ITT as a corporation is today a stumbling, troubled giant, a collection of disconnected and faltering lines of business. ITT itself is rumored to be ripe for a takeover or even liquidation by a corporate raider. Its deep-seated illnesses have their roots in the empire-building efforts of Geneen and Rohatyn.

Felix Rohatyn "was absolutely one of the critical moving forces at ITT," said a Wall Street analyst who follows the company and asked not to be identified. "He saw himself becoming a major partner at Lazard simply because of his work with one company—ITT. He wore two hats. He had two positions, and they conflicted. As an investment banker, he had nothing but massive fees and personal wealth to gain by doing lots of deals for ITT. At the same time, as an ITT director, he represented shareholder interests. In retrospect, I can say very clearly that it is generally believed those two interests were very divergent. It is also believed that Felix did not pursue the shareholders' interests with the same aggressiveness with which he pursued his own."

As early as 1971, congressional investigators could look at the ITT pattern—the suspect accounting practices, the bureaucratization of companies brought under the Geneen management regime—and issue a warning: "Notwithstanding ITT's growth record, in both net income and sales, there are indications that the efficiency and performance of its constituent units deteriorate after they are taken into ITT's system."

Wall Street suspicions of what Geneen and Rohatyn had wrought were reflected most vividly in ITT's terminally disappointing performance on the New York Stock Exchange. From the mid-1960s until 1973, stock in the corporation typically fluctuated between thirty and sixty dollars per share. Then the bottom dropped out. The stock hit a low of twelve dollars per share during the 1973–74 market collapse and eventually reached equilibrium in the twenty-five-to-thirty-five-dollar range. ITT shares have rebounded in recent years, but only after the two chief executives who followed Geneen—Lyman Hamilton, who served as chief executive for roughly eighteen months after Geneen stepped down as CEO in 1977 (he remained chairman), and Rand Araskog, who continues to serve as ITT's chief executive—began to *divest* the corporation of many of its acquisitions, a process *Fortune* dubbed "The De-Geneening of ITT." It might as well have been called the "De-Rohatynization." From 1979 through 1981, ITT sold off thirty-four companies with combined sales of $1.1 billion. In January 1985, it announced plans to sell still more operations, with assets worth $1.7 billion.

Rohatyn was asked to discuss the revisionist thinking on the legacy of Harold Geneen. We were surprised to hear him agree with many of the points raised by critics of ITT. "Clearly, looking back today, conglomeration, if you will, has not been a successful experiment," he said. "People found they couldn't manage as many businesses as they thought they could. Many people overextended themselves, and they learned a useful lesson—they couldn't run everything.

"ITT was a rather special situation," he continued. "By the early 1960s, ITT had seen many of its telecommunications businesses nationalized, the biggest one being the Cuban telephone company," which was expropriated by Fidel Castro soon after he assumed power. "Harold Geneen's basic theory was that this trend would continue, that ITT's European telecommunications companies were in jeopardy, and that therefore the company had to diversify. Since in the United States, it was facing an entrenched monopoly in the phone company [AT&T], it couldn't become an American telecommunications company. That was the genesis [of the merger spree].

"Now, it turned out to be incorrect. ITT's European operations not only were not nationalized, they flourished. The telecommunications monopoly in this country was broken up. Therefore, you could argue that ITT would have been better off putting its money into telecommunications, and putting its money into domestic telecommunications. In retrospect, that is probably correct. Now, that doesn't mean that some of these acquisitions, especially Hartford Fire and the finance companies, over the long haul, are not good, sound adjuncts to a large, credit-hungry company. But [as for] a lot of the other businesses, you could argue that ITT would be just as well off without them, if not better."

This is a remarkable retrospective by someone as intimately involved as Rohatyn in the creation of the crumbling ITT monument. What is even more remarkable is how his professional reputation was built on such a shaky foundation—and how little it has suffered as ITT continues to wither and decline. The man who worries so deeply about the risks of financial excess has carved for himself the enviable niche of risk-free intermediary. Chairman Rand Araskog announced in August 1984 that ITT had retained two investment banks to study strategies to increase shareholder value—studies that led to the divestiture announcements less than six months later. One of the two firms was Lazard Frères.

· · ·

Felix Rohatyn's rise to prominence at Lazard Frères highlights the strange and incomplete criteria on which investment bankers are judged. The number and size of deals they conclude, and the ability to bring into the corporate fold acquisition targets that resist the solicitation of their clients, are valued more highly than the long-term consequences of the transactions for stockholders or employees or communities. Within this world, Rohatyn's success is explained by the unique combination of skills he wields. He is accomplished in the technical dimensions of his business. He has demonstrated a facility with accounting, finance and corporate restructuring that few others possess. He also commands certain personal qualities—a sense of humor, an ability to soothe, flatter or manipulate— that often are as essential to the completion of a merger as the deal's financial merits.

David Margolis, president of Colt Industries, has worked with Lazard Frères on at least two major mergers over the past ten years. He offered this comparison between Rohatyn and other Wall Street figures.

"My feeling with a lot of investment bankers is that they really don't understand their own limitations," Margolis told us. "There are a good number of people on Wall Street who think they understand what business success is all about on the corporate side. They really don't. I don't know what it is about the Wall Street process, but they lose a human dimension. . . . Felix is very good at understanding that equation. He has a very acute sense of what you really need, what you mean, and if he does not have a very good idea, then chances are you are not going to hear from him with a lot of small talk and drivel."

Margolis illustrates Rohatyn's capacity to build on successful negotiating experiences. The Colt president served under Harold Geneen at ITT from 1959 through 1962, about the time Rohatyn was beginning to cultivate his special relationship to the hard-driving ITT chief. Early in the New York fiscal crisis, Rohatyn and Margolis were working on a deal for Colt—a hostile takeover bid for Garlock Inc., an acquisition that Margolis said Rohatyn suggested. At the time, Rohatyn was also looking for business executives to serve on the Emergency Financial Control Board (EFCB), the powerful political institution designed to bring discipline to New York's budget process.

"That was Felix," the Colt president told us when we asked how he came to serve on the EFCB. "They decided they wanted some private-sector, corporate types [for the board], and Governor Carey, I presume, asked Felix to make all of the recommendations involved." Four years after Margolis left the EFCB, the two would team up again, this time on the $1.4 billion bid for Colt by Penn Central. Lazard Frères was advising Penn Central, which emerged from bankruptcy in 1978 and began a hunt for merger partners. "Felix was the point man, if you want to use that word, on the Colt deal," a Penn Central executive said. "He did in fact bring the Colt deal to Penn Central. He knew us, and he knew the principals of Colt."

An example of how Rohatyn's role as a business negotiator can bear fruit beyond the corporate world is his friendship with Bernard Vernier-Palliez, who was named France's ambassador to the United States on January 4, 1982. Rohatyn worked closely with Vernier-Palliez during the ambassador's tenure as chairman of Renault, the state-owned auto maker. He advised the French company on its purchase in 1979–80 of a controlling equity stake in American Motors (AMC), as well as on its acquisition of a 45 percent interest in Mack Trucks. These were extremely sensitive negotiations, given public concern over foreign penetration of the U.S. auto industry and Renault's status as a government-owned company based in a Socialist-run country.

We asked Rohatyn about this dimension of his work with Renault. "The fact that Renault is state owned creates an atmosphere that you have to dispel," he told us. "The people here, the management here, get very nervous when they think they are dealing with a foreign state, especially a Socialist state. So it takes a little while for them to understand that in the case of Renault, they were dealing with a management that was professional and not political."

Rohatyn's role as counselor to Renault, especially with respect to AMC, has gone far beyond consultation on the mechanics of its original investment. He serves as chairman of the finance committee of the AMC board and is one of five directors named by Renault to represent its interests. According to former AMC executives, Renault requested that he be appointed to the board in 1979 after it purchased a 19 percent stake in AMC and became entitled to name two directors. That request was rejected by AMC, which wanted to maintain strict separation between U.S. and French presence in the company. Rohatyn also represented AMC in 1983 when it sold its AM General operation to raise badly needed investment capital. And he worked closely with Renault management in early 1982 when AMC negotiated a concession package with its unionized workforce. The company and the United Auto Workers agreed to treat a three-year, $120 million wage cut as a loan to the company, repayable by 1988 at 10 percent interest. Rohatyn described to us how the deal was struck.

"The thing that I found amazing, and so did [Vernier-Palliez] when we got in to AMC, was really the bad relationship that existed between the company and the union," he said. "We had a dinner that we asked for, early on, with [then UAW president Douglas] Fraser and [Raymond] Majerus [then director of the UAW's AMC department], and with [Gerald] Meyers, who was then still the chief executive. We talked a little bit about Renault's plans for AMC, in terms of the investment and what we were going to do. And it was clear that it was the first time that anyone had brought the union in to tell them what the company was going to do.

"It was clear that AMC had to have some relief," he continued. "Chrysler was getting the relief that was negotiated as part of the loan guarantee agreement. There was no way we could make the kind of investment we were making in the company, and manufacture small automobiles, which are the lowest margin, and be uncompetitive on wages. We could have done [the negotiations] two ways. Since AMC was in very deep [financial] difficulty, we could have hardballed it and demanded a labor concession as part of the package when we made our investment—condition the investment on the concession. And I thought that was probably the way we should have done it. It's easier for a labor leader to make a concession when he can show what he's getting for it, and also what happens if it doesn't happen. At the same time, Renault is a national company, and a foreign company. They thought, and after a while I agreed with them, that from an image point of view, and a policy point of view, it would create the wrong atmosphere to come in as part of a big dramatic negotiation.

"And so we did it the other way. And we told Doug and Majerus that we were conscious that we weren't doing it the way that from a business point of view might have been the most rational, but that we thought that in the long-term interest of relations between the company and the union and the French, [a less confrontational approach] was the best way to do it. Given that we gave up that enormous leverage at the beginning, and that we gave it up deliberately, we did the best we could afterward."

Beyond establishing Rohatyn as a presence in the auto industry, his relations with the French, and with Renault's influential former chairman, have helped to expand his already substantial political contacts here and abroad. "Felix's name is known among important businessmen and policy makers in France," Vernier-Palliez said during a Saturday morning conversation at the French embassy. "The first time Felix met the French finance minister [Jacques Delors, who has since become president of the Commission of the European Communities] was at a dinner I gave when I was still at Renault. He has met many times the president of the Republic, and he is acquainted with politicians on both sides in France. His name is not well known in the country by the average man, but for people who count, he is known."

Since Vernier-Palliez was named ambassador, the two men have kept in touch. Rohatyn was awarded the French Legion of Honor in a ceremony at the French embassy. He has also been a guest at dinners hosted by the embassy at which prominent bankers, economists, and government officials exchange views on issues of the day. "Felix is always an active participant in the conversations," Vernier-Palliez reported. Other participants in the conversations have on occasion included Federal Reserve chairman Paul Volcker, former New York reserve bank president Anthony Solomon, Martin Feldstein, former chairman of President Reagan's Council of Economic Advisors, and Jacques de Larosière, managing director of the International Monetary Fund.

What is so intriguing about this unusually personal dimension to Rohatyn's career is the way it shapes and constrains how the influence that comes with business success can be utilized. There is a caution that seems to grow out of being acquainted with, and well liked by, such a broad range of people. Material success and praise from so many quarters can dull the taste for risk, challenge, and potential failure. It also determines his impact as a negotiator in the public realm. Rohatyn has spent his entire life as a member of, and advisor to, the corporate and financial elite. He has absorbed its values and understands its long-term needs. When he directs his skills toward public crises where the power of the establishment is in jeopardy, his role as honest broker—no matter how impartial in the technical sense—serves ultimately to reinforce the standing of the institutions on whose behalf he has labored for so many years.

The most instructive lesson on this score is Rohatyn's work in New York. The emergence of New York City from the throes of insolvency was an undeniably remarkable achievement—a financial rebirth in which Rohatyn, as chairman of the Municipal Assistance Corporation, played the decisive role. When the investment banker stepped into the crisis in May 1975, the city was groaning under the weight of a short-term debt of $6 billion. It was locked out of the private financial markets. Its budget for the fiscal year beginning June 30, 1975, would register a massive operating deficit. By January 1984, when we traveled to New York for our first conversation with Rohatyn, the city had reentered the financial markets. Its budget was in balance. And Rohatyn was locked in a public squabble with Mayor Koch over how to spend a $1 billion *surplus* MAC had generated.

None of this, however, should obscure a fundamental reality. Powerful institutions that played a critical role in the evolution and precipitation of the fiscal crisis—namely, New York's major commercial banks—were well protected by the program of loan rollovers, stretch-outs, and refinancing devised by Rohatyn during the course of grueling negotiations. Meanwhile, those who over time had the least degree of control over city finances and budget policy—the poor, the elderly, the unemployed, the students—were affected most harshly by the rigid austerity program adopted at the insistence of the banks.

Economist Robert Lekachman, in a review of Rohatyn's book *The Twenty-Year Century,* a collection of his speeches, articles, and congressional testimony, offered a compelling description of the real costs of the New York City rescue:

> As a model of shared sacrifice, New York City . . . severely violates the canons of fairness which [Rohatyn] promulgates. Low income students were compelled for the first time in its history to pay tuition in the City University. Transit fares rose. A fifth of the municipal labor force was laid off and as a result the city became dirtier, even more unsafe, and meaner in its treatment of the sick, poor and the elderly. . . . No bankers or bank stockholders were penalized, although their role in financing the city's mounting deficit was pivotal. Why did the prudent types at the head of Chase, Citibank, and the other money market institutions continue to fund political improvidence? Why should they have been rescued by MAC while the innocent suffered?

Lekachman might have posed a more basic question: What other outcome could have been produced through negotiations between parties with such unequal bases of power? This is not to suggest that Felix Rohatyn simply acted as an agent of the banks in his capacity as MAC chairman. His stature as a negotiator—and his capacity to enter crisis situations, from the near-collapse of Wall Street to the creation of an employee-owned steel company—depends, above all else, on perceptions of him as detached and impartial. During the New York crisis, Rohatyn clashed on several occasions with representatives of the financial world. At least once, when David Rockefeller, Walter Wriston, and others demanded a system of outside monitoring of city finances that Rohatyn found extreme, he sided explicitly with organized labor and the city. "One or two of the banks never forgave us [for adopting that position]," Rohatyn told us. "In fact, we [Lazard Frères] lost the business of one of them." But Rohatyn did not have to be partial to the interests of Chase Manhattan, Citicorp, and Morgan Guaranty to preside over a series of negotiations whose outcome was so partial to them. The constraints of time, as well as the financial realities under which the negotiations were conducted, dictated that the institutions most responsible for the city's insolvency would contribute the least to its financial health.

Donna Shalala, president of New York City's Hunter College, served as an original member of the MAC board. An admirer of Rohatyn, she has also been described as MAC's most independent director. During a conversation in her Hunter College office, she described how MAC functioned and the constraints under which the agency operated. "The one thing about the fiscal crisis was that every constituency was represented," Shalala said. "There is no question the financial people were always in the lead, because the key was, who was willing to do the financing. . . . The question was, how could we get enough credibility to sell billions of dollars worth of bonds? From my point of view, the concerns of low-income people and working people in particular—particularly the unions—were always on the table, and if any of the solutions were sensitive at all, it was because these constituencies were represented. I cannot think of a time when Felix Rohatyn just went with the banks' point of view. He always tried to fine-tune it, so everybody got part of the pain. Now, because the public sector was so heavily focused on low-income people, they were always going to take a larger part of it. But Felix spread it around more than one would have expected someone from the financial community to do."

But Shalala did concede that at the most basic level—the contributions of each constituency to the rescue package—the commercial lenders escaped largely unscathed. "They did incur some liabilities," she said. "But in some sense, through the combination of the bailout and the refinancing, [bank] shareholders were pretty well taken care of."

There were also serious, and troubling, political consequences to the agreement Rohatyn cast. The trauma of the fiscal crisis—and the revelations of incompetence and indecision among elected officials and greed among the city's financial patrons that were an integral part of it—could have given rise to a broad-based movement to challenge privilege and unfair sacrifice and to demand a degree of public accountability the absence of which made possible the fiscal gimmickry that led to the crisis in the first place. Instead, precisely the opposite occurred. Political power was moved further from the public realm and entrusted to two new agencies—MAC and the Emergency Financial Control Board, which in 1978 dropped *Emergency* from its title to reflect its more permanent status. Both of these organizations, whose commanding role has eroded as the city returned to financial health, were dominated by individuals—bankers, lawyers, real estate brokers, corporate executives—whose daily experiences and business pursuits could not possibly have allowed them to represent the vast mass of New Yorkers.

David Margolis discussed with us the democratic implications of what transpired: "The period into which Felix stepped, and he brought me into that, was an incredibly unique period. I don't know that it has ever been duplicated in this country. You had the collapse—the total, utter collapse —of the democratic process in this town. You had a Mayor [Abraham Beame] who had in effect been repudiated. The political process was frozen, and that permitted the private sector—in the shape of Felix Rohatyn and some of the others—to have an incredibly large amount of influence. The elected officials were frozen in their tracks. There was no confidence. They were dead broke. And so what Rohatyn and the rest of us had to say was the only relevant thing being said at that time. It is, in a sense, unhealthy. We weren't elected to anything. But the process, the electoral process, was at the moment immobilized because the elected people had absolutely no influence any longer. They had lost their right to govern in a sense. And so for a few years, between 1975 and 1977, when you had a new mayoral election, the private people in effect substituted for the democratic process."

. . .

The self-imposed caution that is a dimension of Rohatyn's standing and influence was evident during our conversations with the investment banker. Whenever he was invited to challenge key constituencies, it was possible to detect a marked drop in candor and insight. We asked Rohatyn to discuss criticism of corporate management raised in recent years by business school professors and management consultants—hardly an area where others have feared to tread. He began by offering a lengthy, and unsolicited, statement on positive developments in the area of "corporate responsibility" and ended with an uncharacteristically vague reply to the question he was asked.

"I think there has been an enormous change over the past ten or fifteen years in the issue of corporate responsibility and corporate ethics," Rohatyn said. "I think the makeups of boards of directors have changed, not only the attitude of management vis-à-vis their boards, but the attitudes of boards vis-à-vis their management. That isn't to say that on most boards you don't find people who are picked by management. But everybody knows that the rules of the game are different: that audit committees have to audit; that outside directors do pass on who gets invited to serve on the board; that minorities have to serve on boards, that women have to serve on boards. Obviously in the first flush of these things you get a lot of tokenism. But that is the inevitable evolution of these things. In the next generation it won't be tokenism. Women will be on the board as a matter of routine. Blacks will be on boards as a matter of routine. The notion that a director is responsible and liable is much more firmly established then it was ten or fifteen years ago. The notion that the Foreign

Corrupt Practices Act is something serious didn't exist twenty-five years ago. The whole question of insider trading. These are serious issues."

"The question, then, of managing for profit," he continued. "You are always going to have people who are better managers than others, who are smarter executives than others. By and large those people will manage for the long term because they are just better executives. There is at the same time the enormous pressure of the [financial] markets themselves. These companies have to raise money in the market, they have to maintain their credit rating. It is the financial community that demands short-term results, not so much the managers of these companies. . . . And that is not going to go away. The better managers will manage more for the long term, but still will be conscious that it would be nice to have quarter-to-quarter [profit] increases. The second-rate managers will look at the next quarter and not give a damn for the long run."

All told, our conversations with Rohatyn suggested a basic pattern of commentary: Speak no ill of the powerful, on whose behalf you labor. But this reluctance to challenge his friends and allies in the corporate world did not extend to other constituencies with whom Rohatyn enjoys close relations. An example was our discussion of the future of organized labor in the United States.

From the perspective of Rohatyn's effectiveness as a political activist, one of the most important by-products of his work in the New York City fiscal crisis was the entree it provided to the world of organized labor. A working relationship with leaders of the American labor movement provides an important leg up in Rohatyn's campaign to win credibility and broad political support for his various economic proposals. (On this score Rohatyn may have recalled the career of his European role model. Jean Monnet's Action Committee for a United States of Europe, his primary political vehicle, included a number of prominent union leaders. "In a democracy," Monnet once said, "the people who matter are the political parties and the trade unions.")

When he first entered the New York scene, Rohatyn was a stranger to labor leadership at both the city and the national level. "To me, they were like Martians, complete unknowns except for Victor Gotbaum, whose picture I had seen once when he was picketing Citibank," he told the *New Yorker*. "They viewed us [the MAC board], I am sure, as a bunch of businessmen and bankers about to rape the city, and to us they were a bunch of wild-eyed left-wing radicals who were trying to rape the city." Gotbaum's son, Joshua, now works as an understudy to Rohatyn at Lazard Frères. The young Gotbaum was well prepared to assist Rohatyn in pursuit of his industrial-policy agenda. Prior to joining Lazard, he worked as an aide to Sen. Gary Hart, no stranger to the issue. Before going to work for Hart, he was an assistant to Stuart Eizenstat, when Eizenstat was President Jimmy Carter's top domestic advisor. One of Eizenstat's last jobs for Carter was to help launch the Economic Revitalization Board, a tentative step in the direction of industrial policy. The board was chaired by AFL-CIO president Lane Kirkland and retired Du Pont chairman Irving Shapiro.

Victor Gotbaum is a labor leader in the rhetorical tradition of John L. Lewis; fiery oratory is a Gotbaum trademark. But his gruff demeanor melts away when the conversation turns to Felix Rohatyn. For example, Gotbaum is unfazed by the investment banker's reluctance to be as free with his criticisms of corporate America as he is with other sectors of society. "I respect the fact that Felix has a different constituency in terms of his primary concerns," Gotbaum told us. "He feels, and I think with strong justification, that he is an idea man. He is projecting the future. He is also sensitive to the fact that he is a partner in Lazard Frères. That's where he makes his living—that's where his primary constituency is." We asked if Gotbaum has ever disagreed with Rohatyn on issues outside of New York politics. He named two: what he called Rohatyn's "flirtation" with the presidential candidacy of John Anderson in 1980, and his call for "bipartisan" government at the national level. "He still has a lot of the European in him," Gotbaum jokes. "He talks in terms of coalition government and I say, 'Felix, what the fuck are you talking about?' "

Rohatyn also counts among his labor acquaintances several of the central figures of recent union history. He has dined with Douglas Fraser, retired president of the United Auto Workers, at Gotbaum's home. Lane Kirkland has visited Rohatyn at his summer home on Long Island.

These two labor leaders also played a role in one of Rohatyn's most recent efforts to win broad-based support for creation of a Reconstruction Finance Corporation. In January 1984, a high-powered task force of big-business executives, labor leaders, and government officials released, to front-page coverage in the New York Times, a report on industrial policy for the United States that amounted to a near-total endorsement of Rohatyn's agenda, including a proposal to create an Industrial Finance Administration obviously patterned after the investment banker's RFC. Rohatyn chaired the twenty-one-member panel, along with Lane Kirkland and Irving Shapiro, the former co-chairs of the Economic Revitalization Board. Other members of the group included Douglas Fraser, Lee Iacocca, former Treasury secretary Michael Blumenthal, and Sen. Edward Kennedy.

A staff member of the Center for National Policy, a think tank under whose auspices the group convened, told us that Rohatyn initiated the idea of a task force. "The work I did with Kirkland and Shapiro was

. . . obviously an attempt to get a different level of participation in the [industrial policy] idea," Rohatyn added. "And also to test out how valid it is—how many people will go along with it."

For someone with working relations with leading labor figures, Rohatyn is surprisingly ambivalent about the role of organized labor in the United States. During a conversation, we posed a simple question: Do you think it would be a positive development for the United States if labor unions represented a larger share of the workforce? Rohatyn answered with a "qualified yes" and then offered an explanation that might unsettle his friends in the union movement.

"Let me put it in a more general sense," he said. "I think it is in this country's interest to have a prosperous working class, and to have a working class that is involved, and feels involved, and feels secure. I think strong labor leadership is always preferable to weak labor leadership, because you can make agreements with people who are strong leaders. We could never have done what we did in New York City if Gotbaum, [Albert] Shanker [president of the American Federation of Teachers], and the other guys weren't secure in their positions. They couldn't have delivered.

"Now, whether or not that always requires organization—that's why I was hesitating and gave you a qualified yes. There is a big movement in this country to right-to-work laws, and to nonunion states and to nonunion companies. And I think the results have been, by and large, pretty good—for the people working in those companies and for the economy because that has been probably the most rapidly growing sector of the economy. And that has also probably been the sector with the most innovative changes in the relationship between management and labor. It has been the sector that has dealt most heavily in profit-sharing and stock-ownership plans [for workers], probably more flexible in adapting the workplace environment to the needs of the people. So my qualified yes is that today, the answer would be probably no."

.   .   .   .   .

The emergence of Felix Rohatyn as a force on the public stage, and his relationship with figures from organized labor, such as Victor Gotbaum and Lane Kirkland, is bound inextricably to his performance as savior of New York City. And not since the height of the New York fiscal crisis has Rohatyn possessed a comparable degree of authority. Much as he has for years as an investment banker, Rohatyn has used the standing and credibility forged during his tenure as chairman of MAC to shape a new set of alliances and contacts—a network that makes his political activism such a unique phenomenon in the corporate world. That network also established a base from which Rohatyn may again emerge as a commanding presence in a social or economic crisis of national or global significance.

One new branch of the Rohatyn network is a direct outgrowth of the MAC experience. Since the late 1970s, Lazard Frères has functioned as a financial advisor to major urban centers whose fiscal pressures are not unlike the crisis that faced New York earlier in the decade. Eugene Keilin, who joined Lazard Frères on January 1, 1979, after spending two years as executive director of MAC, described developments on this front. "The process of working through the problems [of New York] taught everyone who did it a fair amount they didn't know before about how cities ran, about how they could get in trouble and how they could get out of trouble," he told us. "Toward the end of the crisis period . . . Felix said, 'There are going to be other cities in trouble, and we have learned some things that we might apply to other places. Why don't you come to Lazard and we'll see if we can develop it into a business?' " Keilin obliged, and Lazard inaugurated a municipal advisory service that has immersed itself in the fiscal workings of Washington, D.C., Cleveland, Detroit, and Chicago.

The real significance for Rohatyn of Lazard's work in major cities has not been the fees it generates but the relationships it has allowed him to cultivate with an important force in American politics: big-city mayors. An example in this regard is Rohatyn's work with Coleman Young, mayor of Detroit.

Lazard became involved in the fiscal problems of Detroit in early 1981, after the city, for decades a fiscal basket case, projected a deficit for fiscal 1981 of $150 million in a total budget of less than $1.5 billion. Although Rohatyn actually did little of the day-to-day work to produce a rescue plan (city budget director Walter Stecher told us he never even *met* Rohatyn, for example), the Lazard partner was soon enough appearing on the front pages of local newspapers and being described, in the words of a lengthy *Monthly Detroit* profile, as "the second most powerful man in Detroit." As testimony to Rohatyn's stature, the *Detroit Free Press* devoted the entire op-ed page of its June 4, 1981, edition to a speech Rohatyn delivered to the Economic Club of Detroit.

It was perhaps to be expected, then, that when Coleman Young was named head of the U.S. Conference of Mayors in June 1982, Rohatyn was invited to address a gathering of the group in Minneapolis, where he plugged the RFC along with a broader program for national recovery. Five months later, Young, Rohatyn, and Coy Eklund, chief executive of Equitable Life Assurance, hosted a conference of fifteen big-city mayors, corporate executives, and union leaders on the thirty-eighth floor of the Equitable building in New York. "Coleman was the chairman; it was at Coy's house; and Felix was the main course," said John Gunther, executive director of the Conference of Mayors. The gathering produced a call for "bipartisan support" of a program that included a Reconstruction Finance Corporation. Since then, Rohatyn or Lazard associates, such as Keilin, have maintained communication with the mayors' organization.

"We're in touch with him or someone on his staff," Gunther said. "We are often on panels with him. If he changed his mind about the RFC approach, for example, I'm sure he'd call me so there would be no surprises."

The second obvious consequence of the MAC experience was Rohatyn's elevation to the status of national celebrity. As the fiscal crisis unfolded, lengthy, slavish profiles of the investment banker began to appear in newspapers and magazines across the country. The barrage of favorable press has not abated. In August 1984 the *New York Times Magazine* published a fawning profile of ten days in the life of "an intense, driven man whose mind, even at the height of a weekend spree, is rarely far from the latest deal." A December 1984 profile in *Institutional Investor* went so far as to quantify the history of Rohatyn's fame, an exercise that produced a Felix Index. The magazine went back to 1970 and traced Rohatyn's appearances in the media. Simple mentions in an article rated a 1. A whole article about him rated a 5. Long essays by him were valued at 10. And on and on. The 1984 Felix Index rating was 150, an all-time record.

This brand of high-profile attention was an important development in Rohatyn's ability, in the words of a 1981 *Newsweek* cover story, to "go national" with his political program. Media praise provided a base of credibility and the perception that Rohatyn's agenda is one to be reckoned with. It provided automatic access to political figures. And while the investment banker's exploits in New York warranted much of the attention, another factor in the torrent of publicity was his universally recognized capacity to charm and captivate reporters. *Newsweek*, one year after its breezy profile of Rohatyn, included him, along with such masters of public relations as Jesse Jackson and opera star Beverly Sills, in an article about the distinct styles of "media handlers."

Writer Charles Kaiser, who was a *New York Times* reporter during the fiscal crisis, described the Rohatyn style. "Rohatyn realized right from the start that he would have to control the [press] coverage of the controversy if he was going to determine its outcome," he explained. "He also understood exactly how to do that. The first half of his daily telephone call [with reporters] would always be on the record—almost invariably providing enough fresh information and quotable quotes to put Rohatyn and the reporter on the front page of the next day's *Times*. The second half would be off the record—so the reporter would know exactly what was most important about the story, and Rohatyn would never be quoted out of context. It was a masterly performance."

The investment banker's facility with the press is an endless source of comment among his friends and colleagues. They understand intuitively that it has been a central dimension of his rise to power in the public sphere. Rohatyn "deliberately cultivated" the media, said New York attorney Theodore Kheel. "I don't think there is any question, and I don't say this critically, whether the motive was self-aggrandizement, or whether he recognized the press was an important part of the exercise of power, that Felix recognized that he had to be accepted by the media in order to become as influential as he became. . . . Felix is extremely press minded, public relations minded. What he does he does with that view in mind. And he has been masterful at it."

Donna Shalala agrees. "Out of the MAC experience Felix learned a lot about the press," she said. "We used to have a big joke about him writing the editorials for the *New York Times*. He learned a lot about talking to editorial boards, about talking to reporters, about working with reporters. He loves quotable quotes. He works hard at coming up with public statements. He is an engaging, charming personality, very quotable, and therefore very attractive to the press. In some ways Felix is the Jesse Jackson of the financial world."

Rohatyn has also made skilled use of the media to air his agenda for politics and economic policy. Ever since the late seventies, when the crisis phase of the New York experience drew to a close, he has been a prolific producer of copy for newspaper op-ed pages and magazine opinion columns. Many of these articles directly address the New York experience and its lessons for the nation. Others are simply Rohatyn's musings on world problems. In the pages of the *Wall Street Journal* he made the case for Polish default. In the *Economist* of London he unveiled a program for "America in the 1980s." In *Business Week* he described his program to refinance Third World debt.

How important has media access been to promoting Rohatyn's broader political agenda? "By and large I haven't had any problem getting a forum, whether it's the various op-ed pages or a speech," he said. "Now, it is very different having a piece on the op-ed page of the *Times* or the *Washington Post* as opposed to making news, which has a much bigger impact. These op-ed pieces, they have some kind of cumulative impact. To that extent that I do other things, it's the things that I do that create a climate for my ideas. If I hadn't done anything [in business or politics],

I could write about industrial policy all day and nobody would pay the slightest attention."

It is, of course, not unusual for business executives and political activists to make use of op-ed pages to gain a hearing for their political agenda. But few individuals from the corporate world do so with as much frequency as Felix Rohatyn. Fewer still have produced the sort of lengthy essays he has published over the years in the *New York Review of Books.* Of all of Rohatyn's writings, none have elicited more attention or curiosity than these articles, which have run as long as ten thousand words, and which appear under such dire-sounding titles as "The Coming Emergency and What Can Be Done About It" and "Reconstructing America."

We asked Rohatyn to discuss the origins of his relationship with the *New York Review.* He explained it grew out of his friendship with Random House editor Jason Epstein, one of the founders of the journal, who owns a summer home not far from the Rohatyn's country retreat in Southampton. "Jason saw a speech I gave, somewhere in Texas, and suggested that the *New York Review* ought to look at it," he said. "He gave it to [editor] Bob Silvers, and that's how it started. The nice thing for me about the *New York Review* is that I don't have any space limitations. If I write for the *Times,* it's seven hundred fifty words, a thousand words. If I write for the magazine section of the *Times,* [the publication date] is six weeks away. And if I feel I have something to say, I don't want to wait that long. . . . [With the *Review*] I have the space, and that has been more important to me than doing [an article] in one thousand words and getting the clout of the *Post* or the *Times,* although I have done that also, obviously." Since his first *New York Review* article appeared in December 1980, Rohatyn has published no fewer than nine subsequent pieces for the publication, many of them based on speeches or congressional testimony.

.   .   .

Felix Rohatyn's accumulated stock of credibility, eminence, and personal associations with figures from a range of power centers in American life creates a formidable base for continued public impact. And there is evidence that his influence beyond Wall Street continues to expand, even if it has not made a qualitative advance comparable to his emergence during the New York crisis. Rohatyn has become a close advisor to New York governor Mario Cuomo. He has counseled him on tax policy and the fate of Shoreham, the troubled nuclear power plant on Long Island. His involvement with Weirton Steel, and the labor accord at Eastern Airlines, where he served as a director from May 1977 to November 1980, suggest that there is room in the private sector beyond mergers for application of his skills as a negotiator.

Rohatyn described how Lazard Frères became a paid advisor in the Eastern situation. "When I saw what was happening [between Eastern and its unions], I called Frank Borman [chief executive of Eastern] and suggested that maybe we could help—on the same principles that we worked here in New York," he said. "One, having a credible set of data, and then seeing if we could negotiate a solution. He was very quick to agree to it and support it . . . and finally so were the unions. But I said, 'Look, we're not going to get in there unless everybody wants us. If there is one party that doesn't want us, forget it.'"

Still, for there to be a dramatic expansion of Rohatyn's presence on the world stage, one of two scenarios must unfold. One scenario, admittedly elusive, is the emergence of a financial crisis of the type Rohatyn has warned about. Were the strong dollar, high U.S. interest rates, a default by a Third World borrower, or other factors to combine to produce dangerous instability in the world economy, who better than Rohatyn—who has written and spoken on the issue and who commands the confidence of political leads on both sides of the Atlantic—to serve as a broker and devise new global financial accommodations? A more straightforward scenario is the election of a Democratic president in 1988. Ever since his participation in the New York crisis, Rohatyn has been rumored as a likely cabinet nominee (perhaps secretary of the treasury) in the event a Democrat captures the White House. During our conversations, Rohatyn made it clear that he would not be displeased by such a development, although he emphasized that he has no interest in seeking elective office on the state or federal level.

"I think I would be a poor candidate," he explained. "I mean, I just can't see myself sitting and debating somebody eighty-seven times, in all kinds of places, or shaking people's hands coming out of subway stops. I don't think I would do it well. And if you are not going to do something well, you shouldn't do it." Does Rohatyn plan to campaign actively for an appointed position? "But you can't initiate those things," he said. "What can I do? What can happen? The only thing that can happen someday is that a Democratic president can ask me to serve in his administration. Well, if it happens, it happens. I can't make that happen."

As he sits high above Rockefeller Plaza, marrying companies to companies and dispensing advice and counsel to governors and presidents, Felix Rohatyn is, at this time, a power-in-waiting. He has chosen to be a catalyst and mediator for those who want him to play that role. In the early seventies, Rohatyn was dubbed "Felix the Fixer" by a *Washington Post* columnist writing about the Hartford Insurance scandal. But that moniker, which has stuck to Rohatyn, is more euphonic than accurate. Rohatyn is an arranger or rearranger—a man approached by others in times of stress and conflict. Anthropologists have long been writing of the importance and prevalence of such a role in primitive and folk societies. In our complex nation, too little attention has been paid to the figures who arrange or rearrange relationships between major sectors of the political economy. Such potentates are expected to be less visible, to take little credit, to recede into the background once the bargain has been struck. They are expected to remain on call, to have a passion for anonymity. Not so Felix Rohatyn. He manages to work the cloistered interstices of power surrounded by an aura of publicity and acclaim that is more than a little unique. That aura itself is an independent base of power that lifts him above the taint and greed of the interest groups he serves so profitably.

But the life of a very affluent, derivative human being can have its dissatisfactions. Life is comfortable when one is perched on a well-appointed island in a sea of public praise and removed from the brick-bats and responsibilities that assail those who are on the front lines. But one suspects that Rohatyn must crave the role of initiator on a global or national plane. He must sense frustration from time to time when he encounters individuals with inferior talents but greater initiatory power than he has. His extracurricular life as a pundit of future risks and remedies can scarcely satisfy for long a man prone to being where the action is.

After all, Rohatyn's observations on the U.S. and world economies, while not revolutionary, are nonetheless very serious. He sees a massive and deeply institutionalized gap between those who risk and those who pay, between those who perform and those who profit. He looks with grave concern on the bidding wars that have erupted between states for jobs and investment. "I think it [the bidding] is very unhealthy," Rohatyn said. "It means that states and cities with low social overheads can just keep on raping states and cities with high social overheads. Clearly at some point that is going to be terribly destructive. In order for it to stop, some national legislative initiative has got to come from somewhere." He is also troubled by the lack of public reaction to waste and duplication in the military budget and its deepening effect on the civilian economy.

"I am amazed that the military has had so little backlash," he commented. "That when you have vigilantism in our subways, mass transit that's collapsing, and the kinds of cutbacks in social programs that we are going to see, people don't think, Do we really need the B-1 bomber, or the MX missile?" The fragility of major U.S. financial institutions as a result of the global debt crisis is a subject he rarely omits in interviews.

Given this understanding of the gravities of the modern world, the question arises as to why Rohatyn is so comfortable coasting. He understands that we are living in a period where criticisms of greed, speculation, or financial short-sightedness have become unfashionable, a period when, in terms of economic power, anything goes. "I think we are in an incredible phase, where all the young graduates want to be Lee Iacocca and Bruce Wasserstein," he said. (Wasserstein is a merger specialist at First Boston whose deals have received some press attention.) "Everybody wants the stock market to go up. And investment bankers are like rock stars." Such a period makes it all the more urgent that Rohatyn risk some of his inventory of trust and friendship to act more vigorously on his views. He readily acknowledged to us that his influence has leveled off. But if he has any plans to disrupt his daily routine and networks with a commitment of personal energies in new directions, he is keeping them strictly to himself.

Men in positions of power often refuse to confront the potential inherent in such power to liberate others rather than further enhance their own conventional standing. The requisite courage, restlessness, and changing frames of reference are just not there. But it can be argued that the moral imperative is there—precisely because the admitted capability and the range to deploy it are ever present. Straddling careers as private-investment banker and public-crisis manager can have its strains. So, too, can juggling allegiances to constituencies of widely differing status that comprise the world of mergers and acquisitions and urban decay. The typology of power Felix Rohatyn represents needs much more sorting out, not only for his future's sake but for that of a democratic society as well.

CHARLS WALKER

External Revenue Service

Charls Walker, the most powerful tax lobbyist in Washington, is puzzled, angry, and a bit weary. It is March 1985. Ronald Reagan, the most reflexively probusiness president of the century, the president whose election set the stage for passage in 1981 of the most generous corporate tax cut in U.S. history, the candidate in 1980 to whom Walker served as an economic advisor, the candidate in 1984 who vowed not to raise taxes even in the face of the most massive budget deficits ever recorded by an administration—this same Ronald Reagan has received from the Treasury Department, and is poised to endorse at least in part, a program for fundamental tax reform that has elicited cries of anguish and forecasts of economic doom from many of the big-business executives whom Walker has served as a paid representative since 1973.

The Treasury tax plan, which was released on November 27, 1984, is a document of considerable historic significance. It represents an ambitious blueprint for tax equity produced by an administration whose economic policies have been fashioned for the primary benefit of large corporations and the affluent. The report, whose three volumes run nearly eight hundred pages, proposed that Congress abolish most of the deductions, credits, and exclusions that Charls Walker and his colleagues among the Washington lobbying elite have worked for years to promote and defend. The plan in return would lower the tax rate on corporations from 46 to 33 percent. The final Reagan program, which was released to Congress on May 29, 1985, backed down from many of the reforms proposed in the Treasury draft. It restored tax breaks for the oil and gas industry that Treasury would have abolished. It abandoned a new approach to depreciation that would have increased business taxes by $180 billion from fiscal 1986 through 1990 in favor of a plan that raises only $26 billion in additional revenue. But these concessions are of little comfort to Walker. He is concerned about the fate of the investment tax credit, a lucrative provision of the code he worked to reinstate during his tenure in the Nixon Treasury Department.

The investment credit—which was established in 1962, suspended in 1966, reinstated in 1967, permanently repealed in 1969, reborn in 1971, and made more lucrative in 1975, 1978, and again in 1981—permits corporations to subtract from their tax bills 10 percent of the cost of new investments in machinery and equipment. It is of particular significance to capital-intensive enterprises, such as producers of steel, automobiles, and chemicals. These are the giant corporations that are the core of Walker's client base. Reagan's proposal to repeal the credit would cost business an estimated $124 billion between fiscal 1986 and 1990.

"I'm reading the political tea leaves," the lobbyist despaired during the last of three conversations conducted over a twelve-month period. "This plan is playing like gangbusters in Peoria. All that guy [President Reagan] has to do is get on TV. Maybe have a little flagellating of corporations. Danny [Rostenkowski, chairman of the House Ways and Means Committee] went to New York and said, 'You corporations are not going to stand in the way of this.' We are back to the old word of 1982. Greed. Greedy corporations. Greedy Charlie Walker. But I'll [still] be in business here. And a few years later we'll put it all back together again."

Walker's reference to 1982, when his clients lost badly after a glorious victory on taxes the year before, underscores the imposing stakes of the world in which he operates and the self-renewing quality of much of what he does. That year, unnerved by massive budget deficits fueled by the tax cuts passed in 1981, Congress approved the Tax Equity and Fiscal Responsibility Act of 1982 (TEFRA). This legislation extracted a major financial toll on big business. In effect, TEFRA took back from corporate America a substantial chunk, perhaps as much as 40 percent, of the business tax breaks secured in 1981 through the Economic Recovery Tax Act (ERTA). The ERTA preferences were projected to cost the Treasury a staggering $500 billion from fiscal 1982 through 1990. What transpired in 1982, and what Walker fears may happen again, is that the specter of runaway budget deficits will leave corporate loopholes vulnerable to further reform.

This is not welcome news for the major corporations Walker represents. But it is very good news for Charls Walker—just as it was three years ago. "A lot of oxen were being gored, and, well, we just made a lot of money," the lobbyist told the *Washington Post* in 1983 when asked about TEFRA. Among the clients for whom he and his six associates toiled: pharmaceutical giant Johnson & Johnson, which opposed revision of a much-criticized loophole that exempts from U.S. taxes profits attributed by U.S. companies to their operations in Puerto Rico; the Aerospace Industries Association, a trade group that represents many of the nation's largest defense contractors, which objected to reform of an accounting method used by corporations with long-term contracts, notably Pentagon suppliers, to defer tax payments indefinitely; and a coalition of at least twelve powerful corporations and trade associations, which included ITT, Eastern Airlines, Scott Paper, and Bethlehem Steel, to defend what had become the single most controversial corporate tax break in memory. That program, called safe-harbor leasing, allowed corporations to "sell" their excess tax breaks to other firms.

It is difficult to discuss with precision just how lucrative the new Reagan-inspired turmoil has been for Walker and his firm. He does not disclose his annual compensation or the fees charged to clients. But it is undeniable that business is up substantially. "The most exposed thing in all of this now is the investment credit," Walker told us. "And I'm willing to bet money that if we [repeal] it this time around, which is a real probability, that in five years we'll be reinstating it. And this is the best thing that ever happened, could possibly happen, to our business."

Charls E. Walker Associates, a seven-member firm in which he and his wife, Harmolyn, hold a 40 percent interest and majority voting control, has in essence two categories of clients. Retainer clients, of which there are fourteen on tax policy, pay the firm an annual fee to represent their interests on Capitol Hill and coordinate overall legislative strategies. Project clients, such as the Independent Refiners Coalition, hire Walker Associates to work on their behalf for a specific period (say, the Ninety-ninth Congress) and negotiate a fee before work begins. Walker does not like to use contingency fees, where payment is increased in the event of legislative success, although he has on occasion. Nor does he charge by the hour. Why not go to hourly rates?

"We don't have that leverage," he replied. "We're not a law firm. There are only seven of us. We don't have a hundred guys in the back office working for fifty dollars an hour while we are charging two hundred dollars an hour. That's number one. We don't have that sort of factory and we don't want that sort of factory. Number two, what would I set my hourly fee at? I have got an implicit hourly fee, which right now is seven hundred fifty dollars." Walker explained how he calculates his "implicit" fee. "We just sort of say to a client, just in our own minds, when there are three [associates of the firm] in there, I am a seven-hundred-fifty dollar guy, another is a four-hundred-dollar guy, another is a two hundred dollar guy. And they ask us, 'If we were doing this on a time basis, what would you [charge]?' And I do a few things on a time basis. I'll have a lunch. A foreign banker wants to have lunch and talk about things. I'll charge him a thousand dollars."

Business is even more hectic today than it was in 1982. Walker turned sixty-two on Christmas Eve 1985 and planned by now to have cut back his work schedule. Instead he is speaking, testifying, meeting with clients, and shuttling between congressional offices at a pace that would wear down a man fifteen years his junior. "I'll tell you, I'm working my ass off," Walker said. "The game plan is not going like I wanted it to. I wanted at this stage to be coming in [to the office] about three days a week. But I am working harder now than I have at any time since I was in the Treasury Department."

Speech invitations alone, normally tendered by business groups anxious to hear Walker's forecasts of the politics of tax reform, are beginning to wear on the lobbyist. But at $7,500 per lecture, his standard honorarium, these invitations are difficult to refuse. "One reason I set the fee up there is to ration [lecture requests]," he said. "But they pay it, and I am getting ready to raise it again. . . . I had a *Fortune* seminar that I was invited to in Palm Springs the day before yesterday. It turned out I had to be in New York yesterday for a client. So I flew to Palm Springs on Tuesday night, made my speech, caught a plane at noon to New York, then came back to Washington. I have been to Palm Springs three times in the last six weeks. And I have to go again next week." Such are the demands and rewards of life as a big-business lobbyist.

. . .

Has Charls Walker never met a tax break he didn't like? "No, that's not fair to say," the lobbyist chuckled, amused by the question. "That's not fair to say. We've turned down clients here. We don't take on business we don't agree with. We were approached several years ago to defend tax-exempt mortgage bonds. I don't like that." Mortgage bonds are issued by state governments to finance home construction and have been criticized for years as an inefficient means to that end. "We were approached by the savings and loans to lobby on All-Savers Certificates. No. It wasn't good public policy. It's not that I like or dislike them all that much, it's just that I don't get all that uptight about them. Let me get something here."

Walker rose from his chair, walked to his desk, and returned with a background volume from the president's proposed budget for fiscal year 1985. He turned to "Special Analysis G," a section of the document that details the estimated costs of various tax-subsidy programs.

"Stanley Surrey got into the lingo the concept of a tax expenditure," Walker said. (Surrey, the late Harvard Law School professor, served as assistant secretary of the treasury for tax policy from 1961 through 1968.

He was an influential critic of many of the business tax preferences that Walker champions.) "And the newspapers take these and play them to a fare-thee-well about what an awful thing this is. And then you look and see the analysis on tax expenditures. The biggest, I guess, is employer contributions for employee pension funds. That's pretty good stuff for public-policy purposes. The second biggest one is employer contributions to employee medical plans. Retirement and health. The third biggest is for deductions for mortgage interest and taxes on your home. You're dealing with home, health, and retirement. There are your three biggest loopholes. Now, I cannot say that overriding public-policy concerns say you eliminate them. And you're not going to do it anyway. I just think it's a waste of time. It's not that I love tax preferences; we're just arguing about the wrong thing."

Walker's manner is informal, but his comments are delivered with polished conviction. He takes taxes seriously, not only because it is as a tax lobbyist that he makes a very comfortable living, but because it is the field to which he has devoted much of his professional life. For more than fifteen years—from 1969 through 1972 as undersecretary and then deputy secretary of the treasury, and since 1973 as chairman of Charls E. Walker Associates—he has been a visible and powerful factor in shaping the federal tax code. No figure outside of Congress has had such influence over the direction of tax policy over such a sustained period of time as Charls Walker. And while the legislative faces and specific battles change, his fundamental agenda remains the same.

Robert McIntyre, director for federal tax policy, Citizens for Tax Justice, is one of the few Washington lobbyists who for years has worked to counter the tax agenda of Walker and his business allies. He discussed with us the power of his adversary. "Walker's whole career has been devoted to trying to cut taxes for rich people and corporations," McIntyre said. "The way he has done it is to advocate, with a great deal of success, new loopholes in the tax laws. If there is anybody who can take responsibility for the mess the tax code has become, it is him." According to Stanley Surrey, Walker's goal is "to get the tax system organized in terms of business tax relief. This in turn generally means putting in a lot of tax expenditures that favor business. That's his role in life, and he is very skillful at it."

Much like the office walls of a trial lawyer who frames newspaper accounts of favorable verdicts to impress insurance adjusters, Walker's Pennsylvania Avenue headquarters, situated one block from the White House, testifies to the length of his tenure in Washington and the focus of his activities. On one wall, above a sofa and easy chair, are portraits and personal messages from six past secretaries of the treasury. He has worked for four of them. George Shultz, under whom Walker served in 1972, wrote that he was "a real professional and a great public servant. With my admiration for the breadth and quality of your work and my thanks for the great help you have given to me and your friendship." John Connally, who was Walker's superior at Treasury just prior to Shultz, was no less appreciative. "With gratitude for his loyalty and support, admiration for his ability and deep appreciation for his friendship," the inscription read. On the wall behind his desk, above a plastic bag containing more than a dozen cigars, are letters, most accompanied by photographs, from every Republican president since World War II. There is also a photograph and message from Lyndon Johnson, with whom Walker consulted from time to time after Johnson retired to his ranch and Walker moved into the Treasury Department.

The Johnson photograph is significant not as evidence of Walker's bipartisanship—he is closely identified with the Republican party—but to situate him geographically. Walker is a Texan. He was born in Graham, which has a population of roughly ten thousand and is located ninety miles northwest of Dallas–Forth Worth. Walker's hometown is small, but it is extremely wealthy. According to its finance director, Graham in the late 1970s was home to seventy-two millionaires, more per capita than any other town or city in Texas. The source of this wealth is oil, which fueled two economic booms in the region and played an important role in Walker's own life. The lobbyist's mother, Sammye McCombs Walker, who turned ninety-one in November 1984, still lives in Graham. She told us the family built and operated the Walker Hotel to cater to the truck drivers and field workers attracted to the town by the oil rush of the late 1920s. The hotel had approximately fifty rooms, and rent was fifty cents per day.

"This whole area boomed," she said of the period. "We had only one train a day in here. It would come late in the afternoon. If you came in from the east by train to do business, you had to spend two nights here. People would travel ten or fifteen miles just to find rooms for the night." The Walker Hotel provided an adequate if modest source of income, but the family's financial situation eventually changed for the better. Charls's father, Pinkney Clay Walker, who died soon after his son's fifth birthday, had purchased property in east Texas. This land began to produce oil in the early 1930s. The output was not sufficient to make the family wealthy, but it did provide a margin of security and finance college educations for Charls and his brother and sisters. Mrs. Walker saw to it that her sons would pursue their education by discouraging them from working in the oil fields. "I didn't want the boys to do that," she said. "That paid higher wages than anything else and I wanted them to stay interested in school."

Walker often returns home to Graham when Congress is not in session, especially in August, to visit his mother and fish on Possum Kingdom Lake, where he maintains a cabin.

The lobbyist, during our conversations, was every bit the expansive Texan. He is gregarious, laughs easily, and enjoys using homespun sayings and stories to make his points. Could it be that the Treasury Department issued its tax reform agenda because the intellectual case against corporate tax breaks is so powerful? "Sure," he replied. "And the tooth fairy will walk in here in a minute and bring us all a Jack Daniels and water." Walker's shirt is white and crisply pressed, a tie strung loosely around his neck. His brown pants are supported by red suspenders, and he wears brown penny loafers. Walker is tall, about six foot one, and solidly built. Although he obviously relishes his Texas roots and enjoys the colorful use of language, he is very much in tune with East Coast values and mores. He told us he favors handgun control, mandatory passive restraints in automobiles, and is "strongly pro-choice" on abortion. These are hardly the views of many fellow Texans.

Walker was accompanied during two of our conversations by Mark Bloomfield, executive director of the American Council for Capital Formation. Walker became chairman of the American Council in February 1975. The organization was unfocused and ineffective. He immediately changed its name and began to assemble a high-powered staff. The Council today boasts a board of directors that includes several of Washington's most prominent lobbyists, as well as representatives of many large corporations, several of whom are also Walker clients. It has become a powerful force in support of reduced taxes on capital gains and other proposals to slash taxation on income from capital. Executive Director Bloomfield is in many ways an instructive foil to his chairman. In his mid-thirties, trained as a lawyer, he is representative of the new breed of young professionals that has streamed to Washington to swell the ranks of the thousands of lawyers, economists, and trade association officials who attend to the legislative needs of big business.

Washington lobbyists often promote, and thrive on, an image as political guns for hire, paid hands who are willing and able to represent any client, no matter how unworthy the cause. "Our approach is to take the first case that comes in the door," a lobbyist who specializes in trade policy told the *Washington Post* in 1983. "That means working both sides of the street. And we've been quite successful at it. We've taken the domestic-protection side for some clients, the free-trade side for others." Such talk is anathema to Walker. He has worked diligently over the years to cultivate an image of substance and professionalism. Walker takes pains to defend any tax preference with which he is associated as consistent with his guiding perspective on tax policy and his long career in the field. "The basic ideas that I have, and that I push, I had before I came into the [lobbying] business," he insisted. "I didn't develop my ideas on taxation to be tailored to the client. It's the other way around."

Walker on occasion does play the role of lobbyist-entrepreneur. That is, he develops an independent position on taxes or economic policy and then works to enlist the support of current and potential clients for his game plan. Since 1983 he has advanced a program to raise substantial amounts of new revenue—perhaps as much as $100 billion per year over five years—and create a mechanism, such as a bipartisan presidential commission, to mold a political consensus on spending restraint to reduce and eventually abolish the federal budget deficit. Walker set out this scenario in August 1983 in a paper circulated among politicians, corporate executives, and the media. It revolves around adoption of a value-added tax (VAT) or a similar levy that Walker has dubbed a tax on business transactions (TBT). A VAT is levied on the value added to a product at each stage of the manufacturing and distribution process and is ultimately passed on to the final consumer. Most economists, including Treasury Department analysts, who considered and rejected proposals to adopt a VAT during their deliberations over tax reform, criticize the tax as regressive. Poor and middle-income families spend a larger share of their annual earnings on consumption than do the wealthy and would thus pay a higher percentage of their income in taxes. But a VAT has enormous power to generate new revenues—and replace taxes lost to the Treasury through business loopholes.

Norman Ture, who served as undersecretary of the treasury for tax and economic affairs for part of the first Reagan term, and who is also a board member of the American Council, pointed to Walker's support of a VAT as an example of his tenacity. "I'll say this about Charlie, he's a bulldog," Ture said. "Like all the rest of us, he seldom has an unequivocal victory. But when he gets a notion in his mind and commits himself to it, especially when the commitment is public, he doesn't give up. He insists on ultimate vindication. Charlie has been after a value-added tax at least since 1971 and very likely before then. . . . And I don't know one year when he hasn't been keenly interested in seeing whether or not this wasn't the time for some revival of it. So I think he's going to pursue this, and pursue this until he knows once and for all he can't possibly have it—and I think that's going to take an awful lot of persuading—or until he succeeds."

This is not to suggest that Walker represents the interests of big business any less than does the swashbuckling trade lawyer. Rather, Walker does not wait for clients to walk through the door. Such an aggressive approach to lobbying makes him even more influential, for it gives him an initiatory as well as a facilitating role.

Walker is known to friend and foe alike on Capitol Hill as Charlie, a defeat of sorts for his mother, who deleted the *e* from her son's first name hoping he would not be so addressed. Back in Graham, she said, he is known as Charls. To his office staff the lobbyist is neither Charls nor Charlie but Dr. Walker, recognition of the fact that unlike many of his peers who labor to shape the tax code to the specifications of their clients, Walker is not a lawyer but an economist. He received his Ph.D. in 1955 from the Wharton School of the University of Pennsylvania. He even taught briefly at Wharton and at the University of Texas, from which he graduated with an MBA in 1948. Walker's professional credentials also include three years as vice-president and economic advisor at the Federal Reserve Bank of Dallas and a brief tenure as economist and special assistant to the president of the Republic National Bank of Dallas.

These credentials are important, because tax lobbying often turns on an ability to justify even the most narrow special-interest preference on the basis of broad policy goals: job creation, capital formation, export promotion. Set the terms of the debate over a provision and you are partway to its approval. And it is easier to influence the debate if you can demonstrate that you believe the case you are making. Walker is a master at this dimension of his job. He has been advocating, with a great deal of success, many of the same policies, for many of the same clients, for many years. During a conversation, the lobbyist will actually lean back and close his eyes as he launches into a defense of a particular tax preference or offers a forecast on the political environment for its passage, repeal, or modification. He writes op-ed articles, for which he is usually identified as a former deputy secretary of the treasury or chairman of the American Council, that set out recommendations on tax policy, many of which are of obvious benefit to his paid clients. He is also co-editor of a book, *New Directions in Federal Tax Policy for the 1980s*, based on a 1983 conference of tax experts and politicians convened by the American Council. Walker even distributes a biweekly cassette service, *Charls E. Walker's Washington Economic Report*, in which "Dr. Walker" explains to his listeners developments on Capitol Hill and in the White House and how they affect the business community.

This professional background is important in an organizational and activist sense as well. Beginning in the mid-1970s, debate over tax policy on Capitol Hill fell increasingly under the sway of academics and economic analysts who argued that excessive taxation of business and affluent individuals was contributing to economic stagnation and a perceived shortage of investment capital. The most vocal advocates along these lines were the supply-siders—economists such as Arthur Laffer, Norman Ture, and Paul Craig Roberts. They were joined by less flamboyant figures, such as Martin Feldstein, whose work at Harvard and as president of the National Bureau of Economic Research was used to defend major 1978 reductions in the tax on capital gains and to promote other reductions of taxes on income from capital. By virtue of his status as someone more substantive than a typical Washington hired gun, Walker not only has been able to make use of the proliferation of these theories in his lobbying, but has encouraged and promoted it.

"I am very, very strong on maintaining ties with the academic community and seeing that they are adequately funded on a no-strings-attached basis," he said. "I raise money for them when I can. . . . When I was executive vice-president of the American Bankers Association, I set up an annual conference of top monetary economists, people like Milton Friedman. We commissioned papers, and they would fight to get in it. It keeps you in touch with the academic community. It keeps you on your toes in thinking about things. And if you do it right—on a no-strings-attached basis—it gives you credibility with academicians that are pure, and also with academicians that are moving close to the political arena."

Of course, "strings" are unimportant if one can pick and choose experts whose broad perspective is in keeping with your agenda. The American Council for Capital Formation commissioned supply-side guru Laffer in the late 1970s to develop an econometric model based on his principles of taxation. Walker himself is no supply-sider—indeed, his relations with supply-side activists and politicians have been marked by no small measure of tension—but Laffer's seductive forecast of increased revenues through lower tax rates is of obvious utility to anyone seeking reductions in business taxes. Walker then testified before the Senate Finance Committee in November 1979 and urged the panel to make use of Laffer's "Prototype Wedge Model" as it considered proposals to make radical changes in the system used to depreciate capital assets. Those changes were adopted two years later and represented the largest tax cut in corporate history.

Walker is also not adverse to stacking the intellectual deck. When the American Council convened its conference in January 1983 on future directions of tax policy, the lobbyist asked John Connally, his Treasury Department mentor, to deliver the keynote address. Connally's speech mirrored almost perfectly the Walker agenda for tax reform—lower income taxes on well-off individuals and corporations and the introduction of a tax on consumption to generate new revenues—and Walker made reference to it in his introduction to the book that grew out of the conference. Little wonder. According to Mark Bloomfield, Walker helped draft Connally's address, a convenient technique to manufacture observations by prominent figures that you can later cite as evidence of the wisdom of your agenda.

. . .

An almost automatic question to pose when examining the career of a lobbyist is, How powerful is he? Or, given Walker's prominence, Is he the most powerful? Were influence strictly a function of visibility, the answer to this last question would be unambiguous, and a resounding yes. Walker's personal expansiveness, his flair for self-promotion, and a lobbying style that reveals his capacity to address tax issues at a deeper level than the shallow pronouncements of most garden-variety flaks have created a high profile for him in Washington. He treats the press well—speaking on the record where other lobbyists demand the comforts of anonymity; attending dinners hosted by Mark Bloomfield where leading corporate executives, prominent journalists, and members of Congress chat and exchange opinions—and the press has done well by him. Since the release of the Treasury tax plan in November 1984, Walker's forecasts, and often his photograph, have been featured in magazines and newspapers from *Fortune* to the *New York Times.* Reporters routinely refer to him, as did a May 28, 1984, *Washington Post* editorial, as "the most powerful tax lobbyist in town."

This is not to suggest that Walker is completely satisfied with his access to or influence with the press. He complained to us that the *Washington Post,* the single most important media organ in his line of work, has demonstrated a consistently pro-reform bias in its coverage of the Treasury plan. Walker was livid about the fact that the editorial page, columnists Hobart Rowan and Robert Samuelson, and guest columnists such as Brookings Institution economist Joseph Pechman have all supported tax simplification along the lines of the Treasury model. Walker has gone so far as to write publisher Donald Graham to register his objections. He also expressed deep resentment at the *Post*'s refusal in recent years to publish any of the op-ed articles he has submitted. This represents a major setback for the lobbyist. He used to "grade" *Post* editorials on taxes and economic policy and send his evaluations to the editorial staff.

"Now they get surly about it," he despaired. What explains the turnaround? "I just have to believe it is the people who control the editorial pages," Walker replied. "I was in [the op-ed page] almost once a month back in 1973 and 1974. Meg [Greenfield, the newspaper's editorial page editor] and I got along real good. I used to get a real bang out of it. I called her up when they turned down my piece, which the *New York Times* printed in the premier [op-ed] space on a Sunday, right-hand top of the page, on why the corporate tax is a crazy tax," he continued. "I sent that first to the *Post.* [Editorial staff writer] John Anderson said, 'Hey, this looks good, I'll send it to Meg.' John Anderson calls back and says, 'We're not going to run it.' I called Meg up, and we had some pretty strained words. We haven't talked since then."

Walker's public visibility can also ruffle feathers among his colleagues. John Meagher, Washington vice-president of LTV Corporation and another central figure among business tax lobbyists, discussed the Walker image. "Charlie brings some very obvious negatives to the process," he told us. "He is considered very much the wheeler-dealer, sort of the personification of the corporate, cigar-smoking world. And that has some barnacles attached to it as well as pluses."

One lesson in the hazards of visibility came in January 1978, when Elizabeth Drew, Washington correspondent for *The New Yorker,* wrote a lengthy profile of the lobbyist for that magazine. The Drew piece was highly complimentary. She was allowed to follow Walker as he worked his magic on Capitol Hill and she reported on his doings and musings in great detail. An official of a trade association on whose behalf Walker has lobbied told us he considered the article "a nauseating piece of fluff." But it did include a few revealing personal anecdotes. There was the image of lobbyist Walker, with extensive client interests in pending energy legislation, spending a "pretty liquid" Thanksgiving with Energy secretary James Schlesinger, who is a personal friend. "Jim said something about 'Walker's greed' and 'the greed of his clients,' " Walker told Drew. "And someone said something about 'amazing grace,' and I made up a parody called 'Amazing Greed.' "

Many of Walker's colleagues were aghast when the piece appeared. We asked whether he regretted having agreed to the profile, or whether, as other lobbyists and corporate representatives speculated, the image Drew sketched made Walker all the more attractive to potential clients.

"Number one, I thought it was a very well-done article," he said. "Number two, I don't know whether it brought any more business or not. Number three, on balance I still think it was a plus. I'm glad I did it, even though, and I don't blame her at all, I misunderstood the ground rules. We didn't talk about ground rules. I didn't know it was going to be a stream-of-consciousness thing. And I did have considerable trouble over one or two or three little things that got twisted." Were his peers troubled by the article? "They were pretty down on it," he said. "That wasn't the way they looked at" how to deal with the press. "A lot of them go around and whisper all the time." How serious were their reservations? "Some were saying, 'He's through in this town.' That no client would touch me with a ten-foot pole."

Walker's mixed history of relations with the press, and the occasional fallout from a high profile that for the most part has served him well, may explain why James Smith, a former comptroller of the currency who is president of Walker Associates, was reluctant to rate his partner's influence. "In this town, probably the worst thing that can happen to you in terms of influence is for somebody to get the idea that you are the big kid on the block," he said. "Everybody in this town likes to take a shot at the big kid on the block.

"You go through the [newspaper] morgue files," Smith continued. "The typical Washington influence story is Charlie Walker, Tommy Boggs, Bob Gray, Bill Timmons, J. D. Williams. And there isn't a new goddamn fact in any of the stories. So it becomes the Washington mythology. I think most people in the Congress who are associated with tax policy know this firm and know members of it. So does the staff up there. I would like to think most of them think we know what we're doing. I would suspect there are some who can't stand our intestines."

Ultimately, the question of singular influence—who is the most powerful, on any issue, on any given day—is probably unimportant. Charls Walker is invariably mentioned as a member of the elite cadre of Washington power brokers who have earned consensus recognition as super-lobbyists: Thomas Hale Boggs, Jr., son of the late House majority leader and a senior partner in the law firm Patton, Boggs and Blow; public-relations guru Robert Keith Gray, whose firm, Gray and Company, is headquartered in a Georgetown building called the Power House; William Timmons, who is closely identified with the Reagan White House; and lawyer-lobbyist Jerry Don "J. D." Williams, whose fundraising prowess is well known among Washington insiders. What distinguishes Walker from these lobbyists is not the *degree* of his influence but the path his career has taken, the singular agenda on which he has focused his accumulated power, and the lobbying techniques he has adopted in pursuit of his agenda.

The central distinction between Walker and most other high-priced Washington lobbyists is his ongoing and concentrated focus on the tax code, an interface between government and private economic power whose consequences for distributive equity and economic growth are enormous. Consider the stakes involved in the broad directions and obscure interstices of tax policy: billions of dollars of profits that corporations can retain, rather than mail to Uncle Sam, if their favored provisions become law; creation and promotion of whole industries, from real-estate tax shelters to oil and gas drilling, whose existence is nourished in large part by tax subsidies; the level and allocation of capital investment, which is affected in important ways by the role of taxes in determining relative rates of return among competing uses of assets. What is of singular importance about Walker is not that he operates in this arena—attendance at any hearing of the House Ways and Means Committee or Senate Finance Committee communicates just how many lawyers and lobbyists earn a handsome living off the tax code—but that he has helped to set in motion and perpetuate a political momentum that has ushered in, with occasional interruptions, a golden era for proliferating tax credits, deductions, and exclusions for wealthy individuals and major corporations. This political momentum has left the tax code more unfair and more complicated. But for Walker's clients it is decidedly less burdensome.

Over the years Walker has played, and continues to play, a number of roles that most other lobbyists either will not or cannot. He shapes media coverage of tax policy through extensive dealings with the press, including editorial briefings and the cultivation of personal relationships with reporters. He works with nonprofit but corporate-financed organizations, such as the American Council for Capital Formation, to mold a business consensus on the tax agenda and to advocate the adoption of that agenda through congressional testimony, conferences, seminars, and the promotion of academic studies. He debates, speaks, and writes. Few lobbyists are angered if they are denied access to the *Washington Post* op-ed page. They have no interest in submitting articles. Fewer still are willing to appear on programs such as *This Week with David Brinkley*, as did Walker on November 25, 1984, to describe a proposal to raise hundreds of billions of dollars in additional tax revenue that his clients do not yet support and that was bound to incur the wrath of a substantial segment of the business community.

How is Walker different from most other business lobbyists? "I have the impression that he organizes a lot of business thinking," said Barber Conable, a congressman for twenty years and ranking Republican on the House Ways and Means Committee until he chose not to stand for reelection in 1984. "He is a background person as much as he is a lobbyist. He likes big projects, and he likes to create the kind of environment where decisions will be made that he thinks will be salubrious for his clients generally. Also, he is tireless. He calls a lot, and usually he is taking somebody's pulse. What would you think about this or that? That means my conversations with him are usually about a minute and a half long.

"Walker is an idea man," Conable continued. "He doesn't try to pull the strings of influence the way J. D. Williams or Tommy Boggs would. Their associations are such—they raise money for Democratic candidates and therefore they have a right to expect loyalty from incumbents they own. Walker isn't that way. Walker likes to make of himself an overall business lobbyist. He has lunches for his clients at his office, and they exchange ideas. Charlie throws things out as a devil's advocate, to increase the mix and to encourage the intercommunication of his clients, just the way you would go to a meeting of the chamber of commerce and try to establish a position. He encourages collective decision making."

It is as if Walker plays the role of both lens and prism for the translation of corporate power into political clout. Like the focusing function of a lens, he takes disparate opinions, programs, and technical evidence and adjusts them until he has a consensus on the proper course of tax policy and the appropriate strategy for its implementation. This is perhaps Walker's most critical function. As he well understands, the most serious adversary of corporate power in Washington—particularly on taxes, where organized citizen opposition to business preferences is sparse and underfunded—is division among the corporations themselves. Bitter disagreements among the companies that pushed through the tax reduction of 1981 partially explain congressional approval one year later of legislation that took back much of that cut. Similar divisions have surfaced over the Treasury tax program. The American Electronics Association, the National Federation of Independent Business, and the Food Marketing Institute have all endorsed the plan and are barnstorming the country to enlist support. These associations represent sectors of the economy, such as high-technology manufacturing and supermarkets, that benefit little from current tax preferences and thus pay high effective rates compared with basic industries. Corporations from the steel and chemical industries, sectors of the economy that make extensive use of current loopholes, are horrified by the plan.

Walker functions as a prism in that his reach as a lobbyist is not confined to Washington wheeling and dealing. He speaks to local business organizations, meets with editors and reporters from regional newspapers, and otherwise disperses ideas forged on Pennsylvania Avenue among opinion makers on Main Street. He and Mark Bloomfield traveled widely in 1984 under the auspices of the American Council for Capital Formation, a speaking tour that Bloomfield dubbed the Road Show, to sow the seeds of grass-roots support for Walker's program of consumption taxes and budget cuts as a solution to the deficit crisis. As part of the Road Show, Walker and Bloomfield conducted briefings for *Fortune, Time, Business Week, Newsweek,* and other major newspapers and magazines. They also spent time in six cities—Minneapolis, Houston, Phoenix, Atlanta, Chicago, and Stamford, Connecticut—where they briefed the regional press, addressed a major economic forum, and met with local business leaders.

Walker explained the goal of the Road Show. "You're trying to do two things with the business leaders," he said. "You're trying to raise their conscious understanding of the [tax and budget] issue. You're also trying to acquaint them with the American Council. You follow up and see if you can get them to support the Council and the Road Show. In Houston, John Connally had a breakfast for us with twenty or thirty heavy hitters. Then we went over and met with the *Houston Post* business editor. I spoke to a group called the Houston Forum at lunch. We did the *Houston Chronicle* in the afternoon. And then we had a seminar at Rice University late in the afternoon with students, faculty members, and some business people. Minneapolis was very similar."

This focus on grass-roots activism, an unusual strategy for a Washington lobbyist, reflects one of Walker's favorite cants about political power. He likes to say that real clout is not controlled by big business or well-funded special interests but by the "Great American Middle Class," which he defines as families with incomes in the $50,000 to $70,000 range. This is the constituency Walker believes a lobbyist must harness to be truly effective. There is an obvious self-serving quality to this idea. It obscures the special-interest power of insiders such as Walker. But the point is not completely without merit. Walker and his allies were able to defeat proposals in 1978 to increase taxes on capital gains by playing on the anxieties of middle-income taxpayers who equate low capital-gains taxes with the ability to sell their homes. The corporate tax agenda triumphed in the 1970s and early 1980s in part because Walker and his colleagues were able to tap broad public resentment over automatic increases in personal taxes fueled by bracket creep. Walker said his business clients are now under siege because the middle class is responding with enthusiasm to the rate-cutting objectives of the Treasury program.

"I feel like I understand politicians and what motivates them," he told us in May 1984. "And I feel like I understand people—what their fears are, what their hopes are, their aspirations. I understand. I got into a big argument, never straightened it out, with Norman Ture at our last American Council meeting. I made the remark that I was very impressed that, recently, politicians are telling me that the flat-tax concept is sweeping their constituents. And I said, 'I understand that.' And Norman in effect said, 'Well, do they know what they're endorsing?' I said, 'No, they don't.' Norm seemed to think that blasted the validity of what I said. The validity was still one hundred percent. People are swinging toward the flat tax, and the fact that these politicians are mentioning it only weeks after April fifteenth gives me the answer right there. It's not that they have this great yearning for simplicity [in the tax system], and so on. What's getting them is not "simple," or "fair." *Flat* is what's getting them. Middle-class Americans are pissed when they fill out those returns and say, 'My God, I'm in the 35 percent bracket, and I still can't send my kid to Harvard. I'm working, my wife's working, we're drawing down twenty-five thousand a year apiece, and I'm paying that damn tax.' So somebody comes along and says, 'We'll flatten that out and put on a maximum rate of 14 percent or 26 percent. Just the word *flat*. If it's flat, it's got to be better than it is now. For some reason, I can understand this, and even anticipate that sort of thing. Where a guy like, without any criticism, Norman Ture, can't."

Walker's role as lens and prism is most pronounced in his work with the so-called Group of Fourteen. These are the core tax clients of Charls E. Walker Associates: fourteen major U.S. corporations that pay the firm substantial retainers to represent their interests in the tax code before Congress. The Group of Fourteen includes some of the largest and most powerful corporations in America. IBM and Du Pont became members in 1984. The group has for years included Procter & Gamble, AT&T, and Ford Motor Company.* This stable of clients provides Walker with an enormous reservoir of potential political power. These companies in 1984 together controlled assets of more than $205 billion, generated sales of nearly $260 billion, and employed more than 2 million workers. They have plants, suppliers, and customers in virtually every state and in most congressional districts. Walker's job is to work with these companies, harmonize their positions on taxes, gather documentation of the potential economic repercussions if their positions are not adopted—forecasts of reduced profits or cash flow, and thus fewer jobs—and use this information to win access and plead his case. To this end, Walker Associates hosts meetings of the Group of Fourteen once every four or six weeks. Thirty or so individuals attend: Walker and a few members of his firm, a specialist on taxes, and a Washington representative from each of the client companies. The lobbyist has also offered to spend a day at the headquarters of each client to brief executives and answer questions on the Reagan tax plan and the prospects for reform.

Walker and his colleagues at Walker Associates do much more than attend to the strategic tax needs of blue-chip corporations. The firm is working on protectionist legislation that would insulate domestic chemical companies and independent oil refiners from foreign competition. It has represented utilities from New Jersey and Pennsylvania looking for a

---

*The following corporations are members of the Group of Fourteen: Alcoa, AT&T, Bechtel Group, Champion International, Dresser Industries, Du Pont, Ford Motor Company, GTE, Goodyear Tire & Rubber, IBM, Owens-Illinois, Procter & Gamble, Union Carbide, and Weyerhaueser. Totals for Group of Fourteen assets, sales, and employment are exclusive of Bechtel, which, as a closely held company, does not release such information.

government bailout to defray cleanup costs at Three Mile Island. It was hired by beer giant Anheuser-Busch in 1984 when its executives feared that producers of cigarettes and hard liquor, both targeted for a tax increase, would try to shift some of the burden of higher "sin" revenues to the drink of the working man. They did try, but the brewers resisted successfully.

Walker and his firm even represented the Netherlands Antilles, a chain of six Caribbean islands spread over a five hundred-mile area north of Venezuela, in that country's quixotic 1984 campaign to beat back a tax bill endorsed by a powerful lineup of corporations, investment bankers, and securities traders. The issue in question was a long-standing proposal to repeal the 30 percent withholding tax imposed on interest earned by foreign citizens and companies who invest in U.S. securities. Sponsors of the repeal measure argued that withholding represented a substantial barrier to U.S. access to foreign capital markets. That barrier had been overcome in the past through incorporation by U.S. firms of finance subsidiaries in the Netherlands Antilles, which since 1955 has enjoyed a treaty with the United States that exempts its citizens and corporations from the tax. The proposal to repeal the tax, which did ultimately pass and was signed into law, threatened to dry up the lucrative fees and levies collected by the island government from these finance subsidiaries.

This work on behalf of the Antilles must rank as one of the more unusual assignments of Walker's career, although the $100,000 retainer his firm was paid might explain why he was willing to advance the interests of an island nation of which few people have ever heard. Walker told us he "cleared this with corporate clients" before he agreed to work for the Antilles. He insisted that most companies were indifferent to the choice between repeal of the tax and renegotiation of the Antilles treaty to make less vulnerable the tax status of U.S. finance subsidiaries operating there. But his activities did not sit well with at least one lobbyist who represented two prominent investment banks. "I think people are a little annoyed about [Walker's role]," he told us. "It's one thing to be a hired gun. I'm a hired gun. . . . It's another thing to be a whore."

Clients such as the Netherlands Antilles are very much the exception for Charls Walker. Roy Englert, one of his six partners at Walker Associates, likens his chairman to a "cabinet member without portfolio"—no doubt much too lofty an image, since cabinet members do not get paid to represent the interests of private corporations—but a characterization that suggests the broader political spectrum with which Walker concerns himself. He operates "independently of clients or anyone else trying to achieve consensus in the business community about things that are important," Englert said. "He just does this on his own. In a sense he is working for clients, but he is not working for clients in the sense that he is trying to get some amendment to a piece of legislation. He is not a lobbyist in the traditional sense. He is more interested in looking at the big picture."

.   .   .

There can be little question that "the big picture" on taxes since the mid-1970s has moved in a decisive—and, from the perspective of fairness and simplicity, troubling—direction. Since 1978, the maximum tax rate on long-term capital gains has been slashed from a theoretical 46 percent to 20 percent. This reduction is of particular significance to wealthy taxpayers, who enjoy the bulk of all benefits from capital-gains preferences, and timber companies, who, through an accident of history, have much of their annual earnings taxed as capital gains. The Kemp-Roth rate cut for individuals, adopted in 1981, in large part benefited individuals who earn more than $50,000, despite claims of across-the-board equity still trumpeted by the sponsors of the measure. But nowhere are basic developments in tax policy represented more graphically than in the ongoing demise of the corporate income tax as a source of revenue for the U.S. Treasury. In 1960, corporations paid for more than 26 percent of federal spending outside of Social Security, which is financed separately. In 1969, corporations funded 24 percent of non–Social Security spending. By 1979, however, the corporate share had declined to 17 percent. It fell to less than 9 percent in 1984. In constant dollar terms, corporate America paid lower taxes in fiscal 1983 than it did in any year since Pearl Harbor. Even without adjustment for inflation, corporate taxes fell from $55 billion in fiscal 1977 to just over $37 billion in 1983.

The ongoing erosion of the corporate tax does not stem from reduction of the tax rate on business income but from the willingness of Congress over the past decade to create and broaden new business tax breaks. These special preferences include the investment tax credit; accelerated depreciation, which allows corporations to write off new investments in plants and equipment far more quickly than the rate at which the assets actually wear out; and a dizzying array of loopholes tailored to the tax-reduction needs of particular companies and industries.

Robert McIntyre, of Citizens for Tax Justice, released a study in October 1984 that documents just how deeply the corporate tax has been eroded. His report examined the tax bills of 250 profitable major corporations over the period 1981 through 1983. He found that 128 of these firms —51 percent—paid *no* federal income tax or received rebates from the government in at least one of the three years. Sixty-five of the companies paid a total of zero or received refunds over the period. And 17 paid no taxes or collected refunds in *all* three years. General Electric earned pretax domestic profits of $6.5 billion over this three-year period but, through skillful use of the tax laws, claimed net refunds of $283 million. Six other companies, including Group of Fourteen members Weyerhauser and Union Carbide, collected refunds totaling more than $100 million, despite total profits of nearly $10 billion.

"Getting rid of the corporate tax doesn't seem to me to be an idea that is going anywhere in this society," said former assistant Treasury secretary Surrey. "But undermining the corporate tax is the way to get somewhere." After he left Treasury, Surrey watched with dismay the proliferation of business tax preferences. These preferences are estimated to cost more than $90 billion in lost revenue in fiscal 1986 and, if left unchanged, at least $130 billion by 1990.

Charls Walker has been a central actor in several of the decisive tax battles of the last fifteen years: the Revenue Act of 1971, which was a direct repudiation of reform policies pursued by the Treasury Department through much of the sixties; the Revenue Act of 1978, which cut the maximum tax rate on capital gains from 46 to 28 percent and which reduced the maximum corporate tax rate (from 48 to 46 percent) for the first time since 1964; and 1981's ERTA, which has been recognized as the largest corporate tax cut in history. We asked him to reflect on his power as a lobbyist and his influence on the tax code. Walker was quick to agree that his impact has exceeded that of his Washington peers in "influence, and being willing to get out front, and being willing to take some risks in the process." He then moved the conversation away from a discussion of power.

"You made the first proper amendment to that question when you shifted from the word *power* to *influence,*" he said. "I have absolutely no power whatsoever. People often ask me how George Shultz has been such a success in government. First of all, he was a college dean, who has no power really—he's got to lead, he's got to persuade, he's got to pull people along. Second of all he was a labor negotiator, where you tie everything down. So it is not a matter of power. It is a matter of being able to influence people's attitudes about things.

"Number two, and I think this is most important," he continued. "It may sound immodest, but I really believe this. That is to be able to see the forest instead of the trees, to take a longer range view of the two fields I have gradually grown into—economics and politics—and sit down with yourself and others, and say okay, here are the forces at work. Sooner or later they are going to end up here, and if these things happen along the way, maybe they end up there sooner. Translation: The positive things that have happened from our standpoint, the American Council for

Capital Formation, and the clients of Walker Associates—and there is quite a bit of overlap there—the positive things that have happened since we set up this firm, would in some measure have happened anyway, because of fundamental social, political, and economic events. The American people, sooner or later, would have come to view capital formation as an important goal of public policy that had been neglected. They would have gotten there sooner or later. So we may have been able, through our organization, through our clients, through the work of [now-retired General Electric chairman] Reg Jones and the corporate community, to make some of this happen sooner. In large amount, those basic things would have taken place anyway."

This is a favorite Walker theme. And it hints at another dimension of his lobbying technique and impact. Walker understands that a significant obstacle to the adoption of his agenda is the cloud of special-interest pandering that hovers over business loopholes. It is difficult in raw political terms to make the case that a worker in a General Electric light-bulb factory should pay more in federal taxes than the massive corporation for which he labors. Or that defense contractors such as General Dynamics and Boeing, who do billions of dollars worth of government business, should make no contribution to financing that government. The basic reality is that one dollar less in taxes paid by corporations is a dollar more that must be paid by individuals, borrowed by the Treasury, or squeezed from government through service cutbacks.

These simple facts of life mean that any proposal for corporate-tax relief, even though many are approved by Congress, is tinged with a surface suspicion that puts the burden of proof on its sponsors. The burst of public attention and outrage that accompanied release of the McIntyre report, which was cited widely by newspapers and magazines, quoted by congressmen and tax-reform advocates, is a perfect example of the potential for backlash. Walker has responded to this enduring political challenge by working hard to professionalize and sanitize his way of life. He firmly rejects any suggestion that campaign contributions, personal friendships between lobbyists and legislators, or outright corruption play a major role in decisions made on Capitol Hill. Astonishingly enough, Walker told us he has never encountered evidence of corruption in Congress and that methods of influence peddling that once prevailed—"booze and broads," as he described them—have been rendered nearly extinct with post-Watergate changes in the congressional power structure and the proliferation of trade associations that seem to represent every side of any given issue.

To be sure, such a negation of one's own power is no surprise, coming as it does from an influential lobbyist. But Walker has actively proselytized this view. He served in 1983 as vice-chairman of a task force on political-action committees convened by the Twentieth Century Fund, a New York research foundation. The lobbyist said he spends 40 percent of his time on unpaid activities. He chaired the 1976 presidential debates. He is also a co-founder and chairman of the executive committee of the Committee on the Present Danger, the influential organization whose anti-Soviet activism helped create a climate for major increases in defense spending. These nonprofit endeavors provide Walker with access to a circle of policy-makers and opinion-shapers in which he might not otherwise circulate. Walker has lunch "about twice a year" with AFL-CIO president Lane Kirkland, whom he came to know through the Committee on the Present Danger. These organizations also lend his lobbying practice a patina of professionalism and public service that counterbalances in part the special-interest stigma that attaches itself to any paid representative of big business.

. . .

Charls Walker first came to Washington as a professional in 1959, when he was asked by Treasury secretary Robert Anderson to serve as an assistant and economic advisor. After the defeat of Richard Nixon by John Kennedy, Walker was named to the top staff position at the American Bankers Association. The organization was based in New York, but Walker remained involved in legislative affairs and beefed up substantially the ABA's Washington presence. He then accepted a government assignment that involved him deeply in tax policy. In 1969 Walker entered the Nixon administration, at the age of forty-five, as undersecretary of the treasury. He was second-in-command in the department for all issues other than international monetary affairs. Paul Volcker, with whom Walker lunches every three or four months, had responsibility for this area. Walker remained at Treasury through President Nixon's first term. He served under three secretaries: David Kennedy (January 1969–February 1971); John Connally (February 1971–June 1972); and George Shultz, who succeeded Connally. His tenure was marked by two critical developments on the tax front. One was a matter of policy, one of politics. Both paid dividends when he left the department to begin a more lucrative career.

For eight years prior to the election of Richard Nixon, federal tax policy had been proceeding on a "reform" course. Assistant Secretary Surrey was an aggressive and committed advocate of tax reform. Although his agenda clashed at times with those of the presidents under whom he served—John Kennedy was more interested in cutting taxes than reforming them, Lyndon Johnson in raising revenues to fund the Vietnam War —Surrey set a tone and policy direction at Treasury that was based on a strong presumption against special preferences for corporations and wealthy individuals. Surrey's presence was so decisive, and his perspective so persuasive in Congress, that even after the election of Richard Nixon, the department forged ahead with a tax-reform program whose roots lay in research compiled by Surrey and his associates before they left office. This material soon became known as the Surrey Papers.

Shortly after assuming office, Walker and his colleagues were pressured by Ways and Means Committee chairman Wilbur Mills to introduce a tax-reform program. (One of Walker's responsibilities as undersecretary was to oversee congressional relations.) The proposals eventually submitted became the basis of the Tax Reform Act of 1969. This legislation repealed the investment tax credit, enacted a series of individual reforms through a "limitation on tax preferences," and cut taxes on low-income individuals by $2.2 billion in 1970–71. "I suppose the conventional wisdom would conclude that what a Republican administration–Charls Walker view of what tax [policy] ought to be, and what the 1969 act was, are probably worlds apart," quipped Walker associate James Smith with a smile. Smith is not exaggerating. One amusing way to understand how far the consensus on tax policy has evolved since the Nixon era is to review some of the public statements uttered by Undersecretary Walker in defense of the reform bill:

- *To the House Ways and Means Committee on May 22, 1969:* "Many of our proposals are aimed directly at correcting abuses which permit wealthy people and prosperous businesses to avoid a fair share of the tax burden."
- *On the* CBS Morning News, *April 22, 1969:* "Our priorities today, rather than subsidizing business investment, clearly are in the areas of dealing with our pressing national problems having to do with the cities, the disadvantaged. . . ."
- *To reporters in Rockford, Illinois, June 3, 1969:* "Tax reform is an idea whose time has come. The American people are willing to pay their fair share of taxes but, quite understandably, they become very unhappy when they find out that there are some millionaires who don't pay taxes, there are some corporations who are favored under the present tax statutes."

This is, of course, precisely the brand of rhetoric Walker's opponents wield today to criticize his lobbying agenda. Within two years, however, it became clear that Treasury's "reform" spirit was little more than a recognition of political realities. The Revenue Act of 1971, in which Walker also played a major role, not only reinstated the corporate tax breaks repealed in 1969, but it added even more preferences. It reinstated a 7 percent investment tax credit, labeled euphemistically a "job development credit," and introduced the Asset Depreciation Range (ADR) system, which allowed corporations to write off investments more quickly than before. The Revenue Act of 1971 took the Treasury Department off the reform course it had followed for close to a decade. Beyond the substance of tax policy, the first Nixon administration also marked a subtle change in the process through which tax policy was developed. No longer did staff members working with the assistant secretary for tax policy set the agenda, although they of course remained involved. Tax policy became a focus of Undersecretary Walker and the secretary.

The raising of decisions on tax policy to higher levels in the Treasury Department was a significant development. It helped to transform the politics of taxation. As Treasury departed from its reform-minded ways, and as top-level officials involved themselves more deeply, corporate executives sensed an opportunity to help shape tax policy. Lobbyist Tommy Boggs, with whom we spoke at length about Walker, offered an analysis of Walker's tenure at Treasury.

"Charlie came along at the same time in history that the CEOs [of major corporations] came along," Boggs said. "And their first real interest was turning around the Stan Surrey kind of tax policy. The Treasury was extremely influenced by the people brought in by Surrey. There are still a number of them left. When Charlie got to Treasury, he removed tax policy from the assistant secretary for tax policy, where it had always been —that is, he removed it from the Surrey shop—and moved it to the level of the secretary. And that accomplished two things. It eliminated the Washington representative, who was used to telling his CEO, 'This is a technical tax issue, and I'll deal with the assistant secretary.' What Charlie would say is, 'Look, you are going to see the secretary, and I don't want anybody there, I want the CEO.' And that got the CEOs interested in tax policy. . . . He created a new communications channel on tax policy which did not exist before."

Developments at Treasury under Walker energized the business community on the subject of taxes. Boggs said the "communications channel" opened on tax policy was the genesis of the Business Roundtable, by some accounts the single most powerful corporate lobby in Washington. "The original Roundtable activities were all in the tax area, and it sort of stemmed from Charlie's coordinating role" at Treasury, he told us. The contemporary Business Roundtable began to take shape in March 1972, when Treasury secretary Connally and Federal Reserve chairman Arthur

Burns pressed major corporate executives, led by John Harper of Alcoa and Frederick Borch of General Electric, to organize more effectively in Washington. As a result of these meetings, the March Group was born, an informal organization of about one dozen companies. Within a year, the leaders of roughly a hundred companies had joined, and the March Group subsequently merged with two other business groups to create the Roundtable. The organization is today composed of the chief executive officers of close to two hundred major corporations, whose combined revenues amount to roughly 50 percent of the country's GNP.

Walker said Boggs made a "valid point" when he linked the birth of the Roundtable to developments in the Treasury Department. "John Connally and I were counseling people like John Harper of Alcoa," Walker said. "You guys in the Business Council, you go down to Hot Springs [Virginia] twice a year and talk to each other. Connally's favorite term for that was verbal incest. Then you have a big black-tie dinner. And at the last meeting you had, the speaker was [then-Senator] Jim Buckley. I mean, Jesus Christ—get Russell Long down there, get Charlie Rangel down there. And so they started looking. These corporate executives were driven by what happened to them during the period from the mid-1960s to the mid-1970s, with this gushing out of regulation. And they said we have to get to work on this."

Walker's role in the formation of the Roundtable is significant, because the approach to lobbying adopted by that organization was symptomatic of broader developments in how business conducted its affairs in Washington. It has become a Washington cliché to observe that "coalition lobbying"—in which a group of corporations or trade associations with similar interests coordinate their lobbying and activism on a particular issue—is the single most effective way to influence Congress. Beginning in the mid-seventies, broad-based coalitions were formed by business to beat back legislation promoted by consumer groups and labor organizations. The Roundtable in a sense represents the ultimate coalition. As *Washington Post* reporter Thomas Edsall noted in his 1984 book, *The New Politics of Inequality,* "The willingness of a host of business interests, many of them competing for the same markets in the private sector, to join together on larger issues before Congress . . . has significantly altered the balance of power in Washington."

Charls Walker was one of the earliest sponsors of this full-court press approach to lobbying. John Meagher of LTV has called him the "grandfather of corporate coalition-building." Walker "in the early seventies was the first person that started putting together coalitions," Meagher told us. "He was the first one, as far as I know, to bring groups together, trying to get some consensus among corporations on particular subjects, particularly in the tax area." Coalition lobbying, as represented by the Group of Fourteen, is built directly into Walker's client base and has been from the day he opened for business. It is one of the essential components of his effectiveness as a lobbyist.

"We have been a 'grass-roots' lobbying operation from day one in this firm," Walker told us. "How do you get in to see Congressman X [if] he is antibusiness? After a little experience I said, 'I don't care how antibusiness a member of Congress may be, he or she will listen to me, let me in, when I am coming to talk about jobs, payrolls, economic growth in their districts. Because that is issue number one.' In other words, it is a constituency matter. So, in our business, we have preferred to deal on an issue not with just one corporate client, but with five or ten or fifteen that we represent year in and year out.

"If you [represent] twelve major multinational corporations and you look over the country, you have got operations, employment, in most of the states and many of the congressional districts," he continued. "And so you have a coalition to begin with. People say, how do you get a bill through Congress? You convince a majority of members that what you're for is good for their constituents, and what you're against is bad for their constituents." One particularly effective form of communication, Walker says, is visits or letters to members of Congress by executives of companies rather than by their lobbyists. Is it fair to say, we asked, that one key to influencing is to show members of Congress what will happen if what you are advocating is not approved and to hear these consequences described by credible industrialists in their state or district? "That's a hell of a big part of it." Is a visit by a chief executive officer more persuasive to a congressman than four thousand letters? "Can be, particularly if there is a constituency relationship there."

Call it what you will—corporate blackmail, corporate bluffs, corporate brinkmanship, corporate flight—Walker understands that the ultimate political ace in the hole for business is a four-letter word: jobs. It is the threat of job reduction, or the promise of robust economic growth and job creation, around which the clever lobbyist builds his case. This is precisely the approach Walker adopted in response to the Reagan tax plan. He quickly assembled a new organization, the Coalition for Jobs, Growth and International Competitiveness, in an effort to raise a $1 million war chest. The coalition consists of seventeen utilities, telecommunications firms, and heavy manufacturers, many of whom are already Walker clients. The tax bills of these companies would rise dramatically as a result of the demise of the investment tax credit and other special preferences. But Walker does not argue that these giant firms, which include AT&T and Ford Motor Company, should not be expected to shoulder a higher share of the tax burden. He cloaks his rhetoric with talk of jobs, the national interest, and the threat of foreign competition.

What Walker describes as "the classic case" of coalition lobbying in Washington is the creation of Conrail out of the ashes of the bankruptcy of Penn Central and five smaller railroads. Although it was not a tax issue, he told us he considers formation of the new railroad, which has cost the government more than $7 billion in subsidies over the last decade, one of his greatest victories as a lobbyist. In a development that points up the dizzying cycle of shelters Walker has helped produce, the Reagan administration's decision in 1985 to sell Conrail, now a profitable enterprise, will provide the buyer with tax breaks that may run as high as $1 billion over five years—a legacy of business-sponsored legislation adopted in 1981.

"In 1973, we were approached to work on the Penn Central bankruptcy problem," Walker said. "We ended up with ten corporate clients, [including] Bethlehem and U.S. Steel, National Steel, General Electric and Du Pont, Allied Chemical, Ford and General Motors. Their common characteristic was that they shipped on the Penn Central. A judge in Philadelphia in early 1973 said, 'I'm going to close that railroad down on November 1, 1973, because it is eating into the estates of the creditors.' These clients said, 'God almighty, we're out of business without freight transportation.'" Legislation to the liking of Walker and his clients was introduced by Rep. Brock Adams, who proposed to restructure the bankrupt rail lines over a twenty-month period and provide $85 million of government funds in the interim to keep the system running. Contending legislation was introduced in the Senate by Vance Hartke, who proposed that the Interstate Commerce Commission study the situation and report back to Congress in eleven months. Walker's assignment: to kill the Hartke bill, since it contained no provision to guarantee uninterrupted freight service, even though the bill had already passed the Senate Commerce Committee with a large majority and was scheduled for a vote in the Senate after the Labor Day recess.

"We got our ten clients in and said, 'Okay, we are going to get a flip-card presentation together that consists of two parts: One is a boiler plate for everybody as to why the Brock Adams bill will do it and the Hartke bill won't work,'" the lobbyist continued. "'The second part of this flip chart has to be done by you, Bethlehem Steel, by you, U.S. Steel. You take the state of Pennsylvania and you calculate that if Penn Central stops on November first—no, let's say by Christmas, that's a good hard-ringing date—what happens to your jobs and payrolls.' And it was tremendous. There are not enough trucks in the world to carry all the iron ore. We said to Bethlehem, 'During the recess, you go to Senators Scott and

Schweiker [of Pennsylvania] and just tell them the story. This is what is going to happen if the Hartke bill passes. But you also [have plants] in Maryland, so you do the same thing with Senator Mathias and Senator Beall.' And so on with all ten clients. They operated in seventeen states. That's thirty-four senators.

"When [the Senate] came back after Labor Day, I went up to see Senator [Warren] Magnuson [of Washington]," he continued. "I didn't know Senator Magnuson—but another trick of the trade, one of the clients was Weyerhaueser—and I said, 'What's going to happen with Hartke?' " (Weyerhaueser is based in Tacoma.) "He said, 'Dr. Walker, we've decided to pull it off the calendar and wait for the House bill.' Great influence? Great swat with the chairman? Christ, no. I didn't know the chairman. Great swat with Hartke? I struck out with Hartke. Pure, old grass-roots [lobbying] in that sense, not in the sense of hundreds of thousands of letters, but to show a direct relationship. And that's what our business is all about over here. Sometimes it's hard, when you try to say, 'Here's the relationship between deferral of [tax on] income for foreign subsidiaries and economic progress in your district.' It's easier on the investment tax credit or a failing railroad. But it can be done on the others."

. . . .

What ranks undeniably as the single most lucrative exercise in coalition lobbying was enactment in 1981 of the Accelerated Cost Recovery System (ACRS), the major business tax provision of the Economic Recovery Tax Act. The three-year campaign that led to passage of this provision remains unsurpassed in terms of the unity that prevailed among business representatives, the breadth of the coalition assembled on its behalf, and the sheer amount of corporate muscle brought to bear on Congress and the White House. *National Journal,* the respected weekly on government affairs, described on June 28, 1980, the raw power of the business coalition assembled to draft and push for approval of a preliminary version of ACRS.

"Imagine a small but valuable missile resting hundreds of feet above the ground at a launch site," wrote reporter Richard Cohen. "Poised to lift it into the air is a potent booster composed of several components synchronized to work together flawlessly. Fueling the rocket are hundreds of thousands of power cells creating a force of unmistakable pressure. No, this is not a re-creation of a moon shot at Cape Canaveral. It is one way to describe an unprecedented effort by business lobbyists to gain congressional support for a major tax change." Fourteen months after the Cohen article appeared, the Accelerated Cost Recovery System was law.

The primary forum through which the coalition operated was the Carlton Group, an informal caucus of Washington lobbyists that began to meet regularly in the mid-1970s to coordinate the program and lobbying strategies of the business community on tax policy. Among the dozen or so individuals who regularly attended Carlton Group breakfasts were officials of the Business Roundtable, the U.S. Chamber of Commerce, the National Federation of Independent Business, the Retail Tax Committee, and Charls E. Walker Associates. Thus, the group included representatives of big business, small business, manufacturers, and retailers. Mark Bloomfield, who attended Carlton sessions as an envoy from the American Council for Capital Formation, compared the assembly, which still meets, but less frequently than it did in the late 1970s, to a corporate United Nations.

"It was an attempt to say, 'Look, why do we not have sort of a U.N. and discuss issues of interest to the various business associations?' " he said. "At a minimum, exchange information, so if people are testifying on the Hill, others don't find out about it when they are sitting [in the hearing room]. And it was a way to hassle out differences, because in 1978 there was a debate [among lobbyists] about reducing the corporate tax versus capital gains. The Roundtable opposed the capital-gains reduction initially. Then when [ACRS] came about, that was an issue where the business community was able to put together a package that most people supported. So it was a way not only to exchange information, but to coordinate strategy."

Charls Walker was a factor from the beginning in the evolution, drafting, and battle for passage of ACRS, although given the range of business interests that sponsored the proposal, it is difficult to isolate his role. Conversations with lobbyists and congressional staff members suggest that Walker played three critical roles: using his position as tax advisor to candidate Ronald Reagan to secure his endorsement of the depreciation proposal; intervening with the Treasury Department on behalf of industries, such as auto, steel, and the airlines, that demanded still more tax relief because of their lack of profitability; and, perhaps most important of all, working over the years to create a climate on tax policy that made Congress receptive to a proposal as costly and radical as ACRS.

A preliminary version of ACRS, known among its sponsors by the shorthand reference 10-5-3, was drafted and introduced in 1979. ACRS itself was passed by Congress and signed into law by Ronald Reagan in 1981. But the real roots of the campaign for accelerated depreciation can be traced back to 1978. Tax experts of all persuasions agree that developments that year—more precisely, passage of the Revenue Act of 1978—

influenced profoundly the willingness of Congress to look favorably upon new tax breaks for business and the wealthy proposed in the name of "capital formation" and more robust economic activity. This political momentum came to a head three years later with the passage of ERTA.

As tax bills go, the provisions of the Revenue Act of 1978 were remarkable largely because their benefits were skewed so dramatically toward upper-income taxpayers. "This was the first bill in recent history to provide a very large tax reduction for the wealthiest group of individuals in the country, those with incomes exceeding $200,000," wrote Stanley Surrey in an essay entitled "Reflections on the Revenue Act of 1978 and Future Tax Policy." The focal point of controversy was the bill's provisions on capital gains. Taxes on capital income were cut dramatically. Business also won two important tax breaks: reduction of the corporate income tax from 48 to 46 percent, the first such reduction since 1964, and permanent extension of the investment tax credit, along with its further liberalization.

These were significant issues of tax policy, but the real significance of the Revenue Act of 1978 was political. Legislative action on the bill began in January when President Jimmy Carter unveiled a tax program that was reform-oriented in the classic sense, although it did contain certain provisions, such as a larger cut in corporate tax rates than what was actually approved, that rankled his reformist allies. Carter called for limitations on tax-deductible entertainment, curbs on a number of other corporate loopholes, a mild tightening of capital-gains taxes, and cuts for moderate-income taxpayers. He was, after all, the president who had labeled the federal tax system a "disgrace to the human race" when he accepted the Democratic nomination. By November 1978, however, this same president found himself signing, after a threatened veto, the most regressive tax bill in memory. What is more, the legislation was approved largely on the strength of supply-side arguments advanced by its supporters. Cut tax rates on capital gains, they promised, and the federal government would collect *more* revenue.

"The significance of the capital-gains thing was that it was a turning point in the direction of tax policy," said Bloomfield. "It turned tax policy away from loophole closing to [the creation of] incentives to invest and save. It is also one of the most controversial parts of tax policy. Therefore, if capital gains ever falls, then I think other things are in serious trouble." On a wall of Bloomfield's Washington, D.C., office, perhaps to underscore the significance of the legislation, hangs an oversized, framed cartoon that traces the history of the capital-gains reduction.

The Revenue Act of 1978 was also significant because it focused attention on Charls Walker. The lobbyist played an undeniably pivotal role, as chairman of the American Council for Capital Formation, in shepherding the legislation through Congress. In fact, he and Bloomfield wrote an article in 1979 for *The Wharton Magazine* entitled "How the Capital Gains Tax Fight Was Won."

Walker elaborated for us on the basic theme of the *Wharton* article. Passage of the 1978 legislation was a classic example of the political power of the middle class, he claimed. "I am absolutely convinced that what really gave the capital-gains provision such a strong and surprising push was not Mark Bloomfield or Charlie Walker, or the Securities Industry Association," he said. "It was the great American middle class, and some columns Sylvia Porter wrote that were read all over the country, about what Carter is trying to do to you" in his tax program. Did Walker have anything to do with those columns? "I had a little talk with Sylvia Porter, yes," he replied. "I saw a preliminary column [on the Carter proposals] and I thought to myself, from an experience I had several years before, in 1959, how widely she was read. I called her and said, 'Are you going to do another column on capital gains?' She said, 'Sure, I am. I'm incensed.' I said, 'When?' She told me, and I said, 'Why don't you delay it just a week, when Congress is back in session?' She did, and it was a rouser. I am convinced this middle-class thing was a very big part" of what transpired. Walker also operated at the level of evidence creation. The American Council commissioned Chase Econometrics to forecast the economic effects of a reduction in taxes on capital gains. The report, by Michael Evans, was released on April 17, 1978. It was wildly optimistic. Evans predicted that a reduction of the capital-gains rate to 25 percent would raise stock prices 40 percent by 1982 and produce 440,000 new jobs by 1985.

Charls Walker was by no means the only Washington hand with an interest in capital-gains tax reductions. The American Electronics Association, a high-technology trade group, was an important player from the beginning, as was Wall Street, whose representatives also promised a stock-market boom if the legislation was enacted. But Walker's talk of grass-roots sentiments does have some foundation. President Carter pushed forward with his reform proposal over the objections of most congressional Democrats, who sensed a tax-revolt mood building across the country. Moreover, big business, in the form of lobbying heavyweights such as the Business Roundtable and such prominent executives as Reginald Jones of General Electric and Du Pont's Irving Shapiro, were late to join the capital-gains bandwagon. They were more interested in securing tax breaks for business rather than for individuals—even wealthy individuals—and feared that generous treatment of capital gains would prompt a presidential veto.

"That is a fascinating case study," said Barber Conable when asked about the Revenue Act of 1978. "Carter was so innocent [politically], and there were a few people in the business community who were overly impressed by the chandeliers in the White House. They believed that Carter would veto the bill that had their corporate rate reduction if it also reduced the rate of tax on capital gains. You see, long-term capital gains were not that important to big business. The corporate tax rate was. And so Irv Shapiro and Reg Jones came to me and got absolutely hysterical —'We're going to lose our rate cut.' I told them to shut up and sit down. 'You're going to look pretty greedy if you're willing to sell small business out to get the corporate rate down.' And they did shut up."

Passage of the 1978 tax bill demonstrated that business could learn to speak with one voice. The Carlton Group continued to function as an important force for unity. Walker spoke at length with us about the events of 1981 and the adoption of ACRS. He was uncharacteristically modest. He stressed that personally he had little or no role in the actual drafting of the legislation, that he seldom attended meetings of the Carlton Group —"I had an associate who was in on all of that," he said—and that in general his role as spiritual godfather of this business tax bonanza has been overstated by reporters and editorialists. Walker's comments on this score reflect the profound and, for the lobbyist, very damaging, fallout from the 1981 tax bill. That fallout continues to undermine corporate power and unity on tax policy.

The sheer magnitude of the business tax cuts enacted that year has fueled such enormous budget deficits that business has been on the defensive ever since. The passage of TEFRA in 1982, designed to raise $214 billion from fiscal 1983 through 1987, was an obvious congressional effort to recapture a portion of the revenue it had given away in 1981. Walker understands this political fact of life, and that he now operates in a threatening political environment. His very success in reducing corporate taxes has contributed to massive federal deficits. These deficits are now the basic catalyst in Congress for proposals to increase taxes on business and continue to reclaim revenue lost in 1981. What Walker has worked to do is to devise a remedy to the deficit threat—a consumption tax or VAT—that increases revenue from sources other than his business constituents.

"What he is proposing to do is shift the tax burden from high-income people and corporations to the poor," said Brookings economist Joseph Pechman, author of the acclaimed *Federal Tax Policy*. "He has gutted the income tax, so now he has to make up the revenue. There is a one-to-one relationship." Added Robert McIntyre, "Why does Charlie Walker support a VAT? Because it's a zero tax on corporate income, which is not bad if you can't get negative rates."

The congressional backlash against special preferences since 1981 also ripped apart the political coalition that had been assembled on behalf of ACRS. Giant corporations that marched in lockstep on the merits of accelerated depreciation became adversaries one year later as they rushed to protect parochial interests against the antideficit fervor on Capitol Hill. These new divisions surfaced most dramatically in the bitter controversy over safe-harbor leasing, a controversy that took an especially heavy toll on the prestige and standing of Charls Walker.

The genesis of safe-harbor leasing is bound inextricably to ACRS. Tax breaks are useful to a corporation only if it has taxable income to shelter. Adoption of a system of preferences as generous as ACRS was of little comfort to companies in a number of industries—steel, automobiles, airlines, paper—that were not at various periods profitable enough to take full advantage of it. This same problem had existed for a number of years with respect to the investment tax credit. And Walker had been working since the mid-1970s to do something about it. Suppose corporation A purchases a machine. It is then allowed, through the investment tax credit, to deduct 10 percent of the cost of the investment from the taxes it owes Uncle Sam. Thus, the actual cost of the machine is only 90 percent of the purchase price. If corporation B purchases the same device but has no income—and thus pays no taxes from which to deduct the investment credit—the actual cost of the machine is equal to the nominal price. Walker for many years championed a simple, if politically unpalatable, solution to this dilemma: Why not allow the Treasury Department to write a check to corporation B for the tax break it could not receive? This proposal became known as the refundable investment credit, or refundability.

The likelihood of adoption of ACRS made the potential for disparities between taxable corporation A and nontaxable corporation B even more dramatic. It was the mission of Walker and a small number of other lobbyists to meet the needs of these troubled firms as the 1981 tax bill wound its way through Congress. The Treasury Department actually proposed the remedy that was ultimately adopted. Rather than permit Uncle Sam to write checks to giant corporations, such as U.S. Steel and Ford—an exercise in corporate welfare too noxious even for the Reagan administration—Treasury proposed that these companies be allowed to transfer their unused tax benefits to profitable firms, which would pay for the ability to reduce their taxes even further. Thus was born safe-harbor leasing.

"Back in 1975 I was testifying before a congressional committee and was asked a question on an issue I wasn't even involved with, the investment tax credit," Walker said, when asked to explain the origins of safe-harbor leasing. "The head of the Air Transport Association, Paul Ignatius, was testifying for a refundable tax credit. . . . One of the members said, 'Dr. Walker, what do you think about refundable investment tax credits?' I said it makes all the sense in the world. It's crazy to have a system where a company would invest and has some taxable income and therefore can take the credit, but a company that invests and doesn't have taxable income—and needs the credit more—can't get the credit.

"Well, the association called me up in a couple of weeks and said, 'Will you work for us in trying to get a refundable credit?' " he continued. "This is 1975. Various other lobbyists in town laughed and said you are never going to get a refundable credit. . . . By 1981, when the Reagan tax program was coming down the pike and included 10-5-3, it was quite clear that this issue was coming to the fore. And by 1981 we were representing six major industries with a payroll of, I forget the number exactly, around $70 billion per year. It wasn't just the airlines. It was the railroads. The steel industry was in trouble. The mining industry was in trouble. The paper industry was in trouble. And we were representing all of those. So we went to Treasury and told our story about how 10-5-3 wouldn't help companies that didn't have the earnings to take the credits. Then Treasury invented safe-harbor leasing."

Were the origins of leasing as clinical as Walker suggested, much of the ensuing controversy might not have erupted. A top official of one trade association whose members were active supporters of the leasing concept (the trade association was also a Walker client) described to us the atmosphere of unrestrained greed that prevailed as leasing became law. "Once ERTA got rolling and [Republicans and Democrats] started to outbid one another for the support of the different communities in Washington, it was simply a process of winnowing out those ideas that didn't have the political sex appeal or that were outrageously expensive," this official said. "At that point, the administration had already signed off on a $550 billion tax giveaway program. Congress had anted that up to $750 billion. If you compare that with the tax legislation of today, it's no wonder people were lining up at the trough, so to speak. And we just happened to be standing in the right line. When Treasury came up with the notion of [safe-harbor leasing], we were more than willing to buy it. Frankly, most of the coalition had decided that refundability was not going to fly . . . and we were looking for an alternative."

The compromise was a disaster from the start. Leasing was made retroactive to January 1, 1981. But for corporations to qualify for safe-harbor treatment of assets purchased in the 225 days between January 1 and ERTA's August 13 enactment, they were required to sign leasing deals within ninety days. This deadline touched off a mad scramble to buy and sell tax breaks—and a series of articles in newspapers and magazines that documented the frenzied activity.

Press attention then turned from leasing to the lobbyists who had pushed for its adoption. "It turned into a public-relations fiasco," Walker said when asked about this episode. "I was identified erroneously as the guy who invented safe-harbor leasing and got it done. The Treasury invented it, but I was identified on the front page of the *Washington Post* as the guy who made a $40 billion raid on the Treasury and all that." Erroneous or not, at least some of Walker's clients believed he brought the press attention on himself. He was photographed at Maison Blanche, a fashionable Washington restaurant, for an April 19, 1982, *Fortune* article on the leasing controversy. The photograph "appeared at a very tense, sensitive time period here in town," remarked a former Walker client. "And I think a lot of people said, 'Hey look, this kind of baggage we don't really need.'"

The rise and ultimate demise of safe-harbor leasing was without a doubt the most damaging political episode of Charls Walker's career. Has he ever been wrong? "Sure I have been wrong," he replied. "I should have fought harder against safe-harbor leasing [in 1981] and in favor of refundability. I was reluctant on that until very late in the day." Has he made any other major mistakes? "Well, once you got safe-harbor leasing, there was every reason to make it retroactive to January 1, 1981. It would have been a mistake not to. But you shouldn't have had ninety days when you could cram in all of your safe-harbor leasing for a year. That contributed to the public-relations fiasco."

Not only did the battle over leasing damage relations with certain clients, but it may well have scared off potential clients, who looked upon the lobbyist as too hot to handle. "I think we paid some price, yeah," said James Smith about 1982. "In the real world, in this town, we were doing a very professional job representing our clients. And I think people in Congress and elsewhere who disagreed with us understand that. They are not going to say, 'Hey, that was a bunch of corrupt nitwits.' There was nothing corrupt in what we were doing. So, in terms of how the city accepts us, how the legislators accept us, I don't think there are any negatives. In terms of corporations out there who are looking to be represented, it may occasionally come up. They'll say, 'Gee, wasn't that the firm . . . ?'"

In the process of opposing TEFRA, the 1982 reform bill that phased out leasing, Walker also suffered bruised relations with the Reagan White House. Tensions developed when the lobbyist, searching for a strategy to raise revenue without undoing the business tax cuts of a year earlier, proposed in testimony before the House Ways and Means Committee that Congress consider a "delay" of the individual tax cut scheduled to take effect July 1, 1983. This was the third installment of the three-year, 23 percent reduction of personal income taxes that was the second axis of the Reagan tax plan. It was also the installment of greatest value to moderate-income taxpayers.

"Yeah, there was some egg on faces there," he said, when asked about 1982 and his dealings with the White House. "They reacted negatively to that. I pointed out that I had sent my testimony to them a week in advance, and asked for comments on it. I never heard from anybody. But you can overstate this sort of thing. I'm not all that, well, I don't know quite how to put it. People greatly overrate the importance of 'being very close' to an administration. The action in this town is about two miles up there." Walker gestured in the direction of Capitol Hill. "Administrations come, and administrations go. There's no continuity to administrations. There is a very strong continuity to the U.S. Congress. I just don't put a tremendously high priority on having a great 'in' with any administration. Furthermore, it can hurt you. I've never been all that partisan, but I think there were some people on the Democratic side that thought, as a result of my actions [with the Reagan campaign] in 1980, that I was more partisan than I am."

The events of 1981 remain the subject of intense controversy on a substantive as well as a political level. ERTA represented the most profound transformation in the level and structure of taxation in post-war America. And no single development in tax policy was as radical, and controversial, as the adoption of the Accelerated Cost Recovery System. The simplicity of ACRS obscures its dramatic implications. Prior to 1981, corporations were allowed to write off their investments in plant and equipment based on the projected useful life of the asset. If a firm purchased a lathe, and the lathe was expected to remain in operation for seven years, the firm deducted the cost of the lathe from its taxable income over a seven-year period. The Treasury Department had issued more than a hundred different guidelines to determine the number of years over which assets could be written off. They extended for as long as sixty years. ACRS simply reduced the number of guidelines to four. It in effect severed the connection between the useful life of an asset and its write-off period for tax purposes. Henceforth, short-lived equipment—cars and light trucks, for example—could be depreciated over three years. Most factory equipment was in a five-year class. Certain long-lived equipment, such as railroad cars and machinery used by utilities, could be depreciated over ten years. Buildings were written off over fifteen years. It was estimated that this simple, yet from the perspective of tax policy quite radical, departure would save business $143 billion between fiscal 1981 and fiscal 1986 and reduce the collective tax bill of corporate America by 50 percent.

The unprecedented cost of ACRS was not its only controversial feature. The new depreciation scheme, when combined with the already-existing 10 percent investment credit, produced a system of tax relief so generous that for most assets it actually created *negative* tax rates. The tax savings that flowed from the purchase of a piece of equipment exceeded any taxes on the profits that equipment generated. These tax breaks could then be used to shelter profits from other assets. ACRS in effect made most investments more profitable after taxes than before taxes. It also meant that corporations and industries that made heavy use of equipment, and thus benefited from the tax-reduction consequences of ACRS, paid much lower taxes than industries that made use of labor or other production inputs.

These and other by-products of ACRS help to explain why the new depreciation scheme received at best marginal support—before, during, and after its passage—from the academic tax experts and economists. Joseph Minarik, a senior research associate at the Washington-based Urban Institute, discussed the grave shortcomings of the new system. "The major problem with ACRS, what the academic economists are saying, is that it is extremely non-neutral," he told us. "It does not treat different assets in the same way. It does not treat [industrial] equipment as a class in the same way as buildings. Its effect varies substantially according to the rate of inflation. So it really gives business all kinds of incorrect signals in terms of how they should be behaving. Now, if you are representing a firm and you want the most money after taxes you can possibly get, ACRS does look pretty good. But there is a very strong indictment against it in terms of the kinds of economic incentives it gives to firms."

In June 1981, when ERTA was still under consideration in Congress, more than two hundred economists issued a "Public Statement on Depreciation Reform" that opposed passage of ACRS. Recent statements of reservations about ACRS have not come only from liberal tax analysts. *Business Week* in June 1984 published an article entitled "The Dark Side of the Business Tax Cuts." The magazine reported on concern among business economists such as Alan Greenspan about "unintended side effects [of ACRS] that could undo some of its benefits."

An editorial in the same issue offered a warning. "Combined with recovery in profits, ACRS has so enlarged the cash flow of many companies that they can think of nothing better to do with the surpluses than buy back their own stock or make merger deals that lack any sound economic rationale," the magazine complained. "In addition, new depreciation laws are so advantageous to real estate . . . that they have fostered a precarious boom and a round robin of uneconomical property swaps. The increased demand for credit spurred by this churning has, in turn, helped to raise interest rates and discourage productive investment."

Walker spoke at length with us about the range of criticisms leveled at ACRS. He defended accelerated depreciation vigorously. This is the crowning achievement of the business lobby in Washington—an exercise in raw political force that will not be duplicated for some time. "I've got a very simple answer to those who say ACRS went too far," Walker insisted. "And that is to say, 'Let me rephrase your criticism. You are saying that we are getting too much investment in plant and equipment.' You cannot judge whether ACRS went too far on the basis of an equation [Harvard professor] Dale Jorgenson works up with a bunch of assumptions, a very arcane sort of thing. You've got to ask yourself, 'Is this causing too much investment?' " But the critics of ACRS argue just the opposite. The U.S. economy for part of 1983 and all of 1984 experienced a boom in business spending on plant and equipment. Walker points to this explosion of investment as evidence of the effectiveness of ACRS. But this spending boom came on the heels of a sharp *reduction* in business investment immediately after ACRS was passed, the result of the deepest recession since World War II.

"Essentially, I don't think it's made any real difference," said Joseph Minarik, when asked about the capital-spending response to ACRS. "We are in the middle of a recovery with an incredible net fiscal stimulus. Businesses are running up against their capacity constraints long after people thought they would. So they are beginning to invest. People who say that somehow ACRS had no impact for three years, and now all of a sudden we're seeing the difference it makes and we're getting more investment than we would have—these people are going way beyond anything anyone can say based on the evidence."

.   .   .

Disagreement among economists and tax analysts over the cost and effectiveness of ACRS is more bitter and animated than disagreement over any other feature of the 1981 Reagan economic program. And with good reason. If Congress can be persuaded that a system of tax preferences as lucrative as ACRS failed to stimulate business investment, it will be difficult for Walker and his clients to argue in apocalyptic terms about the job-threatening impact of the new Reagan proposals. But if Walker and his allies can document a cause-and-effect linkage between lower taxes and higher investment, reform of business preferences will be all the more difficult to achieve.

This divergence of opinion and analysis came into sharp focus in a debate between Walker and Robert McIntyre. The debate, which took place in June 1985, was sponsored by Public Citizen. These two adversaries squared off for the first time in their careers. They faced questions from a panel of three reporters and members of the audience. The session did not disappoint. McIntyre discussed the results of a study he released in January 1985. That report, *The Failure of Corporate Tax Incentives*, examined investment behavior from 1981 through 1983 for 238 major U.S. corporations whose tax-relative tax burdens were examined in an earlier study by Citizens for Tax Justice. McIntyre's findings struck at the heart of claims by Walker and his business colleagues that tax incentives —in the form of accelerated depreciation or the investment credit— promote increased spending on new plant and equipment. Consider the single most dramatic finding. According to McIntyre, the fifty lowest-taxed industrial corporations, whose tax rate over the three years averaged minus 8.4 percent, actually *reduced* their investment over this period by 21.6 percent. Meanwhile, the fifty corporations with the highest burden, an average rate of 33.1 percent, *increased* their investment by 4.3 percent. Given this pattern, McIntyre wondered, how could Walker begin to argue that raising taxes on business would reduce corporate investment?

Walker became genuinely exercised over the McIntyre report. He read criticisms of the methodology—criticisms to which McIntyre replied —by a staff economist at the American Council for Capital Formation and an associate of supply-sider Norman Ture. He asked the press why it continued to report on the findings of such a "badly discredited" document. And he insisted that McIntyre's basic argument, that ACRS and its companion tax incentives did not increase business investment, was seriously flawed.

The ninety-minute debate ranged from disagreement over who ultimately pays the corporate tax to specific criticisms of the Reagan tax plan. But the most acrimonious disputes centered on the effectiveness of ACRS. The following exchange characterizes the gulf that divides the two tax activists:

> *McIntyre:* What I'm trying to tell you is that you can't find a correlation [between tax incentives and investment] that some have said the theory would produce. There's a lot of reasons for that. One has to do with the basic issue of demand for product. Another has to do with how interest rates might have a different impact on different companies. Look at Whirlpool [with an average tax rate from 1981 through 1983 of 45.6 percent] and General Electric [which received re-

funds of $283 million]. GE cut its investment. Whirlpool increased its investment. Maybe it's because Whirlpool needed to make some improvement in its products that it couldn't put off. . . . The point is the incentives, which were promised in 1981 that they would produce this big investment, didn't do it. It was promised all through the years that they were going to save the steel industry. They haven't done it. We think they don't work, and all they have done is increase the deficit. . . .

Walker: Let me just throw a quick question at the press here. Does the press understand that according to official government figures, in the recovery after the 1981–82 recession, that the rate of business-fixed investment was up 15 percent a year as contrasted to 7 percent average in earlier postwar recoveries? That is a fact. And how this man can just sit here and look at you and say it's wrong, I do not understand.

McIntyre: Well, I can say it's wrong because investment fell to an all-time low in '81 and '82 and then came back.

Walker: You were in the worst recession since the Depression.

McIntyre: You bet. That's right, exactly right. Despite what the people who told us—and the chamber of commerce was one of them, I don't know if you were—that if these incentives were enacted we wouldn't have a recession.

Walker: The recession started before they were enacted! Well, it did! We had a recession in '80 and '81. The law was signed in August of '81.

McIntyre: And what caused the recession was largely these long-term revenue losses that were projected, that pushed up interest rates.

Walker: It was caused by monetary policy.

McIntyre: Right.

Walker: Well, you can't have it both ways.

McIntyre: Monetary policy was designed to deal with those long-term deficits. You know that.

.   .   .

Charls Walker today enjoys the fruits of a career dedicated to the service of large corporations. But his career raises obvious questions. Why not work to place your hands directly on the levers of power, either through a return to government or by accepting an executive position with a corporation? Why become a lobbyist? Walker offered two explanations:

The life-style is not overly taxing, and the rewards are extremely generous.

"When I came down here as deputy secretary of the treasury, I came out of Connecticut, I thought I just might move back up there and run for the Senate some day," he explained. "I wasn't down here very long when I saw I couldn't last with that life-style. I like people, but I don't like that many people that much. I [also] had opportunities back in the 1960s. The heads at different times of two major New York banks came to me when I was thirty-six, thirty-eight, forty years old. One guy said, 'I want you to come over and be vice-chairman of this bank. You will be my successor.' Another guy said, 'I want you to be executive vice-president of this bank.' And I looked around at the life-style. You have to go out almost every night and entertain customers, even when you're the biggest bank in the world. I said that's just not for me. The same is true with the life-style of a politician."

Walker is an early riser—he often awakens at 5:30 A.M.—and he likes to leave the office by 6:00 P.M. Besides reading, of which he said he does "a tremendous amount," he pursues two extracurricular activities: golf and Pac-Man, the video game. "I play Pac-Man several times a day," he told us. "I get up in the morning, put the coffee on, and play Pac-Man." For relaxation? "My wife says it's amazing, because I'm over there cussing and screaming and saying you dumb ass and so on. Yeah. I guess [for relaxation]. I don't take my blood pressure before and after. I get my exercise by jogging." Walker is also an avid golfer. He is a member of two of Washington's most exclusive country clubs, Congressional and Burning Tree, both of which are located close to his suburban Maryland home. "One Washington rep had a system where if his phone rang twice, [the call] flipped over to Burning Tree," he joked. "I don't have a system that flips over, but in recent years I spend a lot of time out there. I moved out to the country. In the summer I can leave here in the midafternoon and still play nine, eighteen holes of golf on the way home. As long as you can be close to a telephone. And vacations are great. When Congress is out, and they are out a lot in the last few years, we really are dead around here."

Lobbying obviously has been good to Charls Walker. He travels the forty-five-minute commute from his home to the office in a Cadillac limousine. He described himself to the *Wall Street Journal* in July 1985 as a "very diminutive millionaire." Although he would not disclose his annual income, it is safe to estimate that he earns at least $500,000 to $1 million per year. Consider the specifics: $7,500 per speech, of which he delivers one or two each month; an "implicit" hourly fee of $750; a general environment in which lobbyists much less prominent or successful than Walker bring down $500,000 per year almost effortlessly.

We were surprised to hear Walker tell us he does not make extensive personal use of tax shelters to reduce his annual payments to the Internal Revenue Service. We asked why, given the explosion of tax-shelter activity in recent years, much of it by individuals who presumably earn much less than a successful Washington lobbyist. "A lot of those tax shelters are much more advantageous for people with different sorts of income than straight [salary] income," Walker said. "But I'll plead guilty. To me, it's just not worth the time and effort to cut your rates that way. . . . If the maximum tax rate was still where it was when John Kennedy came in, 91 percent, I certainly would [use tax shelters]. One of the biggest achieve- ments I ever was associated with was getting that top [tax] rate of 70 percent on salaries and earned income cut to 50 percent in 1969. Once you get down to the 50 percent level, there's really not much sense in going to tax shelters. Because there is a risk involved. You can get burned awfully, awfully easy. This last year, for the first time ever, I've gone into a tax shelter other than owning some tax-exempt bonds. It is a very modest one, and it's very much associated with public interest. The National Housing Partnership. It's very safe, it's involved in building housing, retirement housing and this and that. So I have gotten into it."

The National Housing Partnership is a congressionally mandated non-profit corporation. It is the largest private producer of low- and moderate-income housing in the United States. By "burned" does Walker mean investigated by federal authorities? "You can either get burned that way, because they're not ultimately legal, or get burned in the sense that the investment is no good," he said. "You go into an oil operation, wildcatting, or this and that, or financing a movie or a play. Jesus Christ, there are more people who bite the dust on that sort of thing."

Walker's relaxed pace is largely the product of his style of operation on Capitol Hill. He has three basic strengths as a lobbyist: his tenure in Washington and his long history of work with the tax-writing committees of Congress; his years at Treasury, which give him a certain degree of credibility; and the economic muscle of his clients. Walker therefore does not bother with many of the more mundane activities that occupy the time of less well-established lobbyists. He is not a big socializer. He believes that wining and dining members of Congress can sometimes harm your cause.

"Now, I do do two sorts of things," he said. "I like good musical comedy. An associate and I took two congressmen and their wives to see a *42nd Street* matinee on Sunday. I wouldn't do it at night; I'll go to a matinee if I really want to do it. And if I do it, I might get some kindred souls to go along with me. The second thing is, I'm the world's greatest barbecuer. A few times each spring or summer we'll have a group of people out, including some members [of Congress]."

Nor does Walker spend much time on Capitol Hill, prowling the corridors and paying courtesy calls on senators and representatives. Tommy Boggs described Walker as "a funny kind of" lobbyist. "He probably doesn't know well more than twenty-five people on the Hill," he commented. Walker said Boggs is basically correct. His personal contacts with legislators are deep, not broad. Walker leaves to his associates, some of whom are well connected with Republicans, others with Democrats, the day-to-day contacts with legislators and agency officials. When does Walker decide to visit Capitol Hill? "When one of my associates says, 'You got to get your ass up there,'" he replied. "Let's suppose we have got a tax issue for a client. And suppose there is a Texas congressman who was a student of mine at the University of Texas thirty years ago. There are some up there, you know. And I've known him forever. Maybe I've supported his campaign. Maybe I'm the godfather of one of his kids. And we've got a corporate client who has a plant in his district that employs five thousand people. That's the person I want to go and see."

Walker's pace is also less taxing than the schedules of his competitors because money is not a decisive factor in his influence. He does not need constantly to host or attend political fundraisers, a Washington ritual that occupies the evenings of superlobbyists such as J. D. Williams or Tommy Boggs. Williams reportedly can be invited to six fundraisers in a single day. He normally donates somewhere near the legal personal maximum of $25,000 a year to House and Senate candidates. Walker, on the other hand, donated a *total* of well under $25,000 from 1977 through 1984, according to records filed at the Federal Elections Commission. Much of that money went to Republican and Democratic party organizations rather than to candidates. Most of Walker's contributions to individuals were in the $125-to-$500 range. Why contribute at all? "Politicians feel kindly toward people, even with a fifty-dollar contribution," he replied. "They say, 'Understand what I'm up against. I gotta run every two years. The goddamn media cost is killing me. I gotta get all the television stuff.' And some hearty soul sends him fifty dollars. There is a kindred spirit that develops there. He understands. If you are in the town, and your business is in the town, in the legislative field, and you don't make even a modest contribution—I make contributions but they are modest—people wonder, where are you?"

. . .

The operations of Charls Walker on behalf of his corporate clients rely on more than his skills, contacts, and ample monetary incentives. The roots of his success and the specific ways in which he prevails grow out of the ideology in which he cloaks large corporations for the lobbying wars on Capitol Hill. This presentation of the corporate imperative is a little-noticed asset, but a vital one, in persuading or inducing the national legislature to favor corporate interests over broader public interests. Walker carries to Congress the concept of the no-fault corporation—an essentially amoral institution fully desirous of providing jobs, goods, and services to the people but vulnerable to impediments placed in its way by government. It is as if these companies, having a generic motivation toward growth, need only to be subjected to properly conceived stimuli in order to advance their contributions to society at large.

This belief in the essentially no-fault corporation reveals itself in the principal tenet of Walker's advocacy. Corporations do not pay taxes, he repeatedly admonishes his audiences, people do. Taxes levied on corporations are transferred onto people. Therefore, taxing corporations is like taxing people, except that this tax also impedes capital formation and economic growth. "The corporate tax is a hidden tax, because we know it is passed on to people some way or other," he told us. "It is either passed on in the form of higher prices or passed back to the capital-formation people [shareholders] or passed back to workers in the form of reductions in wages and benefits." This is the endless Charls Walker drumbeat. The corporation is seen as a helpless transfer agent, unable to absorb any of the incidence of taxation and irresistibly drawn to making others pay instead. Walker concedes that no one can determine what share of any corporate income tax is placed on consumers as compared with shareholders or workers. But he is just as certain that none of this tax, as an added cost of doing business, is absorbed by companies during the process of competition, innovation, and efficiency improvement. After hours of conversation and review of years of Walker testimony and writings, one sees few indications that people, with all their faults and frailties, animate companies. Rather, the transcendent companies strive to work their beneficent will on the economy only if the outside environment is congenial enough.

The corporation as a free-standing artificial entity, not to be judged as are real mortals by the spectrum of ethical standards, lies at the core of the Walker approach to decision makers in government. The simple abacus that registers his political calculations deals not with the profits of his clients but with the jobs of the lawmakers' constituents—jobs that are not just created but can be erased or transported to foreign lands. Jobs connote service and votes. Profits mean greed and improper pressure or temptation to legislators. Walker is wise enough to know the vast difference between the two approaches in fulfilling his designs for the nation's tax laws.

By representing broader tax policy backed by an array of commercial and industrial interests one avoids the patina of special-interest pleading that attaches itself to a single wealthy client or an individual corporation seeking special dispensation. Walker prefers a pattern of advocacy with an intellectual and professional sheen. He arranges conferences attended by professors of economics and tax policy; he helps to fund research by professors who place their academic imprimatur on his chosen directions; he publishes his thoughts; he speaks the language of statistics; he massages budgets and fiscal reports and congressional hearings. With his activities, along with his Ph.D., "Dr. Walker" moves toward a time when he will be seen more widely as a leader of corporations in Washington's often treacherous labyrinths and not merely a handyman, guide, or facilitator. He strains to be both brain and laser for the corporate retainer in between.

Those who know the public Charls Walker are familiar with the importance he attaches to distinguishing between the words *power* and *influence*. Again and again he declared to us that he has no power. But he did concede that he possesses some influence. Power is not consonant with being a professional; it connotes the unsavory or heavyhanded. Influence is cranial; it connotes legislators recognizing their self-interest and that of the nation as being one with the self-interest of Walker's clients. Influence is taking what is right and gaining decisive acceptance. Power is taking what is avarice and turning it into gain. Influence invites the skilled, while power beckons the brutish. In Walker's appraisal, congressional lobbying of the past deployed far greater use of power than does that of the present, which relies more on influence. No more, he claimed, are satchels of cash trundled to Capitol Hill offices. Now political-action committees refine the lobbyists' crass image. Rather than shaping decisions by the lure of personal aggrandizement, PACs succeed by providing better access to congressional offices, Walker said. They have broadened our democracy, he asserts, by diversifying contributions, access, and arguments to members of Congress.

Some observers would call political contributions a form of institutionalized bribery. But not Walker, who became unusually agitated when asked about Common Cause and its ongoing campaign to limit the amount of funds legislators can accept from PACs. "My pet peeve really is Common Cause," the lobbyist said. "I ran into a political scientist today. I didn't know him from Adam. And he started talking about PACs and what a misleading thing Common Cause is doing in the PAC arena. . . . The great leap that Common Cause makes is [to say] that because of the PAC contributions, Congress is bought. And then they're going out to sell this to the American people. It's just not true." Isn't Walker concerned about the explosive growth in PAC donations to congressional campaigns? "I pose this question," he said. "What do we really want in our system of campaign finance? I think we want two things. We want it to be open and above board. We want it to be, in Eisenhower's term, clean as a hound's tooth. Number two, we want a dispersion of influence. . . . You ask whether your system today is open, clean, and more above-board than it was thirty years ago. Well, hell yes. Where are the black bags? Where are the IRS investigations? Number two, look at the dispersion. There are so many PACs out there of all stripes, of all philosophies, of all shapes."

For those who have no PACs and can make no campaign contributions, what are their democratic tools? Walker displays little interest in or tolerance for new means by which these other Americans can communicate and focus their will. When asked his opinion, he expressed reservations about the use of initiatives, referenda, and recalls to make democracy more direct. "That concerns me," he said. "I'm basically for representative democracy. I'm basically for the original idea of representative government and not plebiscite government. It bothers me." He also expressed distaste for a proposal to allow taxpayers to use their form 1040 as a vehicle to join together voluntarily, through a fundraising checkoff mechanism, into a taxpayers' rights-and-reform association.

As a broker, catalyst, and lens for corporate policy in Washington, Walker is a concentrator of economic power at critical junctures. By institutionalizing power, he can insist on calling it influence. The effect of course is the same—more for the haves and less for the have-nots. When his business clients pay less in taxes, others pay more in one form or another. Or their children inherit the effects through more public debt. But are there benefits to Walker's handiwork: more employment, better products, safer workplaces and environment through modern investment? How can any such benefits be quantified to accord Walker his preferred place in history? In brief, can Walker's legislative successes be tested by their consequences? The answer would seem to be no. Economic performance in the United States deteriorated throughout the decade of the seventies, precisely the period when Washington lobbyists scored their most sustained gains in reducing the business tax burden. The passage of ACRS was followed by the most devastating recession since World War II. And the legislation unleashed a host of problems—artificial disparities between returns on assets, a boom in real-estate tax shelters, incentives for short-term rather than long-term investment—that still linger. But can Walker and his colleagues ever lose so long as their propositions are mere articles of faith that can be invoked instead of examined?

In certain ways, Walker can lose. He can unnecessarily choose to engage in the improprieties of power instead of accomplishing the same thing through the institutionalization of influence. Or he can lose by overplaying his influence. Witness the saga of safe-harbor leasing. He can also lose if he finds himself in a serious crossfire of conflicting interests among his covey of clients. Finally, he can lose if some countervailing coalition or force defeats his legislative agenda. This type of loss for Walker is on a substantive level, not a financial one.

What is that group or coalition? Organized labor has ceased to be an effective opponent to corporations on tax matters, except for the labor-financed research organization Citizens for Tax Justice. Small taxpayers have few organized forces speaking for them in Washington. The largest group of them all, the National Taxpayers Union, is not known for its assault on corporate tax privileges or subsidies, though it has recently been active to some extent in this field. Charls Walker makes his impact in large part without having daily to confront an organized civic adversary or contender. To be sure, there are obstacles in the executive branch and among members of Congress and the media. But as an outside advocate, Walker rarely has to worry about any moves by representatives of small taxpayers. In this respect, Walker's power has never really been tested. It is power in what is otherwise a vacuum. Chemical company lobbyists must contend with environmental groups in Washington. Their auto-industry counterparts are challenged by safety activists and on occasion insurance-company lobbyists. But Charls Walker, with a few exceptions, has never experienced such stimulation, such pressure to have his activities and corporate victories made concrete in terms of their effect on millions of other people's lives. The accountability that proceeds from having civic opponents is just not there.

But this does not mean that the man from Graham, Texas, is without worries. Were he of sufficient Shakespearean bent, he could envision a dramatic role for himself in the nation's deepening economic tragedy. He clearly sees this tragedy coming, though it is not his business to talk too much about it. He spoke with us about mounting federal deficits, the exploding national debt, the towering international trade deficit. His canniness did not permit the expression of direct foreboding. But his latent candor emerged in the following exchange:

Q: Do you have anything to say about the shortcomings of President Reagan?
A: Not really.
Q: Not publicly, you mean?
A: He is such a sweet guy. I can't criticize that boy. I would have hoped that we would have seen a little stronger push on deficit reduction. I think the administration is in danger of losing its

focus, like it had in 1981. I would have focused sharply on deficit reduction and tied it into trade. I think those are the two biggest problems. We are heading for a trade war. We don't have any rules of the road for international trade. This president, it's not so much a criticism as it is saying here, at this time and place, this man, the leader of the Free World, with conservative leaders in other governments, a summit coming up where we can go in and say, 'All right . . . we now have a very big problem in that we have no trade policy.' The dogma of free trade is dead. Our country is almost an island in this. . . . A combination of deficit reduction and working for a new regime in international trade. That's what I would like to see as the focus of this administration. Not tax simplification. That's nice to talk about, but it's not numero uno.

Q: . . . Is it because Reagan has a new staff in his second term?

A: Maybe. But the real time to move on this was November [1984] and pull together Tip O'Neill and the Democrats at Camp David. [Senator Russell] Long was ready to go. [Congressman Richard] Gephardt was ready to go. Tip didn't make much difference. We have passed that time now. And he had the old staff then.

Q: So you have no explanation for this inaction?

A: I don't want to talk about my friend Ron. [Voice rising] He's done a hell of a lot of good things.

Ronald Reagan is at the peak of his ideological influence and power within his party. Yet Walker sees a momentous, historic opportunity slipping away into a fiscal abyss, with possible calamitous consequences. And he, Charls Walker, cannot do anything about it. More than any other factor in the formula of how to increase his influence, Charls Walker now needs fewer assured friends and more vulnerable adversaries in positions of government.

WHITNEY
MacMILLAN

Remote Feed

Whitney MacMillan, son and brother of Yale graduates and a member of the class of 1951, by all accounts did not belong to any of the coveted secret societies at the university. He need not have felt deprived. MacMillan was preparing to join what may fairly be called one of the largest secret societies in global industry or commerce—the arcane world of the international grain traders. An amiable, athletic lad who majored in social science and literature, MacMillan played wing on a varsity hockey squad dominated by students from his home state of Minnesota, studied enough to get by comfortably, and, upon graduation, went right into the family business—Cargill, Inc.

He rose, over the course of twenty-five years, to head a corporation established by Will Cargill in 1865 with the purchase of a partial interest in a grain elevator at the end of an Iowa railroad line. John H. MacMillan, Whitney's grandfather, assumed control after the death of Cargill's founder. The company was at the time teetering on the brink of collapse. Grandfather MacMillan did not merely salvage the faltering enterprise— he established a momentum toward expansion and profitability that continues to this day. By 1929, when Whitney was born, the company was confident enough to launch its overseas operations. It established offices in Europe and Argentina. Fortunately, John MacMillan had also married Edna Cargill, Will's daughter. Their bond is the genesis of a legacy of wealth and power that has remained very much all in the family.

John H. MacMillan has been called the savior of Cargill by Minnesota business writer Don Larson. But it was John H. MacMillan, Jr., Whitney's uncle, who as president from 1936 to 1960 sketched the rough outlines of a strategy that has built the world's largest grain trader, one of the nation's largest flour millers, and its second-largest meatpacker. The modern Cargill is a colossus by many definitions. It employs roughly forty thousand people—more than the combined workforces of agribusiness giants ConAgra, Archer Daniels Midland, and Land O' Lakes. Cargill has registered with the U.S. government more warehouses and elevators for grain export than any other corporation or farm cooperative. Its sixteen export elevators in the United States and Canada, from which grain is loaded onto vessels for ocean crossings, can accommodate nearly 130 million bushels. This amounts to more than one-fourth of the registered export capacity in the two countries. Cargill's largest competitor in the trading business, Continental Grain Company, has a registered export capacity of 56 million bushels, 12 percent of the U.S. total.

For the past few years, Cargill's annual sales have ranged between $28 and $32.6 billion, which would rank it above U.S. Steel, Chrysler, and General Electric on the Fortune 500. These revenue figures are approximate because Cargill is the largest private corporation in the United States, with no public shareholders and no obligation to report much of anything about its finances to state and federal agencies. It is also a family-owned business. The Cargills and the MacMillans control 85 percent of the stock in an enterprise whose shareholders' equity is valued at $2.5 billion.

Even as a Yale undergraduate Whitney MacMillan could expect to be a candidate for Cargill's high command. For several years after graduation he dutifully worked the perimeters of the company. He was a vegetable oil merchant in Minneapolis, San Francisco, and the Philippines. He supervised merchandising of barley and oats. By 1959, at the age of thirty, he was an assistant vice-president in the grain division. Three years later he was named an assistant to the president. This early period was sometimes exhilarating and suspenseful, as befits any merchant house that must live by its wits to buy and sell profitably in turbulent markets. The work could also be tedious and heavy with routine. Bob Monnens, a shop steward in Cargill's barge division with whom we spoke during a visit to Port Cargill, the company's huge complex on the Minnesota River, remembers one incident from the chairman's youth. "Whitney worked a night shift at the soybean plant during the summers he was in college," Monnens told us. "He didn't give a shit. He laid down and slept many times."

Such behavior was a temporary deviation from MacMillan's strong desire, at least as described by many of his friends, to reach the top at Cargill by climbing the ladder of meritocracy rather than riding the escalator of nepotism. Of course, his name did not work against rapid advancement. He was elected to the board of directors in 1966, fifteen years after he joined the company. He was named a group vice-president in 1968 with responsibility for grain and commodities, seeds and Cargill's barge division. He became an executive vice-president in 1971, president in 1975, chief executive in 1976, and chairman in August 1977.

Whitney MacMillan today oversees Cargill's global interests from the second floor of a sixty-three-room replica of a French château. The compound is situated on the banks of Lake Minnetonka, twelve miles outside of Minneapolis. The surroundings are plush and comfortable. The chairman's office is part of what was once the château's master-bedroom suite. Elizabeth MacMillan, Whitney's wife, designed and had custom-made a huge bookshelf that covers all of one wall, according to a former Cargill executive who worked closely with the chairman. Easy chairs contribute further to the residential ambience of the office, which looks out over the grounds to the south. Outside MacMillan's window office is a contoured concrete pond that covers one acre and was once used as a swimming pool by employees. A picturesque, undulating pathway connects the Lake Office, as it is called, with the Office Center, a more conventional building for more than twelve hundred Cargill employees.

The château is not meant to resemble an ordinary corporate headquarters. The chairman presumably likes it that way—private, secluded, casual, and tranquil. These surroundings are fit for pondering, reflecting, and digesting the information that flows in daily from all points of the compass and for rendering the decisions that keep the company's many worlds furiously spinning in their profitable orbits. Far from the peace and quiet where MacMillan rules is the other side of Cargill: the huge, steamy, smelly slaughterhouses of Cargill's meatpacking subsidiaries, the uproarious pits of the commodity markets in Chicago and Minneapolis and around the world, where the company never stops hedging, the groans of its cattle feedlots in Kansas, a chain of flour mills that stretches from Jacksonville, Florida, to Buffalo, New York, the seed-crushing facilities, the poultry farms, the vast warehouses and grain elevators, the innumerable barges, the unit trains, the steel and fertilizer mills, the insurance companies, and of course the Cargill men. Its agents are everywhere—in Asia, Africa, North and South America, Europe, and Australia—buying, selling, storing, transporting, and, always, sniffing out information through a network of personal contacts that easily transcends nation-states, with all their conflicting ideologies and timeless antagonisms.

Chairman MacMillan directs this corporate empire within a giant cocoon of secrecy. That cocoon, spun years ago by his elders, continues to infuriate, puzzle, and amaze those who praise or criticize the company. Details of life inside the château remain obscure. What is not obscure is that power in a large privately held corporation is fundamentally different —both in its exercise and in its defense and perpetuation—from power in a publicly held corporation. Cargill jealously guards information that public companies must disclose as a matter of course. This secrecy has weakened the constituencies—farmers, governments, other middlemen—with whom Cargill does business. It is especially consequential in tight markets, when subtle shifts in supply or demand can precipitate wide swings in price and profitability. It has also retarded the growth of countervailing institutions such as cooperatives and structural reforms in the global trading system for agriculture.

Nobody in the world, save perhaps Cargill's brotherly competitors in the international grain trade, understands the advantages of private ownership more fully than Whitney MacMillan. But the Cargill chairman is said to display none of the signs of tension, intrigue, and connivance that a Hollywood melodrama might ascribe to his insular executive role. Vin Weber, a conservative Minnesota congressman, described the Cargill chairman as "patrician, aristocratic, aloof, very removed, and very powerful." That is how he appears to outsiders. Weber has met him only twice. To friends and associates, MacMillan is a study in moderation. He is said to possess an evenness of temperament and a sense of modesty, even in the midst of great wealth.

"My impression is that he is a hardworking, capable person who probably knows his own limitations better than anybody else," said Alex Scott, a Yale classmate of MacMillan who is president of Scott-Atwater Foundry in Saint Paul. "From that standpoint he is able to find people to work with him who complement him. He's certainly concerned about the various inroads that society has decided would be used to circumscribe the free-enterprise system. In the kind of business he's in, where you act on intuition and judgment, you have to be relatively unfettered. In no way does he flaunt his wealth. He could live an entirely different way with a far different approach to life and still get along very well."

Whitney MacMillan was born on September 25, 1929. He is trim and vigorous, although his silver-white hair and ruddy complexion make him look older than his years. One former executive recalled traveling by car with MacMillan and Cargill officials Walter Gordy, Jr., and Sam DeKeyser, who worked in the salt division. "Whitney said, 'It's my birthday today,' so we all wished him happy birthday," this former associate reported. "Somebody said, 'Who's the oldest in the car?' Walt said, 'I'm forty-five.' I was forty-seven. Sam was forty or something. Whitney said, 'I'm forty-five.' With his sparse hair and craggy face he looked older than he was. So Sam said, 'More like fifty-five, I'll bet.' Whitney was not amused."

The Cargill chairman is said to be taller and more fit than his older brother, Cargill MacMillan, Jr., who is a senior vice-president. As an individual, he pursues few things as doggedly as his privacy. MacMillan is not listed in *Who's Who in America.* He seldom becomes personally involved with charitable events in Minneapolis, a city known for its corporate philanthropy. Even less frequently can he or his family be found on the local society pages. The Cargill chairman has many allies in his commitment to anonymity. At times during our research it appeared that protecting the privacy of one of America's major businessmen was a fetish to MacMillan's close friends, even at the cost of not recounting praise.

Connor Fay, a Clairol executive and Yale classmate, put it simply. "I'd like to respect Whit's sense of privacy," he told us. "That really is my reaction. I don't think it's good manners to tell things about Whit that he doesn't want to tell about himself." Brewster Atwater, chief executive of General Mills, and a prep school classmate of the Cargill chairman, also declined an interview. "I know Whitney MacMillan very well," he remarked. "He's a good personal friend, and for that reason I'd rather not be interviewed."

A. Skidmore Thorpe, another prep school chum, was a bit more expansive. "He is a true involved company man," Thorpe said. "He enjoys it. It's in his blood. One thing we do together"—he is referring to the old-boy network from Blake School—"is an investment club. It's called TCIT [Twin Cities Investment Trust]. This has been going on for thirty years. It's just a little thing where we throw in ten dollars a month. We get together eight times a year for dinner. Whitney doesn't attend many of them because he's out of town so much."

As an executive, MacMillan manages to blend his commitment to privacy with a leadership style that is neither reclusive nor understated. He enjoys mixing with employees. "He is most comfortable at social gatherings after hours," said Clayton Tonnemaker, a former all-pro linebacker with the Green Bay Packers who worked closely with MacMillan during part of his tenure at Cargill. "He used to come with me to salt-division regional sales meetings. After dinner and a couple of drinks he would just open up. He was with his people and he was warm, open, friendly. Those were among the few times I ever saw him open up. In company situations he was always kind of aloof."

MacMillan is also known for probing sessions with subordinates. "He was good at and loved to play the role of devil's advocate," said Tonnemaker, who left the company in 1977. He described what it was like to make a proposal to the current chairman: "Whitney would take the position, 'This is bad, this is wrong.' Then, just as soon as you were agreeing with him, he would say, 'Okay.' Sometimes he did it so well that I would think Whitney was indecisive. But he makes you focus on the negative side."

Richard Slade, a friend of MacMillan's who is president of the Minneapolis College of Art and Design, said that this argumentative style can at times be trying. "I'm thinking of him always . . . defending some outrageous position that he has taken, really to the point of antagonizing people sometimes," Slade told us. "That devil's-advocate approach to the world sometimes gets to be aggravating. Whether you're attuned to it or not, if somebody's always taking an opposite position, sometimes you wonder what the point of the conversation is."

But Whitney MacMillan is not personally meanspirited. Nor is he a workaholic. He reads widely and collects rare books. He paces himself. A Minneapolis executive who has hunted quail with MacMillan in South Carolina described a typical trip. "He is not an avid hunter," this executive said. "He goes more to spend time with friends and for the experience. He enjoys the dogs, the scenery, the country ambience. Whether he gets one or ten birds in a day is less important than the experience. That's one of his characteristics. If you think of something you haven't done before, he's anxious to try a new experience. He may not go back and do it a second time, but he'll do it once."

Several of his friends described him as a family man who likes to spend time with his wife, two children, and four grandchildren. Applied to his extended family, this trait is part fealty and part corporate obligation. The head of the company must keep the three dozen or so Cargill and MacMillan shareholders at peace with one another and with their own acquisitive appetites.

MacMillan's most taxing responsibility may well be the travel schedule he maintains. He feels the need to visit Cargill outposts around the world and observe firsthand the company's myriad operations. One Twin Cities executive who has known MacMillan for more than two decades estimates that he spends 25 to 35 percent of his time on the road. "He believes in going out and kicking the tires," this executive said. "My impression is that he believes a good CEO has to know a lot about the business climate, the countries he's operating in, his operations. And that's why he gets around and tries to know as much as possible—so he can judge the recommendations made to him by top executives and so he can feel comfortable approving them. He wants to know enough to say aye or nay."

The chairman has also served with a few select noncorporate organizations that require occasional travel. He is on the Visiting Committee of Harvard University's Russian Research Center, whose acting director is Kremlinologist Marshall Goldman. He is also a director of the U.S.-U.S.S.R. Trade and Economic Council. Minnesota congressman Bill Frenzel flew to Moscow in November 1982 with MacMillan and other luminaries, including Sen. Robert Dole and Archer Daniels Midland chairman Dwayne Andreas, himself a powerful figure in the agribusiness world.

"We were all excited about a big thaw [in U.S.-Soviet relations] coming up," Frenzel recalled. "And Bob Dole asked me to go with him. At the same time, he invited his friend Dwayne Andreas, who was also a member of the council board, and Whitney MacMillan. So we went to Russia on the same airplane, a U.S. government airplane. But I was told by Mr. MacMillan that [the flight] was a bad deal because the rate they had to bill him at was a lot more than [he would have paid] had he traveled commercial. That's the MacMillans—they have deep pockets."

Despite his globe-trotting, the Cargill chairman does manage to find time to play golf and tennis and to ski. A chance Saturday noon telephone call to the pro shop at the exclusive Woodhill Country Club in Wayzata, Minnesota, revealed that MacMillan was walking in from a round on the links. (True to form, Woodhill's golf pro declined to disclose MacMillan's handicap after he asked the Cargill chairman if he would object.) MacMillan takes tennis lessons on Friday evening when he is in Minneapolis and he has vacationed at John Gardiner's Tennis Ranch in Carmel Valley, California, a popular retreat for the wealthy and notable. These pastimes are indications of the man's intense privacy. How does one ski privately? One does what Whitney MacMillan has done—travels a hundred miles across the Canadian border north of Idaho, into British Columbia, and helicopters to passes of virgin snow between the ten-thousand-foot peaks of the Bugaboo Mountains.

"He is a very strong skier," said Richard Slade. He and his children have accompanied MacMillan and his daughter, Betsy, on three trips to the Canadian mountains. "But he has stopped skiing in the Bugaboos. I think there are two reasons. One is that there's a reasonable risk ratio. And he doesn't feel that he skis enough to be strong enough to ski hard for a week in variable conditions."

. . .

Third-party assessments can form a tapestry of useful insights and understandings about a profile subject, but they cannot compare with nor replace dialogue with the principal. We were prepared that our request for an interview with Chairman MacMillan would not be received with immediate approval. An exhaustive literature search turned up only one feature interview with MacMillan, either in print or in electronic journalism. The short article appeared in September 1977 in the *St. Paul Pioneer Press*. Even this rare opportunity for public comment did not inspire profound insights. "Policy is pretty much formulated by people who have the experience to formulate it," MacMillan remarked in a typical statement about his company. (Cargill would not furnish information about any other instances when MacMillan granted interviews as chairman.)

The anonymity of the corporation over which MacMillan presides, and of the chairman himself, even among constituencies whose economic welfare is affected deeply by Cargill's power and policies, can be an endless source of fascination. Whitney MacMillan is a nonentity to a remarkable range of individuals. A few illustrations capture this phenomenon. Lester Brown, the eminent resources analyst and president of the Worldwatch Institute, spoke at length with us about the structure of the grain trade but could not name the chairman of the industry's largest player. James Evans, chairman of the giant Union Pacific railroad, which hauls grain for Cargill, was embarrassed when he could not name the company's chief executive at first. "Don't tell Whitney MacMillan I don't know him, because I should," Evans told us. "I don't want this guy to think that the chairman of Union Pacific doesn't know him."

By chance, we met two bright middle managers from the Dayton-Hudson department store chain, whose headquarters is in Minneapolis. What do you know about Cargill? they were asked. "Cargill is really a mystery company," one replied. "I interviewed someone who worked there for a job with us, and he told me it is organized like a submarine, with separate compartments. The people in one section don't know what the others are doing." Both men were stunned to learn that Cargill's sales exceeded $30 billion per year. Our experience with farmers who sell their crops to the corporate giant and buy their seed and feed from it was no less startling. During a speech in April 1985 at a college in Kansas—wheat country—we asked members of the audience of four hundred whether they had heard of Cargill. A large number of hands were raised. This group was then asked to identify its chairman. Only one person named Whitney MacMillan.

Even this record of corporate insularity did not prepare us for Cargill's unmatched capacity to review and delay interview requests. Formal discussions over access to MacMillan and other company executives began with a letter to assistant vice-president Stuart Baird on November 2, 1983. The letter was followed by seventeen months of intermittent dialogue. There was an afternoon-long meeting at the Cargill Office Center in August 1984. A promised visit to the château was canceled because of construction on the grounds. There were telephone conversations and more correspondence with Baird and William Pearce, vice-president for public affairs. This persistence, which was meant to underscore our sincere interest in communicating the thoughts and experiences of the Cargill chairman, did persuade the company to provide some information: transcripts of speeches delivered by MacMillan, several years of company newsletters, and promotional pamphlets. Frustrated by our lack of progress, we placed a call directly to MacMillan. Surprisingly, he accepted it. What follows is a partial transcript:

Ralph Nader: We've been in touch with Mr. Baird. We have had long interviews with other CEOs. You've seen the correspondence my associate Andrew Moore has had with Mr. Baird, which explains the nature of the book and what will be covered. While we understand you are not known for giving interviews, we have decided to be persistent in order to show our good faith in trying to have your viewpoints and judgments represented. I talked with Peter Dorsey [Cargill's outside attorney] about this matter, whom I'm sure you know—
Whitney MacMillan: That's true.
Nader: And we would like to make this request to you.
MacMillan: It's something I don't ever give much thought to. I prefer to keep those thoughts private. No, I don't think so.
Nader: Is it because I went to Princeton and you went to Yale?
MacMillan: I have a daughter who went to Princeton, and a son-in-law. I don't find that objectionable at all.
Nader: Would you object to interviews with other [Cargill] executives?
MacMillan: I didn't say I would object or not. That request will have to come through the channels.
Nader: Have you ever been interviewed?
MacMillan: Seldom, and certainly not in the area that you're dealing with. I would consider that proprietary information. We have no patents to protect us in our business. Why would one ever give secrets away, if the government wasn't there to protect you? I prefer to pass.
Nader: Thank you for your candor and for entertaining our request.
MacMillan: Super.

Thereupon the mystery man of Cargill vanished from the immediate scenes of our research, along with the rest of the Cargill executive corps. We did find other sources. Cargill is simply too big to be cloistered fully. Production workers hosted an extended tour of Port Cargill, where the company processes soybeans and ships grain, salt, molasses, and fertilizer. Although Cargill must comply with minimal financial-disclosure requirements, specific events and controversies can produce interesting documentation. Acquisitions sometimes trigger reports to the Securities and Exchange Commission (SEC). Court proceedings are often a rich source of information. Even tax disputes, such as a 1969 ruling by the Internal Revenue Service regarding taxes on the inheritance of Whitney MacMillan and his siblings, are sometimes matters of public record. (A former Cargill executive who worked closely with the chairman told us that MacMillan once said he spent fully one-third of his time on family tax matters. It took the MacMillans four years before the $600,000 dispute was resolved in their favor. The claim involved the estate of Edna Cargill, daughter of founder Will Cargill and wife of Whitney's grandfather, John MacMillan.)

The most valuable sources of information and insights on Whitney MacMillan proved to be former company executives, personal friends, competitors, farm activists, and politicians. Some of the people we approached refused to be interviewed. Others insisted on anonymity. A number of them, including several former Cargill officials, were generous with their time and on-the-record insights. Little did we know that this, too, would become a bone of contention. Almost one year after our initial contact, Stuart Baird simply refused to believe that we had succeeded in interviewing at length several former employees. This is a company long 'on loyalty and short on public squabbles and leaks. There is a homogeneity among top executives that seems to produce a lifelong commitment to the enterprise. There is even a word to describe the most loyal of the loyal, those who eat, sleep, and breathe Cargill. They are the "greenbloods," a reference to the color of Cargill's corporate insignia. "The saying is, 'You bleed green,' " said Frank Tonnemaker, Jr., of his most earnest colleagues in the management-training program. (Tonnemaker followed his father into the company and left after three years.) "They will not question any assignment."

.   .   .

The wealth and power of Whitney MacMillan, as with those who preceded him at the helm of Cargill, are founded, in large measure, on the bountiful harvests of the Great Plains of North America. His giant company continues to thrive because certain areas of the world, especially the United States and Canada, produce more food than their citizens and livestock can consume while other regions—the Soviet Union, China, Japan, and most of the developing countries—must satisfy some or much of their demand for specific crops by importing. Cargill is the most powerful force in a sector of the world economy, the international grain trade, that mediates between the plenty of the agricultural haves and the needs of the have-nots. It is a giant enterprise by any standard.

Authoritative figures on Cargill's size and profitability became available in October 1985, when the company had to make public some financial information in order to raise funds on the Eurobond market. Revenues for fiscal 1985 (Cargill's fiscal year ends on May 31) were $32.3 billion, up from $28.4 billion in 1981. Net income in 1985 was nearly $280 million, compared to $207 million in 1981. Release of this data has no precedent in Cargill's recent history, even though the circular devotes only six pages to a narrative and quantitative review of company operations. Reliable figures on market share—the percentage of world trade in wheat, corn, and other commodities Cargill handles—are more difficult to come by. Not even the most seasoned experts, with the exception of those employed by Cargill and its counterparts, can describe with precision just how much of world commerce in a range of vital commodities is controlled by the largest international traders. Many of these operations are as shadowy as Cargill. Continental Grain Company, MacMillan's largest competitor, was founded in Belgium in 1813 and is now based in New York. Louis Dreyfus Corporation, number three, is based in France and has long been a power in European markets. Bunge and Born—first Dutch, then Belgian, then Argentine— is now based in São Paulo, Brazil, and is known in Latin America as "The Octopus." Mitsui and Company, a Japanese corporation, purchased the grain-trading assets of Cook Industries, a publicly held operation, in 1978. Cook was the fourth-largest trader of U.S. grain but was badly mismanaged. Garnac Grain, which was founded in 1937, is controlled by the André family of Lausanne, Switzerland, and in the United States is the smallest of the giants.

The fact that all of the remaining companies are in private hands, and that data reported to governments often raises more questions than it answers, prevents outside analysts from compiling authoritative statistics on the relative power of the Big Six. What can be said is that the control of the giants is decisive. Richard Gilmore, an agriculture consultant and author in 1982 of a book on the grain trade, estimated that the six largest traders account for more than 90 percent of U.S. exports in wheat, corn, and oats and more than 80 percent in sorghum. Cargill has often claimed that such estimates are an exaggeration. But MacMillan himself hinted at the decisive presence of his company when he disclosed partial figures on 1984 grain shipments in a rare public statement issued in early 1985. Cargill exported from the United States nearly 6 million tons of wheat from June through November 1984. That compares with total wheat exports over this period of approximately 22.8 million tons. Thus, Cargill's market share alone was greater than 25 percent. A 1984 company newsletter reported that Cargill handles 15 to 18 percent of all grain shipments from France, which exports ten times more wheat than its closest European rival.

This degree of concentration, in an industry whose performance affects so deeply conditions in so many countries, has for decades produced fear and mistrust among farmers and political leaders. Congressman James Weaver, an Oregon Democrat and a persistent critic of Cargill, worries about the power of the grain traders. "These companies are giants," he told us. "They control not only the buying and the selling of grain but the shipment of it, the storage of it, and everything else. It's obscene. I have railed against them again and again. I think food is the most—hell, whoever controls the food supply has really got people by the scrotum. And yet we allow six corporations to do this in secret. It's mind-boggling."

The top agriculture official in a major farm state captured the mood of his constituents when he talked with us about the traders. "I'm at war with those bastards," he said. "I don't hate the grain companies, but since I've had this job and started to deal with them, it's harder to like them. They dump crap in the grain. They steal from the farmers. They just ain't real nice people."

But no force in the United States—governments, farmers, or new competitors—has been able thus far to challenge the hegemony of Cargill and its competitors or build alternatives to the prevailing corporate marketing systems. Weaver has more than once introduced legislation to establish a National Grain Board, modeled after government agencies in Australia and Canada, to coordinate exports of U.S. grain and set minimum prices. His proposals have been soundly defeated. The American Agriculture Movement (AAM) tried in the late 1970s to develop its own capacity to export grain. This venture, known as Parity, Inc., did manage to ship 29,000 tons of wheat to Portugal in 1979. But the organization soon fizzled out and now is dormant.

Ted Godfrey, an AAM vice-president who supervised the operation, said that demands for bribes shut Parity, Inc., out of important markets. "I know for a fact that if I had handed over $200,000 in South Africa, I could have sold a lot of grain," Godfrey told us. "The same thing is true in Mexico. We were trying to export seed there. If you want to get anything done, you pay in advance under the table."

Farmland Industries, a major cooperative, has managed to ship grain to Mexico and Iraq. But Eugene Vickers, Farmland World Trade's Washington representative, emphasized that the export drive remains in the formative stages. "The biggest challenge is that we don't have an overseas network of agents and representatives," Vickers said. "Cargill not only has agents in major buying countries but also its own offices.

This gives them a tremendous advantage in having an office on the scene to develop contacts and provide information. It takes a long time to get established. We are becoming known, but the Cargills have been around for years."

Part of the reason for the resilience of Cargill and its brethren comes from the nature of the grain trade itself. Conceptually, the world in which Whitney MacMillan operates is straightforward. His company buys grain in surplus regions and transports it for sale in areas of shortage. But that is where the simplicity ends. The global exchange of grain demands construction of an expensive network of physical assets. Country elevators take in and store raw grains during the period between harvest and shipment. Larger facilities—terminals and subterminals—assemble the grain from country elevators for shipment via railroad and barge to ports on the Atlantic, Pacific, or Great Lakes. Here wheat, corn, and other commodities are moved into export terminals, from which oceangoing vessels are loaded and dispatched overseas. These terminals are massive. Two of Cargill's elevators in Duluth, Minnesota, on Lake Superior, together can store more than 14 million bushels of grain and load onto ships nearly 200,000 bushels per hour. Duluth is an important center for wheat and sunflower-seed exports to Europe. Cargill's terminal in Seattle, Washington, loaded in 1984 the single largest grain shipment ever transported on a U.S. vessel. The *Jade Phoenix*, which took forty-three days to make the 12,000-mile voyage from Seattle to Egypt, carried 110,000 tons of soft-white wheat from the Pacific Northwest—enough to bake 378 million loaves of bread.

This physical network of elevators, terminals, ports, and barges is made even more byzantine by the artificial complexities with which Cargill and its handful of competitors conduct their operations. It is unlikely that grain shipped from Kansas to Khartoum would be recorded as having traveled along the most direct geographic route. Shipments more often flow through a dizzying maze of subsidiaries and paper companies that operate around the world. A web of entities based outside the United States provides a number of advantages. It is easier to hedge commodity sales, a critical element of any such transaction, with multiple sources of grain supplies. Foreign subsidiaries allow Cargill to buy and sell to itself, which helps the company profit from short-term price and exchange rate movements. These subsidiaries are also an organizational basis for tax-minimization strategies—an ongoing concern of the traders. W. B. Saunders, now vice-chairman of Cargill, testified before Congress in 1976 and explained why his company uses foreign subsidiaries to minimize tax payments:

Taxes are a critical cost element in our business. Unlike firms involved in manufacturing operations, commodity traders possess no unique advantages like patents, trademarks, brand franchises, technology or product superiority which enable them to absorb higher tax costs. We all buy and sell the same commodities, dealing with the same sellers and the same buyers. To compete on equal terms we had to seek tax costs no greater than those to established foreign-owned competitors.

The hub of Cargill's many-spoked wheel of intracorporate exchange is the shadowy Tradax International. Tradax is based in Panama, but its center of operations is Geneva. It moves grain all over the world, from Buenos Aires to Beijing, from Bangkok to Baghdad. When Cargill sells grain to the Russians, it usually goes through Tradax—which has even been known to buy Russian grain, such as the 100,000 tons of Soviet barley it once sold to Hungary and Italy. Arranging trades between Eastern European countries, such as selling Hungarian wheat to the USSR, is not that unusual, according to testimony at the 1976 congressional hearings.

Robert Benson, a former Cargill trader, provided an appetizing whiff of how this intricate web of transactions promotes tax minimization. "Tradax cost [Cargill] a ton of money," he told us. "They made us subsidize Tradax in a sense. We sold stuff cheaper to them so they could make a profit." *Washington Post* editor Dan Morgan described in his book, *Merchants of Grain*, which is the most authoritative account of the industry's history, other tax strategies that fuel Tradax operations:

> When Cargill sells a cargo of corn to a Dutch animal-feed manufacturer, the grain is shipped down the Mississippi River, put aboard a vessel at Baton Rouge and sent to Rotterdam. On paper, however, as tracked by the Internal Revenue Service, its route is more elaborate. Cargill will first sell the corn to Tradax International in Panama, which will "hire" Tradax/Geneva as its agent; Tradax/Geneva then might arrange the sale to a Dutch miller through its subsidiary, Tradax/Holland; any profits would be booked to Tradax/Panama, a tax-haven company, and Tradax/Geneva would earn only a "management fee" for brokering the deal between Tradax/Panama and Tradax/Holland.

The structure of his industry and the unique collections of assets at his disposal are the foundations of Whitney MacMillan's brand of power. Cargill is a corporation, and MacMillan a corporate leader, whose autonomy cannot be rivaled by, or in, large publicly held companies. Cargill's power to sustain and nurture its lucrative options is of a dual nature—the power to decide for others and the power to prevent others from deciding for it. It manages to grow and profit in a sector of the world economy marked by agony and turmoil. A deadly cycle of drought and famine claimed the lives of 300,000 Ethiopians in 1983 and 1984 and threatens the well-being of another 8 million. Throughout Africa, 150 million people—one-third of the sub-Saharan population—are subject to drought conditions. The United States, breadbasket of the world, is in the throes of a crisis among its family farmers unlike anything since the Great Depression. A bushel of wheat that fetched $4.21 in January 1981 brought a farmer only $3.36 in January 1985, according to the Texas Department of Agriculture. A pound of peanuts that sold for 49 cents in January 1981 sold for only 24 cents four years later. The vise grip of lower prices and other forces—record farm debt levels, high interest rates, that make servicing that debt even more burdensome, declining land values, and an overvalued dollar—is bankrupting the vulnerable and forcing agriculture toward a future of fewer and larger farms.

What is so remarkable is how little attention has been paid to the role of Cargill in the perpetuation of these agricultural crises or how modest are the expectations of its potential role in their resolution. It is a silence that speaks volumes about the power of Whitney MacMillan and the corporation he directs.

MacMillan has no doubt come to expect and enjoy this autonomy, even though he understands it may be disturbed by a few passing challenges. His predecessors all experienced the ups and downs of the grain trade. This sense of history gives the family a perspective that both anticipates these roller coasters and plans for them. Cargill executives are not prone to panic. They have survived too much—too many wars, crop failures, weather disasters, revolutions, boycotts, and embargoes—to warrant unnecessary excitements. Whitney MacMillan was hunting quail when the Carter administration announced its grain embargo on the Soviet Union, one of the wrenching events of recent agricultural history. His reaction? "He stayed out a couple of more days," said a fellow sportsman. "The hunting was successful."

The chairman's cool is at once noteworthy and telling. The Cargills and the MacMillans have faced the competition and intrigues of other merchant houses—the Belgian Fribourgs of Continental, the Dreyfus family of France, the Argentine Borns of Bunge and Born—that operate under equally tight-lipped family control. Whitney MacMillan has drunk deeply from this history, which extends back a century, when Russia and India were major grain exporters. The mantle of leadership wears more comfortably when it comes from such lineage. Now Cargill is number one —the undisputed giant among giants of the world grain trade.

. . .

The effort to understand Whitney MacMillan and the company he directs must begin with a grasp of its status as a private corporation and how such a status facilitates its offensive and defensive strategies. Cargill is a massive entity with no public shareholders. Ownership is shared by three branches of the Cargill and MacMillan families, which together control all but roughly 15 percent of the total equity. An October 1984 report in *Forbes* estimated that each of the three family groups held Cargill shares worth at least $500 million. Whitney and his sister and brother, the children of Cargill MacMillan, represent one branch. Their first cousins, the children of Cargill's brother, John MacMillan, Jr., are a second branch. The third group with a stake in the company is a grandson and granddaughter of Will Cargill, its founder. Company executives control the remainder of the shares, although this stock has no voting rights.

Cargill has no public annual meeting and does not have to submit annual and quarterly reports or other routine filings with the Securities and Exchange Commission. It is chartered in Delaware, since 1901 the least demanding jurisdiction in the country for business incorporation. Roughly one-third of the companies on the New York Stock Exchange, including such giants as General Motors, Ford Motor Company, Citicorp holding company, and ITT, are chartered in Delaware, where laws and judicial decisions heavily favor management over shareholders whenever there is conflict. Cargill's private status adds to the advantages of a Delaware charter.

The lack of public annual reports, annual meetings, and other vehicles for dialogue and disclosure has immediate consequences for accountability. It closes off the possibility of shareholder lawsuits and the depositions and public testimony by top managers such lawsuits often require. It closes off channels of communication and protest that have been used as levers of influence over public corporations. Corporate-responsibility groups, such as religious and environmental organizations, have no shareholders meeting to attend where they can publicize their causes. They cannot offer resolutions through the proxy mechanism and nominate or make demands on the board of directors. These and other access points are unavailable to such shareholders of conscience. So too are derivative conscience-raising endeavors, such as locating, educating, and trying to persuade institutional shareholders—universities, pension funds, and bank trust departments—about the wisdom of proposals for reform of company policies and business practices.

Private ownership has a major restraining impact on a second vehicle of scrutiny—the media. There has been precious little written about the structure, operations, and power of Cargill, and even less about the man and families who control it. What has been published, in the financial press and elsewhere, is often redundant and unambitious—rewrites of rewrites of Cargill press releases or brochures. Several factors contribute to this uninspired media performance. There is the initial problem of very limited access. Reporters also find a reduced incentive to dig out material when there are so few contact points for follow-up once the information is published. Many business stories go to print because of an editor's expectation that an SEC or New York Stock Exchange response will provide material for another story. Reciprocally, law-enforcement agencies often receive leads for inquiry or legal action from material unearthed by daily newspapers or periodicals. No leads, no agency investigations to be covered.

The Minneapolis media are not renowned for their aggressive coverage of the area's largest and most powerful corporate citizen. But WCCO-TV, a leading local station, did produce and air a hard-hitting documentary in March 1980 that examined U.S. agriculture and the impact of the international grain traders. The program, "Feast of the Giants," was one segment of a WCCO documentary series called *The Moore Report.* It communicated at some length the insights of agribusiness critics and reported on specific charges of misconduct against Cargill and Iowa Beef Processors of Iowa City, Nebraska. The program contained no response or rebuttal from Cargill—but not for lack of trying on the part of its producers. According to Greg Pratt, who wrote and produced the segment, WCCO requested in writing an interview with Whitney MacMillan as early as six months before the program aired. As is its habit, Cargill chose not to grant interviews. Company officials claimed that the Soviet grain embargo, announced as the show was being produced, was too great a drain on executive energies. Thus, criticisms of Cargill's power and allegations of misconduct necessarily went unanswered.

"The research we present tonight tells us that the food industry has grown highly profitable, dangerously concentrated, and perhaps monopolistic," said host Dave Moore as he framed the program's theme. "A significant part of what we pay in the store, in other words, may well be an overcharge, an unjustified cost, money that we may be shelling out for a rash of acquisitions and mergers, the high cost of advertising, and the fact that fewer and larger firms are competing for our dollar. Food industry representatives say this new research is far-out, others say it is far-reaching. But if what these researchers say is true, we are faced with a perplexing question: Will this vital food industry in the hands of fewer and larger firms either enhance or threaten our cherished notions of democracy, free enterprise, and a fair deal?"

The reaction at the château, and by Cargill's Minneapolis business colleagues, was immediate and furious. Cargill published in less than a week a sixteen-page pamphlet that responded to twenty-one assertions and charges the company considered false or misleading. Perhaps to underscore the gravity of Cargill's objections, the pamphlet was issued under the signature of Whitney MacMillan, who, in a foreword, described the documentary as "superficial and admittedly biased." MacMillan did not explain how a company whose resources were too strained to cooperate originally in the show's production found time to compose such a detailed rebuttal. The pamphlet was not the only reaction. Cargill vice-president William Pearce met with top WCCO executives soon after the broadcast to communicate the company position. WCCO agreed not to rebroadcast "Feast of the Giants" unless it was edited to include Cargill's perspective. There was still more. Northwestern Bell, a sponsor of *The Moore Report*, quickly announced that it would no longer sponsor the series, a decision that at the time prompted speculation of a link to corporate displeasure with the segment on Cargill.

Dwight Hicks, who was then advertising staff manager for Northwestern Bell, confirmed that this was precisely what transpired. Hicks told us that top Bell executives received telephone calls from "high-level people at other companies" in Minneapolis. "Cargill people were not making those calls," he explained. "The ones who did felt it was a cheap shot at a fellow brother." Bell withdrew its sponsorship "basically because we were totally embarrassed by the content of the show," Hicks continued. "It embarrassed us and the business community. It embarrassed me because I was going to a Cargill wedding a week or two later." For Whitney MacMillan, the fallout may still be continuing. After he viewed the documentary, the Cargill chairman told a company employee he would never again watch WCCO-TV. Cargill has not disclosed whether MacMillan remains true to his vow.

Three years after "Feast of the Giants" the grain company faced a second, if more polite, effort by an outside organization to examine and evaluate its operations. The Priests Senate of Saint Paul and Minneapolis issued, in March 1983, a 179-page report entitled *Daily Bread: An Abdication of Power*. The study, while critical, was moderate in tone. It even included a chapter entitled "Perspectives on the Theology of Food." The authors went out of their way to accommodate Cargill. Project researcher Diane Elwood and a member of the Priests Senate traveled to Minnetonka for conversations with public-affairs officials. They conducted tape-recorded interviews for use in the report. The Cargill executives became concerned after they realized they had failed to tape the conversations themselves or take notes. So they made a request: Would the research team resubmit its questions in writing, accept written answers from Cargill, and use this material, rather than transcripts of the recordings, in the report? The researchers agreed.

This act of good faith did not restrain Cargill executives from later trying to quash or edit the document shortly before it was released. (Cargill was furnished with a prerelease copy.) According to Elwood and Father John Gilbert, who was president of the Priests Senate, top Cargill executives, including its veteran general counsel, John McGrory, initiated a quiet lobbying effort to persuade the archdiocese not to release *Daily Bread.* Several high-level executives, all of them Catholics, sent a letter to Archbishop John Roach that communicated their doubts about the report. "They spoke of it in terms of it [being] a shoddy piece of work," said Father Gilbert, who considers himself a good friend of general counsel McGrory. "The conclusion was that [the report] should not be published." After a debate, and a decision to delete an appendix that described the goals and strategies of a Canadian organization that advocates organized campaigns to check the power of the grain traders, the Priests Senate chose to release *Daily Bread* despite the Cargill objections.

"I tried to propose to him [McGrory] that what we are interested in is feeding the hungry in the world," Father Gilbert continued. "What I suggested [to Cargill] was that they come debate in public. Have a day when the ministers of the Twin Cities could come out and hear different views on the grain trade, including Cargill's. They were worried that they might come off looking as though they were against the church, or antichurch. So it never happened."

· · ·

There is an important distinction to be drawn between privacy and secrecy. Cargill's status as a private corporation is a mode of organization that determines what business information it is required to disclose. Secrecy is an explicit strategy to deny outsiders timely or valuable knowledge. This is an industry where discretion is not only good manners but a critical element of sound business. The company is called upon to serve capitalists, socialists, communists, fascists, democracies, and dictatorships. A corporate code of silence reassures these diverse constituencies.

Cargill's jealous protection of the details of its operations also creates a fundamental imbalance of power vis-à-vis other sectors of the farm economy. Undisclosed agreements with railroads on special rates to haul commodites give the grain giant an advantage over farm cooperatives and rural electric associations, which can neither demand similar rates nor document discriminatory pricing. Tight control of information about profits and losses on specific transactions shields Cargill against detailed claims of excess profits or price manipulation. "Destination Unknown" exports and frequent destination changes on the high seas make it more difficult for regulators to track global grain flows.

Worldwatch Institute president Lester Brown discussed with us the imbalance of power between these information haves and have-nots: "The thing about the grain trade is that it's very difficult for governments to implement their policies when they don't have control of the [food] resources, and in some cases, don't even have the information on the resources. There's an awful lot that happens in the world grain trade that we learn about after the fact and not before," he said. "And that's because the companies thrive on information over which they have much greater control than anyone else. . . . It's that ability not only to have their own information networks which gives them an advantage in dealing with farmers and others—individual farmers can't maintain that kind of global market-intelligence system—but when you add to that the Department of Agriculture working with the grain companies [as a source of data], the farmers really don't have a chance. . . . If prices jump all over the place, they really thrive, because they usually know which way they're going to jump before anyone else."

Cargill's "intelligence network" is an object of frustration and awe, even in its roughest characterization. It is by most accounts without equal. The company maintains a vast infrastructure to collect data on crop prices, production trends, and sales activity around the world. When secrecy is combined with relentless information gathering, Cargill's power advantage becomes even more profound and consequential. Whitney MacMillan presides over a trading empire whose continued autonomy rests in part on its role as an accumulator of knowledge for itself and a perpetuator of ignorance for others.

Business Week reported in 1949 on Cargill's elaborate communications system and its capacity to handle five thousand wires daily. Robert Benson, the former trader, said the company has offices around the United States that file reports on crop conditions. A Cargill bulletin of September 1983, described the workings and capabilities of the Cargill Information Center, "whose art it is to mine Cargill-useful facts and ideas from a growing mountain of information." The information center has access to computerized data banks around the word. It contains for immediate reference more than seven thousand studies compiled by or for

Cargill operating units. Two-thirds of the information searches at the center are done electronically and provide answers to the following sorts of inquiries: "I need five years' figures on catfish production and requirements for making catfish feed"; "I want a potential list of customers for salt, as used to enhance oil recovery in California oil fields"; "Give me Canadian production and consumption figures for high-fructose corn syrup."

These impressive means of data gathering and retrieval are the tip of the iceberg. "Cargill is the best in the business in terms of agricultural intelligence," said Bob Bergland, secretary of agriculture under President Carter. "They beat everybody else hands down." Bergland stated flatly to us that when it comes to agricultural intelligence, Whitney MacMillan knows more than CIA director William Casey, and his company has the capacity to generate more information than the vast data-collection systems of the U.S. Department of Agriculture (USDA). The company has more employees overseas than USDA, and these people are freer "to go around the countryside poking around" than are the department's overseas emissaries, Bergland explained. Texas agriculture commissioner Jim Hightower agrees with Bergland's assessment. "They are not only secretive, they are in a secretive business," he said of Cargill. "They're worldwide. And I'm telling you, they've got more agents than the CIA."

Cargill's chairman understands better than anyone else the value to his company of its information hegemony. His rationale for secrecy is simple. Strategy is Cargill's stock in trade. And strategy, unlike inventions and trademarks, receives no governmental protection. So strategy must remain confidential. In our brief conversation with MacMillan, that was precisely the reason he offered for declining to be interviewed. But we had previously told his aides we would not request disclosure of strategy or tactics. We had no interest in learning how many sales in how many countries Cargill was making in a given commodity. The strategy excuse is a ruse to camouflage broader company operations and impacts. The reality is that the Cargill men view their business as one giant trade secret, its lawful right to secrecy arising from its private-company status.

Bob Bergland spoke at length about Cargill and the uses of secrecy. He emphasized several times that company policies in this regard are not a product of eccentricity but of conscious strategy. "They raise this wall of secrecy, and it raises all kinds of doubts about their integrity," Bergland told us. "And it is part of their strategy. It is not happenstance." Bergland also argued that the strategy is counterproductive, that Cargill would benefit from a policy of more complete disclosure. "Why they maintain this wall of secrecy is beyond me," he remarked. "And I have said this to friends of mine at Cargill. 'Why don't you open up and let the world examine you? It's a very disconcerting thing.' They've got everything to gain by being more open."

But do they? If doubts and suspicions were coalescing to erode Cargill's profit or influence, Bergland would have a point. This is not happening yet. Cargill gains by not talking about its contacts and relationships with communist bureaucrats. Right-wing opponents of U.S. trade with the Soviet bloc, who have focused attention and denunciations on the activities of Control Data, Occidental Petroleum, and Dresser Industries, are largely silent when it comes to Cargill. It gains by not releasing, on a regular basis, detailed information about corporate profits and taxes. Such disclosures have touched off controversies around, and accelerated investigations of, large publicly held companies, such as General Electric and General Dynamics. Secrecy makes it more difficult to link incidents of corporate misconduct to specific officials, never an easy task even in a public company.

Minneapolis assistant U.S. attorney Daniel Schermer, who investigated charges in the late 1970s of tax avoidance by Cargill's Spanish subsidiaries, was asked if Chairman MacMillan figured in his probe. "Cargill is an extremely compartmentalized company," he told us. "To the point where it would be difficult to put your finger on just about anything and say, 'That guy's responsible.' "

Bergland's tenure as secretary of agriculture is itself testimony to the uses and power implications of a sustained policy of secrecy and nondisclosure. When the Carter administration, over the objections of the Agriculture Department, imposed its grain embargo on the Soviet Union, Bergland was forced to turn to the grain traders, who also opposed the embargo, for detailed information on shipping commitments. "When the Russians invaded Afghanistan and Jimmy Carter asked me how much grain the Russians had bought, we couldn't tell him, because we didn't know," Bergland told an interviewer in 1983. "I think Cargill's view is much like the European view, or the Japanese view. They generally regard the United States as a grain colony."

This information gap assured Cargill and its brethren an ongoing role in postembargo policies. On the weekend after Carter announced the trade restrictions, Bergland called representatives of the grain companies into his office to determine who had unfulfilled contracts with the Soviets. He could not find out for himself. "I was authorized to buy up Russian positions in the contracts," Bergland said. "We set up teams. There were Department of Agriculture professionals working with each individual company. They mostly had their information with them. Some had to call or fly back to headquarters to get it."

Despite the traumatic news of the embargo sent through the fields of Kansas and North Dakota, the traders were protected. USDA compensated Cargill and its colleagues for grain they had agreed to, but could no longer, ship. A 1981 report by the Agriculture Department inspector general suggested that the compensation rate, designed to provide traders with a profit, but not a taxpayer-financed windfall, was too generous. The inspector general also described possible manipulation by unnamed companies. Large amounts of grain were reclassified as bound for the Soviet Union and thus made eligible for compensation. "There was an unusual amount of shifting from 'unknown destination' to 'USSR destination' in the two days preceding the announcement of the suspension," the report noted. "Approximately 30 percent (5 million metric tons) of the total undelivered contracts originally assumed by [the federal government] were entered into the USDA Export Sales Reporting System (ESRS) as 'destination USSR' in the two days preceding the grain suspension." Such shifting was facilitated by the fact that a high U.S. official had announced two days before the embargo that U.S. authorities were contemplating trade sanctions against the Soviet Union.

.   .   .

The use Whitney MacMillan makes of the strategic applications of secrecy combined with input from a vast intelligence network insulates Cargill from the demands and dissatisfactions of outside constituencies. There is a pattern of growth and profitability at Cargill, a history of conquest beyond familiar terrain, that has transformed the sweep and character of the corporation. MacMillan and his predecessors have used their unique arsenal of protections to shape an economic organization of expanding impact and decreasing vulnerability to shifting economic forces.

A company pamphlet once quipped, "The Reign It's Plain is Mainly in the Grain." But for more than two decades Cargill has built on its position as trader to move deeply into other sectors of agribusiness and even other whole areas of industry and commerce. Its reach extends across five continents, both under the earth and over the seas. It is a corporate empire of dizzying sweep and scope.

Cargill collects grain in country elevators in the United States, six provinces of Canada, France, Brazil, Argentina, and Thailand. It moves that grain in part with an armada of 420 barges and 11 towboats that operate on U.S. inland waterways; 2 huge vessels that sail the Great Lakes and 12 oceangoing ships; 2,000 railroad hopper cars and over 2,000 tank cars. The company trades, markets, and processes commodities through a network of eight hundred plants and offices in fifty-two countries. It has sugar-trading operations in Central and South America and Great Britain. Tradax markets sugar in Eastern Europe and the Middle East, and in Asia through offices in Singapore, Bangkok, and Tokyo. It purchased in 1981 the cotton-, fiber-, and rubber-trading arms of the London-based Bowater Corp., with interests in India, Pakistan, Turkey, and several African countries. Cargill can process 300 million bushels of corn every year and produce twenty-five different kinds of corn syrup and 800 million pounds of cornstarch. Plants in Great Britain and the Netherlands together can mill nearly 20 million bushels annually and turn corn from the United States into sweeteners for candies and other products. Cargill is the second largest miller of flour in the United States, with thirteen plants (number fourteen is under construction) and the capacity to produce 4.5 billion pounds of flour each year. Shaver Poultry Breeding Farms, in Ontario, sells layer chicks to egg producers and broiler chicks to commercial feeder-growers in more than ninety countries. An orange juice plant in Brazil can ship at least ninety thousand tons of concentrate each year. And this is just the beginning. Cargill has trading, production, or marketing operations in life insurance, steel, cocoa, molasses, coffee, salt, seeds, resins, construction and manufacturing equipment, vegetable oils, and on and on and on.

There has been a consistent and cohesive dimension to the Cargill expansion strategy. It represents classic positioning both in a geographical and in a strategic context. The incomparable productivity of the American Midwest convinced Cargill's leaders to stick largely with food—but to move further along the processing chain in order to integrate backward toward the farmer and forward toward the consumer. Its emergence as the nation's second-largest meatpacker is characteristic of the evolution toward value-added agribusiness built around its traditional core of trading. During World War II, the company acquired an operation to produce and market livestock feed, most often made from soybeans and corn, under a popular brand name. In 1974 it acquired Caprock Industries, one of the country's largest cattle feedlot operations, and began to tap the output of its fed division to fatten its herds. Whitney MacMillan oversaw the 1979 acquisition of MBPXL, a billion-dollar meatpacker based in Wichita, Kansas, and created a market within the corporation for cattle fed by Caprock. (MacMillan was thwarted by a federal judge in December 1983 when he tried to build his company's position even further with the $60 million purchase of Spencer Beef, the country's third-largest meatpacker. In January 1986, the Supreme Court agreed to review the decision.) Cargill thus deployed capital generated through operations in the highly concentrated grain trade to become an integrated presence in another industry, meatpacking, structured as an oligopoly.

Diversification away from grain trading is Cargill's way of hedging the ups and downs of its trading activities. The company is a modern master of risk management. It can make money whether farmers are making money or losing money. Its ability to survive on low margins, together with its relentless drive to reduce handling and transportation costs, means it can profit even in hard times. Its unmatched capacity for grain storage and shipment opens huge windows of opportunity during times of unexpected market surges, such as major purchases by the Soviets or Chinese. An integrated and diversified corporate structure has allowed Cargill to withstand the stagnation of U.S. farm exports since 1980–81 that has devastated farmers in the Midwest, who grow the crops the company sells.

Cargill's aggressive conglomerate strategy, which has flourished under Whitney MacMillan, dates back as far as the reign of John MacMillan, Jr. It has been nourished and sustained in large part by the company's emphasis, referred to by nearly every former executive with whom we spoke, on long-range investment and returns. Cargill has claimed for years that it distributes less than 5 percent of its annual earnings as dividends and reinvests the rest. This patient investment pattern is tied directly to family ownership. Unlike a public corporation, where managers work to increase short-term profits and the current price of company stock, a private firm often prefers to enhance asset value for its owners. Cargill has been willing to risk large short-term costs—costs that would depress the share price of a public corporation—to establish a major presence in industries such as poultry and beef processing. Cyclical downturns allow the grain giant to purchase assets at a discount, a process one friend of MacMillan's compares to "buying straw hats in winter."

There is little evidence that Cargill will be compelled to initiate a public offering. The company is a credit-intensive rather than capital-intensive operation. Its borrowing relations with banks around the world are healthy, and it can generate internally all the capital it needs to pursue its agenda for expansion.

"Cargill is a private company because in agriculture the stock market won't pay true value," said a former high-level company executive. "So Whitney will keep it private. Stock markets won't pay true value because earnings are cyclical and margins are thin. In agribusiness, the quarters flop around, the years flop around, but growth trends over time are usually better than a lot of other companies. Cargill is in a cyclical business—and Whitney preached this. Cargill's philosophy is to expand in the down years of a business's trend, and that's Whitney's philosophy too."

Vice-president William Pearce, in a rare burst of public insight, explained to a reporter in 1983 how Cargill can continue to operate privately:

> The companies you're speaking of [that are held publicly] have very different requirements than we do. They need to sell products to people in the supermarkets. They need to attract people to invest in them. They need to be seen by people who make decisions about their business as prominent and generous and important. Our business is much different than that. We're not in the equity market, we're not out trying to persuade people of our good works and good intentions so they'll invest money in the business. We don't want their money, you know, we don't—we don't need it. Nor are we trying to convey a sense of what we do to people —to people on the street.

The literature on the behavioral differences of executives in private corporations versus public corporations is slim. But it is undeniable that Cargill's status as a family-owned enterprise has been a decisive element in its power and profitability and in its evolution as an agribusiness conglomerate. Consider the business environment of a Fortune 500 chief executive compared with the world in which Whitney MacMillan operates, and the questions these differences raise. Private managers can make decisions and adopt strategies without worries about reaction on Wall Street, forecasts of business analysts, or the appetites of corporate raiders. But does this mean Cargill is more deliberate in corporate planning? With a board free of outside directors and replete with family and loyalists, MacMillan can gather his directors at the château in a few hours, if not a matter of minutes. But does this result in more nimble decision-making? Because it does not have to report significant pending litigation or other damaging information to the SEC, Cargill management is less diverted by external conflict and controversy. Edward Cook, the founder of Cook Industries, complained in 1976 about the handicap under which he operated. "Every time my 10-K comes out, my competitors go to my customers and say, 'Look, if you dealt with us your name wouldn't be in print,' " he said. "This just isn't a high-exposure industry." But does freedom from such outside pressure focus management attention and energies? Interviews with former Cargill executives, many of whom worked alongside or reported to Whitney MacMillan at various stages of his career, suggest they believe all three questions should be answered in the affirmative.

Whitney MacMillan has more control over his time and schedule, and the directions of his corporation, than the chief executives of most Fortune 500 companies. He is firmly in control at Cargill and has few worries about challenges to his authority. As of August 1984 the company's board of directors had thirteen members, according to records on file in the Washington, D.C., Office of Corporations. Of these directors, four are members of the Cargill or MacMillan families. (One is Whitney's older brother, Cargill MacMillan, Jr.) Two others serve with Whitney in the Office of the Chairman. Yet another, a group vice-president, is a prep school and Yale classmate of the chairman. And the family role in Cargill extends well beyond the boardroom. John H. MacMillan III, Whitney's cousin, is a vice-president. Martha MacMillan Bennett is a personnel specialist. Arthur "Buzz" Schmidt, Whitney's son-in-law, and father of his four grandchildren, is a Chicago-based account manager in Cargill's processing division.

This substantial family presence leaves no questions about who runs Cargill. But the current chairman, and family members before him, have not been afraid to tap the expertise of outsiders in their drive to create a larger and more profitable enterprise. Cargill has succeeded for a long time in blending family control, in all its nepotistic manifestations, and professional management for maximum strategic advantage. Nepotism provides the unity, the trust, the continuity of leadership that supply a corporation with motivation beyond that of the immediate dollar. But unrestrained nepotism can demoralize talented outsiders. Cargill's breakthrough has been to maintain ownership and family control without sacrificing management competence.

Several forces have bridged the gulf between the family and nonfamily executives. The company has submitted to nonfamily management when the Cargills and MacMillans could not produce adequately seasoned or talented executives. For sixteen years after the death of John MacMillan, Jr., the top officers of Cargill were outsiders: Erwin Kelm, whom Whitney MacMillan succeeded as chairman; the late president Fred Seed; and former vice-chairman Robert Diercks. The current president, James Spicola, is also from outside the family, as have been the two vice-chairmen since Diercks. Perhaps the most accomplished nonfamily achiever of recent years is M. D. "Pete" McVay, Spicola's predecessor as president. McVay was a driving force behind Cargill's moves into meatpacking and steel and an expanded presence in grain and oilseed processing. Former Cargill trader Robert Benson described McVay as "a go-go-go man" whose standing was unquestioned. "Pete was considered just a quarter of a step away from God," quipped another former executive, who described McVay's relationship with Chairman MacMillan.

A long-standing management-training program also promotes stability and harmony in the executive ranks. Thomas Veblen, a former vice-president for human resources, compares this development program to military training. "It's kind of like the Marine Corps," he joked. "Get 'em before they know the meaning of fear—or before they go off to business school and you have to unteach them everything they've learned." Cargill has also extended the benefits of nepotism beyond its ruling families. Loyalty among outside executives is passed on from generation to generation with the help of a summer-jobs program in which Cargill employs Minneapolis students. Two-thirds of the students hired are children of current employees, some of whom eventually go on to permanent positions in the company.

.   .   .

There is, all told, a serenity within the Cargill executive corps upon which a number of former managers commented. It is a serenity that underscores the chairman's capacity to involve talented outside managers whose loyalties are beyond question. It also reflects his ability to mediate between contending family interests. Few friends and former executives offered theories on why Whitney MacMillan rose to power over his older brother Cargill and his various cousins. But several did agree that there seems to be little or no sharp infighting among the relatives. The chairman's siblings and cousins "all have their niche," said Skid Thorpe. "Over the years they have found what they do best." A former company executive told us MacMillan "got the confidence of the family members and the other management within Cargill" as he climbed the management ladder. "He could relate to and handle the role of being a catalyst in keeping the family's interests together."

This is not to suggest that there are no clashes or tensions among Cargill managers. Clayton Tonnemaker, a twenty-two-year company veteran, reported to Whitney MacMillan for five years when the current chairman was executive vice-president. "There was not much doubt that he was the crown prince," Tonnemaker said. "He had responsibility [as executive vice-president] for salt, grain, and Cargo Carriers [Cargill's barge subsidiary]. That whole period was like a super-training program, although Whitney spent most of his time on the grain-processing side. He and [vice-chairman] Barney Saunders have and have had a close relationship. Whitney always represented the family."

Tonnemaker then related a story meant to underscore MacMillan's authority even before he became chairman—a rare glimpse of executive life at Cargill. "The most dramatic example of family control occurred when the salt division was trying to buy AENCO," Tonnemaker told us. "This was the last acquisition I made. It does solid-waste processing.

. . . When we in the salt management team looked around [for an acquisition] for Whit, it was one of the businesses we identified. He said, 'You've got the skills to run a high-volume, municipal-market business.' And one of them was solid-waste processing. The purchase price was less than $500,000, and it had a small earnings stream and a few key R-and-D people.

"Whitney was the champion of the acquisition, and we could do it for peanuts," Tonnemaker continued. "I was working for him then. The procedure was, Whit and I would go up in front of the executive committee [of the board] and try to sell the idea of the acquisition. We did this several times. They always turned it down, saying it didn't fit, it was too small, and, last, I don't think they liked the idea of being in the garbage business. [Then-chairman] Erv Kelm didn't want to go to the Minikahda Club and have somebody say, 'I hear you're in garbage now.' The last time we made a presentation, we were in the directors room at the Lake Office, sitting in the French Provincial furniture. It was just before lunch, which the senior executives always eat in the executive dining room promptly at twelve-thirty. At twelve-twenty-five after going through it a couple of times, they said, 'No, let's wait.' They clearly didn't want to make the decision—just go to lunch. Kelm starts to get up. Seed and Diercks get up to follow him. Whitney stays seated. He gets all red in the face and says, 'We haven't made a decision yet.' They stop in their tracks, turn around, and sit down.

"John McGrory, being the legal man, calls for a vote," Tonnemaker said. "Seed, Kelm, and Diercks abstained. McGrory says, 'How should this appear in the minutes?' Whitney answers, and he was pretty agitated, 'Just as it happened: one yes and three abstentions.' And it passed. It was the most dramatic example of ownership control I have ever seen. Whitney was the owner, and they were running the business."

It is also safe to say that harmony among top Cargill managers and employees does not extend through all levels of the hierarchy. Consider the company's recent history with respect to hiring and promotion of women and blacks. In October 1984 Cargill settled a lawsuit filed by four former employees and the Equal Employment Opportunity Commission (EEOC). Under the terms of the settlement, Cargill paid a total of $200,000 to the individual plaintiffs and set aside $1 million for distribution among any former employees who qualify as claimants on the fund. It also established targets for hiring and promotion of minority employees. Randolph Staten, a state representative in Minnesota, worked for Cargill from 1971 to 1977 as corporate affirmative-action officer. He left the company because of what he described as "cutbacks in the firm's commitment to affirmative action and its support of minority and civil rights groups."

Staten described to us a recent history of sincere efforts on the part of Cargill management to develop and implement more progressive hiring practices, followed by a period of backsliding just prior to and following his departure. Soon after he joined Cargill, Staten understood that he faced a challenge. "I would describe the personality of the corporation at that time as extremely hostile to the principles and policies of an affirmative-action program," he said. "Its plans and policies did not call for and had not included people of color and women. I could tell that anything that would change that was going to be a major struggle. . . . The perception was that you could hire black secretaries and bring in a couple of token [management] people—that you did not have to have an impact on management."

But the situation gradually improved. According to Staten, Cargill formed an equal-employment committee that included divisional vice-presidents, General Counsel John McGrory, and Chairman Erwin Kelm. Staten called Vice-chairman Robert Diercks "the social force" behind the committee and also said that Whitney MacMillan, then an executive vice-president, attended a number of meetings. "This meant that the affirmative-action effort had very high visibility," Staten noted. "The managers understood that when we established goals, we meant business." Understanding eventually gave way to a hardening of attitudes. Staten said Cargill cut back on the percentages of women and blacks admitted into the fast-track management program, which prior to his arrival had included no blacks and only one woman. The company scaled back a campaign to increase recruitment at minority colleges. The executive monitoring structure on affirmative action began to erode.

Cargill did not provide us the policy statement on affirmative action that was issued by Whitney MacMillan and referred to in a company newsletter. How would Staten describe Chairman MacMillan's personal commitment to progressive hiring and promotion? "I recall one annual meeting of managers from the different [Cargill] divisions," he said. "Someone posed a question to Whitney MacMillan about a commitment to affirmative action. I was less than satisfied with his answer, to say the least. He said, in effect, there are certain people who build this company, those are the ones who will be rewarded, and those are the people who will run this company."

.   .   .

The management discipline in the château, as well as Cargill's evolution away from sole reliance on the grain trade, have bred into its executives an attitude of self-control, self-containment, and self-determination that is not limited to their role in the world economy. Starting with its corporate structure and extending to its apparatus for political influence, MacMillan and his colleagues have developed strategies and tactics to supplement Cargill's market power for the protection and advancement of its global momentum.

Cargill is accustomed to using the political influence that arises from economic size, contacts, and well-developed information resources. But the company operates in a mode of low visibility that reflects the structure of its political environment and suits the personality of its chairman. Unlike the automobile industry, which must contend with the influence of safety advocates and the insurance lobby, or chemical producers, whose Washington agenda is under constant scrutiny by environmentalists, Cargill has few well-organized opponents with whom it engages in direct political combat. It seldom must contend with seismic challenges to its power and interests. Rather, its task is to monitor the political landscape, maintain its hegemony, and head off pesky legislative proposals that emerge from time to time. The company's power in Washington—on issues from grain-elevator safety to commodity-price supports to railroad deregulation to farm-export policies—is undeniable. But its style of influence is subtle.

MacMillan and his colleagues are a background presence on Capitol Hill and in the executive branch. Cargill does make modest use of political-action committees to support its allies, but it does not crusade on their behalf or punish its legislative adversaries. George McGovern, no friend of the grain traders, could not recall any heated encounters or pressures with Cargill or Whitney MacMillan during his entire Senate career. Other congressional activists, such as North Dakota congressman Byron Dorgan and Oregon's Jim Weaver, also reported no pressure on them personally and no support by Cargill for their electoral opponents. Even David Senter, Washington representative of the vocal American Agriculture Movement, said that Cargill has not pressured his organization or criticized it in public. "They're active behind the scenes more so than they are publicly," Senter commented. "In other words, they're not testifying for this or that. It's just that they are hosting cocktail parties and receptions and taking policy-makers out to steak dinners." (Cargill vice-president William Pearce, who was deputy trade representative during part of the Nixon years, and Robbin Johnson, vice-president for public affairs, move easily in farm economy circles and are well known by many influential farm-state legislators.)

Congressional aides and USDA officials often describe Cargill's Washington office as more of a listening post than a lobbying nerve center. The company prefers to work through influential trade associations—whose Washington headquarters apply the standard array of full-time lobbyists, departmental monitors, heavily used mailing lists, and campaign contributions to focus their demands on Capitol Hill. Cargill belongs to more than twenty of these Washington trade groups, from the American Meat Institute to the Corn Refiners Association, the American Iron and Steel Institute, the National Turkey Federation, the North American Export Grain Association, and the National Association of Wheat Growers.* Their state-of-the-art lobbying techniques offer Cargill the advantages of Washington influence without the costs of close company identification with controversial proposals or overt political tactics.

This subterranean approach to political engagement fits Whitney MacMillan's style perfectly. His company never waivers in its determination, though it prefers to forge its levers of influence without sparks. The Cargill chairman seldom travels to Washington for public appearances and does not have a reputation as a back-room power broker. A Freedom of Information Act request for all correspondence between MacMillan and top agriculture officials of the Reagan administration produced only one letter—a September 1981 invitation to Seeley Lodwick, the Agriculture Department undersecretary, to attend a live Washington broadcast of *A Prairie Home Companion*, the popular nationwide radio program sponsored by Cargill. (Lodwick has since been replaced by Daniel Amstutz, a former Cargill executive.) Dale Hathaway, an undersecretary of agriculture in the Carter administration, said he "sees Whitney sometimes at receptions." Congressman Bill Frenzel, who told us that no Minnesota chief executive is a frequent enough visitor to Congress, said that MacMillan has attended dinners of the Wednesday Group, a House Republican club, "a couple of times." These are hardly indications of deep personal involvement on the political front.

But the Cargill chairman did not always maintain such a low profile. MacMillan is a life-long Republican, and at least for a few years as a young executive flirted with business-oriented political action. George Pillsbury, another Minneapolis food-company heir and a former state senator, whose wife is a first cousin to the Cargill chairman, told us that MacMillan had been active in the party along with other Cargill executives during the

*Cargill or a subsidiary is also affiliated with each of the following organizations: American Corn Millers Federation, American Feed Manufacturers Association, American Seed Trade Association, Chicago Board of Trade, Futures Industry Association, Miller's National Federation, National Broiler Council, National Corn Growers Association, National Council for U.S.-China Trade, National Council of Commercial Plant Breeders, National Grain Trade Council, National Institute of Oilseed Products, National Peanut Council, National Soybean Processors Association, Procompetitive Rail Steering Committee, U.S. Feed Grain Council.

1950s. A Yale classmate added that MacMillan did some fundraising at the time for state Republicans. "He was active in the Republican party in Minnesota in the late fifties," said Congressman Frenzel, also a personal friend of MacMillan. "We had a very aggressive state chairman who went out and found guys like Whitney MacMillan and tried to activate them. He got young businessmen signed up, and Whitney was active for six or eight years, and identified with the Republican party. Shortly thereafter, the U.S. Chamber of Commerce had a practical-politics course they tried to merchandise through corporations. Cargill was active, I think, at least partially because of Whitney's interest. But he is no longer active."

The Cargill chairman has also indulged from time to time in politicking on behalf of a member of the family—cousin Wheelock Whitney, a persistent candidate for elected office in Minnesota. "When his cousin ran for [state] senate, and for governor, and for lieutenant governor, Whitney was fairly active," Frenzel recalled. "Making calls, calling around raising money for him. He wasn't the chairman of the operation. In fact, one of the few political calls I ever got from my friend Whitney was when he called up and said, 'Why don't you go to your caucus for my cousin Wheelock and cast a vote for him for lieutenant governor?' I was going anyway, and I did, and that gave Wheelock one vote in my caucus. It was sixteen to one." Alas, such is the stuff of Wheelock Whitney's public career. The cousin of the leader of the state's most powerful corporation has suffered through a long political drought. Wheelock Whitney declined our request for an interview, as did other MacMillan relatives we contacted.

Cargill's subtle but methodical presence in Washington has been supplemented during periods of challenge or controversy by a technique of political action that takes full advantage of its secretiveness. It is a policy of strategic disclosure and is, in many ways, the converse of one that perpetuates ignorance. Cargill has come to understand that turning the information spigots just a bit, particularly at critical political junctures, can confuse or overwhelm congressional critics.

Strategic disclosure has both defensive and offensive functions. When Iowa congressman Neal Smith conducted aggressive hearings in 1980 on the structure of the meatpacking industry, Cargill declined an invitation to send executives. But the country's second-largest meatpacker did send a seven-page single-spaced letter, signed by President Pete McVay, that responded to charges of oligopolistic control and opposed legislation introduced by Smith to promote competition. This "testimony" of course had a special advantage. One-way communication does not provide opportunities for questioning or rebuttal.

What is still the classic example of defensive disclosure was Cargill's response to a 1976 investigation by the Senate Foreign Relations Committee's subcommittee on multinational corporations, the panel that produced dramatic revelations of corporate wrongdoing by ITT, Lockheed, and the oil giants. When the subcommittee decided to set its investigative sights on the grain trade, Cargill decided on a brilliant response. It offered to disclose information nearly all of which is routinely available from a public company, and thus satisfy the taste for an adversarial proceeding. The information included details on sales, income, corporate structure, tax payments, and deferrals of Cargill and its subsidiaries. This was the first time Cargill had made available such a broad selection of material.

The timing of these disclosures worked as much in the company's favor as the disclosures themselves, according to a source close to the subcommittee. Although standard practice called for documents to be submitted forty-eight hours in advance of a hearing, Cargill delivered much of its material less than twenty-four hours before the public session, which took place on June 24, 1976. Still more information arrived the very morning of the hearing.

What took place that day was remarkable; it is hard to believe this was the same body that left few stones unturned in its investigation of allegations of bribery by Lockheed in Japan. Only two senators attended: Dick Clark of Iowa and Charles Percy of Illinois. Clark and Percy went easy on the assembled Cargill executives, who did not include MacMillan but did include then-chairman Erwin Kelm and three other top officials. Even more Cargill representatives were members of the audience. "I have never seen so many representatives of a single company come to a hearing," said a former committee aide. "Cargill likes to make a lot out of thinking that they made us cower. . . . From the point of view of theater, if I were Cargill I would have been quite pleased."

Whitney MacMillan figured in a more recent example of the value of selective disclosure—in this case, information revealed by Cargill for offensive rather than defensive political ends. Cargill stunned the agricultural world in January 1985 when it announced that it had purchased 25,000 metric tons of Argentine wheat destined for sale to U.S. millers on the Gulf Coast. News of the deal sent shock waves through Washington and the farm belt. According to the *Wall Street Journal,* Cargill's plan represented the first time ever that wheat from Argentina, a major U.S. grain competitor on the international stage, would be imported into the breadbasket of the world. It was as if Saudi Arabia were to begin importing oil because it could be produced and transported more cheaply than Saudi crude.

Critics of the deal immediately cried dirty politics. Cargill has long advocated reductions in price supports for U.S. crops. It has identified existing support levels as a factor in recent declines in U.S. grain-export volume. These critics, who included several members of Congress from farm states, said Cargill's claim that it could buy Argentine wheat, ship it to the United States, pay all trade duties, and still deliver it to millers at a lower price than domestic grain, was outright false. The fact that news of the deal appeared as the 1985 Reagan administration farm bill was under congressional consideration encouraged skepticism.

Still, the fact that Cargill controlled all of the critical information on the deal meant that its adversaries could denounce the plan as specious but not prove their case definitively. "We checked into [the deal]," North Dakota senator Mark Andrews said. "My sources indicated to me that [Cargill] didn't have a ship loading in Argentina with a U.S. Gulf port destination and that they didn't intend to make this transaction in the first place. . . . If this was indeed the case, then what we saw was a cheap publicity stunt. . . ." Congressman Byron Dorgan, also of North Dakota, questioned the mechanics of the transaction as well. "Since Cargill is privately held, there's no way to know whether it might have suffered a loss in the transaction while using the transaction to apply political pressure for a farm bill more to their liking," he said.

Soon after Cargill disclosed its import plan, Chairman MacMillan issued a rare public statement to announce that his company would not proceed with the transaction. A measure of the influence of Cargill's adversaries? Perhaps. But U.S. grain competitiveness soon became the talk of Washington farm circles, a development MacMillan no doubt anticipated. A Senate subcommittee held hearings in February to explore precisely this issue. Cargill vice-president Robbin Johnson testified at the hearing.

"They've led the consumers to believe that we ought to cheapen the price of American grain because there's cheap grain in Argentina," Minnesota commissioner of agriculture Jim Nichols said when asked about the impact of the episode. "And it's not true. Initially I was trying to organize a boycott [in response]. We were working it out with farmers. Then Cargill withdrew the sale. Then the opposition dissipated. But they got exactly what they wanted. They wanted to make a statement to the consumer that there's cheap grain in Argentina. Even though it's a goddamn lie, that's what the consumer thinks now. How the hell could he think anything else?"

．　　．　　．

Cargill's decisive market presence, its potent status in Washington, and the unity and loyalty of its executive corps all embolden the corporation against competitors and outside constituencies. But such power also brings risks—particularly given the industry culture in which Cargill operates. The grain trade offers ample opportunities for misconduct and unethical practices that are less tempting in industries where the public spotlight shines more brightly.

Conversations with farmers, farm activists, and politicians produced a number of stories about contamination of grain shipped overseas. Ted Godfrey, the AAM vice-president who supervised Parity, Inc., said his operation declined to participate in what he learned was a standard practice among exporters. "When we were shipping grain through Parity, Inc., a sanding service out of Houston called us and asked if we wanted any sand," he told us. "We weren't running a concrete business, we were trying to export grain, so at first we didn't know why they were calling. But it became obvious—they just squirt beach sand on the [conveyor] belt as the grain goes into the ship. They also have a water service, if you want to add water to the grain."

Former Agriculture secretary Bergland, during his years as a congressman, traveled to Italy, where he met a merchant who complained bitterly about the impurity of grain shipped from the United States. Bergland asked the merchant to take him to the port and offer evidence of his accusations. "I was flabbergasted," he said of what he saw. "I considered it a scandalous betrayal. . . . The system at the time was vulnerable to all kinds of abuse and fraud."

Bergland returned to Washington and began work on remedial legislation. The eventual results were 1976 amendments to the U.S. Grain Standards Act of 1940 and the establishment of the Federal Grain Inspection Service. Bergland told us that Cargill cooperated in his campaign for legislation. Four company executives, including Vice-chairman W. B. Saunders, met with Congressman Bergland and provided him with more "anecdotal evidence" of grain contamination. But even after passage of the 1976 legislation there is still room for suspect, if not illegal, practices in the industry. The Grain Standards Act set tolerances for foreign matter in exported grain. Grain whose purity exceeds these standards is often mixed with inferior grain to produce a passable blend or simply injected with foreign matter until it bumps up against the tolerances.

David Senter, Washington representative of the American Agriculture Movement, described the process of purposeful contamination. "When a farmer goes to a Cargill elevator and sells wheat or corn or whatever, Cargill docks that farmer for any kind of foreign matter, any kind of dirt, cracked grain, high moisture, or anything," he explained. "They dock the farmer's price, so he takes less for that commodity. . . . And then when they get to the export facility, each one of these negotiations with foreign countries—one [customer] might say you can have up to 4 percent foreign matter, one might be 5 percent. In other words, each one of these contracts has a certain percentage of foreign matter it allows. When Cargill loads the commodity on the ship, say, if the moisture content is down at 12 percent, and the contract allows 14 percent, they put water on it as it goes on the ship and bring it up to the 14 percent [level]. They can get corn prices for just water that they're pumping in. If the foreign matter of the grain they're loading is only at 6 percent and the contract allows 8 percent, they will add sand, dirt, screenings, below-grade grain—whatever they have available at that export facility—and bring it right up to the limit with all that trash. All the grain companies operate the same way."

United Press International (UPI) reported on these and other practices in a May 1985 feature on dirty grain. The lengthy dispatch focused on the controversy associated with the type of grain "blending" Senter described and complaints by foreign customers about the quality of U.S. exports. "The Canadians and the Australians, the chief American trade competitors, generally export a higher quality and cleaner grain," the article noted. "Studies indicate part of the reason is that the entire system is in the hands of the government, which balances the expense of cleanup with eventual profits. Cleaning is done at central locations under strict supervision. In the United States, cleanup is haphazard. Sometimes it doesn't happen at all."

We had hoped to ask Whitney MacMillan about these and other exporting practices about which we learned. His refusal to grant an interview made that impossible. But David Senter, Bergland, and the myriad sources cited by UPI were not the only farm experts to discuss contamination and blending. "If we've got a real clean load [of grain], we'll make sure we hold it until we can mix it with something dirtier," a Cargill superintendent told the *Kansas City Times* in July 1982. "Otherwise, we'd be throwing away money."

When a company is a major actor in a fast-track business environment, getting the sale can mean doing what needs to be done if foreign representatives demand bribes. How does a company such as Cargill—sheltered as it is from outside inquiry and challenges—survive in these shark-infested waters? Former secretary Bergland did not address Cargill's behavior directly, but he did describe the waters. "I do know there are opportunities for bribes and payoffs," he said. "In a couple of countries I know precisely how the system works. I am offended as a human being at some of the practices involved. I don't want to defend Cargill, but their defense would probably be: 'Look, we are dealing in this corrupt market.

Either we play the game by these stupid rules or we don't play at all.' "

The dynamics of the grain trade would seem to offer many incentives for payoffs. Competition among the major firms is said to be fierce. Large trading companies are based in the United States, South America, Europe, and Japan—whose governments have different policies on bribery and the conduct of business overseas. The product over which the traders jockey is fairly uniform and sold mainly on the basis of price. And the grain trade has a tradition of respecting a sequence of commission agents that could provide ample cover for payoffs or bribes. According to Congressman Bill Frenzel, who made no allegations against Cargill, the Minneapolis trader, like many corporations with whom he has been in contact, has serious reservations about the Foreign Corrupt Practices Act, which outlaws most payments to foreign officials and was passed in 1977 in response to the furor over bribes paid abroad by multinationals such as Gulf Oil and Lockheed. "Cargill hires a hell of a lot of Bulgarians and Brits and South Africans and Koreans who don't understand our laws, who have to be told what to do all the time," Frenzel said. "I think Cargill probably says [to its representatives], stay as far away from officialdom as you can. Quote proper prices and don't be caught passing canapés at the end of the day. I've asked every company in my district what they think of the Foreign Corrupt Practices Act, and they all think it sucks eggs."

The lines between gifts, entertainment, retrospective commissions, and outright bribery are sometimes finely drawn. Whitney MacMillan issued a statement to employees in November 1975, during the controversies over foreign bribery by prominent U.S. corporations, in which he underscored Cargill's emphasis on ethical practices. But no one has yet disclosed the specific systems and procedures MacMillan has put in place to guard against bribery, and the company would not provide us with a complete text of the 1975 ethics statement.

It is reasonable to question whether endemic secrecy and corporate life in the dark, outside the fishbowl, contribute to temptation and its fulfillment. The more definitive answers will remain for future investigations or unofficial whistle-blowers. What can be said is that Cargill's behavior over the years has been far from spotless. The company admitted in March 1977 that it had made "unusual payments" of $5 million between June 1971 and December 1976. It disclosed the payments in response to an Internal Revenue Service questionnaire distributed to major corporations. (Excerpts from MacMillan's statement on bribery were released on the same day.) All told, Cargill under Chairman MacMillan has compiled an unenviable record of violations and dispositions of prior violations on a number of fronts:

- The company's Canadian affiliate admitted in October 1983 to having accepted 145 truckloads of grain at its elevator in Morris, Manitoba, that were not authorized by the Canadian Wheat Board. A Cargill audit the previous year identified the irregularities, and the company notified the board. Cargill paid a fine of nearly $126,500CDN, and a company manager, who pled guilty to eighteen charges, was fined $8,500CDN.
- In 1982 Cargill settled a lawsuit filed in Sioux City, Iowa, and agreed to pay $5.1 million to the Bryant Beef feedlot company. Feed corn purchased in the late 1970s from Cargill had been contaminated by aldrin, a chemical once used against rootworms but banned by the Environmental Protection Agency as a carcinogen in 1974. An Oklahoma feedlot company received an award of $158,000 in a similar case one year earlier.
- Cargill pled guilty in U.S. District Court in June 1981 to four criminal counts of willfully violating mine-safety laws at its salt mine in Belle Isle, Louisiana. The site was rocked by an explosion in July 1979 that killed five miners. The violations, for which the company was fined $45,000, were not connected directly to the blast. Cargill closed the salt mine, the world's largest, in February 1984.
- The Minnesota Pollution Control Agency fined Cargill $5,000 in December 1980 for excessive emissions of grain dust at the company's Duluth terminal. The company also promised to install new dust-control equipment.
- In September 1978, a federal judge in Louisville, Kentucky, fined Cargill $50,000, the maximum penalty, and assessed against Arthur Klobe a fine of $30,000 and two years of probation in connection with a price-fixing scheme in the resin-coatings business. Resin coatings are used in the manufacture of paint. Cargill pled nolo contendere to the charges, which applied to company behavior between 1971 and 1974. Klobe, who has since retired, was vice-president, chemical products division. He later became secretary of the Cargill Foundation, to which the company makes annual donations, and president of the company's North Star Steel unit.
- Cargill pled guilty in April 1978 to three counts of violating Pennsylvania environmental statutes after a chemical-products plant discharged xylene and ethyl benzene, two toxic chemicals, into Philadelphia sewers. The company was fined $50,000 and charged $5,000 for monitoring costs. At the time, the fine was the largest ever levied under the state's clean-streams law.

This list of violations and misconduct is not exhaustive. Perhaps the most intriguing charges of wrongdoing leveled against Cargill involved accounting practices adopted by two company subsidiaries in Spain, Compañía Industria y de Abastecimientos (Cindasa) and Piensos Hens. These practices reduced tax payments to the U.S. and Spanish governments. And it is important to note that these were not obscure outposts on the fringes of the Cargill empire. The board of Cindasa included Pete McVay, the retired Cargill president; James Spicola, the current Cargill president; and Hendrik Van Veen, then vice-president and head of the international soybean-crushing division.

The public scandal over Cargill's Spanish operations was touched off in March 1977. It continued through November 1981, when Cargill pled guilty in U.S. District Court in Minneapolis to charges that it understated its income by more than $7 million during fiscal years 1975 and 1976. The company paid the back taxes and a modest fine of $10,000. The government agreed not to bring criminal tax charges against Cargill related to ongoing investigations, conducted by the Internal Revenue Service and a special grand jury, of company tax returns from 1972 through 1976. The IRS ended its investigation in August 1983. The extent of civil penalties, if any, is not public information.

The origins of the accusations against Cargill are as interesting as the questionable practices themselves. In March 1977, a courier assigned to the mailroom of Cargill's Minneapolis law firm, now called Dorsey & Windhorst, was asked to deliver a twenty-three-page memorandum to John McGrory, Cargill's general counsel. The memo was a typed version of notes made by a member of the firm during interviews with auditors from Peat, Marwick, Mitchell & Co. and a Cargill tax attorney. The interviews, part of an internal investigation, covered reservations voiced by the outside auditors about a so-called black-peseta operation underway in Spain. The subsidiaries in effect maintained two sets of books, a practice that served to shelter income from tax authorities. The messenger became curious about the contents of his package and decided to stop off in a men's room to examine them. Struck by what he found, he photocopied the document, resealed the envelope, delivered it, and then leaked the memo to the *Minneapolis Star* and the Internal Revenue Service. The *Star* inexplicably chose to bury this explosive story in a longer article on Cargill's disclosure of the $5 million in "unusual payments" abroad.

But the timing of the leak could not have been more convenient for the IRS. The agency had already begun a routine audit of Cargill tax returns from the early 1970s. Its work had been delayed because of Cargill's internal investigation. The memo provided cryptic details of the black-peseta operation and how Cargill's top executives chose to handle it. Peat, Marwick, Mitchell had advocated for several years that Cargill abandon the practice, and the company chose not to do so. The memo recounts statements by Ken Anderson, a Peat, Marwick auditor, about his recommendation to discontinue the double bookkeeping. "Ken Anderson's interpretation of the situation is that Cargill wanted to discontinue black pesetas but could not do so," the memo said. "He felt that the Spanish partners wanted black pesetas and that it was impossible to buy businesses and the like without black pesetas." (Cindasa had used sheltered funds to purchase a chrome mill and pay bonuses to local executives.)

There was even a touch of humor, as the memo recounted a remark by James Cargill, a grandson of founder Will Cargill and a senior vice-president, at an August 1976 meeting of the audit committee. "Ken Anderson said that Jimmy Cargill said, obviously as a joke—if anybody will wear pinstripe [prison] suits, it will be you guys (meaning Peat, Marwick, Mitchell)," the document reported. "It was Ken's impression that the other directors were embarrassed."

James Cargill's defensive humor may well have been inspired by the findings of a journey by Whitney MacMillan two months earlier. Then-president MacMillan went to Spain and met with executives from Cindasa and Piensos Hens. "Whitney took a strong stand there," the memo noted. "This is when they told Whitney that the black-peseta operations were more expansive than we thought. Because of this, Whitney took a strong position. . . . [Cargill official] Jay [Berkley] said there would be no more purchases of companies with black pesetas."

.   .   .

There is a frustration that gnaws at Whitney MacMillan that never seems to go away. For all of Cargill's success as a grain trader, for all of its demonstrated capacity to insulate itself from proposals for reform in how commodities are exchanged between nations, for all of MacMillan's ability to accelerate the company's movement forward and backward along the food-processing chain, Cargill is still not understood by many of its customers and suppliers. Too much of the public, and especially the farmers, harbor serious reservations about the status quo in the grain industry and the role of his family's company. But MacMillan and his associates do not want to go to the public and personally communicate their philosophies and rationales. They want public understanding and privacy and secrecy at the same time.

The Cargill chairman addressed this issue directly in a 1979 speech. The company had surveyed opinion leaders and farmers two years earlier.

The results were unsettling. Fully 94 percent of the farmers had heard of Cargill, but only 49 percent knew what it did. And a large section of the broader population expressed grave misgivings about the power of the traders.

"Among the general public, about as many people believe that grain prices reflect anti-competitive practices as believe that they reflect supply and demand in a competitive market," MacMillan reported. "Only one-fourth of those surveyed think grain export sales should be continued if they raise domestic prices. One person in four felt the U.S. government should regulate grain sales as the Canadian government does. While about 40 percent believe that our grain system is still the best in the world, doubts clearly exist. . . . A lot of factors probably go into explaining these attitudes. Grain prices have fluctuated—sometimes sharply—in recent years. Grain companies have been at the center of several public contro-versies."

There have been a few attempted resolutions of this impasse. Cargill began a Farmer Program in 1981, through which it conducts seminars with planters, teaches company executives how to communicate more persuasively with rural audiences, and distributes information on trends in world trade and agricultural productivity. Cargill released a pamphlet in July 1984 that addressed six "misconceptions" about the industry. Decorated much like a comic book, with caricatures more appropriate for elementary school students than the farmers for which it was intended, the pamphlet argued, among other things, that the traders do not set the price of grain (prices are determined by supply and demand); grain traders do not buy low and sell high (companies hedge their transactions and earn profits by creating markets and taking "controlled risks"); grain companies do not make too much money at the expense of farmers (why, Cargill's profits from grain activities over the last ten years have averaged less than two cents a bushel).

These and other "misconceptions" are irritating to the Cargill men. They do not like to be perceived as bushel barons whose market power allows them to control world trade in food. But there do remain a vast number of friction points between Cargill and the constituencies on which its business is built—points of conflict and controversy that con-tinue to sow the seeds of suspicion and despair. An April 1985 report by the General Accounting Office (GAO) included perspectives on the grain-marketing system from two producer organizations. Both the president of the American Soybean Association and a director of the Colorado Association of Wheat Growers questioned whether supply and demand still govern the international market. Texas agriculture com-missioner Jim Hightower told us that were he U.S. attorney general, he would initiate an antitrust investigation "of the whole grain trade."

These are not just sentiments born of the crisis of the 1980s. George McGovern, writing more than ten years ago, rejected the compatibility of private control of grain flows and stability in supply and price. "The contention that the world can have [food] reserves held in private hands is fallacious on its face," he argued in his preface to a report of the Senate Select Committee on Hunger. "Private traders are in business to turn investment into profit as rapidly as possible. To expect that a multiplicity of private traders would or should manage the acquisition and release of food and feed grains in a manner which will meet the goals of a conscious reserve policy—to flatten the widest upward and downward fluctuations in market prices and to maintain a steady supply against times of shortage —would be contradictory. . . . In reality, a [food] reserve in private hands is no reserve at all."

Jim Nichols, Minnesota commissioner of agriculture, offered a contemporary appraisal of the impact of his state's largest corporation. "Cargill is in the international trade business," he said. "They make a profit on each bushel [of grain] they sell. It figures that the more bushels they sell, the more profit they'll make. So they want American farmers to produce a whole lot of grain and sell it cheap. That helps them. I think they can make a profit whether the product is selling high or low."

It is not difficult to delineate the preferred world of Cargill—and where that world clashes with the interests of producers. Cargill profits most from trading large volumes of grain in a milieu of fluctuating prices. Its unmatched capacity to store and ship commodities, its superior intelligence network, and its abundant lines of credit all mean that Cargill can manage large amounts of grain and thrive in an unstable environment. Farmers prefer an environment of predictable prices that provides a livable return on their costs of production. Cargill benefits from massive production-for-export in the United States, where its infrastructure of elevators, terminals, and port facilities is second to none. Excessive cultivation for export has created an environment for farmers of unreliable foreign demand and vulnerability to political shocks such as the Soviet grain embargo.

Lester Brown, president of Worldwatch Institute, explained why Cargill traditionally has not supported a system of international grain reserves. "The reason they're opposed to a food reserve is because that would tend to stabilize prices," he said. "And Cargill thrives on uncertainty and a decided advantage in market intelligence—they know a lot more about what's going on in the world than almost anyone else, including a lot of the governments. And as a result, they can exploit that information in their grain trading. If grain prices were much more stable, they would have to make a living off of normal day-to-day trading margins rather than speculation."

If there was ever a period when the world of Cargill could be harmonized with the interests of farmers, it was the decade of the 1970s. These were years of record supply, record demand, and record exports of farm products from the United States. World trade in grain soared from 1.5 billion bushels in 1970 to 5.1 billion bushels in 1980. The share of world grain needs met by imports, a measure of global food dependence and the demand for Cargill's services, rose from 9 percent at the beginning of the decade to 14 percent by its close. U.S. farmers eagerly planted "fence row to fence row" and captured the lion's share of the increased global demand for imported commodities.

But even during this era of prosperity the benefits of increased world trade were not shared evenly between producers and those who bought and sold their output. Massive U.S. production led farmers to make huge new investments in land and equipment—investments whose burden began to weigh heavy as interest rates climbed later in the decade. The ethos of maximum cultivation, even on marginal land, meant greater application of pesticides and herbicides and less attention to other pressing environmental threats. And the drive to produce more and more crops for nations dependent on U.S. farm products created an ironic reverse dependence: When export markets stagnated or importers turned to other sources, the U.S. farm economy entered a period of turmoil and consolidation that has wreaked havoc on medium-sized family units. The roots of the farm crisis of the 1980s are planted firmly in the export boom of the 1970s.

Through it all, however, Cargill has reigned supreme. MacMillan's company has maintained and extended its degree of control in rural America despite the turbulent environment in which it operates. Boom times bring large trading volume, enormous profits, and discretionary capital that can be used to integrate further as a supplier to farmers and a processor of their output. Cargill can survive periods of export stagnation more readily than farm cooperatives and its trading-dependent competitors. Size alone is a buffer against hard times. So too is Cargill's diversified structure. The company generates profits from meatpacking, poultry, and steel even when margins on trading in commodities are razor thin.

One example of how the expansion of Cargill has intensified pressures on traditional farm structures—during periods of both expansion and decline—is the ongoing demise of country elevators owned by farm cooperatives. These facilities, long the marketing backbone of rural America, have been under pressure for more than a decade. Cargill and others built massive inland facilities—terminals and subterminals—designed to store large volumes of commodities and load onto "unit trains." These trains can haul more grain, at lower prices, than can the trains and trucks that service country elevators.

Bob Bergland used the word *disaster* to describe recent developments in this sector of the farm economy. "The farmer marketing system is coming apart at the seams," he warned. "Small cooperative [elevators] have been noncompetitive and are closing up in droves. There is no way of competing. Cargill with its great scale and vertical integration—the local coops are no match."

Pressure on cooperative elevators began to build a decade ago. In the late 1960s Cargill developed the unit train, with up to 125 uniform hopper cars that are larger and easier to load than boxcars, and negotiated financial deals with the railroads that further increased the cost savings of this new form of transportation. But these savings had a cost of their own: Country elevators had neither the facilities necessary to service these trains nor the capital to invest in state-of-the-art equipment.

"The unit train was an example of modernization that created both efficiencies and gross inequities," wrote consultant Richard Gilmore in his 1982 book on the grain trade. "It was a development that benefitted the railroads, large traders, and the government in their joint effort to move as much grain as possible into the export stream. Its effects on small traders and producers were less beneficial."

The stagnation of farm exports since 1981 has created a new kind of pressure on cooperative elevators—the burden of overcapacity. According to Michael Turner, a professor of agricultural economics at the University of Nebraska, his state experienced a massive expansion of elevator capacity during the decade of the seventies. But the leveling off of U.S. farm exports in the last five years has left Nebraska with more than twice the storage capacity it needs. Cooperative elevators are selling out, filing for bankruptcy, or merging with other elevators in the face of high interest costs on money borrowed to finance their expansion—a classic shakeout pattern that enhances the market power of the largest and least vulnerable enterprises.

.   .   .

Whitney MacMillan rose to power at Cargill late in the bountiful seventies and has directed the company throughout the crisis-ridden eighties. With a review of his rare public speeches, and the company's even rarer information booklets, it is possible to piece together his perspective on world agriculture and Cargill's role and responsibilities on the global food stage.

March 19, 1980. MacMillan reflects on the export surge of the previous decade and its implications:

> The real change came when farmers no longer had to produce for government programs and could begin producing for markets. Markets, we all learned from the 1970s, can grow. And, the fastest growing market was overseas. Farm exports worth $7 billion in 1970 are today worth $37 billion, five times as much. . . . Farmers have now tasted the benefits of producing for markets. They are learning that it is easier—and more rewarding—to please customers than politicians. They are also learning that they can help build their own markets through market development activities. They see incomes rising around the world, pushing up expectations for better diets. These demand pressures will grow, regularly and reliably. In my judgment, most farmers now want to be part of this growth industry, not a controlled industry. . . .
>
> Today, the government is largely out of the storage business. It has sold off its bins. Grain reserves are now in farmers' hands. Government incentives still influence when that grain is bought and sold, but individual farmers make the final decisions. And, concessional foreign sales are now less than 5 percent of total exports. . . . I think we can see growing recognition of the superiority of economic freedom over control in guiding the marketing of grain. All of us—farmers, marketers and consumers—are better off when people must offer better price and service to earn business. . . . World trade reduced the incidence of famine. It helped millions to improve their diets. And, it revealed that national policies of protection pose a threat to food security.

August 21, 1979. MacMillan responds to proposals for a National Grain Board, modeled on the Canadian agency, that would supervise exports and set prices:

> Threats to the current balance between private initiative and public oversight can take many forms. One of the most beguiling notions is that farmers could improve their lot by changing partners and embracing a government grain board. Proponents of this idea argue that a grain board could use its "food power" to achieve a laundry list of desirable goals—trading bushels for barrels [of oil], achieving fair prices for farmers, guaranteeing stable

prices for consumers. This concerns me for three reasons.

My first concern is the direct effect on Cargill's interests. Putting government in the grain business would mean that we could no longer do what we do best. My second concern is for the farmer. Government cannot be made the sole seller of export grain without becoming the sole buyer of export grain. For farmers, that becomes an unequal partnership. . . . My third concern is that the case for a grain board rests on a false premise. A grain cartel would not succeed the way the OPEC cartel has. The reason is simple: A cartel must control both price and supply to succeed.

April 27, 1982. In his only major published lecture, entitled "The Role of the Private Sector in Agriculture," delivered at Macalester College in Saint Paul, MacMillan outlines his views on comparative economic systems. He cites the writings of Harvard economist John Kenneth Galbraith and explains why private ownership of farmland has proven to be "the most efficient and effective organization of the means of production. . . . Farming is not a 9 to 5 job," MacMillan said. "It requires an exploitation of the worker that, in the end, only works when self-imposed. As John Kenneth Galbraith observed in his autobiography, 'There are limits on the toil that can be demanded in the large firm; the small businessman is at liberty to exploit himself. . . . [That] is why agriculture lends itself badly to socialism.' Galbraith might have added that the self-exploitation required of successful farmers also explains why firms like Cargill don't invest in basic farming activities."

The Cargill chairman also describes the appropriate role of the private sector in a world rife with hunger and starvation:

If market-based food costs are seen as too high for some members of society, then the public must make up the difference in a food subsidy. Examples in the United States include our food stamp, school lunch and other special feeding programs. The same principle applies internationally. Grain companies and farmers are not in a position to provide food aid to poor countries directly. The cost of subsidizing that aid must be born by others. . . . The private sector's role also *is not* to offset disruptions in food supplies caused by political disturbances or crop failures. The private sector can grow and move the food, but it cannot finance this activity.

MacMillan's remarks on food shortages remain perhaps his most direct statements on this issue. He does not believe that the private sector has ignored food emergencies. According to the Cargill chairman, expansion of exports and development of the physical infrastructure to handle them have improved delivery systems to the hungry. This proposition, delivered a few years before the anguish of Ethiopia and other parts of Africa became front-page news around the world, will not enhance his reputation as a forecaster.

The extra grain-handling capacity built during the 1970s "has helped speed up the response time to war-torn displaced people in Kampuchea or crop-devastated regions like the Sahel," MacMillan said. "In other words, the world today can respond faster and at less cost to provide emergency famine relief because of commercial export growth. The severity of famine has declined as a result."

The Cargill chairman has articulated other basic themes in his public speeches. He is opposed to trade embargoes and use of the "food weapon" as an instrument of foreign policy. "Few countries import more than 10 percent of their grain needs and U.S. exports account for less than 10 percent of world grain use and less than 5 percent of world food use," he noted two years after the Soviet embargo. "So, there simply is no leverage in exploiting U.S. grain exports for sustained diplomatic advantage." He rejects supply-management programs, such as government-imposed cutbacks in cultivation and paid land diversions, which are designed to control overproduction in the interests of higher prices and more environmentally sound farming techniques.

Not surprisingly, MacMillan does support certain forms of government intervention in the grain trade. Above all else he advocates market development—creation, particularly in the Third World, of demand for wheat and corn and soybeans through the use of foreign aid and government credit. Since the inauguration of the Food for Peace program in 1954, Cargill has exported grain whose purchase was financed by grants and concessionary loans from the U.S. government. Food for Peace, which today only underwrites a small percentage of U.S. grain exports, accounted for one-third of all shipments in the early 1960s. MacMillan and other Cargill officials have called for rejuvenation of Food for Peace and other market-development programs of the U.S. government. They also advocate the promotion of dietary patterns in the developing world that increase demand for imported grain.

"We must teach industrializing nations how to use feed grains and protein meal to improve diets by producing low-cost meat, milk, and eggs," MacMillan told a North Carolina audience in 1982. "This is market development at its best."

. . .

This is the ideological framework of the chairman of the largest grain trader in the world. But MacMillan's Cargill is considerably more pragmatic than the chief executive's philosophy might suggest. Its pragmatism goes beyond the interesting juxtaposition of MacMillan's endorsement of free enterprise in agriculture and the intimate relationships his company has built with Soviet commissars and Soviet import bureaucracies. It goes beyond Cargill's willingness to accept subsidies, direct and indirect, that make the private sector significantly less private with respect to risks. Cargill's pragmatism is at the core of its corporate being. It animates its strategy and its relentless role in reacting to and shaping global food practices and policies. That strategy centers on the role of the United States as a source of extractive wealth—what former Agriculture secretary Bergland means when he says Cargill considers the United States a "grain colony."

Extraction begins with what Cargill does not put back in the areas from which it benefits so handsomely. Consider its role as a taxpayer in states whose farmers produce the grain Cargill markets. For years, governors have struggled to develop ways to collect in taxes an equitable share of the profits of multinational corporations that operate in their states— corporations whose accountants work long and hard to allocate income to those states and nations whose tax rates are least burdensome. One concept that addresses long-standing grievances that these firms simply have not paid their fair share is unitary taxation. The idea is straightforword: A state should tax a percentage of the worldwide profits of a corporation that reflects the share of the company's business conducted in that state. Calculations to develop an apportionment formula are based largely on the state's share of three measures of overall corporate activity: property, payroll, and sales.

Unitary taxation has proven to be a potent vehicle to boost tax revenues. It has been applied in some two dozen states and has prompted bitter opposition from much of corporate America. But in the case of Cargill, the impact of this conceptual breakthrough has been diluted by grave apportionment problems that state tax officials have not encountered in most other industries. Grain harvested in North Dakota might be stored in Montana and exported from a port in Washington. The state of destination, in this example Washington, would be expected either to tax the grain or attribute it to North Dakota or Montana for taxation. But several important exporting centers—Washington, Louisiana, Minnesota, Texas—neither tax the export-bound grain nor "throw back" the shipment for tax purposes to producing states. This grain is, in effect, not attributed to any state, a phenomenon that auditors have dubbed a "nowhere sale." Such "nowhere sales" give Cargill every incentive to attribute as much grain as possible to Louisiana or Texas and minimize allocations to producing states.

This is precisely the environment Byron Dorgan faced when he served as state tax commissioner prior to his election to Congress from North Dakota in 1980. During a review of Cargill's tax payments in 1974, Dorgan noticed a troubling discrepancy. The grain company reported gross sales of more than $7 billion but had allocated to North Dakota—the country's second-largest wheat producer and a source of barley, oats, and rye—receipts of only $12 million. How could such an important source of grain be credited with such a minuscule share of Cargill's total sales? Dorgan asked to review Cargill's federal tax returns and filings in other states. The company's initial response was to flood his office with paper—and not furnish the information in which he was most interested. Cargill provided access to fifty thousand pages of data, of which eleven thousand pages applied just to the company's grain elevators in the state. The documents could have formed a seventeen-foot paper tower that weighed 550 pounds.

Charles Keller, an accountant in the North Dakota attorney general's office, offered a glimpse of Cargill's brand of cooperation. "I remember being in a Cargill warehouse in south Minneapolis in the dead of winter," Keller told us. "There were thousands of boxes. All we had for heat and light was a sixty-watt bulb. We had to take turns warming our hands around the bulb, and we had to write with our gloves on."

Keller's research was supplemented by additional and more useful tax information supplied by Cargill under the instructions of a North Dakota judge. Robert Kessel, an auditor in Dorgan's office, described the basic findings: Sales figures Cargill reported on a state-by-state basis represented in total only a fraction of corporate revenues reported to the U.S. government on its federal tax return. This discrepancy was facilitated by "nowhere sales" in key exporting states.

"I think for some years Cargill reported only twenty percent of its [total federal] sales to the states," Kessel said. Property and payroll, the other factors in the apportionment formula, "were substantially higher because you can hardly manipulate them as you can sales." Cargill argued that the discrepancy was legitimate in view of the absence of uniform laws in the states in which it does business. The company eventually settled claims arising from the North Dakota audit and agreed to make a payment to the state. The terms of the settlement are confidential.

The apportionment problems identified in North Dakota are replicated across the Midwest. In June 1982, Cargill appealed the results of an audit by the Montana Department of Revenue that covered the years 1975 through 1979. As a result of that appeal, and the attendant filing requirements, we obtained documents that offer an intriguing glimpse into the tax world of Cargill. For example, its income-tax payments to all states and localities in 1978 totaled only $2.2 million. Documents filed with the SEC report that Cargill's aftertax income in fiscal 1978 was more than $121 million. Such are the meager tax burdens of the world's largest grain trader. Cargill's income-tax payments to state and local governments over the entire five-year period were less than $33 million.

Cargill's demonstrated ability to minimize income-tax payments to state and local governments is an example of how the intricacy of its operations allows it to avoid a measure of responsibility that more modest enterprises have to meet. A local grain elevator, without Cargill's capacity for strategic revenue allocation, must shoulder a higher effective tax burden in its state than the MacMillan empire. And this is just one dimension of the Cargill advantage. The federal tax code, with its laundry list of credits, deductions, and exclusions, offers MacMillan's firm still more opportunities for higher profits at the expense of taxpayers.

Cargill's use of DISC as a vehicle to reduce its U.S. tax bill is one example of this. In 1971 Congress enacted legislation to encourage exports with the use of tax breaks. U.S. firms were allowed to establish Domestic International Sales Corporations, or DISCs, and defer income taxes on up to one-half of DISC profits. This loophole has been an important windfall for corporations that ship large quantities of goods overseas. It is impossible to quantify with precision how much Cargill has saved through the DISC mechanism. Unlike public corporations, which under certain circumstances must release data on DISC, Cargill issues no annual report. But the company has made ample use of the program. According to documents obtained in the Montana tax appeal, the grain trader worked through five separate DISCs in 1979, the last year for which information is available. Stevens International was Cargill's DISC for peanuts, Tennant International involved export of metals and electronic components, MBPXL International applied to beef shipments, Hohenberg International was a vehicle for cotton trade, and Cargill Export handled other overseas shipments.

Cargill Export was by far the company's largest DISC. In fiscal 1979 the company attributed earnings of nearly $61 million to this DISC—a substantial figure in light of the fact that Cargill reported taxable income

of $169 million on its federal return. Over the period 1975 through 1979, Cargill attributed to all DISCs earnings of $260 million. It deferred taxes on $102 million. Congress replaced the DISC program in 1984 by another incentive system for exports, known by the acronym FSC. The FSC legislation, which was approved with little debate and even less public attention, not only established a new and improved loophole but forgave repayment of deferred taxes built up under DISCs—a direct windfall worth about $12 billion to corporate America.

Whitney MacMillan's company has also made use of outright subsidies from federal, state, and local authorities. Its $28 million terminal in Duluth, Minnesota, a massive complex from which Cargill ships grain and oilseeds from states including Wisconsin, North Dakota, and Iowa, was financed in large part by industrial revenue bonds and special state and federal funds. Cargill's terminal in Burns Harbor on Lake Michigan in Indiana, with a storage capacity of 5 million bushels, was financed with $18 million in tax-exempt bonds issued by the Indiana Port Commission.

Cargill has even managed to profit from government policies designed primarily to subsidize other sectors of the farm economy. Consider the Payment-in-Kind (PIK) program, the Reagan administration's 1983 plan to address both the problems of overproduction and the abundance of crops already in storage. Under PIK, the Department of Agriculture used existing reserves of wheat, corn, grain sorghum, rice, and cotton to compensate farmers who agreed to withdraw acreage from cultivation. This is where Cargill, which for years had been paid to store government grain purchased under price-support programs, entered the equation. By virtue of its unrivaled network of elevators, unit trains, barges, and trucks, Cargill too was paid in kind to handle the transfer of grain from government ownership to farmers. (PIK became so popular with farmers that the Agriculture Department even had to buy grain from the private sector, including Cargill, to meet its swap obligations.) The total value of the program to Cargill was $55 million, according to a report by the General Accounting Office. The GAO analysis also hinted at the structure of concentration in the grain trade. Cargill received more than one-fifth of the 1,259 contracts to transport and transfer wheat, corn, and grain sorghum—more than any other firm. Cargill and Continental, its largest competitor on the world stage, together received 40 percent of the payments for handling these three commodities.

Minnesota agriculture commissioner Nichols came down hard on the subject of Cargill and government subsidies. "Do you know who the fattest hog is in the public trough?" he asked. "Who got more money than anybody else in the world from the government last year [1984] and every year from time immemorial? Cargill. All surplus grain is stored basically

in private warehouses. Cargill is paid thirty cents to fifty cents a bushel to store it. Who has the most storage in the world? During PIK, they got all the storage. Every time they handled one hundred bushels they kept twelve. They got paid twelve bushels of grain to handle one hundred. It's an unbelievable amount of money they're handling. . . . They cleaned up."

The extractive dimensions of Cargill's operations—greater and greater control in rural areas, minimal tax payments to the states, direct and indirect subsidies from the federal government—are not limited to the realm of prices and profits and output. The commitment to production for export has created problems of physical extraction as well—extraction from the land, through soil erosion, of nutrients that are vital to its continued productivity. Indeed, there are few greater environmental dangers to the future of American agriculture than the threat posed by the loss of fertile topsoil to rain and wind. Environmentalists and resource experts have warned for years that unchecked soil erosion and its implications have been ignored in the hue and cry for greater and greater farm production. One-fourth of the 400 million acres of U.S. cropland is experiencing excessive erosion. Moreover, much of the land at risk continues to support crops—cotton, soybeans, corn, and sorghum—that exact a heavy toll on topsoil.

Worldwatch Institute president Lester Brown explained how this reality places farmers in a quandary. "Narrow profit margins, such as those confronting U.S. farmers during the early 1980s, might well mean that if farmers were to invest in appropriate [soil] conservation measures their profit margins would disappear entirely, forcing them to operate at a deficit," he wrote in 1984. "They would then face the prospect of bankruptcy in the near future. Alternatively, they could continue to follow existing agricultural practices and avoid near-term bankruptcy, but face the prospect of declining productivity over the long term and eventual abandonment of the land, if not by this generation then by the next. In the absence of a governmental cost-sharing program similar to those used so effectively in the past, a farmer's only choice is whether to go out of business sooner or later."

How has Cargill responded to this urgent environmental threat? The title of a November 1982 column by Vice-president Robbin Johnson in a company newsletter says it all: "Exports Have Positive Role in Soil Conservation." Johnson's basic argument for the compatibility of increased exports and progress on soils was to define the problem away. Why worry, he wondered: "Data from the National Resources Inventory taken in 1977 indicate that, of 1.4 billion acres of non-federal land, 1.2 billion acres are stable. Less than 200 million acres suffer actual soil loss rates above average tolerance levels." Johnson did not say that this reassuring

calculation had very little to do with the real problem. The relevant base is farmland—not all land outside of federal ownership—and with that base in mind Johnson's figures are of no assurance at all.

.   .   .

Another important measure of corporate performance, albeit a neglected one, is how a firm connects its charitable skills and resources to the alleviation of contemporary tragedy. Nothing quite frames the extractive character of Cargill like its response to the many millions of Africans in the cauldron of disease and debility as they hover on the brink of starvation. Here is a company that knows food, possesses food, and is surely one of the leading world experts on how most efficiently to handle, ship, and store food so that it reaches point B from point A in good shape. Here is one of the world's leading researchers and producers of the seeds that grow into the staples of life. Here is a company that knows which strains of crops require the least water and can thrive best in harsh African environments. Here is a company that has political and economic influence and leverage. Yet here is Whitney MacMillan telling a college audience in 1982 that "grain companies and farmers are not in a position to provide food aid to poor countries directly. The cost of subsidizing that aid must be borne by others." This assertion is too facile, too categorical, and too incomplete.

We embarked on a search for the charitable Cargill. Jim Nichols, Minnesota's commissioner of agriculture, reported that "we have our own African famine relief program here, asking the farmers to contribute ten bushels of grain. Cargill said they were participating in another program." Stuart Baird, the Cargill assistant vice-president, described that program to us. He said, as of spring 1985, that Cargill had made two donations to Ethiopian famine relief. A mid-February donation went through Save the Children—98,000 pounds of flour. Cargill coordinated the shipping but did not pay the freight. The other donation was in the fall of 1984. Cargill provided 5,800 bushels of wheat via Oxfam, part of a total shipment of 514,360 bushels headed for Ethiopia. Baird said that Cargill helped line up the logistics and the ship and paid cargo, insurance, and freight for its 1.1 percent fraction of the load. "Cargill offered its expertise to make sure everything worked right," he said. The company "tried to ship at the cheapest price." Baird then added an important observation. Cargill was able to ship at much lower costs than the $250 per ton paid by a group of farmers who made a recent relief shipment.

The point is not just that Cargill is wealthy and knowledgeable enough to help significantly more. In addition, its expertise, beyond immediate famine relief, extends to averting future famines. Large regions of Africa desperately need seeds—an area of Whitney MacMillan's managerial expertise and Cargill's prominent capability. Yet Cargill germinates only silence.

What could be running through the minds of MacMillan and his relatives as they watch night after night the horrific television pictures of the expanding African drought? Aside from believing that famine relief and prevention is a governmental function, they must realize that government has been known to respond to the advice of prominent corporate citizens—especially a laggard Reagan administration, which had to be pushed to expand famine relief by members of Congress, by an urgent call to the president from Mother Teresa, and by the public attention given the hungry and dying by musicians and other celebrities. Whether as sponsor, networker, or strategist, Cargill has chosen not to play a leading role. MacMillan may wish not to become involved in a vast open-ended crusade that might sharply increase public expectations about Cargill's ability to help, and drain away executive concentration engaged in building sales and profits. Unfortunately, he does not communicate what he is thinking. And as head of a private corporation, he is exposed to no occasion where he can be expected to answer questions on this major issue.

Cargill's relation to African famine is a business one. Perhaps one restraint on any charitable exuberance can be gleaned by a sample announcement, this one in January 1985, out of the U.S. Department of Agriculture. As reported in *Feedstuffs,* a trade publication, USDA's Commodity Credit Corporation (CCC) that month sold $66.7 million worth of corn, wheat, and rough rice to private exporters for resale to African countries hard hit by severe drought. Cargill and Louis Dreyfus Company received the CCC corn contracts.

As a private corporation with a passion for anonymity, Cargill does not worry about the high-gloss public-relations programs on which many large multinationals spend so much time and money. The one exception is the company's home state, where the connection between charitable display and community acceptance has been given some thought. Personally, his associates told us, Whitney MacMillan and his wife, Elizabeth, have attended fundraisers for the Minnesota-based Mayo Clinic and its hospitals. Along with Paul Volcker and Mobil chairman Rawleigh Warner, MacMillan also serves on the board of the Mayo Clinic, where Cargill's generous health benefits allow many executives to receive an annual checkup.

Judging by documents on file with the Treasury Department, the Cargill chairman and his extended family make their cash contributions go a long way. The Cargill Family Fund, which MacMillan's cousin,

James Cargill, directs, has assets in the $55,000 range. It made three grants in 1983—$250 to Ducks Unlimited, $3,000 to the Minnesota Medical Foundation, and $250 to Trout Unlimited. The Cargill MacMillan Family Foundation has assets in the $126,000 range. (Among its assets is stock in the First National Bank of Palm Beach, Inc., a side venture of Whitney, Elizabeth, and Cargill MacMillan, Jr., and W. John Driscoll, a Yale classmate of the Cargill chairman.) The Cargill MacMillan foundation gave away all of $8,470 in 1983, through a remarkable number of grants—thirty-four. The donations included $700 to the Covenant Theological Seminary, $50 to the Midwest China Center, $200 to the Art Center of Minnesota, $50 to Yale University, and $100 to the Abortion Rights Council of Minnesota. Cargill MacMillan, Jr., and his brother, Whitney, seem to believe in wide dispersal of limited charitable donations.

This philosophy carries over to the larger Cargill Foundation, which traditionally receives an infusion of $1 million a year from Cargill, Inc. The foundation's 1984 tax return reports about $20 million in assets and $1.5 million in donations to 101 grantees. All but 9 of the recipients were from Minnesota. A review of these grants suggests several conclusions. The foundation clearly does not concentrate on heavy funding of right-wing think tanks and causes, as do so many better known corporate foundations. The Cargill Fund did make a grant of $25,000 to the American Enterprise Institute in 1983 and grants in 1983 and 1984, totaling $50,000, to the eminently conservative Department of Economics at the University of Chicago. A partial list of recipients who received $5,000 or more in 1984 reads like a Who's Who of Twin Cities charities: United Way, YMCA, Urban Coalition, Planned Parenthood, Community Crime Prevention, Bridge for Runaway Youth, Twin Cities Public Television, Walker Art Center, Minneapolis Society of Fine Arts, the Minnesota Private College Fund, United Negro College Fund, the Voyageur Outward Bound School, the annual grant to the family's prep school, the Minnesota Children's Medical Center, the Central Institute for the Deaf, and Abbott Northwestern Hospital. Many other grants are in the $1,000 to $5,000 category.

Curiously, Whitney MacMillan is not on the Cargill Foundation's board, although his brother Cargill and his cousin James are directors. John Driscoll, chairman of First National Bank of Palm Beach and a life-long friend of MacMillan, offers a partisan insight into the boss's inclination: "There are those who think they [the MacMillans] don't give enough to the community, but for Whitney, the most important thing he can give people are jobs. Opening fish-processing plants in Brazil is a lot higher on his hit parade than doing things around here."

There are other examples of Cargill's recent charitable activities—contributing to the YMCA's building fund; providing 300,000 pounds of high-protein food, valued at $150,000, for welfare distribution in Minnesota and North Dakota. But the overall percentage of pretax income that Cargill devotes to charitable giving appears to be under 1 percent. (The estimate is based on deductions for charitable contributions reported in tax documents from the Montana case, and income figures filed with the SEC and elsewhere.) This modest record of contributions needs some contextual background. Unlike public companies, Cargill does not have to concern itself with a view that University of Chicago economists would offer—that corporations have no business giving anything to charity. Their business, says Milton Friedman, should be only to make money and leave to shareholders judgments about who receives contributions from their dividends. Since there is no separation of ownership from control at Cargill, such philosophical exhortations against charitable giving have no place. Moreover, there probably is no other metropolitan area in the United States where corporations more consciously reject the Friedmanite position than the Twin Cities.

Prof. William Ouchi, who makes this very point in his 1984 book *The M-Form Society,* described the charitable philosophy of Minneapolis. "In this age of self-centeredness and in our system of free enterprise profit-maximizers, Minneapolis is anomalous," he wrote. "In 1981, 62 local companies gave 5 percent of their pretax profits to charity, creating social endowments. Another 21 were members of the Two Percent Club, giving that level of pretax earnings. For the United States as a whole corporate giving has remained steady at 0.66 percent to 0.75 percent of pretax earnings." Dayton-Hudson, the Minneapolis-based department store and bookstore chain, is a charter member of the Five Percent Club. General Mills, Pillsbury, and Honeywell are Two Percenters. Cargill's annual sales are larger than the combined revenues of these four neighboring giants. A 1982 report on charitable giving in Minneapolis examined one contributing factor in this performance. "The civic involvement of business leaders is by no means entirely a matter of individual choice," it noted. "There is conscious and explicit peer pressure to participate in public affairs; the area sees itself as a community."

Ouchi's chapter on Minneapolis cites dozens of other local companies and their charitable recipients. He also describes approvingly the Downtown Council, the Minnesota Association of Commerce and Industry, the Minnesota Business Partnership, and the Minnesota Project on Corporate Responsibility—all local or statewide business groups. But not once does he mention giant Cargill or Whitney MacMillan. This no doubt disturbed Cargill executives not a whit. The preference for seclusion over exposure, even favorable exposure, has long reached the proportions of a fetish at company headquarters. Peer pressure stops at the shores of Lake Minnetonka.

E. J. Weigle, president of the Winneshiek County Historical Society in Decorah, Iowa, must wonder about just how far this seclusion can go. He wrote a very polite letter in 1982 to Cargill president Pete McVay and invited the company to provide a modest sum to finance an official historical marker at the site of the first Cargill facility. He assured Mr. McVay that the marker, to be placed in Conover, Iowa, would be made of "good quality material of a metal alloy," as were the previous nine markers approved by the Historical Society. Mr. Weigle even enclosed a proposed script for the marker, under the title Conover Site of Cargill's First Business 1865: "In August 1865, William W. Cargill stepped off a Marquette and Western Train in Conover, and within a few days was stacking bagged grain in a storage flathouse," it was to read. "He later became partner and owner of the facility, the first of a network of Cargill elevators. Conover was at the end of the railroad, boasted about 300 people, 32 saloons, 3 hotels and 12 grain storage flathouses. Because the railroad soon built further on, Conover lost its marketing advantage and gradually died out as an important pioneer center."

William R. Pearce, Cargill's vice-president for public affairs, responded to Weigle's suggestion after a long delay. "I regret to say that the consensus here is against our participation in establishing the marker," he wrote. "It is difficult for me to explain why, but the feeling seems to be that it's inappropriate for a business to erect monuments to itself."

THOMAS JONES

Life of a Salesman

Before the late 1950s, the United States gave its allies without an aerospace industry jet fighters free of charge. It also supplied used F-84s and F-86s, aircraft left over from the Korean War, through military grant-in-aid programs. But the men at Northrop Corporation, a California-based manufacturer of missile components, recovery systems for the space program, and the world's first lightweight supersonic jet trainer, thought these allied governments would rush to buy new airplanes—especially if they were designed to meet the special needs of Europe and the Third World.

Thomas Jones joined Northrop in 1953 as assistant to the chief engineer. A rising star in aircraft circles, he became a corporate vice-president four years later. Gilbert Nettleton was named vice-president of Northrop's international division in 1956, ten years after he began work with the company as a test pilot fresh out of the air force. The two executives soon began to travel from country to country—Greece, Turkey, Norway, New Zealand—sounding out generals and defense ministers and soliciting their appraisals of a new fighter Northrop was designing. Their global market research was not as glamorous as it might sound. "When you spend three hundred days a year out of the country, in the days before commercial jets, and you're not home on weekends, you tend to lose your family," Nettleton told us. "And I spent thirty out of the other sixty-five days in Washington."

Vice-president Jones was charged with pitching the concepts of the new fighter to potential foreign customers. His training as an engineer prepared him well for this assignment. Though he was not a seasoned world traveler, he was a quick study—quick enough to assume command at Northrop by 1960.

"Jones had never been to Europe," Nettleton continued. "He had never been to the Far East. His only travel was into South America—

Brazil. But Jones is very sensitive to the fact that people in other countries are different. They speak different languages. He had learned to speak Portuguese, and he spoke it quite well. He didn't try to take a piece of American turf with him everywhere he went, to stand on it and declare, 'I'm an American.' I had traveled a lot with the merchant marine. It was a very natural thing for me. Jones was very quick to understand the differences, to take the time to talk, but also to find out what the other fellow's problems were, what his operating conditions were. In those days I could have told you the salary of every NATO employee. And for the enlisted men, what they were given when they enlisted. How many pairs of socks, how many pairs of shoes. We knew all that stuff. We had to understand these countries."

The plane on whose behalf Jones and Nettleton circled the globe became known as the F-5 Tiger. Northrop engineers modified the design of their T-38 Talon trainer, which the United States first acquired in 1956, to create a lightweight alternative to the Lockheed Starfighter, the preeminent export fighter of the time. The Lockheed jet was selected in 1958 for delivery to the West German air force. A number of other customers, including Holland, Belgium, Italy, and Japan, soon fell into line. But the Starfighter's reputation for crashing led anxious pilots to dub it the "flying coffin" and the "widow-maker." Northrop's Tiger—quick, lethal, and easy to operate—found a welcome market among allied governments that lacked the trained personnel to maintain top-of-the-line aircraft. Anthony Sampson, who examined the international weapons trade in his book *The Arms Bazaar*, described the attractions of an early version of Northrop's F-5.

"The Tiger, as it was to be called, was a sharp-nosed twin-engine plane which was uniquely versatile, whether for Europe or the Third World," Sampson wrote. "It took off with a sexy roar, like a thousand motorbikes; it could fly at Mach 1.4 at 35,000 feet, and then zoom down to fly just above the ground, terrifying tribesmen. More seriously, it could carry missiles on its wing-tips and 20mm guns in the fuselage nose. It was cheaper and safer than the Starfighter, and it was custom built for the Pentagon's program of Foreign Military Sales."

William Lightfoot, a Northrop marketing executive from 1963 to 1975, explained the plane's breakthrough feature: "The idea of a relatively unsophisticated fighter that isn't the most expensive, but is extremely reliable," he told us. "Tom Jones built the Chevy Impala of fighter planes as opposed to the Ferraris or Lamborghinis that other companies were building. Most designers go for the most hi-tech and sophisticated aircraft possible."

Northrop submitted statistics on fighter performance to a House subcommittee in 1984 that quantified the Lightfoot distinction. The F-5E Tiger II, a much-updated version of the original plane, is undeniably slower and less capable than more sophisticated fighters such as the General Dynamics F-16A Fighting Falcon. It has a maximum speed of Mach 1.6—or 1.6 times the speed of sound. The Falcon can fly at Mach 2. The F-5E's combat thrust-to-weight ratio, a measure of engine power, is 0.74; that of the F-16A is 1.15. But the Northrop plane is more reliable, easier to maintain, and quicker to scramble from a standing start to 40,000 feet. Northrop calculates that a fleet of thirty-six F-5Es flying twenty hours each month requires a team of 350 service personnel. A comparable fleet of F-16As needs 484 technicians.

Simplicity and reliability alone could not guarantee the success of the Northrop fighter. So Jones crafted a sales presentation that not only stressed the performance virtues of the F-5 but created a budgetary rationale for its acquisition. "I was in charge of developing the mechanics of marketing," said Gil Nettleton. "Jones was in charge of developing the concepts of the airplane and showing what those concepts meant. It was the first form of systems analysis and operations analysis. He was the first man who really articulated and then put into chart form for briefings— and I went all over the world with him talking about it—what is now called life-cycle costing. The theory is that the initial purchase price [of an airplane] is just a small part of the total cost through its lifetime. You've got to worry about attrition, training cost, and maintenance. You've got to worry about getting the number of hours needed for the pilots to be sharp, not busting up the airplanes. This was put together by Jones and his people. It became a very great theme."

Jones himself explained the inspiration for life-cycle costing to *Time* in 1961. "We must make our new technology the liberator of our resources rather than a ravenous consumer," he declared. "We must recognize the power and value of technical simplicity as distinguished from the complexity that we too often regard as sophistication. We have tended to ignore something that the best Paris dress designers—and Sir Isaac Newton—never forgot: the ultimate of sophistication is simplicity itself." Jones has been sounding that theme ever since.

Nettleton and his companion managed to open a gigantic new market for Northrop as a result of their convincing presentations. The F-5 was first ordered by the U.S. Air Force in 1962. Within five years Northrop had delivered four hundred planes to more than a dozen customers: Iran, Korea, Greece, Vietnam, Canada, Norway, and other countries scattered throughout Asia, Europe, and Africa. The Tiger has since become the most widely used fighter outside the Soviet bloc. Saudi Arabia and Taiwan built their modern air forces on the foundation of the F-5. Iran, South

Korea, and Taiwan together purchased nearly a thousand F-5 fighters.

The profitable ascent of the Tiger also propelled Thomas Jones to a position of unrivaled power inside Northrop. Actually, Jones had made something of a name for himself even before he joined the company. He graduated from Stanford University in 1942 with a degree in aeronautical engineering. He immediately went to work in California for Douglas Aircraft, which turned out thousands of bombers, fighters, and other aircraft during World War II. The young engineer remained at Douglas for the duration of the war. He began to fashion a critique of military production and procurement that later animated his F-5 strategy.

"The military men wanted the highest possible performance—more speed, more altitude, more payload—and the manufacturer thought that delivering anything short of that was unpatriotic," Jones told *Time.* "This not only made for sizeable technical risks, but it stretched out the lead time to three years. For slightly less speed and slightly less range, we could have cut it down to one year. And what would have been the result if we had pushed the state of the art less hard and had thereby tripled our Pacific Fleet bomb load about two years earlier? Somehow, there wasn't any equation between what was needed and the cost—not just in dollars but in time."

The end of World War II touched off a depression in the California airplane industry. Jones realized he needed a change. He left Douglas in 1947 and moved to Brazil, where his economy-minded perspective on contracting dovetailed nicely with the aspirations of that country's influential military leaders. He spent four years as a technical advisor to the Brazilian Air Ministry. Jones became an important force in its development as a self-reliant air power. He wrote budgets, worked on airport planning, and served as a professor at the Brazilian Institute of Technology. In 1951, however, he decided to return to southern California as a staff consultant at the Rand Corporation think tank. Two years later he published a detailed monograph, *Capabilities and Operating Costs of Possible Future Transport Airplanes,* that examined the economics of commercial jet aviation. The study received wide acclaim in the industry.

"Tom Jones got a large part of his reputation when he was at Rand," said Glenn Lord, who worked under Jones at Northrop for twelve years. "He did a study on the economics of jet transport. He determined that it had a more economical cost per seat-mile than rotary engine planes. He went around to companies trying to sell this idea. One time he was allowed to go before executives at Boeing. His presentation was one of the things Boeing grabbed onto to develop its first commercial jets." The first Boeing 707 jetliner was delivered to Pan American World Airways in 1958. Northrop today manufactures the fuselage of the Boeing 747. This arrangement, the largest commercial aircraft subcontract ever, generated revenues of more than $2.2 billion for Northrop between 1966 and 1984.

The Rand consultant was lured to Northrop in 1953 when a college chum, deputy chief engineer William Ballhaus, offered him the job of assistant to the chief engineer. Northrop was still a rather modest operation. Jones accepted the Ballhaus offer on two conditions: that he be allowed to work on "basic problems" and that whatever his title, he have a say in strategic management decisions. His rise through the hierarchy ensured that both conditions would be met. Jones left engineering after three years to direct corporate development planning. There Northrop discovered his real strength—conceptualizing a product and marketing it. He became a vice-president one year later. Whitley Collins, Northrop's chief executive, died in May 1959. The board of directors elected Thomas Jones, then only thirty-eight years old, to be the company's new president. He became chief executive in 1960 and chairman in 1963.

Jones inherited a corporation that had fallen on decidedly hard times. Jack Northrop established the enterprise that bears his name in 1939. It quickly secured a niche as an engineering concern given to inspired technical design in the tradition of its founder. Jack Northrop was responsible for the design work on the Lockheed Vega, which took Amelia Earhart across the Atlantic in the early 1930s. He also masterminded the P-61 Black Widow night fighter used in World War II. After the war, Northrop designed the Flying Wing, an airplane without a fuselage, which is now acknowledged to have been years ahead of its time. The air force canceled the Flying Wing contract in 1949, and the company limped through the next decade by peddling a catalogue of planes, missiles, and navigation equipment to the U.S. government. Northrop's stagnation became especially pronounced in the late 1950s. Revenues in 1960 declined to $234 million—17 percent less than in 1957.

President Jones set out to engineer the first of several corporate transformations at Northrop over which he would preside. In 1960 the company generated 70 percent of its stagnant revenues from the production of missiles, electronics, and communications systems. The F-5 changed all that. Sales doubled between 1960 and 1967. Much of this expansion could be traced directly to the explosive growth of the Tiger. Aircraft shipments accounted for 45 percent of total revenues by 1967, the bulk of which came from the F-5 and its T-38 cousin. Northrop also evolved into an international enterprise. Political and economic developments in Europe or Southeast Asia became as important to Northrop's future as purchasing decisions by the American military.

The global market Jones established was not as easy to retain. Other companies—Dassault of France, Lockheed of the United States—had their own fighters to sell. Gil Nettleton claimed in our conversation, and Jones has hinted publicly, that the marketing practices adopted by these competitors were not as scrupulous as their own. Where life-cycle costing led the charge for Northrop, others reached deep into their pockets to win friends and influence people. The international grease machine was shifting into high gear.

"As far as foreign bribery is concerned, that's a fact of life," Nettleton told us. "Everyone in business knows that the competition is out there. We had lost a large sale in Switzerland because the French had dumped a million dollars into the hands of the commanding officer of the Swiss air force. We had a lot of business taken away from us by those things, and it was apparent that if you were in that arena, you had to consider what was legal in those days."

What was legal, and already standard practice for many contractors, was the use of independent agents, working on a commission basis, who enjoyed close personal relations with foreign leaders. Thomas Jones adapted quickly to this slippery environment. He orchestrated a new approach to airplane sales that he soon refined with as much precision as he had the life-cycle cost method. In 1961, one year after he was named chief executive, Jones worked with James Allen, vice-president and assistant to the president, to establish a secret fund in Paris that was used to launder money for U.S. political contributions. That same year, Northrop purchased a 20 percent stake in a Dutch aircraft manufacturer. Jones served on the board of the Fokker company with the influential Prince Bernhard, who later resigned all of his public positions in the Netherlands as a result of the Lockheed bribery scandals. The Northrop president also began to assemble a stable of well-connected foreign representatives who served as the core of an aggressive international sales force.

Jones even threw himself into the fray. He logged hundreds of thousands of miles a year cementing his personal ties to overseas leaders. He initiated what would become a close relationship with the shah of Iran during a visit by the shah to a Northrop manufacturing complex in 1962. William Weir, Northrop's Far East regional manager from 1971 to 1980, worked with great success to promote F-5 sales to Taiwan. He told us that Chairman Jones met with many Taiwanese ministers, the country's military leaders, and President Chiang Ching-kuo, son of the late Generalissimo Chiang Kai-shek.

A retired Lockheed executive, himself no wallflower when it came to wining and dining foreign leaders, became exasperated when he described Jones's multinational ubiquity. "You always had to deal with the principals" of foreign countries, this executive explained over lunch in Orange County. "And in the Third World they always want to deal with the [corporate] principals too. I remember once when I left the Paris Air Show and flew to Riyadh, Saudi Arabia. I met with the chief of the air force general staff. When I came out of his office, who was sitting there, waiting to go next, but Jones. I went to Tehran. There I met with General Khatami, who was a good friend of mine." (Khatami was chief of the Iranian air force and a brother-in-law of the shah.) "I walked out of his office, and who's waiting there to talk to him next but Jones."

Northrop's long-standing and lucrative relationship with the kingdom of Saudi Arabia illuminates many of the strategies and tactics Chairman Jones has used to extend his company's global presence. It is difficult to overstate the importance of the Saudi connection. Northrop first sold F-5 fighters to the royal family in 1965. The government took delivery of more than 110 planes over the next fifteen years. Northrop has also been prime contractor in the Saudis' Peace Hawk program since it began in 1972. Under Peace Hawk, the company functioned for many years as an overseer of the Saudi air force. It did everything from train pilots to supervise the construction of runways and manage snack bars at Saudi air bases. Peace Hawk generated revenues of more than $2.5 billion from 1972 through 1982—fully 20 percent of Northrop's total revenues. The most recent stage of the program, which ran from 1983 through 1985, carries a price tag of $666 million.

Northrop planes and technicians have clearly performed up to Saudi expectations over the years. A retired air force colonel who was stationed for three years in Saudi Arabia told us that the company "is a superstar in the Saudis' eyes." The royal family demonstrates "a great deal of loyalty to Northrop," he explained. "Trust in Northrop—that's one statement you'll hear from Prince Fahd [a former chief of the air force] and Prince Sultan [the Saudi defense minister]." But performance alone does not account for the company's unmatched history of aerospace business in Saudi Arabia. The importance of the human touch should not be overlooked.

Northrop has over the years made use of a carefully selected network of friends and contacts with the Saudi royal family. The first such agent was Kermit "Kim" Roosevelt, a grandson of President Theodore Roosevelt. Kim Roosevelt is best known as a participant in events that precipitated the overthrow of Iranian premier Mohammed Mossadegh in 1953 and the return of the shah to the Peacock Throne. Jones hired Roosevelt in 1965. Four months later, the former CIA operative convinced the Saudis to cancel their proposed purchase of the Starfighter. Roosevelt reportedly spread the word that Lockheed had bribed its way into a contract, news that did not sit well with King Faisal. The Saudis bought

F-5s instead. Northrop's invaluable consultant accompanied his chairman on every trip Jones made to the Middle East during the mid-sixties, according to a statement by Jones to company auditors in 1974. Roosevelt, who still maintains an office in Washington, declined to speak with us. But the report of the company auditors, which was released in 1975, concluded that the consultant "has been perhaps the key figure in establishing the very high level of activity Northrop now has in the Middle East." He was paid nearly $440,000 between 1965 and 1975.

Roosevelt also introduced Northrop to a second well-known local representative. Adnan Khashoggi, the son of the personal physician to the late King Ibn Saud, briefly attended Stanford and soon thereafter began to work as an agent for Western companies trying to drum up business in Saudi Arabia. Jones hired Khashoggi in 1970. Their relationship was productive—and more than a bit stormy. It became the focus of an embarrassing public scandal over a 1972 attempt to bribe two Saudi generals with $450,000. Khashoggi's work in Saudi Arabia also became the focus of a bitter legal dispute over the size of commissions he was demanding. When Khashoggi's firm, Triad Financial Establishment, brought the dispute to arbitration in 1979, it demanded at least $174 million in back commission payments. An arbitrator awarded Triad $31.5 million four years later. Northrop took a charge against income that totaled more than 10 percent of 1983 operating profits as a result of the judgment.

Experiences such as these may have tempered Northrop's enthusiasm for high-priced influence brokers such as Adnan Khashoggi. As the company has taken it upon itself to sustain its Peace Hawk business, Chairman Jones has occupied a conspicuous position. The retired air force attaché described the chairman's ease of circulation among top officials in the country. "Tom Jones is on a first-name basis with more heads of state than anyone I know," he said. "He is number one a businessman. But he is very savvy politically. He knows how to talk to these people. When he goes to see Prince Sultan, he talks about the general political situation. He knows what it is all over the world—in the Middle East, Thailand, Europe."

A former chief of the U.S. Military Assistance Advisory Group (MAAG) in Saudi Arabia confirmed these observations on the Jones style and presence. MAAG offices function as overseas extensions of the Pentagon agency that administers security assistance. The Northrop chairman "is the most personally involved CEO that I've come across," he told us. "Tom really believes in being on a first-name basis with the key leaders in-country. He believes it is in the best interests of the United States and Saudi Arabia to have good relations. He works the political end of things.

. . . In Saudi Arabia he has a good deal of contact with Prince Sultan. There are also those that he works in the Saudi air force. His contacts are quite broad."

. . .

Thomas Victor Jones, who turned sixty-five on July 21, 1985, does not direct the largest corporation in the aerospace industry. Nor does Northrop rank among the most sizable U.S. military contractors. It was number twenty-six on the Pentagon's list of companies allocated prime contracts from the Defense Department in fiscal 1984, with awards valued at nearly $900 million. McDonnell Douglas, the largest military supplier, received contract awards worth $7.7 billion. But Northrop's ranking is deceptively modest. The Pentagon does not publish comparative data on the *total* value of its business with individual suppliers. Its prime contract statistics do not include the value of subcontracts, even when those subcontracts are quite substantial. In Northrop's case subcontracts represent a major percentage of its Pentagon business.

The Navy's F/A-18 Hornet strike fighter is a case in point. Jones's company manufactures 40 percent of this expensive aircraft—the Navy plans to buy nearly 1,400 planes at a total cost of $40 billion—but because McDonnell Douglas is the prime contractor, Northrop's revenues do not figure into its Pentagon ranking. The F-18 was Northrop's single largest manufacturing project in 1984. It delivered the center and aft fuselage sections and twin vertical stabilizers for ninety-nine Hornets and received $623 million. The Sanford C. Bernstein investment management firm has projected that the Hornet will generate revenues for Northrop of $6.6 billion between 1979 and 1988.

It is also important to understand that size alone does not determine the impact of a company in its industry or the standing of its chief executive among his peers. Thomas Jones has presided over an era of relentless growth and prosperity at Northrop. Its track record testifies to his unrivaled mastery of the intricate and sometimes harsh forces that govern the world of military contracting. The chairman of Northrop cannot deploy the same brand of power and political leverage available to the chief executives of larger contractors that monopolize production of major weapons systems. The navy's capacity to discipline General Dynamics (1984 revenues: $7.8 billion) is circumscribed by the fact that no other corporation manufactures the Trident submarine. And the massive start-up costs associated with submarine production discourage rapid entry by other shipbuilders. Jones has managed to mold an enterprise of staggering profitability without the advantages of massive size and monopoly control that accrue to certain of his rivals.

It is instructive to compare the Northrop of 1960 with the Northrop of 1984. Thomas Jones took control of an enterprise whose inspired history had given way to a bleak and insecure future. Northrop today is riding the crest of a wave of uninterrupted expansion. The company employs more than 41,500 workers in a network of plants that stretches from the arid deserts of the Antelope Valley in southern California to Rolling Meadows, Illinois, and the suburbs of Boston. (Northrop is among the largest defense contractors in Illinois. Some 4,600 employees in Rolling Meadows turn out a range of electronic countermeasure devices, including radar-jamming transmitters for the B-1B bomber.) Total revenues in 1984 were $3.7 billion—more than double sales in 1980 and fifteen times greater than when Jones took control. Profits have soared as well. Northrop earned $167 million in 1984—nearly double its earnings in 1980 and twenty-two times greater than in 1960.

This history of growth and profitability has made Thomas Jones an acclaimed figure on Wall Street. A series of reports on Northrop prepared in 1985 by Bernstein & Co. projected an even rosier future. A May 1985 report estimated that earnings per share would increase at an annual rate of 23.5 percent between 1985 and 1989. That compares with anticipated rates of growth of 19 percent at McDonnell Douglas, 11 percent at Lockheed, and 8 percent at General Dynamics. A March 1985 report by Bernstein analyst David Smith compared Northrop's future with that of its rivals. "Northrop appears positioned to realize exceptional growth," Smith concluded. "Unlike General Dynamics and Lockheed, whose growth will come to a temporary halt in 1987–1989, Northrop is expected to grow at a double digit annual rate through 1989. With the improving outlook" for the Stealth bomber and the F-20 fighter, "high growth should continue into the 1990s. We continue to prefer Boeing and McDonnell Douglas to Northrop because of their excellent prospects from the coming commercial aircraft order boom. But among the pure defense companies, Northrop is clearly the investment of choice."

The Northrop chairman's 1985 address to shareholders suggested that his company has been the "investment of choice" for quite some time. Jones reminded his audience that a stockholder who purchased 100 Northrop shares at the end of 1974 would have spent $2,400. That investment, assuming full reinvestment of dividends, was worth $57,000 by the spring of 1985—a compound annual rate of growth of 33 percent. Jones himself, who is the company's largest individual shareholder, has reaped the fruits of this fantastic appreciation. His 220,000 shares were worth roughly $10 million in July 1981. By July 1985, after a three-for-one stock split in 1984, those same shares were valued at $36.3 million. His total holdings in July 1985, more than a million shares, were worth nearly $60 million.

One important factor in Northrop's explosive growth has been its chairman's unmatched ability to overhaul the character and orientation of the company in response to the emergence of new military doctrines at home or the demise of reliable clients abroad. He revived the company in the 1960s and early 1970s by blanketing the Third World with the F-5 Tiger. Aircraft sales, primarily the F-5 and its T-38 companion, represented 54 percent of total revenues as recently as 1975. The prominence of the F-5 also required that a substantial share of Northrop's business be conducted overseas. Foreign sales accounted for 49 percent of total revenues in 1976 and as much as 64 percent in 1977. Aircraft sales now account for 70 percent of total revenues. But the F-18 fighter and Stealth bomber dwarf the contribution of the F-5. Stealth is a top-secret bomber that is scheduled to succeed the B-1B, whose maiden sortie took place in October 1984. Northrop is the prime contractor for research and development on Stealth, by any standard an incredibly expensive project. Bernstein has estimated that Stealth will generate revenues for Jones's company of $5.4 billion from 1981 through 1988.

Northrop has also become an overwhelmingly domestic corporation. More than 70 percent of its revenue in 1984 represented direct sales to the U.S. government. Another 6 percent came from commercial transactions with domestic customers. Foreign sales accounted for the remaining 22 percent—down from its 1977 high. This profound corporate transformation underlines Jones's instincts for survival in a turbulent environment. The Vietnam War provided initial momentum for the F-5 Tiger. Third World generals could witness firsthand its lethal combat performance and be comforted by the U.S. Air Force's commitment to the plane. The emergence of the Nixon Doctrine, under which the United States flooded strategic outposts such as Iran, Thailand, and Indonesia with expensive weapons, generated a thriving market for fighter aircraft and support services. This export imperative faltered as the 1970s wore on. The collapse of important customers—the fall of South Vietnam in 1975, the overthrow of the shah of Iran in 1979—forced Northrop to shift its sights. The burdens of rising oil prices and massive foreign debts sapped the weapons-buying capacity of the Third World. Meanwhile, the unprecedented Reagan military buildup created immensely profitable markets at home.

Jones adjusted to these destabilizing trends with characteristic agility. Under the Stealth contract, which Northrop was awarded in 1981, the company directs research and development for a bomber whose production costs could approach $50 billion. Northrop produces much of the guidance system for the MX Missile, a contract that generated revenues of more than $730 million from 1980 through 1984. It manufactures electronic components for a number of tactical missiles—the Harpoon, the Phoenix, the Tomahawk—whose procurement has increased significantly under the Reagan administration. Northrop has sold target drones, unmanned aircraft that are used to simulate enemy missiles and fighters during combat training, to the navy, army, and Marine Corps.

Northrop even has a strategy to resume major shipments overseas. Jones claims to have invested more than $800 million since 1978 to engineer and manufacture a sleek new export fighter that can scramble to forty thousand feet in three minutes, race at Mach 2, and destroy an enemy plane with upgraded Sidewinder missiles. The F-20 Tigershark is decidedly faster and more lethal than its F-5 predecessors. It is also considerably more expensive. Northrop has offered to sell the Tigershark to foreign customers at a fixed price of $11.4 million each. It would replace aging squadrons of F-5s, some of which sold for under $2 million per plane.

Paul Nisbet, a respected aerospace analyst with Prudential-Bache Securities, discussed the history and future of Northrop under its current chairman. "Tom Jones played a vital part in the emergence of Northrop as a major aerospace company," Nisbet told us. "He is the premiere foreign salesman. His company will be in the top two or three aerospace contractors if both programs [Stealth and the F-20] come through. Jones has succeeded in putting together a very powerful corporation, with strong management, conservative accounting, high margins, and strong product-support capability in the field."

.   .   .

Northrop's corporate redirections and legacy of global conquest should not obscure the defining reality of its history and operations: its reliance on the U.S. government as a customer for its products or as an agent for sales abroad. Northrop sells the F-18 to the navy, guidance systems for the MX Missile to the air force, and gyroscopes for the Space Shuttle to NASA. Even shipments of Northrop aircraft to Saudi Arabia or Tunisia or Brazil are funneled through the U.S. government. All arms sales to foreign countries must be approved by the State Department, which determines what countries are eligible to buy, the range of weapons contractors may sell, and the volume in which they may sell them. The review process often fuels intense jockeying between contractors; potential foreign customers; and the State Department, Pentagon, and Congress.

There are three distinct categories of exports regulated by two State Department offices. Sales under the Military Assistance Program (MAP), the dominant form of shipments from World War II through Vietnam, and Foreign Military Sales (FMS), the principal category since Vietnam, are both administered by the Office of Security Assistance and Sales. MAP deliveries are not sales at all but grants of military hardware paid for by the U.S. government. Northrop's shipments of fighters to Iran and Vietnam in the mid-1960s were made largely under the MAP program. FMS transactions involve exchanges of substantial equipment or services for cash, taxpayer-subsidized credit or outright grants. By the mid-1970s the vast majority of Northrop's overseas business was administered under FMS guidelines. FMS transactions accounted for 55 percent of Northrop's total revenues in 1977. The third category of international arms shipments involves commercial sales of military and police hardware to governments or foreign companies. These shipments are licensed by the State Department's Office of Munitions Control.

The structure of the market in which Northrop operates shapes in fundamental ways how Chairman Jones approaches his job as chief executive of a major weapons producer. The relationships between a military contractor and its customers differ in several important respects from more traditional buyer-seller interactions. There are a limited number of companies from which the Pentagon can obtain the weapons it plans to deploy or recommend to allied governments. James Fallows, author of *National Defense*, describes military contracting as a "thin industry," since "for any given military product, there are at best a handful of firms capable of accepting the government's business."

The small number of potential military suppliers is an important source of producer leverage. Concentration among manufacturers also contributes to the intensity with which these firms contend for Pentagon awards. When a single contract can generate a backlog of orders worth billions of dollars, a producer will spare little expense to win. The history of aerospace contracting is one of bitter rivalries among the industry's giant corporations. These high-stakes skirmishes are just as often played out in the halls of Congress and through the endless gladhanding of Washington public relations as they are with hard-headed competition on price or quality. But they are very real nonetheless.

Northrop and General Dynamics have been engaged in a form of guerrilla warfare for several years over the F-20. Northrop's campaign to market its fighter in the Third World suffered grave setbacks when the Reagan administration allowed General Dynamics to sell its more glamorous F-16 to South Korea and Venezuela, both of whom were thought to be prime candidates for the Tigershark. Even smaller countries, such as

Singapore, have been allowed to purchase F-16s. For several years it looked as though the Tigershark might rank as the most serious blunder of the Northrop chairman's career.

Jones has fought back with a masterful political and economic offensive. He took advantage of public outrage surrounding cost overruns and improper billings by General Dynamics to orchestrate a torrent of editorial support for his rival F-20. He has worked his allies on Capitol Hill to pressure the Pentagon to embrace the Tigershark. In April 1985 he offered to sell 396 F-20s to the U.S. Air Force and provide spare parts for twenty years at a fixed cost of $15 million per plane—thus moving directly to steal from General Dynamics a substantial chunk of its largest and most profitable contract. General Dynamics responded in June by offering to sell 216 stripped-down F-16s at a discount of $3.5 million each—provided the air force lives up to its commitment to purchase 720 GD fighters.

Jones has also worked diligently to protect appropriations for the Stealth bomber against congressional efforts to expand production of the B-1B beyond its anticipated limit of one hundred aircraft. The B-1B is assembled by Rockwell International. The chairman's activism on this top-secret research program has at times ruffled feathers in Washington. *Armed Forces Journal International,* a respected monthly that covers defense affairs, reported in September 1982 on Pentagon displeasure over Jones's Capitol Hill maneuvering in support of the Stealth. The *Journal* reported Pentagon officials' statements that Jones had "lobbied too hard" and "tried to end run [the air force] in Congress, with some help from Boeing" to secure additional funding for Stealth research at the expense of the B-1B. It also reported that air force officials wrote a letter to the Northrop chairman "emphasizing the need to protect Stealth secrets better" after publication of a celebratory *Business Week* cover story on Northrop. The *Business Week* article, which appeared on April 19, 1982, included a number of pieces of information on the bomber that the Pentagon reportedly considered confidential. In a prepublication letter to *Armed Forces Journal,* Washington attorney Edward Bennett Williams threatened legal action against the journal on behalf of Northrop. The company never made good on its lawyer's threat.

The Northrop chairman also understands when discretion is the better part of political valor. The Lavi fighter (*lavi* means "lion" in Hebrew) is designed to serve as the bulwark of the Israeli Air Force in the 1990s. The program was announced in February 1980. It has been in trouble ever since. Israel has pumped well over a billion dollars into research and development on the Lavi, and the *Jerusalem Post* reported in December 1984 that design and production costs for three hundred aircraft could run as high as $9 billion. Many defense analysts argue that the only way Israel can make the controversial project cost-effective is to spread its enormous costs over a large number of fighters. In other words, export or perish.

Enter Thomas Jones. He considers the Israeli Lion an unfair threat to his F-20 Tigershark—especially since Israel has received grants from the U.S. government worth $1.35 billion through fiscal 1986 to underwrite research on the Lavi. Northrop has dedicated $800 million of its own funds to the F-20 and has already produced three prototypes. But Jones has not gone to bat on these issues with anywhere near the intensity with which he has tackled General Dynamics or the B-1B. West Virginia congressman Nick Rahall introduced an amendment in 1984 that would have forbidden Congress from appropriating Foreign Military Sales (FMS) credits to assist in the overseas development of weapons that compete with U.S. arms. The legislation would of course have applied to the Lavi.

Rahall told us that he never met with the ubiquitous Jones to discuss his amendment, which was defeated by a margin of 379 to 40. "I have not worked closely with Northrop," he said. "It came to their attention that I was going to offer the amendment. I have met some Northrop officials since then. We have discussed my amendment, my efforts on the Lavi, and how much they are for them, but basically it's been a ho-hum type of thing. We all recognize the realities of the votes in the House and what a fruitless effort it would be."

Did Northrop offer any lobbying assistance? "I think it was more of an after-the-fact thing," Rahall replied. "A willingness to come to my aid. Perhaps they did not fully believe I would carry [the legislation] as far as I did. They did come up afterward and profusely thank me."

Jones's apparent calculation of the politics of Lavi funding has not stopped him from putting his position on the record. Early in 1983, soon after news of potential U.S. support for research on the fighter surfaced in the American press, Jones dispatched no-nonsense letters to Secretary of State George Shultz and Secretary of Defense Caspar Weinberger. He has known both men for several years by virtue of their common California roots. We obtained copies of the correspondence under the Freedom of Information Act. Excerpts from two letters capture the tone and substance of the chairman's objections:

- *January 17, 1983:* Recent published reports indicate that the Administration is seriously considering support for the new Lavi tactical aircraft development by Israel, through the use of foreign military sales credits, through the use of U.S. technology transferred to Israel, and possibly through other means. These reports concern me greatly, not just because of Northrop's interests—which are considerable—but because of the implications such a policy change would have for the U.S. aerospace industry and for our Country. Not only would such a course of action result in the development of an aircraft which would undoubtedly duplicate aircraft developed in this Country during this decade, but it would also aid the development of a capability in a foreign country which would enable it to compete directly with U.S. industry. . . .

Israeli Government officials and the past President of Israel Aircraft Industries have told me that even with U.S. support the Lavi program is not economically viable without export sales. The Lavi *will* be competitive with U.S. aircraft, and particularly the F-20, around the world—notably in South America, Africa and other areas where Israel has been active as an arms supplier. While Israel would be expected to accede in principle to U.S. control over sales of the Lavi to third countries, such controls are often uncertain and have been voided by policy exceptions in the past. . . .

By this letter I am therefore asking that you and Secretary Shultz, to whom I am sending a similar letter because of his responsibilities in the area such a decision would impact, to personally involve yourselves in this decision. I am confident that when you do, considering all the factors I have mentioned, the result will be the right one.

• *April 25, 1983:* In view of the Administration's recent decision to grant [25] technical licenses to U.S. companies in support of the development of the Lavi fighter in Israel, I must express my deepest concern over the possibility that further consideration may now be given to some form of U.S. Government funding for this project.

As I stated in my letter of 17 January, continued U.S. sponsorship of this new foreign fighter aircraft program, whether directly or indirectly, is particularly harmful to the Northrop Corporation and to the many companies who have invested with us in the development of the F-20 Tigershark in response to U.S. Government policy. . . .

I cannot believe that direct or indirect funding by the U.S. Government to support or further subsidize the development of a foreign aircraft such as the Lavi that inevitably will compete for sales and international influence with an existing U.S. aircraft, the F-20 Tigershark, would be consistent with U.S. foreign or domestic economic interests.

A clear and immediate understanding is now required as to whether our Government really wishes the Tigershark to exist before I, in good conscience, can allow the resources of Northrop and our team members to be further obligated.

The Northrop chairman received cordial and sympathetic replies to both missives. Defense Secretary Weinberger assured Jones in a May 17 "Dear Tom" letter, "I know of no plan now to permit the use of Foreign Military Sales (FMS) credit funds for research and development (R&D) efforts on the Lavi, whether the R&D is performed in the U.S. or in Israel." Weinberger's intelligence reports proved to be something less than prescient. Congress first approved FMS credits for the Lavi just six months after his letter to Jones.

. . .

Concentration among military producers has its corollary in concentration among buyers. There are a limited number of countries that can finance substantial acquisitions of the products Northrop manufactures. The F-5 has been delivered to thirty countries since it was introduced more than twenty years ago. But by 1980 a handful of countries—Iran, Saudi Arabia, Taiwan, and South Korea—owned 46 percent of the 2,285 planes that had been delivered. Little has changed with respect to F-5 ownership over the last five years. The F-18 Hornet has been sold to the U.S. Navy and only three other countries: Spain, Australia, and Canada. The loss of any major customer for these two aircraft has a major impact on Northrop's financial prospects. The fall of the shah of Iran, a development that sent tremors through the entire U.S. arms industry, is perhaps the most graphic example of the potential for overnight evaporation of boundless markets.

Northrop first sold F-5 fighters to Iran in 1965 when Kermit Roosevelt, its influential agent in the Middle East, began work on behalf of Jones. That sale, for more than 100 F-5As and F-5Bs, set the stage for what would become an intimate and profitable embrace between the weapons-hungry shah and one of America's most aggressive foreign salesmen. Northrop's Page Communications subsidiary won a contract with Iran in 1970 to build a telecommunications system that used five hundred communications stations to link more than sixty urban centers. The deal was valued at $225 million. Iran contracted for a major shipment of F-5Es in 1974. The initial package, 141 planes at $1.2 million each, was worth $170 million before the addition of support services. The total value of the plane-and-service package rose to $377 million by August 1976.

Accounts of individual sales to the shah do not begin to communicate the degree of coordination between Northrop and the Iranian regime. Kermit Roosevelt enjoyed instant access to top military and civilian officials. Northrop established a joint venture with the Pahlavi government in 1971 to develop an indigenous aerospace industry. Jones even enlisted Iran in his campaign, which was ultimately unsuccessful, to build and sell a land-based model of the F-18 Hornet.

The F-18L was designed to serve as an export version of the fighter that Northrop and McDonnell Douglas were building for the U.S. Navy. Iran emerged in the fall of 1976 as a linchpin in Jones's marketing strategy for the plane. Northrop had to demonstrate to the Pentagon that foreign customers were interested in its proposed F-18L. Iran not only expressed a commitment to buy 250 copies of the plane, but also offered to finance its development to the tune of $250 million. (Estimates at the time put the total value of the Iranian F-18L deal at $4 billion.) This remarkable proposal was communicated to Defense secretary Donald Rumsfeld in a September 12, 1976, letter from General Hassan Toufanian, Iran's vice-minister of war. The Carter administration announced that it would withhold approval of the deal nine months later.

William Sullivan, who became U.S. ambassador to Iran in June 1977, saw the letter in the course of briefings he received to prepare for the job. Sullivan hinted that Chairman Jones had a strong hand in the composition of the dispatch. He also reported on Jones's reaction to efforts by the Carter administration to limit overseas shipments of sophisticated weapons. "I saw in the course of my briefings the letter from General Toufanian," Sullivan told us. "It was written in English that was beyond the command of Toufanian or, for that matter, of the shah. I was aware of the letter. But the new Carter policy cut straight across that. I think Tom came to Washington to protest the policy. In the course of that he did talk to me. The principal point he made was that Northrop aircraft were developed without government R & D funding. . . . Our conversation was blunt, but there was no antagonism. I told him that in my reading of the president's [new policy directive] I didn't see that he had a chance, and that therefore that he was wasting his time on the exercise."

Jones also worked the Pentagon and U.S. representatives in Iran. Major General Ken Miles, who was head of the MAAG office in Tehran under Ambassadors Richard Helms and William Sullivan, recalled an animated encounter with the Northrop leader. "Jones visited, but I don't remember exactly when, whether it was in the fall of 1976 or early 1977," Miles told us. "He did come to the MAAG. He came to see me and dressed me down right in my office. He told me I was trying to 'queer' his sale. I was saying I didn't know anything about the F-18L, which was true. I had received nothing from my superiors. But at that time Iranian arms purchases were out of control, and the contractors weren't a hell of a lot better. Tom Jones was as feisty as any of them. When he visited my office, he was feisty with very few pleasantries. I told him, 'I'm flying your F-5s every day.' I was working very diligently to bring his F-5 on line."

Major General Miles soon visited the Pentagon and got another lesson in the attachment of Chairman Jones to his sale. "I was visiting the deputy assistant secretary of defense for international security assistance," Miles recalled. "He wanted me there to pretty much call me on the carpet for trying to not support the sale of the F-18L to Iran. I was told it had been decided at DSARC [the Defense Systems Acquisition Review Council] and I had better get behind it. By that time I had my dander up. I was already a major general and I told him if that's what he wanted, he could send a telex so advising me. . . . It was obvious to me that Tom Jones had a hell of a lot of pull within the building, at least with the civilian guys."

Even this yeoman effort on behalf of the F-18L was not enough to prevail over a White House commitment to limit additional weapons shipments to arms-glutted countries such as Iran. Ambassador Sullivan recalled that both Vice-minister Toufanian and the shah himself "personally mentioned their unhappiness that the F-18L, which they dearly wanted, was not going to be available to them." Less than two years later Thomas Jones would have to adjust to an even more cataclysmic turn of events. His valued customer and proposed engineering partner was overthrown by a revolution that would halt U.S. arms shipments completely.

The market structure of mutual dependence between buyer and seller in military contracting creates an environment where factors beyond those that routinely enter into purchase decisions—cost, performance, reliability—assume a critical role in weapons procurement. Personal friendships and allegiances forged through years of collaboration can taint dispassionate contracting. Both sides develop an overwhelming interest in procurement stability. Sellers struggle to limit the emergence of new competitors and aggressive price and quality demands by their customers. The overriding logic of the system is that status—the standing of a corporation and the individual who directs it—becomes a decisive factor in the military equation.

Failures such as the F-18L or Jones's self-restraint on the Lavi illuminate the limits to power with which a contractor must contend. Major departures in U.S. foreign policy or a Third World revolution can erase overnight years of contact-building and collaboration with foreign governments. Long-standing commitments between the United States and its strategic allies can interfere with efforts to build markets in nonaligned countries.

Within these parameters, however, the room for maneuver is substantial. A military contractor must be trusted—even liked—by the foreign leaders with whom he does business. Or he must hire agents who can supply that trust for a price. Northrop pursued this formula with great success for much of the 1960s and 1970s. A July 1975 report by the executive committee of the Northrop board of directors disclosed that the company distributed $30 million in commission payments to overseas agents between 1971 and 1973 alone. Jones personally supervised much of this activity. His conduct eventually resulted in years of scandal and public scrutiny that must have been a grueling ordeal for someone accustomed to operating quietly in Washington or Tehran or Taipei.

Jones even faced a potential prison term as a result of his conduct. He pled guilty on May 1, 1974, to having violated a statute prohibiting campaign contributions by a government contractor. He made $150,000 in illegal donations to the Nixon campaign at a time when Northrop was pushing to sell a prototype of the F-18 fighter in Europe and the United States. The $150,000 was paid in two installments. The first, for $100,-000, consisted of twenty checks drawn on a Luxembourg bank. The second contribution, made at the behest of Nixon fundraiser Herbert Kalmbach, financed one-third of the hush money paid to the Watergate burglars.

Jones was told by Kalmbach that the money was earmarked for a "special need." He replied, "I trust you Herb. Make certain that my help is known to the White House." The Northrop chairman could have been sentenced to prison for a maximum of five years as a result of his contributions. Instead, he was fined $5,000.

A memorandum from the Watergate Special Prosecution Force, obtained under the Freedom of Information Act, described the circumstances surrounding his second donation. The memo provides a rare glimpse into the world of Thomas Jones during the early 1970s:

> At some point not long after his $100,000 contribution, Jones was meeting with Kalmbach on another matter, probably an effort by Jones to have the President appear before the Los Angeles World Affairs Council. [The Northrop chairman was president of the council from June 1972 to June 1975.] During that meeting Jones suggested to Kalmbach that he was aware that in campaigns there is often at last minute special needs for funds for unforeseen contingencies and that, should such a need arise in the President's campaign, Kalmbach should contact Jones and he would try to help. Jones explains that what he had in mind were such things as a last minute television blitz.

In late July, after receiving his instructions from [John] Dean and [John] Ehrlichman, Kalmbach called Jones and reminded him of his earlier pledge of funds for a "special need," and told Jones he needed additional cash. On July 31, Kalmbach called Jones again to say he was in the area and would like to stop by to pick up whatever cash Jones could make available.

At that time Jones had a total of $50,000 available to him from the Savy fund [which was established in 1961]. He was holding $25,000 of it himself; he had obtained this from [Vice-president James] Allen several months before in part because he thought that he might be called upon to make certain "under the table" payments to foreign sales agents in a country that had recently outlawed commission payments except to the government of the country. He called Allen from a meeting and asked him to put the remaining $25,000 in with Jones' portion. When Kalmbach arrived, Jones had his secretary bring the packet of money in from his safe and handed it to Kalmbach. He sought and received assurances from Kalmbach that the money would be treated as the first $100,000 had been, i.e., anonymously.

That night Jones received a call from Kalmbach who told Jones he had counted the money and it was $75,000. Jones was incredulous and insisted Kalmbach must be mistaken. Kalmbach persisted and offered to return $25,000. Jones said there was no need for that, that Kalmbach should credit this to Jones' "goal."

The status imperative since the dark and worrisome Watergate days has been addressed through more subtle mechanisms of influence. Jones's basic goal has been to restore Northrop's public-relations niche as a paragon of efficient and competitive defense manufacturing. He has been active on the lecture circuit and likes to deliver speeches on procurement reform and Northrop's perspective on contracting. He is an occasional congressional witness, even though it was Sen. Frank Church's Subcommittee on Multinational Corporations that most thoroughly documented his earlier misdeeds. Jones has built a high-powered promotional and lobbying campaign for the F-20 on the premise that the Northrop fighter represents a cost-conscious break with business-as-usual for the Pentagon.

This crusade for corporate resurrection has been remarkably effective. At times it has been so bold as to border on shamelessness. Just over two years after Jones pled guilty to making illegal campaign contributions, he wrote an op-ed piece for the New York Times that criticized cost overruns in the defense industry and suggested that manufacturers who did not

make the grade should be left to fail in the marketplace. Jones dazzled Sen. William Proxmire and the Joint Committee on Defense Production in September 1977 when he testified in support of fixed-price weapons contracts and more aggressive equipment modernization by his defense-industry rivals. Just eighteen months earlier he had appeared before the same committee and faced charges that Northrop had provided lavish entertainment for Pentagon officials.

Jones apparently considers himself so thoroughly rehabilitated that he even feels comfortable making substantial donations to political campaigns. The Northrop chairman and his wife contributed $29,000 between 1979 and 1984. The bulk of the funds, $19,000, was channeled to the Northrop Employees Political Action Committee for subsequent distribution. (The Northrop PAC contributed a total of nearly $400,000 over this six-year period.) The Reagan-Bush campaigns got $5,000; the rest was scattered among half a dozen congressional and Senate candidates.

Of course, considerations of price or performance or military requirements and capabilities are not absent from contracting decisions. Northrop by and large has managed to build weapons that perform the missions they were designed to perform. Jones has recruited to his company thousands of capable engineers. The fact that a company as small as Northrop could be named prime contractor on a program as expensive and strategic as the Stealth bomber is testimony to its technical expertise.

Northrop has occasionally played on the misery of its rivals to increase its stable of scientific talent. According to one prominent Wall Street analyst, Jones scored an engineering coup of the first order when he "raided" the Lockheed Skunk Works during the troubled 1970s. "Lockheed couldn't afford the spending needed to keep its researchers happy," this analyst explained. "Jones hired away some of the more brilliant guys at the Skunk Works and gave them the research bank they wanted. This has led to long-term ill feelings between Lockheed and Northrop."

The career of Thomas Jones and the continued momentum of Northrop underline the fact that accomplished engineering must often be supplemented with—and is sometimes overwhelmed by—less objective forces in the *entente cordial* between military suppliers and their clients. Success as a military contractor requires intimate familiarity and alliances with powerful figures on Capitol Hill; advocates in the Pentagon, where rivalries between branches of the military often spill over into contracting decisions; an intercultural sophistication that allows for seemingly effortless movement between widely divergent societies; and access to decision-making circles in the White House that set the broad parameters of

military doctrine. The chairman of Northrop Corporation has built a thriving enterprise by mastering these demanding requirements.

.   .   .

By virtue of his scandal-tainted legacy, his unrivaled tenure in the aerospace industry and the global reach of his salesmanship, tracking Thomas Jones is an exhausting task. Our research was made even more challenging by the fact that the Northrop chairman refused to cooperate in any way with us. There are two competing philosophies of corporate relations with journalists and the public at work in this profile.

On the one hand, dozens of Wall Street analysts, active and retired military officers, former Northrop executives and business associates of Jones gave freely of their time to discuss the chairman and his career. Four former ambassadors stationed in countries where Northrop has sold fighters and other military equipment consented to interviews. All of them had met with Jones during their tenure. Brigadier General Chuck Yeager spoke with us about his consulting work for Northrop and his friendship with Jones, whom he has known for many years. We spoke with former Northrop consultants, many of whom are still active in the industry. Even the chairman's son, Peter, a television news reporter in Austin, Texas, said he understood the difficulties of constructing a profile without the participation of the principal and agreed to a conversation.

Peter Jones said his father was "absolutely not" suspicious of the press and that he "holds no grudge" about his treatment by the media during the uproar over foreign bribery and illegal campaign contributions. "Ninety-nine percent of the time he feels he has been treated very fairly," young Jones told us. "Any mistakes [by the press] were those of emphasis or judgment."

Certain common themes emerged from our conversations about the Northrop chairman. Friends and military officials with whom Jones has clashed remarked on his relentless commitment to Northrop and its products. Clair Peck, a former Northrop director and Stanford classmate of Jones, called him "a marvelous salesman" who was very persistent. "He always has contingency solutions," Peck told us. "If one sales plan doesn't work, he always has variations to try."

Peter Jones described life at home with his father. "He is always on the phone in the middle of the night," Jones said. "He has that time clock that gets him out of bed to make a call halfway around the world. He works very hard. It is almost his form of creativity. There is always a project he is working on."

Most of our interview subjects also marveled at the growth of

Northrop under its current chairman. "Jones did a phenomenal job with the company," said twelve-year Northrop veteran William Lightfoot. "When I went out there [in 1963], the company had just broken the $300 million mark. Now it sells more than $3 billion. I do think he tends to cut corners a bit ethically sometimes. . . . He'll do absolutely whatever is required for his company. He's a little more racy than the others in the industry."

On the other hand, many individuals whom we tried to contact—in particular, active Northrop executives and members of the board of directors—joined their chairman in silence. Before and during a ten-day visit to California, we made efforts to interview twelve current and former outside directors. Only two of them, Thomas Barger, a retired chairman of the Arabian American Oil Company (Aramco), and Clair Peck, now a wealthy building contractor, agreed to conversations. Other directors either did not return repeated phone calls or declined interview requests. Many former civilian officials responsible for national security policy and retired military leaders also refused to comment on the career of the Northrop chairman. All told, at least forty business executives and military officers who had worked closely with Jones declined our requests for interviews. This deep-seated unwillingness to discuss company affairs, relations with governments, and other dimensions of the aerospace industry—a commitment to silence that surpassed even the sweeping no-comment protections accorded Cargill chairman Whitney MacMillan—is itself testimony to the power Jones wields. It is as though a whole group of men and women are animated by the principle "Mum's the word."

Northrop officials served up a unique rationale for their chairman's refusal to participate: Jones was unwilling to put his stamp of approval on a project that focused on him personally rather than on Northrop as a corporation. "Any way you pursue this, a personality profile is a dead end," insisted Vice-president for Public Affairs Les Daly. We initiated contact with Northrop by letter on October 10, 1983, and restated our interest in an interview at regular intervals through April 9, 1985. There was a meeting over lunch with Daly at a restaurant in Northrop's Century City headquarters building. There were four letters that explained at length the goals of the book and responded to questions and concerns put forth by Northrop. There were numerous telephone conversations with Daly, who did respond to a few specific inquiries about Northrop operations and policies. But through it all, the position on access to Jones was carved in stone.

Could we interview other Northrop executives? "I don't want to beat around the bush," Daly told us. "None of the people in the company feel they want to be interviewed about Jones." Could we submit written questions? "Then you could say he declined to respond to four out of six questions." We sent written questions nonetheless in April 1985. Daly chose not even to present them to Jones, so as to protect his chairman from the claim that he had declined to respond to specific inquiries. "The day we began, I said we're not going to do an interview," Daly said in May 1985. "Mr. Jones didn't refuse to answer questions. He declined to be interviewed."

More than 80 percent of Northrop's 1984 revenues come from sales to, or transactions that must be approved by, the U.S. government. Does the public not have a right to learn more about the man who leads the company? "When I was in government, I saw it as my obligation to grant interviews, because government is essentially public," Daly replied. "I was always surprised and somewhat worried about the people around me who wouldn't grant interviews. But in industry I don't think it's the same thing. We have been careful not to give interviews that would be likely to portray a personality over business affairs." Daly took a leave of absence from Northrop to serve as assistant for public affairs to Charles Duncan, a former Pentagon official who was named secretary of energy late in the Carter administration.

A Democratic party fundraiser and lawyer, prominent in southern California, contacted Northrop on our behalf. He spoke with Daly, Jones himself, and Donald Hicks, senior vice-president for marketing and technology. (Hicks was nominated in June 1985 to replace Richard DeLauer as undersecretary of defense for research and engineering.) The attorney then reported back to explain the Northrop chairman's reticence. "Jones is scared shitless after his shenanigans during the Nixon period," he told us. "They said, 'This is one we can't do. We probably could have gotten Jones to jump out the window more easily than to give you an interview.' I told Jones, 'You are going to get your rear end kicked.' " After we informed Daly that we had interviewed Thomas Barger, who retired from the Northrop board in 1982 for health reasons, he tried to plant doubts about Barger's credibility. "He is a very sick man, and frankly, I don't think he is quite the man he used to be, if you know what I mean," Daly warned.

We could not help but be slightly amused by talk of Chairman Jones's aversion to "personality profiles." The Northrop leader is nothing like the faceless bureaucrats who so often rise to the top of Fortune 500 corporations. Jones's entire career has been marked by a uniquely personal identification with his company. No other aerospace executive can rival his twenty-five-year tenure as chairman of Northrop. No other aerospace executive has shaped so thoroughly the strategies, values, and patterns of conduct that animate his enterprise. Few industry executives elicit such visceral criticism or genuine praise.

Retired Col. G. J. "Salty" O'Rourke, a former deputy budget director for the air force, described his perceptions of management at Northrop during the turbulent 1960s. "Jones ran the company from stem to stern," he told us. "When Tom Jones drops dead, that's going to be the end of Northrop." O'Rourke had little complimentary to add to his assessment. "I never dealt with Mr. Jones because I had absolutely no respect for the guy," he explained. "He could not sell a plane to the U.S. Air Force because everybody knew his tactics and his methods."

Chuck Yeager, the first pilot to break the sound barrier and who later flew the experimental Northrop X-4, offered a different perspective. "I've known Tom Jones for probably twenty-five or thirty years," he told us. "When you're involved in research and development, you associate with all the aircraft manufacturers. Among manufacturers there is an order of integrity. I've noticed over the years that Northrop stands behind its products. Tom Jones has the highest order of integrity in the business. His being the leader of the company, his policies reflect down through the company. Especially his integrity."

.   .   .

There is no more dramatic illustration of Jones's unquestioned standing within Northrop (although Yeager might disagree) than the fact that he remains chairman and chief executive officer despite the scandals and suspicions that dogged him for much of the 1970s. Consider the improprieties to which Northrop admitted. Jones pleaded guilty to having made illegal campaign contributions. He not only paid a $5,000 fine but agreed to reimburse Northrop nearly $175,000. Northrop disclosed illicit payments to Saudi generals and an Iranian tax collector. Pentagon auditors challenged and demanded reimbursement on millions of dollars worth of company charges for overhead expenses, including entertainment of Defense Department personnel. For example, Northrop leased a duck hunting lodge on Maryland's Eastern Shore, where it hosted weekends for Pentagon brass on more than 140 occasions between 1971 and 1974.

To be sure, the mid-1970s was a period of widespread investigation and disclosure of improper corporate practices at home and abroad. Gulf Oil disclosed millions of dollars of questionable payments in Korea, Bolivia, Italy, and to the presidential campaigns of Richard Nixon and Sen. Henry Jackson. American Airlines, which was the first corporation to reveal that it had made illegal contributions to the Nixon campaign, pled guilty in October 1973 to a misdemeanor charge involving a $55,000 donation. Lockheed, perhaps the most notorious case of them all, admitted in August 1975 to having paid $22 million in kickbacks and bribes since 1970. Its trail of payoffs stretched from the Netherlands to Japan to Italy. The list of companies and their wrongdoing could go on and on.

The experiences of Northrop and Thomas Jones bear detailed recounting for several reasons. First, the company demonstrated a pattern of misconduct with which Jones was intimately involved. This was not a case of an otherwise scrupulous operation making a one-time mistake, or of kickbacks by middle-level managers that escaped the attention of the man at the top. Not only did Chairman Jones approve many questionable relationships with foreign representatives, but he also held back much of that information from the board of directors. Second, Northrop's behavior stands in stark juxtaposition to its chairman's running commentary on waste and inefficiency in military production. Jones portrays himself—and by and large he has won a reputation—as something of a maverick in a fraternity of otherwise lethargic and cozy manufacturers. Finally, Jones managed to survive the disclosures of the 1970s and entered the next decade a respected figure in his industry. Many of his aerospace colleagues were less resilient.

The Watergate scandal and reports of overseas bribery claimed a number of corporate victims. Daniel Haughton and Carl Kotchian relinquished leadership at Lockheed after their assorted misdeeds became front-page news. Robert Waters, Lockheed's treasurer, shot himself dead. Gen. Paul Stehlin, a retired chief of the French air force who served as a Northrop consultant in Paris, apparently suffered a similar fate. The Church Committee disclosed in June 1975 that the general had been on the Northrop payroll for eleven years and that he had advocated a French media campaign on behalf of Northrop's F-18 prototype. British journalist David Boulton, whose 1978 book *The Grease Machine* provided a detailed examination of Lockheed bribery, described what happened next.

"An agency reporter, reading the newly released letter [from Stehlin to Jones], telephoned him, and the general realized the game was up," Boulton wrote. "It was the early hours of the morning. Stehlin left his wife sleeping in their new apartment at 6 rue du Cirque near the Élysée Palace, walked to his office near the Opéra, burned his files, left the office, and stepped from the pavement in front of a bus. He was knocked down and died ten days later in hospital, leaving an unsolved mystery as to whether his death was suicide or the accidental result of a state of shock. The tough Tom Jones is said to have wept on hearing the news."

The fallout from the Northrop scandals did transform the company's formal management structure. In response to a shareholder suit over the Nixon contributions, Northrop adopted a series of governance reforms in 1974. It agreed to appoint outsiders to at least 60 percent of the seats on the board of directors. The executive committee was reorganized to con-

sist exclusively of outside directors. The board must now approve contracts with consultants and foreign representatives that are expected to
cost the company more than $200,000. Jones even agreed to step down
as president.

But there is little evidence that adding outside directors or a new
president has eroded the chairman's authority. Soon after the board
agreed to the 1974 reforms, it passed a resolution praising the chairman's
contributions to the corporation. Eight months later, the Northrop
board's newly formed executive committee issued a report on the origins
of the scandal over campaign contributions and foreign bribery that included recommendations for further reform. It remains a truly remarkable
document. The committee found that Chairman Jones in effect shielded
from other directors basic information about the use and payment of
foreign representatives. But it stopped short of recommending his immediate replacement as chief executive. An excerpt from the July 16, 1975,
report, which ran to sixty pages, summarizes the general findings:

> The Committee recognizes the extent to which Mr. Jones has
> contributed greatly to the success of the Company during his
> tenure. Among other things, he deserves credit for the Company's
> initiative and long-range planning in tailoring the Company's pro-
> ducts to the needs of its customers and for ensuring the efficient
> and reliable operation of the Company. His leadership in reorgan-
> izing the Company into autonomous profit centers and in earning
> for the Company a reputation for performing its contracts on
> time, within cost commitments and at a reasonable profit also
> must be acknowledged. Northrop's development of the foreign
> market and its increasing sales and backlogs of the past decade can
> to a large measure be credited to his efforts. Questionable business
> judgments in marketing strategy should, in the Committee's view,
> be evaluated against the background of his extremely valuable
> contributions to Northrop.
>
> Even with this perspective in mind, the Committee has con-
> cluded that Mr. Jones as Chief Executive Officer must bear a
> heavy share of the responsibility for the irregularities and impro-
> prieties noted in this Report, for the atmosphere within Northrop
> which contributed to those shortcomings, and for the failure to
> concern himself with the functional weaknesses and pressures
> within management which have brought the Company to its pre-
> sent circumstances.
>
> The Committee's judgment regarding Mr. Jones is based upon
> its assessment of his personal role in many of the relationships or

transactions studied by the Committee. In several instances, he either actively fostered marketing strategies without recognizing the potential for raising questions of impropriety or he refrained from taking the initiative to supervise effectively the activities of other Company personnel. Mr. Jones's ambiguous role in the improper payments of $450,000 to Northrop's agent in Saudi Arabia is one such example. His personal failures or errors of judgment in connection with certain relationships such as EDC, Weisbrod, Blandford and MTC [other consulting arrangements] also support the Committee's conclusion. More generally, the Committee believes that Mr. Jones created within the Company, by his example and style of management, an atmosphere which discouraged informed discussion of the wisdom and practicality of various arrangements and practices that carried substantial business risks, as well as significant adverse legal consequences for the Company. Northrop and its shareholders are now confronted with the consequences of his actions.

The Executive Committee is not convinced that Mr. Jones has communicated fully and openly with the Auditors, with the Committee and with the Board of Directors itself or recognizes the seriousness of his involvement in the matters addressed by the Committee. The Committee is disappointed that Mr. Jones failed to concede his lack of knowledge regarding certain of the matters discussed in this Report. The Committee also is concerned that Mr. Jones failed to acknowledge his familiarity with matters which the committee is persuaded that he knew or should have known.

The report went on to recommend that Northrop immediately elect a new chairman and select a new president within a year. (The June 1976 deadline for selection of a new president was part of the settlement of the 1974 shareholder suit.) It also stressed that due to "the absence of an apparent successor" to Jones, the new president should be "qualified to become the Company's Chief Executive Officer." Jones's temporary replacement as chairman was seventy-six-year-old Richard Millar, a member of the board since 1946. Thomas Paine, a former administrator of NASA and General Electric executive, assumed the presidency in February 1976. Jones reclaimed the chairmanship at the same time with unanimous support of the board.

Thomas Paine, who now works as a consultant in southern California, retired six years later at age sixty. He declined our requests for an interview. One Wall Street analyst did offer a not-for-attribution reading of

Jones's current degree of control. "Tom Jones has selected recent management from the outside," he told us. "They are not strong individuals in terms of leading charges. They do not have the clout within the corporation to materially alter decisions. Jones is *the* man to make decisions in the enterprise. The company is where it is today because of Tom Jones."

. . .

Despite his track record as a brash and relentless operator, Thomas Jones is in many ways the consummate West Coast executive. His aristocratic manner and comfortable life-style seem out of place relative to the substance of his career. Jones was born and raised in Pomona, a college town located thirty miles east of Los Angeles. Except for his years in Brazil, his life and business career have revolved around an axis planted firmly in southern California. Jones has been married for almost forty years to the former Ruth Nagel, a daughter of the late Conrad Nagel, the Hollywood matinee idol of the twenties and thirties. (Conrad Nagel was a co-founder of the Academy of Motion Picture Arts and Sciences and played a role in the creation of the Academy Awards.) They have two children, Peter and Ruth, who are in their early thirties. Neither has followed their father into the business world.

Jones and his wife raised their family and continue to live in a rambling Bel Air ranch house once owned by King Vidor, another Hollywood luminary. Their home is nestled comfortably at the foot of a hill. A high fieldstone wall opens onto a curving drive. Orange trees, full of fruit at the time of our December visit, dot the surrounding lawns. A shake roof and brick chimneys give the house the feel of a Mediterranean villa. While private—Moraga Drive dead-ends into a barred and guarded complex of houses—it also has instant access to the San Diego Freeway.

The Northrop chairman's long-standing affiliation with Stanford University is in keeping with his California roots. Jones graduated from Stanford in 1942. He was a member of the board of trustees until he was forced to resign in the wake of the bribery revelations. His two children were Stanford undergraduates at the time of his resignation. Even as a college student Thomas Jones exhibited certain high-society instincts, which have blossomed during his tenure at Northrop.

Clair Peck, the former board member, described the chairman-to-be during his student days. "I've known Tom since college," he told us. "We were in the same engineering class at Stanford. We both graduated in 1942. He was a very intelligent student, a popular student. He was in the honor societies. I was his lab partner. He was a good person to work with.

He was a bit different, you know. He had a certain cultural flair. When the rest of us would sit down to drink beer, he would be getting in his car to drive to the Philharmonic."

Jones was featured on the cover of *Time* as early as 1961 as a rising susperstar in his industry. The article overflowed with gushing accounts of his worldly talents. "As much a thinker as a manager, sophisticated Tom Jones can design airplanes, speak fluent Portuguese, pick his way knowledgeably among Burgundy vintages, and discourse easily on modern French paintings (which he collects) or the problems that man will run into on the moon." Two years later, *Newsweek* featured the Northrop leader, along with Thomas Watson, Jr., of IBM and Richard Cross of American Motors, in a lengthy article on "Renaissance Executives." *Newsweek* was taken by Jones's involvement with the arts (it described him as a "Mozart buff") and his membership in the Los Angeles chapter of the Confrérie de la Châine des Rôtisseurs, a gourmet society founded in Europe during the thirteenth century. His daughter, Ruth, who attended film school at the University of Southern California after her graduation from Stanford, now runs a gourmet food store in Los Angeles.

Peter Jones assured us that his father has not lost his taste for fine foods. "He is just as passionate about his private life as he is about his work," said the younger Jones. "He likes to sail and to cook." Does he maintain an active social calendar? "He is not a big partygoer at all. There were parties, but they were small and personal. He used the house for business parties only as the need arose. The house remained a place for the family. A great weekend for him and my mother is just staying home and cooking vegetables from the garden."

Our one opportunity to evaluate firsthand the Jones personality was Northrop's 1984 annual meeting of shareholders. The gathering, which took place in the auditorium of the Hawthorne Community Center, was attended by an associate of the authors' based in California. Hawthorne is a diverse working-class suburb of Los Angeles whose economy and culture are dominated by Northrop's largest manufacturing plant and its myriad suppliers. The forty-five-minute affair, a remarkably brief session by Fortune 500 standards, exuded formality and seriousness of purpose. Members of the board sat in wood and leather chairs with high backs. Chairman Jones was instantly recognizable. He was tall and dressed very conservatively. He was stiff and formal—and very much in control—as he sped through the agenda. The main item of business at the meeting was the same item that has been at the top of the Jones business agenda for much of this decade. The Northrop chairman complained long and bitterly about the U.S. government's failure to promote the jet fighter on which he has staked his reputation.

"The F-20 Tigershark was developed with a new level of advanced technology and, more important, a new approach in advanced technology," he lectured shareholders. "The F-20 will permit [allied] countries to achieve real security. Not only through higher performance, but through greater maintainability, reliability, and economy. The F-20 will permit the United States to achieve a greater level of our own security by permitting these countries to defend themselves by themselves, without outside assistance. That was the original intent of the Mutual Security Act thirty-five years ago. It is the intent today. . . . The F-20 provides a higher level of military security for these countries than any other fighter in the world, at less cost to them and/or to us. Yet, without official [U.S.] government endorsement, without the government taking initiative to disclose the quality of the F-20 as a first-line American complement to other first-line fighters in our inventory, the Tigershark lacks the credibility needed for political acceptance abroad."

A stenographer dutifully recorded the chairman's words. Jones paused only three times during the course of the entire gathering: once so that the corporate secretary could announce results of the board election, twice to screen films about the F-20. The first film, which featured Northrop's chief test pilot, Darrell Cornell, ran only ninety seconds. (Cornell was killed five months later when a Tigershark he was piloting crashed at Suwon Air Force Base in South Korea.) The second, which featured Chuck Yeager, was more substantial. The legendary aviator spoke warmly of the plane. He explained that flying the Tigershark was a lot different from flying in the old days. "Now, you get in, and you fire," he said. "You aim and you fire. The guy who does this first wins, and the guy who doesn't loses." After both films, the audience applauded enthusiastically.

Later, Jones was asked by our correspondent to reflect on the deadly impact of the products his corporation manufactures. Adm. Hyman Rickover, in his farewell testimony to Congress, told legislators that he would sink all of the nuclear-powered ships whose construction he had sponsored were they not a necessary evil. Has the Northrop chairman ever had similar reservations about the wisdom of his work? "I've not had similar thoughts," Jones said with a smile. The auditorium rang with a chorus of approving shareholder laughter.

.   .   .

Wealth, power, and a certain charm bred by success allow Thomas Jones to indulge his predilection for fine food and high culture and to move effortlessly in exclusive social circles. There is also a solid business imperative woven into his elegant life-style. Jones has long been a member of the tightly knit social clique gathered around Ronald Reagan. This set of friendships has been of particular value during Reagan's years in the Oval Office. In February 1981, the Northrop chairman was the only aerospace executive invited to join in a very special celebration—the oldest president's first White House birthday party. Three months later, Jones hosted a private dinner party for Reagan at Washington's fashionable Georgetown Club. This affair brought the president back into high society for the first time since the March assassination attempt at the Washington Hilton. Jones ended the year, as he often does, with the president and his entourage at Walter Annenberg's New Year's Eve party near Palm Springs, in the California desert.

"Tom and his wife, Ruth, are dear friends of ours," said Holmes Tuttle, a California auto dealer who is a prominent member of Reagan's so-called Kitchen Cabinet. "We see him quite frequently. As a matter of fact, I saw him several times over the weekend." We spoke with Tuttle during a visit to California in the first week of January 1984.

Jones is also a member of an intriguing network of social organizations about which little is known, or can be discovered. The contacts made and friendships sealed in these fraternities have direct implications for Northrop's business. The Bohemian Club of San Francisco has been in operation for more than a hundred years. Its members include some of the most powerful figures from government and industry: Gerald Ford, William F. Buckley, Jr., Fred Hartley, Ronald Reagan, George Shultz, and Caspar Weinberger. The club conducts an annual "encampment" on three July weekends at its redwood grove north of San Francisco. These are strictly all-male affairs—even the waiters, cooks, and attendants at the encampment are men—and they are filled with speeches, seminars, and old-boy rituals. Jones attends these summer retreats with great regularity. He stays in a campsite at the grove called "Lost Angels." We spoke with a number of his Lost Angels campmates to understand this singular convocation.

"I would be happier, Tom would be happier, we would all be happier, if you just didn't say anything about Bohemian Grove," protested John Myers, a former chief test pilot and Northrop director. "I was probably one of Tom's sponsors when he got into the club four or five years ago. There is a waiting list for nonresidents about twenty-five to thirty years long. For anyone to get in, it almost takes a special act, a lot of people who are interested in seeing you join. It is preferential treatment, really."

What does the Northrop chairman do at Bohemian Grove? "Jones is as well known as most people in Lost Angels Camp," said D. Tennant Bryan, chairman of Media General Corporation of Richmond, Virginia. "He is a great philosopher, among other things. It is very comfortable [during the encampment]. You do what you want. I love to walk with him. I love to talk with him. He does both with vim and vigor. . . . And somebody always seems to be playing dominoes. It is the state pastime in California."

Albert Casey, retired chairman of American Airlines, spoke about Jones in a telephone interview from his Cape Cod home. "He knows everybody. I don't think he's a card-playing, domino [playing], drinking sort of guy," Casey said. "He's much more interested in serious conversation. . . . He's an interesting man to spend time with because he's so informed. He's always up to date, always current." Another member of Lost Angels Camp, Harry Volk, who is chairman of Union Bank of Los Angeles, explained that "people who go to Bohemian Grove, go with a commitment to make it an experience of relaxation in this redwood grove, and to avoid discussion of business as such. But you can't avoid, with a lot of bright men, talking about politics, social problems, Mexican immigration. It is a therapeutic experience for all of us."

For Jones, however, weekends such as these are more than therapy. They are the kind of meet-and-greet experience upon which he thrives. Along with about a hundred other executives from the aerospace and airline industries, the Northrop chairman also belongs to the Conquistadores del Cielo, Spanish for "Conquerors of the Sky," which meets twice a year. The forty-five-year-old organization convenes on the weekend after Labor Day at the A Bar A dude ranch near Encampment, Wyoming. Gates Learjet Corporation owns the ranch. Early members of the club actually dressed in costumes designed to resemble those worn by the original conquistadores.

"Tom is very much of an outdoorsman," said Albert Casey, who is also a Conquistador. "He is a fine horseman, good with a gun. . . . A great many of the Conquistadores enjoy outdoor activities." The spring meeting usually takes place in a Sun Belt state, often Arizona, according to Donald Douglas, Jr., secretary-treasurer and sports chairman for 1983–84. (T. A. Wilson, chairman of Boeing, was the 1984 president.) Harry Combs, a former president of Gates Learjet, insisted that the club is "absolutely, purely social. It's an interesting bunch of guys. We are all aviation people, all horsemen who like to do these sorts of [outdoor] things." Do Conquistadores talk business at the meetings? "There is no appearance of anything like that," Casey said. "These men share genuine friendships. Most of the airline executives have worked for two or three airlines, and most of the aerospace executives have worked for two or three aerospace companies. These people rotate among the different companies."

.   .   .

Throughout his career, Thomas Jones has used his talent for cementing strategic social and political alliances to supplement the performance virtues of the products he sells and keep Northrop on a growth path. A third distinguishing feature of his tenure as chief executive is the perspective on warfare and national defense he has championed for decades. The leader of any major contractor must be able to identify the strategic perils against which his weapons are designed to protect and make the case for their singular lethality. But Jones has not been content merely to parrot tired industry warnings about the Soviet threat—although he seldom misses an opportunity to do so. Since his days at Rand, he has carved out an analytical niche that often places him in conflict with accepted behavior in military production and procurement. He has not been reluctant to articulate these views publicly.

Has the Northrop chairman instituted procedures at his company that differ fundamentally from industry norms? "I don't think Tom Jones considers himself a maverick," Vice-president Les Daly replied. "He says, 'It can be better. For bureaucratic, or administrative, or inertia reasons, contracting isn't as good as it ought to be. And it can be better.' He is not some guy cutting away from the herd. He takes the herd at its word. His purpose is to galvanize the American defense industry and the American private sector to do better. He believes that, in that sense, the defense process is essentially no different from anything else. He is perhaps more outspoken than those in the mainstream."

The organizing themes of Jones's commentary have been consistent for more than two decades. He abhors the defense industry's failure to design military hardware for reliability and affordability and its obsession with technical sophistication. He has long argued on behalf of more widespread adoption of fixed-cost contracting. He has criticized other weapons manufacturers for failing to modernize their plant and equipment at a rate that keeps pace with civilian industry. We would have liked to develop these insights and criticisms more fully during the course of a personal interview. Although Jones declined, Northrop did provide a selection of speeches by the chairman that communicate his essential philosophies.

"In a period of uncertainty about the future of defense procurement or the defense budget, it was perhaps understandable if the defense industry was not held accountable for its performance, its planning, and individual enterprise in the way that other companies were," he lectured a California banking group in 1976. (Jones was referring to his days at Douglas Aviation during World War II.) "However, with the stability of the defense environment today, the defense industry must be held accountable. Individual companies must be held to their commitments. There is no longer any excuse for failing to invest in modern plant and equipment, just as any other industry does. . . . Competition must be based on the quality of a company's products, its demonstrated ability to commit to cost and schedule guarantees, and to provide sufficient financial strength to back those commitments. Those companies that respond to the challenge creatively and with a resolve to meet their commitments, will be profitable. Those that do not will deservedly fail."

The chairman made much the same point six years later in a Chicago speech before investment analysts. "One of the strongest levers that can be applied to achieve greater efficiency in the defense budget is the leverage of the private sector through technical innovation and manufacturing productivity," he said. "We have always argued that the strengths of the private sector, the entrepreneurial initiatives that have worked so successfully throughout the entire American economy, can—and *must*— be applied to meeting our defense objectives; that the free enterprise system can be used to defend the free enterprise system. We see growing recognition of this in various steps being taken by the administration and the Pentagon to improve the defense procurement system, to provide incentives for investments in productivity, and to eliminate the anachronisms that have turned out to be disincentives."

There is a heavy dose of public relations in these rhetorical exhortations. Jones has traveled the world peddling the F-5 and other weapons in the Northrop product catalogue as *the* resolution of the tension between the hearty military appetites of the Third World and its limited financial resources. His speeches and testimony on efficient procurement helped Jones recover from the scandals of the 1970s by transforming Northrop's image. But there is more to the Jones perspective on contracting than its utility as a publicity tool. He is trained as an engineer, and he proved himself at Rand to be capable of innovating new markets for the aerospace industry. By most accounts, his company makes more limited use of government-owned plant and equipment than the industry norm. Northrop owned or leased 15.8 million square feet of office and manufacturing space in 1984, of which only 2.5 percent was federal property. According to *Business Week*, the industry total is closer to 50 percent. Northrop products—with one important exception— have not been dogged by the serious defects and delays that have plagued missiles from Hughes Aircraft, semiconductors from Texas Instruments, and the Divad antiaircraft gun from Ford Aerospace.

There is no more dramatic example of Thomas Jones putting his money where his mouth is than the recent evolution of the F-20 Tigershark. Military analysts routinely describe the F-20 as the first privately funded U.S. combat aircraft in recent history. Northrop's $800 million investment in the design, production, and testing of three F-20 prototypes represents an unprecedented gamble in a world where taxpayer-financed development money can flow like water. Jones also markets the F-20 on a fixed-cost basis, unusual in the cost-plus military environment. Northrop has made a "binding commitment" to potential foreign buyers that it can deliver the plane and standard support services for $15.4 million per copy. As we have seen, Northrop's F-20 commitment has not translated into immediate sales or vast profits. The Tigershark may well represent the marketing challenge of Jones's career. But it remains by any standard a notable chapter in the history of military aircraft development.

It is also important not to overstate the singularity of Northrop under its current chairman. The company has hung with the industry pack in opposition to legislation sponsored by Republican senator Mark Andrews that requires the Pentagon to secure written warranties when it buys new weapons systems. The Andrews legislation was approved in 1983. Critics charge that the Defense Department, which joined contractors in opposition to the proposal, has since issued enforcement regulations that dilute its impact.

"Warranties are nuts," Les Daly told us. "You buy a TV set, you throw the warranty in a drawer, and you never look at that warranty for ten years. Why? Because the guy built the TV set to work. You don't even think about the warranty. What you wanted was a TV set that worked —not a warranty. . . . Here I like to say that we put the engineers to work at the beginning so the lawyers won't go to work at the end. Jones and Northrop use the levers of the economic system to get that airplane to work. Warranties miss the point. And they confuse the point. Warranties are for lawyers. Warranties are almost a narcotic that make you think you've got something that works. We've got something better [with the F-20]—a fixed price per flying hour for spare parts—that puts the incentive on the manufacturer. He should have the determination and the incentive to make the parts very reliable. That's what you want, a low-cost, reliable system. We don't think that an insurance system is going to give you what you want. If there's a battle, we want to be able to have the generals call up the pilots, not the lawyers. Northrop thinks that warranties are the last act. Northrop thinks the incentives are better [when] built into the system."

Jones's exercise in "free enterprise" defense contracting also has made use of many of the ongoing—and largely unseen—public subsidies that are an integral part of the aerospace industry. One example on this score is a Pentagon program called Independent Research and Development (IR&D). Under this program, the Defense Department grants a firm about 5 percent of the value of its military contracts to pursue research ventures of its own choosing. IR&D is basically a built-in federal dole to military contractors. According to a 1981 study by Gordon Adams of the New York–based Council on Economic Priorities, these research subsidies have been of particular importance to Northrop. Between 1973 and 1978 Northrop received $112.5 million under the program. This level of support, when compared with the $173.1 million worth of company-sponsored research and development disclosed in Northrop financial statements, produced the second highest ratio of government subsidy to company research among fifteen of the largest defense contractors.

Our attempts through the Freedom of Information Act to secure data for the period 1979–83 were denied by the Pentagon. The Defense Department has adopted a procedure under which it asks contractors their opinion of what should remain confidential before releasing company-specific information. After consulting with the contractors, the Department chose not to release the data.

Northrop's opposition to warranties and its use of IR&D funds pale in comparison with the track record of its largest manufacturing project, which stands as a contradiction of its chairman's efficiency-minded creed. The Navy's F-18 Hornet was approved for full-scale development in December 1975. It was meant to serve as a low-cost replacement for aging fighters and attack aircraft. Instead, the dual-mission Hornet has experienced a decade of production delays and cost overruns. Pentagon analysts estimated a decade ago that they could buy a fleet of eight hundred F-18s for a total of $11 billion—less than $14 million per plane. By September 1982 Navy secretary John Lehman was threatening to cancel the program unless Northrop and McDonnell Douglas lowered their price from $24 million to $22.5 million. The Pentagon now plans to purchase nearly fourteen hundred F-18s. The total cost of the program is expected to reach $40 billion—nearly $30 million per plane.

The Hornet has also experienced defects serious enough to have convinced Canada and the United States to ground or restrict their squadrons for several months. Cracks developed in the Northrop-produced tail assembly during the summer of 1984. An outraged Caspar Weinberger insisted that McDonnell Douglas, prime contractor on the F-18, underwrite the repairs out of a contingency fund. The episode cost McDonnell Douglas an estimated $25 million. Throughout its testing period the F-18 experienced problems with leaking fuel cells. The number four fuel cell, located in the center of the fuselage, which Northrop builds, had to be replaced fourteen times in the first nineteen hundred hours of testing.

A number of factors have contributed to this sorry price and quality performance. Inflation during the 1970s outpaced the projections of Defense Department forecasters. Design changes postponed the delivery of aircraft and thus increased their cost. But there is little question that the manufacturers of the F-18 must bear primary responsibility for its troubled history. Excerpts from a series of reports published after investigations by the General Accounting Office (GAO) capture the scale of Northrop's contribution to the F-18 fiasco:

- Northrop Corporation manufactures and assembles the F/A-18 center and aft sections; however, it underestimated the amount of time to do this. For example, to build the full-scale development aircraft sections, Northrop spent more than twice as many assembly hours as originally expected. Consequently, all costs went up. Not only was the additional assembly time costly to Northrop, but its inability to deliver needed aircraft parts caused costly delays to the F/A-18 flight test program. As of October 26, 1979, the estimated program cost growth incurred by Northrop was $159 million. (February 14, 1980)
- Delivery of each developmental aircraft was late an average of 2 months, thus contributing to the flight test program delay. The total program setback caused by the delivery delays, according to the Navy, is from 2 to 3 months.
  Late deliveries were primarily attributed to Northrop's production problems, as indicated by the results of Navy reviews and comments by various officials at Northrop, McDonnell, and the Navy. They felt that Northrop underestimated the production requirements for the F/A-18. Northrop estimated 67,500 production hours per developmental aircraft but actually took between 93,000 and 147,000 hours per aircraft. Contributing to Northrop's production problems were poor plant layout; required major redesign of the F/A-18's environmental control system for improved maintainability; and recurring problems with fit, access, and leakage of the F/A-18's fuel cells. (February 14, 1980)
- Northrop has been experiencing difficulty in installing the vertical tails. As the tails are installed, shims are individually machined to fit between the vertical tail tabs and the aircraft's frame. The problem lies in the difficulty of measuring the gaps so that the shims can be machined to within acceptable tolerance.

To assure proper shimming, Northrop currently has a team that performs special measurements on each vertical tail installed. If the measurements are not within specifications, the vertical tail shimming must be corrected. Northrop officials informed us that although no tail assemblies are being shipped out with improper shimming, this is a time consuming and costly process. They said that tools are being improved to correct installation difficulties, and plans are underway to automate the shim machining process. (February 18, 1981)

• Although F/A-18 production performance appears to be improving, manufacturing problems continue to cause cost increases. For example, Northrop's major production problem has been ensuring that the proper parts reached their assigned place on the production line at the proper time. This creates added concern when considering that most of the parts involved are built by Northrop. While Northrop's parts problem has improved in recent months, it still continues, requiring that some assembly line work be performed out of sequence. This contributes to cost overruns.

According to Navy officials, the contractors will have more incentive to control costs in the future because the 1982 F/A-18 airframe and engine contracts are firm-fixed price. (June 10, 1983)

The selection of speeches we were provided by Northrop suggests that its chairman has not conceded publicly that the F-18 is a monument to the brand of inefficient contracting he denigrates. On several occasions Jones has actually trumpeted the virtues of the Hornet. "The objective was for the F-18 to have three times the reliability and one-half the maintenance required by the F-4J and A-7 aircraft that it was to replace," he boasted on June 13, 1984. "Reports of its fleet operations indicate that the F-18 is meeting this objective." One month later the navy issued fleet-wide restrictions on certain flight maneuvers as a result of the tail cracks. On July 30, 1984, the navy stopped taking delivery of new F-18s until the defect was corrected.

. . .

The development and shifting fortunes of another Northrop aircraft, the F-20 Tigershark, illuminate many of the themes that have characterized Thomas Jones's long career in the aerospace sector. Its distinction as the first privately financed fighter in recent history is in keeping with

Northrop's niche in the industry. Its roller-coaster history of potential marketing breakthroughs and outright rejection by otherwise faithful Northrop customers testify to the range of pressures and forces under which a military contractor operates. The zeal with which Chairman Jones has promoted his pet aircraft in Washington and overseas recalls his early days at Northrop, when he beat the bushes on behalf of a fighter, the F-5 Tiger, that was still on the drawing board. Jones has deployed a remarkable range of weapons in his campaign to sell the Tigershark— congressional maneuvers, access to the White House, strategic media relations, and the cultivation of alliances with the leadership of potential foreign customers, such as Taiwan—that captures his tactical savvy and flexibility.

Northrop's F-20 was born in the wake of a major shift in U.S. foreign policy. The Carter administration came to power convinced of the need to limit transfers of sophisticated arms to the Third World, particularly when the introduction of new weapons could fuel regional arms races. The White House understood that many governments were anxious to replace squadrons of F-5s or to graduate into new fighter aircraft. It also wanted to restrict the proliferation of top-of-the-line fighters, such as the F-16. The State Department unveiled its solution to this dilemma in January 1980. Under its so-called F-X policy (F-X stands for fighter export) the administration announced that it would approve sales of a new "intermediate" fighter designed strictly for shipment overseas. "Intermediate" was defined as an aircraft with capabilities in between the capabilities of Northrop's F-5E and the General Dynamics F-16. Because the plane was to be designed for international sales, the administration announced it would provide no financing for research and development.

The F-X decision was precisely the sort of challenge one might expect Northrop to accept given its profitable history as a manufacturer of export fighters and its chairman's rhetorical posture on defense contracting. The company did rise to the occasion. It had begun engineering and design work on a successor to the F-5E in 1977. The Carter policy created just the right environment for a major push on this new-generation fighter. Investment in development of the F-20, which until 1982 was known as the F-5G, soared during the late 1970s and early 1980s. Wall Street registered its approval. The company's stock rose from $40 a share to $56 a share within three weeks of the F-X declaration. Northrop's fortunes as a manufacturer of fighter aircraft suited to the unique demands of the Third World were about to experience a renaissance.

Or so it seemed. Unrestrained enthusiasm about the future of the Tigershark gave way to bitterness and frustration within only two years. The election of Ronald Reagan, a turn of events celebrated by his good friend Thomas Jones, brought to power an administration that did not share Jimmy Carter's instincts for restraint on arms transfers to the Third World. Although the White House did not overturn the F-X policy, it soon abandoned its spirit. The United States agreed in 1981 to supply Pakistan with F-16 Fighting Falcons, a deal that whet the appetites of other Third World generals. The State Department then agreed to sell the glamorous fighter to Venezuela, Korea, and Egypt—all thought to be prime candidates for the less-powerful Tigershark. Jones came to understand that the environment in which he was working to sell the F-20 had changed fundamentally. No episode better illustrates Northrop's vulnerability to U.S. foreign policy considerations than the demise of its plans for a door-opening sale to Taiwan.

The Republic of China is one of Northrop's crowning success stories as well as one of its most bitter disappointments. Not only did the company sell a substantial number of planes on the island—the Taiwanese air force operated approximately 320 F-5s by 1982, more than any other country—but Northrop and Taiwan actually coproduced portions of the fighter in local plants. The island nation soon became the quintessential Tigershark candidate. Its pilots and technicians had logged thousands of flying and maintenance hours with the F-5. Its generals were thirsting to amass more air power in response to perceived threats from the People's Republic. Its relative prosperity meant it could afford the more expensive fighter.

The State Department and the Pentagon recommended in August 1978 that Taiwan be allowed to co-produce Northrop's F-5G as a successor to the F-5E arrangement, which was due to expire in 1980. Leonard Unger, the last U.S. ambassador to Taiwan (he served from 1974 to 1978) is now a professor at the Fletcher School of International Law and Diplomacy. He explained the situation in Taiwan. "We thought some kind of follow-on [to the F-5E] was necessary," he told us. "I'm sure that at the time industry people were going through the back door to people in Taiwan while we were discussing the possibility with the Taiwanese. The idea was to increase the [production] role on Taiwan. We saw Jones on a fair number of occasions, but there were no lengthy negotiations we took part in. Jones did take a very active interest in it—more than other executives. I remember his being there when I was meeting with the local chamber-of-commerce folks."

Northrop's hopes for a victory with the F-5G were quickly dashed. President Carter decided to table co-production plans two months after he received favorable recommendations from State and the Pentagon. Washington approved the sale of forty-eight more F-5Es in November as a gesture of consolation. There was no great mystery to the Northrop setback. The United States was poised to establish full diplomatic relations with Beijing. It had no interest in antagonizing the People's Republic with a major weapons sale to its offshore adversary.

The demise of the F-5G in 1978 was Northrop's first disappointment on Taiwan. Fifteen months later, when Carter unveiled his F-X policy, the administration once again authorized Northrop to begin talks with Taiwan about the new fighter. The discussions went nowhere. Then came Ronald Reagan, whose years of rhetoric on the evils of communist China and the righteousness of the Taiwanese buoyed Northrop's hopes for its F-5G. Again it was not to be.

Congressional leaders voiced doubts about the wisdom of alienating an important new ally by supplying fighters to a country whose air force was already capable of defending it. Military analysts consider the F-5E more than a match for the Soviet-designed MiG-21, China's best fighter. Members of the House Subcommittee on Asian and Pacific Affairs sent a letter to President Reagan on June 18, 1981, that communicated their disapproval of any F-X sale. It argued,

> Even in terms of the air balance itself, the F-5E, which is the current mainstay of the Taiwanese air force, is technically superior to any of the combat aircraft in the PRC air force. And, even if we were to upgrade the Taiwanese air force by selling them the FX, the chances are that the PRC would still be able to achieve air superiority given the enormous quantitative advantages they have, assuming they were prepared to accept the enormous losses that would inevitably be inflicted upon them. To the extent that the Taiwanese do have a substantial number of planes in their present inventory that will soon become obsolete, we can and should extend our coproduction agreement with Taiwan for the F-5Es which they already have, thereby enabling them to replace the planes they will be retiring without introducing a new generation of military aircraft into the region. In short, Mr. President, it seems to us that, from a purely military perspective, the FX is neither needed nor necessary for the defense of Taiwan at this time.

Congressman Mervyn Dymally, whose southern California district is home to Northrop's largest manufacturing plant, signed the letter to Reagan. He told us that Jones visited his office to express his displeasure —one of only two times the Northrop chairman has met personally with him since his election in 1980. But Dymally's position on Taiwan was the least of Jones's worries. Even the Reagan administration came to understand that the diplomatic costs of approving F-5G shipments would far outweight any benefits in terms of increased Taiwanese military power. The State Department announced in January 1982 that Taiwan would be permitted to buy still more F-5E fighter planes—but no advanced aircraft. Thomas Jones was foiled again.

Northrop's fruitless work on behalf of a fighter sale to Taiwan sapped the momentum of the Tigershark program. But even had that sale gone through, new clouds were beginning to loom on the horizon. It became clear in the early 1980s that Carter's F-X policy was based on a flawed premise. Third World allies were simply not prepared to buy fighters whose capabilities were inferior—or perceived to be inferior—to the capabilities of more sophisticated aircraft in the U.S. arsenal. The status imperative in the arms industry had taken on a new wrinkle. Poor countries were insisting on weapons as lethal and costly as those available in the West. Thomas Jones was quick to appreciate this debilitating variable in the arms-sales equation. He thus set out on a new campaign: to sell the Tigershark to the U.S. Air Force. The Northrop chairman was not anxious for a domestic sale of the F-20, a market that was never envisioned when the plane was on the drawing board, primarily to generate direct revenues. Rather, inclusion of the Tigershark in U.S. squadrons would imbue the fighter with a degree of credibility and prestige in the eyes of Third World generals that it does not now hold.

Jones has waged an all-fronts campaign to secure a domestic sale. His earliest efforts involved Capitol Hill maneuvering to win the F-20 a place in the Air Force Aggressor Squadron. The Aggressor Squadron is a fleet of aircraft that are used in combat training to simulate attacks by Soviet fighters. For years the squadron was composed of F-5s. From 1981 through 1984 there were at least two serious efforts to modernize the Aggressor Squadron by acquiring new aircraft from Northrop. In neither case did the Tigershark initiatives come from the air force itself. A former Washington lobbyist for General Electric, which manufactures the engine for the Tigershark, described the first episode. "In August of 1981, at a big National Security Council meeting in California, President Reagan turned to some of his advisors and basically said, 'Let's see what we can do about getting the F-5G into the air force inventory,' " he told us. "The administration started to make an effort in the Office of Management and Budget (OMB) to get money and stick the F-5G into the Aggressor Squadron. About $180 million went into the budget. The air force was absolutely apoplectic about this. They felt the F-5G inclusion would make it go more toward quantity as opposed to quality. They fought it tooth and nail.

"John Tower sent a letter over from Congress to the air force and to

Weinberger stating that he felt if there was going to be any new Aggressor aircraft, there should be a competition, which means that the F-16/J79 should be considered as well," the former lobbyist continued. (General Dynamics builds this fighter in the home state of the retired Texas senator.) "While all this was going on, somebody leaked a story to a newspaper reporter that Ed Meese and Tom Jones were implicated together in this. It looked like something shady, with a big political favor going to Tom Jones. As soon as it happened, when it got public and implicated some administration officials, it put a little pressure on the president. Boom, the money was gone."

The article to which the lobbyist referred appeared on page one of the *Washington Post* on January 12, 1982. It described the Northrop chairman's long friendship with the president and his advisors. "Thomas V. Jones, chairman and chief executive of Northrop, has known Reagan on a social basis," reporter George Wilson wrote. "He attended, for example, the New Year's eve party at Palm Springs, Calif., given by publisher Walter Annenberg for Reagan. [Defense secretary] Weinberger and Secretary of State Alexander M. Haig Jr. were among the Cabinet members at that party. A spokesman for the Northrop executive said he has no way of knowing whether business has been discussed between Jones and Reagan and other White House officials in social settings." The article also quoted a disgruntled Pentagon source. "This administration feels obligated to help Northrop with its F-5G," the Pentagon official said. "That's why we're trying to find a way to use it even though the Air Force doesn't want it."

Northrop managed to bounce back two summers later. Chairman Jones traveled to Washington and explained his F-20 predicament to California senator Pete Wilson. He apparently made an effective presentation. Wilson soon began a series of maneuvers in a Senate armed-services subcommittee to secure additional funding for the Aggressor Squadron. He made little secret of the fact that he hoped the F-20 would be the squadron's agent of modernization.

A Wilson aide spoke with us in June 1984 and described what transpired. "Tom Jones visited our office last summer," he said. "He told Pete about the F-20: its history, the F-X policy, the near-sale to Taiwan under the Carter administration, and the near-sale to Taiwan under the Reagan administration. This was in August. He suggested that he had received private encouragement from both administration and Pentagon officials. He said Northrop thought the plane was best used for foreign military sales, but it now looked like it was going to require the U.S. government and U.S. Air Force stamp of approval. Pete talked with the president, who listened carefully. But the [fiscal 1985 defense-spending authorization] bill came over without the Aggressor aircraft in it. Pete made it clear that he would only offer an amendment [to the bill] that gave no direction toward Northrop, but with the expectation and hope that Northrop would get the contract."

Wilson's amendment would have added $150 million to the 1985 defense authorization to finance new fighters for the Aggressor Squadron. His proposal met strong opposition from a number of senators, and Wilson agreed to drop it in return for allocating additional funds to the navy's version of the Aggressor Squadron. But even this compromise was of little assistance to Northrop. The navy disclosed in September 1984 that it would lease Israeli Kfirs for use in combat training. Four months later it announced that it would add to its squadron by purchasing fourteen General Dynamics F-16s, a plane only the air force had flown, for $155 million.

. . .

The F-20 represents a wager by Thomas Jones of $800 million. But the fighter is nothing like the inexpensive, bare-bones Northrop aircraft of previous decades. The Tigershark is a compelling piece of evidence that the company has come full circle under its current chairman. Northrop's revenues have increased tenfold since Jones took command in 1960. Its profits have grown even more dramatically. Whether through an extensive network of foreign agents that reported to him, or through skillful maneuvering on Capitol Hill, Jones has met nearly every challenge and overcome every crisis that has crossed his desk. Pentagon analysts are even betting that his frustrating campaign on behalf of the F-20 may bear fruit before long. If so, Thomas Jones will have snatched victory from the jaws of near-certain defeat.

Northrop has been able to force the Tigershark issue as a result of the atmosphere of scandal and mistrust that has plagued General Dynamics since reports of kickbacks and cost overruns at the company surfaced in early 1984. Jones sensed that a window of opportunity had opened. Northrop officials began complaining bitterly in the media and before Congress about unfair treatment at the hands of the Pentagon. Jones himself testified in March 1984 that the air force was not pushing hard enough to explain the capabilities of the Tigershark to potential foreign customers. The company worked feverishly to set off a stream of favorable publicity. *The Atlantic* devoted many thousands of words to the story of "The Airplane That Doesn't Cost Enough." The curious thesis of the article, which drew a sharp reply from Defense secretary Weinberger, was that the Defense Department was refusing to buy the F-20 because it was not expensive enough. Procurement of the Northrop fighter thus would draw attention to the bloated budgets that fund other aircraft.

Sixty Minutes chimed in one month later with another glowing testimonial. All three major newspapers—the *New York Times*, the *Wall Street Journal*, the *Washington Post*—wrote spirited editorials in 1984 and 1985 on the virtues of the F-20. Why this outpouring of sympathetic media attention? Because Northrop has managed to miscast the plight of the F-20 as a case study in Defense Department parochialism. It has portrayed the Tigershark as an affordable complement to the F-16 Falcon that the Pentagon has ignored for reasons of pride or prejudice. Much of the national press has bought this argument.

But Jones and his newfound allies in Congress and the media overlook a number of salient facts. The F-20 was never designed to be purchased by the air force. The U.S. government never suggested it planned to buy it. The Tigershark was manufactured in response to the Carter administration's F-X—fighter export—policy. Should U.S. taxpayers now spend billions of dollars on F-20s so that Northrop can acquire the prestige its fighter needs to generate interest in the Third World? Moreover, the air force contracted for the F-16 only after the plane won a flyoff against a competing fighter. That prototype, the YF-17, was a Northrop model. Jones's April 1985 offer to sell 396 Tigersharks—a proposal the air force is said to be seriously considering—in effect represents a second bite at the air force apple. Such competition is welcome and healthy from the perspective of beleaguered taxpayers. But Northrop's bid should not be perceived, as it has been in much of the press, as a breathtaking departure from the contracting status quo.

A review of Jones's strategy and tactics does not adequately describe and define the human reality of his work. There is a distinction to be drawn between the life of a military contractor and that of any other kind of businessman—a distinction that Jones's business success serves only to obscure. Northrop has not prospered by delivering goods and services that enrich life. Its guiding imperative has been to deliver implements of destruction to and through the United States government. One can imagine that the attributes its chairman has demonstrated throughout his long career—ease of circulation among countries and cultures, an intensity and energy, a capacity to find a niche in a complex industry that others could not—might have been adaptable to promote peace through communication rather than armed confrontation.

With the F-20, it is becoming clear that even his role as a many-gauged force for position in the narrower world of military contracting has begun to erode. Other contractors have observed the Jones style of success and pursue it in a way that diminishes his singularity, even as it pays indirect tribute to his effective modes of operation. Having cast new molds of doing business and winning business, Jones appears content to fill them with as many dollars of profit as possible.

Given his refusal to be interviewed, and the fact that his refusal extends to company associates and subordinates as well, there is no way of knowing what new horizons, if any, Jones has established. He is not persuaded that the chief executive of a defense-industry company—whose bills are paid overwhelmingly by the taxpayer and which is inherently imbued with an obligation for public accountability—needs to answer responsible public inquiries. Whatever the gaps in understanding this driven, privately gregarious but publicly reclusive man, his legacy is likely to have few heirs inside the company. In contrast to the institutionalized industry practices he has helped to shape, Jones has left Northrop in a situation similar to the plight of a business run by a founder who cannot recruit strong successors or provide for a rational process of corporate succession.

The chairman's dominance inside his company does not bode well for a large corporation shouldering central military construction and research responsibilities. Weapons systems are not easily reassigned when the highly centralized management drive reposited in one chief executive disappears. Without provision for stable managerial transfer, Jones's "indispensable man" style of management can be considered something of a national security risk.

The nineteenth-century British legal historian Henry Maine wrote that the progress of civilization is marked by the evolution from transactions based on social position to transactions based on contracts. "The society of our day is mainly distinguished from that of preceding generations by the largeness of the sphere which is occupied in it by Contract. . . ." he wrote in his treatise *Ancient Law*. "Not many of us are so unobservant as not to perceive that in innumerable cases where old law fixed a man's social position irreversibly at his birth, modern law allows him to create it for himself by convention." Northrop's Thomas Jones has carved out a twentieth-century reversal of this dictum. He has choreographed an intricate ballet of corporate status in his company's relationship to governments that transcends its corporate contracts. Know-who is bigger than know-how and, in Jones's strategic approach, is the mother's milk of know-how. Know-who brings the contracts, and when they come, Jones can always hire the know-how.

A private man directing a public company built on the sometimes sandy soil of tax dollars can easily lose touch with future organizational needs because of an overriding personal involvement in the present. When that characteristic is coupled with an insulation from public access, Thomas Jones runs the risk of having festering conditions in his company mount, when a normal public spotlight would have caught them in the bud. Given Jones's closed-door policy, far beyond the structures of military security, only time will tell whether his biggest gamble was with a company known as Northrop Corporation.

WILLIAM
McGOWAN

Monopoly Breaker

On August 9, 1972, William McGowan, chairman and chief executive officer of MCI Communications, and John deButts, chairman and chief executive officer of American Telephone and Telegraph (AT&T), met for the first time in New York City. But for their titles, the two men had very little in common.

The AT&T chairman, fifty-seven, was the consummate organization man and a courtly southern gentleman. Born in Greensboro, North Carolina, he graduated from the Virginia Military Institute in 1936 and that very summer began work with a Bell system affiliate. He became chairman of AT&T in April 1972. McGowan, son of a Pennsylvania railroad engineer and union organizer, graduated in 1954 from Harvard Business School. He turned down job offers from three major corporations (Westinghouse, Continental Oil, and Container Corporation of America) to pursue an eclectic series of ventures that took him from movie production to specialty handbags. He did not enter the world of telecommunications until he founded MCI at age forty.

The conversation went on for roughly two hours and was, at least on the surface, proper and cordial. At times, however, tensions developed. DeButts was chairman of an organization known as "the largest corporation on earth." From the twenty-sixth floor of AT&T headquarters, where the two men met, he supervised a communications empire with revenues in 1972 of nearly $21 billion—generated largely from local and long-distance calls placed on the more than 105 million Bell telephones then in service. But deButts inherited control at a time when the comfortable world in which AT&T had thrived for so many decades was beginning to unravel. Service in major urban centers was faltering. The company's performance on Wall Street was mediocre. Morale among its 1 million employees was sagging. The gradual unfolding of a new regulatory climate was jeopardizing the monopoly status that for decades had defined

AT&T's existence and the structure of telecommunications in the United States.

Two landmark decisions issued before deButts took power had shaken the Bell empire to its foundation. The Federal Communications Commission (FCC) declared in its 1968 Carterfone ruling that the blanket prohibition against attaching non-Bell additions—switchboards, answering machines, and so on—to Bell phone lines was unreasonable. Carterfone amounted to a preliminary birth certificate for companies looking to manufacture telephone equipment to compete with or supplement equipment produced by Western Electric, AT&T's manufacturing arm. Three years later, in the Specialized Common Carrier decision, the FCC approved competition in the provision of one form of long-distance communications —private-line services. Private lines are essential to high-volume users of long distance (corporations, government agencies, hospitals) and for specific communication needs, such as dedicated telephone links between a main office and regional sales outposts.

By August 1972, fourteen months after the ruling that authorized its existence, MCI was still more a proposal than a functioning corporation. The company, which was established in 1968, leased three floors of office space in Washington, D.C. From this command post, William McGowan directed the activities of ninety-five employees and eleven "expert consultants." But with the proceeds of a public stock offering, a multibank line of credit worth $64 million, and additional millions from private placements, MCI had raised more than $110 million—at the time, the largest start-up financing in Wall Street history. The company planned to begin construction of a thirty-four-city system that included New York, Atlanta, Saint Louis, and Los Angeles. A new era of competition in telecommunications had begun. John deButts knew he was meeting with someone determined that it continue. According to McGowan, a portion of the conversation went like this:

DeButts: A problem for us is the reaction of the investment community. We have tried to convince them that the company deserves better treatment but they react emotionally. Every research analyst recommends that they buy [AT&T], but we still go down. Last week we had a meeting with a hundred and fifty analysts and said very strongly that we were going to compete for this new business and they reacted very favorably. A number of them came up and said, "It's about time." As a matter of fact, my last meeting with stockholders was received very well because of my statements about competition. If we hold next year's annual meeting as planned, we will have ten thousand stockholders there, and I must say to them that we will compete vigorously.

McGowan: I don't understand why you need to be that aggressive. Why don't you tell them the facts—that is, there is no way [MCI] will have the majority of any future business, and as a matter of fact the specialized carriers will not only be serving a very tiny market, but by aggressively promoting the industry could even help you.

DeButts: We tried to do that in the Carterfone case. After that decision we announced that it would be good for us, but the investors did not believe it and we can't do that with you. You must understand that the investors react emotionally and not logically. They are convinced that competition will hurt us and I have no choice in this area but to be very explicit about our competitive posture. I have many friends and contacts on Wall Street and I have asked them, "Why does our stock sell so low and why does the public refuse to support us in the [financial] market?" They most frequently mention you as the reason.

Immediately upon conclusion of the meeting, William McGowan went to an office where he had access to a secretary, and dictated a twenty-one-page transcript of the conversation—a transcript that makes it possible to reconstruct the events of August 9. John deButts did not even bother to take notes.

.   .   .

It is the spring of 1984. William McGowan is seated in a conference room on the twelfth floor of MCI's Washington, D.C. headquarters. His surroundings breathe nouveau-riche prosperity. The wood is blond. The lighting is recessed. The conference table has a black top and is surrounded by black leather chairs with stainless steel arms. Behind McGowan are five gold statuettes, including several Clios, that have been awarded to the company for its colorful and smart-alecky advertising campaigns. McGowan grinned as he recalled his first encounter with the now-retired leader of AT&T. Since his 1972 confrontation with deButts, the chairman of MCI has taken on—and helped to take apart—one of the most powerful corporations in the world.

The date of McGowan's final triumph can be fixed precisely: on January 1, 1984 AT&T began a new existence stripped of its twenty-two local operating companies, whose combined assets exceed $100 billion, and the prized Bell name and logo. The breakup of AT&T has left the company smaller and less powerful, although with revenues in 1984 of $33 billion and assets of $40 billion, it remains a huge corporation by any standard. More to the point, dissolution of the Bell System is a watershed in the restructuring of telecommunications in the United States. It represents a decisive chapter in the introduction of an era of competition in the industry, an era whose roots lay in FCC decisions issued during the period in which McGowan and deButts first met. Competition has encouraged the proliferation of new products, new services, and new companies. It has also raised the worrisome prospect of convulsive changes in the pricing and universal availability of telephone service. And it represents a decisive personal victory for the chairman of MCI, who relishes any opportunity to cast doubt on the prospects of his humbled competitor.

"The future of AT&T is [un]clear, because they have got a manufactured-equipment company which frankly is not very good," he told us. "Western Electric lived too long on the monopoly business. Therefore, it has never learned to compete. I have been trying to buy something from Western Electric for two years. And they have been trying to sell us something. Do you think we can get something? I said to our guys, 'Why don't you buy some copper wire?' I was trying to announce [a purchase] to show that the [new] system makes sense"—here his voice rose—"that even MCI is buying [from AT&T], right?" Then he whispered. "Too expensive. Costs too much."

The chairman of MCI could elaborate for hours on the shortcomings of AT&T management. He criticized the company's personnel policies and customer relations. He even poked fun at Bell Labs, AT&T's respected research arm, whose scientists have collected seven Nobel Prizes in physics. "About ninety-five percent of the employees of Bell Laboratories should be put into an engineering department at Western Electric," McGowan argued. "The Bell Labs scientists design [telecommunications] equipment, and not very well. Maybe five percent of the guys at Bell Labs are doing basic scientific research, staring at their navels and worrying about the content of follicles. That's kind of like AT&T's advertising budget. It's great for them and it's helped the country. But you know, they're kidding themselves to pretend that they are something different than that."

McGowan often extends his biting commentary to American business as a whole. "We are a very individualistically oriented company," he said of MCI. "We really look for people who are individuals. We look for people who aren't seeking a home, who do their own bit, who want to be rewarded or damned depending upon the results [of their work]. We are not a very family-oriented business. A lot of companies are very interested in that. They have all kinds of things for family, and they believe that they should. We don't have any of that. We don't have Christmas parties. As a matter of fact, we don't allow family members to join the business. If somebody's here, that's it.

"We try to have the minimum amount of guidelines," he continued. "We don't have rules and regulations, we don't have systems and procedures. It is the worst thing American business has ever done. As a matter of fact, you could probably run a damn good business by figuring out how quote, an American corporation does things, and doing the opposite. We do it that way. Anytime I have a decision that relates to people or organization, I try to figure out how the typical American corporation would do it, and then I do it the other way. And it works. Because everyone in these corporations has figured out how *not* to do everything."

There is an undeniable touch of hubris in the MCI leader's ruminations on AT&T and his Fortune 500 colleagues. ("You won't find anyone in the world who has a bigger ego," one early MCI investor told us.) But McGowan claims to have built a prosperous enterprise based on his unorthodox management principles. He presides over a corporation with revenues in 1984 of nearly $2 billion—29 percent greater than its revenues in 1983 and more than seventeen times its sales five years earlier. The company is the nation's largest, and best known, long-distance competitor of AT&T. In 1984 its network of microwave towers, optical-fiber, and satellite transponders covered almost 80 percent of the United States and serviced 1.8 million residential customers. It also supported more than 360,000 business customers, including many of the country's largest corporations, who purchase long-distance voice, WATS lines, data transmission facilities, and a range of other communications services.

By virtue of its established network and explosive growth since 1980, MCI is recognized as the leading force among the group of companies —GTE Sprint, ITT, and Allnet—that will continue to draw millions of customers, and billions of dollars, away from AT&T. And MCI is expanding the reach and capacity of its network much faster than any of its non-AT&T competitors. This construction agenda cost $1.2 billion in 1984 and more than $900 million in 1985. MCI put into service in March 1984 a 240-mile system of single-mode fiber optics between Washington, D.C., and New York. With fiber optics, information travels via light waves. A laser emits pulses of light at a rate of 405 million per second through hair-thin glass cables. MCI's New York–Washington route is the longest and highest-capacity single-mode system in the world. Each pair of these cables, and there are twenty-two pairs, can transmit six thousand simultaneous voice conversations.

.   .   .

To be sure, for all its expansion in recent years, MCI is still a gangly upstart when compared with its major competitor. The firm accounts for perhaps 6 percent of the market for long-distance communications. The chairman told us MCI will not achieve "critical mass" until it controls 10 percent of the market. AT&T holds roughly 85 percent. But size and market share do not begin to describe the role and power of MCI in its industry. What gives particular gravity to the career of William Mc-Gowan, and what distinguishes MCI from most other entrepreneurial breakthroughs, is the range of second-level consequences associated with or precipitated by the birth of the company. It would be an overstatement to suggest that McGowan is single-handedly responsible for the demise of the Bell System. But it is fair to say that no single individual played a more decisive role in this profound transformation.

The continued expansion of MCI, and its chairman's emergence as a visible and respected figure in telecommunications, has created a base for continued impact on the pace and direction of industry change. MCI can innovate products and services, promote the growth of upstart equipment suppliers and new technologies, and intervene in the regulatory process to balance the enormous presence of AT&T. Or it can settle into the comfortable role of the also-ran, deferring to AT&T on price and service and maintaining enough management discipline to maintain cost and profit advantages over its flat-footed rival. How the company and its leader choose to exercise their unique leverage powers will be a decisive factor in determining whether competition, advocated for so many years by McGowan, becomes a road to more creative and affordable communications, or a path to needless confusion and inequity.

The AT&T divestiture agreement, which was initialed on January 8, 1982, and implemented with important modifications two years later, resolved federal antitrust charges filed on November 20, 1974. The settlement was the product of the advances in technology that made obsolete the monopoly structure that governed telecommunications, the rise to power in Congress of procompetition legislators, and the increasing dissatisfaction with the regulatory status quo among members of the FCC. The experiences of MCI set in motion certain forces, and accelerated others, that galvanized this antimonopoly consensus. Rulings issued by the FCC in the early seventies as a result of filings by MCI, or opposition by MCI to filings by AT&T, set the stage for competition. Court decisions later in the decade, in cases where McGowan and his company were at odds with the commission, extended its scope. The sheer survival of the company, during a period when many other would-be rivals collapsed, reassured legislators and regulators of the feasibility of competition. The government lawsuit itself was shaped in important ways by the history of MCI's relations with AT&T. McGowan and his colleagues documented patterns of illegal AT&T behavior, collected material and insights from the field, and turned their information and expertise over to government lawyers.

Washington attorney Philip Verveer, lead counsel in the AT&T case for the Justice Department from 1973 to 1977, described to us the degree of cooperation early on between MCI, which had filed antitrust charges of its own against AT&T six months before the government suit, and staff attorneys in Justice, who initially focused their investigation on the conduct of Western Electric. "A tremendous amount of the [Justice] Department's case was in fact based on the spadework that MCI's attorneys had done," Verveer told us. "I don't think the department's investigation relied on MCI for political impetus. But what MCI allowed us to do was to give the case a running start. The company provided us with an educational background. In addition, the controversies it was having [with AT&T] kind of fueled the department."

The history of MCI over the past five years has been one of spectacular growth. Our conversations with William McGowan, which were conducted in four sessions over fourteen months, took place under circumstances that capture just how fragile the company's status remains. The long-distance market is characterized by relentless cost pressures, aggressive pricing and saturation marketing by the industry leader, and turmoil in the legal and regulatory environment. MCI can look forward to several years of profit squeeze. Earnings in 1984 actually declined, to under $60 million from more than $200 million in 1983, even as revenues soared. The ongoing pressures associated with lean profits are magnified by investor uncertainty and speculation in MCI stock. MCI has been the most actively traded issue in the over-the-counter market (OTC) for each of the last four years. Its stock price can soar or plummet whenever regulators or the courts issue a decision that may affect the company's competitive position.

On August 23, 1983, for example, a staggering 16.5 million MCI shares changed hands, an OTC record, when the FCC ruled that MCI and other AT&T competitors would have to substantially increase their payments for connections to the local telephone network. MCI's stock price dropped 26 percent. So-called access charges are the largest single expense in long-distance transmission, and investors correctly perceived that a government-ordered increase in the fees would be a blow to the company's profit forecasts. This precipitous decline took place less than one month after MCI had issued $1 billion worth of notes and warrants to fund its network expansion—a debt offering that would have been unthinkable were it proposed after August 23. Since Chairman McGowan owns nearly 5.8 million shares, his net worth shrank over those twenty-four hours by nearly $30 million. All told, McGowan's MCI holdings on a typical day in the spring of 1985 were worth between $45 and $55 million. That compares with the $150 to $160 million his shares could command when MCI stock was flying high in 1982.

McGowan insisted he is unfazed by it all. "Somebody said to me a couple of weeks ago, 'What does it feel like to lose $100 million?' " he told us. "I would love to play poker with that guy, because he must think the money in the pot is his. He would be a terrible poker player. That is Manchurian money. You don't get associated with it. I never had it, so how could I lose it?"

Could he not have sold some of his holdings when the price was especially lofty? "Well, no, if you are in the company, it is different," he replied. "I am not an investor. I am the entrepreneur-manager. I have never sold a share of stock. I have given stock away—to my family, and schools—but I haven't sold it."

There is a certain air of unreality about McGowan's chin-up attitude towards MCI stock. What chief executive would not despair over so severe a fall in his company's fortunes on Wall Street, not to mention the value of his own portfolio? But certain factors do cushion the blow. MCI may be a small and vulnerable enterprise when compared to AT&T. But when stacked up against its other rivals, McGowan's firm is a behemoth and a model of stability. MCI in 1983 accounted for 40 percent of the long-distance market that is not controlled by AT&T. GTE Sprint, its largest non-AT&T competitor, claimed about 23 percent. Allnet, the third-largest, had all of 6 percent of the non-AT&T market. McGowan himself told us the only competitor he worries about is "the one I don't know yet." In other words, the brutal cost pressures and marketing demands of the long-distance business might lead to a combination of weak firms that produces a single corporation with a chance of survival.

The gulf between MCI and its smaller rivals became even more profound in June 1985 when McGowan, much to the surprise of industry observers, announced that IBM had acquired a 16 percent equity interest in his company and had transferred ownership of Satellite Business Systems (SBS) to MCI. SBS, another long-distance rival to AT&T, was owned jointly by IBM and Aetna. It had secured a foothold in data communications for big-business customers—a segment of the long-distance market for which McGowan hungered but MCI had been unable to crack—even though it had never managed to turn a profit. IBM said it would pour an additional $400 million into MCI over the next three years.

The complicated transaction, valued at $1 billion, fueled speculation that the computer giant was preparing to acquire all of MCI. McGowan assured us that this was not the case. He said IBM believed it was important to maintain a foothold in the telecommunications sector, and that a 16 percent interest in profitable MCI was more valuable than a controlling interest in loss-ridden SBS. IBM agreed not to increase its stake in MCI beyond 30 percent without permission. It also agreed to vote its shares at MCI annual meetings in accordance with the vote of non-IBM stockholders. If MCI stockholders split 80–20 on a particular issue, IBM will vote its shares 80–20. The company will thus exercise a neutral role in MCI's governance.

The IBM deal enhanced MCI's standing among its long-distance peers overnight. SBS gives McGowan's firm an immediate injection of new revenues and 200,000 additional customers. SBS also brings with it an impressive collection of space-based technologies that will expand the capacity of MCI's earthbound network. But the real significance of the alliance is the seal of credibility associated with IBM. McGowan explained to us that MCI had managed to win business from more than four hundred members of the Fortune 500, but was generating "like 5 percent to 7 percent" of the revenues it projected it could collect from these heavy-spending customers. A typical Fortune 500 communications manager worries that he might take the fall if his company relies heavily on MCI and technical problems surface. On the other hand, blind faith in AT&T might incur the wrath of the financial kingpins, who are enthusiastic about the cost savings associated with the independent carriers. The solution to this dilemma? Token use of MCI but continued reliance on AT&T.

"The communications manager uses us so that when somebody says, 'Are we using competitive carriers?' he can say, 'Yes sir, we're saving money,'" McGowan argued. "But not so much that his tush is in trouble. These guys have great loyalty to their businesses. But their number one loyalty is to their own tush. They are fearful to expose themselves. So I said how do we penetrate that? We are known as a cheap long-distance company. The guy sees us on television with Joan Rivers. So I figured an affiliation [with an established firm] would do it. I looked at Digital Equipment. I looked at a number of companies. . . . IBM can give the communications manager a lot of courage. Instead of 5 percent [of your long-distance bill with MCI], how about 25 percent? He can now say, 'I'm going with the company that has the IBM connection.' It changes the character of our business."

MCI's history has created additional resilience to setback. The temporary profit squeeze of the mid-1980s is insignificant when compared with the company's condition through much of the 1970s. MCI for years hovered on the margins of solvency. This was during the campaign waged by the Bell System—before the FCC, across a negotiating table, in the courts, before Congress—to limit the range of long-distance services MCI would be allowed to provide. The financial and human costs of this confrontation were enormous. During the first nine years of its existence, MCI lost more than $120 million. There were layoffs, including 25 percent of the workforce during Christmas week 1973, and the departure of top executives, including MCI's first president. But most of all there was uncertainty. The survival of the company was at stake whenever the FCC or the courts issued a major ruling that involved MCI.

There is no question whom William McGowan holds responsible for the years of agony at the company. "Up until 1972, AT&T was headed by a guy named H. I. Romnes, an engineer who had patents in his own name, a gentleman," he said. "He was very humble for a telephone type. When we won that case in front of the FCC [in 1971], he announced, and was quoted in the newspaper as saying, 'We disagree with the Commission, but we understand how it can benefit the public and benefit us, even.' I read what I thought was a very gentlemanly approach to us. It turned out that AT&T's board, in looking for a replacement for Romnes, decided that what was needed was a Mr. Tough Guy, and for several reasons. One, they were having trouble getting rate increases in the states. They were very reluctant to file them, and I think the board felt H. I. Romnes was not insistent enough in pushing through rate increases. The second problem was that the craft unions had basically taken over control of the company, and [AT&T] needed someone who would be tough and get control back. What they usually do in an outfit like that, in most corporations, is to have two or three people kind of groomed [to succeed the chairman]. The people they had were Bob Lilley [executive vice-president of AT&T], William Lindholm [also an executive vice-president], and deButts [vice-chairman since 1967]. They picked the Genghis Khan of the crowd. Tough. John was very tough. It turned out that this was one time in AT&T's life when they should have had someone a lot more pragmatic. He was not. He didn't believe in anything except their way."

The period of confrontation between AT&T and MCI came to a symbolic close on June 13, 1980, when a jury in Chicago ruled that the Bell System had violated the Sherman Act in its behavior toward MCI from 1972 through 1974. The $600 million award to MCI—which under antitrust law was trebled automatically to $1.8 billion—represented the largest antitrust judgment in American history. AT&T immediately appealed the verdict and the award. In January 1983, an appellate court in Chicago sustained the bulk of the jury's findings. But it remanded the case for recalculation of damages. The retrial concluded on May, 28, 1985. Its outcome stunned McGowan and his associates. MCI had decided to raise its damage estimate to $5.8 billion before trebling, an audacious move that in hindsight was a grave miscalculation. The jury, disenchanted by the size of and rationale for the claim, awarded MCI only $37.8 million before trebling. Six months later, MCI's long legal campaign against AT&T, including a second lawsuit filed in 1979, came to a final conclusion. The settlement provided MCI with roughly $200 million in cash, plus products and services whose value is unknown.*

William McGowan has mastered the intricacies of MCI's antitrust case against AT&T. He was the first witness to testify at the 1980 trial and he sat through every day of the lengthy proceeding. He was also the first witness to testify at the 1985 trial. McGowan enjoys recounting speeches, memoranda, and notes of meetings by AT&T officials unearthed in the process of discovery. "We got documents," he said. "He [deButts] had a series of meetings with the presidents of the [Bell] operating companies starting in 1972. . . . One meeting was in Key Largo, at the Ocean Reef Club. What do we do about MCI? It was led by John and there were the various [local Bell] presidents. One I remember, from Northwestern Bell—I liked his name, Nuremberger. He said, 'Why don't we get rid of the bastards before the FCC gets accustomed to having them around?' " McGowan began to chuckle and swivel in his chair. "You had Charlie Brown [the current chairman of AT&T], who was then president of Illinois Bell: 'Those bastards aren't going to take away my business.' "

McGowan's memory of the sentiments expressed in Key Largo is accurate, but he is somewhat mistaken about who said what. According to notes taken at the meeting, which we obtained from the files of the

---

*We conducted a long interview with McGowan nearly six months before the May 1985 decision. He predicted the jury would award "$2 billion or $3 billion" before trebling. According to posttrial analysis, MCI's fatal mistake was to argue that the practices for which AT&T was found guilty in the 1980 trial—conduct directed at its new rival's plans to crack the market for private lines—slowed construction of the MCI network and thus reduced revenues and profits from traditional dial-up service, a business that did not even exist in the early 1970s. Once the jury rejected that argument it was uncertain about how to disaggregate MCI's calculation of damages in the private-line segment (mainly business customers) from its dial-up segment (mainly residential). So it voted instead for an award close to the AT&T estimate.

antitrust case, Nuremberger did not suggest that ATT "get rid of" MCI. That suggestion was made by another official who, according to the notes, said, "Shouldn't we act now rather than wait until they have going business which regulators might not permit us to dislodge?" And it was Nuremberger, not Charles Brown, who issued the declaration of defiance about the loss of business to MCI. Illinois Bell president Brown did say, again according to the notes, that there were "large amounts of revenue vulnerable which we can preserve if we choke off now." Just who was to be "choked off" was not made clear.

.   .   .

William McGowan's current surroundings testify to the emergence of MCI as major corporation and to the work habits of the individual who has presided over the company since it was incorporated in August 1968. McGowan approaches his job with singular intensity. He arrives at the office by 7:30 or 8:00 A.M. and routinely puts in a twelve-hour day. He usually works seven days a week, although he spends only two or three hours in the office on Sundays. His current schedule, which includes extensive travel and work outside the office, is much less grueling than the pace he maintained during the seventies. According to a number of colleagues, McGowan, during the years of confrontation with Bell, demonstrated an unmatched capacity for work. He could be found in the office at all hours of the day or night, on weekends, on holidays. Richard Sayford, a director of MCI and a classmate of McGowan at Harvard Business School, said he never asked the MCI chairman for his home telephone number in the old days because he was never home to answer the phone.

McGowan today labors in spacious, well-appointed quarters, although personally he is an unimposing figure. He is short, almost pear-shaped, and was attired in shirtsleeves for each of our discussions. McGowan is a frenetic conversationalist. His voice can rise from a whisper to a mumble to an outburst in the process of making a single point or telling a single story. Even when seated, he is in perpetual motion: swiveling in his chair, laughing boisterously, pounding the table, lighting a cigarette. He was a chain smoker for many years, and he puffed on Lark Lights and drank black coffee through hours of interviews. (McGowan gave up smoking for Lent in 1985, and during our final conversation went through only five cigarettes, his new daily limit.) Guttural noises, not unlike sounds produced by video games built around images of war, pepper his conversation. He once stuck out his tongue as he mentioned the name of a retired general counsel of AT&T.

The walls of McGowan's conference room, where our first two conversations took place, are lined with framed covers of annual reports, prospectuses, and checks from successful financings. Between the conference room and McGowan's desk is a conversational grouping with sofa and chairs. The furniture is green and white, evidence of the MCI chairman's Irish-Catholic heritage. On one chair is a green pillow. Stitched in white yarn is the slogan "God made the Irish #1." The dominant visual image in this office is paper. It is everywhere. On the floor. On McGowan's desk. On the radiators. On a bookshelf, lined with many books: *In Search of Excellence,* which McGowan has yet to read; *The Best and the Brightest,* David Halberstam's study of Vietnam policy-making in the Kennedy and Johnson administrations; *Financier,* a biography of Wall Street titan André Meyer; and Ken Follett's *On Wings of Eagles,* an account of Texas billionaire H. Ross Perot's mission to free employees of his company held hostage in Iran.

McGowan is a voracious reader who plows through books, business publications, newspapers, general-interest periodicals, and specialized newsletters several hours a day. Richard Sayford recalled when the MCI chairman dropped in unexpectedly for a weekend visit in Florida. Soon after McGowan arrived, a box was delivered to the Sayford home. It was stuffed with magazines, reports, and company memoranda that McGowan perused as he floated in a swimming pool.

"I believe that if you get enough information into your head, you are intuitively, rather than logically, going to make a hell of a lot better decisions," he told us. "I have seen it work so many times. I just read and read and read and talk it out, and read, and I think I make better decisions. I think you have a tremendous advantage over someone who does not do that."

The sweep of McGowan's reading surfaced in our conversations. At one point, during a discussion of the decline of the steel industry, he called out to his secretary for a news clip he had torn out of the *Los Angeles Times* several days earlier. The article reported criticism of David Roderick, chairman of U.S. Steel, by a leader of the Japanese steel industry. At the beginning of our second conversation, the MCI chairman rushed into his conference room, where we were already seated, and waved a long article by management guru Thomas Peters. The article, published as an "exclusive reprint" by *Florida Trend* magazine, examined the quality of customer service at a range of major corporations. He read from the article and then launched into his own discussion of customer relations at MCI.

There is an energy about William McGowan, a certain swashbuckler quality to his personality, that produces a youthful exuberance rare among the chief executives of major corporations. Shareholder meetings of MCI must be seen to be believed. They are nothing like the staid, almost mournful, sessions convened by most large corporations. The 1984 annual meeting, the first since the breakup of the Bell System, took place in the ballroom of the Washington Hilton. Roughly five hundred people attended, and McGowan entertained them from the opening gavel. He had a wisecrack for every item on the agenda. He introduced Chief Financial Officer Wayne English and claimed that "most of the board has lent their hair to him." He referred to an emissary from the company's accounting firm, Price Waterhouse, and said he "has been kept in a sealed envelope in a hotel safe since last night." When shareholders voted to retain Price Waterhouse for 1985, a routine event at annual meetings, McGowan said, "We can let Pat Keller out of the safe now." And on it went.

MCI executives recount story after story about the antics of their chairman. In 1981, McGowan and the advertising agency that has created the company's popular television commercials, Ally & Gargano, hatched a plan to embarrass Kenneth Cox, MCI's reserved senior vice-president. Cox is a former commissioner of the FCC and chairman of the National Advertising Review Board. He suggested revisions in certain MCI ads that he considered to be in bad taste. At a board meeting, McGowan screened a spoof ad based on the premise that MCI's cheap rates could benefit obscene callers. It was inspired by AT&T's slogan "Reach Out and Touch Someone," which was revised to read, "Reach Out and Touch Yourself." At the end of the sixty-second spot, there is the sound of a man breathing heavily into a telephone. A woman at the other end exclaims, "Andy, is that you, son?" Cox reports he was not amused.

During one of our conversations, McGowan demonstrated his personal computer. He dialed MCI Mail, an electronic message service the company unveiled in October 1983, and began to read aloud news headlines the service provides. "Casey Linked to Decision to Train Rebels in Psychological Warfare," the first headline said, a reference to William Casey, the CIA director whose tenure has been marred by controversies over his financial dealings. "Now, isn't that a shock—imagine that," McGowan quipped. He then leaned over and whispered. "You know that red phone in Casey's office? That's not to the president. That's to his broker."

The MCI chairman is also given to an unusual degree of candor and reflection. He is willing, even anxious, to offer opinions on subjects from the future of telecommunications in the United States to the effects of the Cultural Revolution on economic development in China. He exhibited none of the self-censorship and reluctance to mention proper names that was characteristic of so many of the chief executives with whom we spoke.

McGowan denounced in no uncertain terms proposals floated by some right-wing professors and members of the Reagan administration to relax or abolish the treble-damage penalty for antitrust violations. "They're wrong," he declared. "Dead-ass wrong. Because what you have in antitrust is basically someone who gets the profit to himself rather than someone else [getting it]. And in order to do that, you violate the law. And so if they lose [without treble damages], what do they do? They just transfer the money they got. What the hell have you got to lose? You just say, 'Hey man, not a bad deal,' right? If I don't get caught, I keep [the excess profits]. If I do get caught, I give it back. . . . I'm a strong believer in giving messages to the boards of corporate America. They just don't understand. We have a document from AT&T's files where a senior guy went around and did a survey of all the top executives. . . . And the survey came to the conclusion that they were going to treat antitrust as another business risk. Like it was rain! I mean, the arrogance that exists in those companies is unbelievable."

McGowan even offered some critical reflections on IBM, his new partner, although his rhetoric was much more measured than on most other subjects. "I do know they're as human as anybody else," he replied when asked about the performance of the computer giant. "They missed complete major waves in that industry. They missed the most significant thing that ever happened in the industry since its first day, and that was the minicomputer. Whole things and whole concepts—they missed them. They're not omnipotent at all. They happen to have an extremely good merchandising and marketing capability with the big user that gives them a margin over everybody else. They devote enormous amounts of money to research and development. Typically, they're not the massive breakthrough kind of guy. They're the refinement types. But you get refinements and refinements. They're clearly the company you would have to give the most credit to for the hundred-to-one improvement in price-performance ratios every twelve or thirteen years. A $1 million computer twelve years ago is now a $10,000 desktop. IBM has clearly been the most significant factor in that."

What follows is a sample of other observations served up during our conversations:

- On Chrysler chairman Lee Iacocca: "I'm not very much of an Iacocca man. . . . I think Iacocca has done very well for Chrysler, but I think his motivation was to prove to Henry Ford that he made a mistake. Well, maybe I shouldn't be bothered by somebody's motivation. But there is always a sign, whenever you see a guy go on television. Here we call it Potomac Fever. Once a

CEO decides he'll go on television, you don't have a CEO anymore—you have a personality, and somebody has to satisfy that personality. It could turn out bad, or it could be alright. But it changes the whole nature of [the job]. The job is not to do that. You start believing your own press."

• On decriminalization of drugs: "The bad drugs, I mean the really serious ones, like heroin, I would give them away free. Absolutely. I would stop all the horseshit. The thing [the government] has to do is break the [organized crime] infrastructure that has built up, which is an ungodly efficient machine. And frankly, I believe that if you gave it away, the infrastructure would die. It would take a couple of years, but it would go away. There would be no profit in it. And nobody's in [the drug business] except for the money."

• On the economic role of big business: "The Fortune 100 has, over the past five, ten, fifteen years, had a net decrease of jobs in this country. [These companies] have had a decrease in productivity. They have made no positive contribution to this country at all. All of the growth in the United States, all of the development, technologically and otherwise, has been from small- and medium-sized enterprise."

• On business and government: "I think of Washington—the FCC, Congress, and the courts—as kind of a business discipline. Like you think of engineering or finance. . . . But this is not true of most corporations, where it should be true. There is an emotionalism that we don't have that I observe when I meet a lot of these [business] people. . . . Part of it, I think, is the psyche of business executives. They have this little daydream. It is like they are on a horse going across the prairie, the rugged individualist, the look of the Marlboro man. The government is a denial of that dream. The government regulates them, the government has rules, and therefore they don't like it. Emotionalism distorts their reaction to [government policy], their ability to cope with it, their ability to have a decent input into it. . . . I think they are hurting themselves, and hurting the cause they want to espouse, by being so emotional about Washington."

• On Wall Street analysts and the press: "There are two good reasons why you should never pay attention to those [Wall Street] guys. First, they are now being paid vast amounts of money, and in the last two or three years, they are being stolen from one [firm by] another. Because of the amount of money they are getting paid, they must, if anything happens, come out and give a comment on it. Mumble, mumble, mumble mumble. The ones that don't know anything about the subject come out with sweeping statements hoping to get business. It's also partially because the editors of our newspapers insist. They get tired of this spokesperson stuff, an unknown 'high-level source.' So they say to their reporters, 'I want some damn names in this article. You've got to quote names.' And the reporters ask, 'Who the hell am I going to quote?' So they go to a book and look it up. These are the analysts for this industry. They get hold of them and they get some names. *It's a name.* That's why all of a sudden you see analysts you've never heard of quoted as experts."

The MCI chairman spoke at greatest length, and with the least degree of criticism, about the future of telecommunications in the United States —specifically, what he believes to be the evolving merger of computer and telecommunications technologies, and the potential of these developments to transform life at home and in the workplace. Such forecasts are nothing new; the "information economy" and its implications have been debated for years. What is interesting about McGowan is the level of detail with which he discussed these issues and the intensity he brought to the conversation. He projected a future of home communications centers, where families use cable television and personal computers to shop, study, bank, and send messages across town or across the country. He argued that newspaper classified ads will be replaced by electronic bulletin boards displayed on home computers. He emphasized time and again that computers and telecommunications represent an opportunity for top-heavy and unresponsive corporations to streamline decision-making and enhance their international competitiveness.

"We are just starting to get our arms around the implications of telecommunications, information itself, and computing power," he told us. "Take them away from being an administrative-support item, an expense item controlled by a budget, and move them over to a profit-making item. Just like you think of advertising. Just like you think of R&D. If you take information at the moment it occurs and in that instant make it available to whomever should have it, the results are fabulous. The amount of inventory you make is not only reduced but you make the right stuff. You make stuff that people are buying, not what some guy at the beginning of the year said would probably be needed.

"When you do that you change the character of the business, the nature of the business," he continued. "You change your whole management structure. All of a sudden management decisions are quicker and better because they are more timely and accurate with the right information. Now this is horribly threatening to people. Executives are threatened by this. Because you know those eight levels of management in a company? Executives were hiding behind them. It's not only expensive, and slow, but it protected their tush. 'Have them review it'—they institutionalized that attitude. Now all of a sudden, slam, bang, there is something to decide. This is very threatening to those people."

McGowan's perspective on the future is important on two levels. His unrestrained enthusiasm reflects the one-dimensional focus of his strategic world view and business orientation. McGowan puts little stock in warning signs that the evolution of competition in telecommunications, and the acceleration of technological change, may claim as many victims as it creates beneficiaries. Cost-cutting and innovation in long-distance have been unabashed blessings for big business. Major corporations, frustrated for years by the inflexibility and bloated costs of AT&T, have used competition to leverage new services, better prices, and improved standards of reliability from suppliers. But advances for corporate America have been accompanied by confusion and dissatisfaction among residential customers.

The dissolution of the Bell System has fueled enormous actual and projected increases in the cost of local dialing. According to a December 1984 report by the Consumer Federation of America (CFA), local rate hikes in the first year after divestiture totaled $4 billion—a 26 percent increase in the average American phone bill. Consumer organizations such as CFA warn that continued escalation of local rates may price millions of poor families and the elderly out of phone service altogether.

Susan Leisner, a member of the Florida Public Utility Commission, described to a joint hearing of the Senate Commerce Committee and the House Energy and Commerce Committee the distributive consequences of these alarming trends. She delivered her testimony on July 28, 1983, at the high point of public outrage over a pricing departure recommended by the Federal Communications Commission (FCC). The FCC proposal, first issued in December 1982, would have levied a flat monthly "access charge" on all phone users for access to long-distance lines. The $2 residential and $6 business charge, originally scheduled to take effect on January 1, 1984, could have risen to $7 per month by 1991. Congressional objections to the plan, which was designed to transfer costs shouldered by interstate long-distance callers, mainly business, to local customers, largely residential, convinced the FCC to delay the implementation and reduce the size of the charge.

"You must overturn the FCC's access-charge decision and prevent those billions of dollars in costs from being shifted onto the local consumer," Leisner implored. "Second, you must take care to keep as many people as possible on the telephone network, regardless of where they live and what their income might be. The soul of our society is at stake here. We cannot become a nation divided by technology, where business and the wealthy use their computers, their microwave dishes, and their fiber-optic cables, to benefit the world's most advanced communications network, while an entire underclass exists that does not even have the ability to pick up the receiver on a plain black telephone and dial 911 in an emergency."

McGowan testified one day later before the same members of Congress. He appeared as a member of a panel of industry leaders that included AT&T chairman Charles Brown. McGowan's testimony may not have been the first time he echoed the leadership of his archenemy —but it was certainly a rare instance of agreement on major legislation pending before Congress. The MCI chairman, like Brown of AT&T, endorsed the concept of access charges and dismissed concerns about the threat it posed to universal service. He restated this position during our conversations. Years of advocacy on behalf of long-distance competition, and a genuine enthusiasm for the equipment and technologies that are streaming out of commercial labs, seem to have blinded McGowan to the distributive fallout of a turn of events he set in motion.

The MCI chairman is also shaping his company's business strategy based on his analysis of trends in pricing and technology. McGowan now plays a modest role in the day-to-day operations of MCI. He is a legal and regulatory tactician, an employee motivator, a lecturer to industry and government, and a long-term strategist. MCI's evolution as a provider of services that go beyond basic long-distance has been shaped and accelerated by McGowan and his projections. MCI Mail is one example; it offers instant communication between computers or electronic transmission of messages from a sender and their delivery on paper to recipients without computers. This new service was unveiled with great fanfare and talk of creating "a new postal system" for the country. The company has also moved into cellular communications, radio paging, and international long-distance—all of which are built around providing new services to business customers who currently make limited use of these services.

MCI Mail and various companion ventures are in the formative stages of development, and many are experiencing start-up losses. But their rapid proliferation underscores the directions in which the company is moving. These directions are built around two basic trends: the emergence of microcomputers in business and as a standard device in the home, and the rise to adulthood of a generation of individuals and managers weaned on long-distance and the use of computers. The ultimate success or failure of these ventures will do more than test the validity of McGowan's insights. It will determine whether MCI can build on its legacy of innovation—or whether it will settle into a comfortable niche as a me-too player in an industry that evolves from monopoly to tight oligopoly under the umbrella of AT&T.

MCI has already demonstrated its capacity to engage in profitable me-too behavior. AT&T announced in May 1984 that it planned to charge consumers 50 cents for each call for long-distance directory assistance above the two free calls allowed each month. This exorbitant charge, to which consumer organizations objected, presented a classic opportunity for MCI to play a competitive masterstroke. Local telephone companies, which actually provide the operator assistance, charge long-distance carriers only 30 cents per call (25 cents for operator assistance and five cents for other service elements). AT&T's charge is based on the 30-cent payment and a 20-cent markup that covered its own costs, estimated at 11 cents, and a return of 82 percent on that 11-cent cost. Thus, MCI had a window of opportunity to provide a popular service at much more affordable rates than its giant rival or to offer many more free calls each month. Its response? The company announced it would charge 45 cents for directory assistance after the first two free calls each month. That 10 percent reduction, which MCI trumpets as an example of its economy vis-à-vis AT&T, represents a disappointing slide into profitable complacency.

.   .   .

It is impossible to understand the potential and pitfalls of MCI without an appreciation of its past. While the company has grown enormously in recent years (MCI in 1985 had nearly 10,000 employees, compared with only 1,500 in 1980), many of its directors and senior executives lived through the dark days of the early seventies, when MCI struggled even to turn a profit. These executives, and even one-time MCI officials who have moved on to other companies, demonstrate a certain brashness, almost an air of defiance, and a reflexive distrust of AT&T. They also share certain opinions about William McGowan. There is an enduring bond between the MCI chairman and his subordinates, a macho sense of camaraderie and collective struggle forged during the firm's years of confrontation with the Bell System. Part of this bond is explained by the fact that McGowan has never been married. He devoted, and continues to devote, nearly all of his waking hours to MCI. Those who worked under him marveled at his iron discipline and tenacity. Executives who had to balance the pressures of work with the demands of family life came to envy their chairman's independence. The all-night strategy sessions, the weekend meetings, hours and hours at the Black Rooster, a watering hole close to the MCI headquarters that company wags came to call the "Dirty Chicken," created a roller coaster of despair and exhilaration that is recalled today with great fondness.

Conversations with former executives about the company's early years invariably elicited images of war and religious devotion. "Bill McGowan has a brother who is a priest," said Stanley Scheinman, who left MCI in 1975 as senior vice-president and special assistant to the chairman. "But I think Bill himself is a priest—his priesthood being the chairmanship of MCI. The commitment to the company *über alles*, the seven-days-a-week, twenty-four-hours-a-day approach. To understand the man, you have to understand the sheer commitment. The excitement of creation, of course, was an ego trip. And the psychic rewards were spectacular. But so was the amount of time and energy spent on it. No one else could have possibly matched McGowan's bachelorhood-priesthood."

Raymond Miller, who joined MCI in 1974 and is now president of a corporation that designs and builds security equipment for telecommunications, offered a different set of images. McGowan, he declared with obvious pleasure, "is a fucker and a fighter and a wild horse rider."

There is no better evidence of the legacy of the seventies than the attitude and disposition of MCI's chairman himself. McGowan is driven by a profound antipathy for his giant adversary that is tempered only by the fruits of victory. This antipathy continues to define his world as a business executive and even his life outside the office. The cornerstone of McGowan's lavish Georgetown residence, which he purchased in 1981 and had remodeled to suit his unusual tastes, is engraved with the old AT&T logo. A crack runs through the middle of the bell.

Through hours of conversation, McGowan made no effort to hide his opinions of AT&T's leadership. "I think they operated with an absolute feeling of arrogance," he said when asked to describe the most significant mistakes committed by AT&T in its relations with MCI. "By that I mean, their arrogance in thinking that they could deny even what the government told them they had to do. . . . I think they also made a mistake, part of this again is arrogance, in assuming invincibility. They assumed they could solve everything that might arise, they could make anything they wanted to happen. For example, they had no perception of the true implications of the government suing them: 'Ah, we solved that before.' As a matter of fact, in the previous lawsuit"—the Justice Department filed antitrust charges against the Bell System in 1949— "AT&T typed the [1956] settlement in its own office. I also think they misjudged their enemy. They assumed that what they saw in the way of financial strength, and numbers of people, and their backgrounds, meant we could not make it happen."

Were McGowan chairman of the Bell System, how would he have reacted to the emergence of competition in the form of MCI? "Leave us alone," he answered without hesitation. "If John deButts had left us alone, we would be today a $400 million or $500 million business, scratching real hard to raise capital because the margins are so low. We would have had a niche market. That is what he should have done. I mean, that's what the law said. He would have been better off just obeying the law. He didn't sense that. It's one thing if someone says, "Look, those guys are going to take my business and to hell with it, I am going to stop them.' But it wasn't even that. It wasn't even duly protecting the [AT&T] stockholder in that sense. He was protecting some principle. And the principle is based fundamentally on arrogance."

Perhaps the most effective way to explore the history of MCI is to begin at a symbolic end—the antitrust verdict against AT&T. MCI filed its lawsuit on March 7, 1974, in the U.S. District Court in Chicago. The case involved the production and review of millions of documents by both sides, a trial that extended over four months and involved sixty-seven witnesses (eighteen for MCI, forty-nine for AT&T), not to mention a seventeen-day deposition of McGowan by a team of AT&T attorneys. On June 13, 1980, at 10:25 P.M., the jury delivered its verdict. Of fifteen alleged violations it was asked to consider, the jury decided against AT&T on ten.

Nearly all of the specific findings revolved around two dimensions of the relationship between MCI and the Bell System from September 1972 to April 1974. The first was the forms of interconnection AT&T was willing to provide between MCI's long-distance facilities and the local telephone system, which in turn determined the range of services MCI could offer its business customers. The second was the conduct of AT&T in negotiations over these interconnections. All told, the period 1972–74 (the FCC ordered Bell to furnish the disputed interconnections on April 23, 1974) can be considered the first phase of the emergence of MCI. This evolution is reflected in the company's operating statements. In the fiscal year ending March 31, 1975, MCI had total revenues of $6.8 million. During its entire history up to that point, the company had collected less than $1 million from the sale of long-distance services.

The second phase of the company's development began on September 10, 1974. MCI applied for permission from the FCC to initiate a new service, called Execunet, which in effect provided subscribers with the dial-up service most individuals think of as long-distance. Subscribers to this service could reach any telephone—as opposed to predetermined offices, as was true with point-to-point—in areas served by MCI. Execunet was McGowan's boldest stroke as chairman of MCI. And it was launched over the strong objections of at least two of his high-level executives. In regulatory terms, Execunet represented a decisive step in the evolution of full competition in the provision of long-distance telecommunications. With the FCC order of April 23, 1974, MCI was able to enter at full speed the business it had targeted from the day it filed its initial applications—specialized communications for industry. But it was clear that the market for these private lines, in part because of aggressive pricing by AT&T, would not materialize to the degree MCI initially projected. With Execunet, the company opened a vast new market in traditional long-distance. The market was reflected once again in company sales figures. From fiscal 1975 to fiscal 1978, MCI revenues increased more than tenfold.

As with private lines, however, the provision of Execunet was more easily decided upon than implemented. The FCC approved Execunet in October 1974. But it soon decided (after a demonstration of Execunet by Bell representatives) that it had been hoodwinked. The service, described in MCI's applications as a new form of private-line communications, was actually little more than traditional long-distance, the commission concluded. MCI's regulatory midwife and most important ally became an adversary. Twice the commission ordered MCI to cease offering the service. These orders had a convulsive effect on the company. Employees were dismissed. At least one top executive resigned. MCI's lenders, whose goodwill was the lifeblood of the cash-starved company, declared in August 1975 that they would extend no new loans. MCI was forced to turn to the public market for cash in October. It issued new shares of common stock that represented one-third ownership of the company for a paltry $9 million. Orville Wright, who became president and chief operating officer of MCI in May 1975, told us in all seriousness that he began paying morning visits to Saint Matthew's Cathedral, a church located close to company headquarters, before arriving at work.

But MCI relied on more than the power of prayer. Both times the FCC decided against the company, MCI took the commission to federal court and prevailed. To this day, Execunet remains a sore point among regulators who otherwise nurtured the development of MCI.

"I think MCI was totally wrong" on Execunet, said Walter Hinchman, a Washington-based consultant who was chief of the FCC's Common Carrier Bureau at the time the Execunet tariff was filed. "I think they were wrong on the law. I think the courts were wrong on the law. I think MCI was wrong in terms of what [services] it had been authorized to provide, and legally, procedurally, and for every other reason Execunet should not have gone forward." But it did, against the combined opposition of the Bell System and the FCC. In July 1977, a U.S. District judge not only upheld the legitimacy of Execunet, but ruled that MCI and the other specialized carriers were in effect free to provide any long-distance services they chose. This decision, which the Supreme Court declined to review in April 1978, might be considered the wellspring of the contemporary era of competition in telecommunications.

William McGowan described the history of MCI from 1968 to the present as a progression through four stages. "When we first started, our business was raising venture capital, raising money, because if I didn't raise money, I couldn't go on to the next stage," McGowan says. "The next business I went into was lobbying the government. That was our business. We had engineers who could write well—I don't think I would fly in anything they built, but they could write well—and we filed our applications for micro[wave towers]. We succeeded in that business"— in 1971, with the Specialized Common Carrier decision—"and then we went to the next stage—raising a lot of money, building a network, getting customers. That ceased in 1973, and we went into another business—not to our liking, not out of choice—which lasted for five years. That was winning court battles and surviving. It was a dictatorial company in those days, because I couldn't take a chance that someone would spend money. I remember when our personnel department consisted of two people. They came to me and said, 'We really should have some [employee] training programs.' I smiled and said, I'll think about it. Because that wasn't surviving or winning court battles.

"When we won the [Execunet] court decision, it was clear, I think, that we were going into a new business," McGowan continued. "As a matter of fact, I tried to get our lawyers to allow me, at 11:59 one night, to shut the company down and start it again at 12:01 in the morning. It was clear what we had to do. We had a little momentum over [the other AT&T competitors], and it was our job to run like hell before the other guys came in. And to run like hell in what we knew how to do, the long-distance voice business, and not divert ourselves at all until we achieved critical mass. We had to cure our balance sheet. We had a negative net worth of thirty-some million dollars. Someone described it as looking like Rome after the Visigoths had gotten through with it."

·   ·   ·

In his discussion of the formative years at MCI, William McGowan often uses the first-person singular. That is fair enough, since every individual with whom we spoke about the survival and expansion of the company agrees that McGowan played the definitive role as strategist—from the its proceedings before the FCC, to negotiations with AT&T, to its struggle to remain solvent throughout the seventies. This was especially true during the stage of company history that McGowan describes as "dictatorial." When the FCC ordered MCI to refrain from marketing Execunet, McGowan gathered his top managers for a weekend strategy session at an executive retreat in Tuxedo Park, New York. McGowan liked to convene these sessions from time to time to remove his top executives from the office and promote free thinking and blunt talk. On this retreat, all the talk was bad.

"Some of the key banks, some of the key suppliers—Rockwell, Bechtel —said, 'Hey guys, you've got a fucking problem,'" recalled G. Scott Brodey, at the time a vice-president of MCI. "The problem was survival. And so decisions had to be made. McGowan made it a Sunday, ten A.M. meeting. He got up, gave a speech, and said, 'We let things slip, it won't happen again. I apologize to all of you. From now on, I'm running the company. I'm running finance, I'm doing this, I'm doing that. Here's what we're going to do.' That's when the knife came down. 'Monday morning, we will have a 20 percent reduction of headcount. We'll start there. If that's not enough, we'll go to 40 percent. This company is going to make it.' From that point on, his whole approach [to management] was different."

What is also true is that while McGowan incorporated MCI in 1968 and labored to build it into a billion-dollar enterprise, the organizing principle around which MCI was founded—providing more flexible, more affordable, long-distance service—belongs to someone else. That individual is John D. "Jack" Goeken, who became the company's first president in 1968 and who left the firm, in a less-than-amicable parting, six years later. Goeken is no longer affiliated with MCI (other than as the owner of a large block of shares), but he remains an important presence in telecommunications. He is chairman of Airfone Inc. and the developer of the concept on which his new company, a joint venture between Goeken and Western Union, is based—providing telephone service for passengers on commercial airliners. He is also one of the few individuals associated with MCI who said he was disappointed with the performance of the firm under McGowan.

"The biggest disappointment to me is that the original concept of MCI was not to be another long-distance telephone company," Goeken told us during a lengthy conversation in his Washington office. "It was to offer new services." And what of the company's chairman? "He's got a large ego, and sometimes you question whether he is feeding his ego or doing what's good for the company. You can just speculate. You don't know what's motivating a person."

On December 31, 1963, John Goeken filed for permission from the FCC to construct eleven microwave towers between Chicago and Saint Louis. Goeken's company was called Microwave Communications, Inc. Its original purpose was much less lofty than its name implied. Goeken was thirty-two years old and the operator of a mobile radio business based outside of Chicago. His goal was to increase sales of CB radios to truckers who traveled between the two midwestern cities. Establishing a microwave system increased the geographical reach of communications between drivers and their home base, and thus improved the prospects for CB sales. Gradually, from this seed, applications for the microwave system expanded. The idea grew to encompass the provision of services to other customers—namely, corporations with specific communications needs, such as a dedicated line between headquarters in Chicago and a sales office in Saint Louis—that were not being met adequately or affordably. MCI proposed to lease voice channels for half-time use (from 6:00 A.M. to 6:00 P.M.) at a 25 percent reduction in rates; in the evening to combine channels to allow for high-speed data transmission; and to allow up to five subscribers to share voice channels on a party-line basis. According to documents submitted at the time, Goeken anticipated total revenues in the first year of operation of $272,000, to be collected from between 58 and 204 customers.

As modest as it sounds, this is the initial scheme that not only hatched what is today a billion-dollar corporation, but set off the erosion of regulatory obstacles to competition in long-distance telecommunications. Goeken's proposal was not especially well financed. He filed his initial paperwork on December 31 to avoid an increase in FCC application fees scheduled to take effect January 1, 1964, that would have cost him $550. But it immediately attracted the opposition of powerful interests. AT&T, Illinois Bell, Southwestern Bell, and Western Union all argued against the application before the FCC. For the next several years, Goeken, assisted by attorney Michael Bader, defended his proposal.

"If you were going to make a movie, you couldn't cast better characters," Goeken recalled. "The AT&T attorneys were sharp, really spiffy. Unintentionally, I looked the other part. I had holes in my shoes. I didn't have any money. I had cardboard boxes instead of briefcases." Despite the imbalance of resources, Microwave Communications received approval from an FCC hearing examiner on October 19, 1967. Nearly two years later, on August 13, 1969, the full commission, in a vote of four to three, upheld the hearing examiner's opinion in what is now known as "the MCI decision."

Communications magazine, in a lengthy interview with Goeken published in September 1969, described the significance of the ruling. "We have found that many readers view Goeken's struggle as merely a local problem, possibly affecting users in Chicago and St. Louis," the magazine noted. "But it is truly a confrontation of far reaching national significance —as the vigorous opposition of AT&T should indicate. Its national scope is such that, along with the Carterfone decision, the initiation of the MCI-type of service stands to revolutionize the communications structure of the country."

William McGowan entered the picture between the time of the hearing examiner's ruling and the 1969 vote by the FCC—in essence, after the most difficult regulatory struggles had been waged. "We knew that we had the judge's decision, which still had to be fought out before the commission, and that would take a long time," Michael Bader told us. "We also knew that you couldn't sit still. I was urging Goeken quite emphatically to get top-level management and financial capability to do something with [the concept of microwave communication]. Jack had talked about applying for a route to New York, Milwaukee, the Twin Cities, one that went down to New Orleans. I said, 'Jack, that's all very good, but you don't have two dimes to rub together.' He had been living in subpoverty level. Many nights he was able to live [in Washington] only because of his wits. He would spend the night on my office couch. Or he would come to my house. At this point, John Worthington brought in the person we needed—Bill McGowan."

Worthington, an attorney with Chicago-based Jenner & Block, had done some legal work with MCI and was acquainted with McGowan. Worthington is now MCI's general counsel, and Jenner & Block handled the company's antitrust litigation against AT&T. On paper, McGowan looked to be just what the situation called for: a graduate of Harvard Business School, a millionaire by his early thirties, a free spirit with a taste for unconventional projects. Worthington arranged for lunch at an Italian restaurant in Chicago. Jack Goeken was unimpressed. "At the time, McGowan had a company that cleaned buildings, a janitorial service," Goeken said. "So when I first met him, he didn't impress me. Worthington said, 'Hey, I set this up, you have got to go back, you have got to see the guy.' I said, 'There's just something about him I don't feel comfortable with.' "

From this rocky start, Microwave Communications of America (MCA), later renamed MCI Communications, was born in August 1968. The idea was a bit involved: to build a national long-distance network, but to do so by forming seventeen regional companies modeled on the Chicago–Saint Louis link. Each of these firms would be incorporated independently, and MCA would hold a financial interest of 30 to 40 percent. MCA would also be paid fees by the regionals and use the money to underwrite engineering presentations for the FCC and the legal expenses associated with winning regulatory approval. MCA eventually spent $6 million in the effort. Soon after incorporation, Goeken and McGowan hit the road to drum up investor interest. "It was a good marriage," Goeken said. "We did almost everything together. Every time we went to raise money, we would go together. He appealed to some people. Other people thought he was too smooth. Those people liked me. Between the two of us, we got enough people trusting us to put the money in." The "money" came in the form of a complex $110 million financing package that consisted of equity, commercial loans, and credits from equipment suppliers. Every current or former MCI executive with whom we spoke said that, on his own, Goeken never would have been able to complete such a deal.

But even as Goeken and McGowan were successfully raising funds, disputes were beginning to surface. Signs of tension "were there rather quickly after the two of them got together," recalled Thomas Hermes, a retired executive vice-president of Rand McNally who was a director of Goeken's Chicago–Saint Louis carrier. "It was not overt, but you could see the signs. Jack would say something, and McGowan would disagree —in the early stages politely, and in later stages, less so. . . . It got to the point where Jack was no longer an asset to McGowan. McGowan could bring in engineers to present the technical side [to the FCC]. Later, I understand, McGowan would leave Jack out of meetings completely. I think McGowan considered him a source of embarrassment. Occasionally, he would bring Jack to lunch as a curiosity—'Here is the guy who invented MCI.' "

The emerging tensions between Goeken and McGowan were not a function of personality but of philosophy and mission. Where McGowan was an entrepreneur, driven by money, the will to win, and the commitment to build a viable corporate organization, Goeken was an innovator, interested in perfecting new applications of technology and, having done so, moving on to different challenges. "Intellectually Jack is an inventor," said Stanley Scheinman. "He is an entrepeneur in the earliest sense of the word. He never developed the managerial and administrative capacity to take a concept and turn it into a business. That created tremendous tension and conflict between him and Bill." That tension manifested itself in the divergent paths they envisioned for MCI. "There were two philosophies of life," Goeken told us. "One was to duplicate the telephone

company. The other was pioneering, to develop specialized activities."
Among the "specialized activities" Goeken had in mind was Airfone, the
service he is now bringing to market. He even suggested that MCI's
network of microwave towers could have been outfitted with weather-
monitoring devices to track atmospheric fronts as they moved across the
United States.

.   .   .

Whether or not John Goeken's ambitious agenda for MCI would have
become an innovative road to increased profits or a fatal drain on scarce
capital became an impossible question to answer when he left MCI in
1974. Before his departure, however, Goeken did work alongside McGowan—and at times at cross-purposes—during the single most critical
period in the company's history. Had MCI not weathered a debilitating
financial squeeze between 1972 and 1974, Goeken's ideas, not to mention
the future of competitive telecommunications, might well have become
an academic exercise.

To understand the tremendous darkness of those days, it is necessary
first to appreciate the initial promise. The Federal Communications Commission announced the Specialized Common Carrier decision on May 25,
1971, long before McGowan or anyone else associated with MCI expected the FCC to act. MCI went public one year later. There was a sense
of euphoria about the operation. MCI began to acquire sites for and
construct its thirty-four-city network, hire a sales force and create an
image for itself as a major new force on the corporate scene.

McGowan described the atmosphere at MCI in the 1971–72 period
during the antitrust trial nearly a decade later. "It was a complete victory,"
he said of the FCC ruling. "Everything we had proposed and what other
people proposed to them [the FCC]—they said they were going to open
it all up to competition. We had been fearful for a while that they might
decide the concept is good, [but] you would have to have individual
hearings on the individual [company] applications. They said no. Anybody
and everybody can go into this business, and all they need to prove is that
they are financially, technically, and otherwise qualified. . . . It was very,
very encouraging to us and all the people who were supporting us."

The euphoria was to be short-lived. MCI had won the right to compete with Bell, but it also relied on Bell, or more precisely the local Bell
operating companies, to make that competition a reality. Telecommunications executives often describe their business as similar to that of the
airlines. Firms such as MCI, in this analogy, provide transportation from
one airport to another. But a second form of transportation—in telephone

parlance, interconnections—is necessary to carry the traveler from his home to the airport and from the airport to his home. And the telephone industry's equivalent of taxis or buses is the local phone company.

Interconnections would be at the center of a series of negotiations between MCI and AT&T that proceeded for one year, from September 1972, when officials from the Bell System met in New York City with John Goeken and Laurence Harris, whom McGowan had hired from Texas Instruments to lead the discussions, until September 1973, when AT&T broke off the talks and announced it would file proposals on interconnections with the public-utility commissions in states where MCI planned to operate. These were the same public-utility commissions, it should be added, whose national association opposed MCI's applications in the FCC proceedings and then sued the FCC to overturn the decision.

This fundamental disagreement was a matter of life or death for MCI. Interconnections, in effect, determine what services a long-distance carrier can offer. Under AT&T's position, MCI would have been restricted to providing the most rudimentary form of service, point-to-point communications. A corporation might use a point-to-point connection to link a regional administrative office with a sales office in the field. The line would allow for conversations only between those two offices. But point-to-point lines were a minor portion of the total private-line market. MCI insisted it had been authorized to provide two more lucrative forms of private-line communication: FX (foreign exchange), and CCSA (common control switching arrangement). According to testimony at the antitrust trial, FX and CCSA accounted for more than 50 percent of the private-line market at the time of the negotiations.

A brief description of FX demonstrates why these more flexible services were so important to MCI. FX is used extensively by the airline industry. The operations of one MCI customer, American Airlines, explain why. American first purchased FX from MCI in 1978. The service, which it also receives from AT&T and other specialized carriers, connects passengers who wish to make reservations on an American flight with one of four reservation centers the airline operates across the country. Airlines often group reservation clerks in clusters to take advantage of economies of scale. But that presents a problem: how to allow passengers, who are obviously reluctant to place toll calls for reservations, to contact a distant center. This is where FX comes in. A traveler in, say, Columbus, Ohio, dials a local American telephone number, which is actually connected to MCI's long-distance terminal in the city. The call is then transferred over MCI's network to the reservation center in Cincinnati, via a dedicated line. The system works in reverse as well. If a reservation clerk in Cincinnati wants to call back a customer in Columbus, he simply dials the customer's local number and is connected via MCI. American Airlines currently does more than $2 million of annual business with MCI. It consists of FX, CCSA, and a small amount of data transmission. MCI is an especially important provider of FX service for American in the Midwest and between Phoenix and Los Angeles. The firm accounts for up to one-third of American's FX business.

As negotiations over interconnections dragged on, the financial pressures at MCI began to mount. The company was raising money and investing in construction—but generating next to nothing in revenues. This is the period that McGowan's skills as a leader were most taxed. In May 1973, he decided to scale back MCI's construction plans. The proposed network was reduced from thirty-four cities to nineteen. Months later, after AT&T broke off talks, he took even more drastic action: layoffs, totaling 25 percent of the MCI workforce. The timing could not have been worse. The decision was announced during Christmas week. That day is referred to by veterans of the period as "Black Friday."

"I think it's about the only time in my life I've seen Bill McGowan really depressed," said Senior Vice-president Kenneth Cox. Cox was a member of the FCC in 1969 and cast a vote in favor of competition on the "MCI decision." His appointment to the FCC expired soon thereafter, and he joined the new firm.

McGowan himself described the hardships at the 1980 antitrust tiral. "Everything stopped," he said. "We had to cut back on everything we did and cease all activities. I left a whole bunch of towers being constructed west of Texas for four hundred or five hundred miles. I put all of the equipment in a warehouse and didn't spend any more, or the least we could, and said we are going to have to survive."

Survival may have been even more difficult as a result of dissension that was dividing MCI management at the time. McGowan was determined to extract from AT&T all of the interconnections he believed his company was entitled to. Anything less, he reasoned, would amount to a permanent forfeiture of the right to provide those services. Goeken, on the other hand, argued that MCI should in effect take what it could get, begin to generate revenue, and then continue the battle with AT&T.

These and other disagreements were set out in remarkable detail in a memorandum Goeken wrote in January 1974. The memo, obtained from the files of the antitrust case, underscores the grave situation at the company. In a section entitled "State of MCI Today," Goeken declared, "Practically out of money. There is enough to see us through April 1974. MCI is seeking to raise additional capital through loans (debt), equity or a takeover by another company. I am not kept posted or consulted along these lines." He then went on to complain about McGowan's management style. "The reason MCI is out of money is due to several management mistakes, directions, and mismanagement." Among the examples: "First they wanted to create an IBM type of image. Everything MCI did had to be done in a big and expensive way. MCI did not have the revenues nor money to create and maintain such an image." And another: "They believed that AT&T would coexist with us, if our rates were only 10 percent less than AT&T's—they made plans, hired people, spent money on this assumption even though AT&T refused and stated that AT&T would never give MCI the type of interconnection we requested, and on which our marketing and revenue forecasts were based. MCI hired thirty-to-forty-thousand-dollar-a-year people when at the time we had no contracts or agreements with AT&T for interconnections. . . ."

The crisis phase of MCI's existence came to a close four months after Goeken wrote his memo—but as was standard fare for the firm, not without a series of trying developments. In October 1973, Bernard Strassbourg, chief of the FCC's Common Carrier Bureau, wrote to AT&T and instructed the company to provide the disputed interconnections. Bell officials declared that Strassbourg lacked authority to issue such a directive and did not comply. On December 31, 1973, a federal judge in Philadelphia ruled that AT&T was obligated to provide interconnections for FX and CCSA service. Bell complied, MCI's first real victory since the Specialized Common Carrier decision, but appealed the decision. On April 15, 1974, an appeals court overturned the December order, arguing only that such a decision should be left to the FCC. AT&T promptly pulled the plug on MCI—an action that a jury would rule six years later violated antitrust laws. Finally, eight days after the appeals court decision, the FCC ordered Bell to provide interconnections. For MCI, the end of the beginning was at hand.

. . . .

The tortuous early history of MCI raises an obvious question. What motivates an individual to embark on such a perilous venture? Few of McGowan's colleagues or subordinates offered intricate theories about what makes their boss tick. Some talked about his energy and ego. Others said he is easily bored and could not have survived a less hectic career. Richard Sayford, the director and Harvard Business School classmate of the chairman, emphasized the difficulties in dissecting the McGowan personality. "Bill comes forth, but when you go back into Bill, it sometimes can be very difficult to find out a lot about him," Sayford told us. "He has been very devoted to his job. One hundred percent loyal to the executives who are very close to him. The loyalty is unbelievable. I don't think you'll find a chief executive who is more loyal. And you look at the group he has had working closely with him. They were all the original guys. But I think even if you went back to them and said, 'Hey, how well do you really know this guy, deep down?' it would be very difficult. He does not talk about himself. He'll expound about how ants mate, how glass fibers do this and that, but when you go back in, when you pierce under and ask, who is Bill McGowan, he becomes a very complex individual."

McGowan himself offered his own observations. First, he never expected such a sustained hostile reaction from AT&T. "I didn't understand the risks," he said. "People think you probably do, but that's not true. I thought the risk was getting government permission to go into business. If somebody told me in 1968, 'You will not know if you are successful until 1978,' I would have said, 'No way. I'm not a masochist.' "

There was much more to the creation of MCI than an inability to project the future. Money seems almost irrelevant to his work. He refuses to sell any of his 6 million or so MCI shares and seemed genuinely unconcerned about the fate of his personal fortune as a result of the plunge in the company's stock price. Nor did McGowan establish MCI to achieve a broad social vision, such as cheaper communications for the masses. MCI's target customers in the early years were corporations and large nonprofit organizations. While it later focused attention on the residential market to add revenue and tap its underutilized network, MCI is once again turning toward corporate users as it markets data transmission and services such as MCI Mail.

The key to McGowan's motivation can be found in the restlessness and drift that characterized his life prior to MCI. McGowan needs to be challenged. He needs to have a bigger and better adversary against which to take aim. He regards business as a battleground. And he engages in combat as much for the excitement and psychic rewards as for what is being fought over. What kept him at MCI was the exhilaration of taking on—and the prospect of dismantling—an institution as powerful as AT&T.

"I think it's more the personal challenge," McGowan said, when pressed on the question of motivation. "One of the things that was very attractive to me in this business was that it had not been done before. I used to love businesses where *I* hadn't done it before. But finally, I got bored with that. So I took off. I took off a year on the theory that I was going to have the very traumatic experience of turning forty years old. I decided that college professors get sabbatical about then, and those guys don't work near like I work. I got bored out of my mind. I went around the world in one direction. Then I tried it in the other direction. Terrible. So I started looking for new things to get involved in. I got involved in a building-maintenance company. A fellow I knew brought me in, and I helped him out." Then came MCI.

William George McGowan was born on December 10, 1927, in Ashley, Pennsylvania, a small working-class community outside Wilkes-Barre. McGowan is the middle child of five children. He spends a great deal of time with his extended family (he has seventeen nieces and nephews) and he is especially close to his older brother, Andrew, a Catholic priest who is a prominent church figure in the Scranton area. William and Andrew, who is usually called Father Joe, get together at least once a month and often visit more frequently. The entire family likes to gather every summer for a week or ten days at the beach. The MCI chairman recounted how his nephew Danny, who was only eleven years old, grilled him about the business during a family outing several years ago. McGowan gives all of his nieces and nephews shares of MCI to provide for their college education.

"Danny has about two thousand seven-hundred shares now," he told us. "His parents won't tell him that. He thinks he has thirty shares. He saw where we split last year, so now he thinks he has sixty. Last summer he was down with me on vacation. I'm reading, I bring down all these papers, and I'm reading, and he comes over and sits next to me. 'Uncle Bill, how's everything going?' he asks. I say, 'Doing good, Dan.' He says, 'I mean with the company. Everything's okay?' 'Yeah, the company's going fine.' He says, 'You mean, you're not worried?' 'No, no.' Then he goes over and sits next to my brother Joe. He says, 'I was just talking to Uncle Bill.' 'Oh yeah, what happened?' He says, 'I don't understand Uncle Bill at all. He says he's not worried about the company, that everything's going well. But I'm losing my ass.'" McGowan let out a boisterous laugh. "'I'm losing my ass.' He even watches the *Nightly Business Report.* We are usually on the most active list, so he sees it every night."

As a boy, the MCI chairman and his family lived in a ten-room brick house in Ashley that is still owned by his brother Leo, an electrical contractor who runs a small firm in the area. Mrs. McGowan, a schoolteacher, gave up her career to attend to the family. Mr. McGowan, a long-time railroad employee, was active as a union organizer and worked as a union official full time for several years. Both parents are now dead. The McGowan household was staunchly Democratic. It was also quite religious. The MCI chairman still attends Sunday mass, although he never aspired to the priesthood. "We were raised in a family where regular attendance at church was taken for granted," said Father Joe. "There was a sense of religious values that gave you your motivation in life."

The McGowan household was also a competitive place. The children were expected not only to complete hgh school and college, but to go on to successful professional careers. "In our family, you practically had to rehearse before you went to dinner," Father Joe quipped. "We were a very competitive crowd as far as conversation. Bill had all the subtleties. He would let someone else do all the front chatter, and he would quietly point out idiosyncracies [in the argument]. He had a great gift for that."

Even as a boy, William McGowan demonstrated a restlessness and disdain for authority that would come to characterize his professional career. During his sophomore year in high school he decided it was time to work as well as study. So over the objections of his parents he began what would become years of employment on the second shift with the Central Railroad of New Jersey. (The minimum age for employment was eighteen, and young McGowan bluffed his way into his first job. He then hired older brother Andrew, who was also underage.) The railroad extended from Jersey City westward to Easton, Pennsylvania, and then to Scranton via Wilkes-Barre. It was a principal carrier of anthracite coal in the region and a chronic money loser. According to a 1955 edition of *Moody's Railroads*, the line reported a profit only once, with the exception of the war years, from 1931 to 1955.

McGowan laughed when asked about his years on the railroad. "Most of the executives at the Central Railroad of New Jersey taught me an awful lot," he said. "How not to do things. How not to deal with people. That's helpful, when you see bad examples [of management]. How not to run a railroad."

McGowan spent more than two years in the army. He arrived in Europe after hostilities ended. One of his first assignments was to assist with the relocation of concentration camp survivors, grisly work that took him to Yugoslavia, Poland, and Bulgaria. McGowan returned to Ashley and used the G.I. Bill to earn a bachelor-of-science degree from King's College, a small institution that had opened its doors in 1946 in nearby Wilkes-Barre. He majored in chemical engineering but quickly decided against further pursuit of the field.

"I was trained as a chemist because that was a brand-new school, and the only science they had was chemistry," he explained. "I found sciences easy, and I took the easy courses so I could work at night. . . . I figured as a chemist, I had to go to graduate school. So I drove around to chemical factories in Jersey and I would say, 'Who runs this place?' I never met a chemist who ran it. Then I would say, 'Where are the chemists?' They would point to a guy with a white smock somewhere. I couldn't see doing that for the rest of my life."

McGowan entered Harvard Business School in 1952 and there shined for the first time outside the narrow confines of his native environment. He almost never made it to Cambridge, Massachusetts. He had been accepted by the Wharton School of the University of Pennsylvania and rejected by Harvard as a result of a bureaucratic foul-up. But he was admitted eventually and, after a conversation with the president of King's College, decided to attend. He told us one of his concerns about Harvard was its "reputation for being very pinko." He stood out immediately. He was named a Baker Scholar, which meant he ranked among the top 5 percent of his class, and was elected by his "section" to represent the students before the faculty. In short, the stage was set for a successful, if unspectacular, career with a Fortune 500 corporation of the sort whose representatives travel to Cambridge each spring to gather up the best and brightest of the business school.

That is, until McGowan signed up to work a summer as an analyst with Shell Oil. "Business can be one of the most boring professions that God ever created the way it's run in most corporations," he told us. "My God, there's no spark; there's no motivation. I remember working one summer in New York at Shell Oil. Bright people in this department. It was kind of a think tank, and I was just there for the summer. A lot of people who were working there were in their thirties. And they had retired. [The offices] were in the RCA Building at the time. We would go out and look at the girls at noon. They would talk about crabgrass and kids and sports and girls. No one ever talked about the business. They had no more interest. They had retired. They weren't going to tell the company, of course. They weren't going to tell the company for some years, in fact. I was thinking, this is deadly, this is bad. You spend so much of your life in what your profession is, doing something this boring. That's one reason I never went to work for any of those guys."

Unhappy with his summer at Shell and unimpressed by job offers he received upon graduation, McGowan set out on a series of ventures that ranged from unusual to downright bizarre. He worked in the film industry. He ran a building-management company that employed moonlighting firemen and schoolteachers. He became involved in the specialty-handbag business, a job that required him to travel to Florida to buy alligator skins. He worked feverishly in the mid-sixties to market an automatic timing device to alert car owners that their automobiles needed servicing. He traveled to Detroit and pitched his product to auto executives. He flew to Japan and met with officials from Toyota. McGowan eventually gave up on the device.

All of these early ventures differed markedly in substance, but many of them shared several characteristics: They were on the technological cutting edge of their industries; McGowan occupied a high-ranking post in the company; the firms were either start-up operations or in deep financial difficulty. McGowan told us his first job was his most enjoyable. From 1954 to 1956 he worked with Magna Theatre Corporation, a new venture formed by Michael Todd, the hard-driving, free-spending Broadway and Hollywood producer who died in a plane crash in 1958. Magna Theatre was formed to market a new wide-screen movie system developed by Todd, a process called "Todd-AO," and to distribute films that used the process. McGowan was hired directly out of Harvard. Six months after he joined the firm, Todd signed up the musical team of Rodgers and Hammerstein. Thereafter, McGowan worked closely in the filming and distribution of *Oklahoma!*—the company's first major success—and came to know Shirley Jones, the film's star, and Elizabeth Taylor, who married Todd in 1957.

Father Joe McGowan recalled how puzzled his father was when he learned son Bill had decided to leave this glamorous business. "It looked like Bill had a great career [with Magna Theatre], but he left it because he just wasn't interested in it. It didn't seem to be enough of a challenge. One of my father's favorite stories was that he couldn't believe Bill would leave a job that paid him thirty-five or forty thousand dollars a year. He said to him, 'Why did you leave? You must have been fired.' 'No, no,' Bill said. 'I just didn't like it.' And my mother said that for years my father would go around mumbling to himself that in all the years he was a railroad engineer, nobody ever asked him, how do you like your job, Andy? With your arm sticking out of the window in the snow and the cold. Nobody ever said to him, 'Do you like it?' "

What did the MCI chairman think of the legendary producer? "Michael Todd was an egomaniac, and not very intelligent," McGowan said. "He was shrewd. He had street smarts. But he was not very bright. He was just ego driven."

McGowan's most lucrative venture was Powertron Ultrasonic Corporation, a firm he started, with a group of engineers, on Long Island in 1959. McGowan had left Magna Theatre and spent several years in New York as a management consultant. He revived troubled companies by assuming control of them and addressing the business problems himself. Powertron was a defense contractor. The firm manufactured components for control systems for aircraft and guided missiles and produced devices to measure extremely cold materials, such as liquid oxygen. The original owners started the firm with an investment of $25,000. In 1962, with sales of more than $2 million, Powertron was sold to Giannini Controls Corp. for close to $3 million. William McGowan became a millionaire.

.   .   .

William McGowan's range of experiences prior to the birth of MCI, the years spent dissecting the business practices of AT&T, and his current standing as chairman of a corporation that is a major force in telecommunications, combine to give him a unique perspective on business management in the United States and the future of his industry. McGowan is eager to express himself on these topics. He travels extensively, at least twice a week, to address industry and academic forums and to "propose a future" for the development of the telecommunications sector. "I think that one of my jobs is to project what I see in the near future, because I think it will influence the future, especially in an industry that has been so highly structured and is now looking for new structures," he said. "I think I can help the process a little bit by proposing new structures, proposing a future."

In his speeches, McGowan goes well beyond discussions of the future of his industry. He is firmly convinced that developments in computer technology and telecommunications, in the context of a regulatory structure that encourages, rather than restrains, change, means that industrial society is poised on the brink of a major economic and social restructuring. He pointed to two major business developments in 1984—the acquisition of Electronic Data Systems by General Motors and the appointment of young, technology-minded John Reed to replace Walter Wriston as chairman of Citicorp—as evidence that major corporations are at last beginning to understand the role of computers and communications as competitive tools. Ultimately, McGowan's observations on business management, the style he has adopted as chairman of MCI, and his ruminations on developments in telecommunications merge into an overall perspective on the future course of American business. Given his track record as chairman of MCI, it is a perspective worth exploring at some length.

William McGowan's thoughts on management flow from one central axiom: All institutions in the process of aging, corporate or otherwise, tend toward bureaucratization and creative decay. Time and again during our conversations he returned to this theme: American management has been its own worst enemy, and the much-invoked goals of increased productivity and innovation will not be achieved through new forms of organization on the shop floor. The essential ingredient is recognition by executives that their management systems are bloated, wasteful, and, in the final analysis, the source of misguided decisions.

"Everybody builds an empire," McGowan complained. "The way you build an empire is [to create] corporations with ten, twelve, fifteen layers of management. Not only is that very expensive, but it practically kills any chance of good decisions being made. . . . One of the big reasons to have all these levels [of management] is to process information. You need to be informed. You know, a tremendous number of people in American institutions are kind of human message switchers. They collect information, and collate it, massage it, distort it, and pass it on. If you can short-circuit that, you can do a lot to improve the [decision-making] process.

"They [corporations] also worship form so much more than substance," he continued. "I take a look at some organizations, and frankly, by the time the organization, or the division or the department, gets through taking care of its human needs, and there are genuine human needs—vacations, sickness, training, and personnel management—by the time they get through the human needs, and the politics of what's going on, they have no time left over for business. Probably the best thing in the world that could happen is that we require every corporation to dissolve after fifteen years or something like that. Just break it apart, because they stop doing anything and spend most of their time protecting themselves. Not creating things, protecting things. And that permeates the whole organization—departments, systems, people."

McGowan raised his plan for mandatory liquidation in two of our conversations. He insisted it was a serious proposal. He also spoke approvingly of Mesa Petroleum chairman T. Boone Pickens, who has terrorized the oil industry with takeover campaigns directed at giants such as Gulf Oil and Unocal and proposals for dismembering integrated producers to increase shareholder return. "I think a lot of what he says is true," McGowan said of Pickens. "Some of these [oil] companies are better off being liquidated. But we don't have a system for that yet. He is one of the cures for that situation—let's liquidate the bastards. He was right about Gulf. It was sitting there slowly dying and he said, 'Why don't the stockholders benefit?' It's crazy. It's supposed to be a stockholder-owned company. Why don't they benefit? So that part of what he did was good."

MCI celebrated its fifteenth anniversary in August 1983 and there is no sign of its impending dissolution. When asked about this apparent contradiction, McGowan pledged substantive age versus chronological age. The real history of MCI began on January 1, 1984, he claimed, when the dissolution of the Bell System ushered in a market structure driven by competition. Moreover, in August 1984, sixteen years after it was formed, MCI unveiled a reorganization plan that McGowan said was designed to redistribute power inside the corporation. Long-distance telephone operations were dismembered into seven regional units, and senior executives from Washington were reassigned to posts across the country to manage the new divisions.

This reorganization struck a major blow for decentralization. The headquarters staff has been reduced substantially. And each of the new units, which correspond to the geographic boundaries of the seven Bell operating companies, have profit-and-loss responsibility. The leaders of each of the divisions are free to organize their operations as they choose, so long as they abide by two McGowan directives. They must create a distinct marketing organization for major accounts, a reflection of MCI's return to its big-business customer roots, and they must separate the sales and customer service functions, so that the company's legendary marketing zeal does not overwhelm its capacity to respond to problems and complaints. The reorganization also demonstrated how change need not come at the expense of continued executive collaboration and communication. Every Monday morning for the past five years, the top twenty to twenty-five executives of MCI, including, of course, the seven officials who are no longer at headquarters, gathered at 8:00 A.M. to discuss the week's anticipated developments. The reorganization made face-to-face meetings impractical. So these "breakfast" sessions are now conducted electronically. The participants send their reports across the country via MCI Mail (the initial reports are now submitted by Friday afternoon) and comment on and ask questions about their colleagues' reports via their personal computers.

McGowan has developed other ways to retard bureaucratization inside the company. There is a minimum of paperwork. A customer of MCI, the company chairman likes to say, generates no paper until his monthly bill is mailed. All other transactions—initial sign-up, logs of calls placed, payments—are recorded and stored electronically. Internal information is distributed widely and with few restrictions on access. To this end, executives make extensive use of MCI Mail. Company officials send more than 160,000 messages each month, which means not only that reports are available more quickly than with paper, but that internal security is inherently less rigid than in most corporations.

McGowan discounted the risks posed by this situation. "I would much rather err on the side of giving out too much information than not giving out enough," he said. "Because most of the time, it's an ego trip. You know, information is power. If I have it, and you don't have it, I therefore have more power than you do. We don't do that, we just distribute it to everybody." In general terms, what does he consider legitimate trade secrets for corporations? "I think there are a few legitimate trade secrets, but then they [business executives] just elaborate from there on up to the whole world. I think there is a very legitimate one in customer lists. I think companies should be allowed to protect their customer lists. . . . I think there probably are processes that should be confidential in process industries. But other than that, I have a hard time figuring out what should be [trade secrets]."

A second dimension to the McGowan management style is the culture and attitudes that permeate MCI. Much of that culture revolves around what MCI is *not*. The corporation is not a family, McGowan emphasized time and again. MCI does not guarantee job security. MCI does not provide for "human needs" beyond what is required to run a successful business. There is no employee credit union. There are no exercise facilities or counseling services. MCI did not even establish a retirement program until April 1981.

"You find very few people [at MCI] saying 'the company,' as if there is an entity like that," McGowan said. "With this company, there's no such thing. When people go home here, it doesn't exist anymore."

We explored this hard edge to the McGowan philosophy. Is there not a middle ground between the strict individualism he advocates and the paternalism he objects to at other large corporations? "I doubt it," he said. "If you become, or have a family atmosphere, why not have family [in the business]? If you have family in the business, how the hell can you not have the appearance of conflicts or favoritism? . . . Also, you are implying something, you are holding something out to people, you are saying, 'We take care of you.' We have a gymnasium for you, we have this for you— the implication is that there is some entity which is taking on responsibility. And since you can never deliver on that all the time, I think you are holding out a false promise, a false hope. Then people feel as if they have been abused, they have been tricked, they have been misled. . . . The company is not going to take care of your social and financial needs, your entertainment. I mean, that's not our business."

What is interesting about McGowan's perspective on management is that it runs counter to so many prevailing notions about how to motivate employees. The MCI chairman said he does not object to greater cooperation and coordination between management and labor and within management circles. But he dismissed as "gobbledygook" specific approaches such as quality-of-worklife programs. He ridiculed the idea that executives can conduct a few pep talks, coin a few slogans, and change the management climate inside the corporation.

How then does MCI cultivate a motivated and satisfied workforce? McGowan pointed to the company's employee stock-ownership plans. Under one program, which is subscribed to by nearly 70 percent of the eligible participants, employees are allowed to purchase shares of MCI at

85 percent of market value. But he did not seem genuinely persuaded of the importance of such programs. Rather, he relies on a set of simple rules: Hire 50 percent of new management employees from outside the company, which allows for adequate in-house promotion without producing an inbred executive mentality; create structures for individual responsibility and accountability; and do not dissuade dissatisfied employees from leaving the firm and returning in the future if they so choose.

"My feeling is, if you have lower than a ten-percent [employee] turnover, there is a problem," he said. "If you have higher than twenty percent, there is a problem. At indoctrination [sessions] for new employees, I tell them that I don't know how they hit upon this industry, by design or by accident, but they are in the right industry for their entire working lives. It is going to be a very exciting place. They may not be in the right company, however. Maybe they want a company that is more structured. Maybe they get a boss that is a real pain, or there is a problem with personality. I say, change jobs. We'll give you a job change. If you still have a problem, leave. Stay in the industry, but go someplace else for a while. And maybe in four or five years, you have changed a little bit, or the bastard who was your boss [has changed]. I want to create an atmosphere where that's possible. The American business atmosphere where if you leave, you are some kind of pariah, a monster, is ridiculous. If you want to leave a company, leave and go someplace else. Maybe you will come back. We have provisions in all of our fringe benefits for prior service."

William McGowan does not look favorably upon the prospect of unionization of MCI's workforce. Like nearly all of the long-distance carriers that compete with AT&T, the company has actively resisted organizing inroads by the Communications Workers of America (CWA) —behavior which prompted the CWA in the summer of 1984 to launch a $2 million campaign to persuade consumers to boycott nonunion carriers. At present, approximately four hundred MCI employees are affiliated with a union. These workers came to MCI in 1982 when the company purchased WUI International, a telex operation owned by Xerox. Our first conversation with McGowan took place during the course of a bitter strike by Local 111 of the International Brotherhood of Teamsters. The walkout, which lasted for nearly one hundred days, was the first strike at WUI since 1948. McGowan was asked how he would react to a campaign by the CWA or another labor union to organize MCI.

"In this industry's situation, and in this company's position, there is no need for [a union]," he declared. "The implication behind a union is that there is a group of people within an organization who carve themselves out and unite in order to have more benefits, or protection, a set of rules that will protect them. Also, by the way, because of the very nature of [a unionized workforce], it means more rigidity in the organization. It would imply, and does introduce, a certain rigidity. . . . You can't have that in this business, especially with what is happening now. . . . Typically, industries that are in the formative stage, changing, using a lot of new technologies, are not a good environment for a union. I know unions fairly well, being a union man, the son of a union man. It is not suitable for this situation."

McGowan's response is more than a bit self-serving. MCI's nonunion status represents an important competitive advantage vis-à-vis AT&T. This advantage will loom especially large over the next few years, as cost pressures and price wars bear down harder and harder on MCI's profit margins. MCI and AT&T, not to mention the other long-distance competitors, have been engaged in a form of hand-to-hand combat over the residential long-distance market since the summer of 1984. The source of this conflict, which encourages the companies to spend tens of millions of dollars each month on advertising and direct marketing, is the introduction of "equal access" to long-distance communications. From MCI's perspective, equal access is the single most important consequence of the AT&T divestiture. Prior to 1984, using a discount carrier such as MCI could be very complicated. A subscriber had to punch up to twenty-two digits to place a long-distance call: seven digits to be connected with the local MCI terminal, an access code that identifies the caller, and the ten-digit telephone number being dialed. Even this cumbersome process had been available only to one segment of the market—individuals with Touch-Tone telephones or consumers willing to purchase tone generators. The rotary-phone market, which represents more than half of all homes, in effect had been out of the reach of AT&T's competitors.

This inequitable market structure began to change under the terms of the consent agreement negotiated between AT&T and the Justice Department. Individuals and corporations—with rotary or Touch-tone phones—will have the opportunity to choose in advance their preferred long-distance carrier. Once the choice is made, the user need simply dial "1" to place a call. This transformation, which will be phased in across the country by 1987, represents a once-in-a-lifetime marketing opportunity for discount carriers such as MCI. The appearance of tens of millions of new customers, grouped in discrete geographical regions, could mean billions of dollars of new business.

But there are also significant costs to equal access. And this is where the nonunion status of MCI enters the equation. In recognition of the inferior connections provided to MCI and its non-AT&T rivals, the discount carriers have historically been required to pay local telephone companies, which complete the final leg of all long-distance calls, only 30 percent of the fees paid by AT&T for its local interconnections. These charges are the single largest cost in the long-distance business—and MCI's differential represented an enormous competitive advantage. But that cost advantage has already begun to disappear. MCI's interconnection charges rose to $480 million in 1984 from $262 million the year before and $143 million in 1982. This expense alone represented a staggering 24.5 percent of revenue in 1984—compared with 17.2 percent in 1983 and 15.8 percent in 1982. With this kind of margin pressure, on top of escalating advertising bills, labor costs and the operating flexibility of the MCI network make the difference between profit and loss.

Given McGowan's predilection for individual autonomy and responsibility within the corporation, we asked him about Japan and the relevance of developments there for management practices in the United States. He said he did not believe Japan held many lessons for business organizations in this country and that talk of a Japanese threat, at least as it applies to innovative applications of computer and telecommunications technologies, was vastly overdrawn.

He began his discussion of Japan with a joke. "There were three businessmen and they were caught in the crime of espionage and sentenced to be shot," McGowan said. "One was French, one was Japanese, one was American. When they were ready to be shot, they were explained the rules. They would be allowed to say anything they wanted to before they were executed. So they asked the Frenchman, and he said, 'Vive la France.' They said anything else? He said no; just 'Vive la France.' The next guy was Japanese, and he said, 'I want to explain the Japanese management system.' And the American said, 'Pardon me, do you mind shooting me out of turn so I don't need to hear that?' I feel a little bit that way about Japanese management.

"It's a cultural thing. There is a consensus," he continued. "You could do things in the United States in the 1900-to-1940 [period] that you could never do afterward. [After 1940] you could not have gotten people to work those hours for that amount of money. The heavy, labor-intensive, uncomfortable, dangerous businesses always go to the country that has two characteristics: one is that it is literate, and two it is poor. We were that way for so many years. We were literate and poor. I'm second-generation. My grandparents were born overseas. My parents worked their asses off. I was born at a time when they whispered in my ear, they really pushed —get educated, expand [your horizons]. Japan took over a lot of that from us. They were literate and they were poor. But now they are even losing out. They're cranking down their shipbuilding. They're cranking down this, they're cranking down that."

The conversation later returned to Japan and the Japanese challenge. Although there has been much written in the last several years about the race between the United States and Japan to build a fifth-generation "supercomputer," McGowan argued that when it comes to widespread innovation, the United States has a commanding lead over its Pacific rival. "In putting together these technologies, in advancing the state of the art of the merging of the information world, we are ahead," he commented. "And our system, I think, happens to be the best to do it. Japan runs on a control basis. Where the worry is about Japan is in the next generation of mainframes—the big, humongous machines that we [MCI] buy, not people at home, and there is some concern about the small portable computer. Japan has come to the U.S. three times now, and did not make it in the workstation-PC-individual environment."

McGowan then rose from the conference table, entered his private office, and returned, beaming like a proud father, with a portable computer no larger than a standard magazine. "Their [the Japanese] system is one in which you are asking the establishment to do it," he continued. "Our system is one that allows people to borrow their mother-in-law's garage. These people"—he points to his portable computer, which is manufactured by Convergent Technologies—"are a spin-off from Hewlett-Packard. We have venture capital in this country by the billions. Do you know what the Japanese have done? They have become so concerned about this, they see what's happening, they have given something like $6 billion to commercial banks and $6 billion to, I guess you would call them investment banks, just for the purposes of venture capital—to get new businesses going. They are even controlling the process of venture capital." He laughed at the thought. "But it takes a long while to do that. In Europe, there is no venture capital. If you are in France, and you never graduated from Polytechnique, I doubt you could ever get money. It's a caste system, an old-boy system. Herr Doctor in Germany. The establishment."

.   .   .

William McGowan did not slay AT&T all by himself. He had committed partners and associates. But over the long haul, McGowan was the commanding presence for the longest period of time. Consider for a moment what he faced in 1968. A vastly entrenched, seemingly all powerful monopoly whose web of agents and advocates around the Federal Communications Commission left that agency wondering whether it could even make a serious *attempt* to regulate such a behemoth. Every day AT&T would collect every piece of paper—hearings, reports, press releases, and so on—that came out of Congress for immediate transmission that evening to its New York headquarters. This was one company that was right on top of Washington. Representatives of the Bell empire were also back in each congressional district. The company encouraged, even mandated, that its local officials become involved in civic organizations and community activities. To this Goliath, McGowan must have seemed less a threatening David than a speculative speck on the horizon.

McGowan fought the monopoly and, more than any single person, cracked it with a combination of incessant regulatory and court challenges, deployment of new technologies, and the skill to raise financing to keep MCI afloat through the lean years. Once underway he raced ahead of other AT&T competitors to become number two—with the rest of the pack quite a distance behind in terms of sales, profits, and, most important, independent-transmission capacity. McGowan also had to win over business and residential customers and make MCI into a television brand name. His principal resource was the ability to move quickly and decisively around, under, and over the smug, lumbering AT&T elephant—while continually being underestimated by his giant adversary. He built from scratch one of the fastest growing companies in the United States. His company is now expanding in many directions—data transmission, electronic mail, international long-distance—before it has consolidated its chief revenue producer, domestic long-distance. The basic strategy is to invest and invest to build a broad base of capacity and diversity before a more sleek AT&T wakes up and starts swinging its deadly tail.

With such success, and with the amassing of an enormous personal fortune, McGowan seems to have changed his personality very little—a sign of a strong character forged from a variety of pre-MCI experiences and a strong family foundation of hard work and thrift. But his very success, and the thirst for confrontation he has brought to his enterprise, raises fundamental questions for the chairman of MCI. William McGowan sees the future. But is he still in a position to lead its invention? Will he remain one of the most successful entrepreneurs in the country or are he and MCI headed toward becoming part of a profitable, but staid, AT&T-led oligopoly in telecommunications?

McGowan claimed that that oligopoly was a future possibility. "The danger [of oligopoly] is going to be in another generation, not in this one," he said. "I think the momentum, the passion, the need for market position, is going to drive this generation into a very competitive situation. The question later on is, if you end up with x number—four—large, long-distance, facilities-based carriers, [what will the market structure be]?"

We wonder about these assurances.

Jack Goeken, the inventor-innovator with whom McGowan joined forces to form MCI, already worries about the trend toward convention. He argues that MCI is simply becoming another long-distance telephone company, not a company offering revolutionary new services. It is duplicating the big corporation it helped to dismember rather than pioneering new pathways. Samuel Simon, executive director of the Telecommunications Research and Action Center (TRAC), a leading consumer group in this field, has characterized MCI as an echo of AT&T at a 10 percent discount.

But then, how much can one expect a single company to accomplish? How many new venture risks can any company, especially a young one, absorb? That depends on the company's capability and orientation. And MCI may now possess more capability than orientation. After all, the company today has a grand opportunity to build its presence in a fast-growing market for long-distance. Growing from 5 percent of the long-distance market to 10 percent by 1990—at the same time the market itself is expanding—means hundreds of millions of dollars per year in new sales. McGowan believes that the under-thirty generation looks upon long-distance calling the way many older people look upon local calling and that the size of the market may depend only on the industry's capacity. The resistance to reaching out via long distance is melting into a proclivity, a habit.

So the temptation is for MCI to follow the curve, to adopt a heavy advertising budget whose cost may offset a good deal of the price efficiencies consumers are supposed to receive from competition, and to fall prey to a brand-name marketing battle characteristic of the monopolistic competition that governs the sale of detergents, processed foods, and cosmetics. But what of McGowan? Can the entrepeneur really end up as tight oligopolist? Will he be satisfied for much longer in having done what nobody before him has done?

These questions are important for more than William McGowan. He now has the personal capital to explode his impact on the national scene if he plans and implements his available options. Let us briefly examine some of these. McGowan has a unique and very perceptive philosophy of business management, one that has been finely honed and forged in the crucible of experiences both wonderful and woeful. Yet his lessons and views are far less known to the public than the thin "Theory Z's" and similar effusions of recent professor-author best-sellers. McGowan needs a book narrated in his inimitable conversational style, peppered with proper names and episodes and places and dates. He is a natural raconteur, a phrase-maker. He has an earthiness that makes one lose sight of the fact that he is a businessman, much less a chief executive officer. The book can be the catalyst for a broad range of operating principles for business organizations and for a critique of the many conventional ways of running corporations into the ground. A catalyst to start people really thinking instead of mimicking the latest from Tokyo or Osaka. And not just the way McGowan may want them to think. Can McGowan's ideas possibly work in corporations much larger than MCI? Can his belief that unions are too rigid a factor in business organization be extended to older, more established industries without threatening the health and safety and economic welfare of employees?

A second opportunity is revolutionary. McGowan can wake up one morning, look at himself in the mirror, and say, "How long am I going to be just a carrier for other corporations' information, or a redundant transmitter of residential long-distance conversations? Why can't I open new doors for millions of Americans to communicate with one another for community purposes, for agendas of social betterment, and for a general right of access to the new telecommunications and computer networks? Why can't I use this new technology to shift the balance of power away from the Big Boys to the ordinary citizens of this country? Why can't I use MCI to pioneer the voluntary formation of residential rate-payer organizations by permitting an insert in the monthly billing envelope inviting consumers to band together? Am I to be constrained to a role of just becoming an Avis to AT&T's Hertz for the next decade?" The odds are that the answer to the last question is yes.

Already, the pressures and advantages of protective imitation are crowding upon MCI and its leader. No longer is MCI the maverick challenger that sided with consumer groups in the great telecommunications debates of years past. MCI is increasingly siding with AT&T on issues such as the residential-access charge. More and more the trend is moving disturbingly toward increased competition with fewer differences between the competitors because members of the other side—consumers —are not afforded an easy mechanism for banding together to advocate their interests. Like many previous new-company entries in other industries, MCI has discovered that it is easier to make money pressing on consumers than pressing bold new moves vis-à-vis AT&T. The former offers the path of least resistance.

Amid the irrepressible boosterism that accompanies the deployers of the new telecommunications technologies, a disquieting vacuum is beginning to be revealed. Business is vastly expanding the use of this equipment —as in the global use of satellites—far faster than nonbusiness sectors. Workers and consumers are largely communicating as they did thirty years ago. Such differential usage embraces a growing information gap, a timely information-retrieval gap, a new universe of haves and have-nots, with the most serious consequences for the distribution of power in a democracy and an economy. A company that can instantly retrieve your credit history is not a company about which *you* can retrieve much of anything about its mistreatment of customers.

William McGowan is more than a gee-whiz narrator of gee-whiz technologies. Few people can probe the way that imbalanced access to and use of these computerized communications systems can produce injustice, oppression, invasion of privacy, manipulation, and stifled voices. As he observed during our conversations, the release of creative energies in the industry promises to be an unabashed blessing for business, especially big business, which stands to reap lower communications costs and greater technological flexibility, including the ability to bypass the local telephone company. Bound inextricably to these developments are the loading of system costs onto residential users to reduce the likelihood of business bypass, the confusions and gouging and deception now underway, and the growing number of poor people unable to afford a projected tripling of their local telephone rates and the introduction of metered local service.

Congressman Timothy Wirth, chairman of the House Subcommittee on Telecommunications, Consumer Protection, and Finance, voiced the potential distributive consequences to journalist William Greider in September 1983. "If people are priced out of access to the telephone, it's the same as pricing people out of education," Wirth observed. "If you don't have access to the future technology you can't go to college. You can't be literate. The telephone, the wired household, will be so important that without it people won't have access to the rest of society and the culture and the world. You will get a two-class system—the communications haves and have-nots—and we will return to an era when large parts of rural America were isolated from the rest of the country. This is flat wrong. It's what we've been battling for fifty years to overcome."

Of course lawmaker Wirth was just scratching the surface of the hardware issues. He did not mention the truly neglected subject of who decides what information can or will be transmitted via these futuristic lasers, microwaves, and fiber optics. All these new technologies are mere tools, albeit spectacular ones, which receive their animation, direction, and values from the underlying power structure in society. Television, too, was once touted as the messenger of great new public enlightenment. But the underlying mercantile and corporate framework of power controlling television turned it largely into a selling and entertainment medium with no way for the audience to communicate electronically with itself on its own public airwaves. How often do technical innovations occlude policy insights.

There are not many people in any given new industry that possess the confidence, the perception, and the experience to keep asking "to what use? to what end?" questions, or in this industry to engage the applications that enhance diverse access and use and content to that information flow. McGowan has those talents along with the ingrained restlessness that may interest him in these directions. Whether William McGowan ventures into these areas, as either an advocate, networker, or builder, will depend on whether he can avoid having his present successes become his future chains.

WILLIAM NORRIS

Revolutionary Without a Movement

Control Data Corporation celebrated its twenty-fifth anniversary in September 1982 with a two-day conference in Minneapolis. Such gatherings are a common ritual among large corporations, especially among those that can boast as robust a track record of growth and profitability as Control Data. The firm was established in 1957 with a handful of employees and rented offices on the second floor of an aging newspaper warehouse. By 1982 it was generating revenues of more than $4 billion and employing a global workforce of more than fifty-six thousand. But its anniversary celebration, whose participants included Harvard economist John Kenneth Galbraith; Archbishop John Roach, then president of the National Conference of Catholic Bishops; and San Antonio Mayor Henry Cisneros, hinted at the considerable gulf that separates Control Data, the fourth-largest computer manufacturer in the United States, from nearly all of its counterparts in American industry.

The focus of the conference, convened under the title "Social Needs and Business Opportunities," was a keynote address by William Norris—Control Data's founder, chairman, and chief executive officer. Norris has been a leading figure in the U.S. computer industry for more than four decades. The company he directs has operated on the frontiers of several computer technologies. Control Data has developed and manufactured some of the most powerful mainframe computers in the world. Its Cyber 205 supercomputer, which was unveiled in 1980 and sells for more than $10 million, is used in seismic exploration by the oil industry, in forecasting weather, and in designing nuclear power plants and atomic weapons. Virtually all of the supercomputers delivered over the past twenty years have been produced by Norris's firm or by Cray Research, which is also based in Minnesota. This small company, which now dominates the supercomputer market, was established in the early 1970s by Seymour Cray, a mercurial engineering genius who left Control Data to strike out on his own. Control Data is also a world leader in the production of sophisticated computer peripherals (printers, disk and tape drives, memory systems) and a major force in data services for the scientific and engineering market, a segment of the computer industry it pioneered.

But in Norris's address, and over the entire anniversary gathering, there was little talk of grueling weeks and months in the laboratory, of the hand-to-hand combat with IBM, the computer giant Control Data had to subdue to earn its high-powered niche in the industry, or of a brave new world of robotics, artificial intelligence, and machine vision. The speeches and seminars focused instead on the crisis of American education, the future of U.S. agriculture and the survival of small farmers, urban poverty and strategies for job creation in the inner city, economic development in the Third World. The conference agenda can be explained by the business agenda Norris has established for Control Data. He is convinced that these chronic human and social needs, and Control Data's ability to design profitable business initiatives to address them, will determine the fate of his company over the next twenty-five years.

Since the late 1960s, William Norris has articulated a philosophy of business and designed a corporate strategy that have made him one of the most unconventional and controversial business leaders in America. He is worshiped inside his company, loathed by many executives who have left, and ridiculed by some corporate peers and on Wall Street. But if Control Data can successfully implement the business philosophy its chief executive has set in motion, he may also come to be known as the most revolutionary figure on the modern corporate stage.

The Control Data chairman has expanded far beyond prevailing boundaries the basic assumptions and principles that govern the social role of private enterprise. He is designing a business response to several of the most enduring challenges of capitalism. In so doing, he is struggling to give new and deeper meaning to the often-invoked, but seldom-defined, concept of corporate social responsibility and to apply the massive human, technical, and financial resources of corporate America to segments of society that up to now have been abused or ignored by the business establishment.

Norris articulated his perspective at length in a November 1984 speech. He distinguished the Control Data strategy from the traditional corporate approach to social responsibility, which he said emphasizes greater concern for employee welfare, product quality, and participation in philanthropic activities. "Social responsibility thus defined was an appropriate place to start twenty-five years ago," he lectured. "It has been good in numerous ways. But it is not nearly good enough, because our society has been going downhill. For more than a decade, unemployment has remained at unacceptably high levels. . . . As a result of a deteriorating educational system, many high school graduates lack science and math skills at a time of growing need for technically trained workers. Even worse, large numbers of students leave high school functionally illiterate, and millions of handicapped persons in our society don't have access to adequate education and training. Less costly ways are needed for the maintenance of health. Urban decay continues. Rural poverty abounds. There are thirty-five million people living below the poverty line. A high level of small-business failures continues. And the list goes on.

"Corporate social responsibility, as generally perceived at present, is on the periphery of these and other major unmet societal needs," Norris continued. "Hence, corporations are addressing symptoms more than their root causes and doing so with a minuscule proportion of their vast resources. . . . Deterioration in our society will continue unless and until substantial corporate resources are invested to help meet major needs as profit-making opportunities in cooperation with government and other sectors. In other words, that action must be part of the mainstream of business backed by a significant investment of resources, and it will impart a broader meaning to corporate responsibility."

Norris's address captured the essential elements of the Control Data approach. This approach has manifested itself in a number of specific products, services, and business ventures. By far the company's most ambitious undertaking is PLATO—Programmed Logic for Automatic Teaching Operations—an elaborate system of computer-based education and industrial training whose development traces back more than two decades, and on which Control Data has staked much of its credibility and prospective financial health. PLATO underscores the guiding dimensions of the Norris philosophy. Control Data's cumulative investment in the system, an estimated $1 billion, is based on a conviction that "labor-intensive" education as practiced in the United States has drained state and local government budgets, leading to a learning environment of unsatisfactory quality. Through PLATO, which Control Data has marketed since 1976, courses on subjects from elementary-school mathematics to the operation of nuclear power plants are delivered over terminals connected via telephone lines to a distant mainframe computer or through hardware purchased outright from Control Data.

The system has taken hold in a number of different settings. The navy has adapted PLATO's Basic Skills Learning System, a program that offers remedial instruction in reading, language, and mathematics, at the Navy Recruit Training Center in Orlando, Florida. The citizens of Forest City,

Iowa, a small rural community in the north-central part of the state, have embarked on a $1 million program to computerize education in their elementary school, middle school, high school, and at a two-year private college. The program was the handiwork of Norris and John K. Hanson, the crusty founder and chairman of Winnebago Industries whose recreational vehicles are the lifeblood of Forest City. Hanson introduced PLATO to his own company in late 1982 to train blue-collar and administrative employees. He and Norris met on several occasions, discussed the Control Data chairman's perspective on computer-based education, and designed the $1 million plan. Students in the public school system have access to 155 microcomputers—one to each 8.3 students—six of which will be connected via dedicated telephone lines to a mainframe computer in Minneapolis. PLATO is used in the high school for instruction in languages, math, science, social studies, and industrial arts.

Meanwhile, at the University of Delaware, which spent nearly $2 million in 1978 to purchase a Control Data mainframe to deliver PLATO, students use the system for instruction in accounting, organic chemistry, criminal justice, and more than one hundred other credit and noncredit courses. The Cyber computer powers 230 on-campus terminals and by 1982 had delivered more than a million hours of instruction. Control Data mainframes also deliver PLATO at Florida State University, the University of Nebraska, and the University of Brussels in Belgium.

PLATO technology, and the application of computers to education, is only the first stage of the Norris strategy and vision. As is true with so many areas in which the company is involved, computer technology is expected to drive fundamental institutional change. Institutional change in education means the emergence of private, for-profit schools to complement and compete with the current regime of public schools. Control Data in August 1984 formed a new subsidiary, United School Services of America (USSA), to market PLATO in all grade levels from kindergarten through secondary school. Walter Bruning, president of USSA, described the ultimate goal of USSA.

"Let me tell you what I think Bill Norris's fundamental education philosophy is," Bruning said during a conversation in his Minneapolis office. "His fundamental philosophy is to operate the schools. He cares a lot about PLATO, the name. He cares a lot about courseware and what we have learned [about education technology]. But when Bill talks about educational delivery, what he is really talking about is running the schools. . . . We are on a novel and maybe even revolutionary path. We are after the privatization of one of the largest public services in this country—the privatization of the public schools."

Many companies do business with public school systems. Textbook sellers and producers of audio-visual equipment are obvious examples. But few of them base their marketing strategy around fundamental criticisms of the education system itself, or expect their products to transform that system in fundamental ways. This is precisely the Control Data approach with PLATO. And this structural critique is at the heart of a number of company initiatives. It also begins to explain the ambivalent social and political character of much of what William Norris says and Control Data does. The assumptions and ethos that animate its programs in education could be considered profoundly conservative—a perspective on the proper roles of government and private enterprise that gives to the corporations responsibility for a service that traditionally has been the function of public institutions. Yet Norris has designed programs in other sectors that his business colleagues might consider dangerously radical and a threat to their market position and power.

Rural Venture, which was unveiled by Control Data in 1980, is one such initiative. Rural Venture is a for-profit consortium, capitalized at $3 million, whose shareholders include several corporations; Land O' Lakes, the sizable farm cooperative; and the archdiocese of Saint Paul and Minneapolis. Its members share a common goal: promotion of viable, small-scale agriculture during a period of heightened concentration in land ownership, record farm foreclosures, and proliferating misery across rural America.

Rural Venture has sponsored projects from Alaska, where it is working to establish the first integrated small-farm operation in an Eskimo village, to New England, where it has provided marketing and production expertise to revive the sheep industry in a six-state area. It is also active in Control Data's backyard. In Princeton, Minnesota, a town of 2,500 sixty-five miles northwest of Minneapolis, ten families are participating in a program that has been underway since 1980. These families, many of whom arrived in Princeton with little or no farming experience, are growing small fruits and vegetables—raspberries, strawberries, potatoes, peppers—and raising sheep, hogs, and dairy cows on tracts of land no larger than 160 acres. The land is owned by Control Data, and the farmers pay an annual rental fee that ranges from 5 to 15 percent of its capitalized value. The company also built livestock facilities and farmhouses—handsome, roomy structures that are earth-sheltered and solar-tempered.

At the center of the experiment are computerized data bases designed to promote more sophisticated financial management by small farmers and to provide technical advice on crop production, choices of farm equipment, and livestock diseases. The ultimate goal of the Princeton project is for each of the families to develop the financial wherewithal to purchase the land they farm. Thus far, that goal has been elusive. The project has been plagued by major setbacks, including a lawsuit filed by a farm couple who withdrew from the experiment after the husband was maimed by a corn picker. Control Data anticipated that the participants, whose arrivals on the farms were staggered, would be prepared financially and technically to purchase their property after three years. None of the eligible families had achieved that objective when we visited Princeton in the summer of 1984.

Still, the significance and implications of the Princeton project and its companion Rural Venture experiments do not rest solely with their success or failure. Also important are the economic assumptions under which they are organized. These assumptions flow directly from William Norris. The Control Data chairman is convinced that sound agriculture in the United States must be built around a rebirth of small-scale family farms and a reversal of the trend toward increased farm size and intensive use of petroleum-based inputs. He is supportive of organic cultivation techniques. He advocates greater self-reliance and cooperation among farmers to reduce their dependence on the corporations that manufacture pesticides and the handful of traders who buy and ship their commodities. Rural Venture data bases such as AgTech and Advantage, which are delivered in Princeton via microcomputers located in a converted pool hall, advise farmers to limit the use of pesticides and implement alternative energy technologies, such as wind power. The location of the Princeton project close to Minneapolis, and the crop diversification that characterizes each farm operation, reflect Norris's concerns about the economic and ecological consequences of crop specialization and the effects of rising transportation costs on farm income.

Norris has spoken for years on U.S. agriculture and the social costs of energy-intensive, corporate-sponsored farming. He is skeptical about claims of increased efficiency pressed by large-scale farmers whose policies of maximum production and intensive application of chemicals have led to environmental degradation and long-term threats such as soil erosion. During our conversations, Norris went so far as to endorse a lawsuit filed in 1979 by California Rural Legal Assistance, a public-interest group, against the University of California. The suit, which went to trial several months before our first interview, charges that large agribusiness dominates the research priorities of the university and that the development of new technologies and machines to harvest more crops with fewer workers represents a violation of the university's obligation to serve the public interest.

"I think there is merit to that lawsuit," he told us. "I think that the land-grant universities have forgotten who it is they serve. They [are supposed to] serve the maximum number of people. And they were serving a very small segment. So I think there is a basis for that lawsuit. And I think it will be meritorious regardless of how it turns out because it illuminates all the issues."

This perspective is of course anathema to leaders of the major chemical companies, food processors, and shipping firms, who have an important stake in the agricultural status quo. Norris told us that despite repeated efforts, he was unable to convince any of the large food and agriculture companies headquartered in Minneapolis—Pillsbury, Cargill, General Mills—to participate as members of Rural Venture. The organization also encountered resistance when it established a project several years ago in Jamaica, Norris said. The resistance did not come from Jamaican officials but from U.S. ambassador William Hewitt, a retired chief executive of Deere & Company, the farm-equipment giant. Hewitt was "just as hostile as hell" because Rural Venture "was down there advocating small-scale agriculture, and that was just against anything he believed," Norris complained. "That was several years ago, and you see what has happened to John Deere. Farmers can't afford the big machinery. They can't afford all those big investments. Agriculture has got to change."

.   .   .

Because William Norris has articulated a corporate mandate that is so broad in scope, and because he is not reluctant—indeed, he is often anxious—to apply his business perspective to areas where Control Data has little direct experience, the company's initiatives are far-flung and often confusing. The Control Data business strategy began to unfold in 1966–67, when Minneapolis was torn by riots in its Northside neighborhood. The disturbances stunned and worried the city's corporate establishment. Norris decided to construct a major manufacturing facility in the heart of the depressed area and provide jobs for inner-city residents while maintaining standards for production efficiency and profitability. The Northside assembly plant, which began operation in early 1968, was the first of seven manufacturing facilities Control Data has established in poverty areas that include the Selby-Dale neighborhood of Saint Paul, Washington, D.C., and rural Kentucky. According to company estimates, these plants employ more than two thousand people.

From this modest beginning, which remains the most successful dimension of the Control Data business strategy, Norris has extended the reach of his company along four distinct paths. The construction of inner-city plants and initiatives, such as City Venture Corporation, an urban development consortium established in 1978, represent Control

Data's programs to create profitable markets among, and deliver services to, segments of society whose needs have traditionally been ignored by corporate enterprise. Organizations such as Rural Venture are designed to revive constituencies such as small farmers that have been ravaged by structural economic forces over which they have no control. Norris is also convinced that the corporate sector can deliver "public services" more efficiently and effectively than government. PLATO is the most important element of this strategy. Control Data has even announced plans to develop a for-profit program to manage prisons. The company is already a joint owner of a plant that assembles computer peripherals in the Minnesota Correctional Facility at Stillwater. It has delivered computer-based education to inmates at more than thirty correctional facilities in the United States and Great Britain.

Finally, Norris has designed programs and policies that reflect his belief that large corporations must behave in ways that promote the health of communities in which they operate and nurture the development of small business, the primary source of job creation and innovation in the economy. He has campaigned for more than a decade to restrict the proliferation of hostile mergers among giant firms. He has also developed ventures, such as its Business and Technology Centers (BTCs), to promote, at a profit to Control Data, the growth of entrepreneurial businesses. BTCs have been built in Baltimore, Maryland; Charleston, South Carolina; Providence, Rhode Island; and more than ten other cities across the country. They range in size from 40,000 to 400,000 square feet and function as incubator facilities for small business. Entrepreneurs can secure office and manufacturing space in a BTC as well as access to a receptionist, secretarial services, and various computer-based services—payroll, inventory control, management consulting—at prices that are said to reflect the cost advantages of providing such services to a large number of individuals under one roof.

Despite this array of initiatives, it is important to understand that the programs for which Norris is so controversial represent a minuscule percentage of the company's revenues, profits, or capital investment. PLATO is by the far the largest of any of these projects. It generated revenues of approximately $200 million in 1983, less than 5 percent of total revenues. Control Data remains, above all else, a conventional actor in the computer industry that is struggling, as are most large producers of mainframe computers and peripheral equipment, to maintain prosperity in an environment dominated by the awesome marketing and pricing pressures of IBM and the rapid pace of technical change. But the future, according to Norris, rests fundamentally on the shoulders of these nascent enterprises. He offered several startling projections during our conversations. By the year 2000, he said, business initiatives inspired by Control Data's "social needs" strategy will account for 80 to 90 percent of the company's total revenues. Within ten years, PLATO alone will generate revenues of $1 billion in the public-school sector, he projected.

It is difficult to find anyone beyond Norris and his disciples at Control Data who endorses such ambitious forecasts. Indeed, it is difficult to identify any of the "social needs" ventures, including PLATO, that can be called an unabashed success. The troubled performance records of these programs have prompted criticism on Wall Street and fueled division and doubt inside the company. They have also exacerbated the financial pressures that now dog Control Data. Never before has Norris faced business conditions as severe as those in the crisis that materialized in late 1984 and continued through 1985. Not only did bankers declare Control Data in technical default on its short-term loans, but the company was forced to withdraw a $300 million public-debt offering in September 1985 after disclosing that it expected a large loss for the year. The evolution of Control Data's business strategy has been as stormy as the career of the man who engineered it. It is a case study in the triumphs and agonies of corporate mold-breaking.

.   .   .

William C. Norris, who turns seventy-five on July 14, 1986, does not look the part of corporate pioneer. He is of average height, under six feet, and of spare build. But for his chalk-white hair he could be mistaken for a man fifteen years his junior. Norris exercises regularly. At two-thirty every weekday afternoon when he is in Minneapolis, he rides the elevator from his fourteenth-floor office to the third floor of Control Data headquarters and walks briskly up eleven flights of stairs. He also takes long walks in the evening (associates say he always carries a notepad, on which he scribbles ideas and reflections) and vigorous swims in his pool. Norris maintains a grueling work schedule. He spends much of his time writing, lecturing, and testifying about Control Data and its programs. At our request, the company produced a list of all speeches, interviews, and articles by Norris from 1979 through 1983. It ran to thirteen pages. His public appearances included a lecture on prison reform at a conference sponsored by the Brookings Institution; speeches at General Mills and Mead Corporation on technology and innovation; a review of Control Data programs and policies at a seminar sponsored by the MIT Laboratory for Computer Science; and a presentation to the committee of

Catholic bishops that prepared the pastoral letter on the U.S. economy. Norris has also written a book, entitled *New Frontiers for Business Leadership,* based on his articles and speeches. The book, which was released in 1983, describes the evolution of Control Data and its business strategy.

The range of issues to which the Control Data chairman addresses himself can at times seem staggering. On February 19, 1982, less than two weeks after he delivered an address in Nebraska on how to rescue the family farm, Norris convened and chaired a meeting in Florida of top executives from sixteen high-technology companies. The organizations represented included United Technologies, Digital Equipment, and National Semiconductor, as well as MIT and the Department of Defense. This gathering set the stage for the formation one year later of Microelectronics and Computer Technology Corporation (MCC), a vast industry consortium that represents the most significant U.S. effort to date to keep pace with Japanese research in artificial intelligence, software design, and so-called fifth-generation computer architecture. Norris has been outspoken on what he perceives to be the Japanese threat to continued U.S. technological supremacy. Three months, and many speeches, after the MCC conference, Norris was in Washington, D.C., to lecture on precollege education in science and mathematics. Such is the business agenda he has carved out for himself.

The Control Data chairman has no plans to retire, although there is pressure from outside the company, in particular from Wall Street, that he do so. He also has no stomach for the retirement policies followed by many large corporations, such as IBM and Dow Chemical, that require executives to relinquish line responsibilities at age sixty or sixty-five. "It's kind of stupid, isn't it?" he asked us. "If someone has a capability, you don't just turn it off and waste it. It doesn't make any sense. It seems to me that most of these retirement rules just make it easy to get somebody the hell out [of their executive position]. Well, there are other ways to do that. It just doesn't make any sense any way you look at it."

Norris was born and raised on a farm in Inavale, Nebraska, a small town on the Republican River close to the Kansas border. The area is known as "Cather Country" after its most famous resident, author Willa Cather, who moved with her family to neighboring Red Cloud as a young girl. Cather was a friend of Norris's mother, Mildred. Norris spent his entire youth on the farm. He was educated in a one-room schoolhouse and then attended a small high school in Red Cloud. He became enthralled with electronics and ham radios and still speaks fondly of *The Boy Mechanic,* a thick do-it-yourself guide to building model airplanes, boats, and other gadgets. He and his twin sister, Willa, earned money as children by trapping skunks and badgers and selling the hides. "I would pull a skunk out of a hole and he would kill it," said Willa, who is a retired professor from Michigan State University. "One time we caught a badger. I don't know if you know how large a badger is, but we had a difficult time getting it on the pony. Bill always skinned them." Norris and his two sisters still own the farm, which is now occupied and managed by the children of long-time Nebraska neighbors.

One legacy of this rural background seems to be a certain disinterest in material comforts—which is not to suggest that the Control Data chairman has not profited handsomely from the growth of his company. He earned more than $670,000 in 1984 and controls, with his wife, Jane, more than 700,000 Control Data shares. The market value of these holdings fluctuated between $17 million and $34 million in 1984. But Norris maintains a modest personal style at work and at home. The family lived in the same Saint Paul home for twenty-five years until his wife persuaded him to build a more spacious residence in the suburbs in 1980. His office is decorated mainly with reminders of his unconventional pursuits. There is an elaborate model of a covered wagon made by inmates at an Oklahoma prison where Control Data has delivered PLATO. There is a miniature dogsled from Alaska. Along one wall are photographs of American farmers.

One former high-ranking company executive, who is in profound disagreement with the Norris business strategy, remains intrigued by his personal qualities. "We're talking about a very complex character," he told us. "He is a highly intelligent, hardworking guy. He doesn't give a damn about money. He wears old suits. He drives old cars. I used to think it was an affectation, but it is genuine. He looks like Carl Sandburg, he acts like Carl Sandburg. He's a farm boy. He doesn't want anything to do with people from New York. He has a dislike for securities analysts, MBA's."

During our first conversation, which took place in October 1984 at the Baltimore headquarters of Commercial Credit, a Control Data finance subsidiary, Norris was attired in a well-tailored gray suit that showed signs of wear. By his side was a brown leather briefcase affixed with a faded decal from the Bahamas. Norris likes to travel to the Caribbean during the winter, often accompanied by his wife and sister Willa, to pursue the one activity outside of business about which he is passionate—fishing. He has a large family (six sons, two daughters, and fourteen grandchildren), and his children and grandchildren often join him on warm-weather fishing expeditions to Canada. He also communicates with them through regular letters that chronicle his business activities, travels, and speeches. Norris typically photocopies these letters, encloses press clippings about Control Data, and sends them to Willa and his children.

.   .   .

In light of his background, his long career in a turbulent industry, and the range of issues and ventures to which he has applied himself over the past decade, the personality of William Norris and his style of conversation are somewhat disarming. Norris is not unfriendly, but he is a decidedly sullen presence. He typically sat motionless, gesturing only to let his fingers glide slowly over his hair or to jot down brief notes, during several hours of interviews conducted in two separate sessions. His answers to provocative questions, many of which elicited uncomfortable silence or evasion from other chief executives, were often more pointed than the questions themselves. Do you think most Fortune 500 executives are unnecessarily staid, dull, uncreative? we asked. "Yes," he said. "I think they largely manage by the book." Are you surprised by the writings of retired ITT chairman Harold Geneen, who has criticized the impotence of boards of directors vis-à-vis management? "Oh yeah, God," he said with a chuckle. "He must be going senile." Several months before our second conversation, Norris testified before a House subcommittee investigating hostile acquisitions. He appeared alongside corporate raider Carl Icahn, who has mounted takeover campaigns against Uniroyal, TWA, and other major corporations. Did Norris meet one-on-one with Icahn to discuss their differences? "No, why would I do that?" he stressed. "I mean, do you go out at night and talk to thugs on the street?"

At times, Norris's abrupt manner can obscure the gravity of his insights. During our first conversation, the Control Data chairman offered a remarkable opinion on U.S. trade with the Soviet Union—an issue on which he and Control Data have crossed swords with the Pentagon since the company began to cultivate business contacts with the Eastern bloc in the mid-sixties. The Carter administration vetoed, on national-security grounds, the 1977 sale of a Control Data computer, valued at $13 million, to be used by Soviet weather forecasters. Under pressure from the late Sen. Henry Jackson, Carter officials also blocked a smaller deal two years later. That decision prompted Norris to label Jackson "a loud-mouthed obstructionist who only knows how to oppose things—in this case jobs."

Norris holds a particular antipathy for Pentagon hard-liner Richard Perle, who worked for more than a decade as Henry Jackson's chief national-security assistant. Perle has acquired a reputation as the Reagan administration's most rabid internal opponent of serious arms negotiations with the Soviet Union. "I think you mentioned Richard Perle,"

Norris said in response to a question on East-West trade. "I think he's done an enormous disservice to this country. You know, when he worked for Jackson—God, he was a thorn in our side. But goddamn, suddenly he winds up over there in the Pentagon. He has had enormous influence on these export controls."

Were he in a position to determine government policy, Norris told us, he would permit U.S. corporations to sell weapons, short of the most technologically advanced systems, to the Soviet Union. He did not set out his opinion with a lengthy rationale or extensive qualification, but as part of a rapid-fire dialogue. Excerpts from the conversation capture the Norris personality:

Q: Do you remember the computer that was detained by the Swedes? It was on its way to Russia. Is that an example of foolish [export] controls?

A: Yes. Yes.

Q: Why do the authorities do that? Is their intelligence faulty?

A: No. I really believe they falsely think they can hold back Russian military technology advances five or six years by denying them access to virtually all [Western] technology. Maybe they have some minor effect, but the Soviets don't seem to lack for military technology.

Q: The conventional view is that we are always ahead of them in computer technology, on the real frontiers.

A: That's true, because we are market-oriented. We complete the innovation process. They don't.

Q: So does that provide a reasonable area for export controls?

A: Yes.

Q: It does?

A: Well, the reasonable area for export control is simply anything that is classified secret, that has a military classification on it. Fine, exclude it. Nobody would ever consider exporting it, not even Control Data. But anything outside of the military, unless it's very, very unusual technology, export it. But don't sell it, get back from the Soviet Union technology of equivalent value.

Q: Would that be forthcoming from the Soviet Union?

A: Yes. Yes.

Q: You mean, they are less hung up on shipping to us?

A: They're not hung up at all. In fact, they'll sell [technology] to you for cash.

Q: Do you think they would sell us missiles?

A: Yes. Hell, they'll sell you anything.

Q: I mean real weaponry. . . .

A: Yes. Yes.

Q: Now, in this respect, would you have anything against us selling them our weapons?

A: Yes. I think it would be very difficult. . . . Because the politicians would just kick that from hell to breakfast.

Q: But if you made the decisions, would you do that?

A: Yes. If I were making the decisions, and didn't have to worry about getting reelected.

Q: But you would stop at the frontier, the latest weapons?

A: Yes.

Q: That would be quite a breakthrough, wouldn't it, if we sold each other weapons?

A: Well, what would you lose?

Norris's comments could be dismissed as the intemperate rhetoric of a frustrated trader. But they are based on an extensive history of business dealings with the East and a well-developed perspective on the benefits of U.S.-Soviet economic exchange. Since 1973, Control Data has participated with Rumania in the manufacture of disk drives and other peripheral equipment for computers. Its operation was the first, and remains the only, joint manufacturing venture between a U.S. corporation and a Soviet-bloc government. Norris has traveled to Rumania twice in connection with the plant, which employs more than four hundred people, and has entertained Rumanian leaders in the United States. Robert Schmidt, who retired in 1983 as vice-chairman of Control Data, supervised the company's business ventures with the East. He has traveled to Moscow roughly forty times. Schmidt estimates that were it not for restrictive U.S. export policies, Control Data could generate annual sales of $500 million through trade with the Soviet Union and its allies.

But trade volume alone does not explain Norris's enthusiasm and aggressive advocacy on this issue. He and Schmidt are convinced that the Soviets, by virtue of their huge scientific establishment, have made important technological advances that their industrial managers are incapable of applying. They argue that U.S. companies, if granted access, could commercialize technologies now trapped in the laboratory. Norris therefore stresses the importance of East-West technology transfer, rather than trade in its most basic form.

"I feel very strongly that we could benefit immensely by getting access to Soviet research results," he explained. "They don't know what to do with a lot of the scientific work they do. They are not market oriented. They have innovations, ideas, that languish because there is no place to exploit them." These opinions are not based on simple conjecture. The *Wall Street Journal* published a long article six months after our conversation with Norris that described how Kaiser Aluminum and other corporations are applying Soviet industrial processes and how some of those technologies have even found their way into U.S. military programs. According to Schmidt, Control Data officials have been allowed to inspect more Soviet manufacturing facilities and laboratories than executives of any other U.S. corporation. Prior to the deep chill in U.S.-Soviet relations, Control Data had licensed thirty energy-saving technologies developed by the Soviets and planned to market them in the West. The firm successfully transferred to U.S. companies a process to harden industrial tools with titanium nitrite and a stone-crushing technology used by the construction industry.

Our dialogue with Norris on East-West trade underscores his general approach to business. He is blunt, at times to the point of being undiplomatic, convinced of the unimpeachable wisdom of his initiatives, and reluctant to consider in any depth the opinions of those with whom he disagrees. Part of his caustic personality reflects the depth of Norris's convictions and commitment. He has written and acted on issues and problems about which many of the chief executives with whom we spoke had not even thought. Someone as serious as Norris about the potential impact of his programs and philosophies has neither the time nor the inclination to toss rhetorical bouquets to his colleagues or to join them in evading difficult questions. Norris told us he realized long ago that the strategies he has articulated are "alien to most CEOs" and that the pressures for peer approval constrain their willingness to look seriously at the Control Data experience.

"I think that if you're a member of the Business Roundtable, or the Bohemian Club, you want the acceptance of your peers," he commented. "And if you get out in left field, you don't have that." Did Norris make a conscious decision to ignore barbs hurled in his direction from the business community? "No, I never made that decision," he replied. "I just did what I thought was in the best interests of Control Data and what I wanted to do. But I was also aware of the fact that this created a certain amount of conflict."

This combative disposition can also give rise to questionable and heavy-handed behavior. Norris has cultivated an ethos of persistence and tenacity inside Control Data that emphasizes the company's unique social mission and its years of competition against larger and more powerful computer manufacturers. On the ninth floor of Control Data headquarters is a wall covered with photographs of the chairman shaking hands with employees who have been awarded one of the company's most coveted honors: membership in the Bill Norris Shark Club. Norris personally decides who will join this elite group, which is restricted to individuals who have demonstrated singular resourcefulness and determination. One-time inductees are known as Sharks. Two-time winners are Tiger Sharks. Three-time honorees, of which there were only nine as of summer 1984, are Bull Sharks. Norris hosts lavish celebrations for these corporate superstars. Shark Club ceremonies have been held in Acapulco, in a hotel in Greece overlooking the Parthenon, and in a castle in Amsterdam.

A former Control Data employee and Shark Club nominee, who is now a marketing official with a rival computer manufacturer, worries that programs such as the Shark Club have fostered an anything-goes atmosphere inside the company. "I believe in competition, but competition has rules of conduct," he said. "I believe that coaching marketing, and Bill Norris is a marketing coach, is very similar to coaching soccer, which I do. You can tell your players to play well, to play hard, and teach them how to do things the right way. But there's a point beyond which you don't excite them any further. When you start bending the rules and asking them to go beyond their skills, you've gone too far. And that's what the Shark Club is designed to do. To excite people so much that they'll do anything."

Control Data has on occasion found itself mired in scandal and controversy over suspect marketing practices. The company reported in 1976 that it had made nearly $4.6 million in questionable payments in twelve foreign countries over the previous decade. A special committee of the board concluded that three officers of the company and one director, none of whom were named, had "expressly or tacitly authorized" some payments. "Substantially all of the $4.6 million in questionable foreign payments by the computer business appears to have been to foreign government employees for the purpose of obtaining favorable treatment in securing or retaining business," its report noted. Control Data pleaded guilty in April 1978 to federal criminal charges arising from the revelations and was fined nearly $1.4 million.

More recently, Norris's firm has become involved in a widely condemned exercise in pork-barrel spending. The controversy surrounds creation of a Supercomputer Computations Research Institute (SCRI) at Florida State University. Seventy percent of the costs for the supercomputer center, which are expected to run to $63 million, will be provided by the Department of Energy. This federal largesse is the political handiwork of Congressman Don Fuqua, chairman of the House Committee on Science and Technology, who labored quietly to secure a $7 million down payment for the center during the fiscal 1985 budget process. By targeting research funds to a specific facility located in his district, Fuqua in effect preempted the peer-review process that traditionally governs such grants. The maneuvering around the Florida State center has been criticized widely in the scientific community and by university administrators. Nathan Dean, vice-president for research at the University of Georgia, described the center to a Florida newspaper as "a waste of taxpayers' money" and "counter to the nation's best interests." An editorial in *Electronics* magazine declared that "Florida State University takes the prize for brazenness." And the supercomputer center was featured prominently in a "Pork Barrel Scorecard" that appeared in *Science* magazine, which is published by the American Association for the Advancement of Science, in November 1984.

The agreement to provide the supercomputer itself, a contract worth tens of millions of dollars to the supplier, was awarded to Control Data on a no-bid basis. Norris's firm was commissioned to supply a Cyber 205 even though Cray Research, its arch-rival in the field, had won a competitive bidding process at Florida State in 1982. The university dropped its contract with Cray when financing plans for its supercomputer did not materialize. It is not difficult to understand Florida State's cozy relationship with Control Data. FSU was one of the first universities to become deeply involved with PLATO and has continued to make extensive use of the system. Norris himself was awarded an honorary degree by the university in 1983, one year before it awarded its no-bid supercomputer contract to his company. Howard Huff, a former director of the computer center, estimated that Florida State represented "at least $25 million" in computer business for Control Data between 1967 and 1983. He objected deeply to the no-bid award to Control Data. "I think Control Data's marketing approach is, you find the key decision makers and you wine them and dine them," Huff complained.

Norris reacted with remarkable nonchalance when asked to address misgivings about the turn of events at Florida State. How does he explain the scientific criticism? "Well, just that these other guys lost," he told us. "And when there are not very many of those plums [federal grants] around, if you don't get yours, you're not very happy. And that procedure has been used since George Washington's day." What procedure? "Well, somebody in Congress decides that he wants to do something for his home state. And as most of them do, they somehow manage to do it. It's just in this instance he [Congressman Fuqua] picked on the supercomputer. From our point of view, that's alright. I'm not condoning the system, but there it is, I can't change the system. I'm sure as hell not going to turn my back on it." As a long-time advocate of the strategic value of supercomputing, would he not have preferred a more rational, merit-based process to distribute government funds? "Well, sure, but that's not our decision," he said. "Florida State is a long-time customer of ours. If they choose to go that way, well, fine, that's their business."

Control Data's heavy-handed tendencies have also surfaced when the company is faced with criticisms of its initiatives from outside observers. "I think of Bill Norris like I think of Jerry Falwell," said Calvin Bradford, director of the Cooperative Community Development Program at the University of Minnesota's Hubert H. Humphrey Institute of Public Affairs. "He is a religious zealot. He is intolerant of people who don't agree with him. He bludgeons them; he beats them down. If they don't believe in his religion, they are evil."

Bradford speaks from experience. From June 1981 through October 1982, he coordinated an exhaustive study on the performance of City Venture Corporation, a program in urban development designed by Control Data and chaired by Norris. Company executives soon became worried about the research project. So they intervened with top university officials to influence how it was conducted. Control Data deputy chairman Norbert Berg and general counsel Lawrence Perlman, who has since been promoted, met with university administrators, fired off heated letters, and extracted an agreement, which was never carried out, that company officials would be allowed to review Bradford's work prior to its publication.

Harlan Cleveland, director of the Humphrey Institute, wrote a memo in March 1982 to university president Peter McGrath in which he described the "high degree of sensitivity" at Control Data to Bradford's research. He said the sensitivity extended "all the way up to and including Bill Norris." Cleveland wrote the memo less than two weeks after Lawrence Perlman sent him a four-page letter that set out Control Data's objections. Perlman was especially upset that Bradford's researchers had been in contact with officials of governments then negotiating with City Venture about proposed projects. "Put simply, they appear to be carrying out a vendetta against Control Data, and they are using the Institute as a cover to carry out this vendetta," Perlman claimed.

Control Data's intervention became a cause célèbre at the University of Minnesota. An editorial in the *Minnesota Daily,* the campus newspaper, described Cleveland's initial decision to permit a prepublication review by company officials as "an egregious violation of academic freedom." Bradford's report, which remains the most comprehensive independent evaluation of City Venture, was released on October 30, 1982. A condensed version was published in the Summer 1983 issue of the prestigious *Journal* of the American Planning Association.

The rough edge to the Norris personality became apparent during our conversations. When presented with complaints expressed by executives who have left Control Data, many to form successful high-technology enterprises of their own, he questioned the legitimacy of their insights. "When you talk to me about former executives, you are not talking about a credible source," he said. "Because some of these guys didn't make it [at Control Data]. And hell, they'll give you most any reason as to why." Norris was also asked to identify the most serious management mistakes committed during the company's history. We expected this to be fertile ground for reflection. Control Data has experienced a string of technical setbacks in the laboratory, layoffs as a result of weak demand for its core products and services, and criticism of its social ventures from citizen activists and Wall Street alike. But the chairman conceded only one misstep over nearly three decades: failure to phase out production of IBM-compatible peripheral equipment sooner than the company did. Control Data announced a $70.3 million aftertax write-off in September 1984 in connection with this troubled product line.

·   ·   ·

Rock-solid faith of the sort exhibited by William Norris can be a source of strength as well as a debilitating weakness. Because the strategic path down which he is leading Control Data is so unprecedented, Norris and his company continue to generate doubt, controversy, even ridicule among business observers—and little or no support from Wall Street or the chief executives of other major corporations. Operating for so long in an atmosphere of skepticism and hostility has toughened Norris and reinforced the rough edges of his personality. When asked what chief executives he most admired, he was at a loss to respond. "I really can't say," he snapped. "That's not something I'm interested in. I don't give a damn what they do. I've got plenty to keep me occupied."

Even in Minneapolis, whose business community prides itself on its philanthropy and traditional social responsibility, Norris is looked upon by corporate executives with a mixture of curiosity and suspicion. He in turn is decidedly unenthusiastic about many of their initiatives. While Control Data does contribute to some charitable causes, it has not embraced the Five Percent Club, one of the most celebrated business institutions in Minneapolis. The Five Percent Club was created in 1976 by the Minneapolis chamber of commerce and promoted by powerful business leaders, such as Kenneth Dayton, retired chairman of Dayton-Hudson, the giant department store chain. Corporations are honored each year with enrollment in the club if they donate to nonprofit organizations 5 percent of pretax profits. The average for all U.S. corporations is less than 1 percent.

"I have had arguments with Ken Dayton [about the Five Percent

Club]," Norris said. "Ken knows it's not going any further as far as having a major effect on the United States. One day, I pointed out to him that [philanthropy] was fine for twenty-five years ago, but that it's not enough today. You have got to have investment. He often says, 'Bill, why do you piss on my concept? I don't piss on yours.'" Norris let out a hearty laugh. "I say, 'Ken, I'm not pissing on your concept. It just doesn't get us where we have to go.'"

The Control Data chairman smiles easily about encounters such as these. But the pressures that accompany his position as a corporate loner are often no laughing matter. His philosophy of business has required that he engage in magnitudes of risk on untested programs and unprecedented policies that most of his Fortune 500 colleagues would not even begin to contemplate. These risks and their consequences are especially evident on Wall Street, where Control Data or, more precisely, William Norris, has been locked in mortal combat for years with securities analysts over the strategic direction and performance of the company. These analysts are puzzled, frustrated, and amazed. They complain that management has overextended itself by striking out in so many directions—health care, urban development, computer-based education—even as the environment for its core operations experiences traumatic change. Norris in turn blasts the financial community for its one-dimensional evaluations. Few chief executives use their annual meeting as a forum to launch an attack on Wall Street. That is precisely what Norris did in 1984.

"Wall Street, of course, has been hammering the price of our stock," he complained in his address to shareholders. "That's not a new experience by any means, even though it is not justified by any careful analysis of Control Data's fundamentals. However, the financial world continues to be influenced by short-term events and overemphasis on quarter-to-quarter performance. This is especially disconcerting in view of the success of Japan, Inc., due in considerable part to their lesser concern for short-term performance."

The distaste of the Control Data chairman for the ways of Wall Street is intense. How does Wall Street affect what you do because of the importance of the share price? "It doesn't," he replied. Most companies are very sensitive to the judgments of analysts. Is that oversensitivity? "Yes. Great oversensitivity." How or when is a company's stock price important? "The day before you go to market with a public offering." Norris described to us his Innovation Budget, an annual allocation of funds over which he has personal control and through which he sponsors long-term projects he considers of special interest or strategic value. But he would not specify the size of the fund other than to say it totals "millions" of dollars each year. The reason? Disdain for analysts. "Regardless of what [the allocation] is, it won't be right [in the judgment of Wall Street]," he complained. "If they don't know what it is, they can't be critical of it."

The significance of these disagreements goes well beyond verbal sparring and colorful denunciations. It goes to the very survival of Control Data as an independent organization. Conversations with several analysts point to a deep-seated lack of faith in the basic competence of company management. This lack of faith translates directly into a depressed price for Control Data stock, which has been undervalued for several years. When the company's financial performance deteriorated in 1984, its share price plummeted even further. This decline made it a prime candidate for a hostile takeover bid. Michael Metz, a senior vice-president of Oppenheimer and Co., calculated in the winter of 1984 that Control Data was worth more dead than alive. A raider could acquire the company, dismember it, sell the disparate pieces, and receive more from the liquidation than the price he paid. "In the hands of a corporate buyer this is terribly attractive property," Metz told us. "In the hands of the present management its value may never go any higher."

Takeover rumors routinely swirl around companies whose share prices are deeply undervalued. In the case of Control Data, acquisition talk has become a cause for genuine alarm. Norris disclosed during our conversations that he had learned of maneuvering to gain control of Control Data by a company he would not name. An official of this firm approached a senior vice-president of computer giant Honeywell, which is also based in Minneapolis, and suggested that Honeywell initiate a hostile tender offer for Control Data. This company would then present itself to Norris as a "white knight" to acquire Control Data without the stigma of having done so on unfriendly terms. "The chief executive officer of Honeywell just about tore that [senior vice-president's] ass off" for even considering the proposal, Norris told us. "He said, 'You damn fool, you don't know what it is that company is after. They may be after Honeywell.' And once you get into one of these [takeover] situations, things get wild."

It is a safe bet that Norris himself would make a battle for control even more "wild" than it might otherwise become. He has worked long and hard to install an arsenal of antitakeover weapons. Norris likes to boast that his firm invented the generous executive-severance packages that have come to be dubbed golden parachutes. Shareholders approved a management incentive plan in 1985 that will distribute an additional 2 million shares, roughly 5 percent of the outstanding stock, to 250 key executives. Such vast new holdings obviously enhance management control. And Norris promises fierce resistance on many other fronts. "I have been working at this for ten years, and I can tell you that somebody trying to take over Control Data would get into one hell of a fight," he said. "They would be so goddamn deep in lawsuits that it would take them ten years to untangle the whole thing."

If the defiant personality of William Norris allows him to persevere in the face of doubt and suspicion, it has also insulated him from the realities of Control Data's performance in recent years. Norris claims to have presided over a tenure almost free of error. Yet it is difficult to identify one major initiative associated with his "social needs" strategy that can be declared an unambiguous success. Certain programs, such as City Venture and Rural Venture, are controversial in terms of effectiveness but not a major drain on company resources. Still others, most notably PLATO, have proven modestly successful in the marketplace, but represent major investments of capital and management resources. And there *have* been unmitigated disasters. The most recent fiasco to wound the company was the rise and demise of Control Data Business Centers.

The Business Centers first appeared in 1980. They were designed to serve one of Control Data's target constituencies, small business, whose needs for financing, management assistance, and access to markets have not been addressed by federal programs despite its role as the primary source of innovation and new employment in the U.S. economy. Control Data opened Business Centers across the country to provide computer hardware, data services, and small-business financing. But the venture was plagued by problems from the start. Bureaucratic conflicts inside Control Data produced an ineffective strategy for marketing and product offerings. Surveys did not suggest that small-business executives really wanted "one-stop shopping" for products and services as diverse as a personal computer and a $100,000 loan. The high fixed costs of acquiring, renovating, and maintaining storefronts across the country overwhelmed operating profits. But the Business Centers mushroomed in an atmosphere that one former Control Data executive described as "hysteria." There were "guys literally running up and down the halls," he said. "It was like a scene out of a Charlie Chaplin movie."

Control Data had opened nearly 150 Business Centers from coast to coast by the end of 1983. This proliferation of offices soon caught the critical attention of Wall Street, which had reservations about the wisdom of the program and urged Control Data to proceed slowly on such an involved undertaking. "Most of us were saying, and I think quite correctly, 'Why do it all so quickly?' " remarked Wall Street analyst William Easterbrook. "They announced the Business Centers three years ago and said they would go to four hundred offices. I think they got up to a hundred and fifty. Most contended, 'Why go from zero to a hundred and fifty so fast? Why not try twenty offices, see if they work, and gradually expand?' " The fears of Wall Street ultimately proved prescient. Control Data announced in 1984 that it was scaling back dramatically on the Business Center strategy. According to *Business Week*, the failure of these centers cost the company $63 million in combined operating losses in 1982 and 1983. Former managers of the operation, who spoke to us on the condition that they not be named, estimated the losses at closer to $60 million *per year.* "The losses were huge, just huge," said one former executive who was hired to help establish Business Centers.

Overall, Control Data has reported unspectacular financial results with grim regularity since 1979. It has seldom outperformed IBM or the major competitors of IBM—Burroughs, Sperry, NCR, Honeywell—with which it is traditionally compared. Over the past five years it has been the *least* profitable member of this group of companies as measured by return on shareholder equity. According to calculations by the *St. Paul Pioneer Press*, which published an exhaustive special report on Control Data on September 24, 1984, the company's return on equity from 1979 through 1983 ranged from a low of 9.2 percent in 1983 to a high of 11.6 percent in 1980. Comparable returns for IBM over this period exceeded 20 percent each year. The performance of NCR, a non-IBM competitor, fluctuated from a low of 11.7 percent in 1981 to a high of nearly 17 percent in 1979. Financial results for Control Data were especially poor in 1984. Profits dropped to under $32 million, down more than 80 percent from 1983, even as revenues passed $5 billion for the first time in company history.

Aggregate financial indicators begin to suggest the depth of Control Data's current difficulties. But they are only part of the story. The company has experienced destabilizing management turnover and turmoil—departures of key executives, demotions of others—and layoffs of thousands of clerical and hourly employees. It has been frustrated by technical setbacks in the lab and on the assembly line. It has been forced to shed product lines and divest itself of real estate to raise cash for new product development. It has even been battered by exogenous disasters, such as the savings-and-loan crisis that wracked Ohio in early 1985. Control Data lost $21.4 million when a perfectly healthy string of banks owned by Commercial Credit had to forfeit its funds on deposit with the overextended state insurance fund.

The erratic performance of specific Control Data programs, and the turmoil that continues to grip the corporation as a whole, raises an obvious set of questions about the wisdom and impact of the "social needs" strategy. What is the relationship between the course charted by Norris and the troubled condition of the company? Would money spent on PLATO or City Venture, if it were invested in the peripherals division, have helped to overcome or avoid some of the failures in new product development? Is top management spending excessive time studying and worrying about education and the demise of the family farm as the businesses in which it generates billions of dollars experience revolutionary changes? It is not difficult to assemble a wide range of answers to all of these questions.

"The social programs clearly took tens, probably hundreds, of millions of dollars out of the company over a period of years," complained one executive, who left Control Data in 1980. His speculation is characteristic of the bitter dissatisfaction of many former managers with whom we spoke. They charged that initiatives such as PLATO and the Business Centers have drained the company of investment funds that could have been applied to new products and services in more conventional lines of business. All told, we found a level of criticism, even anger, among executives who left Control Data that simply did not exist in any of the other companies whose executives we interviewed. One former manager, who came to Control Data from another major computer manufacturer, said the realities of life inside the company demoralized legions of bright young managers who were attracted by the Norris philosophy. "These kids wanted to believe there is a Santa Claus," this former executive said. "Not only is there no Santa Claus, but Santa Claus turned out to be Jack the Ripper."

Norris and his colleagues take strong exception to these attacks. They argue that Control Data's recent performance is symptomatic of the turbulent environment for all computer manufacturers and that critics of the "social needs" strategy overstate the amount of capital these programs have claimed over the years. Deputy Chairman Norbert Berg, Norris's closest associate inside Control Data, agrees with outside estimates that suggest that Control Data has pumped $80 million into social ventures above and beyond PLATO. This level of investment, while not trivial, is hardly enough to make or break the company's fortunes in peripherals or supercomputers.

"In any company, I don't care who you are, you never have the resources that you want if you are a division manager," said Berg during an interview in his Minneapolis office. "And the more far out, if you will, some of the [social needs] projects are, the more people are going to say, 'I should have more money for my technology.' But nobody outside the company ever complains about Control Data's technical efforts." Berg also estimated that seventy-five of the company's one hundred top executives fully understand and endorse the strategic direction designed by Norris, while 25 percent dissent from it. Norris said the Berg estimate "was probably about right."

The actual state of affairs at Control Data probably lies somewhere in between the animated criticisms of former managers and the reassurances of Norbert Berg. It is undeniably the case that the company has been plagued, as have other competitors of IBM, with traumatic changes in the business environment for its major product lines. The market for mainframe computers has been characterized in recent years by fierce competition. Control Data's peripherals line, traditionally a source of strength, has suffered from vicious price cutting in a glutted market. The need for data services, a segment of the computer industry Control Data pioneered in the 1960s, has been transformed permanently by the proliferation of powerful microcomputers and minicomputers that perform many of the operations once handled for a fee by Control Data's giant computer centers. These are the competitive challenges under which the company has struggled—and to which it has been unable to respond. These challenges have nothing to do with PLATO or City Venture or any of the other social initiatives. But Norris's social agenda has intensified the pains of adjustment.

Perhaps the most compelling example of the costs of the "social needs" strategy is the slow deterioration of Commercial Credit, a finance subsidiary that makes personal and mortgage loans, writes property-casualty insurance, and leases aircraft, vehicles, and computers. Problems at Commercial Credit became so intractable that Control Data put it on the auction block in November 1984. The proposed sale of Commercial Credit, which never came to pass, was also part of Control Data's strategy to defend itself against a hostile takeover. Part of the $850 million management expected to collect through the divestiture would have been used to buy back Control Data shares and boost the price of outstanding stock, making the company less attractive to a raider.

Control Data purchased Commercial Credit in 1968 when it intervened as a white knight to rescue the Baltimore-based finance company from a hostile takeover. For years it was the company's star performer. Control Data used Commercial Credit as an internal bank to lease its giant computers to customers who could not afford outright purchase. Commercial Credit contributed a stable stream of profits during periods when earnings in the computer segment fluctuated wildly. But the performance of the finance arm began to erode in the mid-seventies. Profit growth first slowed and then turned negative. A number of factors contributed to this turn of events: intense price competition in property-casualty insurance, high and volatile interest rates, a lack of management discipline that produced a rising expense base. But another undeniable element in the demise of Commercial Credit was the fact that in the mid-seventies, precisely because it was so profitable, the finance company began to shoulder the financial burden of several Control Data programs designed by Norris as part of his "social needs" strategy. Commercial Credit bore much of the expense of PLATO courseware development. It marketed Technotech and Worldtech, international technology-transfer services with operations from Israel to Costa Rica. Even the Control Data Business Centers, which had been designed by managers from four different segments of the company's operations, were collapsed into Commercial Credit in December 1981.

These business ventures became an enormous financial drain on the finance subsidiary. It is possible to quantify the burden with some precision because Commercial Credit files separate financial statements with the Securities and Exchange Commission. And these statements, unlike the filings of Control Data, offer some insight into the profit-and-loss performance of individual programs. From 1976 through 1980, a segment of Commercial Credit described as Education, Technology, and Related Services—which included PLATO, Technotech, and Worldtech, and in 1980 a small number of business centers—lost $32.5 million. It was the only division of Commercial Credit to lose money every year over this period. And with the exception of 1978, the losses increased from year to year. Commercial Credit began to offer different profit breakdowns in 1981. The relevant category became Small Business Services, whose operations beginning in December of that year reflected the dismal performance of Control Data Business Centers. From 1981 through 1983, Small Business Services, which also included the results of Electronic Realty Associates (ERA), a nationwide real-estate network acquired in 1981, lost $67 million. All told, the cost to Commercial Credit of programs designed by Control Data as part of the "social needs" strategy totaled at least $100 million from 1976 through 1983, compared with combined profits during this period of $360 million.

. . .

The Commercial Credit experience notwithstanding, it is difficult to offer authoritative judgments on the success or failure to date of the Control Data experiment. Part of the problem is the nature of the programs themselves. Norris and his top subordinates repeat over and over again that the development of business programs to address urban decay or promote small business requires time. They are prepared to accept losses, even tens of millions of dollars of losses, for a number of years as the necessary price for ultimate success. Norris and his colleagues also insist that because so many of these ventures represent voyages into uncharted waters, mistakes and missteps are to be expected—and should be accepted more readily than they might be in less creative business undertakings. Norbert Berg explained this unusual tolerance of failure. "We went out and did some things in the agricultural area," he told us with respect to Rural Venture. "What the hell did we know about it? What did anybody know about it? Providing computer services and agricultural [data bases] to farmers is a brand-new ball game. So we got out there and we found out about the distribution channels that farmers have confidence in, what their real needs are. You adapt your packages, your products and services. Over and over again we get into areas and then find out how to do it. That is a very strong and persistent mode for Norris to push the company in."

A second, and perhaps more important, factor that makes it difficult to evaluate the Control Data experience is the disturbing degree of secrecy and imprecision that surrounds so many of these programs. Control Data is in many respects a very open corporation. Company officials allowed us to request material from corporate archives. We received several documents: an internal history of Control Data's founding and first year of operation; a study of the company's early experiences with inner-city plants; an internal history of its efforts, unsuccessful for many years, to establish a data-services beachhead in Japan. Not all of this material reflected favorably on the company. In "Risking Credibility," the review of Control Data's first poverty-area factories, the reader learns the name of the study committee formed in early 1967 to explore the feasibility of such facilities. The group was called the Special Corps for Utilizing Marginals—the SCUM team for short—hardly the most sensitive name one could imagine for such a panel. By summer the group had been renamed SPUD, Special Project for Utilizing the Disadvantaged.

When it comes to reporting on the financial performance of many of Control Data's controversial initiatives, candor gives way to a remarkable degree of inexactitude. Norris in particular has a tendency to make sweeping claims about the effectiveness of his programs. These claims are at times overstated. In a February 17, 1984, presentation to the Catholic bishops, Norris discussed City Venture and its performance in the Warren-Sherman area of Toledo, Ohio. According to local estimates, City Venture helped to create one thousand new jobs in the depressed neighborhood. After reading a lengthy endorsement of the program by George Haigh, chief executive of Toledo Trust, who has worked closely with City Venture in Warren-Sherman, Norris assured his audience that "the Toledo experience is being duplicated in other locations in which City Venture is operating." But City Venture's Toledo operation is anything but typical. The project is far and away the most successful ever undertaken by the organization. No city to date has been able to "duplicate" its results.

Thomas Anding, associate director, Center for Urban and Regional Affairs, University of Minnesota, is conducting an ongoing review of City Venture Corporation. He is reluctant to offer definitive opinions on the success or failure of the program. But he does suggest that the promises of City Venture have not always matched its performance. "It's clear the wildly optimistic notions that the City Venture people had were crazy right from the start," Anding said. He also offered a more general observation. "The one tendency Control Data has is to be honestly overoptimistic about its products. There is a kind of naive enthusiasm in that company that is unusual. It doesn't come out of the marketing people. It's not a marketing strategy. It's real. These damn people are believers. If there were still dragons, they would be the first people going out on horses" to slay them. This "naive enthusiasm" has on occasion attracted the attention of regulatory authorities. Control Data signed a consent decree with the Federal Trade Commission in January 1981 over exaggerated claims made in advertising for Control Data Institutes, vocational schools that train students for entry-level employment as computer operators, programmers, and technicians.

A more significant example of Control Data's tendency toward inexactitude is PLATO. In speeches to educators, academics, and business leaders, Norris routinely claims that Control Data has invested more than $900 million in the development of hardware and software for PLATO. This is a huge sum in light of the fact that PLATO generated revenues of only $200 million in 1984 and that it did not reach profitability until the fourth quarter of 1983. Yet there is evidence that the Norris estimate may be grossly inflated. Few of the analysts with whom we spoke accept the Control Data figure. No less an authority than Robert Price, who became president of Control Data in 1980 and who presides over the day-to-day operations of the company, told *Business Week* in October 1983 that the $900 million Norris estimate "isn't within a cannon shot" of the true investment figure. "Bill likes to have fun," Price continued. "People wouldn't call him a visionary if they didn't think he was dealing in big numbers."

.   .   .

The effort to understand the strengths and weaknesses of William Norris goes beyond a simple interest in personality. If there is one issue on which everyone associated with Control Data—former executives and current officers of the company, independent critics and supporters—can agree, it is that Norris dominates the firm to a degree that transcends the power wielded by the chief executives of nearly any other major, publicly owned corporation. Control Data is molded decisively in the image of its founder and chief executive. This commanding position has allowed Norris to lead his company on a strategic path that encounters ongoing internal and external resistance. It is a prerequisite for continued movement in this direction. His leadership style also brings certain costs. The fact that Norris has ruled Control Data so thoroughly, for so long, has produced a pervasive corporate ethos—a mythology of sorts—that emphasizes his indispensability and creates, intentionally or otherwise, a climate in which dissent and open debate are stifled.

The remarkable authority wielded by the Control Data chairman becomes immediately evident with a visit to the company's headquarters in the Minneapolis suburb of Bloomington. Norris's presence can be felt throughout this imposing fourteen-story structure, whose opaque glass exterior is a vivid contrast to the windmill that stands in a front parking lot. There is the Shark Club portrait gallery on the ninth floor. Scales in all the restrooms are a reminder of the company's—and the boss's—commitment to fitness and health. Outside of Norris's own office is the wheel of a large sailing ship. This gift was presented to him in 1973 after Control Data reached a lucrative settlement with IBM of an antitrust suit filed five years earlier. He has called the suit one of the most important management decisions in the history of the company.

The suit charged that IBM, in a campaign to slow the growth of upstart Control Data, had promised to deliver computers that in effect did not exist. By holding out the prospect of these "paper machines and phantom computers" IBM made customers reluctant to take the plunge and buy equipment designed by Norris and his colleagues. The lawsuit against IBM was a critical chapter in Control Data's history. And it was filed by Norris without the public support of other computer firms and against the advice of certain Control Data managers and directors. The resolution of that suit on such favorable terms is still cited, more than a decade later, as evidence of Norris's leadership genius. Control Data was allowed to acquire IBM's data processing subsidiary, Service Bureau Corporation, at book value, and received other cash and noncash benefits that brought the value of the settlement to more than $100 million.

Dedicated to "Our Helmsman," the words inscribed on the captain's wheel capture the loyalty of Norris's lieutenants—and the standing he still enjoys inside Control Data:

> He chose a course that had no charter
> No other Helmsman dared be the martyr
> He steered the ship and brought us through
> This Wheel for him—is from his crew.

But there exists much more than anecdotal evidence of the power of William Norris inside Control Data. James Worthy, a Control Data director and professor of management at Northwestern University, wrote an unpublished essay in 1979, part of which explored Norris's leadership style. His observations are as relevant today as they were six years ago. "Despite its very large size, its widely distributed ownership, and its able and responsible board, Control Data is as effectively under the control of its chief executive officer as it would be if it were an independent owner-managed business. . . ." he wrote. "There are few heads of major corporations in the country that have anything like this degree of autonomous power."

A former Control Data executive, who left the company in 1981 after more than fifteen years in management, explained the Norris presence in different terms. "Norris had several objectives for how the world would remember him," he said. "One was to be the man who introduced computers to the world of education. One was to be the leading Western entrepreneur in opening business dealings with the Eastern-bloc countries. And one was to be recognized as either one of the leading, or the leading, socially responsible executives in the world. When we had meetings with him, he would talk about how 'our names will be carved in stone.' And that's what he was thinking. It was never an issue with Norris to make money. What he had above all else was a total and complete grasp of power: how you get it, how you keep it, how you use it. And I think any summary of him has to conclude that he was very talented in that area. The man had a grasp of power that is unmatched."

This argument may be extreme, but it is not an uncommon sentiment among former Control Data executives. The sheer length of Norris's tenure, and the fact that he is identified so closely with every aspect of the company's business and history, can create resentment within executive ranks, particularly among managers who question the wisdom of Control Data's business strategy. Norris himself is not unaware of these sentiments. He concedes that he does wield an unusual degree of authority inside the corporation. We read to him the James Worthy passage. He agreed—with a simple yes—that it accurately described his status as chief executive. But he was quick to add that he has *earned* such power and that he is careful not to abuse it.

"I spend a lot of time working with the board [of directors] of Control Data, and I lecture my associates on how you deal with a board fairly," he told us. "One principle is, don't ever surprise them. Don't ask them for decisions, get them involved in decisions. As a consequence, while Jim Worthy may interpret that as authority, I think of it as a common-consent sort of thing. They give me that right [of leadership autonomy] simply because they are comfortable. And boy, I tell you, there is nothing more uncomfortable than an edgy director."

What makes Norris's authority such a unique commodity in corporate America are the mechanisms through which it is exercised. The Control Data chairman has for many years played little or no role in the day-to-day operations of the company. Unlike Harold Geneen, who ruled ITT for two decades by immersing himself in the details of the company's performance and using his knowledge to cross-examine and discipline subordinates, Norris delegates oversight responsibilities to Norbert Berg and Robert Price. The chairman is a remote figure inside Control Data even as his presence is pervasive. According to Berg, Norris does not, on a routine basis, review divisional budgets, product development plans, or capital equipment authorizations—the traditional turf on which struggles for corporate control are waged. His presence is felt and communicated on different planes, of which three seem to be especially important. There is his unusual degree of financial independence. Every year, Norris receives an allocation of funds, over which he has personal control, and through which he finances long-term innovation projects. The relationship between the Control Data chairman and his board of directors, which is more complex than Norris suggests, is another important dimension of his internal authority. Finally, and perhaps of greatest significance, Norris and his colleagues have used company ceremonies, incentive programs, and tales from the corporate past to instill unshakable faith and loyalty to the chairman among rank-and-file employees.

One of Norris's more unconventional sources of power is his so-called Innovation Budget. As a concept, the Innovation Budget is roughly five years old. It serves several purposes. First, it allows Norris to invest in projects and product development without imposing a financial burden on operating divisions—an approach that would affect divisional profits, and thus executive bonuses, and thus management morale. "Norris with his vision always wants to do this, that, and the other thing, to try future-oriented things," Berg explained. "And he was taking money from people's budgets to do it. Several years ago, I said, 'Bill, you can't do that to people because you are affecting their bonuses, among other things.' It might well be the right thing to do. It is much more future-oriented. This way, we give him some money and he plays with it . . . but he doesn't affect anyone's current operations."

Under the Innovation Budget, Control Data employees apply for grants with a one-page form (a copy of which Control Data supplied us) that requires a description of the project, an elaboration of its benefits to the company, and an estimated budget. Norris has used his Innovation Budget to fund Stay Well, an impressive preventive health care program that it now markets to other corporations, and the Advantage agricultural data base. Norris has also used the Innovation Budget to fund the development of projects, such as PLATO courseware, that lower-ranking executives resist because of doubts about their potential returns or viability. He described to us his commitment to the development of Control Data's Lower Division Engineering Curriculum, which instructs students in calculus, physics, chemistry, thermodynamics, and computer science and is delivered via PLATO to engineering schools. To prepare the curriculum, Control Data assembled a "faculty" of engineering professors from several major universities.

"As the next step in our education program I want to offer engineering education, deliver it into engineering schools. . . ." Norris said. "So, Control Data is setting up an engineering faculty. Well, nobody [inside the company] wants to fund that at all." Norris let out a chuckle. "They don't really know if it's ever really going to pay off or not. I don't know either, but I do know that the big payoff is in continuing education, and if we don't get it at the academic stage, we won't have it at the industrial end. So I am willing to take the risk of very little profit, or no profit, in the academic part in order to get the much bigger return in continuing education." With the Innovation Budget, Norris can pursue—and has pursued—this strategy even if his PLATO managers do not support it.

A second source of authority for Norris inside Control Data, and one that is more controversial than the Innovation Budget, is the relationship between Norris and the board of directors. The role of the Control Data board is a source of bitter disagreement between allies and critics of Norris. To his supporters, Norris has groomed a board of directors whose involvement with, and responsibility for, company affairs is a model of sound corporate governance. To his detractors, he has surrounded himself with a rubber-stamp body, staffed with weak individuals or hired hands, that allows him to pursue ventures that would be rejected as unprofitable or unsound by a more independent board.

Harold Hammer, executive vice-president and chief administrative officer of Gulf Oil, served as a high-ranking Control Data executive from 1966 to 1972. He continues to follow developments at the company. "If you examine the board carefully, you will see that he has stuffed it with sycophants," Hammer said of Norris. "They are under his thumb. He gives them bonuses, salaries, stock options. When there isn't a board meeting, they are working for him as consultants. Well, you know, if you pay somebody fifty thousand or sixty thousand dollars a year, they are indebted to the chairman who appoints them. Why should they cross the chairman? Why should they fire the chairman? Why should they even raise their voice to the chairman when that's the hand that's feeding them?"

Leroy Stutzman, an outside director since 1975, is aware of the board's reputation. He resents it. "I realize that since Norris is a strong figure, it is commonly assumed that he, like Carnegie, Mellon, and other people in the past, runs [the board] with an iron hand and people rubber-stamp things," he said. "But that's not true. It's just not true. . . . I will make a general statement here. People are people. And most people, whether they are on the board of directors or some other forum, don't have enough guts to really make a decision. And that's unfortunate. But some people do, and Norris encourages anybody who will stand up to stand up, and he tries to educate them so they will be able to do so. So this would really be a bad rap, to indicate that he handles a rubber-stamp board."

To document his argument, Stutzman pointed to one of the unique features of the Control Data management structure. The company has a set of internal committees, which might be considered "subboards," whose members include managers and outside directors. These internal boards review specific dimensions of the company's business, including food systems (relevant to Rural Venture), education and health strategy, and a corporate research advisory committee that oversees research and development in computer hardware and peripherals. But other aspects of the structure of the board suggest less-than-vigorous oversight. Until 1984 the executive committee was composed exclusively of insiders or quasi-insiders: Norris, Berg, Price, and a retired vice-chairman. William Keye, the former vice-chairman, left the board at the end of 1984 and was replaced on the executive committee by Richard Lareau, who has been a director since 1971. The Minneapolis law firm in which Lareau is a partner collected legal fees of nearly $1.4 million from Control Data in 1984. This stacking of the executive committee hardly maximizes the impact of independent directors.

The board as a whole, of which there were eighteen members in 1985, gives the impression of being an aging and stable group that receives an injection of new blood only rarely. And several members are in fact paid consultants or lawyers for Control Data—a dual identity that could temper their independence. Stutzman, for example, received consulting fees of more than $230,000 from 1982 through 1984. James Worthy, who has written extensively about Norris and Control Data, has also been paid consulting fees, as were Walter Mondale, who resigned from the board to pursue the presidency, and at least two other outside directors.

Norris was asked about his relationship with the board. Has he ever been outvoted, overruled, or compelled to scale back a program at the insistence of his directors? "Well no, because I brought them into the decision-making process early," he said. "By the time the decision was made, there was a consensus. I guess the one that was the most difficult was the decision to sue IBM. There was great concern by one or two members that IBM would just turn around and kick the hell out of Control Data. In fact, one of them told me that, and I wrote it down. But he still voted [to sue]. Years later, when we were celebrating the settlement, I reminded him of [his warning] and he denied that he ever said it. Having gone through a few experiences like that, I think it helps in the long run to get a relationship where there is confidence."

One positive consequence of Norris's authority inside Control Data is that he is free to express opinions that are at odds with prevailing wisdom among his business peers—opinions that other CEOs, even if they did share, might censor for fear of antagonizing outside directors who disagreed with them. This independence is reflected most dramatically in Control Data's business strategy. But throughout much of his career, Norris also has spoken out and been active on a range of critical issues facing big business as a whole. His positions on these issues, in turn, shape Control Data policies and often set the company apart from traditional norms of conduct.

During our conversations, for example, Norris discussed the behavior of IBM since the Reagan administration dropped long-standing antitrust charges against the company in January 1982. This is a sore subject for the Control Data chairman. His company's private antitrust action against IBM prompted the Justice Department to file its suit during the closing hours of the Johnson administration. Control Data has continued to reel from the price and marketing power of the newly unleashed IBM. It was the computer giant's new aggressiveness that forced Control Data out of the plug-compatible market in 1984.

"It was just too damn hard to keep up," Norris said. "By the time you can find out how to make your interconnections [to IBM equipment], two or three years had gone by. And IBM could just take another step or [increase] their production volume and cut their price. There's just no way you could get in there."

"I don't think the government should have dropped the suit," Norris continued. He then proposed two limitations on IBM's power that he said Justice Department attorneys could have extracted in a negotiated settlement: a pledge by the company to disclose its hardware standards prior to the introduction of new products, so that competitors could design compatible equipment, and a system of constraints on IBM pricing inside the United States. "The way it is now, IBM can just knock the shit out of any company it wants to," Norris warned. "And they will." He also argued that the computer giant may come to regret its Reagan-sponsored freedom. "IBM would still be the IBM of today" had it agreed to the sort of restraint structure Norris proposed, he said. "And maybe eventually it would escape the fate of AT&T. Because probably what will happen, and it won't be under the Reagan administration, but the next administration will go after IBM on new antitrust charges.

There is perhaps no better example of how Norris's authority translates into public advocacy, and how this advocacy conditions company policy, than the Control Data chairman's years of activism on another issue: the wave of hostile mergers and acquisitions that continues to grip corporate America.

William Norris has been campaigning for ten years—publicly, aggressively, and with little support from his CEO peers—against a proliferation of corporate mergers and acquisitions whose value in 1984 exceeded $122 billion. Norris's concerns go well beyond the traditional worries over offensive and defensive maneuvers that occupy the debates of business leaders who voice any public alarm over the merger wave. He does not bother discussing the intricacies of PAC Man defenses, two-tier tenders, poison pills, and crown-jewel lockups. Norris instead focuses on the economic and social consequences of the transactions. In 1976, long before the issue reached the level of visibility it commands today, the Control Data chairman published an essay in the *Wall Street Journal* that set out in detail his objections to the nascent trend. He described hostile mergers as "one of the most damaging vestiges of the notorious 'robber baron' era of American business." He even conceded that Control Data, which has acquired a large number of companies, although none of them on unfriendly terms, "would have been wiser" in many cases to have pursued joint ventures or other forms of cooperation with its merger partners.

On March 28, 1984, Norris appeared before a House subcommittee examining the offensive and defensive maneuvers that have been spawned by the increasing ferocity of many of these takeover battles. "We maintain that hostile takeovers frequently have a negative impact on: the competitive environment, employees' jobs and careers, the productivity and innovation of the companies involved, customers, suppliers and, indeed, entire states and communities," he told subcommittee members. "The bottom line is that the role and impact of hostile takeovers is *devastating* in societal terms [emphasis in original]."

What gives genuine weight to Norris's strong views on hostile takeovers is that his activism goes beyond the realm of speeches or testimony. Norris works to enlist other chief executives to join him and adopt a stance of public opposition to developments on the merger front. Here he has met with only modest success. The Control Data chairman has had unhappy experiences with the Business Roundtable, the powerful association of chief executive officers. Several years ago, Norris met with Robert Hatfield, who was then CEO of Continental Group and chairman of the Roundtable's task force on economic organization. Norris complained to us that Hatfield "lectured" him on the importance of free markets and did not evaluate seriously the arguments he set out.

"I was damned unimpressed at their lack of real perception, looking at things in depth," he said of his experience with the Roundtable. "They just had a committee set up and they had a closed mind, and that was that. It was a waste of time." Lately the Business Roundtable has been inching toward a more activist position against the rampant takeover movement. This change of heart is largely the work of Andrew Sigler, chairman and chief executive of Champion International, who is chairman of the Roundtable task force on corporate responsibility. Norris has met with Sigler and reported to us that Sigler's views "are hard to distinguish" from his own.

The Control Data chairman is more understanding about the dilemma of individual CEOs who choose not to express their opinions in public. "The average chief executive officer does fear the possibility of a hostile takeover," he explained. "They think that something ought to be done. But they're very reluctant to stand up and be counted on this subject for two reasons. One, maybe five years ago the feeling wasn't as universal as it is today and there was peer pressure. The average chief executive likes to have the approbation of his peers. That's changing, because they're all scared now. The other reason is, and it is still present, that they are afraid that if they speak out, they will attract the attention of a corporate raider and become the target of a takeover."

On occasion, Norris has convinced chief executives to testify with him against hostile acquisitions (he has appeared before congressional committees at least five times to discuss the issue) only to find that the individual fails to show up. As another example of the power of peer pressure, Norris cited John Whitehead, who retired in 1984 as co-chairman of Goldman, Sachs & Company, one of Wall Street's most profitable investment banks. Goldman Sachs for years has served as Control Data's financial advisor, and Norris said that Whitehead has serious reservations about the merger trend. Yet he has not been willing to speak out in public. The reason? "That is peer pressure from his partners," Norris said. "They make money out of the business." Goldman Sachs has a policy of not advising acquirors in unfriendly takeover battles, but it does design defensive strategies.

William Norris is not the only corporate executive who has spoken out as a critic of the merger wave. Samuel Bronfman, chief executive of the

Seagram Company, proposed in September 1982 that Congress restrict the tax-deductibility of interest on credit assumed to finance hostile takeovers. His views appeared on the *New York Times* op-ed page. Felix Rohatyn has written, lectured, and testified on his opposition to many of the acquisition tactics that have evolved in recent years. The Control Data chairman differs fundamentally from executives such as Bronfman and Rohatyn for one simple reason: His company practices what he preaches. Bronfman published his *New York Times* article after Seagram had participated in two high-profile merger battles—an attempted acquisition of St. Joe Minerals and the acquisition of a 20 percent stake in Du Pont. Rohatyn advised Bronfman on both deals and earns millions of dollars every year as an advisor to other acquisition-minded CEOs.

Norris, on the other hand, has sponsored codes of conduct at Control Data that institutionalize his criticisms of the behavior of other corporations. At Control Data's 1978 annual meeting, shareholders approved a "Social Justice Policy" that governs how company directors must respond to an offer to buy Control Data. In addition to evaluating the offer's fairness to shareholders, this policy statement declares, directors must "without limitation" consider "the social and economic effects on the employees, customers, suppliers . . . and on the communities in which the corporation and its subsidiaries operate or are located." When Control Data itself considers an action that involves potential dislocation—acquisition of another company, a plant closing, divestiture of a product line —company officials must prepare a "Social Impact Statement" that examines the effects of the transaction on the corporation's non-shareholder constituencies.

Outside the company, Norris has on occasion taken his opposition to hostile acquisitions beyond the stage of speech making and quiet persuasion of his peers. He has intervened directly on the side of target companies to help them fend off unwanted suitors. The most recent case involved a small data processing company based in Minneapolis.

On September 21, 1984, Edudata Corp., a Princeton, New Jersey, firm that had gone public less than two months earlier, initiated a hostile tender offer for Scientific Computers, Inc., an established, Minneapolis-based company with revenues in 1983 of $15 million and a workforce of 250. The takeover attempt, financed with a $10 million bank loan, did not attract even a paragraph's worth of attention from *Business Week* or *Fortune.* After all, in the first six months of 1984, corporate America witnessed fifteen mergers with a value of $1 billion or more. But the unwelcome bid by Edudata did attract the attention of William Norris, who intervened early in the process on the side of Scientific Computers.

The Norris presence was at first felt indirectly. The Edudata tender offer was governed by a Minnesota statute, adopted in August 1984, that sets out strict conditions on attempts to acquire control of corporations based in the state. Actually, Edudata chose to challenge the law on the same day it embarked on its takeover attempt. The challenge was unsuccessful. The new legislation had been adopted at the urging of Minnesota Wellspring, an advisory organization composed of leaders from business, organized labor, government and the academic world. Norris is the godfather of the influential organization, and the takeover statute was proposed by a Wellspring task force he chairs.

As the Edudata offer proceeded, Norris chose to inject himself more directly into the battle. On October 1, he sent an angry letter to Albert Angrisani, chief executive of Edudata, whom Norris had come to know during Angrisani's tenure as assistant secretary of labor in the Reagan administration. Norris sent a similar letter to William Simon, the former Treasury secretary, who is an Edudata director. The Control Data chairman let it be known that he would not be a passive observer of Scientific Computer's efforts to resist Edudata's bid:

> The hostile takeover attempt of Scientific Computers by Edudata is of great concern to me as well as many others in Minnesota. I was amazed to learn that as the CEO of Edudata your company would embark on such a mission. Having served in the Department of Labor as a guardian of working men and women and then to engage in a practice which disrupts careers and jobs of employees in a company through a hostile takeover is entirely inconsistent and abominable. There doesn't seem to be any justification for the hostile takeover of Scientific Computers. Even the tired, lame reason that hostile takeovers replace entrenched incompetent management doesn't apply here, because your company has no track record and relatively little in the way of assets. . . .
>
> I urge you to reconsider and back off from your attack on Scientific Computers. That would be the socially responsible decision. If you persist, you can be assured that Scientific Computers will be receiving assistance from many organizations in Minnesota to survive as an independent company.

It is difficult to know how decisive a role either the Wellspring legislation or Norris's personal intervention played in Edudata's decision to withdraw its tender offer twenty-four days later. Scientific Computers agreed to buy back its stock at a premium from raider Edudata. What is clear is that few CEOs have the inclination or the internal power base to strike out so aggressively in a situation with no direct bearing on the health of their own company.

.   .   .

There is a temptation, when one examines the range of business ventures and issues into which William Norris has thrust Control Data, to impute a scattershot quality to much of it. Any company that can build supercomputers, work with Eskimo farmers north of the Arctic Circle, and deliver remedial instruction in mathematics to prison inmates is not an organization with a narrow strategic focus. One former executive described the company to us as "a random collection of projects all going in different directions." Salomon Brothers analyst Stephen McClellan, in a 1984 book on the computer industry, titled a section on Control Data "Too Many Fingers, Too Many Pies." In fact, the company's bewildering agenda of "social needs" initiatives and Norris's activism on issues such as hostile takeovers and East-West trade grow out of a well-defined perspective on the forces that move business enterprise, as well as the mechanisms through which corporations can maximize their social impact. The Norris world view is undeniably eclectic. But it is bound inextricably to his career as a business executive and the rise of Control Data from a shoestring operation to a business firm of global power. It also explains in part the difficulties and controversies that have plagued several of the company's recent endeavors.

The single most important feature of the Norris world view is his relentless focus on technology and innovation as a primary engine of economic growth and social progress. This preoccupation is evident in his speeches, in the pages of his book, even in his personal life. And it embraces a confusing range of productive and destructive technologies. Norris is a vocal advocate of renewable energy and conservation. He is a trustee of Appropriate Technology International. His home in suburban Minneapolis is earth-sheltered, and its swimming pool is heated by solar collectors and electricity from a wind generator. Norris is also a majority investor in FastGrow, a company managed by his son Roger, that conducts research in hydroponics, the cultivation of vegetables in greenhouses with nutrient-rich water. Control Data paid FastGrow $820,000 in 1983 to promote commercial cultivation and sale of culinary herbs, and the small company manages Control Data's own programs in this area.

Norris also spoke enthusiastically with us about several of the most controversial elements of the Reagan military buildup—the Star Wars missile defense system and the Strategic Computing Initiative, a five-year $600 million research program sponsored by Defense Advanced Research Projects Agency (DARPA) to promote breakthroughs in computer technologies for military applications. Both initiatives have generated extensive criticism from scientists and engineers who regard them as expensive drains on scientific talent and research funds that could be applied to civilian projects and as dangerous steps toward increased reliance for military decision-making on computers rather than humans. Given Norris's commitment to the development of solar and wind energy, and other appropriate technologies, one might expect him to share some of these reservations. Instead he dismissed criticisms of the programs on both counts.

"We would be crazy to get out of it and rely on getting an agreement with the Soviet Union," he said with respect to Star Wars. "We have to go ahead, and at some point, when the Soviets perceive that they can't outspend us, you are going to get meaningful arms control." What of doubts about the system's technical feasibility? "Look, I can remember when I used to go to the [navy's] Bureau of Ordnance and try to sell them on the idea of putting a computer, a digital computer, on shipboard. They looked at me like I was crazy," he commented. "I got into a hell of a fight with the director of research at Sperry Corporation over [the merits of] an airborne digital computer. He told me, 'Goddamn it, go back to Saint Paul and tend to your business.' . . . So [technical misgivings] about Star Wars don't surprise me."

Infatuation with innovation and technology in all forms has been characteristic of Norris since his days on the farm with *The Boy Mechanic*. He graduated from the University of Nebraska in 1932 with a degree in electrical engineering. He has spent his entire adult life as a participant in, or leader of, enterprises working on the frontiers of technological development. Much of his career before Control Data was tied to the military establishment. During World War II, Norris was a lieutenant commander in the Naval Reserve and part of a navy-sponsored operation known by the acronym CSAW, for Communications Supplementary Activity—Washington. This group of scientists and engineers, which has been described by computer historians Arnold Cohen and Erwin Tomash as a predecessor of the National Security Agency (NSA), had top-secret responsibilities for breaking enemy codes, and coordinated its activities with civilians working on state-of-the-art computer technology. Between the end of the war and the incorporation of Control Data twelve years later, Norris remained involved with computer research and development —first as a founding executive of Engineering Research Associates (ERA), established with support from the navy in July 1946 to continue the work of CSAW, and later as vice-president and general manager of Univac operations at Sperry Rand. During this period, Norris labored at the center of the computing universe.

But it is the rise of Control Data that most clearly underscores the decisive role of technology in Norris's career. He and a group of disaffected colleagues left Sperry Rand in 1957 (they were soon joined by other defectors) to establish a corporation whose only real asset was the technical competence of its founders. Their objective was to design and build the most powerful computers in the world—computers such as the CDC 6600, which was announced in 1963, delivered in 1964, and carried a price tag of $5.5 million, a huge sum for the time—and secure a profitable niche in an industry that had already fallen under the dominance of IBM. In 1966, *Fortune* labeled Control Data "one of the boldest ventures in modern business history." The description was a touch hyperbolic, but it communicated the technical challenge the company faced. Norris and his co-founders could not expect to survive, let alone prosper, through financial strength or market power. They had little of either. Success or failure rested, above all else, on developments in a laboratory in Chippewa Falls, Wisconsin, where Seymour Cray worked with a staff of fewer than thirty-five people to design and, in the earliest days, assemble the computers that were the lifeblood of the company. Those machines—first the CDC 1604, then the CDC 3600, then the CDC 6600 —were faster and more powerful than any commercial computers available elsewhere.

The inexorable growth of Control Data taught William Norris a second lesson that continues to influence his approach to business. Innovation is expensive, and fraught with risk, and the most effective way to benefit from investment in research and development is to spread that risk among a number of partners. Hence, his emphasis on "cooperation." From his earliest days as chairman of Control Data, Norris has championed the merits of joint ventures between his company and competitors in the industry. This was by and large a survival strategy. As advances in computer technology became more expensive to obtain, the only way for a newcomer such as Control Data to keep pace with industry giant IBM was to pool its financial and technical resources.

Norris for many years failed to convince his industry peers of the wisdom of this strategy. He approached NCR in 1962, and Honeywell in 1963, with proposals for technical cooperation in the development of new products. He was turned down both times. Eventually, however, he won corporate converts—and the use of joint ventures and technology transfers with competitors has played a decisive role in the company's expansion. There is no better example of this phenomenon than the emergence of Control Data as a major force in the production of computer peripheral equipment. In terms of sales growth and profitability, no segment of the company's business has outperformed peripherals over the past two decades. Disk drives, tape drives, printers, rotating-disk memories, and other peripheral equipment generated sales of approximately $1.3 billion in 1983, nearly 30 percent of the company's total revenues. Most of that revenue can be traced to three joint ventures in which Control Data holds controlling interests, and whose other participants include computer giants such as NCR, Honeywell, and Sperry. Magnetic Peripherals, Inc., which was formed in April 1975 and manufactures rotating-disk memories, is the largest of the three joint ventures. Control Data owns 67 percent of the operation, which employs twelve thousand employees in twenty-two plants and warehouse operations in the United States and Western Europe. The other participants include Honeywell, which owns 17 percent, and Sperry, which joined in 1983 and controls 13 percent.

This disposition toward industrial cooperation and technology exchange also explains the intensity with which Norris approached the formation of Microelectronics and Computer Technology Corporation. MCC represents the joint-venture model applied across an entire industry and directed at a common adversary—Japan. During our conversations, the Control Data chairman expressed deep-seated resentment of Japan and its policies on trade and technology transfer. His opinions were especially striking in light of his hospitable views on technological cooperation with the Soviet Union.

"They don't give us the same access to their technology and their markets that we provide them," Norris complained. "Most of their research, or a large part of their research, is done by private companies. Japan doesn't have the large research universities that we have. That is not one of the resources. This [research] is our great resource. And that's why they are buying in [to U.S. universities]. And I say, goddamn it, unless they give us equivalent [technology], they don't buy in." At Control Data's 1983 annual meeting, Norris proposed that until Japan eased its restrictions on U.S. access to technology, its firms be barred from access to university research in the United States. In a *New York Times* column published two months later, he went so far as to suggest he would support restrictions on study by Japanese graduate students in the United States until a commercial accommodation is reached. "I think the Japanese haven't forgotten fundamentally who won the war," Norris told us. "You know, I'm supposed to be a racist and all these sorts of things. I'm just a realist, I'm not a racist. And I really think that's part of it from their point of view."

The final dimension of the Norris world view—and one that takes on particular gravity in light of the direction he has designed for Control Data—is his attitude toward government. Unlike many of his colleagues in industry, the Control Data chairman does not demonstrate a knee-jerk antigovernment disposition. This orientation also grows out of his career. ERA was largely a creature of the military establishment. It was founded with active support from the navy, and nourished by cost-plus military contracts. During its formative years, Control Data, too, was a ward of the state. The military, federal agencies, and research institutions funded with government grants were target markets for the powerful computers it manufactured. According to a 1963 *Business Week* cover story, Control Data sold 70 percent of its total output to the federal government during the first five years of its existence.

This history of collaboration with, and financial support from, federal authorities has produced in Norris a tolerance of—even an enthusiasm for—government activism in the economy. He was the only big-business executive to testify in favor of the Humphrey-Hawkins Full Employment Act of 1978, whose passage, he said at the time, "must be considered as a top priority." Control Data is a powerful political force in its home state of Minnesota, and it has clashed on occasion with other corporations that advocate traditional antitax, antispending positions on public issues. For example, the company resigned in 1982 from the Minnesota Association of Commerce and Industry, the state's largest business lobby, in a dispute over its strident antigovernment posturing. Norris has been a key figure in the emergence of Minnesota Wellspring. The organization's agenda reflects Norris's disposition toward cooperation between business and the public sector—at times, in fact, it appears that Wellspring is his personal vehicle for political influence. According to the *St. Paul Pioneer Press*, Norris chairs the only standing Wellspring task force, whose members normally gather at Control Data headquarters for meetings.

Minneapolis deputy mayor Jan Hively, described the dominant Norris role. "You keep going to meetings [at Control Data] and you keep finding that you're in this terribly impressive room with lots of good food," she told the *Pioneer Press*. "And someone [from Control Data] stands up at the podium and proclaims. They are announcing their dogma. It's very difficult to have a healthy, two-way conversation." Over the past several years, Wellspring has convinced the Minnesota legislature to adopt a number of its recommendations: the creation of model centers in high schools to demonstrate the use of education technologies; tax credits for corporations that invest in, or transfer technology to, small business; the establishment of a fund to provide grants to communities and small businesses to support small-scale agricultural processing and marketing programs; the allocation of nearly $4 million to create a Supercomputer

Institute at the University of Minnesota. This last program benefits Control Data directly, since university officials have agreed to purchase a Cyber 205 for use in the institute.

. . .

The legislative agenda pursued by Wellspring is characteristic of the Norris approach to government. Norris basically defines activism by the public sector as tax breaks, subsidized financing, or outright subsidies provided by government to promote specific social and economic objectives. The "social needs as business opportunities" strategy revolves in fundamental ways around direct and indirect financial subsidies by government and the development of close working relationships between Control Data executives and public officials. With PLATO, government is a market. School systems contract for the delivery of computer-based education or spend millions of dollars, as have Toledo, Ohio, and Richmond, Virginia, to purchase Control Data mainframes. With City Venture, municipal, state, and federal authorities are expected to provide tax incentives, low-interest financing, and grants to fund social services such as counseling and remedial training, as an integral dimension of the consortium's economic-development program. When Control Data builds manufacturing facilities in depressed areas, it expects local authorities to compensate it for the increased training and employment costs it must assume, by turning over property at below-market rates and providing tax credits and other subsidies.

This public dimension of Control Data's programs has on occasion generated media controversy, resistance among target constituencies, and allegations of conflicts of interest and improprieties. On October 9, 1981, the *Minneapolis Star* published a special report on a massive development program in downtown Minneapolis. The project involved two consortiums with overlapping corporate memberships: Industry Square Development Co., which was organized in 1978 by twenty-five local companies to promote construction of a domed sports stadium; and City Venture, whose $149 million Urban East project was unveiled in March 1979 and abandoned less than two years later. The proposals for Urban East generated bitter protest by many residents of the city's Elliot Park neighborhood, the target for much of its job-creation activities. The overall program, which applied to a fifty-block area whose development rights were controlled almost exclusively by Industry Square, was criticized in the *Star* report as unprecedented in scope, vague in terms of commitments from the development consortium, and shrouded in potential conflicts of interest. Several public officials at the city, state, and national levels who worked closely with City Venture and Industry Square left government, either voluntarily or as a result of electoral defeats, and assumed positions as employees of, or consultants to, the consortiums.

"The Industry Square and City Venture companies needed—and received—assistance from influential government officials to obtain valuable development rights for land surrounding the Hubert H. Humphrey Metrodome," *Star* reporter Jeff Brown wrote. "Later, several of those officials were hired by some of both companies' investors after they left public office. The following relationships among Industry Square and City Venture, their investors and government officials illustrate the often-blurred lines between the personal interests of government officials and their public obligations." Brown went on to trace the activities and allegiances of five leading players in the development scenario.

Norris wrote a lengthy response to the *Star* report, which he dismissed as "a colossally stupid array of half-truths, misrepresentations and erroneous inferences." But it is undeniable that Control Data has made a major effort, particularly in Minnesota, to win support from political figures whose allegiance can make or break many of its "social needs" programs. Walter Mondale became a Control Data director after his electoral defeat in 1980 and was paid handsome fees (nearly $80,000 in 1982, for example) for his services as a consultant. When the Democratic Farm Labor party (DFL) was turned out of government in 1978 in a massive Republican sweep, Control Data hired ousted Gov. Rudy Perpich and four high-level members of his administration and gave consulting contracts to defeated U.S. Sen. Wendell Anderson and his top aide. According to the *Minneapolis Tribune*, Control Data came to be known among Minnesota political insiders as the "DFL Government in Exile" and the "Shadow Government." That status changed in 1982 when Perpich returned to office. He and Norris have since worked closely on various projects. They traveled together to a number of states in July 1984, on an aircraft supplied by Control Data, to stump for creation of a multistate consortium that would conduct high-technology research and exchange it for technology controlled by foreign firms.

If Norris's relationships with public officials in Minnesota are more personal than most, they are certainly not unprecedented. But they do underscore a critical dimension of the company's operations that distinguish them from more traditional forms of commerce. Control Data's marketing, on a for-profit basis, of services such as education that have traditionally been provided by government, or its provision of new services that rely on political accommodations in the form of special legal or financial treatment for Control Data, means that the corporation will be expected to conform to strict norms of conduct. The new frontiers for business that Control Data has developed must be matched by new standards of public accountability if the agenda of the company is to be reconciled with the imperative of democratic control. To date, Control Data's track record on this score has proved to be the most troubling aspect of its performance.

Norris himself has done little to resolve these concerns or promote new standards of responsiveness to public constituencies. His angry dismissal of the Industry Square episode is one example. During our conversations, he criticized the Minnesota open-meeting law, which applies to the operations of Minnesota Wellspring, as "for the birds." The open-meeting law requires that most gatherings of public or quasi-public bodies be open to all citizens. We asked whether the proliferation of for-profit schools and privately managed prisons would erode citizen access to officials and information through mechanisms such as the Freedom of Information Act, or state and local equivalents. "We're going into the operation of prisons," Norris replied. "I don't see any reason why we would change our management style, or have open meetings. Jesus Christ, if there is something that's stupid, it's an open meeting.

"I think there will be an erosion," he continued. "For example, we are operating schools, and I don't envision having requests for information and so forth. But I can tell you, I have not thought about it a lot."

The evolution of City Venture Corporation, which was organized by Control Data in 1978, captures the strengths and weaknesses of the Norris world view and the nature of the accountability demands posed by the company's operations. City Venture is a for-profit consortium whose members include twelve corporations and two church organizations—the American Lutheran Church and the United Church of Christ. But it is clearly a Norris initiative. Control Data designed the program and solicited the cooperation of other actors. It is the largest shareholder, with a 35 percent stake, and Norris has chaired the consortium since it was formed.

City Venture is, in essence, an urban-planning-and-development vehicle. It contracts with municipal governments—Toledo, Ohio; Philadelphia; and Charleston, South Carolina are three of more than twenty cities in which it has made proposals or initiated projects—and develops plans to create jobs, promote small business, and deliver remedial education and training in target neighborhoods. These plans are normally paid for with combinations of city, state, and federal funds and can cost taxpayers from $500,000 to $1 million. Most City Venture projects share several features: construction of a Business and Technology Center (BTC) to promote the growth of neighborhood enterprise; a Fair Break program, part of the PLATO curriculum, that prepares individuals to receive a high-school-equivalency degree and provides computerized counseling on employment attitudes and job-search skills; creation of a Seed Capital Fund and Cooperation Office, designed to develop a pool of venture capital and technical expertise for local entrepreneurs; and, on occasion, the location of a Control Data assembly plant or Commercial Credit bindery in the neighborhood to anchor the development effort.

Although it is by no means the largest "social needs" initiative sponsored by Control Data (the entire City Venture staff numbers no more than thirty people), its operations have attracted critical scrutiny because of their broad implications. The arrival of City Venture in a community implies a transfer of authority from government planners and community organizations, traditional sponsors of economic-development proposals, to an outside organization operated on a for-profit basis. The plans for training and job creation in a typical City Venture project revolve around the sale of Control Data products and services. This linkage, which is a critical part of the "social needs as business opportunity" strategy, has been interpreted in some communities as a conflict of interest and has produced resistance and controversy.

Calvin Bradford's 1983 article on City Venture in the *Journal of the American Planning Association* discussed the tensions inherent in the program:

> The most common complaint [by municipal officials] was that City Venture simply delivered to the city a cut and paste version of existing *city* plans. However, the City Venture plans did bring together some existing plans and projects into a single process. Second, City Venture worked into this integrated plan selected elements of the City Venture package, as was expected. However, it was the inclusion of a wide range of other Control Data educational and human service programs that most upset local officials and agency professionals. As one development professional in Florida put it, "We all resented the [City Venture] management plan pushing Control Data Corporation products. Virtually everything they came up with had a Control Data product."

This is not to suggest that City Venture has always met with negative reactions. The organization received a contract in Toledo, Ohio, in April 1979 and for five years sponsored an ambitious, and largely effective, development program in the city's Warren-Sherman neighborhood. Not only did it sponsor construction of a BTC (which houses a diverse group of small companies that includes a manufacturer of automotive safety glass, a health care consultant, and a producer of wire harnesses for computers), but Control Data located a bindery and a Magnetic Peripherals assembly plant in the neighborhood. These facilities on their own produced hundreds of new jobs for local residents. The consortium was also able to convince Owens-Illinois Corporation to locate a box-fabrication plant in Warren-Sherman. All told, according to City Venture estimates, the consortium created more than four hundred jobs within three years after it initiated its activity and one thousand jobs by 1984, when it began a planned phaseout of its presence.

City Venture's Toledo operation also paid handsome dividends for Control Data. The company received large government grants during the course of the project that financed delivery of PLATO's Fair Break program and other computer-based social services. In 1984, the Toledo school system announced that it would purchase a Cyber 170 mainframe to deliver PLATO in city high schools and provide continuing education for adult residents. The 1984 PLATO budget for Toledo totals more than $1 million. According to Herbert Trader, a former president of City Venture who now serves as a Control Data vice-president, the company's successful marketing efforts in Toledo can be traced directly to the goodwill generated as a result of the Warren-Sherman experience.

"This goes right to the heart of our philosophy as a company, and it is something that certain people criticize us for," Trader said during a discussion in Minneapolis. "There was something there for us. In Toledo, we have sold about $3.5 million worth of computer-based education. It would defy any sense of probability that we would have had business there without the City Venture program. Overall, we have done about $7 million worth of business that we can track directly to City Venture's involvement with Control Data. That was always the concept when I started in the business. I didn't divorce the two."

At times, however, the symbiotic relationship between City Venture and Control Data—and the transfer of responsibility for development initiatives to the for-profit consortium—has produced division and failure. The most powerful example of this phenomenon is the experience of City Venture in its own backyard. The consortium withdrew from Minneapolis in February 1981, less than two years after it unveiled a $149 million development project called Urban East.

Minneapolis Star reporter Jeff Brown examined the roots of City Venture's demise. "The Urban East plan was abandoned largely because Elliot Park residents and neighborhood leaders felt that the neighborhood itself should control any widespread development there," he wrote. "Many residents were concerned that the power of public agencies to move people out of buildings, demolish structures and engineer a new economic base in the area would, in effect, be surrendered by the city government—which the neighborhood could influence—to a privately held, profit-motivated corporation, over which the neighborhood would have no control."

What accounts for the differential performances by City Venture in Toledo and Minneapolis? The Bradford report suggests a critical element. "In implementing the programs, the community, government, and other private sector actors all played active, cooperating parts that were consistent with their own images of their roles and capacities," it concluded with respect to Toledo. City Venture has failed, Bradford argued, when "the government agencies that contracted with City Venture transferred their own public planning and management functions to a private corporation. The private sector initiative defined both the ends and means, thus co-opting the public planning processes."

City Venture Corporation's ultimate success, which will be measured by the ability to repeat performances such as its planning and organizational effort in Toledo, will reflect in important ways on the merits of the Control Data business strategy. But the failure of City Venture—and even a decision to dismantle the operation—would have no noticeable impact on Control Data's bottom line. The consortium is capitalized at $3 million, and Control Data has recovered its investment several times over through sales of computer-based services and hardware promoted by City Venture operations. The same cannot be said of PLATO, Control Data's system of computer-based education. More so than any of the other "social needs" endeavors, PLATO has for years claimed an enormous amount of management attention and hundreds of millions of dollars of investment capital. The performance of PLATO in the marketplace for education and training—and the ability of Control Data to penetrate the one segment of this market, public education, that has thus far eluded PLATO—may well determine not only the company's future financial health but the legacy of William Norris as a corporate pioneer.

On several levels, the two-decade history of PLATO is a microcosm of the history of Control Data itself. Norris has devoted himself to promoting and furthering development of computer-based education. Much of his 1984 address to shareholders focused on the merits of PLATO and its potential as a major source of revenue for Control Data. He has used the Innovation Budget to fund development of specific courses and curricula about which he feels strongly. United School Services of America (USSA), the new subsidiary that markets PLATO to elementary and secondary schools, reports directly to Norris and his colleagues in the Office of the Chairman.

We asked Norris whether the success or failure of PLATO will determine his standing as a corporate leader and Control Data's reputation as a force for innovation. He replied "certainly" without hesitation and projected that "there is no question about the outcome." But former executives responsible for computer-based education complained that Norris's personal involvement with PLATO has at times created as many problems as it has solved. Because marketing and development strategies for PLATO are in an ongoing state of flux—a reflection of structural shortcomings in the Control Data system as well as the rapidly changing conditions of computer-based education—sound management requires open communication and quick decisions. The pervasive presence of Norris seems to have detracted from both.

Robert Linsenman, who left Control Data in April 1984 after more than a decade of work on PLATO, compared being assigned to the division with "being a point man" in Vietnam. "It was phenomenal," he said during a conversation in Minneapolis. "PLATO being such a central part of Norris's thinking and such a central part of his attention, it was a very political part of the company. People were moved in and out sometimes on a whim. . . . Some people considered being assigned to the education division as punishment." Linsenman argued that the fallout of Norris's presence was felt most deeply in courseware development. He described the company's courseware strategies as erratic and unstructured —and therefore more expensive than they needed to be. "Norris is not an unreasonable man," he continued. "But people try so hard to please him that they don't give a shit if the business falls apart. A lot of the senior executives in Control Data hate to give him bad news. They hide the truth from him."

It is also the case that the development of PLATO speaks to Norris's qualities as a genuinely farsighted business leader. School districts across the country today are scrambling to install computers in their classrooms. According to Talmis, Inc., a Chicago-based market-research firm, U.S. public schools had installed 720,000 personal computers by the end of 1984. Houston, Texas, whose school system has received extensive attention in the national press, has hired a full-time associate superintendent for technology and installed more than 1,500 computers in 200 of its 235 schools. It is virtually impossible to pick up an education magazine or newspaper without reading about some new software program or yet another campaign for computer literacy.

Norris and Control Data have been on the frontiers of computer-based education since 1962, when the company became involved in research conducted by Dr. Donald Bitzer at the Coordinated Science Laboratory (CSL) of the University of Illinois. Like the formation of Control Data itself, the growth and evolution of PLATO has its roots in the U.S. military. Initial research on PLATO began at CSL in 1959 and was funded by the army, navy, air force, and the Pentagon's Advanced Research Projects Agency. All of these branches of the defense establishment had an interest in promoting inexpensive ways to train and educate soldiers. Control Data entered the research equation when it donated one of its earliest mainframes, a CDC 1604, to be used as the main source of computing power for the system. The company has maintained close ties with Bitzer and the University of Illinois ever since. Bitzer's current research operation, conducted at the Computer-based Education Research Laboratory (CERL), is the largest program for development of computer-based education in the United States.

Given this history, Norris approaches the fervor with which computers have been embraced by the education community with an understandable ambivalence. The proliferation of personal computers in elementary and secondary schools vindicates his years of crusading on the merits of computer-based education. But the thought of millions of high-school sophomores pecking away at an Apple computer does not begin to conform to his broader vision for the use of computers in schools—a vision that is based on the belief that computers can not only deliver instruction but should *manage* the process of education itself. It is this vision, which is shared by Bitzer and his staff at CERL, that has animated development of PLATO from the beginning.

"What computers can do, will do, and are doing is to manage the education process so that teachers have more time to spend with students in creative learning situations," said USSA president Walter Bruning. "The requirements on our schools not only to define minimum competency and see that basic skills are taught but to deal with the whole intellectual development of the youngster requires the use of computers to manage the environment. To do the drill and practice things that are done best by computers. To do the simulation things"—such as computerized versions of chemistry experiments—"that are done best by computers. PLATO is not just a terminal. It is not just a mainframe. PLATO is a discipline to manage a school."

The future of PLATO remains perhaps the most open of all the questions that surround the future of the corporation William Norris directs. Control Data's system of computer-based education is superior on a technical basis to any rival on the market. Its sophisticated graphics and touch-sensitive screen, which allows students to operate the machine without using the keyboard, makes it accessible and interesting to children of all ages. Its thousands of hours of courseware, and its testing and record-keeping capabilities, mean that it has the potential to become more than a glorified piece of audio-visual equipment. Operating PLATO via telephone connections to a Control Data mainframe allows interested subscribers to communicate with users around the world and share new courses and ideas.

But for every strength and selling point, PLATO has a corresponding weakness. The sheer size and sophistication of the system mean that it is extremely expensive. Is a board of education that is hard-pressed to meet teacher salaries more likely to spend $1 million on PLATO, even if it is convinced of the system's technical merits, or thousands of dollars on personal computers to satisfy demands by parents that their children be exposed to the computer age? Its integrated curriculum implies a reduction in the autonomy of teachers. Is it realistic to expect human instructors to turn over their classrooms and lesson plans to a computer manufactured by some giant corporation thousands of miles away? Even Control Data's decades-long experience with PLATO has its costs. Being first with a technology does not always mean being successful. Other large corporations, including IBM and Digital Equipment, are entering the education market after having studied and learned from Control Data's adjustments and growing pains.

Andrew Molnar, an expert on computer-based training with the National Science Foundation, compared PLATO to the ill-fated Vanguard missile. The Vanguard crashed whenever it was launched. But its solid-fuel propulsion system represented a radical advance over the liquid-fuel systems then in use. Insights developed in the struggle to perfect Vanguard trickled down to many other missile programs. "I think PLATO still has probably the largest collection of innovative ideas with regard to instructional computing anywhere," Molnar said. "Much of it is not transferable. Much of it is not usable in other systems. But PLATO just abounds with all sorts of compelling ideas."

One of Norris's remaining challenges as chairman of Control Data is to turn the "compelling ideas" and technological virtues of PLATO into a growing and profitable business that will justify his massive investment in the system.

. . .

William Norris, by his concepts and by his practice, is a businessman seeking a future in old rejected markets through the application of new technologies. He looks upon large areas of decay in cities and the countryside not as jettisoned, expendable sectors of the economy but as challenges that should inspire companies to rethink their marketing strategies and product innovations. His industry peers, in contrast, seek new market tiers on top of established markets and ignore low-income consumers. These managers are relieved, if not eager, to see government move into those unprofitable and forbidding vacuums where people have near-desperate needs for food, housing, and health and educational services. They prefer to service the frontiers of buyers' wants rather than to find rigorous ways of meeting the subsistence needs of "the other economy."

The evolution of have and have-not economies in the United States has long troubled Chairman Norris. And when Norris is troubled, he starts thinking. His observations have led to the creation of a variety of projects, which are in various stages of maturity and the sum total of which still defies final judgment. Consider one facet of the Norris approach—displacement of public schools and public prisons with corporation-owned-and-run institutions. Will these functions be universally accessible or will they skim off the top clientele, commercially speaking? Will these services be held accountable to the public and governmental institutions or will the umbrella of trade secrecy and other shields of the private sector obscure their internal activities? If Norris yearns for a pure laboratory experiment for his ideas, he will have difficulty ever finding or affording such a rigorous testing ground.

Perhaps the missing link is not a mythical laboratory but the absence of more effective ways to involve and excite the target constituencies. Given the present crisis in the small-farm economy, Rural Venture might be expected to be spreading like wildfire across the landscape. It is not. It might be expected that hundreds of Control Data organizers are operating throughout the country to develop a public consensus in small towns and a movement for desired actions. Or that the local television, radio, and newspapers would be communicating up-to-date reports on this ecologically, technologically, and economically jolting approach to small-farm prosperity and self-reliance. They are not.

It could be that the missing seed is charisma—something that Norris does not possess and would not seek to develop. He is outspoken and critical and persistent, like many charismatic leaders or managers or founders of institutions. But he cannot seem to add the sizzle to the steak. It is hard to imagine him selling PLATO on television the way Lee Iacocca markets cars. And he has recruited few people who do. Important new economic approaches have at times attracted political supporters or champions. Norris has had limited success here as well. Whatever one thinks of the Norris vision, there is a base of facts and experiences to evaluate. But those facts are little known outside Norris's Minneapolis headquarters, let alone digested and dispersed by sympathetic advocates. North Dakota congressman Byron Dorgan, who has been a vocal advocate of the family farm, told us he has never heard or read of Rural Venture.

Norris does work closely with Minnesota governor Rudy Perpich, once an employee of Control Data, and with the mayors of certain cities in which Control Data has built plants or delivered services. But even his friend and former company director Walter Mondale, upon hitting the hustings as a presidential candidate, did not find room in his campaign proposals for the Norris economic gospel, at a time when people were searching for social and business strategies that would directly touch the neglected and forgotten rather than merely feed the aggregate indices of economic growth that hide "the other economy." Mondale's silence is the more remarkable because Norris means to expand Control Data's operations, and the reach of its impact, by breeding more small businessmen, farmers, and skilled workers who would further diversify and energize the economy against the tides of conglomeration and stagnant productivity he finds so abhorrent.

One can disagree with the Norris business strategy and yet sympathize with his desire to fracture the rigid paradigm imposed by Wall Street analysts to evaluate corporate performance. Norris wants yardsticks other than just sales and profits. He is a lone voice in the upper echelons of big business who is searching for *qualitative* measurements of corporate output and behavior. Sales of equal dollar amounts can have widely varying economic impacts. Constructing plants in the inner city, as Norris has done, is more than just a way to make use of available low-wage labor. It is a way to help revive a depressed local economy and produce there a faster velocity of market exchange—the multiplier effect. Dollar sales and profits from such a plant may amount to the same as sales and profits from a plant in a suburban industrial park; but Norris would argue that the similarities end there. It is this kind of assault on the conventional models that has brought Norris critical or cynical reviews from business analysts and writers. It is as if these observers are upset with Norris's crusading with shareholder dollars—even though these same analysts and writers hardly bat an eye when Exxon or ITT pours hundreds of millions of dollars down a conventional investment rathole.

Control Data's current financial troubles can deal a severe blow to the dreams of William Norris. As profits diminish from quarter to quarter, and the inexorable pressures from IBM increase, his most cherished ventures will attract heightened outside attention and blame. Already the most recent round of management turnover and layoffs has given rise to finger-pointing and second-guessing inside and outside the company. This newly exposed Achilles heel may lead to further internal and external perturbations that could send Norris into retirement or seriously stay further elaboration of his projects. Norris has regularly asserted that these projects need time—time for the company to learn and time for the ventures themselves to work their way into the rigid or forlorn subeconomies for which they were designed. Quarter-to-quarter performance evaluations mix with Norris about as well as oil does with water. Nonetheless, to succeed, the Control Data chairman needs company profits and an even longer tenure as chief executive. He also needs a public mobilization that can build a broader movement behind him. But the breakthrough that spells such a momentum does not seem to be at hand.

Conclusion

Shortly after *The Big Boys* was released, a columnist for the *Detroit News* wrote an article objecting to the book's "dark portrayal" of General Motors chairman Roger Smith. Our profile documented Smith's many campaigns to flex GM's corporate muscle against defenseless workers and communities, questioned his infatuation with automating the production of automobiles rather than promoting meaningful advances in their quality and durability, and explored his personal shortcomings as a leader and motivator. Auto writer James Higgins was not alone in his misgivings about our critical analysis of Smith's performance as chief executive of the world's mightiest industrial corporation. After all, the business press had been overflowing for at least two years with flattering, at times giddy, reports on the chairman's commitment to organizational innovation and competitive renewal. However, Higgins did grudgingly concede, towards the end of his column, that "a reassessment of Smith's performance probably is overdue."

Over the past eighteen months, the reassessment has resonated from Wall Street to Detroit to the financial pages of every major newspaper in the United States. Roger Smith has been recast from industrial savior to mega-corporate bumbler. In April 1985, the *New York Times Magazine* wrote a glowing profile on Smith titled "The Innovator." By March 1987, a *Business Week* cover story would examine the question "General Motors: What Went Wrong." Inside and outside GM, the loss of confidence in Smith's leadership has become so profound that a shareholder's suggestion at the company's 1987 annual meeting that the chairman announce his resignation met with hearty applause.

What is so remarkable about Roger Smith's fall from praise is that the painful human consequences of his seven years in power—the plant closings, the consistent inattention to quality control, automobile safety, pollution control, and fuel efficiency, the physical destruction of whole neighborhoods to make way for factories, the threats to the quality of life of communities across Michigan as a result of GM's property-tax-reduction gambit—played a relatively modest direct role in his transformation from corporate hero to goat. Instead, it was the failure of Smith to measure up to the dollar yardstick. His months-long spat with EDS founder and GM director Ross Perot, which ended in December 1986 when Smith agreed to pay $742.8 million in what Perot called "hush-money" for Perot's shares, infuriated other shareholders, who were not eligible to sell their holdings at the generous premium offered Perot. Shortly thereafter, when it was confirmed that Ford Motor Company would register higher annual earnings than its vastly larger rival for the first time since 1924, Smith's credibility with Wall Street and the financial press reached a low from which it has yet to recover.

In addition to outearning General Motors, Ford was also much more efficient in 1986 by having $160,000 in sales per employee, to GM's $120,000. (It is interesting to note that when Roger Smith took over as chairman, the two companies' sales-per-employee figures were almost identical). Market share also has continued to drop under Roger Smith from a high of 46 percent when Smith took over as chairman of General Motors to the present figure of 41 percent. This drop occurred even despite GM's program of record low financing discounts. According to most analysts, GM's market-share decline is expected to continue. Investment analyst David Healy of Drexel Burnham Lambert has predicted that GM's market share will fall to around 36 percent by the end of 1987.

In fact, Roger Smith earned the distinction of being placed on *Forbes* magazine and the *New York Times* poll lists of the ten worst chief executives for 1986 and was given the lowest ranking in the annual awards dinner of the *Gallagher Report,* a New York weekly newsletter for management executives. Some of the reasons for this unenviable judgment of GM's CEO are reflected in the following candid comments by H. Ross Perot—the recipient of Smith's generous buyout.

- "The whole problem is at the top. Only in America can you blame the guy on the factory floor. It's the GM system that produces an inability to make good products."
- "I was in every possible way encouraging the company to stay competitive and urging it to move heaven and earth to improve the quality of its cars and the competitiveness of its prices. . . . You've got to move Roger and the rest of those people out of the fourteenth floor of the GM building and down to real places where people are doing the real work of building cars."

- "GM management will not communicate with dealers. Cadillac dealers are angry at GM."
- "Roger Smith turns blue when Ford is mentioned. He goes nuts. Iacocca drives him nuts because he makes more money than Roger." He also added that "Smith has an uncontrollable temper where he gets blue in the face, tears in his eyes, and trembling hands, and is totally out of control."
- "At GM board of directors meetings, we never discussed safety as a safety problem, of people getting hurt. It was always discussed as a legal problem. To hear Smith on the air-bag thing was nauseating."
- Perot relates that one time, in exasperation, he told a group of GM executives: "You hate your customers, you hate your dealers, you hate your workers and your shareholders, you even hate each other—how can you have a bright future?"

Depending on what is controversial at the time, the passage of a few years can change many of the external standards used to evaluate executives. In one of our interviews with U.S. Steel (now USX) chairman David Roderick, we noted that if the conversation had been conducted ten or fifteen years ago, the topics would have been quite different. In the early 1970s, we would have talked about environmental pollution, occupational health, corporate concentration, consumer abuse, and issues of corporate governance. These problems have not disappeared. But today, as a result of surging imports, continuing unemployment, high interest rates, huge budget deficits, and the Reagan administration's commitment to crippling the regulatory programs and the antitrust laws, the focus of executive concerns has shifted appreciably. Leaders of the automobile industry no longer spend much time debating new standards for pollution control or safety. Very few are being proposed. Steel-industry executives have little reason to conduct a dialogue with the leaders of the United Steelworkers. Much of organized labor is in a period of broad retreat, with its bargaining efforts more often directed at giving up less than getting more. Big business now sets the agenda.

In the ebb and flow of competing power centers in the 1980s, big business finds the federal government more accommodating and organized labor less capable of resisting than they have been in decades. It is stark testimony to the dominant power of large corporations in this country that while our economic conditions become more perilous, these companies and their leaders grow even more supreme. Over the past decade, our economic activity has deteriorated, as shown by such key indicators as poverty, debt, productive investment, public infrastructure, and corporate-tax payments as a percentage of profits. The power of the countervailing institutions to business has declined. There have been fewer Justice Department investigations, fewer enforcement actions by the Securities and Exchange Commission (SEC), and fewer Congressional hearings in recent years than at any time since the early 1960s—all in the face of widespread corporate crimes, scandalous business failures, and environmental damage. As the greatest wave of mergers and acquisitions in U.S. history swells—1984 saw more than 2,500 deals, worth a staggering $122 billion—the U.S. Senate no longer has the subcommittee on antitrust and monopoly to examine the social and economic implications of these momentous changes. The panel was abolished at the end of 1980. The philosophy guiding our political institutions is that when times are tough, we should leave the wealthy and powerful alone, or succor them with fruits from the public treasury. For only they can lead the country out of the valley of economic despair to the hilltops of recovery.

The multinational corporate model has no serious challengers on the horizon, either in conception or operation. Except for the continued proliferation of consumer-driven institutions, which advance energy conservation, cooperative buying and advocacy, self-help and do-it-yourself programs, the corporate model is at its highest point of hegemony and ideological supremacy in this century. Harvard University professor Robert Reich explored the standing of big business in a 1985 essay:

> Nothing so exemplifies the unfettered position of today's large corporations as the autonomous power enjoyed by their chief executive officers—"CEOs" in business-speak—notwithstanding the continuing poor performance of the companies they run. . . . [W]e are faced with a major paradox. Our corporations are stewards for a sizable chunk of our national wealth. The long-term performance of these corporations is abysmal, and continues to worsen. But at the same time we—the citizens and the shareholders—are willing to grant these companies, and their CEOs, ever greater license to act in any way they wish.

One result of the paradox is that theorists who have written reassuringly of the enduring power of countervailing forces in the political economy, and the analysts who saw political pluralism taming excessive concentration of economic power, must rethink their appraisals. This is not to suggest that corporations have broken free of many of the constraints forged over the past fifty years. Even in their present dominant position, companies must still adhere to many governmental standards of conduct vis-à-vis workers, consumers, and the environment. But as long as large corporations control the jobs, the investments, the public's savings, and public resources, there is no guarantee that even these fundamental safeguards are secure.

Douglas Fraser, president of the United Auto Workers from 1977 to 1983, told us in 1985 that he believed General Motors chairman Roger Smith would like to abolish the UAW if he could. Fraser also assured us that Smith could never succeed in disabling one of America's most powerful unions, even if he tried. But there is little doubt that GM's strategy is to obtain so many layers of shop-floor concessions and production alternatives—global sourcing and automation are only the most potent weapons—that the UAW will be well on its way to indentured status.

The survival of other forces of restraint is also in question. Corporate lobbies such as the Chamber of Commerce and the Business Roundtable are pushing for major revisions in federal laws designed to curb business fraud and bribery. They also want to weaken the Clayton Antitrust Act and the treble-damage rights of plaintiffs. (Antitrust law specifies that victims of anticompetitive business practices be compensated for three times the value of the damages they suffer. The provision is meant as a deterrent.) Although business executives who have experienced first hand the sting of monopoly abuse do not support such revisions—MCI chairman William McGowan is one such executive—the Reagan administration has embraced them.

It is under conditions of extreme stress or extreme license that the makeup of the nation's corporate leadership can best be discerned. This is an age of extreme license, although the long-term consequences of corporate domination are, under Reagan's permissiveness, beginning to manifest themselves. Even many of the business leaders with whom we spoke registered grave concerns about the structural health of the U.S. economy. Felix Rohatyn worries deeply, as does Paul Volcker, about rampant speculation on Wall Street. David Roderick objects to many of the practices of U.S. banks in lending to the Third World—objections echoed almost verbatim by Dow president Paul Oreffice. "The banks lent their money," Oreffice said. "My problem comes in if a bank says somebody owes them a guarantee. Nobody owes them a guarantee. They took their own risk."

Firestone chairman John Nevin criticized the reckless use of bank debt to finance takeovers and leveraged buyouts. "Responsible business executives don't make bets they can't afford to lose," he told us. "It's that simple. Now, do you make bets? You're damn right you do. It's part of the game. With $1 billion in debt when I got here in 1979, and $1.2 billion in equity, this company was faced with a major risk of absolute economic disaster. An inability to service the debt, which would have led to bankruptcy or some kind of reorganization. I just view that as the kind of bet that responsible business executives don't make. Now, will I bet $100 million on a new venture, like a new roofing plant? Sure, because we can lose it and the corporation survives. But I think when you talk about some of these acquisitions—where people are financing, with bank debt, $600 million or $700 million of a $800 million or $1 billion purchase price, [to buy] a company that six weeks before sold on the market for $600 million—unless you're dealing with an organization of enormous financial strength, it's a bet that you just can't afford to lose. And you don't make bets that you can't afford to lose."

All of these men of wealth and position are connected with others of wealth and position who share their views. Yet how have they all responded to these hazardous and destabilizing trends? Furrowed brows perhaps, private luncheon jeremiads, and an occasional speech or article that reflects just the tip of their real apprehensions. Business leaders are much more likely to create groups that protect and expand their own power than to establish institutions that curb or diminish the undue influence of other segments of the business community. Certainly, none of these men believes that their Washington trade associations or the government will take bold moves to forestall any rush to financial collapse —although the government will certainly be expected to pick up the pieces and bail out an economy that deals more and more in speculation than in investment. America's leading business executives must face up to a fundamental question: Are they and like-minded peers capable of catapulting the power they deploy every day to areas of statesmanship and leadership beyond their routine maneuverings?

The patterns of commentary and public advocacy by investment banker Felix Rohatyn, and the self-imposed caution that shapes and constrains roles outside Wall Street, underscore the urgent need for greater courage and personal risk-taking among the corporate elite. During our interviews, Rohatyn was churning with criticism of the speculative abuses, the excessive pay, and the competitive one-upsmanship that have come to dominate contemporary investment banking. Since the book's publication, Wall Street has been rocked by its most serious financial scandals in memory. The confessed wrongdoings of arbitrageur Ivan Boesky and investment bankers Dennis Levine and Martin Siegel, and the charges of insider trading leveled against other junior and senior members of the investment-banking fraternity, have led many observers to suggest that Wall Street is rotten to the core—or, at the very least, that the feverish rush to profit from the relentless wave of mergers and acquisitions has created an industrywide atmosphere in which respect for the spirit and the letter of securities laws and regulations is valued less than the ability to deliver billion-dollar deals.

This period of turmoil and public outrage presents an unrivaled opportunity for a Wall Street figure with the visibility and credibility of Felix Rohatyn to make a major contribution to a process of industry cleansing and reform. Such a contribution would require bold and decisive action —action that risks offending recalcitrant colleagues and present or potential clients. Instead, Rohatyn has approached this urgent issue much as he has the Third World debt crisis and urban recovery: testifying before Congress, writing op-ed pieces in which he despairs of the current scandal and proposes tepid reforms; delivering commencement addresses that exhort graduates to aspire to goals loftier than the pursuit of quick riches that so consumes their peers on Wall Street.

At times, Rohatyn's business-as-usual approach to insider trading has rung especially hollow. For example, a March 1987 article in *The New York Review of Books,* in which he devotes several thousand words to an analysis of the Wall Street scandals, never mentions the fact that two young associates in his own firm were among the first individuals to plead guilty to criminal charges stemming from the Dennis Levine confession. Rohatyn could perform a major service by documenting to the public how inside information was passed with such reckless disregard for the law by professionals at Lazard Frères, why it went undetected, and what steps Lazard has adopted to make sure such illegal behavior does not occur again. These or other bold steps, such as Rohatyn using a few of his accumulated millions to fund an independent organization to critique and monitor Wall Street ethics and professional practices, would require a break from the have-it-both-ways style of public involvement he has perfected over the past decade. Such a break does not seem forthcoming.

Professor James MacGregor Burns has drawn a useful distinction between two kinds of political leaders. His categories apply to the economic sphere as well. There are, he observes, "the transactional leaders who thrive on bargaining, accommodating, manipulating, and compromising within a given system," and "the transforming leaders who respond to fundamental human needs and wants, hopes and expectations, and who may transcend and even seek to reconstruct the political system, rather than simply to operate within it." There is little in the long climb up the company ladder to prepare the chief executive for such an encompassing tranformational role. For years these businessmen acted as individual maximizers. Organization men, yes—but always looking out for number one in their vaulting ambition to reach the top. As chief executives, their daily work is mission-specific, measured above all else by the number of dollars they bring in for the companies. There is very little time, and even less reward, for contemplating or advocating systemic responses to any deepening economic fragility.

Michael Maccoby, in his book *The Gamesman,* writes of the "profound emotional costs of corporate life, especially the loss of spirit in the pursuit of career." The work of the gifted managers he studied "was incompatible with developing deeper knowledge about themselves and others." Given these limitations of the workplace, to whom else would these executives concede responsibility for anticipating and forestalling the serious economic fissures that are the product of many disparate transactions in a complex marketplace? There were few indications, among the executives we interviewed or in the business literature we searched, that the responsibility would be conceded to the government. As Wharton School professor Edward Herman has noted: "Despite the increase in size of government in the United States, the government has been confined to support functions and excluded from participation in primary economic activities. This role limitation helps make government a hostage to the business community. . . . Government can move only a limited distance in opposition to business desires, otherwise incentives will fail and the pace of economic activity will slacken."

The "support functions" of government are manifested in scores of subsidy programs, tax expenditures, R&D transfers, and protections from competition worth tens of billions of dollars annually. Uncle Sam has become the guarantor, insuror, and bailer-out of last resort for increasingly larger sectors of private enterprise. Federal Reserve chairman Paul Volcker made just this point in a 1985 speech at Harvard University: "We rail at government inefficiency and intrusion in our markets, while we call upon the same government to protect our interests, our industry, and our financial institutions."

There was little doubt in our mind that the businessmen who rule the commanding heights of the economic government in this country believe that it is the function of the political government to facilitate and follow the "regime of capital." It was also our distinct impression that residents of the executive suite are less and less able to understand the dollar-valued economy or predict its future. They are not alone—as prominent economists should be the first to attest.

The upside-down economy (reduced inflation despite record deficits) has many variables and treacherous hidden currents. It would take business executives of unusual substance, all coordinating their policy activities, to assume the mantle of responsibility that their mind-sets and powers have denied governmental institutions. But such will and talent are simply not there. To go beyond their day-to-day orientation means connecting with major, long-term shifts in the political economy that invite broader audiences and different risk patterns than does sticking to their business. Questions of contaminated groundwater and radioactive wastes are on a different scale from a company's use of water or energy. Corporate power exercised at the frontier of turbulent economic and social issues, even if widely applauded by civic constituencies, may jeopardize that same power when used in conventional business activities.

The reluctance of leading corporate figures to take a public stand on the threat of nuclear war illustrates their unwillingness to accept any possible zero-sum relation in the deployment of power between the public and corporate domains. Businessman Harold Willens, author of *The Trimtab Factor,* found this to be the case with many of the executives he has urged, without success, to join the arms-control movement. We experienced hesitations similar to those reported by Willens. None of the executives with whom we spoke was comfortable with the notion that business leaders, as the single most powerful group in American society, have a special responsibility to educate the public on the most urgent issue of our time.

Firestone chairman John Nevin discussed the political disposition of his peers. "I think CEOs are like other people," he told us. "They are going to respond to issues like violence on television, the abortion controversy, the nuclear-arms race, the apartheid problem in South Africa, much more on the basis of their personal convictions than on their corporate role. Their corporate role will put them in a situation where many times they will have to take positions on certain issues as part of the job. But they don't differ an awful lot from the rest of the American public in the sense that many of the issues I listed may seem too far away for them to get distraught over. I think there are compelling arguments to say they are issues we ought to be damned concerned about. . . . I'm old enough to remember when guys used to come around and say they would build a bomb shelter in your backyard for $3,000. Do you remember that? Hell, the risk of atomic war is at least as great now as it was then, and you couldn't sell anybody a bomb shelter today."

But even Nevin believes it would be inappropriate for him to speak out on arms control in his corporate capacity. "If I am chairman of Zenith and I think the company is being cut to pieces by dumping or customs fraud or unfair import practices, then I think it is perfectly fair for me to go to Washington and testify as chairman of Zenith and express my views," he said. "If I'm the chairman of Ford, and I think airbag legislation is wise or unwise, I think it is very appropriate that I go to Washington and testify. Now, if I want to talk about whether drunk drivers should go to jail, about abortion, about whether church schools should be supported with tax funds, about the nuclear arms race—where I have no reason to believe that there is a community of interests among my corporation's employees or shareholders—then I think I'm out of line trying to use my title as a basis for getting a wider audience." Most business leaders can't envision life as an active citizen outside of the corporate structure.

We came away from our conversations more impressed than ever with the importance of analyzing when and why business leaders choose *not* to exercise their power. When major centers of influence do not apply that influence in matters of grave public importance, vacuums are created that result in defaults. There are many issues short of nuclear war in which similar vacuums have existed. For years insurance companies consciously avoided prodding or confonting the auto industry to produce more crashworthy vehicles or even to install seat belts, despite the insurers' interest in loss prevention. But in the late 1960s, companies such as Liberty Mutual criticized unsafe vehicle engineering, and later Allstate, State Farm, and United Services Automobile Association (USAA) also became critical of the auto industry by promoting air bags. And the anticipated auto-company backlash did not amount to much. Abdication of power can itself be a form of corporate irresponsibility and a breach of implied trust on behalf of consumer or worker protection. Conglomerates with many subsidiaries tend to build in stronger inhibitions than single-line companies do. And single-line companies have even fewer inhibitions when the founder is still in charge.

This dynamic is illustrated in the careers of Control Data's William Norris and MCI's William McGowan. In their public candor and their business agendas, through their testimony, dreams, and disputatiousness with businessmen, these two men represent a singular resource—however much their uniqueness has depreciated in time, through success or fatigue. The distinction between these executives and the organization men who are their counterparts is vast. Throughout his quarter-century as chairman of Control Data, Norris took more business risks in a year than most CEOs would take in their term. In the struggle to build MCI, McGowan experienced intensity of frustration, anger, and confrontation that would break lesser executives. During our conversations, both men demonstrated a degree of critical insight and candor, a forthrightness in their observations on business trends, that distinguished them from their reticent peers.

There is perhaps no more compelling evidence of the critical roles played by both of these executives than the course of their companies since their departures from active duty. Since Norris's retirement in January 1986, Control Data has embarked on a program of retrenchment and retreat. The company has closed plants, laid off thousands of workers, and divested itself of 80 percent of its Commercial Credit finance subsidiary. Many of these moves were a recognition of business realities, and represented rationalization of the company's core business operations, such as peripherals and mainframe computers. There is no doubt that much of this streamlining would have taken place had Norris remained in charge. But there is also no doubt that the era of innovation and experimentation at Control Data outside the company's core businesses is over. Chairman Robert Price has disposed of many of Norris's most creative ventures, and there is faint prospect of movement into new areas. As Price told *Business Week* in Febuary 1987, "We don't have any visions. We have a damn job to do, and that's to make the company profitable."

Norris himself remains active in retirement—continuing to speak out against hostile takeovers, proposing new strategies to aid family farms, pushing for more unfettered international technology transfer. But any future impacts on the political and economic debate will be through the force of Norris's individual personality and history. As an enterprise, Control Data now has little in any new departures in corporate responsibility.

The changes at MCI since William McGowan's heart attack in December 1986, and subsequent transplant surgery, are more subtle than the drastic retrenchments at Control Data. But they are no less real, and no less attributable to the absence of the company founder. A May 1987 report in *Business Week* offered this perspective on the post-McGowan MCI: "McGowan's seat-of-the-pants supervisory style is long gone. It has been replaced by a bureaucratic, conservative approach more in tune with [IBM], which owns 17 percent of MCI and has one of its eleven board seats."

Indeed, there has been talk among Wall Street analysts that MCI would now consider a merger with Sprint—a deal that would give rise to oligopoly in long-distance telecommunications much sooner than even consumer-oriented critics of the AT&T breakup might have imagined. Such a course of action would be anathema to McGowan, who liked to ridicule his leading non-AT&T competitor and nicknamed it "Splint." Without his return to active duty (and it is simply too early to judge the likelihood of his return) MCI seems destined to accelerate the trend towards corporate conformity that had begun to surface late in McGowan's own tenure, and against which the self-confident founder might have struggled successfully.

In our study, however, the worst excesses of inhibition were not found among the corporate leadership, but in the upper ranks of labor unions. There, party-line, repressed, platitudinous speech was the norm—when union leaders spoke at all. The institutionalization of corporate accommodation, festooned by a don't-rock-the-boat mutuality, has nearly silenced organized labor as a vital force in the battle over ideas, values, and social conditions. We were astonished that the leaders of the United Auto Workers and the United Steelworkers did not grant interviews on the CEOs of the largest corporations in their respective industries, although Steelworkers president Lynn Williams cautiously answered written questions. Actually, their behavior was not unusual. Anyone who wants to learn more about corporate power by talking to most union leaders should expect to be disappointed in today's United States.

In his 1824 essay "On Corporate Bodies," William Hazlitt offered an important distinction between personal accountability and corporate accountability. "Corporate bodies are more corrupt and profligate than individuals, because they have more power to do mischief, and are less amenable to disgrace or punishment," he wrote. "They feel neither shame, remorse, gratitude, nor good-will." To put the point another way, suppose a village blacksmith in old Vermont had to recall all the horseshoes he forged in a year to correct defects in them. How long would his reputation or credibility remain intact? General Motors has known years when it has recalled a comparable volume of its products. Yet chairman Roger Smith's image-makers—with no audible objections from the media or regulators—continue to insist that "Nobody Sweats the Details Like GM." Artificial entities such as corporations seem garnished with an immunity that can be breached only by a sustained civic focus on the personal development and accountability of their executives. Business leaders need to be recognized as the powerholders they are.

Nearly all the executives we spoke to denied their power. We eventually began to ask them if they considered themselves powerful just so we could gauge the reflexiveness with which they said no. Paul Oreffice does not consider himself the most powerful man in Midland, Michigan. He deferred on that score to retired Dow chairman Carl Gerstacker and certain members of the Dow family. He also argued that organized labor is more powerful in Washington than organized business, and that small business has more political influence than big business. Charls Walker, one of Washington's most accomplished lobbyists, insisted he had "absolutely no power whatsoever," although he did admit to possessing some "influence."

We asked David Roderick whether he worried that any segments of the business community had more power than they could exercise responsibly. "I don't think that it really can be abusive," he replied. "I really don't. Not in a large corporation. And I mean this. You have to remember that you are under public scrutiny. Number one, you have to obey the law. You cannot operate outside the law. You just start with that. Secondly, you can't do things that are morally wrong. Because you get nailed equally fast for that, and you should. Thirdly, you are not a total power in and of yourself. I believe in selecting powerful board members because I believe it's a healthy thing. I like a board member that's man enough and has had position enough to handle authority over time. If he sees Dave Roderick doing something he doesn't think Dave Roderick should be doing, he's going to tell me because he's not the least bit afraid of Dave Roderick. He's not awed by Dave Roderick. . . . Those controls are in place. So I don't think you have runaway power. And I think the people that would try to exercise it would end up with a rather tattered organizational fabric."

While the U.S. Steel chairman may question the existence of "runaway power," he has not hesitated to deploy it—even in the most literal sense. But he is expressing the public stance adopted by most executives on this issue. For to deny power is to affirm the constraining imperative of the marketplace, the regulatory decrees of government, and other external pressures on the corporation. Under this enduring mythology, the corporation merely responds to the market and to other forces whose rewards and sanctions serve to legitimize its position.

We asked Firestone's John Nevin about the nature of executive power. His reflective comments turned the historic formula around. "I don't think there is any way you can head up a corporation of this size without describing yourself as having power," he said. "I will now express the view that power is amoral. It can be used for moral or immoral purposes, but in and of itself it is amoral. Now, when somebody says to me, has somebody got excessive power, you've got to tell me how they're using it. . . . Did Gandhi have excessive power to influence the world? Levels of power that are incredible in the case of Gandhi—but you don't talk about them as excessive because it was used for what most people would perceive as a moral purpose. . . . I think the controls over my power are very substantial. Yes, I can go on an ego trip. But if the company loses market share in Detroit because I get arrogant in terms of what quality level I need, or if I get arrogant with dealers, there is a very quick response in terms of shareholders, the board of directors. There is a judgment that can be imposed on me by the press. . . .

"I have substantial power," he continued. "But I think it can't be used except overtly. The minute I use it overtly I attract attention. And I better be able to defend using it—whether it's the press, whether it's lawsuits, whether it's a strike, the board of directors, or what. Now when I compare that to the kind of unseen power—You know, one of the funniest cartoons I have seen in a long time is the one about the arms manufacturer [for the Pentagon] that has made an indestructible weapon. A part of it is made in every Congressional district. . . . I think generally that corporate executives in large corporations have enormous power. I think relative to the people who work in them, chief executives in any corporation have enormous power. But I think that society is enormously ahead of where it was ten years ago, certainly enormously ahead of where it was thirty years ago, in terms of the responses it has available to it to deal with abuses of power."

Nevin acknowledged that he has a personal responsibility for the power he exercises. Throughout our work on this book, it became increasingly clear that the leaders at the top of these corporations are more than just consensus managers. They can make major changes. The oft-described and widely touted grip of the corporate technocrats can be redirected. Wall Street has always factored in the arrival or departure of key executives when it appraises a company's stock. What is not recognized as widely as the profit-or-loss turnaround role of top officials is their power to change long-held public policies of the company. Who can doubt that Paul Oreffice can personally redirect his company toward strong advocacy against the chemical contamination of the biosphere, just as he has maintained Dow's no-layoff policy during difficult economic times? Or that Roger Smith can single-handedly reverse GM's opposition to air-bag installation? It was the direct personal commitment of CEOs Archie Boe of Allstate and Edward Rust of State Farm that led to their companies' active championship of air bags while their counterparts in other large insurance firms did not.

Decisions made at the top can be changed at the top. Even corporate approaches insinuated for years throughout seemingly entrenched bureaucracies can be reversed by the top. In 1980 the new chairman of Ford Motor Company, Philip Caldwell, declared to his associates that the company was going to excise $1 billion of waste each year. When a Ford executive told us this story in 1984—adding that the goal had indeed been reached each year, leaving middle-management offices empty by the gross —we recalled how many times we had heard corporate vice-presidents testify that their companies just could not afford to meet health and safety standards for their workers, consumers, and communities.

The human values of life and health did not have the kind of perturbing effect to force large corporations to recognize how many layers of fat they were building up in their organizations. It took the Japanese commercial challenge and a series of best-selling books on Japanese management and efficiency to push big business in the United States to examine its hidden lard. Over the years of observing and contrasting executive behavior, we have noted a few revealing instances where business leaders have managed to see beyond the balance sheet and income statement. J. Paul Austin, then-chairman of Coca-Cola, told us in the early 1970s that it was a visit to his company's Florida orange groves that influenced him to improve the harsh conditions of his migrant workers. A few years later, we were told by a director of Armco Steel that the chairman once decided to provide some diversity for a board of directors' meeting by taking the members into one of the company's coal mines. After just thirty minutes inside the cold, dark shaft, this director decided he would not again claim that the miners were overpaid. The abstractions of corporate leadership can become pitiless convictions when unchallenged by exposure to the pain of the afflicted.

Consider the case of Roger Smith. The GM chairman pays far more personal attention to the annual science awards of the General Motors Cancer Research Foundation than he does to the cancer and cancer risks his own factories inflict on GM workers. By being identified with a foundation with less than $2 million in assets, Smith has reaped considerable amounts of favorable publicity. The annual awards ceremony for the honorees takes place in an elegant dining room at the U.S. State Department. Formal dress, classical music, fine food and wine, and an assortment of celebrities mix easily during the gala evening. How far away this world must seem to the workers at GM's wood-model shops in the greater Detroit area. The Michigan Cancer Foundation discovered a rate of cancer in these facilities 50 percent higher than that among a matched group of males taken from the general Detroit population. The findings were disclosed in 1980, after GM workers, feeling that neither the union nor the company would listen to their cancer worries, visited the *Detroit News*. The newspaper in turn published a series of verifying articles.

In 1984, following other worrisome health surveys, GM and the UAW announced a five-year study of the effects of exposure to cutting fluids used in machine-tooling plants. Even this dilatory response would not have materialized without employees such as Michael Bennett, a journeyman pipefitter at GM's Fisher Body plant in Flint, Michigan. In 1977 Bennett began to suspect that the number of his fellow employees dying from cancer was unusually large. Analyzing the available data, he confirmed his suspicion: among his sample of workers, the death rate from cancer, especially lung cancer, was much higher than that for the comparable population. Although he demonstrated there was a problem, he had no resources to establish the cause. General Motors did have the resources —but chose not to follow up. Bennett, the amateur epidemiologist, was one of the 1981 winners of the Michigan Citizen of the Year Award sponsored by the *Detroit News*.

The story of GM workers sounding the alarm on high cancer risks is an instructive lesson in the style of CEOs such as Roger Smith. He honors scientists for advancing cancer detection and cancer prevention; he ignores his own workers who have helped alert his company about the need to engage in the same task. There may be many explanations for this contrast, and many remedies for it, but the one departure that could bring results is straightforward: Smith needs to rub shoulders with GM plant workers. If Whitney MacMillan, chairman of the world's largest grain trader, were to visit the famine fields of east Africa, would he return to the château on Lake Minnetonka and resume his detached attitude toward a scourge that Cargill could help alleviate? Would David Roderick, the nonnegotiable man, have exercised a more sensitive response to his plant shutdowns if he had spent a few days in the affected communities, among their residents? These questions are not whimsical, even though they are seldom asked. It is of immeasurable significance for a chief executive to have the qualities of a person, and engage the personal growth that touches conscience, while at the helm of that impersonal, artificial entity we call the modern corporation.

As so often happens with systems of power, when external constraints wither, internal strains begin to appear. The most visible current threat to the power and autonomy of corporate leaders is the emergence of Wall Street as a contending power center. The capital markets have found many ways to flex their muscle and check managerial autonomy. They have also prompted many questions about the incentives thus created for shortsighted business conduct. Institutional money managers now send stock prices soaring or plummeting overnight. Investment bankers charge outrageous fees for a few weeks' counseling on a merger, and executives obligingly write out a check. The unprecedented takeover wave has instilled a degree of paranoia, if not outright panic, in executive suites across the country. Reshuffling of assets, billion-dollar loans to finance the repurchase of common stock, massive layoffs—these and other maneuvers reflect the business response to the ever-present threat of the corporate raiders.

Wall Street's new assertiveness has affected major decisions by most of the men profiled in this book. David Roderick, whose company's outdated and inefficient steel operations could occupy the full-time attention of several top executives determined to turn them around, has instead devoted his most focused energies to dressing up his company's assets and fending off the advances of hostile suitors. In July 1986, Roderick approved a symbolic step intended to ratify in the eyes of Wall Street the strategic redirection he had set in motion upon assuming office: the name U.S. Steel was officially changed to USX Corporation. Several months later, in the midst of what would become the longest steel strike in U.S. history, Roderick's attention was focused not on the bargaining table, but instead on Wall Street, as rumors swirled that Australian raider Robert Holmes à Court and New York corporate raider Carl Icahn had accumulated large blocks of USX stock.

These rumors soon proved to be true, and there ensued a tendentious battle for control of the giant firm. Roderick and his adversaries danced the now-familiar takeover shuffle: angry cries of greenmail from Pittsburgh, allegations of managerial incompetence from New York, promises of financial restructuring in the interests of shareholders, eventual accommodation. While the ultimate outcome of this currently dormant struggle for USX remains open (Icahn still controls a large block of company stock), it is fair to say that Wall Street was able to command the attention of Chairman Roderick in a way that the anguished protests of unemployed steelworkers and their suffering communities could not hope to match.

William McGowan spoke with us about the roots and implications of the volatile stock market. "The one extreme for a hundred years was that you always gave your [corporate] pension money to the bank," he said. "And the bank would take the pension fund and abuse it unmercifully. They'd invest you in forty-year railroad bonds, at four percent or something. When inflation started to get bad, everybody started realizing, This is ridiculous. Gradually over the last ten years we've gone to the other extreme, where every money manager is now measured through a computer against every other money manager and against every [stock-performance] index. And he's got to perform. So they're like lemmings. Once there's a favorite [stock] and everybody's on it, well, I've got to get on it. And once everybody gets off it, then I've got to get off. That's their business, and I understand. They all admit to me that it's wrong, that what they do is wrong. But I have to deal with it [as a businessman] anyway."

Mesa Petroleum chairman T. Boone Pickens personifies this new force on the corporate scene. He has tapped Wall Street's enthusiasm for acquisition battles, and the money managers' willingness to invest heavily in junk bonds, to mount campaigns to take over Cities Service, Gulf, Phillips Petroleum, and Unocal—all companies many times larger than the enterprise Pickens directs. Whatever the ultimate effect of his controversial deals—and there is persuasive evidence that the corporate backlash to Pickens's threats has robbed from shareholders more rights and potential economic value than he and other raiders have created—his impact has been felt well beyond these particular takeover gambits. And his experiences reflect the severe pressures brought to bear on anyone that dares challenge the corporate status quo.

During a long conversation in June 1985, well before the publication of his autobiography, Pickens described some of the opposition tactics of his targets. "You won't even believe the pressures that are involved here," he told us. "For instance, I knew I had a block of stock that was with us in the Gulf deal. And then there was pressure put on that particular investment advisor to [vote] with Gulf management. This pressure was totally removed from Gulf. It was another company. The CEO called the investment advisor up and said, 'vote with Gulf management because we're thinking of putting some of our pension funds around and we're looking at your firm.' It's that kind of pressure that is coming to bear on these money managers."

We asked Pickens to describe other obstacles that target companies and their allies place in his way. What follows is a portion of our conversation:

Ralph Nader: They put pressures on banks not to lend you money?
Boone Pickens: Oh, yeah. That goes on all the time.
Nader: In your book are you going to name names?
Pickens: Oh, yeah. I'll have it all in there. It's worse than that. The Business Roundtable puts pressure on you.
Nader: How do they do that?
Pickens: That's real easy. I can tell you how. They'll tell them, "You quit doing business with this guy or we're going to quit doing business with you."
Nader: Does it work?
Pickens: Sure. They eliminated some of our banks that way.
Nader: So it's like the old-boy network.
Pickens: Absolutely. Totally.

Pickens has faced challenges of a more personal sort. He has been vilified by the business establishment, in the press, and before Congressional committees. With a touch of humor, he recalled testimony delivered hours before our interview by Unocal chairman Fred Hartley, who successfully resisted a Mesa-led takeover attempt. "They had Hartley up there [on Capitol Hill] today," Pickens said. "He went on for about twenty minutes in just a rambling diatribe. He called me a jackass. He said that any jackass can do what Pickens has done, something like that. . . . He pointed over at [New York Senator Alfonse] D'Amato and said, 'You have to do something about these barbarians! They are destroying America!' And D'Amato laughed at him. He said, 'What do you have in mind for us to do, Mr. Hartley?' You know, as if it was a joke."

Pickens also told us that Phillips hired a private investigative firm— Jules Kroll & Associates—"to dig up dirt" on him. "We sued them finally," he said. "They called an ex-employee who they thought was an enemy of mine. And the irony of the thing was, yes, I had fired him. But we weren't really enemies, and it so happened our families were good friends. They asked him if he would talk about me, and he said yes. And they said, 'Can you tell me where his children are located?' And he said, 'That's the end of this interview,' and hung up the phone. He then called me and told me what happened." Does Pickens believe Phillips wanted to play rough with his family? "I really don't think they were going to do any harm to them," he replied. "I think what they were going to do was to harass them. I think they were going to start calling them up and say, 'Your dad's a bad guy,' and stuff like that."

The Business Roundtable is doing its business not only privately—"it's all done at lunch," Pickens said—but also publicly, with a legislative campaign on Capitol Hill to secure passage of various antitakeover measures. The premier lobbying arm of big business knows what it wants in the legislative arena because thousands of corporations in the United States have approved bylaw and charter changes to defend against the raiders—supermajority provisions, reincorporation in Delaware, staggered elections of directors, new stock with special voting rights—even though the vast majority of the companies are not under a remote threat of a hostile offer. While these charter provisions may never be directed against a raider, they will make it more difficult for shareholder advocates to prevail against management on nonacquisition issues. There is little doubt that for now, the net effect of the celebrated takeover moves by Pickens and his colleagues has been a dilution of shareholder rights and a dramatic increase in the debt-servicing burden for many large and middle-sized companies. The latter development reflects a conscious decision by some CEOs to make their companies' balance sheets less sound, and thus less attractive to the raiders.

T. Boone Pickens portrays his takeover attempts against Gulf, Unocal, and the other targets as part of a grand campaign to promote greater management accountability with respect to shareholder value. "You can forget the individual [takeover] deals," he told us. "Individual deals are somewhat insignificant compared to the main event. The main event is, Who the hell is it that owns the company?" What are the concrete manifestations of the main event? "I haven't thought about it," he replied. And that is the problem in a nutshell.

Pickens told us he has no plans to take a portion of his handsome profits and join with other prominent raiders to establish an advocacy institution that would challenge the backlash forces they have unleashed, and build political momentum to preserve and extend shareholder rights.

Such an institution could educate shareholders on the impact of the "defensive" charter amendments they are approving in droves. It could organize on Capitol Hill in favor of the much-threatened principle of one share, one vote. It could propose ways to make annual meetings a more effective forum for shareholder participation. That was July 1985. By August 1986, Pickens was unveiling, with great fanfare, United Shareholders of America (USA), a research-and-lobbying group formed to pursue precisely the brand of shareholder activism we had described thirteen months earlier.

The forces of opposition to Pickens are not unlike the corporate reaction to the rise of the consumer movement in the 1960s. The independent-minded oilman has been exposed to assaults on his motives and integrity, intervention by forces in the business community outside the realm in which he operates, and the unified pressures of corporate lobbies such as the Business Roundtable. Large corporations also have more escape clauses than ever before to avoid accountability and reduce financial uncertainty. CEOs have few worries about losing authority or directive power from within the corporate structure. It is still relatively rare for boards of directors or shareholder demands to exert specific reshapings of policy, behavior, or direction. To be sure, should a CEO be running the company into an annual sea of red ink, these usually passive control mechanisms would assert themselves. But the overwhelming norm is unchallenged control of the board by the chairman, who has a major say in the nomination of directors—not to mention the other advantages of controlling information and stafftime, which tilt the balance of power decisively in his favor.

The board of directors, the public shareholders, SEC disclosure rules, and other accountability requirements all mask one final reality: There is nothing in law to stop any public corporation from going private and evaporating these conventional claims for corporate legitimacy. Cargill, of course, has never been a publicly owned firm. It seems to be none the worse in terms of sales, profits, and financial strength. The number of companies going private by means of leveraged buyouts is rising rapidly, and so is their size. The $6.2 billion leveraged buyout of Beatrice Foods is but the largest example of how the special powers and privileges at the disposal of Whitney MacMillan are proliferating.

The corporation, which began in the early nineteenth century as a capital-investment organization under government charter that accorded shareholders limited liability, has now become, in its larger forms, an institution seeking limited liability for itself and unlimited privilege for its managers. We need broader, popular standards of managerial performance based on the essential needs of people. These standards should be shaped by growing numbers of citizens who care how much damage is done to the human environment, to workers' health, to the rights and hopes of future generations.

Before laws, before regulatory standards and company self-restraint, comes the quality of the public's knowledge and expectations. These are the twin reservoirs for good business conduct. If they are not continually replenished, the hazardous divergence between corporate power and responsibility will widen. This is history's lesson for the advancement of worker and consumer justice.

Chief executives have to have a wider perspective than the one described in the conservative magazine *Public Opinion*, published by the American Enterprise Institute. There, in the August–September 1985 issue, Walter Guzzardi, a member of the board of editors of *Fortune*, offered this capsule of the ethos: "In fact, top executives of big corporations have always taken good care of themselves, and they always will. In a crunch, they come first. Good times or bad, right or wrong, they get rich —and what's shocking about that, unless you have a code that says they shouldn't."

The ideology and structure of large firms have not kept up with the accelerating impact of their activities over generations and geographies. Executives feel comfortable with the belief that their companies are producing for the "invisible hand" of the marketplace. It relieves them of accountability for how the overall system is working and where it is heading. Sidney Harman, former undersecretary of commerce and a successful entrepreneur, observes that while top executives know their specialties, they are "without a sense of the whole." He went on to say: "They know how to work the system—as distinguished from knowing how to make the system work. Most of them deal with financial symbols and models in abstract terms, leaving them incapable of thinking in human terms or grasping human conditions. They think vertically, are organized vertically, and are so locked up in a homogenized pyramid, which requires them to be infallible, that they can never say they blew it. So they have little opportunity to learn and grow. They are often surrounded by sycophants. Yet they have to confront new situations all the time."

Adam Smith knew that the ideology of the "invisible hand" was an idealization quite removed from market reality. This is very far from the way modern corporations plan to reduce risks through market power and to get the public to help pay their costs through tax breaks and other subsidies. Smith's "invisible hand" of 1776 has been joined two centuries later by the "invisible atom," the "invisible gene," the "invisible currency," the "invisible pollutant," and the "invisible bureaucrat."

Working at high levels of abstraction, pampered executives can distance themselves from everyday life, limiting their ability to deal with reality. The need for distance grows more insistent every day—the mounting challenges of doomsday weapons, mass famines, artificial intelligence, and genetic engineering are added to the stresses of conventional chemical, production, and marketing technologies. To induce more managerial foresight and honesty, those at the peaks of corporate power need to have their thoughts and actions better known to the public. If people think more about how major business executives work, then those executives may think harder about how their work affects people.

The "Go-for-It" drive, reflected in unprecedented golden parachutes, greenmail, executive salaries, bonuses, and perquisites, is symptomatic of deeper patterns of avariciousness in the Reaganite era of corporate permissiveness. The erosion of traditional self-restraints and prudence—whether in such areas as commercial bank lending, military contracting, conflicts of interest, or merger mania—most worry executives who pause long enough from the rat race to reflect. Indeed, the "private" thoughts and fears come out in frequent bursts of candor or concern during interviews. Seismic fissures and contradictions in the global and national economy do not go unnoticed. CEOs know that the very precariousness of the nation's economy, which gives the multinational corporations such major global influence, can suddenly turn into economic calamity for their highly leveraged firms. There are cycles in the public's tolerance of overreaching or underdelivery by business. There are limits to awarding large corporations public subsidies, guarantees, and immunities without receiving commensurate public accountabilities, disclosures, and performances in return.

In these times, with business and government converging toward a kind of corporate statism, who will be left to counterbalance this new alliance? The country's corporate leaders should not assume that the public will continue to be passive and resigned, that people will continue to feel aggrieved but unable to react. No leaders, in any society, can afford to disregard the signs of growing decay, of a breakdown in confidence. A people who feel betrayed by those they have trusted may turn to alternative solutions, to new allegiances.

Sources

Some magazines and newspapers were so frequently consulted that, to save space, we have abbreviated their titles in the notes that follow:

BW: Business Week

CEN: Chemical and Engineering News

CR: Corporate Report

CW: Chemical Week

NYT: New York Times

WP: Washington Post

WSJ: Wall Street Journal

For each chapter, certain periodicals were so central that all issues from the relevant time periods were consulted; it would be pointless to list all the pertinent articles in them. These periodicals are noted at the beginning of the published sources for each profile.

DAVID RODERICK

Ice Ingot

David Roderick granted two interviews, on Sept. 12 and Oct. 10, 1984, and a telephone interview on Mar. 22, 1985.

In 1984 and 1985, more than forty-five other individuals were interviewed, including nine former U.S. Steel executives, five current or former executives of other steel producers, seven labor officials, five industry analysts, nine public-interest representatives, and two congressmen. Six of the interviews were off the record.

Published Sources

Important Periodicals: *Crain's Chicago Business*, 1983–84; *Chicago Tribune*, 1983–85; *Pittsburgh Post-Gazette*, 1980–85; *Pittsburgh Press*, 1980–85.

Adams, Walter, *The Structure of American Industry* (New York: Macmillan, 1982).

Allegheny Conference on Community Development, *A Strategy for Growth: An Economic Development Program for the Pittsburgh Region* (Pittsburgh, 1984).

American Iron and Steel Institute, *Steel at the Crossroads: The American Steel Industry in the 1980s* (Jan. 1980); *Steel at the Crossroads: One Year Later* (June 1981); *Steel and America: An Annual Report* (May 1983; all Washington: Amer. Iron and Steel Inst.).

Arenson, Karen W., "U.S. Steel and National Drop Plan to Link Steel Divisions," *NYT*, Mar. 10, 1984.

Barnett, Donald F., and Louis Schorsch, *Steel: Upheaval in a Basic Industry* (Cambridge, Mass.: Ballinger, 1983).

Bensman, David, and Roberta Lynch, "Lessons in Loyalty," *Commonweal,* Feb. 24, 1984.

"Big Steel's Liquidation," *BW,* Sept. 17, 1979.

Borrus, Michael, "The Politics of Competitive Erosion in the U.S. Steel Industry," in *American Industry in International Competition: Government Policies and Corporate Strategies,* ed. John Zysman and Laura Tyson (Ithaca: Cornell, 1983).

Buss, Terry F., and F. Stevens Redburn, *Shutdown at Youngstown* (Albany: SUNY Press, 1983).

Buss, Terry F., and F. Stevens Redburn, with Joseph Waldron, *Mass Unemployment: Plant Closings and Community Mental Health* (Beverly Hills: Sage, 1983).

Carnegie-Mellon University, Physical Technical Systems Project, *Milltowns in the Pittsburgh Region: Conditions and Prospects* (Pittsburgh: Carnegie-Mellon, May 1983).

Crandall, Robert W., *The U.S. Steel Industry in Recurrent Crisis* (Washington: Brookings Institution, 1981).

Fallows, James, "America's Changing Economic Landscape," *Atlantic,* Mar. 1985.

Feasibility Study of the Duquesne Works' Blast and Basic Oxygen Furnaces for United Steelworkers of America (New York: Locker-Abrecht Associates, Jan. 28, 1985).

Greenhouse, Steven, "U.S. Steel's Oil-Pipe Gamble," *NYT,* Nov. 14, 1983.

Hogan, William T., *Steel in the United States: Restructuring to Compete* (Lexington, Mass.: Lexington Books, 1984).

Hymowitz, Carol, and Thomas F. O'Boyle, "U.S. Steel to Let Aide Go, Reassigns Others in Reorganization of Labor Relations Unit," *WSJ,* Aug. 13, 1984.

Ignatius, David, "Who Killed the Steel Industry?" *Washington Monthly,* Mar. 1979.

Investor Responsibility Research Center, *Proxy Issues Report: Plant Closings: United States Steel Corp.* 1984 Analysis E, Supp. 2 (Washington, Apr. 16, 1984).

Kirkland, Richard L., Jr., "Steel's New Luster," *Fortune,* Apr. 6, 1981.

Longworth, R. C., "A Betrayal on South Works," *Chicago Tribune,* Jan. 11, 1984.

Loomis, Carol J., "U.S. Steel and LTV Find Hidden Charms in Losers," *Fortune,* Mar. 5, 1984.

Lynd, Staughton, *The Fight Against Shutdowns: Youngstown's Steel Mill Closings* (San Pedro, Calif.: Singlejack, 1982).

MacNeil-Lehrer Report (NET-TV), May 24, 1983.

Melnick, R. Shep, *Regulations and the Courts: The Case of the Clean Air Act* (Washington: Brookings Institution, 1983).

Miles, Gregory L., and William J. Powell, Jr., "The Toughest Job in Business," *BW,* Feb. 25, 1985.

O'Boyle, Thomas, "David Roderick Tries to Recast U.S. Steel by Redeploying Assets," *WSJ,* Feb. 1; "U.S. Steel's Graham Must Balance Need to Improve Sites with Union Relations," *WSJ,* May 2; "Laid Low by Recession, Big Steel Companies Consider Major Change," *WSJ,* May 27, 1983. "U.S. Steel Corp. Discussing Link to Korean Firm," *WSJ,* Apr. 3, 1985.

Plotkin, Sid, and Bill Scheuerman, "Lessons of the Pastor Roth Affair," *Nation,* Feb. 23, 1985.

Roderick, David, various speeches, to: Cleveland Soc. of Financial Analysts, Oct. 20; N. Y. Soc. of Security Analysts, Nov. 1; Commonwealth Club of Calif., San Francisco, Nov. 5, 1982. Cong. Steel Caucus, Washington, Apr. 19; Amer. Iron and Steel Inst., NYC, May 25; Nat. Press Club, Washington, Nov. 10, 1983. Inst. of Scrap Iron and Steel, Las Vegas, Jan. 18; Wharton-AISI Conf., Phila., Mar. 1; 83d Annual Stockholders' Meeting, Birmingham, May 7; Nat. Conf. on the Dislocated Worker, Detroit, June 12; Grad. School of Business, Univ. of Pittsburgh, July 27; Press Conf.,

Pittsburgh, July 31; N.Y. Soc. of Security Analysts, Sept. 10, 1984. Can Mfrs. Inst., San Francisco, Feb. 12; Ohio C. of C., Columbus, Mar. 13, 1985.

Schorsch, Louis, "The Abdication of Big Steel," *Challenge*, Mar.–Apr. 1984.

Sease, Douglas R., "At Three Steelmakers, New Chief Executives Try for Turnarounds," *WSJ* July 22, 1980.

Serrin, William, "Two Views of Steel's Future," *NYT*, Feb. 13, 1985.

"A Steelman Steps Up the Pace at U.S. Steel," *BW*, Mar. 9, 1974.

Steelworkers Research Project, *Chicago Steelworkers: The Cost of Unemployment* (Chicago: Hull House Assoc. and United Steelworkers of America, Jan. 1985).

Symonds, William, "Interview with David Roderick," *BW*, June 13, 1983.

Tuma, Gary, "David M. Roderick," *Sky*, June 1984.

"U.S. Steel Settles Pollution Cases for $74.3 Million," *WSJ*, June 17, 1977.

United Steelworkers of America, *A Report: The Future of Steel: 1983 Basic Steel Agreement* (Pittsburgh, Mar. 1983); *Report of the Convention Committee on Future Directions of the Union* (Cleveland, Sept. 24–28, 1984).

Wayne, Leslie, "Big Steel's Puzzling Strategy," *NYT*, July 10, 1983.

Wines, Michael, "Steel: Managing Decline," *Nat. Jour.*, Mar. 31, 1984.

Yanowitch, Murray, "Embattled Steel," *Challenge*, May–June 1978.

Government Documents and Legal Proceedings

Deposition of David M. Roderick, *Lyle Williams, et al.* v. *U.S. Steel Corp.* (Mar. 12, 1980).

Deposition of William R. Roesch, *Lyle Williams, et al.* v. *U.S. Steel Corp.* (Mar. 11, 1980).

U.S. Congress, House, Comm. on Banking, Finance and Urban Affairs, Subcomm. on Economic Stabilization, *Industrial Policy, Part 2* (July 13, 14, 18, 26, 27, 28, 1983).

U.S. Congress, House, Comm. on Energy and Commerce, Subcomm. on Health and the Environment, *Health and the Environment Miscellaneous, Part 5* (Mar. 25, 1981); Subcomm. on Oversight and Investigations, *Capital Formation and Industrial Policy, Part 3: Crises in the Steel Industry* (Mar. 22, 26, 29, Apr. 23, 26, 1982).

U.S. Congress, House, Comm. on Foreign Relations, Subcomm. on International Economic Policy and Trade, *H.R. 600: Foreign Investments in the United States* (Sept. 15, 1983).

U.S. Congress, House, Comm. on Public Works and Transportation, Subcomm. on Economic Development, *Economic Health of the Steel Industry and the Relationship of Steel to Other Sectors of the Economy* (Dec. 7, 1981).

U.S. Congress, Senate, Comm. on Environment and Public Works, *Steel Industry Compliance Extension Act of 1981* (Mar. 3, 1981).

U.S. Congress, Senate, Comm. on the Judiciary, *The Domestic Steel Industry and the Antitrust Laws* (July 1, 1983).

U.S. Congress, Cong. Budget Office, *The Effects of Import Quotas on the Steel Industry* (July 1984).

U.S. Congress, Office of Technology Assessment, *Technology and Steel Industry Competitiveness* (OTA-M-122, June 1980); *U.S. Industrial Competitiveness: A Comparison of Steel, Electronics, and Automobiles* (OTA-ISC-135, July 1981).

U.S. Dept. of Labor, Occupational Safety and Health Admin., Case File No. Y1496/145 (Calumet City Area Office—Region V) (obtained under FOIA).

U. S. Environmental Protection Agency, "Environmental News: American Industry: We

Need Your Help" speech by John R. Quarles, Jr., to the Conference Board, Feb. 5, 1976.

U. S. Federal Trade Commission, *In the Matter of U.S. Steel Corp., et al.: Request* (Docket No. 760, May 13, 1985).

U.S. General Accounting Office, *New Strategy Required for Aiding Distressed Steel Industry* (EMD-81-29, Jan. 8, 1981); *The Steel Industry Compliance Extension Act Brought About Some Modernization and Unexpected Benefits* (RCED-84-103, Sept. 5, 1984).

U.S. Securities and Exchange Commission, *SEC Docket* 18 (Oct. 10, 1979), pp. 497–509.

Unpublished Sources

Correspondence of Donald Clay with A. M. Rosenthal, Sept. 28, 1984.

Correspondence of David Roderick with U.S. Steel management, Oct. 11, 1982; with Joseph Cardinal Bernardin, Jan. 18, Feb. 1, 8, 13, 1984.

Correspondence of Edgar Speer with U.S. Steel management, Feb. 23, 1976.

ROGER SMITH
Detroit Iron in Orbit

Roger Smith did not grant an interview.

More than eighty individuals were interviewed in 1984 and 1985, including four former GM executives and two outside directors, seven industry executives, seven labor leaders, three congressmen and one U.S. senator, six current and four former regulatory-staff officials, eight consumer activists, and ten lawyers. Thirty-one of the interviews were off the record.

Published Sources

Important Periodicals: *Automotive News*, 1980–85; *Consumer Reports*, 1980–85; *Detroit Free Press*, 1980–85; *Detroit News*, 1980–85; *Flint Journal*, 1985; *Kansas City Star*, 1984–85; *Korea Herald*, 1985; *Youngstown Vindicator*, 1985.

Altshuler, Alan, et al., *The Future of the Automobile* (Cambridge, Mass.: MIT, 1984).
Auerbach, Joseph, "The Poletown Dilemma," *Harvard Business Rev.*, May–June 1985.
Automotive News, GM 75th Anniv. Issue, Sept. 16, 1983; "GM and EDS," Mar. 18, 1985.
Crandall, Robert W., "Import Quotas and the Automobile Industry," *Brookings Rev.*, Summer 1984.
Cray, Ed., *Chrome Colossus* (New York: McGraw-Hill, 1980).
Phil Donahue Show, May 10, 1982 (Cincinnati: Multimedia Program Productions).
Duthie, Stephen, and Richard Willing, "GM: A Portrait," *Detroit News*, Sept. 1982 series.
Face the Nation (CBS-TV), Mar. 15, 1981.
Katz, Harry C., *Shifting Gears* (Cambridge, Mass.: MIT, 1985).
Kraft, Joseph, "The Downsizing Decision," *New Yorker*, May 5, 1980.
Power Newsletter, J. D. Power and Associates, Sept. 1980–84.

Salter, Malcolm, Alan Webber, and Davis Dyer, *The Big Three: Struggling for Renewed Competitiveness* (Cambridge, Mass.: Harvard Business School, n.d.).

Shaiken, Harley, "Detroit Downsizes U.S. Jobs," *Nation*, Oct. 11, 1980.

Smith, Roger B., various speeches, to: Colo. Bankers Assoc., Colorado Springs, Colo., May 29, 1971. GM Diesel Equipment Div., Detroit, Apr. 3, 1973. GM Management Clubs, New Orleans, Mar. 25, and Jacksonville, Fl., Mar. 26, 1975. Anderson C. of C., Anderson, Ind., May 6; Intercollegiate Marketing Competition, Detroit, May 18; Cold Finished Steel Bar Inst., Washington, June 2; Grand Rapids, Mich., C. of C., June 17; Vanderbilt Univ., Nashville, Tenn., Sept. 28; Civic Leader Luncheon, Louisville, Ky., Sept. 30; Future Farmers of America, Kansas City, Mo., Nov. 12, 1976. LBJ Library, Austin, Tex., Mar. 2, 1979. Nat. Auto Dealers Assoc. Conv., New Orleans, La., Feb. 10, 1980. Indianapolis C. of C., Feb. 26; Nat. Petroleum Refiners Assoc., San Antonio, Tex., Mar. 30; Detroit-Hamtramck Assembly Plant Ceremony, May 1; Austrian-American C. of C., Vienna, Aus., June 3; Amer. C. of C., Tokyo, Japan, July 14; Engineering Soc. of Detroit, Sept. 15; Soc. of Automotive Engineers, Detroit Sec., White Sulphur Springs, W. Va., Oct. 9; City Club of Cleveland, Dec. 11, 1981. Economic Club of Pittsburgh, May 11; Assoc. of Iron and Steel Engineers, Chicago, Sept. 28; Austin Area Urban League, Austin, Tex., Oct. 16; GM España Zaragoza Plant, Zaragoza, Spain, Nov. 5; GM Christmas Prog., Dec. 23, 1982. New Detroit City–Suburban Forum, Mar. 17; Better Business Bureau/Adcraft Club of Detroit, Dearborn, Mich., May 6; "Flint Salutes GM," Flint, Mich., Sept. 15; Amer. Assoc. of State Highway and Transportation Officials, Denver, Colo., Oct. 4; Conf. on Worksite Health Promotion and Human Resources, Washington, Oct. 11, 1983. Knights of Charity Dinner, Detroit, Feb. 25; Automotive Industries Luncheon, Detroit, Feb. 28; Univ. of Chicago Management Conf., Chicago, Apr. 9; Nihon Keizai Shimbun, Tokyo, Japan, Apr. 20; GM Cancer Research Awards, Washington, June 13; Anderson Area C. of C., Anderson, Ind. June 25; Orion Township Plant Dedication, Orion, Mich., July 5; GM Steel Buyers Conf., Detroit, Aug. 1; Mich. Automobile Dealers Assoc., Mackinac Island, Mich., Aug. 7; Management Briefing Seminar, Traverse City, Mich., Aug. 13, 1984. International Assoc. of Business Communicators, NYC, May 21, 1985.

Sobel, Robert, *Car Wars: The Untold Story* (New York: Dutton, 1984).

Stepanek, Marcia, *Detroit Free Press*, May 1983 series.

UAW-GM Report, Sept. 18, 1979; Mar. 1982; Sept. 1984.

Wines, Michael, "Reagan Plan to Relieve Auto Industry of Regulatory Burden Gets Mixed Grades," *Nat. Jour.*, July 23, 1983.

Wright, J. Patrick, *On a Clear Day You Can See General Motors* (New York: Avon, 1979).

Yates, Brock, *The Decline and Fall of the American Automobile Industry* (New York: Empire, 1983).

Government Documents

U.S. Congress, Cong. Res. Serv., *Prospects of Non-Compliance with the Automobile Fuel Economy Standards: Some Policy Options and Assessment of Their Likelihood* (Dec. 21, 1984).

U.S. Congress, House, Comm. on Energy and Commerce, Subcomm. on Commerce, Transportation, and Tourism, *Future of the Automobile Industry* (Feb. 8, 1984); Subcomm. on Oversight and Investigations, *FTC Rev. 1977–84* (Sept. 1984).

U.S. Congress, House, Comm. on Ways and Means, Subcomm. on Trade, *Fair Practices in Automotive Products Act* (Sept. 28, 1982).

U.S. Congress, Senate, Comm. on Commerce, Science and Transportation, *Highway Safety Act of 1983* (May 26, June 14, July 13, 1983); Subcomm. on Transportation, *Motor Vehicle Safety and the Marketplace* (Feb. 17, Mar. 10–11, 1983).

U.S. Congress, Senate, Comm. on Energy and Natural Resources, Subcomm. on Energy Regulations and Conservation, "Responses of General Motors Corporation to Questions . . . at a Hearing on Fuel Economy, May 14, 1985" (submitted June 19, 1985).

U.S. Congress, Senate, Comm. on Finance, Subcomm. on International Trade, *Issues Relating to the Domestic Auto Industry* (Mar. 9, 1981); *State of the U.S. Automobile Industry* (June 27, 1984).

U.S. Dept. of Commerce, *The U.S. Automobile Industry,* Reports for 1982 (June 1983) and 1983 (December 1984); International Trade Admin., *A Competitive Assessment of the U.S. Automotive Parts Industry* (Mar. 1985).

U.S. Dept. of Transportation, *Actions to Help the United States Auto Industry* (Apr. 6, 1981); Nat. Highway Traffic Safety Admin., Filings (Docket No. 81-02-NPRN-NO1, High-Mounted Stop Lamp; Docket Nos. FE-85-01-NO1 and FE-84-02-NO1, Corporate Average Fuel Economy).

U.S. Federal Trade Commission, *Dissenting Statement of Commissioner Pertschuk: GM-Toyota Joint Venture* (FTC File No. 821-0159).

Corporate Documents

Transcript, GMC Annual Meeting, 1981–85.

"Actions to Influence the Outcome of Bargaining," A. S. Warren, Jr., Presentation to Personnel Directors, Oct. 11, 1983.

"Assembly of 1984 'S' Car," Memorandum to F. J. McDonald from J. E. Godfrey, July 25, 1980.

"North American 1987 CK Pickup Program Proposal."

Unpublished Sources

Correspondence of Roger Smith with Neil Goldschmidt, Oct. 5, Nov. 23, 1979; Feb. 15, 1980; Andrew Lewis, Jan. 28, Feb. 9, 13, 25, Mar. 26, Apr. 2, 29, May 7, Jun. 25, Aug. 25, 28, Oct. 12, Nov. 5, 1981; Jan. 18, Feb. 10, 1982; Elizabeth Dole, Aug. 25, 26, Sept. 19, 1983; May 4, 22, 1984; Bill Brock, Mar. 4, Apr. 2, 1981; Ronald Reagan, Jan. 18, 1982. (Obtained under FOIA)

PAUL OREFFICE

Chemical Warrior

Paul Oreffice granted two interviews, on Sept. 26, 1983, and Dec. 5, 1984, and a telephone interview on Dec. 6, 1983.

In 1983 and 1984, forty other individuals were interviewed, including eight former Dow executives, five lobbyists and environmental activists, five lawyers, three labor officials, three industry analysts, and three government regulators or public-health specialists. Four of the interviews were off the record.

Published Sources

Important Periodicals: *CEN,* 1978–85; *CW,* 1978–85; *Midland Daily News,* 1978–84.

American Cancer Society, *Cancer Facts and Figures 1984* (New York: Amer. Cancer Soc., 1983).

Arruda, Marcos, Herbet de Souza, and Carlos Afonso, *Multinationals and Brazil: The Impact of Multinational Corporations in Contemporary Brazil* (Toronto: Brazilian Studies Latin America Res. Unit, 1975).

Blumenthal, Ralph, "Files Show Dioxin Makers Knew of Hazards," *NYT,* July 6, 1983.

Blustein, Paul, "Dow Chemical Fights Effect of Public Outcry Over Dioxin Pollution," *WSJ,* June 28, 1983.

Brandt, Ellis N., "Napalm—Public Relations Storm Center," *Public Relations Jour.,* July 1968.

Burnham, David, "Dow Says U.S. Knew Dioxin Peril of Agent Orange," *NYT,* May 5, 1983.

Commoner, Barry, "The Promise and Peril of Petrochemicals," *NYT Mag.,* Sept. 25, 1977.

"The Cracks in Dow's Theory of Dioxins," *CW,* Apr. 13, 1983.

"Dioxin: Special Issue," *CEN,* June 6, 1983.

"Dow Cleans Up Pollution at No Net Cost," *BW,* Jan. 1, 1972.

"Dow Faces Up to Its New World," *CW,* Apr. 22, 1967.

"Dow Pushes New, High-Profit Lines to Put It on Top," *CW,* Nov. 19, 1980.

"Driving Down Debt," *CW,* May 26, 1982.

Duerksen, Christopher J., *Dow vs. California: A Turning Point in the Envirobusiness Struggle* (Washington: Conservation Found., 1982).

Evans, Peter, *Dependent Development: The Alliance of Multinational, State, and Local Capital in Brazil* (Princeton, N.J.: Princeton Univ. Press, 1979).

Feeney, Andy, and Jim Jubak, "Dow and Dirty," *Environmental Action,* May 1983.

Gerstacker, Carl A., "The Structure of the Corporation," White House Conf. on the Industrial World Ahead, Washington, Feb. 7–9, 1972.

Hamilton, Martha M., "Dow Tries Burning Its Toxic Waste," *WP,* Oct. 25, 1984.

Harvard Business School, *The American Industrial Health Council,* case no. 0-383-047, 1982.

Holusha, John, "Dow Halts Fight to Sell Herbicide," *NYT,* Oct. 15, 1983.

Lepkowski, Wil, "Paul Oreffice: Optimist at Dow's Helm," *CEN,* Sept. 11, 1978.

Lernoux, Penny, *Cry of the People* (Garden City, N.Y.: Doubleday, 1980).

Levin, Doron P., "Dow Chemical Will Buy Unit from Thiokol," *WSJ,* Nov. 16, 1984.

Loomis, Carol J., "Richardson-Merrell Unswallows a Pill," *Fortune,* Jan. 12, 1981.

Meyer, Herbert E., "Dow Picks Up the Pieces in Chile," *Fortune,* Apr. 1974.

Milstein, Susan, "The Crusader Who Lost His Way," *American Lawyer,* Apr. 1984.

Morner, Aimee L., "Dow's Strategy for an Unfriendly New Era," *Fortune,* May 1977.

Oreffice, Paul F., "EPA Is Doing a Better Job," *CW,* July 7, 1982; "Chemical Industry Medal Address: Law and the Threat It Poses to the US Chemical Industry," *Chemistry and Industry,* Jan. 2, 1984. Various speeches, to: Advertising Council Panel on Energy Conservation at the White House, June 22, 1977. Commonwealth Club of Calif., Jan. 27; Economic Club of Detroit, Sept. 18; Indiana C. of C., Indianapolis, Oct. 12, 1978. Ariz. Business Forum, Phoenix, Mar. 29; Town Hall of Calif., L.A., Apr. 3, 1979. Amer. Business Press Seminar, Boca Raton, Fla., Apr. 29; College Placement Council, Chicago, May 21, 1980. Stockholders' Meeting, May 8; International Palladium Medal Award Dinner, NYC, Nov. 17, 1981. Stockholders' Meeting, May 13; American Grad. School of International Management, Glendale, Ariz., Dec. 16, 1983. South Dakota School of Mines and Technology, May 12, 1984.

Pasternak, Judy, "Grim Trade: Jobs for Health Fears," *Detroit Free Press*, May 15, 1983.

Peck, Keenen, "A Company Town Makes Peace with Poison," *Progressive*, June 1983.

Pirages, Suellen, "Hazardous Waste Disposal: Compliance with Increasingly Stringent Regulations," International Solid Wastes Cong., Phila., Sept. 15, 1984.

Rawls, Rebecca L., "Dow Finds Support, Doubt for Dioxin Ideas," *CEN*, Feb. 12, 1979.

"Restructuring for Future Profits," *CW*, July 28, 1982.

Rohter, Larry, "Retired Brazilian Officers in Industry Link Rulers to Civilian Power Centers," *WP*, July 25, 1978.

Ross-Skinner, Jean, "Dow's Continental Coup," *Dun's*, Mar., 1972.

Severo, Richard, "Eight Religious Orders Join in a Stockholders' Drive Against Herbicide," *NYT*, Feb. 17, 1980.

Seward, William B., *Up from Brazosport*, Midland, Mich.: Dow Chemical Company, 1974.

Shabecoff, Philip, "Dow Has Refused to Give EPA Data," *NYT*, Mar. 17, 1983; "Dow to Cover Soil Tainted by Dioxin," *NYT*, Nov. 6, 1984.

Siekman, Philip, "When Executives Turned Revolutionaries," *Fortune*, Sept., 1964.

Sinclair, Ward, "Chemical Industry to Have Powerful Voice About New EPA Chief," *WP*, Jan. 15, 1981; "Dioxin Brings Dow under Fire," *WP*, Apr. 24, 1983.

Smith, Lee, "Dow vs. Du Pont: Rival Formulas for Leadership," *Fortune*, Sept. 10, 1979.

Storck, William J., "Paul Oreffice: Dow and the Chemical Industry," *CEN*, Nov. 23, 1981.

Sylvester, Susan L., "Dioxin, Discharges, and Dow," *CBE Environmental Rev.*, May–June 1982.

Tarnoff, Stephen, and Stacy Shapiro, "Monsanto and Dow Paying 65% of Agent Orange Pact," *Business Insurance*, May 14, 1984.

Today (NBC-TV), Mar. 21, 1983.

Trost, Cathy, *Elements of Risk: The Chemical Industry and Its Threat to America* (New York: Times Books, 1984).

Whiteside, Thomas, *The Pendulum and the Toxic Cloud: The Course of Dioxin Contamination* (New Haven: Yale Univ. Press, 1979).

Government Documents and Legal Proceedings

Council on Environmental Quality, Dept. of Agriculture, Dept. of Energy, and Environmental Protection Agency, *Public Opinion on Environmental Issues: Results of a National Opinion Survey*, 1980.

Executive Office of the President, Council on Environmental Quality, Toxic Substances Strategy Comm., *Toxic Chemicals and Public Protection* (Washington: G.P.O., May 1980).

Michigan, House of Representatives, Fiscal Agency, *Review of the Economic and Public Role of Dow Chemical in Michigan*, n.d.

Natural Resources Defense Council, *Comments on the Proposed Regulations for Identification, Classification and Regulation of Toxic Substances Posing a Potential Occupational Carcinogenic Risk* (29 CFR Part 1990, Docket No. H-090, Feb. 28, 1978).

U.S. Congress, Cong. Budget Office, *Environmental Regulation and Economic Efficiency* (Washington: G.P.O., Mar. 1985).

U.S. Congress, House, Comm. on Education and Labor, Subcomm. on Labor Standards, *Use and Control of the Fumigant Ethylene Dibromide* (Sept. 13, 1983).

U.S. Congress, House, Comm. on Energy and Commerce, Subcomm. on Oversight and Investigations, *EPA: Investigation of Superfund and Agency Abuses, Part 1* (Feb. 17, Mar. 7, 18, 21, 1983); *Investigation of the Environmental Protection Agency: Report on the President's Claim of Executive Privilege over EPA Documents, Abuses in the Superfund Program, and Other Matters* (Aug. 1984).

U.S. Congress, House, Comm. on Science and Technology, Subcomm. on Natural Resources, Agriculture Research and Environment, *EPA Oversight on Dioxin Contamination* (Mar. 23, 1983).

U.S. Congress, Joint Economic Comm., Subcomm. on Economic Growth and Stabilization, *The Cost of Government Regulation* (Apr. 11, 13, 1978).

U.S. Congress, Senate, Comm. on Environment and Public Works, Subcomm. on Toxic Substances and Environmental Contamination, *Contamination from Ethylene Dibromide* (Jan. 27, 1984).

U.S. Court of Appeals for the Sixth Circuit, *Dow Chemical Company* v. *United States of America,* No. 82-1811, Nov. 9, 1984.

U.S. Dept. of Commerce, Bureau of Industrial Economics, Office of Regulatory and Federal Program Analysis, *An Assessment of the Relative Effect of Certain Federal Regulations on the International Competitiveness of the U.S. Petrochemical Industry* (BIE-SP83-1, Apr. 1983).

U.S. Environmental Protection Agency, *Citizens Petition for an Investigation and Enforcement Action* (Mar. 16, 1983).

U.S. General Accounting Office, *EPA's Efforts to Identify and Control Harmful Chemicals in Use* (RCED-84-100, June 13, 1984); *Assessment of New Chemical Regulation under the Toxic Substances Control Act* (RCED-84-84, June 15, 1984).

Unpublished Sources

Correspondence of Paul Oreffice with Anne M. Gorsuch, May 18, June 31, July 28, Sept. 10, Nov. 1, 1982; and Feb. 8, 1983. (Obtained under FOIA)

FELIX ROHATYN

The Interstitial Man

Felix Rohatyn granted three interviews, on Jan. 9 and Feb. 21, 1984, and Jan. 15, 1985, and a telephone interview on Jan. 22, 1985.

In 1983 and 1984, thirty other individuals were interviewed, including three active or retired Lazard partners, nine executives and directors of Lazard clients, and four officials of other investment houses. Five of the interviews were off the record.

Published Sources

Important Periodicals: *Institutional Investor,* 1975–85; *Village Voice,* 1975–77.

Alpern, David M., et al., "Mr. Fixit for the Cities," *Newsweek,* May 4, 1981.
Altman, Roger C., and Jeffrey E. Garten, "The Fallacy of a Modern-Day R.F.C." *NYT,* Oct. 9, 1983.

Auletta, Ken, "The New Power Game," *New York*, Jan. 12, 1976.

Behr, Peter, and Merrill Brown, "A Wider Role for the Consultant," *WP*, Oct. 11, 1983.

Bernstein, Jeremy, "Allocating Sacrifice," *New Yorker*, Jan. 24, 1983.

Blumenthal, Sidney, "Drafting a Democratic Industrial Plan," *NYT Mag.*, Aug. 28, 1983.

Brody, Michael, "The Crunch at ITT," *Fortune*, Feb. 18, 1985.

Brooks, John, *The Go-Go Years* (New York: Weybright and Talley, 1973).

CBS Evening News with Dan Rather (CBS-TV), Jan. 9, 1984.

CBS News (CBS-TV), Nov. 16, 1981.

CBS News Special Report (CBS-TV), Nov. 23, 1975.

Citizen Program to Eliminate the Gap: Financial Plan, City of New York, Fiscal Year 1984 (New York: The City Project, 1983).

Cockburn, Alexander, Jack Newfield, and James Ridgeway, "The ITT-Lazard Affair: A Dirty Deal That Will Not Die," *Village Voice*, Feb. 14, 1977.

Cohn, Gary, "Labor's Big New Role Inside Eastern Airlines Seems to Be Succeeding," *WSJ*, Oct. 31, 1984.

Colvin, Geoffrey, "The De-Geneening of ITT," *Fortune*, Jan. 11, 1982.

Cook, James, "A Case for Reindustrialization: An Interview with Felix G. Rohatyn," *Forbes*, Jan. 30, 1984.

Curtis, Charlotte, "Politics, but Not as Usual," *NYT*, June 7, 1983.

Face the Nation (CBS-TV), Dec. 14, 1980.

Fallon, Pierre, "The Making of Lazard's Michel David-Weill," *Euromoney*, Mar. 1981.

Feinberg, Phyllis, "The Rise of the Megadeal," *Institutional Investor*, May 1982.

Fireman, Ken, "U.S. Is Key to Bail-Out of City, Consultant Says," *Detroit Free Press*, June 4, 1981.

Gargan, Edward A., "M.A.C. Chief Says City Economy Faces Obstacles," *NYT*, Dec. 12, 1983.

Glynn, Lenny, and Elizabeth Peer, "Felix: The Making of a Celebrity," *Institutional Investor*, Dec. 1984.

"The Gold Rush to Lazard," *Fortune*, Sept. 11, 1978.

Goldstein, Don, "Saving Jobs, but at What Price?" *Nation*, Dec. 10, 1983.

Goodwin, Michael, "Rohatyn Sees Political Struggle Over Surplus," *NYT*, Dec. 3, 1983.

Goolrick, Robert, *Public Policy Toward Corporate Growth: The ITT Merger Cases* (New York: Assoc. Faculty Press, 1978).

Gottlieb, Martin, et al., "Back from the Brink: The Enduring Legacy of New York's Fiscal Crisis," *NYT*, June 30, July 2, 4, 6, 8, 1985.

"Harold Geneen's Tribulations," *BW*, Aug. 11, 1973.

Hayes, Samuel L., III, "The Transformation of Investment Banking," *Harvard Business Rev.*, Jan.–Feb. 1979.

Hellman, Peter, "The Wizard of Lazard," *NYT Mag.*, Mar. 21, 1976.

Henry, Sherrye, "Felix Rohatyn and the Mandates of Fortune," *Vogue*, Jan. 1985.

Hoffman, Paul, *The Dealmakers: Inside the World of Investment Banking* (Garden City, N.Y.: Doubleday, 1984).

Industrial Policy Study Group, *Promoting Economic Growth and Competitiveness* (Washington: Center for National Policy, Jan. 1984).

"ITT: The View from Inside," *BW*, Nov. 3, 1973.

Jensen, Michael, "The Lazard Frères Style," *NYT*, May 28, 1972; "Merger Mastermind," *NYT*, June 23, 1974.

Kaiser, Charles, and Lucy Howard, "How to Handle the Press," *Newsweek*, Apr. 19, 1982.

Kaus, Robert M., "Can Creeping Socialism Cure Creaking Capitalism? *Harper's*, Feb. 1983.

Kinsley, Michael, Review of *The Twenty-Year Century* by Felix G. Rohatyn, *New Republic*, Mar. 26, 1984.

Kraar, Louis, "Seagram's Sober System for Buying Big," *Fortune*, May 18, 1981.

Labor-Industry Coalition for International Trade, *International Trade, Industrial Policies, and the Future of American Industry* (Washington, Apr. 1983).

Lekachman, Robert, review of *The Twenty-Year Century* by Felix G. Rohatyn, *New Leader*, Dec. 12, 1983.

Levin, Hillel, "Felix the Fixer—Detroit's Newest Power," *Monthly Detroit*, May 1981.

Loomis, Carol J., "ITT's Disaster in Hartford," *Fortune*, May 1975.

Louis, Arthur M., "The Bottom Line on Ten Big Mergers," *Fortune*, May 3, 1982.

McClintick, David, "How ITT Maneuvered to Get a Tax Ruling in the Hartford Deal," *WSJ*, Oct. 12, 1972; "Life at the Top: The Power and Pleasures of Financier Felix Rohatyn," *NYT Mag.*, Aug. 5, 1984.

Maier, Mark H. "Felix Rohatyn's Double Standard," *Progressive*, Feb. 1983.

"Making Money—and History—at Weirton," *BW*, Nov. 12, 1984.

"The Man Who Is Reuniting Lazard's Empire," *BW*, June 18, 1984.

Metz, Tim, and Gary Putka, "After Some Slow Years, Lazard Frères Regains Its Drive, Profitability," *WSJ*, Sept. 6, 1984.

Newfield, Jack, "The Unaccountable Elitist: Rohatyn Is Our New Robert Moses," *Village Voice*, Aug. 2, 1976.

Newfield, Jack, and Paul DuBrul, *The Permanent Government: Who Really Runs New York?* (New York: Pilgrim Press, 1981).

Peterson, Iver, "Cleveland Testing Advice of Rohatyn," *NYT*, Feb. 15, 1981.

Pileggi, Nicholas, "The Thirty-six Who Run New York," *New York*, Jan. 9, 1978.

"The Power of a Fertile Mind," *Fortune*, Oct. 1975.

Putka, Gary, "Lazard Houses Plan to Forge Closer Links," *WSJ*, May 21, 1984.

Reich, Cary, *Financier: The Biography of André Meyer* (New York: Morrow, 1983).

"The Remarkable Felix G. Rohatyn: Wall Street's Merger Maker," *BW*, Mar. 10, 1973.

Robertson, Wyndham, "Passing the Baton at Lazard Frères," *Fortune*, Nov. 1977.

Rohatyn, Felix, "A New R.F.C. Is Proposed for Business," *NYT*, Dec. 1, 1974; "Public-Private Partnerships to Stave Off Disaster," *Harvard Business Rev.*, Nov.-Dec. 1979; "A Better Way to Bail Out Chrysler," *NYT*, Jan. 13, 1980; "The Older America: Can It Survive?" *N.Y. Rev. of Books*, Jan. 22, 1981; "A Matter of Psychology," *N.Y. Rev. of Books*, Apr. 16, 1981; "New York and the Nation," *N. Y. Rev. of Books*, Jan. 21, 1982; "Rx for Healthy Cities: Cooperation of Business, Labor and Governments," *Governmental Finance*, Sept. 1982; "Alternatives to Reaganomics," *NYT Mag.* Dec. 5, 1982; "How About Domestic Cooperation?" *NYT*, July 7, 1983; "Junk Bonds and Other Securities Swill," *WSJ*, Apr. 18, 1985; "Lessons of the '75 Fiscal Crisis," *NYT*, June 10, 1985. Various speeches, to: N.Y. C. of C. and Industry, NYC, Sept. 21; Nat. Council for Urban Economic Development, Nov. 11, 1976. Deadline Club and N.Y. Assoc. of Financial Writers, Feb. 23, 1977. Harvard Business School Club International Dinner, Apr. 5, 1978. 1980 Financial Conf. of the Conf. Board, NYC, Feb. 28, 1980. The Conference Board, NYC, Mar. 16; Southern Methodist Univ. Public Admin. Luncheon, Dallas, Mar. 23; Milwaukee Sentinel Forum for Progress, May 3; U.S. Conf. of Mayors, June 21; 92d St. YMHA, NYC, Oct. 27, 1982. Fordham Univ., NYC, May 22; Labor Industry Coalition for International

Trade, Akron, Nov. 29, 1983. Amer. Soc. of Newspaper Editors Conv., Washington, May 10, 1984.

Rustin, Richard E., "Wall Street's Rohatyn Emerges as a Key Man in New York's Rescue," *WSJ*, Oct. 10, 1975.

Sampson, Anthony, *The Sovereign State of ITT* (New York: Stein and Day, 1973).

Schoenberg, Robert J., *Geneen* (New York: Norton, 1985).

Senate Democratic Caucus, *Jobs for the Future: A Democratic Agenda* (Nov. 16, 1983).

Shalala, Donna E., speech to League of California Cities, San Francisco, Oct. 22, 1975.

Shalala, Donna E., and Carol Bellamy, "A State Saves a City: The New York Case," *Duke Law Jour.*, 1976: 1119–1132.

"The $16 Billion Bootstrap," *Forbes*, Oct. 15, 1976.

Smith, Geoffrey, "A Prominent Wall Streeter Defends His Proposal for a Revived Reconstruction Finance Corporation," *Forbes*, Feb. 15, 1975.

Sobel, Robert, *ITT* (New York: Times Books, 1982).

Solow, Robert M., review of *The Twenty-Year Century* by Felix G. Rohatyn, *NYT Book Rev.*, Jan. 1984.

Starr, Roger, review of *The Twenty-Year Century* by Felix G. Rohatyn, *New York*, Jan. 9, 1984.

Steinbreder, H. John, "Deals of the Year," *Fortune*, Jan. 21, 1985.

Stone, I. F., "Behind the ITT Scandal," *N.Y. Rev. of Books*, Apr. 6, 1972.

Tabb, William K., *The Long Default: New York City and the Urban Fiscal Crisis* (New York: Monthly Rev. Press, 1982).

Tracy, Eleanor Johnson, "The Clash of Styles in Investment Banking," *Fortune*, Sept. 25, 1978.

Watkins, Alfred J., "Felix Rohatyn's Biggest Deal," *Working Papers for a New Society*, Sept.–Oct. 1981.

Wayne, Leslie, "ITT: The Giant Slumbers," *NYT*, July 1, 1984.

Weirton Joint Study Committee, Inc., Weirton Steel Corp., *Disclosure Document Regarding . . . the Establishment of the Weirton Steel Corp. Employee Stock Ownership Plan*, Aug. 19, 1983.

"What Edgar Bronfman Wants at Seagram," *BW*, Apr. 27, 1981.

Wise, T. A., "In Trinity There Is Strength," *Fortune*, Aug., 1968.

"Would Industrial Policy Help Small Business?" *BW*, Feb. 6, 1984.

Government Documents

U.S. Congress, Cong. Budget Office, *The Industrial Policy Debate* (Dec. 1983).

U. S. Congress, House, Comm. on Banking, Finance, and Urban Affairs, Subcomm. on Economic Stabilization, *New York City Seasonal Financing Act of 1975* (Dec. 16, 1977); *New York City's Fiscal and Financial Situation, Parts 1 and 2* (Feb. 21, Mar. 8, 1978); *Industrial Policy, Part 4* (Sept. 14, 1983).

U.S. Congress, House, Comm. on Energy and Commerce, Subcomm. on Oversight and Investigations, Cong. Res. Serv. Economics Div., *Merger Tactics and Public Policy* (Mar. 1982); Subcomm. on Telecommunications, Consumer Protection, and Finance, *Takeover Tactics and Public Policy* (May 23, 1984).

U.S. Congress, House, Comm. on Small Business, *Conglomerate Mergers—Their Effects on Small Business and Local Communities* (Oct. 2, 1980).

U.S. Congress, House, Comm. on Ways and Means, *Tax Aspects of the President's Economic Program* (Mar. 5, 1981).

U.S. Congress, Senate, Comm. on Banking, Housing, and Urban Affairs, *Oversight on New York City Loan Program* (Dec. 21, 1976); *Oversight on the New York City Seasonal Financing Act* (Dec. 14, 1977); *Hearings on New York City Financial Aid Legislation* (June 7, 1978); *New York City Loan Guarantee Act* (Feb. 7, 1980).

U.S. Congress, Senate, Comm. on Foreign Relations, Subcomm. on International Economic Policy, *Global Economic Outlook*, Jan. 19, 1983.

U.S. General Accounting Office, *New York City's Fiscal Problems: A Long Road Still Lies Ahead* (GGD-80-5, Oct. 31, 1979).

CHARLS WALKER

External Revenue Service

Charls Walker granted three interviews, which took place on Feb. 7 and May 7, 1984, and Mar. 8, 1985.

In 1984 forty other individuals were interviewed, including three partners of Charls Walker Associates, ten other Washington lobbyists, four current or former Congressmen, six congressional aides, and five tax policy analysts. Four of the interviews were off the record.

Published Sources

Important Periodicals: *Capital Formation*, 1981–85; *People and Taxes*, 1982–85; *Tax Notes*, 1980–85.

ABC News: This Week with David Brinkley (ABC-TV), Nov. 25, 1984.

Baldwin, Deborah, "Hired Guns," *Common Cause*, Mar.–Apr. 1985.

Baughn, William, and Charls E. Walker, *The Banker's Handbook* (New York: Dow Jones, 1978).

Blustein, Paul, and Jane Mayer, "Business Lobbyists Celebrate Reagan's Dislike of Higher Corporate Taxes in Treasury Plan," *WSJ*, Feb. 11, 1985.

Bonafede, Dom, "Charls E. Walker: The Gentle Persuader," *Washington Dossier*, Feb. 1985.

"Charls E. Walker," *District Lawyer*, July–Aug. 1981.

Choyke, William J., " 'I Am No Expert,' " *Dallas Morning News*, Feb. 13, 1982.

Clark, Timothy B., " 'Sin' Taxes Won't Be Spared by Capitol Hill Revenue Raisers," *Nat. Jour.*, May 5, 1984.

Cohen, Richard E., "The Business Lobby Discovers That in Unity There Is Strength," *Nat. Jour.*, June 28, 1980.

Common Cause, *People Against PACs* (Washington, 1983).

Coopers & Lybrand, *An Analysis: 1982 Tax Legislation—Tax Equity and Fiscal Responsibility Act of 1982* (Washington: Nat. Tax Organ., Coopers & Lybrand, 1982).

Cowan, Edward, "When Tax Experts Confront Taxpayers," *NYT*, Oct. 3, 1982.

De Witt, Karen, "Business Wins Friends and Influences Washington," *NYT*, Jan. 7, 1979.

Drew, Elizabeth, "Charlie," *New Yorker*, Jan. 9, 1978.

Dunn, Mari Lee, and Margo Thorning, *Expenditure Tax Options* (Amer. Council for Capital Formation, Center for Policy Res., Washington, Mar. 2, 1984).

Edsall, Thomas B., "Three Who Sowed Tax Provision Reap Its Business Bonanza," *WP*,

Oct. 5, 1981; "How a Lobbyist Group Won Business Tax Cut," *WP*, Jan. 17, 1982; Interview with Charls Walker, *WP*, Aug. 22, 1982.

Gerth, Jeff, "A Power Broker's Many Roles," *NYT*, Oct. 29, 1980.

Glynn, Lenny, "The Talleyrand of the Tax Code," *Institutional Investor*, Apr. 1983.

Hershey, Robert D., Jr., "Battle Over Revising Income Tax Law Begins to Take Shape," *NYT*, Nov. 13, 1984.

Independent Refiners Coalition, *U.S. Energy Security Implications of the Crisis in the Nation's Petroleum Refining Industry*, (Washington, Feb. 1985).

Kieschnick, Michael, *Taxes and Growth: Business Incentives and Economic Development* (Washington: Council of State Planning Agencies, 1981).

Langley, Monica, "Frenzied Sign-Up of Lobbyists on Tax Proposal Is Boon for Ex-Aides, Others with Capitol Ties," *WSJ*, Feb. 6, 1985.

Large, Arlen J., "Battle Opens on Paying $1 Billion Cleanup Bill for Three Mile Island," *WSJ*, Oct. 21, 1981.

McIntyre, Robert S., "Companies Enjoy Too Many Loopholes," *NYT*, Jan. 29; "The Loopholes Distort Incentives," *NYT*, Nov. 4, 1984.

McIntyre, Robert S., and Dean C. Tipps, *Inequity and Decline* (Washington: Center on Budget and Policy Priorities, 1983); *The Failure of Corporate Tax Incentives* (Washington: Citizens for Tax Justice, Jan. 1985).

McLure, Charles E., Jr., *Must Corporate Income Be Taxed Twice?* (Washington: Brookings Institution, 1979).

McQuaid, Kim, "The Roundtable: Getting Results in Washington," *Harvard Business Rev.*, vol. 59, May–June 1981.

Meyer, Richard, *Running for Shelter: Tax Shelters and the American Economy* (Washington: Public Citizen, Jan. 1985).

Minarik, Joseph J., "Income Versus Expenditure Taxation to Reduce the Deficit," *Tax Notes*, Mar. 19, 1984.

Nightly Business Report (WETA-TV, Washington), Charls Walker's commentaries on Apr. 19, 1982–Jan. 23, 1984.

Pechman, Joseph A., *Federal Tax Policy* (Washington: Brookings Institution, 1983).

Reilly, Ann M., "Washington's Super Lobbyists," *Dun's Business Month*, Aug. 1983.

Russakoff, Dale, and Anne Swardson, "Tax Plan Splits Lobbies," *WP*, June 14, 1985.

Shanahan, Eileen, "Economist Picked as Treasury No. 2," *NYT*, Jan. 10, 1969.

Sheppard, Lee, "Charls Walker Spreads the Word," *Tax Notes*, July 16, 1984.

Surrey, Stanley S., "Our Troubled Tax Policy: False Routes and Proper Paths to Change," *Tax Notes*, Nov. 17, 1980; "Reflections on the Revenue Act of 1978 and Future Tax Policy," *Georgia Law Rev.*, vol. 13, Spring 1979.

Twentieth Century Fund, *What Price PACs?* (New York, 1984).

Vise, David A., "Lobbyists Fault Tax Plan," *WP*, Nov. 28, 1984.

Walker, Charls E., "Federal Reserve Policy and the Government Securities Market," Ph.D. dissertation, Wharton School, Univ. of Pa., 1955. "Needed: A Dialogue on the Corporate Income Tax," *Nat. Jour.*, June 5, 1982; "Eliminate Corporate Tax," *NYT*, Apr. 3, 1983; "Consider a U.S. Sales Tax," *NYT*, Nov. 29, 1984. Speech, Wharton School, Univ. of Pa., Philadelphia, Jan. 29, 1981.

Walker, Charls E., and Mark Bloomfield, "How the Capital Gain Tax Fight Was Won," *Wharton Mag.*, Winter 1979; "The Political Response to Three Potential Major Bankruptcies: Lockheed, New York City, and Chrysler," in *Toward a New U.S. Industrial Policy?* ed. Michael L. Wachter and Susan M. Wachter (Phila.: Univ. of Pa. Press, 1981).

Walker, Charls E., and Mark A. Bloomfield, eds., *New Directions in Federal Tax Policy for the 1980s* (Cambridge, Mass.: Ballinger, 1983).

Walker, Charls E., and Henry S. Reuss, *Major Tax Reform: Urgent Necessity or Not?* (Washington: Amer. Enterprise Inst. for Public Policy Research Rational Debate Series, 1973).

Government Documents

President of the U.S., *The President's Tax Proposals to the Congress for Fairness, Growth, and Simplicity* (Washington: G.P.O., May 1985).

U.S. Congress, Cong. Budget Office, *Federal Support of U.S. Business* (Washington: G.P.O., Jan. 1984).

U.S. Congress, House, Comm. on Government Operations, Subcomm. on Commerce, Consumer, and Monetary Affairs, *Tax Evasion Through the Netherlands Antilles and Other Tax Haven Countries* (Apr. 12, 13, 1983).

U.S. Congress, House, Comm. on Interior and Insular Affairs, Subcomm. on Energy and the Environment, *Financial Implications of the Accident at Three Mile Island* (May 4–5, 1981).

U.S. Congress, House, Comm. on Ways and Means, Subcomm. on Trade, *Proposed Amendments to the Countervailing Duty Law* (Oct. 20, 1983).

U.S. Congress, House, Committee on Ways and Means, *Tax Aspects of the President's Economic Program, Part 2* (Mar. 1981); *Administration's Fiscal Year 1983 Economic Program, Part 1* (Feb. 19, 1982); Subcomm. on Oversight and Subcomm. on Public Assistance and Unemployment Compensation, *Background Material on Poverty* (Oct. 17, 1983). *Summary of the Provisions of H.R. 4170 (Tax Reform Act of 1984)* (Apr. 16, 1984).

U.S. Congress, House, Comm. of the Whole House on the State of the Union, *Trade Remedies Reform Act of 1984* (May 1, 1984).

U.S. Congress, House, Office of Records and Registration, "Reports Pursuant to Federal Regulation of Lobbying Act: Charls Walker Associates, Inc.": Aerospace Industries Assoc. of Amer. (I.D. No. 03895090, Jan. 8, 1983); Mead Corp. (I.D. No. 03895084, Jan. 8, 1983); Amer. Telephone and Telegraph Co. (I.D. No. 03895048, Jan. 8, 1983); Amer. Guild of Authors and Composers (I.D. No. 03895091, Jan. 10, 1984); CBS, Inc. (I.D. No. 03895106, Jan. 10, 1984); COPIAT (I.D. No. 03895108, Jan. 10, 1984); Nat. Payments System Coalition (I.D. No. 03895104, Apr. 9, 1984); Agrico Chemical Co. et al. (I.D. No. 03895050, Jan. 9, 1985).

U.S. Congress, Joint Comm. on Taxation, *General Explanation of the Revenue Act of 1978* (Mar. 12, 1979); *General Explanation of the Economic Recovery Tax Act of 1981* (Dec. 29, 1981); *Analysis of Safe-Harbor Leasing* (June 14, 1982); *General Explanation of the Tax Equity and Fiscal Responsibility Act of 1982* (Dec. 31, 1982); *Study of 1982 Effective Tax Rates of Selected Large U.S. Corporations* (Nov. 14, 1983); *Description of Provisions of S. 1992 Relating to Life Insurance Products and Policyholders* (Jan. 27, 1984).

U.S. Congress, Senate, Comm. on the Budget, *First Concurrent Resolution on the Budget, Fiscal Year 1983* (Mar. 10, 16, 17, 1982).

U.S. Congress, Senate, Comm. on Energy and Natural Resources, and Comm. on Environment and Public Works, Subcomm. on Nuclear Regulation, *Financing the Cleanup of the Three Mile Island Nuclear Powerplant* (Oct. 20, 1981).

U.S. Congress, Senate, Comm. on Finance, *Tax Cut Proposals* (July 24, 1980); *Tax*

Reduction Proposals (May 19, 20, 1981); Subcomm. on Savings, Pensions, and Investment Policy, and Subcomm. on Taxation and Debt Management, *1983–84 Miscellaneous Tax Bills—VI: S.1066, S.1550, S. 1557, and S. 1666* (Sept. 19, 1983).

U.S. Congress, Senate, Comm. on the Judiciary, *The Antitrust Equal Enforcement Act* (Apr. 22, May 11, Dec. 7, 1981; Feb. 10, 1982).

U.S. Dept. of Justice, *Foreign Agent Registration Statement, Charls E. Walker Associates, Inc.* (Regis. No. 3538, Nov. 10, 1983).

U.S. Dept. of the Treasury, Office of the Secretary, *Tax Reform for Fairness, Simplicity, and Economic Growth,* 3 vols. (Washington: Nov. 1984).

Firm Documents

Amer. Council for Capital Formation, Center for Policy Res., *Capital Formation Folio* (Washington, Oct. 1981); *1983 Annual Report.*

H.R. 2331: To Increase Minority Ownership of Telecommunications Properties (Washington: Charls E. Walker Associates, Inc., 1983).

Walker, Charls E., "Dealing with Federal Deficits," Discussion Draft, Aug. 15, 1983; "The Case for Fundamental Tax Reform: Questions and Answers," Discussion Draft No. 2, Apr. 10, 1984; "The Great Tax Debate: Is the Fourth Estate Doing a Proper Job?" Discussion Draft, Jan. 23, 1985.

WHITNEY MacMILLAN

Remote Feed

Whitney MacMillan did not grant an interview, although he spoke briefly with the authors over the telephone on Nov. 30, 1984.

In 1984 and 1985, more than one hundred seventy-five individuals were interviewed, including thirty-five Minneapolis community leaders and activists, seventeen former Cargill executives and three executives from Cargill subsidiaries, twelve federal regulatory officials, twelve state regulators, eight farm group representatives, eight grain industry officials, eight congressional aides, seven former classmates of MacMillan, seven professors, six industry analysts, five former U.S. Dept. of Agriculture officials, and five congressmen. Sixteen of the interviews were off the record.

Published Sources

Important Periodicals: *CR*, 1975–85; *Feedstuffs*, 1975–85; *Manitoba Co-operator*, June 1983; *Milling and Baking News*, 1975–85; *Minneapolis Star and Tribune*, 1945–85; *North American Farmer*, 1984–85; *Reporter*, Amer. Agriculture Movement, 1984–85; *St. Paul Pioneer-Press*, 1975–85; *U.S. Export Sales*, Foreign Agricultural Serv., U.S. Dept. of Agriculture, 1984–85; *Western Producer*, June–November 1983; *Winnipeg Free Press*, October 1983.

Brooks, Geraldine, "What's Worse Than a Salt-Free Pickle? A Balmy Winter," *WSJ*, Feb. 24, 1984.

Brown, Lester R., et al., *State of the World 1985* (New York: Norton, 1985).

Brown, Terry, "The Cargill Combination," *CR*, May 1983.

Busch, Lawrence, and William B. Lacy, eds., *Food Security in the United States* (Boulder: Westview Press, 1984).

"Cargill Cancels Wheat Plan," *NYT*, Jan. 10, 1985.

"Cargill: Preparing for the Next Boom in Worldwide Grain Trading," *BW*, Apr. 16, 1979.

"Cargill Reaps New Harvest," *BW*, Apr. 16, 1949.

Caufield, Catherine, "The Rain Forests," *New Yorker*, Jan. 14, 1985.

Caves, Richard E., "Organization, Scale, and Performance of the Grain Trade," *Food Research Institute Studies*, vol. 16, 1977–78.

Conklin, Neilson C., and Reynold P. Dahl, "Organization and Pricing Efficiency of the U.S. Grain Export System," *Minnesota Agricultural Economist*, no. 635, May 1982.

"The Corporate Report Private 100," *CR*, Jan. 1983.

Donahue, Christine, "Revenge of the Frostbelt," *Forbes*, Nov. 5, 1984.

Egerstrom, Lee, "Cargill, BN Reap Most Benefits of U.S. Farm Aid," *North American Farmer*, June 27, 1984.

"Feast of the Giants," *The Moore Report* (WCCO-TV, Minneapolis), March 2, 1980.

"Forbes 400," *Forbes*, Oct. 1, 1984.

George, Susan, *How the Other Half Dies: The Real Reasons for World Hunger* (Montclair, N.J.: Allanheld, Osmun, 1977).

Gilmore, Richard, *A Poor Harvest: The Clash of Policies and Interests in the Grain Trade* (New York: Longman, 1982).

Higgins, Harold, "Cargill: A Giant 'Growing with Agriculture,' " and "Cargill Growth Is from Within," *St. Paul Sunday Pioneer Press*, Sept. 11, 1977.

"The Incredible Empire of Michel Fribourg," *BW*, Mar. 11, 1972.

Insel, Barbara, "A World Awash in Grain," *Foreign Affairs*, Spring 1985.

Kahn, E. J., Jr., "The Staffs of Life," *New Yorker*, June 18, Nov. 12, Dec. 17, 1984, Mar. 4, 11, 1985.

Kay, Hubert, "The Two-Billion Dollar Company That Lives by the Cent," *Fortune*, Dec. 1965.

Larson, Don W., *Land of the Giants: A History of Minnesota Business* (Minneapolis: Dorn, 1979).

MacMillan, Whitney, various speeches, to: 1979 Seminar, Bloomington, Ill., Aug. 21, 1979. West Suburban C. of C., Minneapolis, Jan. 30; Nat. Grain and Feed Assoc. Annual Conv., San Francisco, Mar. 19, 1980. Amer. Soc. of Farm Managers and Rural Appraisers, Louisville, Nov. 1981. Macalester College, St. Paul, Apr. 27; North Carolina Agribusiness Council, Raleigh, Sept. 11, 1982.

McGrath, Dennis J., "Embargo Startled Dealers, Farmers," *Minneapolis Tribune*, Jan. 6, 1980.

Mesdag, Lisa Miller, "The Fifty Largest Private Industrial Companies," *Fortune*, May 31, 1982.

Minard, Lawrence, "In Privacy They Thrive," *Forbes*, Nov. 1, 1976.

Morgan, Dan, *Merchants of Grain*, (New York: Penguin, 1980).

North American Congress on Latin America, "Cargill: Harvest of Profits," *Latin America and Empire Report*, Oct. 1975.

Schell, Orville, "A Kind of Commons," *New Yorker*, Apr. 23, 30, 1984.

"Secret Harvest," *First Camera*, NBC News (NBC-TV), Nov. 13, 1983.

Senate of Priests of St. Paul and Minneapolis, *Daily Bread: An Abdication of Power—The Joseph Project Report on Hunger, Grain, and Transnationals* (St. Paul: Archdiocese of St. Paul and Minneapolis, Mar. 1983).

Senior Classbook, Class of 1951 (New Haven: Yale Univ. Press, 1951).

Shellenbarger, Sue, "Bigness Counts in Agribusiness, and Cargill Inc. Is Fast Becoming a Commodities Conglomerate," *WSJ,* May 7, 1982.

Sinclair, Ward, "Cargill's Proposed Import of Grain Reaps Criticism," *WP,* Jan. 9, 1985.

Tamarkin, Bob, "What—And Who—Makes Cargill So Powerful?" *Forbes,* Sept. 18, 1978.

Wall, Wendy L., "Cargill Set to Import Wheat; Some Believe Move Is Political Ploy," Jan. 8; and "U.S. Isn't Any Longer Cheapest Source of Some Kinds of Grain for Domestic Use," Jan. 14; both *WSJ,* 1985.

Wall, Wendy L., and Kathleen A. Hughes, "Soviet Union Emerges as a Big, Clever Player in Commodities Game," *WSJ,* Jan. 29, 1985.

Wessel, James, *Trading the Future: Farm Exports and the Concentration of Economic Power in Our Food Economy* (San Francisco: Inst. for Food and Development Policy, 1983).

Youngblood, Dick, "Sales Soar, Nearly Triple Cargill Profits," *Minneapolis Tribune,* Dec. 2, 1973.

Zielenziger, Michael, "Grain: A Harvest of Danger," *Kansas City Times,* July 1982.

Government Documents

Equal Employment Opportunity Commission, "Consent Decree," Oct. 1984, *EEOC* v. *Cargill Inc.*

Insurance Dept. of the District of Columbia, *Annual Statement of the Summit National Life Insurance Company of Akron in the State of Ohio,* Dec. 31, 1983. (Obtained under D.C. FOIA)

National Commission on Agricultural Trade and Export Policy, *Interim Report to the President and the Congress* (Mar. 1985).

Office of the Commissioner of Banking, *Eighty-Ninth Annual Report* (Madison, Wisc., Dec. 31, 1983).

Oregon Tax Court, No. 1999, *Cargill, Inc.* v. *Dept. of Revenue, State of Oregon,* Complaint and Request for Refund, June 27, 1983; Answer, July 25, 1983.

Securities and Exchange Commission, *Notice of Special Meeting of Stockholders* (Chestnut Hill, Mass.: Seaboard Allied Milling Corp., Dec. 11, 1981).

Securities and Exchange Commission, *Offer to Purchase for Cash Any and All Shares of Common Stock of MBPXL Corporation by Cargill Holdings, Incorporated* (New York: First Boston Corp., Dec. 7, 1978).

State Tax Appeal Board, Mont., STAB, No. CT-82-4, *Cargill Inc.* v. *Dept. of Revenue of the State of Montana,* Appeal, June 24, 1982; Answer, July 26, 1982; Stipulation, Nov. 24, 1982.

United States Attorney, Minneapolis, *Information* (26 U.S.C. 7206[1]), Nov. 12, 1981; *Plea Agreement,* Nov. 13, 1981.

U.S. Congress, Cong. Res. Serv. *Farm Price and Income Support Programs: Background Information* (83-2 ENR, May 1982 and Jan. 1983).

U.S. Congress, Cong. Res. Serv., *Federal Farm Programs: A Primer* (84-232 ENR, Dec. 1984).

U.S. Congress, House, Comm. on Agriculture, Subcomm. on Dept. Operations, Research and Foreign Agriculture, *Hearings* (Apr. 4, 1985); Subcomm. on Wheat, Soybeans, and Feed Grains, *Review of Grain Elevator Safety* (July 21, 1982).

U.S. Congress, House, Comm. on Small Business, *Small Business Problems in the Marketing of Meat and Other Commodities, Part 3* (Staff Report, Oct. 1980).

U.S. Congress, Senate, Comm. on Agriculture, Subcomm. on Foreign Agricultural Policy, *Hearing on the Competitive Position of U.S. Agriculture in the Current World Market* (Feb. 7, 1985).

U.S. Congress, Senate, Comm. on Foreign Relations, Subcomm. on Multinational Corporations, *International Grain Corporations* (June 24, 1976).

U.S. Dept. of Agriculture, *Report of the Secretary's Meat Pricing Task Force* (June 15, 1979), *Official List of Warehouses Approved under the Uniform Grain Sales Act* (1985).

U.S. Dept. of Agriculture, Agricultural Stabilization and Conservation Serv., *Warehouses Licensed Under U.S. Warehouse Act as of December 31, 1984;* Economic Res. Serv., International Economics Div., *Sources of Recent Changes in U.S. Agricultural Exports* (ERS Staff Report No. AGES831219, Jan. 1984); Federal Grain Inspection Serv., Compliance Div., Regulatory Branch, *Export Elevator List* (March 1985); Office of Inspector General, *Report of the Inspector General on the Suspension of Agricultural Exports to the USSR (1-4-80 to 4-24-81)* (Audit Report No. 5099-1-FO, Nov. 1981) and *Supplemental Report of the Inspector General on the Suspension of Agricultural Exports to the USSR (1-4-80 to 4-24-81)* (Audit Report No. 5099-1-FO).

U.S. General Accounting Office, *Grain Marketing Systems in Argentina, Australia, Canada, and the European Community; Soybean Marketing System in Brazil* (ID-71-61, May 28, 1976); *Lessons to Be Learned from Offsetting the Impact of the Soviet Grain Sales Suspension* (CED-81-110, July 27, 1981); *Market Structure and Pricing Efficiency of the U.S. Grain Export System* (CED-82-61, 1982); *The SICEA Brought About Some Modernization and Unexpected Benefits* (RCED-84-103, Sept. 5, 1984); *Information on the Department of Agriculture's Commodity Exchange Contracts for the 1983 Payment-In-Kind Program* (RCED-85-62, Mar. 11, 1985).

U.S. Internal Revenue Service, "Return of Private Foundation," Form 990-PF, for: Cargill Family Fund, 1983; Cargill MacMillan Family Foundation, 1983; and Cargill Foundation, 1980–84 (all obtained under FOIA).

U.S. Tax Cases 73-1, p. 81,318, *Keinath, et al. v. Commissioner of Internal Revenue* (U.S. Court of Appeals, 8th Circuit, Nos. 72-1647–1651, 5/8/73.

U.S. Tax Court, Dockets 4646–69—4650–69 and 3636–67—3641–67.

"Weekly Report of the USDA Coordinating Office for Monitoring the Suspension of Grain and Soybean Exports to the USSR," Report No. 65, May 29, 1981 (obtained under FOIA).

58 U.S. Tax Court Reports 352. *Keinath et. al. v. Commissioner of Internal Revenue*.

480 F.2d 57 (1973). *Keinath et al. v. Commissioner of Internal Revenue*.

483 F.Supp. 1070. *U.S.A. v. Harold Bonnell and Charles Rice*.

Corporate Documents

Cargill (Jan. 1984).

Cargill Bulletin (1982–85).

Cargill Crop Bulletin (1980–82).

Cargill Limited/Cargill Limitée and Its Subsidiary Companies: Consolidated Financial Statements (Canada: 1977–84).

Cargill News (1983–84).

Cargill Newsletter (1984).

Cargill World Headquarters (n.d.).

Chucker, Harold, *The Role of Markets in the World Food Economy: Summary of Papers Presented at the World Food Economy Conference* (Oct. 14–16, 1982).

"Export Administration Act Renewal" (Cargill position paper, contained in Robert Fahs letter to William Lesher, Apr. 13, 1983). (Obtained under FOIA)

Grain Exports in Focus, (Cargill Corporate Relations Dept., Nov. 1, 1981).

"Let the US-USSR LTA Lapse, Sanctify Contracts" (Cargill position paper, contained in Robbin Johnson letter to John Block, May 14, 1982).

A Look at Grain Industry Misconceptions (Cargill pamphlet, July 1984).

MacMillan, Whitney, *A Perspective of the Food Industry, the Grain Business and Cargill* (Mar. 7, 1980).

Notice of Annual Meeting of Shareholders (Palm Beach: First Nat. Bank of Palm Beach, 1985).

"A Proposal for a New U.S.-USSR LTA" (Cargill position paper, contained in Robbin Johnson letter to John Block, May 18, 1981).

"A Proposal for Resolving the Embargo Impasse" (Cargill position paper, contained in Robbin Johnson to John Block, Mar. 23, 1981).

"Summary of Conference at PMM [Peat Marwick Mitchell] on Feb. 14, 1977."

"U.S.-USSR LTA" (Cargill position paper, contained in Robbin Johnson letter to Seeley Lodwick, Sept. 15, 1981).

World Grain Trade in Focus (Community Relations Dept. 1982).

The World of Cargill (n.d.).

Unpublished Sources

Correspondence obtained under FOIA from U.S. Dept. of Agriculture: Whitney MacMillan with Seeley Lodwick, Sept. 21, 1981. Robbin Johnson with John Ochs, Mar. 9, 17, 1981; with John Block, Mar. 23, Apr. 24, May 18, July 7, 1981; May 14, June 21, 1982; with Thomas Hammer, Nov. 24, 1981; with Seeley Lodwick, Sept. 15, 1981; with William G. Lesher, May 18, 1984; with Richard E. Lyng, May 14, 1984; with Daniel Amstutz, Jan. 17, 1984. Robert Fahs with William G. Lesher, Apr. 13, 27, 1983; with Alan T. Tracy, May 17, 1983; with John Block, Apr. 13, 1983; with Daniel Amstutz, Apr. 13, 1983; with Richard Lyng, Apr. 13, 1983.

Correspondence of William R. Pearce with E. J. Weigle, Oct. 1, 1982.

Correspondence of M. D. McVay with E. J. Weigle, July 19, 1982; with Joaquin Guardiola, Dec. 20, 1979; with Neal Smith, Apr. 2, June 4, 1980.

Correspondence of Gordon W. Hoff with G. L. Foster, May 26, 1982.

Correspondence of Jim Nichols with Rudy Boschwitz, Feb. 4, 1985.

THOMAS JONES

Life of a Salesman

Thomas Jones did not grant an interview.

From 1983 to 1985, more than eighty-five individuals were interviewed, including fifteen former Northrop executives, fourteen former Northrop consultants, nine former Pentagon officials, six securities analysts, five defense industry analysts, and two Congressmen. Fifteen of the interviews were off the record.

Published Sources

Important Periodicals: *Aviation Week and Space Technology*, 1975–85; *Washington Star*, 1974–77.

Adams, Gordon, *The Iron Triangle: The Politics of Defense Contracting* (New York: Council on Economic Priorities, 1981).

Aerospace Industries Association, Electronic Industries Association, and National Security Industrial Association, *Technical Papers on Independent Research and Development and Bid and Proposal Efforts* (Washington, 1974).

Barnett, A. Doak, *The F-X Decision* (Washington: Brookings Institution, 1981).

Boulton, David, *The Grease Machine* (New York: Harper and Row, 1978).

Clogher, Rick, "Weaving Spiders, Come Not Here," *Mother Jones*, Aug. 1981.

Davenport, Andrew, Leon Howell, and Michael Morrow, "The Fallout from a Corporate Watergate," *Far Eastern Economic Rev.* Jan. 16, 1976.

Easterbrook, Gregg, "The Airplane That Doesn't Cost Enough," *Atlantic*, Aug. 1984.

Egan, Jack, "Northrop: Know the Right People," *WP*, June 15, 1975.

Fallows, James, *National Defense* (New York: Vintage, 1981).

Fialka, John J. "Easy U.S. Credit Helps Sell Arms; Repayment Can Be Another Matter," *WSJ*, June 13, 1984.

Gansler, Jacques, *The Defense Industry* (Cambridge, Mass.: MIT Press, 1980).

Goodwin, Jacob, *Brotherhood of Arms: General Dynamics and the Business of Defending America* (New York: Times Books, 1985).

Gordon, Michael R., "No Tigersharks for Taiwan—The Tale of an Arms Sale That Didn't Sail," *Nat. Jour.*, Jan. 16, 1982; "Selling the F-20, or How Northrop Corp. Turned a White Elephant into a Prize Bull," *Nat. Jour.*, July 13, 1985.

Harris, Roy J., Jr., "Unglamorous Northrop Got 'Stealth' Job on Its Record for New, Simplified Designs," *WSJ*, Nov. 20, 1981; "Coproduction Boost U.S. Arms Sales," *WSJ*, July 12, 1984; "Aviation Bosses Belong to Secret Club Where Dressing in Pink Frocks Is Okay," *WSJ*, Sept. 17, 1985.

Hollie, Pamela G., "Northrop's Product Strategy: Simplify," *NYT*, Feb. 4, 1980; "Here Comes Tom Jones Again," *NYT*, Aug. 2, 1981.

Jones, Thomas, "For a Sound Defense Industry," *NYT*, Nov. 23, 1976; "Stabilizing Defense Budgets," *Aviation Week and Space Technology*, Jan. 3, 1977. Various speeches, to: Annual Shareholders' Meeting, Hawthorne, Calif., May 20, 1981. New York Soc. of Aerospace Analysts, NYC, Mar. 9; American-Swiss Assoc., NYC, Apr. 6; ABA/FBA/NCMA Joint Symposium, Los Angeles, Apr. 15; Investment Analysts Soc. of Chicago, Apr. 22; L.A. C. of C., July 14; Nat. Contract Management Assoc., Nov. 4; International Logistics Symposium of the National Security Industrial Assoc., Arlington, Va., Nov. 30, 1982. AFSC Horizon South Conference, Ft. Walton Beach, Fla., Mar. 10; Seidler Amdec Securities 1983 Meeting, Beverly Hills, Calif., Apr. 14, 1983. Bottom Line III Conf., Nat. Defense Univ., Washington, June 13, 1984.

Klare, Michael T., "The Unnoticed Arms Trade: Exports of Conventional Arms-Making Technology," *International Security*, vol. 8 (Fall 1983); *American Arms Supermarket* (Austin: Univ. of Texas Press, 1984).

Kolbenschlag, Michael, "High Roller," *Forbes*, Mar. 2, 1981.

Kraar, Louis, " 'Everyone at Northrop Is in Marketing,' " *Fortune*, Apr. 10, 1978.

"Look Who's Heading for No. One in Defense: Northrop," *BW*, Apr. 19, 1982.

Maine, Sir Henry, *Ancient Law* (London, 1885).

Noonan, John T., Jr., *Bribes* (New York: Macmillan, 1984).

"Northrop's Punishment for Campaign Giving," *BW*, Feb. 24, 1975.

Paine, Christopher, and Gordon Adams, "The R&D Slush Fund," *Nation*, Jan. 26, 1980.

Pauly, David, "The Comeback of Tom Jones," *Newsweek*, Jan. 31, 1977.

"A Place in Space," *Time*, Oct. 27, 1961.

Redman, Christopher, "Northrop Aims for a Killing with the Tigershark," *Fortune*, June 24, 1985.

Salpukas, Agis, "Talking Business—with Jones of Northrop," *NYT*, Nov. 17, 1981.

Sampson, Anthony, *The Arms Bazaar: From Lebanon to Lockheed* (New York: Viking, 1977).

Schemmer, Benjamin F., "Pressures Build for DoD to Buy and Help Sell Northrop F-5G as Its Business Prospects Look Bleaker than Advertised," *Armed Forces Jour. International*, Sept. 1982.

Sick, Gary, *All Fall Down: America's Tragic Encounter with Iran* (New York: Random, 1985).

Sobel, Lester A., ed., *Money and Politics: Contributions, Campaign Abuses, and the Law* (New York: Facts on File, 1974).

Sutter, Robert, "U.S. Arms Sales to Taiwan: Implications for American Interests," *Jour. of Northeast Asian Studies*, Fall 1982.

Tyrrell, C. Merton, *Pentagon Partners, The New Nobility* (New York: Grossman, 1970).

Weinstein, Henry, "Northrop's Solo Act," *NYT*, June 11, 1975; "Jones Intends to Stay on Top at Northrop," *NYT*, July 18, 1975.

Weiss, Elliott J., proj. mgr., *The Corporate Watergate* (Washington: Investor Responsibility Research Center, 1975).

Williams, Winston, "Bungling the Military Buildup," *NYT*, Jan. 17, 1985.

"The World of the 'Renaissance Executive,'" *Newsweek*, Nov. 18, 1963.

Government Documents

Gerard, Francis R. *Vista 1999: A Long-Range Look at the Future of the Army and Air National Guard*, Mar. 1982; and *First Report of the Tactical Fighters Task Force*, Feb. 2, 1985 (both Washington: Nat. Guard Assoc. of the U.S.).

U.S. Congress, House, Comm. on Appropriations, Subcomm. on the Dept. of Defense, *Department of Defense Appropriations for 1983* (June 16, 1982).

U.S. Congress, House, Comm. on Foreign Affairs, Subcomm. on International Security and Scientific Affairs and Asian and Pacific Affairs, *Review of Administration's Policy on Sales of Advanced Fighter Planes to ASEAN* (Mar. 28, 1984).

U.S. Congress, House, Comm. on International Relations, Subcomm. on International Economic Policy, *The Activities of American Multinational Corporations Abroad* (July 29, 1975); Subcomm. on International Security and Scientific Affairs, *Review of the President's Conventional Arms Transfer Policy* (Feb. 2, 1978); *Foreign Assistance Legislation for FY83 (Part 2): Review of Security Assistance Programs Worldwide* (Apr. 20, 1982).

U.S. Congress, Joint Comm. on Defense Production, *DOD-Industry Relations: Conflict of Interest and Standards of Conduct* (Feb. 2, 1976); *Defense Industrial Base: DOD Procurement Practices* (Sept. 29, 1977).

U.S. Congress, Senate, Comm. on Foreign Relations, Subcomm. on Multinational Corporations, *Multinational Corporations and U.S. Foreign Policy* (June 9, 1975).

U.S. Dept. of Defense, *Report for the Secretary of Defense on the Implementation of the United States Foreign Military Sales Program in Iran*, Submitted by R. Kenly Webster, Sept. 19, 1977; Defense Contract Audit Agency, *Audit Report No. 4721-99-6-0007* (Aug. 6, 1975) (obtained under FOIA); Inspector General, *Report on the Audit of Financial and Program Management of the F/A-18 Program* (Apr. 14, 1983).

U.S. Dept. of the Navy, *Operational Test and Evaluation Force Report: F/A-18* (Oct. 4, 1982) (obtained under FOIA); *OPTEVFOR Evaluation Report: F/A-18 Weapon System (U)* (July 21, 1983) (obtained under FOIA).

U.S. General Accounting Office, *Evaluation of the Navy Air Combat Fighter Source Selection* (PSAD-76-77, Mar. 4, 1977); *Operating and Support Costs of New Weapon Systems Compared with Their Predecessors* (LCD-77-429, Oct. 17, 1977); *Defense Department Is Not Doing Enough to Maximize Competition When Awarding Contracts for Foreign Military Sales Programs* (PSAD-78-147, Oct. 17, 1978); *An Unclassified Version of . . . "Need to Demonstrate F-18 Naval Strike Fighter Weapon System Effectiveness Before Large-Scale Production"* (PSAD-79-25, Feb. 27, 1979); *F/A-18 Naval Strike Fighter: Its Effectiveness Is Uncertain* (PSAD-80-24, Feb. 14, 1980); *Operational and Support Costs of the Navy's F/A-18 Can Be Substantially Reduced* (LCD-80-65, June 6, 1980); *F/A-18 Naval Strike Fighter: Progress Has Been Made but Problems and Concerns Continue* (MASAD-81-3, Feb. 18, 1981); *Navy's F/A-18 Expected to Be an Effective Performer but Problems Still Face the Program* (MASAD-82-20, Feb. 26, 1982); *Navy's F/A-18 Program Faces Budget Concerns and Performance Limitations as Aircraft Enter the Fleet* (MASAD-83-28, June 10, 1983); *The Navy Can Reduce Its Stated Requirements for F/A-18 Weapons Tactics Trainers* (NSIAD-84-84, Apr. 11, 1984).

Watergate Special Prosecution Force, Record Group 460, Campaign Contributions TF, Northrop #332 (obtained under FOIA): Legal and Factual Analysis; Witness Statements; Memoranda; Planning and Coordination; Recommendations.

Corporate Documents

Report to the Board of Directors of Northrop Corporation of the Special Investigation of the Executive Committee (July 16, 1975).

Unpublished Sources

Correspondence of Thomas V. Jones with Alexander Haig, June 15, 1982; with George Shultz, Jan. 17, Apr. 25, 1983; with Caspar Weinberger, Jan. 17, 31, Apr. 25, May 17, 1983 (obtained under FOIA).

WILLIAM McGOWAN
Monopoly Breaker

William McGowan granted four interviews, on May 3 and 30, and December 3, 1984, and July 10, 1985.

In 1984 more than seventy other individuals were interviewed, including twelve former MCI executives, seven current MCI executives and three outside directors, six former Federal Communications Commission officials, six telecommunications analysts, four former business associates of McGowan, two executives with MCI corporate customers, and three officials of MCI's suppliers. Three of the interviews were off the record.

Published Sources

Berg, Eric N., "Setbacks in Long Distance: Competitors Feel Squeeze," *NYT,* Apr. 22, 1985.

Bernstein, Jeremy, *Three Degrees Above Zero: Bell Labs in the Information Age* (New York: Scribner's, 1984).

"Breaking Up the Phone Company," *Fortune,* June 27, 1983.

Cooper, Mark, Gene Kimmelman, and Pamela Gilbert, *Ringing Off the Wall: An Alarming Increase in Residential Phone Rates 1984–1986* (Washington: Consumer Federation of Amer. and U.S. PIRG, May 12, 1985).

Edersheim, Peggy, "Electronic Mail Hasn't Delivered, But Backers Say It Is on the Way," *WSJ,* July 23, 1985.

Elia, Charles J., "MCI Communications Is Facing Key Quarter in Firm's Effort to Bring Cash Flow into Black," *WSJ,* Apr. 9, 1976.

Frierich, Otto, "Seven Who Succeeded," *Time,* Jan. 7, 1985.

Greenya, John, "The Revenge of the Long-Distance Inventor," *Regardie's,* Jan.–Feb. 1981.

Greider, William, "Reach Out and Crunch Someone," *Rolling Stone,* Sept. 15, 1983.

Hoffer, William, "Giant Killer," *Success,* Jan. 1984.

Inman, Virginia, "MCI Races the Clock, Bets Billions of Dollars in Phone Competition," *WSJ,* June 14, 1983.

Isikoff, Michael, "Unions Organizing Boycott Against MCI," *WP,* June 26, 1984.

Johnson, John Paul, "The Un-Telephone Company," *Communications,* Sept. 1969.

Kimmelman, Gene, and Mark Cooper, *Divestiture: One Year Later* (Washington: Consumer Fed. of America, Dec. 19, 1984).

Louis, Arthur M., "The Great Electronic Mail Shootout," *Fortune,* Aug. 20, 1984.

Makower, Joel, "The Maverick Mogul of MCI," *United Airlines Mainliner,* June 1983.

McGowan, William, various speeches, to: Alexander Brown and Sons Telecommunications Conf., Baltimore, Md., Jan.; Commonwealth Club, San Jose, Calif., May 5; Telecom 83 Forum, ITU, Geneva, Switz., July 5; Annual Stockholders' Meeting, Washington, July 19; George Washington Univ., Washington, Oct. 12, 1983. Symposium 1984 European Management Forum, Davos, Switz., Feb. 1; Annual Stockholders' Meeting, Washington, July 17, 1984. Annual Stockholders' Meeting, Washington, May 16, 1985.

"MCI's Newest Strategy: Shooting for a Broader Spectrum," *BW,* Oct. 10, 1983.

Miller, Gregory, "MCI's Struggle for Survival," *Institutional Investor,* Sept. 1983.

Moody's Industrial Manual, 1963.

O'Reilly, Brian, "More Than Cheap Talk Propels MCI," *Fortune,* Jan. 24, 1983.

Patterson, William Pat, "Would You Take on Ma Bell?" *Industry Week,* May 3, 1982.

Pollack, Andrew, "Jostling in the Overcrowded Phone Market," *NYT,* Oct. 21, 1984.

Rosenfeld, Steven P., "MCI Shares Battered in Wake of FCC Decision," *WP,* Aug. 24, 1983.

Sanger, David E., "The Changing Image of IBM," *NYT,* July 7, 1985.

Shook, Robert L., *The Entrepreneurs* (New York: Harper & Row, 1980).

Shooshan, Harry M., III, ed., *Disconnecting Bell: The Impact of the AT&T Divestiture* (New York: Pergamon, 1984).

Simon, Samuel A., and Michael J. Whalen, *Teleconsumers and the Future: A Manual on the AT&T Divestiture* (Washington: Telecommunications Res. and Action Center, 1983).

This Week with David Brinkley (ABC-TV) Aug. 7, 1983.

Tydeman, John, et al., *Teletext and Videotext in the United States: Market Potential, Technology, Public Policy Issues* (New York: McGraw-Hill, 1982).

White, Eileen, "MCI Communications Face Pitfalls in Bid to Solidify No. Two Spot," *WSJ*, May 31, 1985.

White, Eileen, and Janet Guyon, "MCI Awarded $37.8 Million in AT&T Case," *WSJ*, May 29, 1985.

Government Documents and Legal Proceedings

Federal Communications Commission, *In Re Applications of Microwave Communications, Inc* (Docket No. 16509, File No. 4615-C1-P-64, F.C.C. 69-870, Aug. 13, 1969); *In the Matter of . . . Consideration of Application to Provide . . . Public Point-to-Point Microwave Radio Service and Proposed Amendments. . . .* (Docket No. 18920, FCC 70-768, July 17, 1970, and Docket No. 18920, F.C.C. 71-547, June 3, 1971); *In the Matter of MCI Telecommunications Corporation* (Docket No. 20640., F.C.C. 76-622, July 13, 1976); Office of Plans and Policy, *Social Objectives and Competition in Common Carrier Communications: Incompatible or Inseparable?* (Washington: U.S. Dept. of Commerce, Nat. Technical Info. Serv., Apr. 1980).

U.S. Congress, House, Comm. on Energy and Commerce, Subcomm. on Telecommunications, Consumer Protection, and Finance, *Telecommunications Act of 1982: HR 5158, Parts 1–3* (Mar. 9, 1982); *Prospects for Universal Telephone Service* (Mar. 22, 1983).

U.S. Congress, House, Comm. on Energy and Commerce; and Senate, Comm. on Commerce, Science, and Transportation, *Universal Telephone Service Preservation Act of 1983* (July 28, 29, 1983).

U.S. Congress, House, Comm. on Interstate and Foreign Commerce, Subcomm. on Communications, *H.R. 12323* (Sept. 28–30, 1976); *H.R. 13015* (July 27, 1978); *Communications Act of 1979, Vol. 1, Part 1* (Apr. 24–26, May 1, 1979).

U.S. Congress, House, Comm. on the Judiciary, Subcomm. on Monopolies and Commercial Law, *Telecommunications Act of 1980* (Sept. 9 and 16, 1980).

U.S. Congress, Senate, Comm. on Commerce, Science, and Transportation, *Amendments to Communications Act of 1934, Part 2* (Apr. 30, May 2, 1979); *Telecommunications Competition and Deregulation Act of 1981: S. 898* (June 15, 1981); *Universal Telephone Service Preservation Act of 1983: Report on S. 1660* (Oct. 7, 1983).

U.S. Congress, Senate, Comm. on the Judiciary, *The Industrial Reorganization Act, Part 5.: The Communications Industry* (June 20, 1974); *Monopolization and Competition in the Telecommunications Industry* (July 23, 1981). Subcomm. on Antitrust and Monopoly, *The Industrial Reorganization Act (S. 1167) Part 2: The Communications Industry* (July 30, 1973); *Competition Improvements Act of 1975* (Feb. 5, 1976).

U.S. Dept. of Commerce, Nat. Telecommunications and Info. Admin., *Issues in Domestic Telecommunications: Directions for National Policy* (NTIA Special Pub. 85-16, July 1985); *Teleconference on Productivity* (La Jolla, Calif.: Western Behavioral Sciences Inst., Oct. 20, 1983, Grant No. RED-795-G-82-13 [99-7-13603]).

U.S. District Court, Chicago, *MCI v. AT&T: Trial transcript; Defendant's exhibit 80*, transcript of Aug. 9, 1972, meeting between John DeButts and William McGowan; *Defendant's exhibit 567*, Jan. 7, 1974, memorandum; *Judge's instructions and special verdict*, 1980.

U.S. District Court, Washington, D.C., *U.S. v. AT&T, Trial transcript.*

U.S. General Accounting Office, *Legislative and Regulatory Actions Needed to Deal with a Changing Domestic Telecommunications Industry* (CED-81-136, Sept. 24, 1981).

WILLIAM NORRIS
Revolutionary Without a Movement

William Norris granted two interviews, on Oct. 2 and Nov. 23, 1984.

In 1984 and 1985, nearly ninety other individuals were interviewed, including eleven current Control Data executives and outside directors, fifteen former company executives, fifteen university professors and administrators who have purchased Control Data products and services or studied the operations of the company, six state and local government officials, and ten journalists with expertise on the Minneapolis business community or the computer industry. Five of the interviews were off the record.

Published Sources

Important Periodicals: *Contact for Control Data People*, 1982–84; *Datamation*, 1981–84; *Corporate Report* 1978–84; *Minneapolis Star and Tribune*, 1980–84; *St. Paul Pioneer Press-Dispatch*, 1984.

Armstrong, Scott, "Reflections on America's Technology Future," *Christian Science Monitor*, Sept. 4, 1984.

Bamford, James, *The Puzzle Palace: A Report on NSA, America's Most Secret Agency* (Boston: Houghton Mifflin, 1982).

Barlas, Stephen, "Giving the Corporation a Conscience," *Express*, 1983.

Bartholomay, Thomas G., *Control Data Corporation's PLATO Computer and South Africa's Apartheid Education System* (Minneapolis, 1984).

Bean, Ed, "Booker T. Whatley Contends His Program Will Help Small Farms Make Big Money," *WSJ*, Oct. 4, 1984.

Bemis, Judson, and John A. Cairns, "In Minnesota, Business Is Part of the Solution," *Harvard Business Rev.*, July–Aug. 1981.

Bendick, Marc Jr., and Mary Lou Egan, "Providing Industrial Jobs in the Inner City," *Business*, Jan.–Mar. 1982.

Berg, Eric N., "Control Data's Fall from Grace," *NYT*, Feb. 17, 1985.

Boffey, Philip M., "The Race for Computer Supremacy: Who's Ahead?" *NYT*, Oct. 23, 1984.

Bradford, Calvin, "Private Sector Initiatives and Public Sector Accountability," *APA Jour.*, Summer 1983.

Bradford, Calvin and Mihalio Temali, *The Politics of Private Sector Initiatives: The Case of City Venture Corporation* (Minneapolis: Univ. of Minn. Hubert H. Humphrey Inst. of Public Affairs, Oct. 30, 1982).

Branan, Karen, "City Venture and the Metrodome Land Grab," *Twin Cities Reader*, Oct. 17, 8–14, 15–21, 1981; "Control Data's Venture into the Cities," *Minneapolis Tribune*, Oct. 10, 1982.

Brooks, Harvey, Lance Liebman, and Corinne Schelling, eds., *Public-Private Partnership: New Opportunities for Meeting Social Needs* (Cambridge, Mass.: Ballinger, 1984).

Brown, Jeff, "Land, Power, and the Dome," *Minneapolis Star*, Oct. 9, 1981.

Burger, Chester, *The Chief Executive* (Boston: CBI, 1978).

Burnham, David, *The Rise of the Computer State: The Threat to Our Freedoms, Our Ethics and Our Democratic Process* (New York: Random House, 1983).

Carley, William M., "Were IBM's Tactics Against Control Data Unfair or Just Tough?" *WSJ*, May 19, 1982.

CBS Weekend Evening News (CBS-TV) Mar. 13, 1983.

Chapman, Margaret, and Carl March, eds., *Common Sense in U.S.-Soviet Trade* (Washington: Amer. Comm. on East-West Accord, 1983).

"Chief Executives Who Won't Let Go," *BW*, Oct. 8, 1984.

Christensen, Wayne, "Life in the Bill Norris Shark Club," *CR*, June 1979.

Clark, Don, "Norb Berg: He's the Guiding Force of Control Data's Innovative People Programs," *St. Paul Sunday Pioneer Press*, Feb. 15, 1981.

Clark, Don, and Linda McDonnell, "Control Data: A Special Report," *St. Paul Pioneer Press*, Sept. 24, 1984.

Connery, Thomas B., "Guns & Butter," *CR*, Sept. 1983.

"Control Data Confirms Disk-Drive Problems, Sees Effect on Profit," *WSJ*, Sept. 21, 1984.

"Control Data Corp. Penalized $1,381,000 after Pleading Guilty to Foreign Bribe," *WSJ*, Apr. 27, 1978.

"Control Data: Is There Room for Change after Bill Norris?" *BW*, Oct. 17, 1983.

"Control Data Starts a Painful Retrenchment," *BW*, Oct. 22, 1984.

"Corporate Winners in the Lottery Boom," *Fortune*, Sept. 3, 1984.

Cowen, Robert C., "Grant Awards Should Be Based on Merit, Not on Political Clout," *Christian Science Monitor*, Aug. 16, 1984.

Cox, Meg, "Control Data Puts Its Computers to Work Helping Farmers Make It on Small Plots," *WSJ*, Oct. 14, 1980.

Dornfeld, Steven, "Where Have All DFLers Gone? Control Data, Nearly Everyone," *Minneapolis Tribune*, Feb. 10, 1979.

Export and Import Controls in East-West Trade (Cambridge, Mass.: Harvard Univ. Russian Res. Center Corporate Sponsor Seminar, Nov. 2, 1981).

"Factories with Fences": Five Task Force Reports from the Wingspread Conference, Jan. 27–28, 1984—"An Idea Too Important to Give Up" (Washington: Office of Prog. Evaluation and Corrections Div., Nat. Inst. of Justice).

Friedrichs, Guenter, and Adam Schaff, eds., *Microelectronics and Society: A Report to the Club of Rome* (New York: NAL, 1982).

Galaskiewicz, Joseph, Wolfgang Bielefeld, and Patti Mullaney, *Corporate-Nonprofit Linkages in Minneapolis–St. Paul: Preliminary Findings from Three Surveys* (Minneapolis: Univ. of Minn., Nov. 1982).

Gardner, W. David, "CDC's Scrappy Chairman," *Datamation*, June 1981.

Gibson, Richard, "Control Data Intends to Sell Its Credit Unit," *WSJ*, Nov. 8, 1984; "Control Data Plans to Sell Some Businesses," *WSJ*, Apr. 1, 1985; "Control Data Unit to Close Consumer Lines," *WSJ*, June 21; "Control Data's Comeback Faces Rough Road: Slide Raises Questions on Chairman's Once-Magic Touch," *WSJ*, June 27, 1985.

Gibson, Richard, and Brenton R. Schlender, "Control Data Decides to Keep Finance Unit," *WSJ*, June 13, 1985.

Gilpin, Kenneth N., "Top Corporate Positions Added at Control Data," *NYT*, July 1, 1985.

Greenhouse, Steven, "Cooperation in Industry: Talking Business with Norris of Control Data," *NYT*, July 3, 1984.

Greenwald, John, "Minnesota's Magic Touch," *Time*, June 11, 1984.

Gustafson, Thane, *Selling the Russians the Rope? Soviet Technology Policy and U.S. Export Controls* (Santa Monica, Calif.: Rand/Defense Advanced Research Projects Agency, Apr. 1981, R-2649-ARPA).

Hagelberg, Marilyn, "Upward Bound," *CR*, Dec. 1982.

Harrar, George, "An Interview: William C. Norris, Control Data's Maverick Chairman," *Computerworld*, Sept. 12, 1983.

Hershey, Robert D., Jr., "Stiff Antitrust Laws Called Rein on U.S.," *NYT*, Aug. 1, 1983.

Hofstetter, Fred T., speech to Assoc. for the Development of Computer-Based Instructional Systems, Columbus, Ohio, May 17; *The Ninth Summative Report of the Office of Computer-Based Instruction* (Univ. of Delaware, Newark, July 1, 1984).

"The IBM Deal: A Windfall for Control Data," *BW*, Jan. 20, 1973.

Ingrassia, Lawrence, "Control Data and Cray Start Feuding Again," *WSJ*, May 25, 1982; "Seeking to Aid Society, Control Data Takes on Many Novel Ventures," *WSJ*, Dec. 22, 1983.

Inskip, Leonard, "Control Data's Norris: After Twenty-five Years, He's Still a Prime Component," *Minneapolis Tribune*, Sept. 30, 1982.

Interfaith Center for Corporate Responsibility, *Proxy Issues Report; U.S. Corporate Activity in South Korea*, 1984 Analysis K (Apr. 9, 1984), and Supp. No. 2 (Apr. 11, 1984).

Iversen, Wesley R., "Where Joint Ventures Are the Rule," *Electronics*, June 16, 1983.

Johansen, Gary, "From Farm Boy to Computer Giant," *Mag. of the Midlands, The Omaha World-Herald*, Aug. 9, 1981.

Johnson, Jan, "Counting on the CDC 205," Oct. 1981; "Tracking a Centipede," June 1982; "Cray & CDC Meet the Japanese," Apr. 1984; "America Answers Back," May 1984; all from *Datamation*.

Levine, Ronald D., "Supercomputers," *Scientific American*, Jan. 1982.

Lippman, Thomas W., "Competitive Boon or Monopoly? Electronics Firms' Joint Research Venture Ignites Antitrust Debate," *WP*, May 8, 1983.

McClellan, Stephen T., *The Coming Computer Industry Shakeout: Winners, Losers, and Survivors* (New York: Wiley, 1984).

McDonnell, Lynda, "Norris, Perpich Pair Ideas, Resources," *St. Paul Pioneer Press/Dispatch*, Sept. 24, 1984.

McLellan, Vin, "CDC Emerging Strategy," *Datamation*, Dec. 1980.

Marcom, John, Jr., "School Supercomputer Centers Promise to Lift U.S. Research," *WSJ*, Mar. 15, 1985.

Meter, Ken, "Early Stages: Deer Valley Farms," *CR*, July 1982.

Minneapolis Task Force on Research and Technology, *Recommendations to the Mayor and City Council*, Aug. 15, 1983.

Mullinix, Patricia M., Ralph T. Heimer, and Diane Skinner, *A Pilot Study of a Spanish Version of the PLATO Basic Skills Learning System Mathematics Curriculum* (Phila.: Courses by Computers, Inc., 1981).

Mundale, Charles I., "Bill Norris: the View from the Fourteenth Floor," *CR*, Jan. 1978.

Murphy, Richard T., and Lola Rhea Appel, *Evaluation of the PLATO IV Computer-based Education System in the Community College* (Princeton, N.J.: Educ. Testing Serv., June 1977).

NARMIC/American Friends Service Committee, *Automating Apartheid: U.S. Computer Exports to South Africa and the Arms Embargo* (Phila.: NARMIC, 1984).

National Commission on Industrial Innovation, *Annual Report 1983* (Los Angeles, 1984).

National Institute for Personnel Research, Council for Scientific and Industrial Research,

The Programming of Psychological Tests on the PLATO System (Johannesburg, So. Africa: CSIR Contract Report C/PERS 303, Mar. 1981).

NSF Working Group on Computers for Research, *A National Computing Environment for Academic Research* (Washington: Nat. Science Found., July 1983).

Noble, Douglas, "The Underside of Computer Literacy," *Raritan*, vol. 3 (Spring 1984); "Computer Literacy and Ideology," *Teachers College Record*, vol. 85 (Summer 1984).

Norris, William C., *New Frontiers for Bussiness Leadership* (Minneapolis: Dorn 1983). "Via Technology to a New Era in Education," *Phi Delta Kappan*, Feb. 1977; "Limiting Japan's Access to Our Research," *NYT*, July 24, 1983; "South Africa: The Case for Selective Investment," *Minnesota Daily*, Mar. 1, 1984; "Employing the 'Unemployable,'" *Electronic Engineering Times*, Sept. 10, 1984. Various speeches, to: Special Symposium on Res. for Small Farms, Beltsville, Md., Nov. 17, 1981. Microelectronics and Computer Technology Enterprises Meeting, Feb. 19; Baltimore PSI Task Force Meeting, May 25, 1982. Wellspring Task Force Meeting, Minneapolis, Jan. 11; Brigham Young Univ., Mar. 31; Baltimore BTC, June 29; Frontiers of Supercomputing Conf., Los Alamos Nat. Lab., Aug. 18; Rotary Club of Minneapolis, Dec. 2, 1983. Bishop's Committee, Feb. 17; NYC Conf., Apr. 5; CDC Annual Stockholders' Meeting, Minneapolis, May 2; Japan Soc., June; Small Business Assoc., Chicago, Aug. 29; 1984 Annual Corporate and Business Law Inst., Nov. 1, 1984.

"Open House Monday Night for Model Computer City Project," *Forest City Summit*, Oct. 20, 1983.

Ouchi, William G., *The M-Form Society* (Reading, Mass.: Addison-Wesley, 1984).

Panel on Large Scale Computing in Science and Engineering, *Report of the Panel.* Washington, Dec. 26, 1982.

Papa, Mary Bader, "Terms of Inducement," *CR*, Mar. 1984.

Perlman, Larry, speech to Investment Community Meeting, Minneapolis, June 1984.

Pine, Carol, and Susan Mundale, *Self-Made: The Stories of Twelve Minnesota Entrepreneurs* (Minneapolis: Dorn, 1982).

Pollack, Andrew, "The Daunting Power of I.B.M.," *NYT*, Jan. 20, 1985.

Report to the Federal Coordinating Council on Science, Engineering and Technology Supercomputer Panel on Recommended Government Actions to Provide Access to Supercomputers and . . . to Retain U.S. Leadership in Supercomputers. (Washington, 1984).

"Reshaping the Computer Industry," *BW*, July 16, 1984.

Rosenberg, Ronald, "High-Tech Do-Gooder Speaks Up," *Boston Globe*, Nov. 29, 1983.

Rothschild, Matthew, "Women Beat Up at Control Data, Korea." *Multinational Monitor*, Sept. 1982.

Rowen, Hobart, "U.S. Ignoring Available Japanese Technical Information," *WP*, July 8, 1984.

Sanger, David E., "Bailing Out of the Mainframe Industry," *NYT*, Feb. 5; "Computer Consortium Lags," *NYT*, Sept. 5, 1984.

Schuyten, Peter J., "The Battle in Supercomputers," *NYT*, July 22, 1980.

Skinner, Diane, and Betty L. Brown, *1980–81 PLATO Computer-Based Instruction Project Final Report* (Tallahassee, Fla.: Computing Center, Fla. State Univ., Aug. 1981).

"Small, Smart, Sharp," *BW*, May 25, 1963.

Sobel, Robert, *I.B.M.: Colossus in Transition* (New York: Bantam, 1983).

Stavig, Vicki, "Minnesota's Wealthiest Business Leaders," *CR*, Aug. 1984.

Stephenson, Frank, "The Supercomputer Computational Research Institute: A Mission, A Machine—Florida State Joins the Supercomputing Race," *Fla. State Univ. Bull.: Research in Rev.*, Spring 1985.

"Supreme Court to Review Strikers' Right to Picket Neutral or Secondary Locations," *WSJ*, Jan. 8, 1980.

Swinton, Spencer S., Marianne Amarel, and Judith A. Morgan, *The PLATO Elementary Demonstration Educational Outcome Evaluation: Final Report* (Champaign, Ill.: Univ. of Ill. Computer-based Educ. Research Lab., Nov. 1978).

Taper, Bernard, "The Bittersweet Harvest," *Science 80*, Nov. 1980.

Tarrant, Bert, "Private Business Stealing March on Government—and at a Profit," *Alaska Journ. of Commerce*, Aug. 6, 1984.

Temali, Mihailo, and Candace Campbell, *Business Incubator Profiles: A National Survey* (Minneapolis: Univ. of Minn. Hubert H. Humphrey Inst. of Public Affairs, July 1984).

Tice, D. J., "Tomorrow the World," *CR*, Feb. 1981.

Toffler, Alvin, *The Adaptive Corporation* (New York: McGraw-Hill, 1985).

Tomash, Erwin, and Arnold A. Cohen, "The Birth of an ERA: Engineering Research Associates, Inc. 1946–1955," *Annals of the History of Computing* Oct. 1979.

Traub, James, "Control Data Goes Public," *United*, Feb. 1983.

Ward, Margaret, "South Africa: The Case for Universal Disinvestment," *Minnesota Daily*, Mar. 1, 1984.

"Why Bill Norris Is Smiling," *BW*, Nov. 10, 1973.

"William Norris: Only Big Business Has Resources to Address Unmet Social Needs," *Woodlands Forum*, Sept. 1984.

Williams, Winston, "Control Data's Drive to Stay in Front," *NYT*, June 13, 1982.

Wirtzfeld, Roy, "Control Data: From Mystery to Legend," *Upper Midwest Investor*, Nov. 1961.

Wise, T. A., "Control Data's Magnificent Fumble," *Fortune*, Apr. 1966.

Worthy, James C., "An Entrepreneurial Approach to Social Problem-Solving: William C. Norris and Control Data Corporation," in *Business and Economic History*, ed. Jeremy Atack (Champaign, Ill.: Univ. of Ill., 1983).

Government Documents and Filings

Congressional Research Service, *Supercomputers: Foreign Competition and Federal Funding* (Order Code IB83102, Sept. 21, 1984).

Federal Trade Commission, *In the Matter of Control Data Corporation, et al.* (97 FTC 84, Docket 8940, Jan. 9, 1981).

U.S. Congress, House, Comm. on Banking, Finance and Urban Affairs, Subcomm. on International Trade, Investment and Monetary Policy, *Export-Import Bank and Trade with South Africa* (Feb. 9, 1978).

U.S. Congress, House, Comm. on Energy and Commerce, Subcomm. on Telecommunications, Consumer Protection, and Finance, *Takeover Tactics and Public Policy* (Mar. 28, 1984).

U.S. Congress, House, Comm. on the Judiciary, *Joint Research and Development Act of 1984: Report* (Apr. 6, 1984).

U.S. Congress, Joint Economic Comm., *Local Economic Development Strategies* (Nov. 23, 1981).

U.S. Congress, Office of Technology Assessment, *Informational Technology and Its Impact on American Education* (OTA-CIT-187, Nov. 1982); *Technology and East-West Trade: An Update* (OTA-ISC-209, May 1983).

U.S. Congress, Senate, Comm. on Foreign Relations, *International Development Assistance Act of 1979* (Mar. 14, 15, 21, and 23, 1979)

U.S. Congress, Senate, Comm. on Governmental Affairs, Permanent Subcomm. on Investigations, *Transfer of United States High Technology to the Soviet Union and Soviet Bloc Nations* (Nov. 15, 1982).

U.S. Congress, Senate, Comm. on Human Resources, *Comprehensive Employment and Training Act* (Mar. 8, 1978); Subcomm. on Employment, Poverty, and Migratory Labor, *Full Employment and Balanced Growth Act of 1978* (Feb. 8, Mar. 7, 8, 1978, pt. 2).

U.S. Congress, Senate, Comm. on the Judiciary, *The National Productivity and Innovation Act: Report* (May 3, 1984); Subcomm. on Antitrust and Monopoly, *Mergers and Industrial Concentration,* (July 28, 1978); Subcomm. on Antitrust, Monopoly and Business Rights, *Mergers and Economic Concentration* (Mar. 8, 23, 30, Apr. 25, 1979.

U.S. Dept. of Agriculture, Economics and Statistics Service, *Economies of Size in U.S. Crop Farming* (Washington: G.P.O., Agricultural Economic Report No. 472, July 1981).

U.S. Dept. of Defense, Defense Science Board Task Force on Export of U.S. Technology, *An Analysis of Export Control of U.S. Technology—a DOD Perspective* (Washington: Office of the Dir. of Defense Res. and Engineering, Feb. 4, 1976).

U.S. Dept. of Justice, Nat. Inst. of Corrections, *Guidelines for Prison Industries* (Washington: Nat. Inst. of Corrections, Jan. 1984).

Corporate Documents

"Chronology of Key Events in Control Data's History" (Aug. 1984).

City Venture Corp., *Base Report: Park Heights, Baltimore* (Dec. 1980).

"A History of Control Data's Founding and First Year of Operation."

Investment Community Meeting (New York, Nov. 1981 and Nov. 1983; Minneapolis, June 1984).

N.Y. Soc. of Securities Analysts Meeting (Aug. 1982).

Fall Securities Analysts Meetings (New York, Nov. 9, 1979, and Nov. 6, 1980).

Report from the "Social Needs and Business Opportunities" Conf., Minneapolis, Sept. 22–23, 1982.

Report to Stockholders on Activities in South Africa, Jan. 1983.

Risking Credibility: A History of Control Data's First Inner City Plants.

Unpublished Sources

Documents, *United States* v. *Control Data Corp.,* Criminal Docket 78-210. (Obtained under FOIA, No. 11,985).

Index

Abel, Harold, 151
Accelerated Cost Recovery System
  (ACRS), 271–73, 275, 276,
  279–83, 289
Adamkus, Valdas, 192
Adams, Brock, 270
Adams, Gordon, 387
Advantage database, 454, 480
AENCO, 319–20
Aerospace Industries Association,
  245–46
Aetna Life & Casualty, xv, 406
Agnelli, Giovanni, 217
Agriculture Department, U.S.,
  311, 312, 313–14, 323, 343,
  346
AgTech database, 454
Airfone Inc., 423, 427
Air Products & Chemicals, 153
Air Transport Association, 277
Alcoa, 260n, 268
Allen, James, 355, 370
Allende Gossens, Salvador, 221
Allied Chemical, 138, 270
Allied Corporation, 153, 214
Allstate Insurance, 137, 514
Ally, Michael, 5, 25, 29
Amalgamated Association, 52–53
American Agriculture Movement
  (AAM), 303, 322, 327
American Airlines, 375, 383, 429
American Bankers Association, 253,
  265
American Council for Capital
  Formation, 250, 251, 252, 253–54,
  257, 258–59, 263–64, 272, 274,
  282
American Electronics Association, 258,
  274
American Enterprise Institute, 525

American Iron and Steel Institute
  (AISI), 35, 36, 41, 42
American Lutheran Church, 494
American Medical Association (AMA),
  138
American Motors, 228–29, 380
American Telephone and Telegraph
  (AT&T), 152, 226, 260, 269–70,
  399–402, 403, 404, 405–6, 407,
  408–10, 416, 417, 418, 419–20,
  424, 427, 428, 429–30, 441–42,
  443–44, 446, 515
Amin, Idi, 212
Amstutz, Daniel, 323
Ancient Law (Maine), 397
Anderson, Jack, 222
Anderson, John, 255
Anderson, Ken, 332
Anderson, Robert, 265
Anderson, Warren, 132
Anding, Thomas, 476
Andreas, Dwayne, 297–98
Andrews, Mark, 326
Anglo American Corporation, 197, 217,
  218
Anheuser-Busch, 261
Annenberg, Walter, 78, 382, 394
Appleyard, Robert, 52
Appropriate Technology International,
  487
Araskog, Rand, 225, 226
Archer Daniels Midland, 293, 297
Armco Steel, 29, 519
Armed Forces Journal International,
  363
Arms Bazaar, The (Sampson), 351
AT&T, *see* American Telephone and
  Telegraph
Atlantic, 395–96
Atwater, Brewster, 296

559